Theology in America

THE AMERICAN HERITAGE SERIES

THE

American Heritage

Series

UNDER THE GENERAL EDITORSHIP OF
LEONARD W. LEVY AND ALFRED YOUNG

Theology in America

The Major Protestant Voices

From Puritanism to Neo-Orthodoxy

EDITED BY

SYDNEY E. AHLSTROM

Yale University

THE BOBBS-MERRILL COMPANY, INC.
INDIANAPOLIS

FOREWORD

Theology has been called one of the three speculative sciences, the queen of study, and the mother of philosophy. But it has also been labeled the dullest field of thought, a monumental illusion, and an invention of the devil calculated to scare believers from the church. Characterization aside, theology purports to be systematic and rational thought about religious belief, centering mainly on God, and his relationship to man, nature, and the universe.

In a nation that traces its origins to the Pilgrim fathers and proclaims its trust in God by the most profane of all media, that root of all evil—money, it is curious that theology is one of the most neglected of subjects. Theologians abound, but historians who poke into every nook and cranny of our past, and who have not neglected religion, pass over theology without much more than a literary genuflection. For proof one need only glance at the standard works in American thought: Parrington's *Main Currents in American Thought,* Beard's *The American Spirit,* Curti's *Growth of American Thought,* Commager's *The American Mind,* Boorstin's *The Americans,* and Miller's *The Life of the Mind in America.*

Sydney E. Ahlstrom has boldly introduced and compiled this volume in a true revisionist spirit. His intention is to demonstrate—contrary to the hoary assumption that theology is bankrupt in America—that the study has enjoyed a remarkably vital and creative history. America's theological achievement has, indeed, been outstanding. The evidence is amply mustered here with astute commentary by Professor Ahlstrom. He finds theology one of the most ambitious and exciting of human enterprises—a system of thought that has impregnated our intellectual tradition, commands our respect, and merits our study. The editor's concern here is with the various representative Protestant theologians, from the time of the Puritans, the Great Awakening, and the Enlightenment, to the Social Gospel and Neo-Orthodoxy of our own time. Ahlstrom sees his subject in the broadest terms, and brings such luminaries as Jefferson and Lincoln as well as Hawthorne and Melville within the periphery of his ambit. For making so intelligible and restoring to importance an area of speculation that we have mistakenly assumed to be merely arid, excessively difficult, and sectarian, Ahlstrom has earned our gratitude. Here in this unique collection that spans Thomas Hooker to H. Richard Niebuhr we have not only the "major Protestant voices"; we have also the clarity, passion, and intellectual rectitude that Ahlstrom himself brings to his subject.

This book is one of a series created to provide the essential primary sources of the American experience, especially of American thought. The series, when completed, will constitute a documentary library of American history, filling a need long felt among scholars, students, libraries, and general readers for authoritative collections of original materials. Some volumes will illuminate the thought of significant individuals, such as James Madison or Louis Brandeis; some will deal with movements, such as the Antifederalists or the Populists; others will be organized around special themes, such as Puritan political thought, or American Catholic thought on social questions. Many volumes will take up the large number of subjects traditionally studied in American history for which surprisingly there are no documentary anthologies; others will pioneer in introducing new subjects of increasing importance to scholars and to the contemporary world. The series aspires to maintain the high standards demanded of contemporary editing, providing authentic texts, intelligently and unobtrusively edited. It will also have the distinction of presenting pieces of substantial length which give the full character and flavor of the original. The series will be the most comprehensive and authoritative of its kind.

Leonard W. Levy
Alfred Young

EDITOR'S PREFACE

"The American mind was thrown at the start into a stern and rough medium." So runs the century-old analysis of Count Adam de Gurowski. And his next words, we can be sure, will be that inevitable verbal exercise of European commentators on the United States, a description of the pragmatic cast of American civilization. But let us hear him further: "It was obliged to direct all its intensity to struggles with nature, with destructive matter; was forced to choose and decide swiftly, to act, and not to remain in musing contemplation."[1] Of course, with regard to American theology this same truism has been uttered over and over again. Richard Hofstadter in a recent work of great excellence devotes three lengthy chapters to the "strength and pervasiveness" of anti-intellectualism in American Protestantism. "Here," he says, "enthusiasm and revivalism won their most impressive victories."[2] A church historian describes the inevitable corollary to revivalism: the accent on doing things, which made "Work for the Night is Coming" a national anthem of the American churches. "Our activism," he writes, "is not a substitute for our religious faith; it is an expression of that faith."[3]

[1] Adam G. de Gurowski, *America and Europe* (New York, 1857), as given in Henry S. Commager, ed., *America in Perspective* (New York: New American Library, 1947), p. 116.

[2] *Anti-Intellectualism in American Life* (New York: Alfred A. Knopf, 1963), p. 56.

[3] Ronald E. Osborn, *The Spirit of American Christianity* (New York: Harper & Brothers, 1958), p. 89.

Because such observations are made so often, and because they contain a large element of truth, it has been widely believed that a substantial American theological tradition simply does not exist. Even American church historians have done more to enforce this conception than to correct it. This volume, therefore, is informed by a positive revisionist intention. Its purpose is to exhibit a sustained theological achievement—an achievement that is, in fact, made all the more remarkable by the immense obstacles that were raised up for a new nation of immigrants and their descendants who migrated westward to tame and people a continent.

The obstacles that beset the editor of an anthology of American theology are similarly awesome, however; and more than one purpose is served by a brief exposition of his problems and the principles of selection by which he has sought to solve them. They have to do, first, with the nature of theology itself and then with the special characteristics of the American scene.

Theology is intrinsically one of the most ambitious and most exciting of human enterprises; it is not the tinder-dry preoccupation of hair-splitters so often depicted. Technically, it is the scientific ordering of the faith which a church confesses and teaches.[4] Actually it moves out from the religious acceptances of a community or a person and moves toward momentous questions of life and death, goodness and truth, time and eternity. The most difficult problems of nature, man, and God come within its purview. Theology deals with the human situation in its totality, historical and cosmic. It reflects man's ultimate concerns, and seeks to speak the truth about ultimate reality. It demands a grappling with virtually all of the philosopher's traditional problems, calls for an historical grasp of the church's long involvement with the major issues, requires an understanding of

---

[4] See the definitions of two of the most widely read systematic theologians of this century: Gustaf Aulén, *The Faith of the Christian Church* (Philadelphia: Muhlenberg Press, 1948), pp. 3–22; and Karl Bath, *Dogmatics in Outline* (New York: Philosophical Library, 1949), pp. 9–14.

contemporary science, art, and culture, and presupposes an understanding of the nature and situation of the men it addresses. Indeed, its scope is almost boundless.

Theology, however, is not uninhibited speculation, for it is controlled in distinct ways: by the biblical witness, by the doctrinal tradition, and by the living faith of the people. Yet even in this respect there are complications, for scholars correct the biblical text, scriptural interpretations alter as one climate of opinion yields to another, and changing currents of piety, sensibility, and devotion modify the popular faith. Doctrines, too, are inelectably adapted to new circumstances. Theology is thus a continuous effort to relate the apostolic faith to the conditions, needs, and temptations of men. Regardless of whatever else may be said about this discipline, it is a vast and expansive activity that does not lend itself to the anthologizing of snippets. Short extracts do not reveal its genius. In the present volume, accordingly, the number of selections has been kept to a minimum and each theologian is allowed to speak through a characteristic mode of expression and at a respectable length. Here is exhibited the work of creative thinkers who provided important intellectual leadership during successive periods of stress and transition.

Yet the scene in which these thinkers did their work was American, and in this circumstance lie two other difficulties for the editor. Most obvious is the extraordinary heterogeneity of the American religious tradition. Almost from the start there have been several major religious movements each of which has responded to times of crisis in its characteristic way. It is obvious that a compromise of some sort is required. My own solution rests on two decisions: (1) to emphasize periods rather than denominations, but wherever possible to select theologians of diverse and representative backgrounds; and (2) to accent the theological activity of the "mainstream" tradition which flows through the churches stemming from the Reformation experience in Great Britain, yet without ignoring other traditions.

A second difficulty inherent in the American experience is the unusual degree to which religious interests impregnate the country's entire intellectual tradition. In the study of American history the two cannot be disengaged, even for analysis, except with great arbitrariness. John Winthrop, Thomas Jefferson, and Abraham Lincoln are major figures in the history of American religious thought; the scientists Benjamin Silliman, Asa Gray, and S. F. B. Morse play prominent roles in church history; and a similar status can be claimed for John Fiske and Henry George, or for a dozen great writers from Thoreau to Eliot. By the same token theology and philosophy in the United States are continually blended even though the two disciplines are theoretically distinct.[5] Since the late 1920's, moreover, a massive movement of research and reevaluation has made the entire field of American intellectual, literary, and religious history much more complicated than it once was. Melville, Hawthorne, and Jonathan Edwards have been restored to the canon; the enormous richness and power of Puritanism has been rediscovered; the close interrelationships of the religious and the secular have been emphasized anew. My assertions expound my solution: despite the complexities, I have not drawn a sharp line between theology and the philosophy of religion. This collection would have seemed distorted and incomplete had Emerson, James, and Royce been excluded.[6]

No formula, however, could possibly solve the problem of selecting the limited number of representative thinkers which a single volume can contain. Considering their influence, or intel-

---

[5] In distinction from what has been said above about theology, philosophers have at least professed a commitment to no tradition other than that of reasonableness, to no group but mankind, and to no institution other than human society; yet many problems of theology remain in their domain and they have almost always felt obliged to examine the claims of the historic religions and to deal with many "religious" questions.

[6] On the other hand I have decided with many regrets not to include works of biblical criticism and the history of religions though Americans made important contributions in these realms.

lectual distinction, at least two-thirds of those who have been chosen here would seem positively to defy exclusion, but for the remaining places at least a score of theologians and philosophers of religion crowd in upon an editor, clamoring for space and presenting credentials on their reputation and historical significance.[7] Having made his choices and explained them in the Introduction, the editor must take consolation in two facts: that the themes and traditions that *are* represented certainly deserve inclusion, and that the reader's interest may warrant a companion volume in which other claimants can be presented.

The Introduction is an account of the historical context in which the American theological enterprise was carried on, and the issues that from time to time occasioned controversy and reformulation.[8] The dialectic of liberal and conservative ten-

---

[7] Among the eminently worthy thinkers whose works have long been considered for inclusion in this volume are the following: John Cotton, Roger Williams, William Penn, Increase and Cotton Mather, John Witherspoon, Samuel Johnson, Samuel Hopkins, John Woolman, Thomas Jefferson, Timothy Dwight, Andrews Norton, Henry Ware, Theodore Parker, James Freeman Clarke, Orestes Brownson, Philip Schaff, James Marsh, James H. Thornwell, Samuel S. Schmucker, Charles G. Finney, William P. DuBose, William A. Brown, William N. Clarke, George Angier Gordon, Borden P. Bowne, Augustus H. Strong, Francis E. Abbot, Octavius B. Frothingham, Edgar Y. Mullins, William R. Huntington, Francis G. Peabody, Shailer Mathews, Edward S. Ames, Benjamin Warfield, Theodore E. Schmauk, D. C. Macintosh, Henry Nelson Wieman, Rufus Jones, J. Gresham Machen, Reinhold Niebuhr, Paul Tillich, and, among men whose published work falls almost entirely after World War II, Joseph Sittler, Edward J. Carnell, and Schubert Ogden.

[8] In a previous essay I treated the history of American theology in a manner that foreshadowed the present volume. The reader is referred to it for a consideration of certain themes and theologians necessarily excluded here. Because my basic interpretation has not materially changed, I have not felt obliged to traverse this difficult terrain along entirely new paths. Cf. "Theology in America: A Historical Survey," in *The Shaping of American Religion,* I, *Religion in American Life,* 4 vols., James W. Smith and A. Leland Jamison, eds. (Princeton: Princeton University Press, 1961), 232–321.

dencies, therefore, inevitably emerges; but to clarify its results I have accented certain unifying themes and discussed the development of the later liberal theology from Emerson to Rauschenbusch in a connected narrative. The selections themselves, on the other hand, are placed in chronological order, though not in accordance with the precise date of the selection chosen but with regard to the historical place of the author's career in American theological history. The headnote preceding each selection seeks to provide information on the author, the circumstances of his writing, and some aspects of the issue with which the selection is concerned. Invitations to further reading are provided in the Selected Bibliography and in certain cases by annotations.

The selections have been edited in the conventional manner, with all omissions and interpolations clearly indicated. Except where otherwise noted in the appropriate headnote, only misprints, confusing or outdated punctuation and capitalization, and incorrect or obsolete citations have been silently corrected. Slight liberties that authors have taken in their quotations have not been corrected if the result would be awkward and if they did not distort the sense of the source. Parentheses are the author's own; editorial additions are placed in brackets. Footnotes are the author's own unless an indication to the contrary is given. All the authors in this volume, with the exception of Rauschenbusch, uniformly use the King James Version in quoting Scripture; the editor's footnotes, where applicable, do the same.

The occasion for acknowledging those who have generously given of counsel and assistance finds me unwilling to risk the omissions that a full enumeration might entail. Special gratitude is due, however, to my colleagues, Professors Hans W. Frei and David D. Hall, for their critical reading of the manuscript and their many helpful suggestions, though of course I would not implicate them in such flaws and errors that remain. I also wish to thank Professor Thomas A. Schafer for allowing me to use his meticulously edited transcriptions from Jonathan Edwards' manuscript notebooks, Professors Bard Thompson and George H. Bricker for permitting me to consult page proof of their edition of John W. Nevin's *The Mystical Presence,* and Helen Kent, DeAnn Martin, Vera Houghtlin, and my wife, Nancy Ahlstrom, for their very valuable assistance in preparing the manuscript. To Sanford W. Wylie, Jr., for aid in compiling the Index I am also indebted. Finally I am grateful to Leonard W. Levy, General Editor, for his interest and counsel. The generosity of publishers who have permitted use of copyrighted materials is acknowledged in connection with the appropriate sections.

S. E. A.

CONTENTS

INTRODUCTION

Christian theology exists in the context of history. Just as the European philosophical tradition, in Whitehead's famous phrase, consists of a series of footnotes to Plato,[1] so Christian theology is a series of footnotes to St. Paul, and back of him stretches still another series of rabbinic footnotes on the Law and the Prophets of Israel. In this sense *American* theology, properly speaking, does not have its own beginning. It is like a conversation being continued by people as they walk into another room.

In the millenium during which Europe as we know it came into existence, western Catholicism shaped the prevailing outlook and attitudes. Social structures and the intellectual life were formed and interpreted in the context of the piety, teachings, and activities of the Church. Lines between state and church were indistinct. This interpenetration of the sacred and the secular, moreover, was only partially mitigated by the Reformation, or even by the founders of American colonies. Only very slowly during the colonial period were mediaeval presuppositions opened to challenge. In like manner the theological interpretation of life's perennial problems long continued to be understood in basically scholastic terms. The works of Thomas Aquinas, as well as his later critics, Catholic and Evangelical, found their way into the library of newly-founded Harvard College; and Jonathan Edwards wrestled with ancient problems of Being in ways that link him not only with the Cambridge and

---

[1] Alfred North Whitehead, *Process and Reality* (New York: The Macmillan Company, 1929), p. 63.

Renaissance Platonists but with St. Augustine as well. The United States itself has no mediaeval period, but in Puritanism we confront more than faint vestiges of that era.

The Reformation, too, made its mark. In fact the country that declared its independence in 1776 was more clearly a product of Protestantism than any other country in the world. Not only were more than 95 per cent of its people of Protestant background, but its social life and institutions had been formed in the wilderness where ancient mediaeval precedents and perrogatives could not be long maintained. Moreover, France and Spain had, from the start, forced this English "empire" to intensify, even to exaggerate, its Protestantism. During the years when the Counter Reformation was at its height, Queen Elizabeth, ironically, was the very palladium of evangelical religion. In positive moral and intellectual terms colonial America was shaped by the English Reformation and, more specifically still, by the dramatic rise of Puritanism. If these factors are not duly weighed, American church history and theology, especially in the colonial period, remains an insoluble conundrum.

THE PURITANS

Puritanism in the broadest sense is a perennial tendency. "Woe to those who are at ease in Zion," cries the Prophet Amos. "Woe to those who lie upon beds of ivory . . . but are not grieved over the ruin of Joseph!" (Amos 6:1-7). Perry Miller touched on another Puritan theme of ancient origin when he spoke of the "Augustinian strain of piety," with its inwardness and utter dependence on the gracious work of God.[2] Yet Puritanism was also a concrete Protestant movement, and it is best understood by examining two quite specific relationships. It

---

[2] Perry Miller, *The New England Mind: The Seventeenth Century* (New York: The Macmillan Company, 1939), p. 4. Reprinted as Beacon Press paperback, 1961.

was, first of all, one of the major variations within the family of "Reformed" churches which during the 1520's began to differentiate themselves into a more radical break with Rome than that which Luther was leading. Secondly, its chief distinguishing characteristics derive from the impact of Reformed teaching on the *English* experience.

The Reformed tradition is perhaps best traced to the reformation inaugurated in Zurich in 1519 by Huldrich Zwingli. It quickly spread to neighboring Swiss cantons and to France, where other stirrings had been manifest for some time, and so traveled down the Rhine through Germany, and then branched out into the Netherlands. John Calvin was soon caught up in this movement; and after the publication of his *Institutes of the Christian Religion* (1536) and his move to Geneva in 1541, he became its most prominent theologian. The term "Calvinism" has been used much too broadly, however; for many other men contributed to the great Reformed consensus which was somewhat tardily documented (and then perhaps too explicitly documented) at the Synod of Dort in 1618–1619.[3]

The distinguishing feature of this consensus (and a major reason for its attractiveness during the Reformation's turbulent decades) was the logical thoroughness with which it repudiated the mediaeval religious and ecclesiastical tradition and replaced it with a clearly defined alternative. In theology this Reformed alternative showed large concern for the historic creeds of the

---

[3] This synod was an international council of Reformed divines that met to deal with modifications of strict predestinarian doctrine proposed by Jacobus Arminius (1560–1609). Since then the term "Arminianism" has become a generic term for Reformed theologies that accent man's freedom rather than total depravity and absolute divine sovereignty. See Philip Schaff, *The Creeds of Christendom*, 3 vols. (New York: Harper and Brothers, 1877; reprinted, 1931), III, 550–597. This is an invaluable work on the history of symbolics, including most of the confessions referred to in this volume. Even more germane is Williston Walker, *The Creeds and Platforms of Congregationalism* (1893), reissued with an Introduction by Douglas Horton (Boston: The Pilgrim Press, 1960).

early Church; but it made God's ordered and absolute sovereignty its central principle, drew out the doctrine of predestination in unambiguous terms, and in matters of worship, vestments, church furnishings, and ecclesiastical polity it purged the church of all "popish" accretions by stripping away everything for which it could not find explicit warrant in Scripture. In ethics it prescribed an austere "this-worldly asceticism."[4] Wherever possible, moreover, it was willing to enlist the authority of the state in the advancement of this program of reform and renovation.

The Puritans of England and America understood themselves to be participants in this Reformed advance; yet they entered into the work as Englishmen, and their distinctive program of reform—even their piety and theology—was shaped by the remarkable fact that England had an independent national church before it had a reformation.

From the time of England's separation from Rome there were men who sought a more thorough reformation of the English church, clergy, and people than Henry VIII had ever planned. Many of these proto-Puritans fled from England during the later years of Henry's reign. They returned to power and influence under Edward VI—only to be exiled or burned during Mary Tudor's reign (1553–1558). After the accession of Elizabeth, however, their cause waxed stronger, and for almost a full century their efforts to redefine Anglicanism gave England what was virtually a second reformation. At its core was a rigorous program for the application of biblical precepts and a revolutionary kind of experiential piety. The legalism which it sponsored—a "precisionistic" effort to apply God's law to every aspect of the world's affairs, private and public, personal and institutional—opened the way to the party spirit and harsh

---

[4] Max Weber, *The Protestant Ethic and the Spirit of Capitalism* (New York: Charles Scribner's Sons, 1930), pp. 148–154; John T. McNeill, *The History and Character of Calvinism* (New York: Oxford University Press, 1954).

sectarianism that shattered the movement and made Puritanism, in many eyes, a synonym for all that was narrow and divisive in Protestantism. But the new tradition of Christian inwardness which it forged served, on the other hand, as a powerful uniting bond among contending ecclesiastical parties, and became the chief basis for the movement's vast international influence.[5]

Puritan theology was formed in the context of the great doctrines of Reformed Christianity: God's awful sovereignty, man's utter depravity, the irresistibility of God's predestinating grace, and the justice of his withholding thereof. Yet it took its rise not in ecclesiastical assemblies but in the work of shepherding souls in turbulent times. It was therefore to a unique degree a *pastoral* theology, designed to console the fearful, convince the hesitant, set aright the erring, guide the unsure, and above all bring assurance of salvation to the Elect. Two components of its message always strained for predominance: a desire to clarify the nature of true Christian experience, and a concern for drawing out man's duties in the church and the world. The distinctive motif in Puritan religion was its combination of an unprecedented emphasis on the need for an inner experience of God's regenerating grace as a mark of election, and a conviction that all men must walk in the light of God's law. This same double motif helps to explain the prominence and persistence of covenant concepts in theologies of Puritan derivation.

The idea of covenant is so fundamental a feature of the Old and New Testaments that no Christian community could ever

---

[5] Because of its pervasive influence on subsequent Protestantism, the revolutionary character of the Puritan movement is often unappreciated. It was the first movement in Christian history to propose that a comprehensive, majesterial, government-supported, national church (not a withdrawn "sect") should yet have a membership limited to "visible saints" who could witness to a specific experience of God's regenerating grace. Even its tests of saintliness (or election) were almost without precedent. During the 1630's, moreover, such establishments were effected in the nearly autonomous commonwealths of Massachusetts and Connecticut. Later, the Puritan movement had large influence on Continental Pietism.

long be alien to it, but Puritanism has always been especially so identified. Indeed, by many scholars, the term Covenant or Federal Theology is taken to be synonymous with Puritan Theology. In part this identification is an exaggeration, yet it points to a distinct reality. That many Puritan Christians would consider themselves a "people of the Covenant" was almost inevitable. Persecuted, ridiculed, and abused during their formative period, and driven to the Old Testament by their need for historical precedents and specific legal guidance, they ineluctably came to identify their situation and their goals with those of the Chosen People, God's Israel. The victorious example of Scotland's covenanting people gave further support to such ideas. At a crucial point in the English Civil War, moreover, Scottish Presbyterians were able to impress covenant concepts into the heart of the movement's chief doctrinal symbols—the Westminster Confession and Catechisms.[6] In the American wilderness, the Puritan's situation and its parallel with Israel's role in history became even more striking.

In this context many Puritans went to elaborate lengths to define regeneration in covenantal terms. Claiming an old strand in Reformed—and pre-Reformation—theology, they understood conversion as culminating in a personal or internal covenant with God that validated the external covenant made in baptism. Reflecting the importance attached to this experience, they often conceived true church fellowship as existing when "visible saints" covenanted one with another. And finally, given their concern for moral order, civic duty, and the general welfare, they sometimes envisaged the body politic or commonwealth as

---

[6] The Westminster Confession fathered a whole family of influential symbols: the Congregationalist Savoy Declaration (1658) and its derivative confessions adopted in Massachusetts (1680) and Connecticut (1708), the London Baptist Confession (1677, 1688) and, derived from it, that of the Philadelphia Baptist Association (1724), and even *An Apology for the True Christian Divinity* by the Presbyterian-turned-Quaker, Thomas Barclay (Latin, 1676; English, 1678).

being collectively in covenant with the Lord for a special corporate task in the world.[7]

The danger of speaking of Puritanism in general terms, however, is that its unity will be exaggerated or that only some one part of it will be accepted as truly Puritan. Considering the years between 1558 and 1689, therefore, we would do well to imagine English history as a mighty prism through which the various emphases and passions of Puritanism were refracted— the temper of each passing period, and the dynamics of the movement itself, being discernible in the changing nature of the spectrum. And even the most casual students of either English or colonial American history are familiar with many aspects of this spectrum. On the right were those who, though satisfied with the *episcopal* government of an established national church, wished to make (or keep) its theology rigorously "Calvinistic" and its practice correspondingly austere. They worked to extend a Bible-oriented form of personal piety into all sectors of the clergy and laity, and sought to purge the Church of all but the most sober reminders of its mediaeval and Romish past. In this sense, Archbishop James Ussher (1581–1656) was a Puritan.

Somewhat more extreme than this group were the *Presbyterians* who proposed a different form of ecclesiastical hierarchicalism for governing a comprehensive national church, one in which Scottish example was especially strong. Though promi-

---

[7] On covenants in Puritan faith and practices see Perry Miller's several works on Puritanism; Edmund S. Morgan, *Visible Saints* (New York: New York University Press, 1963); Geoffrey Nuttall, *Visible Saints* (Oxford: Basil Blackwell, Ltd., 1957); and Norman Pettit, *The Heart Prepared: Grace and Conversion in Puritan Spiritual Life* (New Haven: Yale University Press, 1966). On the continuing force of covenantal thinking in America, see Perry Miller, "From the Covenant to the Revival," in James W. Smith and A. Leland Jamison, eds., *The Shaping of American Religion*, I (Princeton: Princeton University Press, 1961); Miller's posthumously published *The Life of the Mind in America* (New York: Harcourt, Brace & World, 1965); and Morgan's *Puritan Political Ideas* (Indianapolis, Ind.: The Bobbs-Merrill Company, 1965).

nent for a time after 1558, and dominant briefly in the 1640's, this "party" was ultimately of far more consequence for Scotland and North America than for England. Yet its intense doctrinal and theological concerns bore widespread fruit. The Westminster formularies are a great memorial to its high water mark in English history.

The Puritanism which gained ascendancy under Cromwell, and which became most securely institutionalized in America, was *Congregational* in its central proposals on church-order but was widely varying in other respects. Its distinguishing mark was a conviction that the local church was a self-sufficient ecclesiastical entity containing the essential "matter" of the Church and possessing all of the Church's historic powers (including ordination and excommunication). The more conservative Congregationalists accepted the idea of national responsibility, legal establishment, and infant baptism. They held that "separation" from fellowship with England's church was unpardonable fanaticism. A more radical group, the *Separatists*, felt conscience-bound to leave the national church and carry on their reformation without "tarrying" for king, parliament, or bishops. Still more radical among the congregational groups were the *Baptists* who found infant baptism inconsistent with the idea that the church must be separated from the state and consist of only regenerate "visible saints." In still other ways they adopted less objective conceptions of ordination, the ministry, and the sacraments. To the left of the Baptists many other groups began to take shape, especially during the Cromwellian period, when the army, far from assuring conformity, became itself a seedplot of radicalism. The Society of Friends, which began to form itself around the testimonies of George Fox in the 1650's, is by far the most famous of these left-wing groups, but there were many others (Ranters, Familists, etc.); and in defending themselves from their more radical critics, the *Quakers* in due course made clear that they held to a kind of highly spiritual congregationalism as against various extreme forms of individualism.

These years of Puritan ferment were also, and by no accident, the years of England's great imperial expansion in the New World; and given her permissive colonial policies (contrasting so sharply with those of Spain, France, and even Holland), almost every element in the "Puritan spectrum" gained a place on American soil in one or another of the colonies.[8] The overwhelming majority of the settlers who came later (even when they were Dutch, German, French, or Scottish) would only accentuate the basically Reformed character of the American colonial population. Since colonial times, therefore, a powerful Reformed and Puritan influence has shaped the moral, intellectual, and religious life of Americans.[9] This tradition also defines the character of the country's main theological developments.

Within a few years of the founding of the Massachusetts Bay Colony in 1630, New England became the world's most exemplary flowering place of Puritanism. Nowhere else did its genius express itself in so unhindered a fashion. Here Puritan statecraft and political theory were practiced in ways never open to Cromwell. Puritan ecclesiology had free rein. Puritan piety and morals shaped the private and public life of society. Theology, the intellectual life, and institutions of learning developed and revealed all the latent strengths and weaknesses of a powerful evangelical movement. And in all of these respects the New

---

[8] Puritanic Episcopalians in Virginia; Presbyterians as minorities everywhere but, in time, especially in the Middle Colonies; nonseparating Congregationalists in Massachusetts and Connecticut; Separatists in Plymouth and Rhode Island; Baptists first in Rhode Island but soon everywhere; Quakers first in Rhode Island then everywhere, but especially in New Jersey and Pennsylvania; and also radical individualists of various sorts, including Anne Hutchinson and (in some of his later moods) Roger Williams. In some cases there were strange inversions of English relationships: Episcopal dissenters in New England, Quaker governors in several colonies, Protestant dissenters under Roman Catholic governors in Maryland, and so on.

[9] Because of its wide effects on American culture, morals, thought, and church practice, some communions far removed from English ecclesiastical history (notably the Roman Catholics and Lutherans) have in America been profoundly "Puritanized" in various periods of their history.

England colonies became especially important because they did not remain tiny, isolated "utopian" communities. From the first they were nourished by an extensive emigration, which included many individuals of great and diverse gifts. Very rapidly the region became both populous and prosperous. In its characteristic way, therefore, New England faced the many social, economic, political, religious, and intellectual problems that agitated all of western Christendom. Indeed, not only did it *face* these problems, it *dealt* with them. By the time a centennial retrospect was possible, the New England churches could proudly (perhaps too proudly) claim a score of men who had achieved genuine, though sometimes quite unsung, theological eminence. Eminence, to be sure, is often transient. Yet one may confidently say of the early fathers of New England—whether, like Thomas Hooker, they emigrated permanently and became founders of colonies, or, like William Ames and Richard Sibbes, they merely lived in America through their books and their students—that they had an enduring influence not only on American theology itself but on the institutions and popular attitudes that have formed its matrix through the centuries.

The nature of Puritan influence is a controversial matter. At one time or another it has been condemned for nearly every latter-day evil or thanked for nearly every real or imagined American virtue. Yet all this praise and blame serves, at least, to emphasize the movement's enormous shaping power. One need not pause here to evaluate its significance for the country's economic and political development; but in the realm of theology we must remember at least three elements of the Puritan legacy. It awakened Protestant concern for the experiential dimension of God's grace. It promulgated a conception of personal and public duty, and of life under God's law that is the effective origin of the American "Social Gospel." It put a high premium on public literacy, the general diffusion of knowledge, a learned clergy, and a reasoned understanding of the faith. It thus conveyed to posterity a deep-seated resistance to the temptations of intellectual sloth and moral indifference (see Selection I).

THE GREAT AWAKENING

Cotton Mather, son and grandson of distinguished leaders in the New England churches, died in 1728, disappointed by signs of declining zeal on every hand and unable to know that the isolated revivals already occurring were heralds of a great spiritual resurgence. In four years Jonathan Edwards would publish the first element in his monumental corpus, and a new era in American theological history would be at hand. These were years of transition. Indeed, the European *crise de la conscience,* which Paul Hazard has so brilliantly described with special concern for his native France, had its New World counterpart.[10] The turn-of-century decades (1680–1720) were a critical turning point in New England's spiritual history.

The simple yet enormously complex element of growth was the primary factor. Between 1630 and 1730 New England was transformed from a series of insecure settlements scattered between Cape Anne and Cape Cod to a bustling provincial society.[11] The "American Revolution" was rapidly becoming a reality: a free, individualistic, democratic society was taking shape. As in the other colonies, an absence of aristocratic privilege, the availability of land and other natural resources, and the immigrant's characteristically ambitious set of mind were creating a new kind of culture that was Western but not European. The social diversification of "early bourgeois civilization" was strongly in

---

[10] Paul Hazard, *La crise de la conscience européene, 1680–1715* (Paris: Voivin & Cie., 1935), in translation as *The European Mind, The Critical Years* (New Haven: Yale University Press, 1953).

[11] By 1689 the population of British America was already 180,000, and by the accession of Queen Anne (1702) the figure had risen to 270,000. New England in this later period was by far the most homogeneous and unified region. Even by 1775 only 5 per cent of its population was non-English. See maps in Curtis P. Nettels, *The Roots of American Civilization* (New York: F. S. Crofts & Co., 1940), pp. 226, 227, 394–397.

evidence, most markedly in the larger commercial centers on the coast. Sectional feelings between this maritime area and the agricultural towns were not only intensifying but were being deepened by cultural differentiation. New England, in short, had achieved a kind of robust adolescence—but not without practical ecclesiastical problems of a very serious kind.

These problems stemmed from an anomaly of the original settlements, namely, that congregations were organized in a "sectarian" manner with the membership restricted to "visible saints" while at the same time these churches played a "churchly" role in society, being established, supported, and defended by the state. The churches were encharged, as the sole bearers of orthodoxy, to carry out in an essentially mediaeval manner all of the classic ecclesiastical functions for all of the people. Membership problems ensued, with the Half-Way Covenant (1662) as the single largest milestone along a course that led to an increasingly widespread acceptance of all professed Christians as members.[12] Inevitably, this meant that the piety of the churches was no longer that of a fervent elite called out of the multitude, but

---

12 In Massachusetts and Connecticut the churches had generally baptized, or accepted into membership, the baptized children of duly covenanted members, citing Israel's practice of circumcision as their legal precedent. But what if (as inevitably happened) these children, when adults, had not had this external covenant confirmed by a conversion experience, that is, by a "circumcision of the heart"? The Massachusetts Synod of 1662 answered the question by underlining the importance of the external covenant (against the Baptists) and came to terms with social reality by recommending that duly baptized adults be regarded as church members if they professed the faith and lived uprightly. They could, in turn, have *their* children baptized, but these *Half-Way* members were denied full privileges. They could not receive the Lord's Supper or participate in churchly decisions such as excommunications. By 1700 both the original requirements and the Half-Way Covenant had been very widely modified. Later the Great Awakening would bring further reversals and innovations. But the effects of this dual conception of membership were felt in New England in various ways for two centuries. The Unitarian Cyrus A. Bartol attacked the perpetuation of the dual-membership tradition in his *Church and Congregation: A Plea for Their Unity* (Boston: Ticknor and Fields, 1858).

simply that of a cross section of a provincial English people. A whole literature of lamentation inevitably arose, and the "Jeremiad" became a major literary form. The entire idea of a national covenant was jeopardized; legislative and synodical efforts to strengthen orthodoxy, tighten organization, and reawaken old ideals were undertaken. Most fateful of the new strategies was the resort to a kind of revivalism in which the Puritan's historic fear of unbridled "enthusiasm" and his demand for rationally controlled experiences of conversion gradually yielded to more productive measures. Solomon Stoddard of Northampton, Massachusetts, was the first to announce and deliberately employ these revivalistic strategies, and his repeated successes between 1680 and 1720 heralded the New England phase of the Great Awakening.

Behind Puritan declension, however, lay much more than population growth and economic diversification. Perhaps most fundamental of all was New England's participation in that profound shift of world-view that announced the Age of Reason. Nor was this a late development. We must remember that men such as Cotton, Hooker, and Winthrop were contemporaries of John Milton, separated by a century from Calvin, affected by the logical and rhetorical reforms of Petrus Ramus as well as other humanistic thinkers, and in touch with many currents of thought stemming from the Renaissance. With the passing years a latent concern for rational order became increasingly apparent in their writings. They were prepared for Isaac Newton's sensational demonstration of universal orderliness, and they moved with regular steps toward an accommodation of natural law concepts and an acceptance of John Locke's defense of the Glorious Revolution of 1688–1689. In 1721 Cotton Mather, the supposed defender of the Old Order, published a work called *The Christian Philosopher* which a later historian rightly saw as the starting point for his history of American Deism![13]

---

[13] Herbert M. Morais, *Deism in Eighteenth-Century America* (New York: Columbia University Press, 1934).

The combination of these intellectual developments with practical problems of church-order would lead during the turn-of-century decades to ecclesiastical disruption and to the emergence of what were, in effect, two New Englands. In eastern Massachusetts the organization of the Brattle Street Church (1699), the ousting of Increase Mather as president of Harvard, and his subsequent replacement by John Leverett (1708) are three signs among a cluster of others that different men and new ideas were prevailing. Solomon Stoddard's provocative departures, the founding of Yale College in 1701 with covert support from the Mathers, and in 1708–1709 a legal presbyterianizing of the Connecticut churches illustrate the contrary tendency. As social and economic differentiation became increasingly prominent, a kind of ecclesiastical sectionalism resulted, with one region moving toward reasonable moralism, and the other toward experiential orthodoxy.

Then in 1734 came that small but momentous event in Northampton—another season of spiritual harvest. But this time Stoddard's grandson, Jonathan Edwards, occupied the ministerial office. What followed is one of the best known episodes in American church history: a brief and fairly solemn "frontier revival," chiefly in the Connecticut Valley towns; a lull, and then a resurgence of enthusiasm through which the New England revival became part of a colonial awakening, which was in turn but the New World phase of the great evangelical revival that was sweeping Great Britain and Protestant Europe. The Age of Reason, after all, was also the Age of Pietism. The threads of connection within this vast international phenomenon were many and various,[14] but none takes on greater significance for

---

14 The interweaving of diverse influences is a fascinating feature of the international evangelical revival: the Puritan William Ames' teaching in the Netherlands; Spener's reading of Dutch and Puritan devotional works; John Wesley's heartwarming contacts with German Moravians as well as his reading and republication of Edwards' account of the Northampton revivals, and so on.

Americans than the labors of John Wesley's highly independent cohort, George Whitefield (1714–1770), who found time for no less than seven missionary journeys to the colonies.

Whitefield's second journey, during the years 1739–1741, was especially important. Not only did his arrival in the Middle Colonies bring decisive support to a Presbyterian revival party just as their efforts were reaching a peak, but he also carried this fervor northward with a whirlwind tour of New England. On his way he preached from the Northampton pulpit and reportedly moved Edwards to tears. More than any other, Whitefield bound together various regional revivals into a single Great Awakening. He became the first truly "national" American figure, and in the process also something of an American church father. For at least a century and a half his kind of revivalism would remain the major evangelistic strategy of the Protestant mainstream. Next to the planting of diverse strands of the Puritan movement in America during the period of colonization, no other force exceeded the Great Awakening in its shaping power on the institutions, piety, preaching, and thinking of the American churches.

In the midst of the anxieties and conflicts which this Awakening provoked, Jonathan Edwards lived out his brilliant and tragic career. But with the lengthening of our historical perspective the scope of his achievement becomes clearer. Though he appears as a solitary colonial pastor caught between the contradictory demands of Pietism and the Enlightenment, his total work can now be seen as a magnificent effort to transcend that dichotomy. He looms as *the* theologian of a vast international revival and the chief intellectual ornament of its American phase (see Selection II).

ENLIGHTENED RELIGION

What in 1710 had been a discernible rift in the precarious unity of Puritan New England was transformed into open rupture by the Great Awakening. By 1750 contrary-minded theologies had taken root and the region became a kind of double seedplot of revivalism and rationalism. What Yale and Edwards were to the one, Harvard and Channing would be to the other—but that is to get ahead of the story.

Charles Chauncy (1705–1787) was the leading champion of Christian rationalism in the post-Awakening years. During a sixty-year ministry at Boston's First Church he gave voice to nearly every major facet of the new liberalism: Arminianism, universalism, antitrinitarianism, and a strong hostility for enthusiastic religion. Jonathan Mayhew (1720–1766), his contemporary at the desk of West Church in Boston, also lent his eloquence to the cause, adding to it a distinct political animus and a sharp anti-Anglican edge even before the Stamp Act crisis of 1765–1766. With the next generation, a self-conscious movement of both clergy and laymen would give "the neighborhood of Boston" its fame (or notoriety) as a cockpit of advanced thinking in both the political and the theological realms.

More clearly than most other movements, moreover, this one illustrated how closely the cause of reasonableness and moralism in religion was linked with the growing demands for a political order based on natural law and self-evident principle. By 1800, after four decades of continual concern with American constitutional problems, almost the entire social establishment of the Boston area had undergone a quiet religious revolution. When accused, as it would be, of having become Unitarian, it found itself willing, after a brief show of outrage, to take pride in the fact.

Between the outrage and the pride there took place a major American theological controversy, with the forces of orthodoxy —now ensconced in their new bastion at Andover Seminary (1809)—joined in argument with the Unitarians who had taken over in Boston and at Harvard. Questions of the Trinity loomed large in this great debate but the central issue was the nature and destiny of man, with orthodoxy relying chiefly on its Edwardsean arsenal, and Unitarians relying on Enlightened convictions as to God's benevolence and man's freedom, goodness, and rationality. In this conflict several distinguished liberal leaders emerged, but none of them equaled William Ellery Channing in influence or persuasiveness.[15] His famous Baltimore Sermon on "Unitarian Christianity" became the movement's manifesto, and as other more organization-minded men founded a new denomination, he came to personify the movement's highest ideals. Under his long ministry the Federal Street Church in Boston became, after Harvard College, the main intellectual and moral center of the "liberal faith."

When Lyman Beecher came to the American Athens in 1826 as a crusader for revivalistic orthodoxy, he was appalled by the prestige and power of the phalanx that confronted him: "All the literary men of Massachusetts were Unitarian; all the trustees and professors of Harvard College were Unitarians; all the *elite* of wealth and fashion crowded Unitarian churches; the judges on the bench were Unitarian . . ."[16]

What Lyman Beecher did not do, and what no historian has attempted in any thorough way so far, is to answer the deeper historical question: Why did America's earliest organized movement of explicit religious liberalism take shape almost exclu-

---

[15] The origins of the Unitarian Controversy are beyond tracing; in a sense they go back to (but are by no means to be identified with) the Christological controversies of the early Church. Jedidiah Morse's accusations and Channing's public letter to Thacher mark its formal opening in Boston (1815). Channing's Baltimore Sermon in 1819 was the next major pronouncement, though Andrews Norton's attack on Trinitarians came out in the same year. Two orthodox replies followed in 1819 and 1820 by Moses Stuart and Leonard Woods, both of Andover Seminary, and to these came rejoinders, the most important that of Henry Ware, Sr., which led on to the lengthy "Wood 'n Ware" debate. Nobody has counted, much less read, the total published yield of the Unitarian Controversy. Yet on both sides, there were dignified and important contributions that merit close study.

[16] Lyman Beecher, *The Autobiography*, Barbara Cross, ed., 2 vols. (Cambridge, Mass.: Harvard University Press, 1961), II, 82.

sively in the oldest Puritan congregations? Obviously no full
answer will be attempted here, but three vital factors can be
suggested. The fact of congregationalism is primary; it provided
a church-order that allowed the doctrinal position of local
churches to undergo gradual alteration, in the words of one
early church-covenant, "according as [God] is pleased to re-
veale himself unto us . . ."[17] Alarm over spiritual "declension"
and widespread doctrinal deviation did lead the Connecticut
churches in 1708 to adopt a confession and to establish a presby-
terial system of control; but in Massachusetts similar proposals,
advanced by the Mathers, were defeated, in part because the
charter of 1691 had put a royal governor in Boston. As a result
there was no way of enforcing allegiance to the Confession of
Faith which the "Reforming Synod" had belatedly adopted
in 1680.

Certain elements in Puritan theology constitute a second
factor: it was from the start pervaded by Platonic or other
rationalistic elements as well as a profound fear of unrestrained
enthusiasm. Puritans prized the intellect and easily recoiled
from excesses such as those the Great Awakening encouraged.[18]
In eastern Massachusetts, moreover, the social and economic
situation provided a third factor of significance: a maritime
society with an increasingly prosperous, urbane, and decorous
"ruling class," open to British influences and naturally inclined
to flattering views of human nature and to optimism about
man's earthly destiny. Given the power of this merchant elite
to shape the churches and Harvard College to their inclinations,
pressures for modifying the institutions and thought-patterns of
the old order were very efficacious. It was understandable and

---

[17] Walker, *Creeds and Platforms of Congregationalism*, p. 116.

[18] Undeniable grounds for the opposite trend to enthusiasm and revivalism also existed. Puritanism was an unstable movement both in practice
and theory. Separation of its component elements was the price of equilibrium.

natural, therefore, that congregational church-order, Puritan theology, and a prosperous commercial society should lack many of the historic hindrances to doctrinal drift, and should prosper the growth of liberal religion and ultimately even that flowering of New England Unitarianism which some would designate a veritable "American Renaissance" (see Selection III).

MODERN PURITANISM
AND THE NEW HAVEN THEOLOGY

While movements of theological liberalism were taking their course in eastern Massachusetts, the "orthodox" tradition established itself elsewhere in New England. The evangelical religion that dominated this "hinterlands province" received its chief theological inspiration from Edwards and its institutional vitality flowed from the Great Awakening. But the later French and Indian Wars, and then the conflicts culminating in the War for Independence provided an extremely inhospitable climate for either theology or evangelism. The revival fires sputtered out. Meanwhile even the strictest of Edwards' followers found irresistible the temptation to translate theological ideas into political, legal, and governmental terms. An important work did go on, however, and despite many distractions a genuine "flowering of New England" also occurred in this region during the age of Channing, Longfellow, and Emerson.

In theology, the essential history of the area and period is an unfolding of the Edwardsean tradition—the growth of what historians have called the New England Theology. First among these Edwardsean successors were two men who studied with the master in his own manse: Joseph Bellamy (1719–1790) and Samuel Hopkins (1721–1803), and then their pupil, Jonathan Edwards the Younger (1745–1801). These men, and the dozens of dedicated men whom they trained, succeeded in taking over most of the orthodox Congregational parishes of New England during the last half of the eighteenth century.[19] The "Consistent Calvinists" or "New Divinity men" who led this party were penetrating, even brilliant thinkers but they lacked Edwards' sublime vision of God's glory as well as his versatility of mind. And because they were usually dour in outward manner and strict in their views on doctrine and church-membership, their congregations were often small. During the 1790's, however, their parishes began to be visited by a continuing series of somber revivals which they interpreted as a providential reward for their Edwardsean loyalty. Between 1800 and 1820 what had been sporadic became general; a second Great Awakening had come to New England and there was great evangelical joy.[20]

Timothy Dwight (1752–1817), grandson of Edwards and president of Yale from 1795 to 1817, was at the center of the New England phase of this great revival. Aside from this institutional station, Dwight was involved in many of the voluntary associations which proliferated during these decades to advance humanitarian, reformist, and missionary causes. He was also a revisionist in theology, and can almost be reckoned the founder of the highly moralistic, reform-minded, and activistic forms of Modern Puritanism that became a dominant element in nineteenth-century evangelicalism. Because his theological works

---

19 See maps charting the advance of orthodox Yale graduates as ministers in the churches of New England for the years 1740, 1775, and 1804 in Conrad Wright, *The Beginnings of Unitarianism in America* (Boston: The Beacon Press, 1955), pp. 34, 257.

20 The "western phase" of this great revival began independently and under quite different auspices in Kentucky; but gradually as the raw frontier ethos changed, East-West distinctions yielded to those of North and South. The presuppositions and strategies of revivalism, nevertheless, remained the most powerful normative forces in the Protestantism of all sections during the ante-bellum half-century. See Charles A. Johnson, *The Frontier Camp Meeting: Religion's Harvest Time* (Dallas: Southern Methodist University Press, 1955); Timothy L. Smith, *Revivalism and Social Reform* (Nashville, Tenn.: Abingdon Press, 1957); and Sidney E. Mead, *The Lively Experiment: The Shaping of Christianity in America* (New York: Harper & Row, 1963), pp. 90–133.

were widely read for a generation and because his followers were legion, he played a large role in clouding over the average American's understanding of both the Edwardsean and early Puritan traditions.[21] Shortly after Dwight's death, his dream of a divinity school at Yale was realized and one of his protégés, Nathaniel William Taylor (1786–1858), was appointed to the key professorial chair. Another of his admiring students, Lyman Beecher (1775–1863), went on to become an enormously influential field campaigner for the evangelical counterreformation. With such leadership the New Haven Theology became a major force on the American scene. Taylor made his mark as an effective revival preacher at New Haven's Center Church, but it was through his later writings and as a professor of theology addressing large classes of future ministers and missionaries at the Yale Divinity School that he earned Frank H. Foster's praise as "the most original, powerful, and widely influential mind which New England theology ever possessed."[22] The chief key to his success was his provision of an extremely plausible "common-sense" rationale for the revivals that were sweeping the country during his lifetime.

Taylor did not use the term "common sense" in its general meaning only, however, but in a special way that places him in an intellectual movement that dominated American religious thought for over a century. The chief philosophic pillar of Tay-

---

[21] Dwight's metaphysical talent was limited, but his accent on human agency and his legalism became important elements in the New Haven Theology. Believing that no Christian who "learns and performs his duty to the utmost of his power . . . will fail of being finally accepted," he gave an elaborate "system of duties" unprecedented prominence in his theology. See *Theology, Explained and Defended in a Series of Sermons*, 4 vols. (1818), I, Sermons 16, 268. On the "System of Duties," see III–IV, Sermons 91–162.

[22] Frank Hugh Foster, *A Genetic History of the New England Theology* (Chicago: University of Chicago Press, 1907), p. 246. Foster's large work is the only study of the Edwardsean tradition as an organic whole. In *The Modern Movement in American Theology* (New York: Fleming H. Revell Company, 1939) Foster describes the disintegration of that tradition.

lor's theology was the Common-Sense Realism that was developed during the eighteenth century in the Enlightened atmosphere of the Scottish universities by Thomas Reid and Dugald Stewart. Taylor, to be sure, was only one among the hundreds of American exponents of this crisp, rationalistic way of explaining things. But he was a potent factor in extending the life of "Scottish Philosophy" in American Protestantism just at the time when a wide variety of new countercurrents were winning acceptance in other spheres.[23] While taking the role of defender of evangelical religion from Unitarian error, he could use these philosophic tools to fit his theology to the aspirations of democratic Americans by underlining the essential freedom and moral agency of man. With his intellectual emphasis and praise of decorum he could also counteract the new kind of high-pressure revivalism which Charles G. Finney was spreading across the country.[24]

The chief representative significance of Dwight, Taylor, and

---

23 See my "The Scottish Philosophy and American Theology," *Church History*, XXIV (September 1, 1955). Taylor's works would not lead one to suspect that Rousseau, Kant, Schleiermacher, Coleridge, or Emerson had made any impact on Western religious thought whatsoever.

24 Charles Grandison Finney (1792–1875) was born in Connecticut, but as a child moved with his parents to upstate New York. He was practicing law in 1821 when his conversion led him into the Presbyterian ministry and then to a career that brought him international fame as a revivalist. He offended many with his "New Measures" for getting conversions and provoked accusations of heresy from the Old School by stressing human freedom, perfectionism, and the need for socially significant commitment (notably on the slavery issue). In 1835–1836 he began a second career as a Congregationalist, as a professor of theology, and later as president of Oberlin College. His *Lectures on Systematic Theology* (1846) validated his new calling and made clear that he had carried Reformed teaching well beyond Taylor and almost into the Methodist camp. Though derivative and intellectually unimpressive, Finney's theology stands very near the center of the popular evangelicalism of his day. His *Lectures on Revivals of Religion* (1835) in like manner document his role as the founder of modern revivalism. See William G. McLoughlin, *Modern Revivalism* (New York: The Ronald Press, 1959) and Perry Miller, *Life of the Mind in America*, pp. 3–98.

Beecher consists in the impetus they gave to a broad New School tradition of Reformed theology and practice. As expounded by various Congregational, Presbyterian, Methodist, and Baptist theologians, "New Schoolism" became, in effect, the ecumenical theology of nonsectarian revivalism, the Sunday School movement, foreign and domestic missions, and a wide array of organized reform activities, notably the temperance crusade. One can almost speak of it as the theology of American Evangelical Protestantism during its nineteenth-century heyday. It was frankly Arminian in its modifications of predestinarian dogma, vigorous in its emphasis on conversion and personal holiness, immensely moralistic in its definition of the good life, strong in millenial fervor, determined to make a model of America's Protestant democracy, and belligerently suspicious of Roman Catholicism both as a rapidly growing church and as a possible influence on Christian belief and practice.

The activistic evangelical tradition in which Taylor found his audience was often narrow in its vision and fiercely anti-intellectual. To a tragic degree its rank and file became alienated from the century's revolutionary developments in science, scholarship, and philosophy. They created the simplistic outlook from which latter-day Fundamentalism would develop.[25] Taylor's mental stance and philosophic allegiance undoubtedly contributed to this situation. On the other hand, he also did much to inspire an interest in cultural reform among those who joined the great "Yankee exodus" to the West; and many of his students became prominent as educators and intellectual leaders (see Selection IV).

THE PRINCETON THEOLOGY AND CONSERVATISM

The New Haven Theology, like the several variants of New School theology that developed in other denominations, was

---

[25] On Fundamentalism, see p. 70.

undeniably liberal in its departures from classic Reformed theology; and neither support of revivalism nor strict personal ethics could veil the fact. Conservative critics, therefore, were quick to complain. One major attack emanated from the Andover Seminary which had considered itself a veritable "West Point of Orthodoxy" ever since the Unitarian Controversy had led to its founding. In Connecticut a long and bitter controversy finally resulted in semi-schism. In 1834 Bennet Tyler led a large group of churches to found Hartford Seminary as another orthodox bastion.[26] It was among the Presbyterians, however, that the most enduring and powerful alternative to Taylorite heresy and all similar departures was formulated and defended.

Men of Presbyterian inclination had made their way to America from earliest times. In New England they had continuously and successfully steered Congregationalism toward more connectional forms of organization. But the first true presbytery was not formed until 1706 in Philadelphia. New England influences soon rose to prominence in this new church, however, and after the Great Awakening became predominant.[27] In 1758 Jonathan Edwards was called to the presidency of the young Presbyterian college at Princeton. The increased flow of Scottish and Scots-Irish immigration gradually overcame this tendency, but even then the Second Awakening weakened traditionalist power by stimulating a strong New School impulse in Presbyterianism. Only with the founding of a general seminary for the denomination at Princeton in 1812 were the possibilities for countervailing influence put into effect, and Archibald Alexan-

---

[26] This seminary was founded at East Windsor by the Connecticut Pastoral Union and it moved to Hartford in 1865. See Curtis M. Geer, *The Hartford Theological Seminary, 1834–1934* (Hartford, Conn.: The Case, Lockwood and Brainard Company, 1934).

[27] See Leonard J. Trinterud, *The Forming of an American Tradition* (Philadelphia: The Westminster Press, 1949) on the Great Awakening in the Middle Colonies, its impact on Presbyterianism, and the founding of the College of New Jersey (Princeton).

der, the first professor in the seminary, set about to realize these possibilities. He is the founder of the Princeton Theology. But it was his pupil and colleague, Charles Hodge (1797–1878), who became the chief architect of Reformed confessionalism at the seminary. And long before his combative career drew to a close, his son, Archibald Alexander Hodge (1823–1886), was active in the role. Benjamin Warfield (1851–1921) and J. Gresham Machen (1881–1937) maintained the institution's reputation for unbending but erudite conservatism down to 1929–1936, when both the seminary and the denomination were disrupted by conservative secessions.[28]

During this century-long period, when the Presbyterian Church was divided first by a New School-Old School schism and then by North-South separations, the Princeton theologians led the attack on Taylorism in their church, resisted Finney's New Measures in revivalism, defended a strict interpretation of polity against Congregational inroads, and discouraged Presbyterian support for interdenominational evangelism. In the face of biblical-critical studies, Darwinism, and the rise of new forms of theological liberalism they continued to draw strength from Scottish, Swiss, and Dutch dogmatics and also propounded their own characteristic defenses—most famously an inflexible doctrine of Scriptural inspiration. They did all of this, moreover, with a sense of theological and scholarly responsibility, with a genuine concern for thoroughness and excellency. As a result they became almost the official spokesmen on these matters for a large sector of American Protestant conservatism. During the long bitter years of the Fundamentalist Controversy (1890–1930)[29] they thus performed an important stabilizing role not unlike that of the Scottish Presbyterians during the

---

[28] See Lefferts A. Loetscher, *The Broadening Church: A Study of Theological Issues in the Presbyterian Church since 1869* (Philadelphia: University of Pennsylvania Press, 1954).

[29] On the Fundamentalist Controversy, see p. 70.

English civil war of the mid-seventeenth century. Part and parcel with their positive contribution, however, was an extraordinarily brittle and literalistic view of biblical infallibility and confessional subscription which tended to isolate later adherents from much twentieth-century theological discussion (see Selection V).

ROMANTIC CURRENTS IN THE REFORMED TRADITION

During the nineteenth century, American theology was increasingly affected by movements and church traditions not arising from the turbulent post-Reformation history of Great Britain. One obvious explanation for this change is the crescendo in immigration which began to alter the overwhelmingly "Anglo-Saxon" texture of the population. By World War I the entire denominational equilibrium was transformed. Not only were the four largest colonial churches (Congregational, Presbyterian, Episcopal, and Quaker) eclipsed by the sensational rise of revivalistic demoninations (Methodist and Baptist), but also Roman Catholics and Lutherans were numbered among the nation's four largest communions. One ugly result of this phenomenon was the outbreak of Nativism and violent anti-Catholicism during the years 1830–1855 and again after 1880.[30] Along with immigration, however, there was a steady influx of European ideas, particularly from Germany. The printed word was the main bearer of these new intellectual currents, with such British thinkers as Coleridge and Carlyle serving as major media-

---

[30] The Puritan's fierce antipathy for things Roman Catholic became one of his most enduring legacies to American Protestantism, including its theology. See Mary Augustina Ray, *American Opinion of Roman Catholicism in the Eighteenth Century* (New York: Columbia University Press, 1936); Ray A. Billington, *The Protestant Crusade, 1800–1860* (New York: The Macmillan Co., 1938); John Higham, *Strangers in the Land: Patterns of American Nativism, 1860–1925* (New Brunswick, N.J.: Rutgers University Press, 1955); and Edward D. Baltzell, *The Protestant Establishment: Aristocracy and Caste in America* (New York: Random House, 1964).

tors. Some influential European theologians and scholars came to America, however; and even more important were the Americans who, after 1815, in ever increasing numbers pursued advanced studies in German universities. Upon returning, they usually became enthusiastic renovators of the methods and presuppositions then prevailing in American seminaries and universities.[31]

Accompanying these various developments, in Europe as well as in America, was a vast change of intellectual temper and spiritual outlook, which has often been labeled "romantic."[32] In America nearly all of these trends challenged the assumptions and practices of the Protestant mainstream, intensifying some old controversies and undercutting others. Some romantics were highly critical of tradition and even radical in their reform programs, Emersonian Transcendentalism being perhaps the most famous American instance. Others were emphatic in their defense of ecclesiastical traditions and conservative in their plans for church renewal. Whereas doubts about the Lord's Supper led Emerson to leave the ministry, a desire to restore the Church's sacramental life led Nevin to the threshold of Rome. And if some liberals used history to ground their confidence in the future, conservatives often made historical study a means for reclaiming tradition.

Certainly the most familiar American romantic manifestation was that storm in a Boston teapot whipped up by the Transcendentalists between 1830 and 1860, with Ralph Waldo Emer-

---

[31] See Jurgen Herbst, *The German Historical School in American Scholarship* (Ithaca, N.Y.: Cornell University Press, 1965); Henry A. Pochmann, *German Culture in America* (Madison, Wisc.: University of Wisconsin Press, 1957).

[32] Some critics consider the word "romanticism" meaningless, but I believe the scholarly literature on the subject does deal with a reasonably distinct phase of Western spiritual history. See René Wellek, "The Concept of Romanticism in Literary History" and "Romanticism Re-examined," in *Concepts of Criticism* (New Haven: Yale University Press, 1963), pp. 128–255.

son (1803–1882) indisputably at their head. By the time of his death a half century after the initial call to arms, the Concord Seer had become an august figure in the American pantheon, and domesticated forms of his leading doctrines had won wide acceptance. Emerson's theological significance, however, is more appropriately considered later—in connection with the rise of religious liberalism.[33]

For the English-speaking world the most sensational outbreak of conservative romantic theology occurred in Oriel College, Oxford, were John Henry Newman and his fellow "Tractarians" sought to lead the Church of England away from its subservience to the state and from its Reformation heritage. Newman himself entered the Roman Catholic Church in 1845, but John Keble and Edward B. Pusey continued to lead the "Catholic revival" in the Anglican communion. In the meantime a parallel and outwardly more successful movement emerged at Cambridge University, where interest centered chiefly on the revival of gothic architecture and mediaeval liturgical practice.[34] In the United States feelings were especially aroused because this reawakening of the "church question" happened to come just when anti-Catholic agitation was at its height. The Episcopal Church became embroiled very soon in internal controversies which even after a century remained very much alive. Theologically speaking, however, the "Oxford movement" had little or no productive result in American Episcopal theology, possibly because Newman had said so magnificently all there was to say—and then had gone on to say too much for an officially "Protestant" church.[35]

---

[33] See pp. 58-64, 293-316.

[34] See Eugene Fairweather, ed., *The Oxford Movement,* (New York: Oxford University Press, Library of Protestant Thought, 1964); James F. White, *The Cambridge Movement* (Cambridge, England: Cambridge University Press, 1962).

[35] See N. P. Williams and Charles Harris, eds., *Northern Catholicism, Centenary Studies in the Oxford and Parallel Movements* (New York: The Macmillan Company, 1933), including an essay by Edward R. Hardy, Jr., on the American movement.

On the European continent there flowed a far wider and deeper current of romantic thought, scholarship, and religious renewal—one in which Catholic, Protestant, and laic influences were often blended. This vast spiritual revolution was in many ways a repudiation of the major tenets of the Enlightenment. More positively, it was a call to the heart, a critique of formalism and artificiality, a plea for warmth, sentiment, and honest subjectivity, a summons to self-consciousness and authentic expression of a person's (or a nation's) genius. On philosophic questions, these religious thinkers tended toward monistic, dynamic, and idealistic modes of construing reality, and often to mystical and pantheistic views. A movement of disciplined historical scholarship also arose and it, in turn, led to the "discovery" of many thinkers, movements, and even whole epochs that, because of ignorance or Enlightened bias, had been repudiated or nearly forgotten.

The most striking American response in this realm emerged in the German Reformed Church, a small denomination whose single, half-extinct seminary in Mercersburg, Pennsylvania, seemed little capable of appropriating the powerful new religious forces which the century was releasing. Every indication suggested that the denomination would soon be absorbed by the revivalistic and virulently anti-Catholic evangelicalism that was sweeping the country, and which by 1830 had led to the organization of three separate revivalistic churches among the Pennsylvania Germans.[36] Yet it was in this unlikely context that the Mercersburg Theology rose to prominence.[37] It was particularly ironic that the movement's leader, John Williamson

---

[36] These churches were the Evangelical Association (1803–1807), the United Brethren in Christ (1800–1815), and the Winebrennerian Church of God (1830). In 1946 the first two of these merged and in 1966 this united body merged with the Methodist Church.

[37] James H. Nichols, *Romanticism in American Theology: Nevin and Schaff at Mercersburg* (Chicago: University of Chicago Press, 1961), also deals extensively with the European background.

Nevin (1803–1886), was a product of Union College and Princeton Seminary, and a star pupil of Charles Hodge himself. He was joined on the Mercersburg faculty in 1844 by another young mediator of German church-historical scholarship and post-Kantian theology—Philip Schaff (1819–1893)—who had recently completed his advanced studies at the University of Berlin. Through their efforts the *Mercersburg Review* became a distinguished journal and the seminary an exciting center of church renewal. Nowhere else in the country did idealistic philosophy, modern biblical study, historical scholarship, and intense practical concern have such a creative theological result.

During its most flourishing period the Mercersburg movement was so controversial that schism in the German Reformed Church was only narrowly averted. Countermovements were launched from two new educational institutions, some opposition leaders moved to the Dutch Reformed Church, and after the Civil War most of the movement's distinctive claims were gradually sacrificed to the cause of denominational unity. Amidst the renewal of Catholic-Evangelical dialogue inspired by Pope John XXIII and the Second Vatican Council, however, the works of Nevin and Schaff have been found to have more relevance and provocative power than those of any other American theological impulse of the nineteenth century (see Selection XIII).

LUTHERANS AND THE CONFESSIONAL RENEWAL

Nevin often directed warnings to the "German churches"—and in the Pennsylvania of his day such wording was meant to include the Lutherans. This was appropriate, since both churches, even though linguistically separated from Anglo-Saxon America, had been yielding to American forms of evangelical faith and practice ever since the Great Awakening. There were, of course, important differences between Lutherans and the Ger man Reformed,[38] but in the colonial period they had been so far subordinated to ethnic considerations that union congregations had become common. During the nineteenth century, however, new currents of theology and a great increase in immigration began to reverse this trend. Thus, Lutheranism came to experience tensions very similar to those provoked at Mercersburg among the German Reformed, except that they were compounded by the organization in the West of new Lutheran communions reflecting the Saxon, Bavarian, Prussian, Swedish, Danish, or Norwegian origins of their membership. An extended crisis of self-definition resulted, with the most memorable events being concentrated in the years between 1855 and 1870.

The Americanizing position was expounded best by the man who dominated nearly a half century of Lutheran history, Samuel S. Schmucker (1799–1873). In his early years, however, when trying to end the sway of the Enlightenment's rationalistic theology, he did much to arouse the Lutheran loyalties of the older eastern churches which had organized themselves in a General Synod in 1821. He also helped to found a Lutheran college and seminary at Gettysburg. But with the passing years he became increasingly identified with the many voluntary associations of the "evangelical united front," and in 1838 published a *Fraternal*

---

[38] The most basic difference between these two churches stems from the reason that the Augsburg Confession of 1530, the chief Lutheran symbol, was expressly an irenicon designed to minimize differences with Rome. Lutherans, therefore, were not programatically antitraditional in liturgical practice and sacramental theology. Also important were long-standing differences on Law and Gospel, in which the Lutherans expressed a wariness of "legalism." No work in English surveys Lutheran-Reformed polemical theology; but compare two excellent nineteenth-century works of historically oriented dogmatics, recently reissued: Heinrich Schmid, *The Doctrinal Theology of the Evangelical Lutheran Church* (Minneapolis, Minn.: Augsburg Publishing House, 1961), and Heinrich Heppe, *Reformed Dogmatics* (London: G. Allen and Unwin, 1950). The Lutheran confessions are contained in *The Book of Concord* (1580), recently published in a new translation by Theodore G. Tappert, ed. (Philadelphia: Muhlenberg Press, 1959).

Appeal for denominational confederation.[39] His theology, expressed in a steady stream of books and articles, was an effort to amalgamate Lutheran Pietism and the New School views of American mainstream Protestantism. This was, of course, precisely the opposite trend from that for which the Mercersburg reformers were hoping. Indeed, Nevin declared that America's Reformed and Puritan churches actually needed to confront the authentic Lutheran witness before they could even contemplate their ultimate ecumenical task:

We look upon Lutheranism, in the present stadium of Christianity, as a necessary part of the constitution of Protestantism. Our idea of Protestantism is, that the two great confessions into which it was sundered from the start, the Lutheran and the Reformed, grew with inner necessity out of the movement itself, carrying in themselves thus a relative reason and right . . . which is destined, accordingly, in due time, to pass away in their inner amalgamation; a result which will involve also, no doubt, a full conciliation of the Protestant principle, as a whole, not with Romanism as it now stands, . . . but still with the deep truth of Catholicism, from which, by abuse, the Roman error springs.[40]

In the meantime a "Confessional" opposition to "American Lutheranism" had arisen, and in 1849 William M. Reynolds of Gettysburg College founded the *Evangelical Review* to provide a scholarly means for recovering the church's Reformation bearings. Of special portent in this effort was the editorship of Charles Philip Krauth of the Gettysburg Seminary faculty and the learned contributions written by his son, Charles Porterfield Krauth (1823–1883). Before long a widening circle of scholars and theologians were speaking and publishing; and a small but

---

[39] See Samuel S. Schmucker, *Fraternal Appeal to the American Churches*, Frederick K. Wentz, ed. (Philadelphia: Fortress Press, 1965).

[40] "The Lutheran Confessions," *Mercersburg Review*, I (September 1849), 468–470.

significant theological renaissance, parallel to those progressing at Mercersburg and on the Continent, began to take shape.

By 1855 the situation had so changed that Professor Schmucker and several sympathetic leaders among American Lutherans concluded that the time for a positive confrontation should be delayed no longer. They employed the extreme and dubious tactic of publishing (anonymously) a "Definite Synodical Platform" and proposing its adoption by the General Synod. It was a revision of the Augsburg Confession in which virtually all of the characteristically Lutheran affirmations had been exchanged for those of American New School Protestantism. The reaction was naturally rather violent; and a great stream of counter literature was published.

In each of the major Lutheran synods there arose at least one conservative theologian of considerable distinction, but two seminaries in particular became strong centers of national influence. Concordia Seminary in St. Louis was an institution of the "Missouri Synod" which had its origins in the emigration from Saxony of a small but dedicated company of Confessional Lutherans. This seminary and synod were dominated by the learning and dialectical skill of a single great theologian, C.F.W. Walther (1811–1887), who also wielded wide influence in the country's other Lutheran synods.[41] More closely related to the American situation was the English-language seminary at Philadelphia. It was founded in 1864 as a result of the doctrinal crisis, and Charles Porterfield Krauth became the seminary's professor of theology. By that time the General Synod had been riven both by the Civil War and by the conflict over American Lutheranism. In 1869 the Pennsylvania Ministerium, with its seminary at Philadelphia, became the nucleus of a General Council of autonomous synods adhering to the unaltered Augsburg Con-

---

[41] See Carl S. Meyer, ed., *Moving Frontiers: Readings in the History of the Lutheran Church-Missouri Synod* (St. Louis, Mo.: Concordia Publishing House, 1964), and Walter O. Forster, *Zion on the Mississippi* (St. Louis, Mo.: Concordia Publishing House, 1953).

fession. During the eventful decades between the Civil War and World War I the General Council played an important role, bringing the newer western synods to a larger awareness of their American status, and deepening the confessional commitment of the older eastern churches. To this task Krauth devoted his best talents, and his great work, *The Conservative Reformation and Its Theology* (1871), documents his understanding of what was most needful. It is a powerful exposition of the Lutheran Reformation's distinctive character and a creative theological statement—probably the single most influential work in the history of the Lutheran Church in America.[42] By giving impetus to the "confessional principle" it hastened the mergers which by 1965 had brought nearly 95 per cent of the country's Lutherans into only three separate church bodies, each of which was formally committed to the task of seeking the removal of all remaining barriers to fellowship through a new national council founded in 1966.

A distinguished non-Lutheran church historian recently concluded his survey of American Protestantism with a remarkable statement on the future role of Lutheranism:

The final prospect for a vigorous renewal of Protestant life and witness rests with the Lutheran churches which had overcome much of their fragmentation by 1960. . . . They have been less subject to the theological erosion which so largely stripped other denominations of an awareness of their continuity with a historic Christian tradition. . . . Among the assets immediately at hand among the Lutherans are a confessional tradition, a surviving liturgical structure, and a sense of community . . . without which Protestants are ill-equipped to participate effectively in the dialogue of a pluralistic society.[43]

---

[42] See C.F.W. Walther, *The Proper Distinction Between Law and Gospel* (St. Louis, Mo.: Concordia Publishing House, n.d.; trans. from German edition of 1897); James W. Richard, *The Confessional History of the Lutheran Church* (1909); Theodore E. Schmauk and C. Theodore Benze, *The Confessional Principle* (1911).

[43] Winthrop S. Hudson, *American Protestantism* (Chicago: University of Chicago Press, 1961), p. 176.

This estimate of strength may be excessive, but whatever elements of truth it holds only underline the importance of the movement of recovery spurred by Krauth and his many theological colaborers (see Selection IX).

Episcopalians, German Reformed, and Lutherans were not alone in their preoccupation with the church question during the mid-nineteenth century. The excesses of nonsectarian revivalism and the dramatic rise of many powerful extraecclesiastical voluntary associations aroused fears and revulsion in many minds. Despite the "common-front" mentality provoked by the rising tide of Roman Catholic immigration, a marked increase in denominational self-consciousness became noticeable everywhere during the decades after 1830. Presbyterians, Baptists, Congregationalists, and Methodists tended to close their organizational ranks. Among Baptists the "Landmark" movement developed new doctrines of a "Baptist succession" to justify their independence from the Reformation tradition. In this general context, and full in the face of Nativist activities, even the non-liturgical churches showed a strong, often very romantic fascination for things Catholic. The Unitarian Henry Wadsworth Longfellow softened many antipathies with his sympathetic "Catholic" poems and translations; and a steady flow of converts to Rome created both headlines and a significant body of Roman Catholic literature.[44]

The tendency of these several churches each in its own way to "return to tradition" was not by any means the only way in which revivalistic evangelicalism was subjected to pressure and criticism during the nineteenth century. Indeed a broad and vigorous current of religious liberalism had even greater conse-

---

[44] The two most famous converts were Orestes Brownson (1803–1876) and Isaac Hecker (1819–1888). Both had been active in the Transcendentalist movement; both were prolific and effective apologists for Roman Catholicism, though in very different ways.

quences, not least in those very churches that had been finding new resources in the past. For both its creative contributions and for its disruptive effects, this liberal movement merits extensive consideration.

THE RISE OF LIBERALISM

Liberalism became a powerful force in American Protestantism only after the Civil War, but it had by then a venerable and distinguished lineage. Indeed, if we designate by the term any movement that seeks to moderate orthodox doctrines by an individualistic emphasis on man's rational and moral powers, liberalism is a perennial aspect of church history. Its chief American roots, nevertheless, lie in the Enlightenment and above all in the impressive witness of the Founding Fathers. Just as the Declaration of Independence is almost a theological document, so patriotic idealism in the United States, as well as the prevailing rationale for democratic institutions, has always been invested with elements of Enlightened religion—whether with the Federalist accents of John Adams or the Republicanism of Jefferson. The great presuppositions of the Age of Reason have consequently conditioned American religious thought in each succeeding epoch, even though organized "Republican Religion" enjoyed only a brief and fitful existence.[45] Nowhere in the world do liberal doctrines have such firm rootage in the national origins and the "canonical scriptures" of the country itself.

William Ellery Channing is an excellent representative of this early rationalistic form of American liberalism. The Unitarian churches, moreover, not only gave Enlightened theology an enduring institutional base but nourished an exceedingly

---

[45] See Gustav A. Koch, *Republican Religion: The American Revolution and the Cult of Reason* (New York: Henry Holt & Co., 1933), and Norman Cousins, ed., *In God We Trust: The Religious Beliefs and Ideas of the American Founding Fathers* (New York: Harper & Brothers, 1958).

popular literary movement that appealed to sentiments and convictions which the country's struggle for independence had heightened. The great Unitarian "parlor poets" (Bryant, Longfellow, Lowell, etc.) were thus certified in ways that led Americans to ignore heresies on the Trinity. The Transcendentalists, too, benefited from this same certification even when they expressed a still more radical disdain for the orthodoxy of their Puritan ancestors.

Looming above every other American Transcendentalist, however, and standing as by far our most important prophet of a new and defiantly antirationalistic form of religious liberalism is Ralph Waldo Emerson, whom John Dewey would later refer to as "the one citizen of the New World fit to have his name uttered in the same breath with that of Plato."[46] Yet Emerson suffers from overfamiliarity. He needs to be seen again as a vigorous, independent innovator who not only attacked his own heritage but challenged many major themes of the romantic movement of which he was a part. He did this, moreover, without losing contact with the ordinary people who flocked to his lectures and read his words.

Emerson began his essential career after resigning from the ministry at Boston's Second Church in 1832. Four years later he revealed the direction of his thinking in *Nature,* an anonymous little volume, almost lost in the great Transcendental outpouring that made 1836 a veritable *annus mirabilis.* Whether by intention or not Emerson produced quite a different result two years later with his address at the Harvard Divinity School which was almost at once recognized as a manifesto of a new "spiritual party" in the Unitarian churches (see Selection IV). Unlike *Nature* or "The American Scholar" (his Phi Beta Kappa Address of 1837), he now dealt unambiguously with controver-

---

[46] John Dewey, "Ralph Waldo Emerson," in Milton R. Konvits and Stephen E. Whicher, eds., *Emerson: A Collection of Critical Essays* (Englewood Cliffs, N.J.: Prentice-Hall, Inc., 1962), p. 29.

sial questions of doctrine and church practice. Henry Ware, Jr.,
and Andrews Norton led the Unitarian establishment's counter-
attack on this "latest form of infidelity"; George Ripley, Orestes
Brownson, and Theodore Parker came to the defense of Transcendentalism, each of them soon getting into an imbroglio of his
own. Ripley left the ministry to become the leading spirit of the
Brook Farm experiment. Brownson founded a radical quarterly
and later became a Roman Catholic. Parker left his West Rox-
bury parish to take up a popular preaching ministry and antislavery career in Boston. Emerson's lectures and writing continued to set the tone of the new movement; but editions, translations, and interpretations of English, German, and French
romantics provided a solid accompaniment, and the new movement soon put an indelible mark on American thought and religious life.

Unquestionably the most prominent aspect of Transcendentalist influence was its reiteration of the Old Puritan and Edwardsean emphasis on the "religious affections." Perry Miller
has stated this important idea clearest of all: Transcendentalism
is "most accurately to be defined as a religious demonstration."[47]
An attack (justified or not) on the "corpse-cold" religion of the
Unitarians and the "ossified dogmas" of orthodoxy exposed its
negative side. On the affirmative, its votaries propagated Coleridge, Carlyle, and a rediscovered Swedenborg. They also
shared the fervency of German romantic thought, including its
strong idealistic and pantheistic tendency. Calling men away
from the fleshpots of sense, they proclaimed the powers of the
religious intuition, a Reason far above the humdrum, common-
sense concerns of the Understanding. Subjectivity gained in
respectability; faith and feeling were given a new warrant.
And among many of them—Emerson a major exception—one

---

[47] Perry Miller, ed., *The Transcendentalists: An Anthology* (Cambridge,
Mass.: Harvard University Press, 1950), p. 8.

could note a renewed concern for human history and religious continuity. Their intellectual life exhibited a dramatic enlargement of intellectual and aesthetic horizons. They also discovered a new kind of rapport with Nature; and this, in turn, aroused apprehensions about commercial and industrial encroachments. But their optimism as to America's potentiality for literary, spiritual, and moral progress remained almost boundless.

These manifold concerns, strengthened as they were by a philosophical concern for religion itself and a characteristic romantic interest in the remote or exotic scene, led also to major contributions in the study and confrontation of other religions, especially those of Asia. Emerson, in his New England way, became a Brahmin of sorts. Parker, Thoreau, and Bronson Alcott showed an equal avidity for Hindu and Buddhist wisdom, while two men in the main Transcendental lineage became pioneers of American scholarship in this area. James Freeman Clarke (1810–1888) was a conservative Transcendentalist who fought consistently to maintain Unitarianism's specifically Christian commitment. As an active minister he also was an effective reformer of parish practice. But he is best remembered as the country's first academic lecturer in the history of religions and as the author of *Ten Great Religions* (1871), almost certainly the country's most influential work in comparative religion during the nineteenth century. Samuel Johnson (1822–1882) was a founder of the Free Religious Association and a critic of Clarke's conservative program for Unitarianism, but his great studies of Oriental religion show even greater sympathy and considerably more erudition.[48]

All of these several passions and interests culminated in still another important contribution made by Transcendental poets,

---

[48] See my *The American Protestant Encounter with World Religions* (Beloit, Wisc.: Beloit College, 1962).

philosophers, historians, and theologians: their insistence that religion and religiosity could be disassociated from specific historical traditions. In this respect they shared—and absorbed— a conviction very dear to Enlightened thinkers. But just as surely they differed from their rationalistic predecessors by stressing the sentimental, intuitive, and mystical aspects of the religious life and by showing a tender warmth for the lessons of Nature. Despite the persistent religious concerns of this American Renaissance, however, it did not issue directly in important theological activity, in part because the movement directed so much of its attention to the problems of New England Unitarianism and more directly because so few of its leaders were concerned with specific doctrinal questions. For both reasons the American churches found it easy to ignore Transcendentalism even though its literature was becoming part of the country's spiritual heritage.

Horace Bushnell of Hartford's North Church, in orthodox Connecticut, was the theologian who best gathered in the Transcendental harvest. As disaffected by revivalism as Nevin, as romantic as Emerson, and as dedicated to the memory of his New England forebears as Beecher, he became in his way the American Schleiermacher. This is to say that more than any other one theologian he stands at the head of the main current of American theological liberalism. Committed to the covenantal notions of Puritanism, sharing his own age's optimistic vision of a Christian (but thoroughly Protestant) American republic, yet deeply worried about the difficulties of preaching traditional doctrines in their traditional forms with the traditional language and in the context of the traditional concept of the parish, Bushnell began rethinking his fundamental categories almost as soon as he entered the ministry and continued to do so with singular determination and flexibility until his death. Like so many of his American contemporaries, he received specific inspiration from Moses Stuart's publication of Schleiermacher's thought on the Trinity and James Marsh's

edition of Coleridge's *Aids to Reflection*.[49] Yet Bushnell's need
for theological substance and his instinctive loyalties kept him
in close dialogue with his own Congregational heritage—his
professors at Yale, his colleagues in the ministry, and his parishioners. One of the most important characteristics of his
thought, in fact, was its conciliatory, comprehensive spirit and
its apologetic motivation. He was never iconoclastic.

Bushnell ranged widely over the theological field, even into
a social gospel of sorts, where he invariably expounded con-
servatively on the issues in question. In addition to central
doctrinal questions, he showed continuous concern for the
problems of cosmology, science-and-religion, language, revivalism, conversion, and nurture. One could argue as to which was
most appropriate to his genius, but undoubtedly the heaviest
repercussions followed from his second published book, *God in
Christ* (1849), which contained his "Preliminary Dissertation
on Language" followed by three addresses recently delivered
in New England, on the Divinity of Christ and the Trinity, on
the Atonement, and on the primacy of spirit over dogma in
the reviving of religion. This work announced not only the
chief preoccupations of his own life but of the liberal movement itself (see Selection VII).

Bushnell was vigorously attacked in his lifetime; North
Church even withdrew from the Hartford–North Congrega-

---

[49] James Marsh (1794–1842), a Congregational minister and later president of the University of Vermont, published in 1819 an American edition
of Coleridge's *Aids*, with a discerning preliminary essay; and in 1833 came
his translation of Johann G. Herder's *The Spirit of Hebrew Poetry*. In 1835
Professor Moses Stuart of Andover published his translation of a section
on the Trinity from Schleiermacher's *The Christian Faith*. Many American
thinkers testified to the influence of these publications. Friedrich Schleiermacher (1768–1834), whose work inaugurates a new epoch in Western
theology and religion, is the subject of an enormous scholarly literature.
His major works are available in paper editions. See Richard R. Niebuhr,
Schleiermacher on Christ and Religion (New York: Charles Scribner's
Sons, 1964).

tional Consociation to save its pastor from possible heresy proceedings. Yet the kind of "progressive orthodoxy" which he preached made steady headway in his own denomination and far beyond. More than anyone, therefore, he can be remembered as the "father of American religious liberalism." In the earlier twentieth century the pioneering thoughts that took shape in his book *Christian Nurture* (1847) made him the patron saint of the religious education movement. By this time, however, liberalism had become far too variegated a movement to be described as simply Bushnellian, and certain major distinctions must be drawn in order to understand its character and to clarify the main lines of its development.

THE NEW THEOLOGY

To be a liberal was and is to be in some way interested in greater freedom. Liberals called for religious liberation—liberation from what they (each in his way) considered to be unwarranted ecclesiastical, doctrinal, or social bondage. Emerson and Bushnell, nevertheless, represent only an early response to a disquietude that would be brought to an entirely different order of magnitude by problems emerging later in the century. Intellectually the Victorian age was not a time of complacency but of revolution; it provided an "ordeal of faith." Decades of pressure from historical, sociological, and psychological study combined with the rise of subjectivistic and idealistic philosophical ideas, had gradually extinguished the old rationalistic Deism of the Revolutionary era and of the early Unitarians. The resulting relativism placed all creeds, systems of thought, and human institutions in a new perspective. The same processes transformed older conceptions of both "natural" and "revealed" religion. Along with these scholarly developments came spectacular advances in the natural sciences and a marked growth of confidence in scientific method as a sovereign mode of approaching human problems. New discoveries and theories in geology, paleontology, and biology had, in addition, created a series of specific intellectual crises. In their early stages these problems were only mildly disruptive, but the publication of Charles Darwin's *Origin of Species* (1859) and the ensuing growth of general evolutionary theories put traditional philosophical and theological categories under acute stress.

The situation of revivalistic Protestantism was especially critical. It had become so alienated from the intellectual forces that were altering the world that the nature and seriousness of the issues could not be widely appreciated. Because of the superficiality of its theological concerns and the anachronistic character of its church practice, moreover, revivalistic Protestantism was losing its appeal for large sections of the population. Its obscurantism meanwhile was forcing many theologians and scholars into exile and provoking a steady exodus of the lay intelligentsia from the churches. The resolution of these conflicts was made especially difficult by the economic problems, social anxieties, and political tensions created by industrial expansion and urban growth. The churches thus had to meet the most difficult intellectual challenges in Christian history while struggling with the problems of institutional disruption.[50]

In the midst of this intellectual and social turbulence, theological liberals became bolder and more numerous. As they became an increasingly self-conscious movement they advanced along two fronts: they attempted to achieve an increase in factual and theoretical understanding of the human situation,

---

[50] See Francis P. Weisenburger, *The Ordeal of Faith: The Crisis of Church-Going America*, 1865–1900 (New York: Philosophical Library, 1959). Specially concerned with the "incoming tide of positivistic naturalism" is John C. Greene, *The Death of Adam: Evolution and Its Impact on Western Thought* (1959), and *Darwin and the Modern World View* (1961), both reissued in paperback by the New American Library. In the American Heritage Series Robert D. Cross, ed., *The Church and the City* (1967), greatly illuminates the problems of urban adjustment.

past and present; and they began to rethink the meaning of the Christian tradition in the context of the age's several revolutions. The liberals were by no means alone in this endeavor, as the preceding section on romantic conservatism has indicated. But they did make vast contributions to a more dynamic conception of religion in the lives of men, to the general assimilation of modern thought and knowledge, to the renewal of seminary education, and to the development of an indigenous scholarly tradition.

Liberalism in nearly all of its later nineteenth-century aspects was committed to a nonsectarian theology much as had been the evangelical revivalism from which so many of its leading theologians had personally fled. This commitment was closely related to the central place of experientialism in both movements and their mutual suspicion of dogmatic concerns. Yet liberals shared a cluster of acceptances and a recognizable doctrinal tendency. At the core of their theology was an optimistic conception of human nature which involved in the first instance a repudiation or modification of the orthodox doctrines of original sin and human depravity.[51] As an almost inevitable consequence, liberals also held optimistic views as to mankind's earthly destiny. The Enlightened idea of progress, reinforced by later evolutionary ideas, received a fervent Christian blessing. Despite the reign of tooth and claw which Darwinian biologists described and which laissez-faire economists prescribed, liberals tended toward the cosmic optimism of John Fiske: God was seen as working to his glory through the entire evolutionary process—in nature, society, and the human conscience.[52] The coming of his earthly Kingdom was confi-

---

[51] See H. Shelton Smith, *Changing Conceptions of Original Sin* (New York: Charles Scribner's Sons, 1955).

[52] John Fiske (1842–1901) was America's most prolific and widely read popularizer of Darwinian and Spencerian theory, which he reconciled with theism by conceiving God as imminent in a cosmic process whose end was the ultimate perfection of all things. Rarely has optimism reached such

dently worked for and expected. Henry George notwithstanding, history seemed to promise ever greater peace, prosperity, and human felicity—not least because of the new reformation that the liberals themselves were inaugurating in Christendom. Christian hope thus had a tangible, this-worldly basis.

The solidarity of the liberal movement should not, however, be exaggerated. Even aside from denominational differences, it was profoundly if not always belligerently divided over two extremely basic issues: first, the understanding of religion; second, the interpretation of biblical revelation.

On the question of *religion* liberals were divided into those with an ethical emphasis and those who were chiefly concerned with other questions. Members of the first group were mainly concerned with man's relation to his neighbor. When thinking about the spiritual life or philosophical questions this group usually relied on custom and common-sense answers. Many of them were not even interested in framing a theological or biblical basis for ethical discourse. Rather, they sought to direct attention to actual social problems. The second group regarded religion primarily as a disposition of mind and soul, or a spiritual and intellectual relation to nature, ultimate reality, Being, or God. Recognizing widespread human anxiety on these matters, they sought to illuminate the human predicament and deepen the religious consciousness. In pursuing this

---

heights: ". . . it is Darwinism which has placed Humanity upon a higher pinnacle than ever. The future is lighted for us with the radiant colours of hope. Strife and sorrow shall disappear. Peace and love shall reign supreme . . . and as we gird ourselves up for the work of life, we may look forward to the time when in the truest sense the kingdoms of this world shall become the kingdom of Christ, and he shall reign for ever and ever, king of kings and lord of lords." *The Destiny of Man Viewed in the Light of his Origin* (Boston: Houghton, Mifflin & Company, 1884), pp. 118–119. Christian liberalism was deeply influenced by such views but compared with Fiske's effusions it seemed sober and realistic. See Milton Berman, *John Fiske, The Evolution of a Popularizer* (Cambridge, Mass.: Harvard University Press, 1961); Henry B. Pannill, *The Religious Faith of John Fiske* (Durham, N.C.: Duke University Press, 1957).

end, however, the second group became itself divided in an immemorial way. On the one hand were those who accented intuition, the feelings, and the subjective dimensions of life. These thinkers were often nostalgic for the piety of their youthful family life; they were moved by Schleiermacher's conception of man's dependence and later by Rudolf Otto's "idea of the holy." On the other hand were those who eschewed philosophic irrationalism and sought a more integrated conception of man's total situation. They accented reason and logic, felt a relish for systematic thinking, and showed recurrent interest in philosophical idealism.

Thus we end up with three major ways of understanding religion. Like all classification schemes, this one has its limits, in part because no individual has only one concern, yet it provides useful categories for the historian. The ideas of each of the three fin-de-siècle liberals represented in this volume, for example, can justifiably be placed in one of the three groups. Walter Rauschenbusch represents the first. His ideas were so persuasive that he almost converted the entire Social Gospel movement to this view. William James, with his consuming interest in the varieties of religious experience, fits into the second, and the great idealist philosopher of religion, Josiah Royce, can be placed in the third.

As for the other great issue—*biblical revelation*—Kenneth Cauthen has distinguished two broad tendencies—modernistic and evangelical liberalism.[53] With the term "modernism" Cauthen refers to those thinkers (not all of whom would wish to be called theologians) whose primary commitment was to the prevailing views of contemporary philosophy and the findings

---

[53] Kenneth Cauthen, *The Impact of American Religious Liberalism* (New York: Harper & Row, 1962). As modernistic liberals he discusses Shailer Mathews, D. C. Macintosh, and Henry Nelson Wieman; as evangelical liberals, William Adams Brown, Harry Emerson Fosdick, A. C. Knudson, Eugene W. Lyman, and Walter Rauschenbusch. John Fiske (see footnote 52) would also exemplify the modernist position.

of science and scholarship. These views and findings were then allowed—in varying degrees—to dictate the content of the Church's teaching. To them the Bible was an historical record of two religions that in turn exhibited the influence of several other religions. Aside from being specially honored in Christendom, and possessing certain intrinsic merits that overcame other equally intrinsic shortcomings, the Bible wielded no more authority than other similar records. Modernism, in other words, was Christian in only a vague and sentimental way, though inevitably there were modernists whose views were shaded closely to Cauthen's other category.

Evangelical liberalism refers to the far less revolutionary and much larger school of liberal thought which understood its task to be that of reinterpreting Christian doctrine only insofar as modern developments, especially in science and scholarship, seemed to require. The term "Progressive Orthodoxy" expresses their intention. These liberals often disagreed as to the amount of innovation required, yet their basically conservative aims made them extremely influential, a fact which calls for a brief review of their leading doctrines.

Jesus remained the theological center for evangelical liberals, especially when the influence of Schleiermacher and, even more, Albrecht Ritschl (1822–1889) began to be felt. "Back to Christ" became something of a slogan for them, and perhaps for this reason nuances of Christology often provide the main clue to any given theology.[54] On two points there was widespread concurrence. First, they tended to be unsympathetic with nearly the whole tradition of doctrinal speculation— from the "mystical flights" of St. Paul, through the metaphysical ventures of the Nicene fathers, on to and including the Reformation. Second, as against these "deviations," they tended

---

[54] For an American liberal's comparison of Schleiermacher, Hegel, and Ritschl, see William Adams Brown, *The Essence of Christianity: A Study in the History of Definition* (New York: Charles Scribner's Sons, 1902).

to prefer the "religion of Jesus," believing that the Master's example and teachings, as revealed by rigorous historical research, provided faith with a far more reliable foundation. A moral theory of the atonement, furthermore, became so prevalent a feature of liberalism that Fundamentalists invariably made an affirmation of the "substitutionary theory"—an essential criterion of orthodoxy.[55]

Ethics, the Christian conscience, and the Kingdom of God moved to the fore as subjects of preaching and theological construction. The Church was understood less as a supernatural agency, less as "the Body of Christ," and more as an agency for the propagation of an ethical message and the advancement of the Kingdom. The great best seller concerned with this issue was Charles M. Sheldon's edifying novel *In His Steps* (1896),

---

[55] "Fundamentalism" is the name usually given to the militant and often obscurantist movement of ultraconservatives in American Protestantism who have sought by various means to preserve the "fundamentals" of Christian orthodoxy and the principle of Scriptural infallibility from the encroachments of modern science, historical scholarship, and social optimism. The Fundamentalists also attempt to preserve revivalistic views of conversion, personal morality, and church membership from the inroads of complacency and worldliness. So long as liberalism was a small minority impulse and revivalism a mighty power in the churches, Fundamentalism was for the most part simply latent. However, after the Civil War it became an increasingly overt movement—both within denominations and as an organized interdenominational movement. In addition to more traditional doctrines, premillenialism, dispensationalism, and above all a very strict doctrine of Scriptural inspiration were prominent elements in its advocacy. The decade of the 1920's was probably its time of peak activity, and the "Monkey Trial" of 1925 was the most publicized event in its long campaign. But even in the mid-twentieth century the Fundamentalist Controversy accounts for the chief rift in American Protestantism. Because of the extremism and aggressive tactics of Fundamentalists a kind of battlefield psychology pervaded American theology and religious scholarship for almost a century. The history of this conflict has yet to be written, but see C. Norman Kraus, *Dispensationalism in America* (Richmond, Va.: John Knox Press, 1958); Norman F. Furniss, *The Fundamentalist Controversy, 1918–1931* (New Haven: Yale University Press, 1954); and Louis Gasper, *The Fundamentalist Movement* (The Hague: Mouton & Co., 1963), which covers the period since 1930.

but liberalism's intense moral concern found its ideal expression in and through the Social Gospel movement.

In the context of so strong an ethical emphasis, it goes without saying that conversion, faith, and holiness tended to be preached as human options, not as divine gifts. God's grace tended to be understood as an indwelling principle of the Creation. Union with God was usually treated in terms of moral obedience, though one may also discern in liberalism an occasional recurrence to the mystical categories which some romantic thinkers had revivified. The doctrine of Last Things was generally harnessed to programs for building the Kingdom of God on earth. All things considered, therefore, the terse summary of liberalism given by H. Richard Niebuhr is not inaccurate: "A God without wrath brought men without sin into a kingdom without judgment through the ministrations of a Christ without a cross."[56] Yet as other works of Niebuhr amply show, there was far more spiritual energy and creative vitality in the best liberal theology than this epigram would suggest.

As with every other major American theological tendency, liberalism, too, was expounded systematically and with considerable attention to the philosophy of religion. The *Outline of Christian Theology* (1898) by the Baptist, William Newton Clarke, probably won the widest and most enduring acceptance. But his popularity was rivaled by William Adams Brown (Presbyterian), by Lewis F. Stearns (Congregational), and somewhat later by A. C. Knudson (Methodist). A careful reader could detect denominational emphases in the words of each of these men but the common ground they occupy is impressive—and far more revealing of the liberal spirit.

The liberals also contributed powerfully to a deep shift in

---

[56] H. Richard Niebuhr, *The Kingdom of God in America* (1937). Reprinted in paperback (New York: Harper & Brothers Publishers, Torchbook, 1959), p. 193.

the philosophical understanding of religion and doctrine. Most decisive were their attacks on rationalistic systems of thought. They demanded the exchange of static conceptions of reality for new and dynamic views. Mechanistic metaphors yielded to the organic ones. Life, growth, spontaneity, and evolution became the master concepts. Indeed the major theological event of the half-century after the Civil War may have been the quiet demise of the Scottish philosophy with its common-sense views and its self-assured demonstrations. But this is not to say that liberals worked in a destructive spirit. They showed a strong apologetic interest and made impressive constructive efforts in theology. In this connection probably none had a more numerous and devoted following than Borden Parker Bowne (1847–1910) of Boston University, whose personal idealism was almost the official philosophy of American Methodism for nearly a half-century.[57]

One of the anomalies of liberalism, however, is the fact that two Harvard philosophers who never considered themselves theologians express the movement's genius most brilliantly. They do so, moreover, in the context of a fruitful and lifelong polarity of views that not only illustrated both the experiential and the speculative aspects of liberal thought, but also recapitulated, at a century's remove, the less friendly relationship of Schleiermacher and Hegel at the University of Berlin. William James (1842–1910) opened his career with a monumental work, *Principles of Psychology* (1890), and culminated it with his classic, *The Varieties of Religious Experience* (1902). Josiah Royce (1855–1916) made his debut with *The Religious Aspect of Philosophy* (1885) and summed up his lifelong concern with religion in *The Problem of Christianity* (2 vols., 1913). Royce took his stand with Reason and an insistence on

---

[57] Bowne is representative of the widespread American receptiveness to Rudolph Hermann Lotze (1817–1881), who sought to bring a scientific and mechanistic view of nature into an idealistic and pantheistic synthesis.

the corporate nature of thought and knowledge; James was an individualist with a deep, relativistic respect for sentiment —even "the sentiment of rationality"—and the will to believe. The First World War and the changed intellectual atmosphere of the 1920's conduced in both philosophy and theology to quite different—and more naturalistic—modes of thought. For this reason both James and Royce are often remembered for summing up rather than for inaugurating an epoch. Yet they stand in the lineage of Edwards, Emerson, and Bushnell as great representative figures in the American theological tradition: Royce as a comprehensive idealist (see Selection X), James as the pragmatic champion of life's possibilities (see Selection XI).

THE SOCIAL GOSPEL

Theological liberalism is commonly and almost inevitably associated with social-political liberalism. This identification, however, is largely the residue of a situation which prevailed among the ministers in many Protestant churches during the 1920's. To continue to think in these terms, therefore, is to obscure the long-term history of social Christianity in America as well as the origins and creative contribution of what is properly remembered as the Social Gospel. The Church's plea for human compassion and moral concern is immemorial; its concern for public issues and the general welfare is at least as old as the mediaeval quest for a "Christian society" or the Puritan effort to create a "Holy Commonwealth." Social involvement continued to be intense during the entire Revolutionary epoch and on into the early national period. The churchmen who began to demand social reforms in the Age of Enterprise, therefore, are best imagined as so many battle-scarred "Christian soldiers," veterans of the humanitarian and reform campaigns launched by the "evangelical united front" earlier in the century. The nineteenth century's greatest evangelical revivalist, Charles G. Finney, was a major forerunner.

The antislavery crusade provided the movement with count-less tactical lessons while the ending of slavery yielded a bound-less measure of optimism.[58]

Insofar as the Social Gospel is understood as the convic-tion that Christians must "speak out" on social issues and not limit their concern to personal salvation, other problems of in-terpretation arise. In order to illustrate the link between aboli-tionism and postwar social concern, for example, one thinks almost immediately of Henry Ward Beecher, the great liberal preacher, whose words from the pulpit (or should one say the stage?) of Brooklyn's Plymouth Church reached across the nation. Beecher's postwar program for America was basically a version of Andrew Carnegie's Gospel of Wealth. Yet it was emphatically a *social* gospel—even though it stood in stark op-position to the agrarian radicals who would soon be led by that Joshua of American Fundamentalism, William Jennings Bryan. Yet neither Beecher nor Bryan are remembered as So-cial Gospel preachers! Where, then, is the special character of the Social Gospel?

The phenomenon usually referred to by this term was, in its most creative period, not really a movement at all, but a mi-nority impulse within the larger movement of religious liberal-ism. Like all liberals, its leaders were searching for new kinds of Christian relevancy. They were also appalled by the human misery, brutality, and injustice that accompanied the country's industrial expansion during the half-century after the Civil

---

[58] On the pioneer social-Christian advocate of Unitarianism, see Daniel T. McColgan, *Joseph Tuckerman, Pioneer in American Social Work* (Wash-ington, D.C.: The Catholic University of America Press, 1940). On later evangelicalism in this respect see Timothy L. Smith, *Revivalism and Social Reform* (Nashville, Tenn.: Abingdon Press, 1957); Chester C. Cole, *The Social Ideas of the Northern Evangelists, 1826–1860* (New York: Columbia University Press, 1954); Gilbert H. Barnes, *The Anti-Slavery Impulse, 1830–1844* (New York: Appleton-Century Company, Inc., 1933); and Wil-son Smith, *Professors and Public Ethics: Studies of Northern Moral Philoso-phers before the Civil War* (Ithaca, N.Y.: Cornell University Press, 1956).

War. Their policy recommendations usually reflected those of various secular reformers. Some advocates of the Social Gospel went no further than a cautious defense of labor's right to organize and a demand for charitable negotiation. A few committed themselves to the specific proposals of Henry George or Edward Bellamy. Some took recent German social legislation as their standard. Others devised adaptations of English Christian Socialism. A few showed Marxist influence. All of them sought to stir the American conscience by publicizing the facts, and their greatest historical importance stems from their making church-going America more aware of the new social problems created by industrialism and unregulated urban growth. (Agricultural dislocations, the racial caste system, ethnic prejudice, religious intolerance, and civil rights were not prominent among their concerns.) Theologically they did almost nothing more, as a group, than modernize the application of characteristic Christian imperatives, except that as liberals they tended to motivate their hearers by an appeal to the "teachings of Jesus" rather than by preaching holiness or sanctification. Except for Rauschenbusch, very few of the men who gained a wide hearing for the cause or became denominational social-action leaders are remembered for especially creative theology. Only a few (notably Richard Ely and Albion Small) made significant contributions to economic or social theory.[59]

The Congregationalist Washington Gladden (1836–1918) is often designated the Father of the Social Gospel and deservedly so. Both as a prolific writer and as a powerful preacher in socially prominent churches he did much to expose the cruelties, corruption, and inequities that tarnished the Gilded Age.

---

[59] See John R. Everett, *Religion in Economics: A Study of John Bates Clark, Richard R. Ely, Simon N. Patten* (New York: King's Crown Press, 1946), and on Small, see Cynthia Russett, *The Concept of Equilibrium in American Social Thought* (New Haven: Yale University Press, 1966). Francis G. Peabody at Harvard and others elsewhere did much to awaken and organize scientific and academic approaches to social issues.

He also popularized modern biblical scholarship and liberal theology in such works as *Who Wrote the Bible?* (1891), *How Much Is Left?* (1899), and *The Ruling Ideas of the Age* (1895). Gladden's contemporaries, meanwhile, extended the work in diverse ways: by inaugurating courses in the seminaries, by activating denominational agencies, by opening programs of social service in individual churches, and by stirring governments and secular organizations to action. Shailer Mathews and Francis Greenwood Peabody gave a sharp social edge to biblical study in such books as *The Social Teaching of Jesus* (1897) and *Jesus Christ and the Social Question* (1900). The Episcopalian W. D. P. Bliss not only experimented with a revolutionary type of urban parish, but also edited the massive *Encyclopedia of Social Reform* (1897). And there were, of course, countless others from many denominations and representing several very different theological orientations.[60]

In the midst of this ferment, the Baptist Walter Rauschenbusch (1861–1918) emerged as the Social Gospel's chief prophet and leading theological voice, especially with the publication in 1907 of his stirring book, *Christianity and the Social Crisis.* He continued to heighten the movement's motivation with a profusion of writings during the next decade; and shortly before his death, with World War I as a chastening background, he systematized his thought in *A Theology of the Social Gospel* (1917). In the social Christianity of American Protestantism during the decade after World War I, Rauschenbusch's thought played a dominant role. And the warm reception that his ideas received no doubt depended on his greatest achievement: he took the trite and, in that day, overworked concept of the "Kingdom of God on earth," added to

---

[60] A history of the theology (or theologies) of either the Social Gospel per se or of the larger movement of social Christianity from 1880 to 1929 is yet to be written.

it an opposed concept, the Kingdom of Evil, and then freighted both with biblical content, genuine social passion, and trenchant applications to the contemporary situation of the country. He gave the Social Gospel two living social concepts.[61] Because of the realistic spirit of his last work, moreover, he alone of the Social Gospel's major advocates had some shaping power on the later efforts of "neo-orthodox" theologians to revive the Church's social witness in the context of more traditional doctrinal positions (see Selection XII).

By the time this later work of reconstruction was begun, liberal theology and social preoccupations had become so pervasive that the evangelical consciousness itself had been seriously threatened in many sectors of American Protestantism. Some kind of rescue was needed if social advocacy was to have any specifically Christian rootage.[62] Protestantism stood on the threshold of another era.

THE NEO-ORTHODOX TURN OF MIND

Liberalism as an invigorating new movement of religious thought, scholarship, and heightened moral concern probably reached its zenith between 1890 and the First World War. Its largest numerical triumphs came later, during the great re-

---

[61] Rauschenbusch's concept of the Kingdom of Evil gave his thought a realism often lacking in the social criticism of liberal theology; but anticipations of this idea in earlier American thought should be noted. Bushnell, for example, developed the idea in his book, *Nature and the Supernatural*, with greater theological depth than Rauschenbusch went into. The evangelical antislavery movement, however, had done even more to delineate the notion of "organic sin"—as against the virtue or sinfulness of individuals, North and South—with Edward Beecher (Harriet's brother) making a specially significant contribution.

[62] On this debt and its limitations, see Donald B. Meyer, *The Protestant Search for Political Realism, 1919–1941* (Berkeley and Los Angeles: University of California Press, 1960).

ligious depression of the Twenties.[63] But this victory was neither profound nor durable and the Great Crash of 1929, the continuing Depression, and the news of terrible political calamities abroad soon created an inhospitable atmosphere for an outlook that required a daily diet of visible human progress. It was in this time of crisis that a new theological epoch began to take shape, and for better or worse neo-orthodoxy is the term by which it has come to be known.[64]

Neo-orthodoxy broke into the American consciousness with powerful stimulation from a great number of European thinkers whose experience of a crisis in Western civilization was far more acute. Even before World War I Jacob Burckhardt, Nietzsche, and Albert Schweitzer had, in their special ways, put the ax to the previous century's bourgeois assumptions. With the guns still booming or barely silent, Oswald Spengler, Ludwig Wittgenstein, and Karl Barth dropped their now famous bombshells almost simultaneously. In 1936 a Norwegian pastor-scholar (a student of Royce and Kierkegaard whose words also bore the marks of Barthian influence) sent "an unpretentious book . . . across the Atlantic as a greeting from a continent in fatal crisis. . . . The Unknown Europe [he said] is the living communion of believers throughout all the nations of what seems to be a dying continent. . . . They have not been rethinking Christianity, or been busy remodeling its message. They have *heard* a Word, coming from the Other side of mere human possibilities."[65]

---

[63] See Robert T. Handy, "The American Religious Depression, 1925–1935," *Church History*, XXIX (March 1960), 3–16. On Rauschenbusch's own denomination during these years see Eldon Ernst, "American Baptists and the New World Movement, 1918–1924," *Foundations*, VIII (April 1965), 161–171.

[64] On some limitations of the term, see my article, "Neo-Orthodoxy Demythologized," *Christian Century* (May 22, 1957).

[65] Sverre Norborg, *What is Christianity?* (Minneapolis, Minn.: Augsburg Publishing House, 1936), pp. vii–viii. The "bombshells" referred to are Spengler's *Decline of the West*, Wittgenstein's *Tractatus*, and Barth's *Commentary on Romans*.

As the postwar crisis increased, a few Americans, even during the Twenties, were led to similar convictions by these diverse European voices and by their own analysis of the times. After 1929 their numbers increased, and before long one could observe the emergence of a definite theological tendency. In terms of publications the years 1932 and 1934 (remembered also for the election of Franklin D. Roosevelt in America and Adolf Hitler's establishment of the Third Reich in Germany) were especially notable. These years and those that followed witnessed what was at once a renaissance, a reformation, and a revolution in American theology, ethics, and religious scholarship. Most prominent among the American theologians were the two brothers, H. Richard Niebuhr at Yale and Reinhold Niebuhr at Union Seminary in New York. Between them they left very few of the period's major issues unexplored; and they spoke brilliantly on several central problems.

The new theological movement, however, did not have a precise doctrinal orientation. At all times it embraced thinkers and scholars who widely disagreed on a great many traditional issues. Quakers, Lutherans, Congregationalists, and Episcopalians contributed to the rediscovery of Kierkegaard. Questions of authority in the Church and related issues of Scriptural inspiration, which had been hotly contested in the Fundamentalist Controversy, were approached in differing ways. In Christology, ecclesiology, and liturgics similar diversities appeared. With regard to foreign missions and other world religions sharp disagreements were manifested. European theologians as different as Anders Nygren, Nicolas Berdyaev, Jacques Maritain, Martin Buber, Rudolf Bultmann, William Temple, Karl Barth, and Emil Brunner, each had their defenders and critics. There were also sharp disputes on foreign policy and domestic social problems—as well as on the questions of ethical theory that preceded *any* Christian discussion of such matters. Finally there were important differences in emphasis even among thinkers who otherwise had much in common (for example, the Niebuhr brothers). In what, we may ask, did their unity consist?

One can answer this question, but it must be with the insistence that the uniting elements of neo-orthodoxy were not doctrinal tenets so much as a way of approaching the Church's message and task. Individual thinkers were thus related to each other by sharing certain trends of thought much as Maimonides, Averroës, and Aquinas (Jew, Arab, and Christian) were related to each other in the Middle Ages by a common Aristotelianism. One can, therefore, suggest at least five elements that figure prominently in this very important intellectual concurrence.

The first element is signaled by the degree to which the history of American neo-orthodoxy can be gathered into a biography of Reinhold Niebuhr, namely, a strenuous involvement in developing a realistic, viable, and dynamic way of addressing social and political problems—both domestic and international. The movement was in large measure a kind of *aggiornamento* of the older Social Gospel. Essential to this objective was a repudiation of the prevailing liberal estimate of man's altruistic propensities. This has often been interpreted either as pessimism or as a reassertion of the doctrines of original sin, but it was not necessarily either one or the other, but often simply a preference for an old and honorable realistic tradition in political philosophy. Reinhold Niebuhr's use of Luther's notion of man as saint and sinner, for example, was based less on the categories of Reformation theology than on his own acute analysis of human nature.[66] As in any coherent philosophy, moreover, a view of man's nature involved a theory

---

[66] "*Homo simul justus et peccator est:* man is simultaneously saint (justified) and sinner." Among "realistic" precursors of Niebuhr one might cite Machiavelli, Hobbes, Alexander Hamilton, and Marx. See especially Niebuhr's most provocative book, *Moral Man and Immoral Society* (New York: Charles Scribner's Sons, 1932).

of man's destiny, in this case a thoroughgoing critique of the idea of progress and the notion that "history is the Christ" or the bearer of inevitable earthly felicity.

A second element of the neo-orthodox concurrence lay in the unqualified respect shown for all genuine scholarly, scientific, and artistic endeavor, including those pursuits that created theological problems. In this respect they affirmed the classic interests of liberalism. Indeed, their opposition to obscurantism of every sort was an essential feature of their effort to transcend the futile quarrels of the Fundamentalist Controversy. For this reason the full implications of historical, sociological, and psychological investigation became a major concern. In theology and ethics neo-orthodox thinkers never questioned the historicity and finitude of man and all his works. The moral ambiguity of most human predicaments was conceded. Relativism was accepted as a deterrent to moral pride, dogmatism, and absolutistic pronouncements. In dealing with this "relativistic predicament," moreover, the dialectical character of neo-orthodox thought became very apparent. This meant on the one hand a certain glorying in the paradoxes of St. Paul and of Reformation theology (especially Luther), and on the other, a willing employment of Hegelian and Marxist modes of analysis. Dialectical categories also enabled them to view the Church and its history both in theological and in mundane "scientific" perspectives. Probably no other aspect of neo-orthodoxy led to so much confusion in the American churches with their long tradition of unambiguous, rationalistic moralism, their literal, propositional understanding of revelation, and their insulation of "Christian history" from world history.[67]

---

[67] Fundamentalism can almost be said to *be* an organized effort to keep the Bible and Christian history insulated from world history. Here lies the major difference between *its* critique of liberalism and that of neo-orthodox theologians.

The unfamiliar vocabulary of existential philosophy added
to this confusion, for here in a third respect neo-orthodox critiques of speculative systems and of legalistic ethics ran counter to the characteristic thought of both liberalism and the
country's older Puritan and Enlightened heritage. Kierkegaard
did, nevertheless, become a living element in American theology and a powerful factor in providing a Christian basis for a
pragmatic, contextual understanding of the moral situation, a
new way of justifying the Christian faith, and an additional
provocation to religious seriousness. These new modes of understanding what it meant to be and to behave like a Christian
also involved a basic revision of both Modern Puritan and liberal attitudes toward piety and religion. Neo-orthodox thinkers
were persistently critical of Pietism and of all romantic efforts to
make man religious. They criticized aestheticism in religion
and showed little interest in Nature. Only in the kind of agon-
ized self-analysis that they learned from existential thought
(assisted by Freud) did they make contact with older conceptions of Christian inwardness, and even then in a way that was
often fundamentally secular, psychological, and almost clini-
cal. In all this, moreover, there was a widespread acceptance
of Karl Barth's distinction between being religious and being
Christian.

Despite all of these essentially nondoctrinal elements in the
neo-orthodox consensus, the movement did have vast doctrinal
significance; and herein lies a fourth major element in its influence. Its theologians effected a major overhauling of liberal
dismissals and a genuine renewal of appreciation for the
Church's whole experience. To start with, biblical study was
rescued from the historian's workshop; with no disparagement
of scholarly thoroughness, exegetical labors assumed new importance for both preaching and theological construction. By
the same token successive periods in church history were re-
claimed, especially the early Church and the Reformation. In

the United States, the 1930's also saw the beginning of a remarkable rediscovery of the Puritans and Jonathan Edwards.[68]

The modern ecumenical movement constitutes a fifth factor that is essential to an understanding of neo-orthodox theologians. To a remarkable degree they participated not only in the great world assemblies which culminated in the formation of the World Council of Churches in 1948, but also in the innumerable committees where the movement's most vital work was carried out during the preceding decade or two. Here it was that Americans experienced Europe's neo-orthodoxy face to face, and out of these encounters came a new kind of catholicity as well as a new conviction that both the nonsectarianism of the revivalists and the antidoctrinal spirit of the liberals were superficial evasions. And from this conviction, in turn, there flowed an unmistakable readiness to face the issues which in the past had broken the Church's visible unity.[69]

Amid these many tendencies, and with Luther, Calvin, and Augustine becoming nearly contemporary theologians again, there came a profound change in the theological climate. The nature and mission of the Church was critically reexamined (see Selection XIII). The classic themes of Christian theology again found brilliant expositors. As a result many church leaders gained a kind of self-awareness that stood them in good stead during the decade of superficial "religious revival" that followed World War II. And in the second postwar decade the neo-orthodox legacy served in still another way to strengthen the

---

[68] Several of Perry Miller's major studies of Puritanism appeared in the 1930's; so also Joseph Haroutunian's *Piety versus Moralism* (1932) on the post-Edwardseans and H. Richard Niebuhr's *The Kingdom of God in America* (1937). See bibliography.

[69] Between the first Faith and Order Conference in Lausanne (1927) and the organization of the World Council of Churches (1948) American theology not only was drastically altered in spirit but gained much in breadth and depth.

churches' understanding of their role in the country's racial crisis. By this time, however, the neo-orthodox period in American church history was a thing of the past. New problems and another generation of scholars and theologians were coming on the scene.

AFTER NEO-ORTHODOXY

"Neo-orthodoxy" is a satisfactory name for the distinctive theological movement that burgeoned in the 1920's and reached a brilliant culmination in the 1930's. But this movement is best understood as a response to the circumstances of a specific period in a specific country. The various kinds of orthodoxy advanced by its proponents were new only in the sense that they were marked by the mood of a specific historical epoch. The movement's influence, to be sure, extended into the years after the Second World War, many of its major thinkers continue to be heard, and some of its leading ideas will be felt for decades. Quite inexorably, however, new conditions created new theological needs and gave rise to new movements of thought and practice.

In postwar America the anxieties of the Thirties lost their urgency. For example, the old liberal campaign to gain the churches' acceptance for the work of scientists and scholars no longer retained its old form. The cruder aspects of the Fundamentalist Controversy had been altered in at least two respects. Fundamentalists discovered a very different kind of opponent—one who was often committed to a tradition and to fundamentals that were far older and richer than those brought forth in America's "old-time religion." The Fundamentalist movement, on the other hand, was significantly altered by the emergence of a "new evangelicalism" that sought to give a responsible theological voice (and scholarly support) to the large sectors of American Protestantism that remained hostile to the ecumenical movement and to many implications of modern thought.[70] For a full decade after 1948, moreover, the country was swept by a remarkable surge of religious interest which conveyed a false notion of institutional health to the churches. The superficial intellectual accompaniments of this revival served, meanwhile, to delay any widespread grappling with changed conditions.[71] During the late Fifties, however, one may note a distinct return to reality in American thought generally and also a marked transformation of the prevailing religious outlook.

The most basic shift in the religious situation was wrought by a vast social, economic, intellectual, and moral revolution which makes it no exaggeration to speak of a post-Protestant and, in certain respects, post-Christian America. Beneath (or accompanying) this change were the technological developments that have produced the "affluent society" and the "ghetto city." At this level an American can almost become an avant-garde thinker simply by fully developing his awareness of the new industrial society that surrounds him. The situation is complicated, however, by the emergence from accepted minority status of the Roman Catholic, Eastern Orthodox, Negro, Jewish, and "humanistic" communities. The election of a popular Roman Catholic president in 1960 and his assassination in 1963 documented and strengthened the new pluralism. Meanwhile the end of one era and the beginning of another was announced by a series of revolutionary Supreme Court decisions, notably those

---

[70] See Ronald H. Nash, *The New Evangelicalism* (Grand Rapids, Mich.: Zondervan Publishing House, 1963). American Protestantism, however, remains deeply riven by the old issues, especially that of biblical inerrancy. Perhaps a third of its constituency is hostile to such ecumenical institutions as the National Council of Churches. See Robert Lee, *The Social Sources of Church Unity* (Nashville, Tenn.: Abingdon Press, 1960), pp. 187–216.

[71] The vast literature on this "revival" is well summed up in Martin E. Marty, *The New Shape of American Religion* (New York: Harper & Brothers, 1959); Will Herberg, *Protestant-Catholic-Jew* (New York: Doubleday & Company, 1955); and William Lee Miller, *Piety Along the Potomac* (Boston: Houghton Mifflin Company, 1964).

pertaining to race relations, electoral reapportionment, censorship, and lingering types of religious establishment. Of paramount importance was the new social and political situation created by the Negro Revolution, the attendant civil rights movement, and still more recently—with the Viet Nam war in the foreground—the desperate militancy suggested by terms such as "black power" and the "new left." In the realm of morals and mores, especially as related to marriage and sexual relations, other unmistakable signs of change have aroused much confusion, anxiety, and a need for ethical rethinking. The resultant literature and discussion, whether at the popular or the most elevated level, make apparent the prevalence of a "new morality" both in theory and practice. American culture, in other words, has also entered a distinctly post-Puritan phase.[72] Among ecclesiastical theorists these changes have been followed by a widespread attack on "morphological fundamentalism." Especially in the cities theorists have questioned the traditional parish and its conventional ministry as the proper form for manifesting the Church locally. The idea of a "placed" or territory-occupying church is criticized as an inflexible mediaeval vestige; and creative search for new forms of ministry has gone on.[73]

In the midst of these transitions, and to a degree stemming from them, came important changes in the theological atmos-

---

[72] These developments have provoked a deluge of discussion in all of the mass media and in many widely read books. See Harvey Cox, *The Secular City* (New York: The Macmillan Company, 1965); Robert R. Ball, *Premarital Sex in a Changing Society* (Englewood Cliffs, N.J.: Prentice-Hall, Inc., 1966); Joseph Fletcher, *Situation Ethics: The New Morality* (Philadelphia: Westminster Press, 1966).

[73] See Gibson Winter, *The Suburban Captivity of the Churches* (New York: Doubleday & Company, 1961); Martin E. Marty, *Second Chance for American Protestants* (New York: Harper & Row, Publishers, 1963); Walter J. Ong, S.J., *American Catholic Crossroads: Religious-Secular Encounters in the Modern World* (New York: The Macmillan Company, 1959); Edward Wakin & Joseph F. Scheuer, *The De-Romanization of the American Catholic Church* (New York: The Macmillan Company, 1966).

phere. Revived with special urgency was the question of the
historicity of human existence, revelation, and the Church—a
concern which neither the old liberal nor the newer "kerygmatic" solutions seemed to satisfy. Heinz Zahrnt bluntly stated
the case in 1961: "It is clear . . . that the fundamental problem
of all theological work is history. The impact of 'dialectical
theology' [neo-orthodoxy] succeeded in repressing it for a time,
but it could not be dismissed completely. The attempt to use
dogma as it were to overrun history has proved a failure."[74] As
a result, the general thrust and intention of Rudolf Bultmann
rather than Karl Barth has come to provide a more widely
accepted starting point. *The Historian and the Believer* and
Christian Faith and History are but two of the many recent
titles that reveal such interests.[75] The most important characteristic of this new atmosphere is an altered understanding of
what, for two millenia, has been habitually referred to as the
secular and the world, or secularism and worldliness. In recent
theological parlance the negative nuance of such terms has been
transferred to their opposites: religion, religiosity, and the sacred. Martin Luther, Barth, and the Niebuhrs all contributed to
this modern awareness of the virtues of secularity. But the
most provocative new stimulus came from ideas expressed in
the letters of Dietrich Bonhoeffer, written during the last few

[74] Heinz Zahrnt, *The Historical Jesus* (New York: Harper & Row, Publishers, 1963), p. 13.

[75] Van A. Harvey, *The Historian and the Believer* (New York: The Mac-
millan Company, 1966); Thomas W. Ogletree, *Christian Faith and History:
A Critical Comparison of Ernst Troeltsch and Karl Barth* (Nashville, Tenn.:
Abingdon Press, 1965). "Kerygmatic solutions" would shift the emphasis
in New Testament interpretation from the historical Jesus to the message
or proclamation of the early Christian community. See page 548, note 23.
The classic demand for reinterpreting mythological elements in the New
Testament came from Bultmann over two decades earlier—in 1941! His
statement is republished, together with critiques and a reply, in Werner
Bartsch, ed., *Kerygma and Myth* (New York: Harper & Brothers, Publishers, Torchbook, 1961).

months before his execution by the Nazis in 1945. Just as he had earlier applauded Bultmann for "letting the mythological cat out of the bag," he now spoke of a "world come of age" that was no longer in need of "religion" and which must be given a "nonreligious interpretation of biblical terminology."[76] Unquestionably, an important shift in the prevailing theological mood is marked by the way these posthumous works of Bonhoeffer have played an activating role in theological seminaries, parsonage studies, and the discussion-groups of the laity. In the train of this reevaluation of the secular and the present-day role of religion, a large and stimulating literature has arisen—in the United States and Canada as well as in Great Britain, Europe, and Asia. Bishop Robinson's *Honest to God* (1963) and Harvey Cox's *The Secular City* (1965) have been the best sellers of this impulse; but many other works have appeared, some confessedly journalistic, others very laboriously argued. These writers have often tended to exaggerate their radicalism, and hence have veiled their continuity with numerous older traditions—not least, with America's first "death of God" theologian, Ralph Waldo Emerson. H. Richard Niebuhr's *Radical Monotheism* (1960), moreover, anticipated many favorite themes of the "secular" theologians, above all their contention that religiosity, supernaturalism, and traditional theistic arguments are not essential or necessarily desirable elements of a Christian outlook. Another long-term factor in the reshaping of theology was the accumulating influence of logical empiricism and linguistic analysis, as best illustrated perhaps in the earlier and later works of Ludwig Wittgenstein. The net effect of these trends is uncertain, yet many important lines of inquiry have been opened.[77]

---

[76] See Dietrich Bonhoeffer, *Prisoner for God: Letters and Papers from Prison* (New York: The Macmillan Company, 1953), pp. 145–181.

[77] See Gabriel Vahanian, *The Death of God: The Culture of Our Post-Christian Era* (New York: George Braziller, 1961); Thomas J. J. Altizer and William Hamilton, *Radical Theology and the Death of God* (Indianapolis,

Another demand for a new kind of theological enterprise arose from the nearly total *bouleversement* of the world situation of historic Christendom. The decline of Europe in the global balance of power and the world-wide resurgence of nationalism, communism, anticolonialism, and the ethnic religions have turned the whole world into a New World. Along with this disruption of the nineteenth century's arrangement of the world has come an even greater revolution in which the scientific, technological, and analytical attitudes of the West are rapidly transforming and unifying the thought-world, ways of life, and future hopes of all mankind. It is this trend that provokes a great contemporary Dutch scholar to assert that the process of secularization is the present form in which the non-Western world is meeting biblical history! "Technocracy," as he puts it, "has ousted ontocracy."[78] In this New World the United States has become the prime example of the new technological civilization and the arsenal of one competing ideology. By a strange paradox it has become almost isolated; it is now the Old World in a New World that it, in so many ways, nudged into being.[79] The crisis of the so-called "foreign" missionary enterprise is only one striking symbol of this transposition. And in this situation the

---

Ind.: The Bobbs-Merrill Company, 1966); Thomas W. Ogletree, *The Death of God Controversy* (Nashville, Tenn.: Abingdon Press, 1966); Kenneth Hamilton, *God is Dead: The Anatomy of a Slogan* (Grand Rapids, Mich.: Wm. B. Eerdmans Publishing Company, 1966); and in a more metaphysical vein, Schubert M. Ogden, *Christ without Myth* (New York: Harper & Brothers, 1961). On Emerson in this context see Selection VI, especially pp. 305–311.

[78] Arend T. van Leeuwen, *Christianity and World History* (London: Edinburgh House Press, 1964). His term "ontocracy" refers to the situation in which the pattern of society is identified with the immemorial order of the cosmos.

[79] The conservatism of the popular consensus in the United States is probably unequaled anywhere in the world. In other ways as well the country now almost fits H. Stuart Hughes' description of the new Byzantium. See his *An Essay for Our Times* (New York: Alfred A. Knopf, 1950), pp. 131–148.

churches are making the anomalous discovery that some of their most valid precedents are those that were laid down in the pre-Constantinian era when the early Church, despite persecution, was extending its witness into the Hellenized cultures of Asia, Africa, and Europe—and despite its Hebraic background was venturing boldly to reshape its theology for those stupendous undertakings.

On the ecumenical scene, finally, there are equally striking developments, though they are largely derivative from this twentieth-century revolution. Of largest portent is the transformation of historic Roman Catholic attitudes dramatized by Pope John XXIII, and the Second Vatican Council that he convoked. In this atmosphere the "Counter Reformation" has, in effect, been brought to a close. The image of Rome as modernity's most implacable foe has been altered. The commencement of genuine theological exchange between traditions separated since the Reformation or longer has already made clear that a major watershed has been crossed. A basic change in the nature and spirit of the Protestant-Catholic relations has become noticeable. This new encounter has had far more than social and institutional results. Indeed, even more important than its contribution to improved interfaith relations is the rejuvenating effect of the ongoing dialogue on theology itself. The likelihood seems great that this trend will continue to have a profound effect on both the subject matter and the methodology of Christian theology.[80]

Perceptive observers often remark that no American theologian of the post-World War II generation has attained anything approaching the significance of Paul Tillich or the two

---

[80] See George Lindbeck, ed., *Dialogue on the Way: Protestants Report from Rome on the Vatican Council* (Minneapolis, Minn.: Augsburg Publishing House, 1965); Gregory Baum, ed., *Ecumenical Theology Today* (Glen Rock, N.J.: Paulist Press, 1965); G. C. Berkouwer, *The Second Vatican Council and the New Catholicism* (Grand Rapids, Mich.: Wm. B. Eerdmans Publishing Co., 1965).

Niebuhrs. The observation is substantially correct, as is its parallel that in poetry and the novel Eliot, Hemingway, and Faulkner lack successors of equal stature. American philosophy since John Dewey shows a similar dearth of public eminence. Genius is rare. While waiting for it to appear, however, we would do well to interpret the crucial alternation of circumstance that has occurred since the "religious revival" of the 1950's when Norman Vincent Peale's *Guide to Confident Living,* Bishop Fulton J. Sheen's *Peace of Soul,* Rabbi Joshua Loth Liebman's *Peace of Mind,* and Billy Graham's *Peace with God* were providing the keynote. The "secular awakening" of the 1960's is marked by an entirely different temper—one that is marked by a questioning spirit, an openness to interfaith dialogue, and a sense of moral urgency. Harvey Cox's *The Secular City* and Martin Luther King's *Why We Can't Wait,* not to mention Billy Graham's *World Aflame,* suggest the new dimensions of popular concern. What will emerge from the mood thus signified, and which American theologians will most effectively focus the rampant earnestness of the times, remains to be seen. Prognostication, fortunately, is not a task of the historian. The reader can simply be counseled to become himself an interpreter of the signs of the times.

Sydney E. Ahlstrom

New Haven, Connecticut
July 1966

SELECTED BIBLIOGRAPHY

The literature of and about American religious thought and its background is unimaginably vast. This bibliography is thus painfully abbreviated. Listed below, however, are guides to the general scene (I), to major periods and movements (II), and to the theologians represented in this volume (III). In IV a few representative works of the post-World War II period are given. Recent works with bibliographies and useful annotation predominate. Except for those by the editor—which are listed chiefly because they amplify or explain judgments made in the Introduction and notes—*all* works listed are very valuable or even indispensable. Editorial comments on individual entries, therefore, are sparingly made. Space limitations also preclude a generous listing of works by individual theologians; but much of this information is available in the Introduction, headnotes, secondary works cited, standard reference works such as the *Dictionary of American Biography*, or in any good library catalogue. Almost all of these men have some works currently in print, and recently reprinted editions, often in paperback, are constantly appearing. Throughout the bibliography works known to be in paper editions are marked by an asterisk (*), though the reader is reminded that these are often not issued by the original publisher. All good booksellers have catalogues of paperbound books in print.

I   *General Works*

AHLSTROM, SYDNEY E. "Theology in America: A Historical Survey," in *The Shaping of American Religion*. James W. Smith and A. Leland Jamison, eds. Princeton: Princeton University Press, 1961. See Smith and Jamison entry below.

BLAU, JOSEPH L., ed. *American Philosophical Addresses, 1700–1900*. New York: Columbia University Press, 1946.

_____. *Men and Movements in American Philosophy*. Englewood Cliffs, N.J.: Prentice-Hall, 1952.

GAUSTAD, EDWIN S. *A Religious History of America*. New York: Harper & Row, Publishers, 1966.

HUDSON, WINTHROP S. *Religion in America*. New York: Charles Scribner's Sons, 1965.*

OLMSTEAD, CLIFTON E. *History of Religion in the United States*. Englewood Cliffs, N.J.: Prentice-Hall, 1960.

SCHAFF, PHILIP, ed. *American Church History Series*. 13 vols. New York: The Christian Literature Co., 1893–1900.

SCHNEIDER, HERBERT W. *A History of American Philosophy*. New York: Columbia University Press, 1946.*

SMITH, HILRIE SHELTON, *et al. American Christianity: An Historical Interpretation with Representative Documents*. 2 vols. New York: Charles Scribner's Sons, 1960, 1962.

SMITH, JAMES W., and A. LELAND JAMISON, eds. *Religion in American Life*. 4 vols. Princeton: Princeton University Press, 1961. Vols. I and II contain many relevant essays. Vols. III and IV are an invaluable bibliography, edited by Nelson R. Burr.

II   *Works on Periods and Movements*

ABELL, AARON I. *The Urban Impact on American Protestantism, 1865–1900*. Cambridge: Harvard University Press, 1943.

AHLSTROM, SYDNEY E. *The American Protestant Encounter with World Religions*. Beloit, Wisc.: Beloit College, 1962.

————. "The Scottish Philosophy and American Theology," *Church History*, XXIV (September 1955), 257–272.

ANDOVER REVIEW, Editors of. *Progressive Orthodoxy; A Contribution to the Christian Interpretation of Christian Doctrines.* Boston: Houghton Mifflin Company, 1886.

BARNES, GILBERT H. *The Anti-Slavery Impulse, 1830–1844.* New York: D. Appleton-Century Company, 1933.*

BILLINGTON, RAY A. *The Protestant Crusade 1800–1860: A Study of the Origins of American Nativism.* New York: The Macmillan Company, 1938.*

BOORSTIN, DANIEL J. *The Lost World of Thomas Jefferson.* New York: Henry Holt and Company, 1948.*

BUCKHAM, JOHN WRIGHT. *Progressive Religious Thought in America: A Survey of the Enlarging Pilgrim Faith.* Boston: Houghton Mifflin Company, 1919.

CAUTHEN, KENNETH. *The Impact of American Religious Liberalism.* New York: Harper & Row, Publishers, 1962. Includes chapter on Rauschenbusch.

COUSINS, NORMAN, ed. *In God We Trust: The Religious Beliefs and Ideas of the American Founding Fathers.* New York: Harper & Brothers, 1958.

CRAGG, GERALD R. *From Puritanism to the Age of Reason: A Study of Changes in Religious Thought Within the Church of England, 1660 to 1700.* Cambridge: Cambridge University Press, 1950.

CROSS, ROBERT D. *The Church and the City.* The American Heritage Series. Indianapolis, Ind.: The Bobbs-Merrill Company, 1967.*

ELLIS, JOHN TRACY. *American Catholicism.* Chicago: University of Chicago Press, 1956.*

FAIRWEATHER, EUGENE R., ed. *The Oxford Movement.* Library of Protestant Thought. New York: Oxford University Press, 1964.

FOSTER, FRANK H. *A Genetic History of the New England Theology.* Chicago: University of Chicago Press, 1907.

_____. *The Modern Movement in American Theology*. New York: Fleming H. Revell Company, 1939.

FURNISS, NORMAN F. *The Fundamentalist Controversy, 1918–1931*. New Haven: Yale University Press, 1954.

GASPER, LOUIS. *The Fundamentalist Movement*. The Hague: Mouton & Co., 1963.

GLAZER, NATHAN. *American Judaism*. Chicago: University of Chicago Press, 1957.*

HAROUTUNIAN, JOSEPH. *Piety Versus Moralism: The Passing of the New England Theology*. New York: Henry Holt and Company, 1932.

HEIMERT, ALAN E., and PERRY MILLER. *The Great Awakening*. The American Heritage Series. Indianapolis, Ind.: The Bobbs-Merrill Company, 1967.*

HEIMERT, ALAN E. *Religion and the American Mind: From the Great Awakening to the Revolution*. Cambridge: Harvard University Press, 1966.

HOFSTADTER, RICHARD. *Anti-Intellectualism in American Life*. New York: Alfred A. Knopf, 1963.*

HUDSON, WINTHROP S. *American Protestantism*. Chicago: University of Chicago Press, 1961.*

KOCH, GUSTAV A. *Republican Religion: The American Revolution and the Cult of Reason*. New York: Henry Holt and Company, 1933.

KRAUS, C. NORMAN. *Dispensationalism in America: Its Rise and Development*. Richmond, Va.: John Knox Press, 1958.

LEE, ROBERT. *The Social Sources of Church Unity*. Nashville, Tenn.: Abingdon Press, 1960.

MCLOUGHLIN, WILLIAM G., JR. *Modern Revivalism: Charles Grandison Finney to Billy Graham*. New York: The Ronald Press, 1959.

MEAD, SIDNEY E. *The Lively Experiment: The Shaping of Christianity in America*. New York: Harper & Row, Publishers, 1963.

MILLER, PERRY. *The Life of the Mind in America; From the Revolution to the Civil War.* New York: Harcourt, Brace & World, 1965.

MORAIS, HERBERT M. *Deism in Eighteenth-Century America.* New York: Columbia University Press, 1934.

POCHMANN, HENRY A. *German Culture in America: Philosophical and Literary Influences, 1600–1900.* Madison, Wisc.: University of Wisconsin Press, 1957.

SMITH, HILRIE SHELTON. *Changing Conceptions of Original Sin: A Study in American Theology Since 1750.* NewYork: Charles Scribner's Sons, 1955.

SMITH, JOHN E. *The Spirit of American Philosophy.* New York: Oxford University Press, 1963. Includes chapters on Royce and James.*

SMITH, TIMOTHY L. *Revivalism and Social Reform in Mid-Nineteenth-Century America.* Nashville, Tenn.: Abingdon Press, 1957.*

SMITH, WILSON. *Professors and Public Ethics: Studies in Northern Moral Philosophers Before the Civil War.* Ithaca, N.Y.: Cornell University Press, 1956.

TRINTERUD, LEONARD J. *The Forming of an American Tradition: A Re-Examination of Colonial Presbyterianism.* Philadelphia: The Westminster Press, 1949.

WALKER, WILLISTON. *The Creeds and Platforms of Congregationalism.* Introduction by Douglas Horton. Boston: Pilgrim Press, 1960.*

WILLIAMS, DANIEL DAY. *The Andover Liberals; A Study in American Theology.* New York: King's Crown Press, 1941.

WILLIAMS, NORMAN P., and CHARLES HARRIS, eds. *Northern Catholicism, Centenary Studies in the Oxford and Parallel Movements.* New York: The Macmillan Company, 1933.

WOLF, WILLIAM J. *The Almost Chosen People: A Study of the Religion of Abraham Lincoln.* Garden City, N.Y.: Doubleday & Co., 1959.*

III   *Studies and Editions Related to Selections*

Note: Works by the authors of the selections are not listed except for reprints of volumes from which selections have been taken and a few noteworthy editions.

THOMAS HOOKER

AHLSTROM, SYDNEY E. "Thomas Hooker, Puritanism, and Democratic Citizenship," *Church History*, XXXII (December 1963), 415–431.

HALLER, WILLIAM. *The Rise of Puritanism, 1570–1643.* New York: Columbia University Press, 1938.*

HOOKER, THOMAS. *Redemption: Three Sermons, 1637–1656.* Introduction by Everett H. Emerson. Gainesville, Fla.: Scholars' Facsimiles & Reprints, 1956.

MILLER, PERRY. *Errand Into the Wilderness.* Cambridge: Harvard University Press, 1956. Chap. 2 on Hooker; Chap. 3 on Puritan theology.*

————. *The New England Mind: The Seventeenth Century.* New York: The Macmillan Company, 1939.*

————. *The New England Mind: From Colony to Province.* Cambridge: Harvard University Press, 1953.*

————. *Orthodoxy in Massachusetts, 1630–1650.* Cambridge: Harvard University Press, 1933.

———— and THOMAS H. JOHNSON, eds. *The Puritans, A Sourcebook of Their Writings.* Bibliographies revised by George McCandlish. 2 vols. New York: Harper & Row, Publishers, 1963.*

MORGAN, EDMUND S. *The Puritan Dilemma: The Story of John Winthrop.* Boston: Little, Brown & Co., 1958.*

————. *Visible Saints: The History of a Puritan Idea.* New York: New York University Press, 1963.*

NUTTALL, GEOFFREY F. *The Holy Spirit in Puritan Faith and Experience.* Oxford: Basil Blackwell, Ltd., 1946.

————. *Visible Saints: The Congregational Way, 1640–1660.* Oxford: Basil Blackwell, Ltd., 1957.

SIMPSON, ALAN. *Puritanism in Old and New England*. Chicago: University of Chicago Press, 1955. Valuable survey with bibliography.*

WALKER, GEORGE L. *Thomas Hooker: Preacher, Founder, Democrat*. New York: Dodd, Mead, and Company, 1891.

JONATHAN EDWARDS

CHERRY, CONRAD. *The Theology of Jonathan Edwards*. New York: Doubleday & Company, Anchor Books, 1966.*

DAVIDSON, EDWARD H. *Jonathan Edwards: The Narrative of a Puritan Mind*. Boston: Houghton Mifflin Company, 1966.*

ELWOOD, DOUGLAS J. *The Philosophical Theology of Jonathan Edwards*. New York: Columbia University Press, 1960.

FAUST, CLARENCE C., and THOMAS H. JOHNSON, eds. *Jonathan Edwards, Representative Selections*. Bibliographies revised by Stephen S. Webb. New York: Hill and Wang, 1962.*

GAUSTAD, EDWIN S. *The Great Awakening in New England*. New York: Harper & Brothers, 1957.

HOWARD, LEON. *"The Mind" of Jonathan Edwards: A Reconstructed Text*. Berkeley and Los Angeles: University of California Press, 1963.

MILLER, PERRY, ed. *Images or Shadows of Divine Things*. New Haven: Yale University Press, 1948.

————. *Jonathan Edwards*. New York: William Sloane Associates, 1949.*

TOWNSEND, HARVEY G., ed. *The Philosophy of Jonathan Edwards from His Private Notebooks*. Eugene, Ore.: University of Oregon, 1955.

WINSLOW, OLA E. *Jonathan Edwards, 1703–1758*. New York: The Macmillan Company, 1940.*

WILLIAM ELLERY CHANNING

AHLSTROM, SYDNEY E. "The Interpretation of Channing," *New England Quarterly*, XXX (1957), 99–105.

CHANNING, WILLIAM ELLERY. *Unitarian Christianity and Other Essays*. Irving H. Bartlett, ed. American Heritage Series. New York: Liberal Arts Press, 1957.*

————. *The Works of William E. Channing*. Boston: American Unitarian Association, 1895. Includes *The Perfect Life*.

CHANNING, WILLIAM HENRY. *The Life of William Ellery Channing*. Boston: American Unitarian Association, 1880. The one indispensable biography.

EDGELL, DAVID P. *William Ellery Channing; An Intellectual Portrait*. Boston: Beacon Press, 1955.

FROTHINGHAM, OCTAVIUS BROOKS. *Boston Unitarianism, 1820–1850; A Study of the Life and Work of Nathaniel Langdon Frothingham*. New York: G. P. Putnam's Sons, 1890.

PATTERSON, ROBERT L. *The Philosophy of William Ellery Channing*. New York: Bookman Associates, 1952.

WRIGHT, CONRAD P. *The Beginnings of Unitarianism in America*. Boston: Beacon Press, 1955.

————. "The Rediscovery of Channing," *Proceedings,* Unitarian Historical Society, Vol. XII, Part II (1959), pp. 8–25. Contains bibliography of recent scholarship.

NATHANIEL WILLIAM TAYLOR

BEECHER, LYMAN. *The Autobiography*. Barbara M. Cross, ed. 2 vols. Cambridge: Harvard University Press, 1961. An invaluable window on the ethos of New School Protestantism.

FISHER, GEORGE PARK. *Discussions in History and Theology*. New York: Charles Scribner's Sons, 1880.

KELLER, CHARLES R. *The Second Great Awakening in Connecticut*. New Haven: Yale University Press, 1942.

MEAD, SIDNEY E. *Nathaniel William Taylor, 1786–1858, A Connecticut Liberal*. Chicago: University of Chicago Press, 1942.

MORGAN, EDMUND S. *The Gentle Puritan; A Life of Ezra Stiles, 1727–1795*. New Haven: Yale University Press, 1962. Illuminates the "age" between Edwards and Taylor.

CHARLES HODGE

DANHOF, RALPH J. *Charles Hodge as a Dogmatician.* Goes, The Netherlands: Oosterbaan & Le Cointre, c. 1930. An appreciative view from an even stricter standpoint than Hodge's.

HODGE, ARCHIBALD A. *The Life of Charles Hodge.* New York: Charles Scribner's Sons, 1880.

HODGE, CHARLES. *Systematic Theology.* 3 vols. Reprint edition. Grand Rapids, Mich.: Wm. B. Eerdmans Publishing Co., 1952.

KERR, HUGH T., ed. *Sons of the Prophets: Leaders in Protestantism from Princeton Seminary.* Princeton: Princeton University Press, 1963.

LOETSCHER, LEFFERTS A. *The Broadening Church: A Study of Theological Issues in the Presbyterian Church since 1869.* Philadelphia: University of Pennsylvania Press, 1954.

SANDEEN, ERNEST R. "The Princeton Theology: One Source of Biblical Literalism in American Protestantism," *Church History,* XXXI (September 1962), 307–321.

RALPH WALDO EMERSON

BISHOP, JONATHAN. *Emerson on the Soul.* Cambridge: Harvard University Press, 1964.

CARPENTER, FREDERIC I. *Emerson and Asia.* Cambridge: Harvard University Press, 1930.

————. *Emerson Handbook.* New York: Hendricks House, 1953.

CHRISTY, ARTHUR E. *The Orient in American Transcendentalism: A Study of Emerson, Thoreau, and Alcott.* New York: Columbia University Press, 1932.

FROTHINGHAM, OCTAVIUS BROOKS. *Transcendentalism in New England; A History.* New York: G. P. Putnam's Sons, 1897. Torchbook edition with an Introduction by Sydney E. Ahlstrom. New York: Harper & Brothers, 1959.*

HUTCHISON, WILLIAM R. *The Transcendentalist Ministers: Church Reform in the New England Renaissance.* New Haven: Yale University Press, 1959.*

KONVITS, MILTON R., and STEPHEN E. WHICHER, eds. *Emerson: A Collection of Critical Essays.* Englewood Cliffs, N.J.: Prentice-Hall, 1962.*

MILLER, PERRY. *The Transcendentalists: An Anthology.* Cambridge: Harvard University Press, 1950.

RUSK, RALPH L. *The Life of Ralph Waldo Emerson.* New York: Charles Scribner's Sons, 1949.

WHICHER, STEPHEN E. *Freedom and Fate.* Philadelphia: University of Pennsylvania Press, 1953.*

_____. *Selections from Ralph Waldo Emerson.* Boston: Houghton Mifflin Company, 1957. A major interpretation by means of selections and annotation.*

WOODBERRY, GEORGE E. *Ralph Waldo Emerson.* New York: The Macmillan Company, 1907.

HORACE BUSHNELL

AHLSTROM, SYDNEY E. "Horace Bushnell," in *A Handbook of Christian Theologians.* Martin E. Marty and Dean G. Peerman, eds. Cleveland: The World Publishing Company, 1965. Pages 36–49.

BUSHNELL, HORACE. *The Spirit in Man.* Mary Bushnell Cheney, ed. New York: Charles Scribner's Sons, 1903. Containing unpublished sermons and other writings and a valuable bibliography of his works.

CHENEY, MARY BUSHNELL. *The Life and Letters of Horace Bushnell.* New York: Harper & Brothers, 1880.

CROSS, BARBARA M. *Horace Bushnell: Minister to a Changing America.* Chicago: University of Chicago Press, 1958.

JOHNSON, WILLIAM A. *Nature and the Supernatural in the Theology of Horace Bushnell.* Lund, Sweden: C W K Gleerup, 1963.

MUNGER, THEODORE T. *Horace Bushnell, Preacher and Theologian.* Boston: Houghton Mifflin Company, 1899.

SMITH, HILRIE SHELTON, ed. *Horace Bushnell.* Library of Protestant Thought. New York: Oxford University Press, 1965.

JOHN WILLIAMSON NEVIN

APPEL, THEODORE. *The Life and Work of John Williamson Nevin.* Philadelphia: Reformed Church Publication House, 1889.

BINKLEY, LUTHER J. *The Mercersburg Theology.* Lancaster, Penn.: Franklin and Marshall College, 1953.

NEVIN, JOHN WILLIAMSON. *The Mystical Presence and other Writings on the Eucharist.* Bard Thompson and George H. Bricker, eds. Lancaster Series on the Mercersburg Theology, IV, Philadelphia: United Church Press, 1966.*

————. *The Mystical Presence, A Vindication of the Reformed or Calvinistic Doctrine of the Holy Eucharist.* Introduction by Richard E. Wentz. Archon Books. Hamden, Conn.: The Shoestring Press, 1963. An unedited reprint.

NICHOLS, JAMES HASTINGS. *Romanticism in American Theology: Nevin and Schaff at Mercersburg.* Chicago: University of Chicago Press, 1961. Excellent on both European and American developments.

SCHAFF, DAVID S. *The Life of Philip Schaff.* New York: Charles Scribner's Sons, 1897.

SCHAFF, PHILIP. *The Principle of Protestantism.* Bard Thompson and George H. Bricker, eds. Philadelphia: United Church Press, 1964.*

ZIEGLER, HOWARD J. B. *Frederick Augustus Rauch, American Hegelian.* Lancaster, Penn.: Franklin and Marshall College, 1953.

CHARLES PORTERFIELD KRAUTH

AHLSTROM, SYDNEY E. "The Lutheran Church in American Culture," *Lutheran Quarterly*, IX (November 1957), 321–342.

FERM, VERGILIUS T. A. *The Crisis in American Lutheran Theology.* New York: The Century Co., 1927.

KRAUTH, CHARLES PORTERFIELD. *The Conservative Reformation and Its Theology.* Reprint Edition. Minneapolis, Minn.: Augsburg Publishing House, 1963.

SPAETH, ADOLPH. *Charles Porterfield Krauth.* 2 vols. New York: Christian Literature Co., 1898–1909.

STEFFENS, DIEDRICH H. *Doctor Carl Ferdinand Wilhelm Walther.* Philadelphia: Lutheran Publication Society, 1917.

WENTZ, ABDEL R., *Pioneer in Christian Unity: Samuel Simon Schmucker.* Philadelphia: Fortress Press, 1967.

WOLF, RICHARD C., ed. *Documents of Lutheran Unity in America.* Philadelphia: Fortress Press, 1966.

JOSIAH ROYCE

BROWN, STUART G., ed. *The Religious Philosophy of Josiah Royce.* Syracuse, N.Y.: Syracuse University Press, 1952.

BURANELLI, VINCENT. *Josiah Royce.* New York: Twayne Publishers, 1964.*

COTTON, JAMES H. *Royce on the Human Self.* Cambridge: Harvard University Press, 1954.

FUSS, PETER. *The Moral Philosophy of Josiah Royce.* Cambridge: Harvard University Press, 1965.

ROYCE, JOSIAH. *The Sources of Religious Insight.* New York: Charles Scribner's Sons, 1963.*

————. *The Spirit of Modern Philosophy.* Boston: Houghton Mifflin Company, 1892. A masterful account of the idealistic tradition.

SMITH, JOHN E. *Royce's Social Infinite: The Community of Interpretation.* New York: Liberal Arts Press, 1950.

WILLIAM JAMES

BIXLER, J. SEELYE. *Religion in the Philosophy of William James.* Boston: Marshall Jones Company, 1926.

BOUTROUX, ÉMILE. *William James.* London: Longmans, Green, & Co., 1912.

BRENNAN, BERNARD P. *The Ethics of William James.* New York: Bookman Associates, 1961.*

JAMES, WILLIAM. *The Varieties of Religious Experience.* Reprint Editions. New York: New American Library, n.d.,* and The Macmillan Company, 1961.*

PERRY, RALPH BARTON. *The Thought and Character of William James.* 2 vols. Boston: Little, Brown, and Company, 1935. Profound, fascinating, and thorough.*

WIENER, PHILIP P. *Evolution and the Founders of Pragmatism.* Cambridge: Harvard University Press, 1949.*

YOUNG, FREDERIC H. *The Philosophy of Henry James, Sr.* New York: Bookman Associates, 1951.

WALTER RAUSCHENBUSCH

HANDY, ROBERT T., ed. *The Social Gospel in America, 1870–1920; Gladden, Ely, Rauschenbusch.* Library of Protestant Thought. New York: Oxford University Press, 1966.

HOPKINS, CHARLES H. *The Rise of the Social Gospel in American Protestantism, 1865–1915.* New Haven: Yale University Press, 1940.

LANDIS, BENSON Y., ed. *A Rauschenbusch Reader.* New York: Harper & Brothers, 1957.

MAY, HENRY F. *Protestant Churches and Industrial America.* New York: Harper & Brothers, 1949. A history of the Social Gospel.

RAUSCHENBUSCH, WALTER. *Christianity and the Social Crisis.* Reprint edition, with an Introduction by Robert D. Cross. New York: Harper & Row, Publishers, 1964.*

————. *A Theology for the Social Gospel.* Reprint edition. Nashville, Tenn.: Abingdon Press, 1961.*

SHARP, DORES R. *Walter Rauschenbusch.* New York: The Macmillan Company, 1942.

H. RICHARD NIEBUHR

AHLSTROM, SYDNEY E. "Continental Influence on American Christian Thought since World War I," *Church History,* XXVII (September 1958), 256–272. The Bobbs-Merrill Reprint Series in History, No. H-5.

_____. "H. Richard Niebuhr's Place in American Thought," *Christianity and Crisis*, XXIII (November 25, 1963), 213–217. One of three essays in a memorial issue.

_____. "Theology and the Present-Day Revival," *Annals* of the American Academy of Political and Social Science, Vol. 332 (November 1960), 20–36.

CARTER, PAUL A. *The Decline and Revival of the Social Gospel, 1920–1940*. Ithaca, N.Y.: Cornell University Press, 1954. Valuable for its accounts of the prohibition, fundamentalist, and ecumenical movements as well as the social concerns of Neo-Orthodoxy.

HOEDEMAKER, LIBERTUS A. *Faith in Total Life: The Style and Direction of H. Richard Niebuhr's Theology*. Groningen, The Netherlands: V.R.B., 1966.

MEYER, DONALD B. *The Protestant Search for Political Realism, 1919–1941*. Berkeley and Los Angeles: University of California Press, 1960.

RAMSEY, PAUL, ed. *Faith and Ethics: The Theology of H. Richard Niebuhr*. New York: Harper & Brothers, 1957. Critical and historical essays on his thought by former students.*

IV   *After Neo-Orthodoxy: Some Representative Departures*

BAUM, GREGORY, ed. *Ecumenical Theology Today*. Glen Rock, N.J.: Paulist Press, 1965.*

BERKOUWER, GERRIT C. *The Second Vatican Council and the New Catholicism*. Grand Rapids, Mich.: Wm. B. Eerdmans Publishing Co., 1965.

BONHOEFFER, DIETRICH. *Prisoner for God: Letters and Papers from Prison*. Eberhard Bethge, ed. Reginald H. Fuller, trans. New York: The Macmillan Company, 1953.*

CHRISTIAN, WILLIAM A. *Meaning and Truth in Religion*. Princeton: Princeton University Press, 1964.

Cox, Harvey. *The Secular City: Secularization and Urbanization in Theological Perspective.* New York: The Macmillan Company, 1965.*

King, Martin Luther. *Why We Can't Wait.* New York: Harper & Row, Publishers, 1964.*

Lindbeck, George, ed. *Dialogue on the Way: Protestants Report from Rome on the Vatican Council.* Minneapolis, Minn.: Augsburg Publishing House, 1965.

Nash, Ronald H. *The New Evangelicalism.* Grand Rapids, Mich.: Zondervan Publishing House, 1963.

Marty, Martin E., ed. *The Place of Bonhoeffer.* New York: Association Press, 1962.*

Ogden, Schubert M. *Christ Without Myth, A Study Based on the Theology of Rudolf Bultmann.* New York: Harper & Brothers, 1961.

Ong, Walter J. *American Catholic Crossroads: Religious-Secular Encounters in the Modern World.* New York: The Macmillan Company, 1959.*

Robinson, James M., ed. *The Later Heidegger and Theology.* New York: Harper & Row, Publishers, 1963.

———— and John B. Cobb. *The New Hermeneutic.* New York: Harper & Row, Publishers, 1964.

Vahanian, Gabriel. *The Death of God: The Culture of Our Post-Christian Era.* New York: George Braziller, 1961.*

————, ed. *The God Is Dead Debate.* New York: McGraw-Hill Book Co., 1966.*

Theology in America

I

THOMAS HOOKER

Puritan Pastor and Preacher

Thomas Hooker (1586–1647)[1] was a prophet greatly honored in his own land, whether that be regarded as the Commonwealth of Connecticut which remembers him as its founder, or as early New England whose leaders in both the church and state praised him as the Chrysostomus-Nov-Anglorum and "the chief light of the western churches," or as Old England from which he fled but where fellow Puritans, whether in triumph or despond, continued to esteem him as a great physician of the soul and a veritable doctor of the Church. With remarkable fullness he exhibits the tribulations, anxieties, and glory of the Puritan movement.

Born to a family of modest situation in Leicester County, he nevertheless received in youth such nurture and education as enabled him to enter Cambridge in 1604, a time when the Puritan spirit waxed strong in that University and especially so in Emmanuel College from which Hooker received his B.A. in 1608 and his M.A. in 1611. A few years later, while still a Fellow at Emmanuel, the event came that changed the course of his life. He received that "experimental knowledge of Christ" that he would henceforward examine so minutely in his sermons. He was now a Puritan divine and around 1620 he began his career as a

---

[1] See Introduction, pp. 24–33.

parish minister. So effective was he as Lecturer at St. Mary's, Chelmsford, however, that the authorities were aroused, and in 1630 he fled to Holland. On Dutch soil he was associated with emigré Puritan congregations in several cities, most notably in Rotterdam, where he saw through the press the last work of the late William Ames, A FRESH SUIT AGAINST HUMAN CEREMONIES IN GODS WORSHIP (1633). Later in that year, upon his arrival in Massachusetts, he was reunited with many of his former parishioners from Chelmsford. In 1634 he was ordained as their pastor in a duly covenanted congregation at Newtown (Cambridge).

Historical controversy has always surrounded the further history of this congregation, which seems from the first to have been restive in the proximity of Boston and its celebrated minister, John Cotton. In 1635 exploration of the possibilities for removal to the West began, and in the following year the congregation with its two ministers made its famous trek to the Connecticut River valley. In 1638 Hooker delivered his celebrated sermon before the convention assembled to provide a Frame of Government for the new communities in the Hartford area. Until his death he continued to play an important role—as an eloquent preacher and sensitive spiritual guide for his own flock, as an active participant in the civil and religious controversies that disturbed New England's peace, and as a formally appointed spokesman for the Congregational Way during the years when Parliamentary victories in Old England, for a time, enabled Puritans to carry out their long-pondered proposals for reforming England's church.

Hooker's genius expressed itself best at precisely the point where Puritanism made its largest and most permanent impact on Anglo-American church life and society—the pulpit. He was a master preacher, and except for A SURVEY OF THE SUMME OF CHURCH-DISCIPLINE (1648), a treatise on polity, Hooker's entire published work is a sermonic literature. Its subject matter is devoted to the two main foci of Puritan concern. Hooker concentrated on the way of salvation, the process by which the wayward sinner moves through the stages of preparation, penitence, and humiliation to assurance of grace in Christ, accompanying these expositions with discourses on man's personal and public responsibilities. Perhaps no man better symbolizes at their uncorrupted fountainhead the two traits that the American churches and the American people owe to their Founding Fathers of the seventeenth century: an intense emphasis on religious experience and a sense of moral duty.

The sermon that follows appeared posthumously in a volume of seven sermons, each with a separate title page and probably for sale separately. It was published in London in 1651 under the title The Saints Dignitie, and Dutie. Together with the Danger of Ignorance and Hardnesse, and included a preface by Hooker's son-in-law and successor at Cambridge, Massachusetts, Thomas Shepard (1605–1649).

The Activitie of Faith illustrates in a remarkable manner the characteristic features of Puritan preaching. It is from start to finish an "opening" of the Scriptures—not only the immediate text but dozens of other related passages from the New Testament and the Old. It shows constant awareness of the preaching situation by its illustrations from the common life, its "plain style," its orderliness, and its attainment of emphasis through repetition. Though solid in substance and with obvious bearing on a great many issues, it is free from exhibitions of learning, rhetorical flourish, and the kinds of argumentation appropriate to a written theological essay. It employs the tripartite form so dear to Puritan preachers that consists of: (1) clarification of the meaning and context of the Scriptural lesson, (2) delineation of the doctrine(s) taught therein, and (3) amplification of the "use" or practical import of these instructions. Seen as a whole the sermon is directed at what was to all Puritans the primary scandal of the Church of England and one constantly to be guarded against in New England: to wit, complacency and the reliance on externals. Yet characteristically it goes on to warn against the dangers of overconfident inwardness, demanding that faith have footsteps in the world.

In this edition only the spelling, capitalization, and punctuation have been modernized; a few headings have been added, but Hooker's language is unaltered, including his italicizing of Scripture passages. It is completely unabridged.

The Activity of Faith:

or,

Abraham's Imitators

Romans 4:12.

And the Father of Circumcision to them who are not of circumcision only, but also walk in the steps of that faith of our father Abraham, which he had, being yet uncircumcised.

The blessed Apostle Saint Paul, from the 20th verse of the former chapter, to the end, disputeth that great question of justification by the free grace of God; and after many arguments alleged to prove that it is by grace, and not by works, he con-

---

From *The Saints Dignitie, and Dutie. Together with the Danger of Ignorance and Hardnesse. Delivered in Severall Sermons:* By that Reverend Divine, Thomas Hooker, Late Preacher in New England (London, Printed by G. D. for Francis Eglesfield, and are to be sold at the Sign of the Marigold in Pauls Church-yard, 1651), Sermon V, pages 155–187.

cludeth in the 28th verse, *Therefore we conclude, that a man is justified by faith without the works of the law.*[1]

Having dispatched this, and settled his assertion by strength of argument in this fourth chapter, wherein my text is, he laboureth to make the truth yet more clear and evident by way of example, and to the end he setteth it forth in the lively color of that faith of Abraham, giving us an instance of this truth, in the example of him who was the father of the faithful, a father not by natural generation but by imitation, the Lord having appointed him to be the copy to all the believers of succeeding ages, that as he believed and by faith was saved, so they that do expect to receive salvation must walk in that way if they purpose to partake of that end.

Now touching this example of Abraham, that I may not be long before I come to that which is the principal point I intend to deliver at this time; the Apostle doth two things. First, he layeth down the pattern itself clearly, both in God's vouchsafing justification to Abraham, and also in God's sealing this by the seal of circumcision, and this he doth in the 11th verse.[2]

And as he hath propounded it thus, both in God's gift, and in God's sealing thereof, so in the words of the text he maketh an application of both, applying it to all Abraham's children that shall live to the end of the world, whether Jews or Gentiles; and in effect it is as if he had said thus: Abraham when he was uncircumcised did believe, and so was justified, therefore they that are uncircumcised may believe, and be also justified. Abraham when he did believe was circumcised, and that hindered

---

[1] Hooker nearly always quotes from the King James Version; in this case perhaps from memory. Both the Geneva and King James versions read "deeds" rather than "works" in Romans 3:28. The Roman Catholic Douai version reads "works." [Ed.]

[2] "And he received the sign of circumcision, a seal of the righteousness of the faith which he had yet being uncircumcised: that he might be the father of all them that believe, though they be not circumcised; that righteousness might be imputed unto them also." Romans 4:11. [Ed.]

not; so those that are circumcised may believe and be justified; that is, the Jews and the Gentiles have both liberty to come into the Covenant of grace, and so also to be happy by that Covenant, as Abraham was.

In the words therefore, you have an application of the former pattern to the particular use of every faithful servant of God that look [or perceive] what good Abraham had and what he received by faith. They that believe as he did may expect the selfsame mercy that he had.

Now the faithful of God and sons of Abraham are here described two ways: I say, every faithful man that is the son of Abraham, that imitateth the faith of Abraham, is discovered in two ways.

First, negatively, what will not suffice to make a man the son of Abraham.

Secondly, affirmatively, what God specially looks for at the hands of those that are to be the children of Abraham.

First, negatively thus, Abraham *is the father of circumcision, not only to them who are of the circumcision;* that is, not only [is he] theirs who have the privileges of the Jews, the Word, and the Oracles of God, Circumcision, and the Passover. 'Tis true, Abraham is their father, but not only theirs that have no more but those privileges, but also theirs that walk in the footsteps of the faith of Abraham. So that by circumcision you must here understand all these prerogatives and privileges which the Jews had above any other nation; and consequently that none of all those privileges then could, [and] that none of ours, as to be in the Church, to be baptized, etc., now can make a man to be the son of Abraham. Abraham *is the father of the circumcision, not to them who are of the circumcision only;* but he is the father of the circumcision if they have faith. They that have bare circumcision only may indeed applaud themselves therein, but they shall never receive thereby those things God hath promised. This is the negative.

Secondly, the affirmative part shows who they be indeed that shall truly be partakers of the comforts and graces of Abraham, namely, those *that walk in the footsteps of that faith of Abraham*. If a man believe as he did, work as he did, walk as he did, so only he may come to have title unto, and interest in the promises God hath vouchsafed in his Word. Thus much for the opening of the words.

[THE NEGATIVE]

Come we now in the first place to speak of the negative part, in which the Spirit of God is pleased to exclude all outward privileges and prerogatives, and to say thus, Abraham *is the father of circumcision to them who are not of the circumcision only;* that is, if they enjoy only outward privileges, they are not the children of Abraham. The point we learn hence is thus much:

That all outward privileges, as the hearing of the Word, the partaking of the Sacraments, and the like, are not able to make a man a sound Saint of God.

The point is clear in the text that if a man had circumcision, that is, if he had all those preferments that God vouchsafeth to a people in the face and bosom of his Church, this would not do him any good at all. He hath no title to the promises because of these, if he rest in them: Abraham *is not the father of those that are circumcised only.* So that I say again, all outward privileges are not able to make a man a true Saint of God. Our Saviour Christ, speaking of Capernaum, saith, *And thou Capernaum, which art exalted unto heaven, shalt be brought down to hell; for if the mighty works which have been done in thee had been done in Sodom, it would have remained until this day* (Matt. 11:23). Capernaum was *lifted up to Heaven;* how? In all those spiritual helps and excellent means that God vouchsafed them above many others; they were highly advanced in the enjoyment of heavenly privileges, they heard the Word of God, and they saw the miracles of Christ; and yet, *thou Capernaum* shalt be deep in punishment; *thou wert lifted up to Heaven* in regard of excellent privileges; *but thou shalt be cast down to Hell* in regard of thy impenitency and stubborness under them. The Apostle Paul disputeth the point, and makes the case clear (Rom. 2:28,29), where he plucks away all these hopes and vain props, which men raise to themselves from the having of outward privileges: *He is not a Jew,* saith he, *that is one outwardly,* that is, he is not therefore a true child of God and a faithful man, he hath not therefore saving faith, because he is circumcised, because he enjoyeth the liberties and privileges of the people of God, and liveth in the bosom of the Church; *but he is a Jew which is one inwardly, and circumcision is that of the heart, in the spirit and not in the letter, whose praise is not of men but of God.* You know that it was an ancient proverb in Israel, *Is Saul also amongst the prophets?* (1 Sam. 10:12 and 19:24). Yes, Saul was amongst the prophets, and he that was once amongst the prophets is now amongst the devils in hell. Judas was highly promoted; he lived as an apostle amongst the disciples, heard our Saviour continually, sat at table with him, and yet for all this, is now damned in hell forever. These were high privileges, and if these would have done the deed, Judas had never perished. Ishmael was circumcised, and yet he was excommunicated out of Abraham's family, the then Church of God, and was a cast-away. Instances are many in the Scriptures to this purpose, but I list not to dwell longer upon the proof of the point; you see it is evident enough, that bare privileges, be they never so high and excellent, are not able to make one indeed a faithful man before the Lord, nor the son of Abraham.

I should have showed the reasons. Alas! outward matters never work upon the heart. That which makes a man a Saint must work upon the soul. Now the Word and the Sacraments barely considered cannot work upon the spirit unless the Lord work a new frame inwardly by the infusion of Grace: *Circumcision and uncircumcision profiteth nothing, but faith that worketh by love* (Gal. 5:6). These outward things are too shallow to reach the inward man, too weak to work so powerfully upon the soul of a Christian man, as to bring the heart to God. But I leave the strengthening of the point by reasons, and because I would not be prevented, I come to the uses.

[FIRST USE OF THE NEGATIVE: THE USE OF REPROOF]

The first use I will hence raise is an use of reproof. This doctrine confoundeth the carnal confidence of those professors that, living in the bosom of the Church, place all their hopes and assurance of being saved upon this bottom: because they have been baptized, and come to Church, and hear the Word, and receive the Sacrament, therefore of necessity (they presume) they must be accepted of God. This was the old plea of the Jews in Jeremiah's time. When the prophet came to them to reprove them for their sins and press them to repentance, they began to quarrel with him and to take up bucklers against him, and cried out, *The Temple of the Lord, the Temple of the Lord, are these* (Jer. 7:4). These are the fig-leaves wherewith poor and ignorant Christians think to hide themselves at this day. Tell them of their faults, bid them walk humbly and holily before God, reprove them for their strange practices against God and his truth, in profaning his day, blaspheming his name, contemning his Word, despising his ministers, etc. And they presently cry out against us: What will you make pagans of us? What do you think we are heathens? Have we not received Christian baptism? etc. This is a bottom that beareth up many: but oh poor silly creatures, this will not do it. Be not deceived, you will shrink under this shelter; you will fall notwithstanding these props, when you come to trial; you may have all this, and yet perish; this will not make you saints in the sight of God. You that are tradesmen, is it a good argument, that because you have good ware in your shops, therefore you have no refuse, no drug commodity? Or you that are husbandmen, because some good corn grows upon your ground, is it therefore all good corn?

Who knows not that there is cockle amongst corn, and bad wares even in your best shops. So it is true here, as there are many hearers in hell, and many receivers in hell, so there are too many in the bosom of the Church, enjoying the outward privileges of God's people, that shall never receive good by all that they partake of.

Therefore I beseech you be not deceived, trust not to these lying words and vain hopes, the Sacrament of Lord, and the Church. I say, trust not to these *lying vanities.* A man may, as Judas, not only have the Sacrament in his hand, but Christ in his mouth, and go to hell notwithstanding. Alas, at the day of judgement, if thou hast nothing to say but this, Lord, I was a hearer of thy Word, a receiver at thy Table, a frequenter of thy house, thou canst expect no other answer, but *Depart from me, I know thee not.* He is not the son of Abraham that hath circumcision only, but *that walketh in the steps of the faith of Abraham.*

[SECOND USE OF THE NEGATIVE: THE USE OF EXHORTATION]

In the second place, here is a word of exhortation, and that is this: we ought hereby to be instructed and provoked to stir up our souls, and not to content ourselves with, or settle ourselves in these outward shadows, but to labor to go further, and beyond all that these outward privileges barely, as outward privileges, can make us; not only to enjoy these, but to strive to be bettered by them; not only to have the Word and the Sacraments, but to improve them; to get more than the outward shell, to labor for the kernel, for the comfort of them. Therefore I would advise a Christian man that liveth in the bosom of the Church where the Lord is pleased to continue helps and means to him, to esteem them great privileges (for so they are), so not to content himself with the outward enjoyment of them, but to call upon himself, and to look inward, to see what the heart saith. Outward things will not do the deed; look we therefore

for somewhat more, that will stand us in stead when the Lord
cometh with *his fan in his hand, thoroughly to purge his floor*
[Matt. 3:12], and to make a division between the *wheat* and
the *chaff*. Take notice of it therefore, and understand for your
spiritual good: when thou comest to the house of God, and
bringest thine hands to receive the Sacrament, and thine ears to
listen to the Word, think with thyself, I have heard the Word, I
have received the Sacrament, but O heart what sayest thou?
Have I embraced these promises? Have I closed with those precepts that have been delivered? Have I eaten Christ in the Sacrament? Hath my faith pitched on him exhibited there, under
the elements of Bread and Wine?[3] How often have I already
lived under the call of God, and yet have rejected it? My soul is
not yet humbled; I only come and hear, and return without any
benefit; therefore now I will go further, and dig deeper, that my
heart may be brought to the obedience of the truth. Mark what
our Saviour Christ saith (John 6:49), provoking the Jews to believe in him and so to receive mercy by him, he speaks on this
manner, forcing them to go further than outward things: *Your
fathers* (saith he) *did eat manna in the wilderness, and are
dead.* Who are those fathers? Those stubborn and rebellious
Jews that fell in the wilderness: *These entered not because of
unbelief,* saith the Apostle to the Hebrews. Now Christ saith,
Your fathers did eat manna, and are dead (Heb. 4:6); he
meaneth are damned, for he saith afterward (verse 51), *If any
man eat of this bread, he shall live forever;* thereby showing a
difference between the faithful and unbelievers, though both
die a natural death; I say, making a difference between the rebellious Jews that did not believe, and those that did believe.
Your fathers did eat manna in the wilderness, a type and a Sacrament indeed to them, as St. Paul expresseth it; but that would
not do the deed. Though the manna came from heaven, yet it
could not bring them up to heaven, it could not free them from

---

[3] See Nevin on early Puritan sacramental theology, pp. 386–398. [Ed.]

eternal death. But here is the privilege of believing and of right receiving: he that doth not only receive bread, but Christ, he that eateth this food, this bread, he shall never die any more, he cannot perish. Labor therefore for this evermore: as when the woman of Samaria heard our Saviour speak of *living water* that would continue forever, she cried out presently, *Oh Sir, give me of this water, that I thirst no more* (John 4:15). So labor for this food above all: labor to settle your souls and to rest your hearts still upon these resolutions. Oh what have I that a carnal man may not have? What do I that a carnal man cannot do? I would have a Christian man, to go beyond all those that live in the bosom of the Church. I say therefore, let this be the question, and examine thine heart: What do I more than the damned in hell have done, I pray? The truth is, the foolish Virgins knocked too. I preach, so did Judas. Do I reform many things, so did Herod. Was I baptized? So was Simon Magus. In a word, am I resolved to confess my sins and to make satisfaction for them? Alas Judas did all this, and yet this would not serve the turn; he sorrowed, and repented, and when he had done, he went and hanged himself. It was not godly sorrow that caused repentence to salvation; he repented only for the gall of sin, not for the soul of sin. Labor we therefore, and let us every one provoke another to go further than ever reprobates went; in praying, and hearing, and professing, labor for something that will stand us in stead in the day of trial, *when the heavens shall be rolled together as a scroll* (Isaiah 34:4), that we may appear before the Lord, and receive a reward from him in his appointed time and season. So much for the Negative Part.

[THE AFFIRMATIVE]

I proceed now to the affirmative: Who those are that may, and do indeed, receive benefit as Abraham did? The text saith, *They that walk in the steps of that faith of Abraham.* That man that not only enjoyeth the privileges of the Church, but yieldeth the obedience of faith according to the Word of God revealed, and walketh in obedience, that man alone shall be blessed with faithful Abraham.

Two points may be hence raised, but I shall hardly handle them both, therefore I will pass over the first only with a touch, and that lieth closely couched in the text,

[I FAITH CAUSES FRUITFULNESS]

That, *Faith causeth fruitfulness in the hearts and lives of those in whom it is.*

Mark what I say, a faithful man is a fruitful man: faith enableth a man to be doing. Ask the question, by what power was it whereby Abraham was enabled to yield obedience to the Lord? The text answereth you, *They that walk in the footsteps not of Abraham, but in the footsteps of the faith of Abraham.* A man would have thought the text should have run thus, *They that walk in the footsteps of Abraham,* that is true too; but the Apostle had another end, therefore he saith, *They that walk in the footsteps of the faith of Abraham,* implying that it was the grace of faith that God bestowed on Abraham, that quickened and enabled him to every duty that God required of him, and called him to the performance of. So that I say, the question being, whence came it that Abraham was so fruitful a Christian, what enabled him to do, and to suffer what he did? Surely it was faith that was the cause that produced such effects, that helped him to perform such actions. The point then you see is evident, faith is it that causeth fruit.

Hence it is that of almost all the actions that a Christian has to do, faith is still said to be the worker. If a man pray as he should, it is *the prayer of faith* (James 5:15). If a man obey as he should, it *is the obedience of faith* (Rom. 16:26). If a man war in the Church militant, it is *the fight of faith* (1 Tim. 6:12; 2 Tim. 4:7). If a man live as a Christian and holy man, he *liveth by faith* (Gal. 2:20). Nay shall I say yet more, if he die as he ought, he *dieth by faith* (Heb. 11:13. *These all died in faith.*)

What is that? The power of faith that directed and ordered them in the course of their death furnished them with grounds and principles of assurance of the love of God, made them carry themselves patiently in death. I can say no more, but with the Apostle, *Examine yourselves, whether ye be in the faith.* Why doth not the Apostle say, *Examine whether faith be in you,* but *whether ye be in the faith?* His meaning is, that as a man is said to *be in drink,* or to *be in love,* or to *be in passion,* that is, under the command of drink, or love, or passion, so the whole man must be under the command of faith (as you shall see more afterwards). If he pray, faith must indite his prayer; if he obey, faith must work; if he live, it is faith that must quicken him; and if he die, it is faith that must order him in death. And wheresoever faith is, it will do wonders in the soul of that man where it is; it cannot be idle, it will have *footsteps,* it sets the whole man on work, it moveth feet, and hands, and eyes, and all parts of the body. Mark how the Apostle disputeth, *We having the same spirit of faith, according as it is written, I believed, and therefore have I spoken, we also believe, and therefore speak* (II Cor. 4:13). The faith of the Apostle which he had in his heart, set his tongue agoing; if a man have faith within, it will break forth at his mouth. This shall suffice for the proof of the point; I thought to have pressed it further, but if I should, I see the time would prevent me.

[THE USE]

The Use therefore in a word is this: If this be so, then it falleth foul, and is a heavy Bill of Indictment against many that live in the bosom of the Church. Go thy ways home, and read but this text, and consider seriously but this one thing in it: *That whoever is the son of Abraham, hath faith, and whosoever hath faith, is a walker, is a worker;* by the footsteps of faith you may see where faith hath been. Will not this then, I say, fall marvelous heavy upon many souls that live in the bosom of the Church, who are confident and put it out of all question that they are true believers and make no doubt but that they have faith? But look to it, wheresoever faith is, it is fruitful: if you art fruitless, say what you will, you have no faith at all. Alas these idle drones, these idle Christians, the Church is too full of them. Men are continually hearing, and yet remain fruitless and unprofitable; whereas if there were more faith in the world, we should have more work done in the world; faith would set feet, and hands, and eyes, and all on work. Men go under the name of professors, but alas they are but pictures, they stir not a whit; mark where you found them in the beginning of the year, there you shall find them in the end of the year, as profane, as worldly, as loose in their conversations, as formal in duty as ever. And is this faith? Oh faith would work other matters, and provoke a soul to other passages than these.

But you will say, May not a man have faith, and not that fruit you speak of? May not a man have a good heart to Godward, although he cannot find that ability in matter of fruitfulness?

My brethren, be not deceived; such an opinion is a mere delusion of Satan; wherever faith is, it bringeth Christ into the soul. Mark that whosoever believeth, *Christ dwelleth in his heart by faith* (Eph. 3:17). And, *If Christ be in you,* saith the Apostle, *the body is dead, because of sin, but the spirit is life, because of righteousness* (Rom. 8:10). *If Christ be in you,* that is: whosoever believeth in the Lord Jesus, Christ dwells in such a man by faith. Now if Christ be in the soul, the body cannot be dead; but a man is alive, and quick, and active to holy duties; ready, and willing, and cheerful in the performance of whatsoever God requireth. Christ is not a dead Saviour, nor the Spirit a dead Spirit; *The second Adam is made a quickning spirit* (I Cor. 15:45). And wherever the Spirit is, it works effects suitable to itself: The Spirit is a spirit of purity, a spirit of zeal, and where it is, it maketh pure and zealous. When a man will say he hath faith, and in the meantime can be content to be idle and unfruitful in the work of the Lord, can be content to be a dead Christian, let him know that his case is marvellously fearful. For if faith were in him indeed, it would appear; ye cannot keep your good hearts to yourselves. Wherever fire is, it will burn, and wherever faith is, it cannot be kept secret. The heart will be enlarged, the soul quickened, and there will be a change in the whole life and conversation, if ever faith take place in a man. I will say no more of this, but proceed to the second point, arising out of the Affirmative part.

[II ON THE IMITATION OF FAITHFUL ABRAHAM]

You will say, what fruit is it then? Or how shall a man know what is the true fruit of faith indeed, whereby he may discern his own estate? I answer, the text will tell you: *He that walketh in the footsteps of that faith of Abraham.* By *footsteps* are meant the works, the actions, the holy endeavors of Abraham; and where those footsteps are, there is the faith of Abraham. So that the point of instruction hence is thus much (which indeed is the main drift of the Apostle),

That *every faithful man may, yea doth imitate the actions of faithful Abraham.*

Mark what I say, I say again, this is to be the son of Abraham, not because we are begotten of him by natural generation; for so the Jews are the sons of Abraham; but Abraham is our father because he is the pattern for the proceeding of our faith. *Thy father was an Amorite,* saith the Scripture (Ezek. 16:3). That is, thou followest the steps of the Amorites in thy conversation. So is Abraham called the *father of the faithful,* because he is the copy of their course, whom they must follow in those services that God calleth for. So the point is clear, *Every faithful man may, yea, doth, and must imitate the actions of faithful Abraham.* It is Christ's own plea (John 8:39), and he presseth it as an undeniable truth upon the hearts of the scribes and pharisees, that bragged very highly of their privileges and prerogatives and said, Abraham is our father. No, saith Christ; if ye were Abraham's children, ye would do the works of Abraham. To be like Abraham in constitution, to be one of his blood, is not that which makes a man a son of Abraham, but to be like him in holiness of affection, to have a heart framed, and a life disposed answerably to his. The Apostle in like manner presseth this point (Heb. 13:7) when he would provoke the Hebrews, to whom he wrote, to follow the examples of the saints, *whose faith* (saith he) *follow, considering the end of their conversation.* So the Apostle Peter presseth the example of Sarah upon all good women, *whose daughters ye are* (saith he) *as long as ye do well* (I Pet. 3:6).

For the opening of the point, and that ye may more clearly understand it, a question here would be resolved: what were *the footsteps of the faith of Abraham?* which way went he? This is a question, I say, worthy the scanning, and therefore (leaving the further confirmation of the point, as being already evident enough) I will come to it, that so you may know what to pitch and settle your hearts upon.

[THE SIX FOOTSTEPS OF ABRAHAM'S FAITH]

I answer therefore, there are six footsteps of the faith of Abraham, which are the main things wherein every faithful man must do as Abraham did, in the work of faith, I mean, in his ordinary course: for if there be any thing extraordinary, no man is bound to imitate him therein; but in the work of faith, I say, which belongeth to all men, every man must imitate Abraham in these six steps, and then he is in the next door to happiness, the very next neighbor, as I may say, to heaven.

[THE FIRST STEP]

The first step which Abraham took in the ways of grace and happiness, you shall observe (Gen. 12:1) to be a yielding to the call of God. Mark what God said to Abraham, *Get thee out of thy country, and from thy kindred, and from thy father's house, unto a land that I will shew thee: And Abraham departed,* saith the text (verse 4), *as the Lord had spoken unto him,* even when he was an idolater. He is content to lay aside all, and let the command of God bear the sway. Neither friends, nor kindred, nor gods can keep him back, but he presently stoopeth to the call of God. So it is, my brethren, with every faithful man. This is his first step: he is contented to be under the rule and power of God's command. Let the Lord call for him, require any service of him, his soul presently yieldeth, and is content to be framed and fashioned to God's call, and returneth an obedient answer thereto. He is content to come out of his sins, and out of himself, and to receive the impressions of the Spirit. This is that which God requireth, not only of Abraham, but of all believers: *Whosoever will be my disciple,* saith Christ, *must forsake father, and mother, and wife, and children, and houses, and lands; yea, and he must deny himself, and take up his Cross, and follow me.*[4] This is the first step in Christianity, to lay down our own honors, to trample upon our own respects, to submit our necks to the block as it were, and whatsoever God commands, to be content that his good pleasure should take place with us.

Nay, yet further, Abraham was not content only to leave his country, and kindred, and father's house, but he left his goods also. The text saith (Josh. 24:2), *Your fathers dwelt on the other side of the flood in old time, even Terah the father of Abraham, and the father of Nachor; and they served other Gods.* Abraham was an idolater before God called him; but as soon as God called him he left his gods behind him, and God only should be his God, to exercise rule and authority over him in every particular.

And this is not all yet, my brethren, I beseech you observe it: Abraham did not this as one constrained and forced thereunto, but so as he would not return anymore; and that is a passage very observable: *Truly,* saith the Apostle (Heb. 11:15), *if he*

---

[4] A paraphrase of Luke 14:26–27. [Ed.]

had been mindful of the country from whence he came out, he might have had opportunity to have returned. If he would have gone back again, he had liberty enough; but he would have no more kindred, nor no more father's house, nor no other gods, because he knew the command of God was otherwise. Therefore he would not return though he might, intimating that he was not drawn from his country by a kind of force; but he so voluntarily yielded up himself to the command of God, and that so prevailed with him, that he would never return any more. But the people of Israel, though they were brought out of Egypt, yet they returned back thither in their hearts. So the text speaks: *They thought of the fish which they did eat there freely; the cucumbers, and the melons, and the leeks, and the onions, and the garlick* (Numb. 11:5), and their minds ran after *the fleshpots of Egypt* (Exod. 16). Many a time a carnal wretch cometh so far as that; when God knocks his fingers off his sins, he lets them go for a time; but his heart is still bent after his former courses, and he lingereth after them still. So was it not with Abraham: and this is the first *step of the faith of Abraham,* that he was content to yield to the call, and to be under the command of God, to let his good pleasure take place in his heart, to leave all, kindred, country, father's house, and never return anymore. And this is that first step that God looks every faithful man should take, that he be willing, that the command of God take place in his heart, that God should make room there for himself, that he should pluck away his dearest sins, that are as near to him as his right hand, and as his right eye. If the adulterer were converted, he would be contented that God should take away his lust, that is as dear to him as his very soul; nay, he would fain, and that with all his heart, have God make way in his soul for his own majesty, by beating down all the holds of Satan, and tumbling that Dagon[5] to the ground which standeth before him. This is the first step of faith.

---

[5] Dagon was the national idol-god of the Philistines. Judges 16:23. [Ed.]

[THE SECOND STEP]

The next step that Abraham, and so every faithful soul, sets forward is this: that whenever faith cometh powerfully into the heart, the soul is not content barely to yield to the command of God, but it breatheth after his mercy, longeth for his grace, prizeth Christ and salvation above all things in the world, is satisfied and contented with nothing but with the Lord Christ; and although it partake of many things below, and enjoy abundance of outward comforts, yet it is not quieted till it rest and pitch itself upon the Lord, and find and feel that evidence and assurance of his love, which he hath promised unto, and will bestow on those who love him. As for all things here below, he hath but a slight, and mean, and base esteem of them. This you shall see apparent in Abraham (Gen. 15:1,2): *Fear not Abraham,* saith God, *I am thy shield, and thy exceeding great reward.* What could a man desire more? One would think that the Lord makes a promise here large enough to Abraham: *I will be thy buckler, and exceeding great reward.* Is not Abraham contented with this? No; mark how he pleadeth with God. *Lord God,* saith he, *what wilt thou give me, seeing I go childless?* His eye is upon the promise that God had made to him of a son, of whom the Saviour of the world should come. *Oh Lord, what wilt thou give me?* [It is] as if he had said: What wilt thou do for me? alas nothing will do my soul good, unless I have a son, and in him a Saviour. What will become of me, so long as I go childless, and so saviourless, as I may so speak? You see how Abraham's mouth was out of taste with all other things, how he could relish nothing, enjoy nothing in comparison of the promise, though he had otherwise what he would, or could desire. Thus must it be with every faithful man. That soul never had, nor never shall have Christ, that doth not prize him above all things in the world. No, certainly, a faithful soul breatheth after nothing so much as mercy in Christ; looks after, and longeth for nothing so much as the assurance of the love of God. Though all the comforts of this world were afforded a faithful man, yet still he would plead with the Lord, Oh Lord, what will become of me notwithstanding all this, so long as my soul is comfortless? What availeth it me to live here? Oh thy mercy! Oh thy salvation! Oh the Lord Christ! These are the things my soul breatheth after. This, my brethren, is the nature of faith, if it be rightly wrought in the soul, as you shall see and find by ordinary experience. For take a man that is truly awakened, and whose conscience is thoroughly touched, and offer him crowns, and scepters, and honors, and all the delights of the sons of men; alas, his soul will care nothing for them, but as Esau said (Gen. 25:32), *Behold, I am at the point to die, and what profit shall this birthright do to me?* So will the poor soul say, what will it avail me, to be high in the favor of men here, and to be a fiend of hell hereafter? What are all these profits and pleasures to me so long as I am not in the favor of God? What good can these outward contentments afford me when I am without Christ? Oh Lord, what wilt thou give me, unless I have my Saviour, and mercy in him, and pardon in him, and all in him, and through him? Still thus beateth the pulse of a faithful soul; and this is the nature of saving faith, the faith of God's elect. As for these things here below, these matters of the world, they are little in the regard and esteem of a Christian man. If he have them, he seeth God in them; if he want them, he is never a whit the worse. The Apostle speaking of believers, and the faithful people of God, saith, that they let their hold go of all these things below; let the world take the world if they would, let the dead bury their dead; but as for them, *having seen the promises afar off, they were persuaded of them, and embraced them, and confessed that they were strangers and pilgrims on the earth,* even in that country that God had promised them (Heb. 11:13).

[THE THIRD STEP]

The third step of Abraham's faith was this: he casteth himself and flingeth his soul (as I may say) upon the all-sufficient power and mercy of God for the attainment of what he desireth;

he rolleth and tumbleth himself, as it were, upon the all-sufficiency of God. This you shall find there, saith the Apostle speaking of Abraham, *Who against hope, believed in hope* (Rom. 4:18). That is, when there was no hope in the world, yet he believed in God even above hope, and so made it possible. It was an object of his hope that it might be in regard of God, howsoever there was no possibility in regard of man. So the text saith (Rom. 4:19), *He considered not his own body now dead, when he was about an hundred years old, neither yet the deadness of Sarah's womb,* but was strong in faith. He cast himself wholly upon the precious promise and mercy of God.

This then is the third step of true justifying faith: that when the believer is informed touching the excellency of the Lord Jesus, and [of] that fulness that is to be had in him, though he cannot find the sweetness of his mercy, though he cannot, or dare not apprehend, and apply it to himself, though he find nothing in himself, yet he is still resolved to rest upon the Lord, and to stay himself on the God of his salvation, and to wait for his mercy till he find him gracious to his poor soul. Excellent and famous is that example of the woman of Canaan (Matt. 15:22, 27) when Christ, as it were, beat her off and took up arms against her, was not pleased to reveal himself graciously to her for the present: *I am not sent* (saith he) *but to the lost sheep of the house of Israel;* and, *It is not meet to take the children's bread, and to cast it to dogs.* Mark how she replied, *Truth, Lord,* I confess all that; *yet* notwithstanding *the dogs eat of the crumbs that fall from their master's table.* O the excellency, and strength, and work of her faith! She comes to Christ for mercy; he repelleth her, reproacheth her, tells her she is a dog; she confesseth her baseness, yet is not discouraged for all that, but still resteth upon the goodness and mercy of Christ, and is mightily resolved to have mercy whatsoever befalleth her. Truth Lord, I confess I am as bad as thou canst term me, yet I confess, too, that there is no comfort but from thee, and though I am a dog, yet I would have crumbs: still she laboreth to catch after mercy, and to lean and bear herself upon the favor of Christ, for the bestowing thereof upon her. So it must be with every faithful Christian in this particular; he must roll himself upon the power, and faithfulness, and truth of God, and wait for his mercy.

[THE FOURTH STEP]

I will join them both together for brevity's sake, though this latter be a fourth step and degree of faith. I say, he must not only depend upon God, but he must *wait* upon the holy one of Israel. The text saith of Abraham (Heb. 6:15) *that after he had patiently endured, he obtained the promise;* he received the performance after he had a little waited for it. So the Prophet David (Psalm 101:2), *I will walk in the uprightness of my heart till the Lord come to me:* as if he should say, if the Lord will absent himself from me, and not reveal himself to me, yet wait I will, and desire I will, and still I will be hoping for the mercy of the Lord till he comes to me. So it was said of Simeon, the good old man, *that he waited for the consolation of Israel,* (Luke 2:25). *Mine eyes,* saith David (Psalm 119:123), *grow dim for the looking for thy salvation. He that believeth makes not haste* (Is. 28:16). He makes haste to obey, but makes not haste to bring mercy from God.

[THE FIFTH STEP]

Abraham's faith appeared in this: he counted nothing too dear for the Lord; he was content to break through all impediments, to pass through all difficulties. Whatsoever God would have, he had of him. This is the next step that Abraham went; and this you shall find when God put him upon the trial (Gen. 22). The text saith there, *That God did tempt Abraham,* did try what he would do for him, and he bade him, *Go, take thy son, thy only son Isaac, whom thou lovest, and slay him;* and straight Abraham went and laid his son upon an altar, and took a knife to cut the throat of his son. So that Abraham did not spare his Isaac, he did not spare for any cost, he did not dodge with God in this case. If God would have any thing, he should have it whatsoever it were, though it were his own life, for no question Isaac was dearer to him than his own life. And this was not his case alone, but the faithful people of God have ever walked the same course. The Apostle Paul was of the same spirit (Acts 20:22–24): *I know not*, saith he, *the things that shall befall me, save that the Holy Ghost witnesseth in every city saying, That bonds and afflictions abide me; but none of these things move me, neither count I my life dear unto myself, so that I might finish my course with joy, and the ministry which I have received of the Lord Jesus, to testify the Gospel of the grace of God.* Oh blessed spirit! Here is the work of faith. Alas, when we come to part with anything for the cause of God, how hardly comes it from us? But I, saith he, *pass not, no, nor is my life dear unto me!* Here, I say, is the work of faith indeed, when a man is content to do anything for God, and to say, if imprisonment, loss of estate, liberty, life come, I pass not, it moveth me nothing, so I may finish my course with comfort. Hence it was that the saints of God in those primitive times (Heb. 10:34) *took joyfully the spoiling of their goods.* Methinks I see the saints there reaching after Christ with the arms of faith, and how when anything lay in their way, they were content to lose all, to part with all, to have Christ. Therefore, saith Saint Paul. (Acts 21:13), *I am ready not to be bound only, but also to die at Jerusalem for the name of the Lord Jesus.* Mark, rather than he would leave his Saviour, he would leave his life; and though men would have hindered him, yet was resolved to have Christ howsoever, though he lost his life for him: Oh let me have my Saviour, and take my life.

[THE SIXTH STEP]

The last step of all is this: when the soul is thus resolved not to dodge with God, but to part with anything for him, then in the last place there followeth a readiness of heart to address a man's self to the performance of whatsoever duty God requireth at his hands. I say, this is the last step: when without consulting with flesh and blood, without hammering upon it, as it were, without awkwardness of heart, there followeth a pressedness to obey God, [then] the soul is at hand. When Abraham was called, *Behold,* saith he, *here I am* (Gen. 22:1). And so Samuel, *Speak Lord, for thy servant heareth* (1 Sam. 3:9). And so Ananias, *Behold, I am here Lord* (Acts 9:10). The faithful soul is not to seek, as an evil servant that is gone a roving after his companions, that is out of the way when his master should use him; but is like a trusty servant that waiteth upon his master, and is ever at hand to do his pleasure. So you shall see it was with Abraham (Heb. 11:8). When the Lord commanded him to go out of his country, *he obeyed, and went out, not knowing whither he went.* He went cheerfully and readily, though he knew not whither. As who should say, if the Lord call, I will not question; if he command, I will perform whatever it be; so it must be with every faithful soul. We must blind the eye of carnal reason, resolve to obey, though heaven and earth seem to meet together in a contradiction. Care not what man or what devil saith in this case, but what God will have done, do it. This is the courage and obedience of faith. See how Saint Paul, in the place before named (Acts 21:12, 13), flung his ancient friends from him when they came to cross him in the work of his ministry. They all came about him, and because they thought they should see his face no more, they besought him not to go up to Jerusalem. *Then Paul answered, What mean ye to weep, and to break my heart?* As who should say, it is a grief and vexation to my soul, that ye would hinder me, that I cannot go with readiness to perform the service that God requireth at my hands. The like Christian courage was in Luther, when his friends dissuaded him to go to Worms: *If all the tiles in Worms were so many devils,* said he, *yet would I go thither in the name of my Lord Jesus.* This is the last step.

Now gather up a little what I have delivered. He that is resolved to stoop to the call of God; to prize the promises, and
breathe after them; to rest upon the Lord, and to wait his time
for bestowing mercy upon him; to break through all impediments and difficulties, and to count nothing too dear for God;
to be content to perform ready and cheerful obedience; he that
walketh thus, and treadeth in these steps, peace be upon him.
Heaven is hard by; he is as sure of salvation as the angels are.
It is as certain as the Lord liveth, that he shall be saved with
faithful Abraham, for he walketh in the steps of Abraham, and
therefore he is sure to be where he is. The case you see is clear,
and the point evident, that every faithful man may, and must
imitate faithful Abraham.

[THE DOCTRINE CLARIFIED]

It may be here imagined that we draw men up to too high a
pitch; and certainly, if this be the sense of the words and the
meaning of the Holy Ghost in this place, what will become of
many that live in the bosom of the Church? Will you therefore
see the point confirmed by reason? The ground of this doctrine
standeth thus: every faithful man hath the same faith, for nature
and for work, that Abraham had; therefore look what nature
his faith was of, and what power it had; of the same nature and
power every true believer's faith is. Briefly thus: the promises of
God are the ground upon which all true faith resteth; the Spirit
of God it is that worketh this faith in all believers; the power of
the spirit is that that putteth forth itself in the hearts and lives of
all the faithful. Gather these together: if all true believers have
the same promises for the ground of their faith, have one and
the same spirit to work it, have one and the same power to draw
out the abilities of faith, then certainly they cannot but have
the very selfsame actions, having the very selfsame ground of
their actions. Every particular believer (as the Apostle Peter
saith, II Pet. 1:1) *hath obtained the like precious faith.* Mark
that there is a great deal of copper-faith in the world, much

counterfeit believing, but the saints do all partake of the *like precious faith*. As when a man hath but a sixpence in silver, or a crown in gold, those small pieces for the[ir] nature, are as good as the greatest of the same metal; so it is with the faith of God's Elect. And look as it is in grafting; if there be many scions of the same kind grafted into one stock, they all partake alike of the virtue of the stock; just so it is here: the Lord Jesus Christ is the stock, as it were, into which all the faithful are grafted by the spirit of God and faith. Therefore whatsoever fruit one beareth, another beareth also; howsoever there may be degrees of works, yet they are the same for nature. As a little apple is the same in taste with a great one of the same tree, even so every faithful man hath the same holiness of heart and life, because he hath the same principle of holiness. The fruit indeed that one Christian bringeth forth, may be but poor and small in comparison of others, yet it is the same in kind; the course of his life is not with so much power and fulness of grace, it may be, as another's, yet there is the same true grace, and the same practise in the kind of it for truth, however in degree it differ.

Here by way of caution I will suggest two things to you.

1. That howsoever all believers have the selfsame nature of faith, yet all must not look to have the same measure of faith, and the same degree of works. 2. That faith doth not perform all its works at one time, but groweth to a ripeness upon several occasions. A child is a perfect man in regard of parts, though not of degrees: he is able to eat, and to see, though he cannot walk and talk; yet because he hath a reasonable soul as well as others, he will walk and talk like others in due time. So howsoever many of the saints of God have not attained to those great actions of grace that others have, yet having the same spirit and principle of grace within, they shall be enabled hereafter to a further discharge of those holy services that God requireth. Thus you see the point confirmed by reason; if all the saints of God are ingrafted into Christ indifferently, if all have the same ground of faith, and the same spirit to work it, and to make it

work, they must needs have the same actions and fruits of faith, because (I say) they have the selfsame causes of their faith.

[THE FIRST USE OF THE DOCTRINE: FOR SELF-EXAMINATION AND DISCERNMENT]

Let us now come to see what benefit we may make to ourselves of this point, thus proved and confirmed; and certainly the use of this Doctrine is of great consequence. In the first place it is a just ground of examination, for if it be true (as it cannot be denied, the reasons being so strong, and arguments so plain) that every son of Abraham followeth the steps of Abraham, then here you may clearly perceive who it is that hath saving faith indeed, who they be that are true saints, and the sons of Abraham. By the light of this truth, by the rule of this doctrine, if you would square your courses, and look into your conversations, you cannot but discern whether you have faith or no. That man whose faith showeth itself, and putteth itself forth in its several conditions agreeable to the faith of Abraham, that man that followeth the footsteps of the faith of Abraham, let him be esteemed a faithful man; let him be reckoned for a true believer. But if any man's faith do not this, but be contrary unto, or fall short of this in the truth (I say, not in the measure) of it, certainly it is counterfeit, it is copper-faith.

O the world of counterfeit faith then, that is in the Church at this day! It was the complaint of our Saviour Christ, that *when he should come, he should scarce find faith on the earth* (Luke 18:8), as if he should say, it will be so little and so rare that one shall hardly know where to find a faithful man. It was the complaint of the Psalmist of old, and is most true of these times, that *the faithful fail from among the children of men* (Psalm 12:1). Many a man *hath a name, that he is alive, and yet he is dead* (Rev. 3:1). Many have a fancy of faith, yet upon the trial we shall find that there are but few, even of those that are interested in the title of Christians and live in the bosom of the

Church, that have any right or title to the Lord Jesus and the promises of God revealed in the Church. Let us try a few.

And first, this falleth marvellous heavy upon, and casteth out all ignorant persons, that were never enlightened, never quickened, never had their minds informed touching Christ and the promises. Alas, they know not what faith meaneth, and what Christ meaneth; and how can these walk in the footsteps of the faith of Abraham, when they never saw the way of Abraham? But let them go; my heart pitieth them. I rather choose to grapple with those that think themselves in a better estate and condition.

[1   OF PROFANE PERSONS: CHILDREN OF THE DEVIL]

And the first of this rank are profane persons, those that live and lie in sin, in Sabbath-breaking, swearing, drunkeness, adultery, and the like. The case of such is clear and evident: these are so far from treading in the steps of Abraham that they hate purity, and holiness, and goodness. And as for these (if any such be here) let them not be deceived, but let me tell them out of God's Word, that as yet they have not faith; as yet they are not the sons of Abraham. What they may be, I know not; I leave them to the Lord, and with them a sight and apprehension of their own condition, and that they may be brought out of that gall of bitterness wherein they are; but as yet, I dare say, they are not the sons of Abraham. Whose sons are they then? My brethren, I am loathe to speak it, and I will not; men will not bear these words from us, but think that we go beyond our commission. For my own part, my soul trembleth to think of them, their case is so fearful. The Lord therefore shall speak, and I will say nothing. Look into John 8. The scribes and pharisees came to Christ, and began to quarrel with him, and to provoke him to say many things, that they might catch him in his speech, opposing our Saviour in the course of his ministry, and laboring to suppress his doctrine. Mark how Christ reasoneth there: *I do,* saith he, *the works of my Father; ye do the deeds of your father.* But, say they, *Abraham is our father;* and again, *We be not born of fornication; we have one Father, even God.* But mark our Saviour's answer (verse 44), *Ye are of your father the Devil, and the lusts of your father ye will do.* Thus Christ speaks to the scribes and pharisees, great men of place, and of great abilities; *You, of your father, Abraham? No, you are of your father the Devil.* My brethren, I will not say it; I beseech you be not offended; it is the Lord that speaks, and I would fain know that man that dare contradict his word. The case is clear, and the Lord will make it good upon his soul in another world. *His lusts,* saith Christ, *you do.* What are those? He is an accuser of the brethren; so are these. He crieth out against and opposeth the purity of religion; so do these men exclaim against the niceness and preciseness of Christians, and blame those that are holy and sincere.[6] The Devil continued not in the truth; no more do these; they are not governed by the truth, they stoop not to it, they yield not obedience to it. The Devil is a liar, and speaketh not the truth; so these men are contented to lie shamefully of their brethren, to broach scandalous things of those that they know to be holy and sincere. In a word, the Devil is malicious and envious; so are all these profane ones, desperate, unreasonable creatures, that cast off God's commands, that neglect the ordinances and wallow in the mire of their sins, that hate the sincerity and power of religion, that envy and malign the true professors of godliness. If the Devil himself were incarnate he could do no more; and surely if there were ever a child like the father, these are like him. I will say nothing, the Lord himself speak to your consciences.

---

6 An early synonym for Puritan was "Precisian," a term suggesting an unduly meticulous concern for the fine points of God's law. Hooker, who was very "precise" in these matters, was understandably sensitive. Worth noting, however, and also characteristic of him, was his relatively gentle extension of hope even to his most profane listeners. [Ed.]

Yea, but you will say, it is true, Christ knew who were the children of the Devil; but can you discern them?

I say nothing, but I can tell you how you may discern them: a child of the Devil doth not go invisible, but may be known, and the Apostle tells you (1 John 3:10), *In this the children of God are manifest, and the children of the Devil.* Mark that *Whosoever doth not righteousness is not of God, neither he that loveth not his brother.* I observe three things in this text: 1. That there are children of God, and children of the Devil; 2. That a man may know them. (The text saith so plainly; they are not my own words. Consult, I beseech you with the place: *In this the children of God are manifest, and the children of the Devil.*) 3. How a man shall know a child of the Devil: *He that worketh not righteousness, and he that hateth his brother, is of the Devil. He that worketh not righteousness;* that is, he that is not willing and contented constantly to take up a Christian course, to walk according to the rule of God's word, to abstain from all filthiness of the flesh and spirit, to live in all holiness of conscience in all things both towards God and towards men; *and he that loveth not his brother,* that is, he that hateth holiness where he sees it, that hateth a good man and one that is sincere, whose color riseth at such a one wherever he meets him; who can brook a drunkard, or a swearer, or an adulterer, but cannot endure a righteous man, a holy man, one that makes conscience of his ways. If there be any such in this congregation, I desire to speak a word to them in the name of the Lord. Let them consider that what I speak is not my own, and I profess that what I say is not out of passion, or a desire to slander any; but the desire of my soul is that they may come to the knowledge of the truth, that they may be saved.

You therefore that are given to these sins, and are walking in this way of death, consider and bethink yourselves, and say to yourselves: Oh Lord, how nearly doth this I have heard this day concern me! Alas, I thought not of this before. I am one that never was a worker of righteousness in all my life; I am one that has hated the servants of God, that has scorned and loathed the purity of religion, and now the Lord hath said it, Christ hath spoke it, his word hath spoke it, that I am the child of the Devil. Alas, it is too manifest to myself, that such a one I am, and God knoweth it much more. What shall I do? Now I pray thee, go thy ways home, break off thy sins by repentance, and labor to make thy peace with God forthwith, and of the son of the Devil to be the son of God. Be mighty with God in prayer to make you his child. And this is all I have to speak to these.

[2   OF CIVILIZED PROFESSORS]

Let me go further, and you shall see more than these cut off from being the sons of Abraham; and surely if Abraham should come down from heaven, he might complain that there were very few of his sons to be found upon the earth. In the next place therefore take a taste of the civilized professors, such as are not as other men: no common swearers, no profaners of the Sabbath, no drunkards, and the like. These men think that they go near indeed to the steps of Abraham, yet give me leave to scan these a little, I pray, and to try them.

Abraham (you know) did not stick with God when he called him, but was content to be under the command of God, and to yield to him in everything. Take now one that hath not the power of godliness in his heart; he keepeth, it may be, his fingers from filching and stealing, abstains from the gross acts of sin and from open profaneness; but what strength of grace is there in his soul? What mortification shall you find of his secret lusts? What subduing of sin within? Alas, ask him what ruleth him, at whose command he is, at whose call he cometh. I appeal to the souls and consciences of all such men; the command of God calleth, and covetousness calleth, which of these is followed? The Lord saith to the worldling, come out of thy countinghouse, and go to prayer; come and hear my Word; the Lord calls to the gentleman, forsake thy pleasures and thy sports, and humble thyself in sackcloth and ashes. The Lord calleth for these things, the times call for them. Who is obeyed? Whose commands do you stoop unto? Is there any command disobeyed but God's? If a man presume on any, it is on the Lord; profits, pleasures, worldly business must be attended, whether the Lord be pleased or no, or whether the duties he requireth be performed or no. You that are gentlemen and tradesmen, I appeal to your souls, whether the Lord and his cause is not the loser this way. Doth not prayer pay for it? Doth not the Word pay for it? Are not the ordinances always losers when anything of your own cometh in competition? Is it not evident then, that you are not under the command of the word? How do you tremble at the wrath and threatnings of a mortal man? And yet when you hear the Lord thunder judgements out of his word, who is humbled? When He calls for fasting, and weeping, and mourning, who regards it? Abraham, my brethren, did not thus, these were none of his steps; no, no, he went a hundred mile off of this course. The Lord no sooner said to him, *Forsake thy country, and thy kindred, and thy father's house,* but he forsook all, neither friend nor father prevailed to detain him from obedience, but he stooped willingly to God's command.

Look again to the fifth note and step of Abraham's faith, and try yourselves a little by that. Are you content to run any hazard for the cause of God? To spare nothing from him? As Abraham withheld not Isaac from God when he required him, so are you contented likewise to withhold, no, not the dearest thing you have when God calls for it. If the Lord put you to the trial, to undergo trouble, loss of goods, imprisonment, banishment, are you content to stoop to these things? To give way and to break through all impediments? Judge yourselves; if it be so, it is well. But let your consciences speak, nay, let your lives and conversations speak; do they not show the contrary? Doth not the very name of danger, the sight of it afar off, the voice of some great man dash all your forwardness out of countenance? Nay, if an Isaac come and complain that those and those things must be provided for, and cry out, *Alas, if you take this course, what will become of wife and children and family, all must to ruin,* you presently give over your profession. Did Abraham do thus? No, he did not so; and I beseech you, think of it; if you were the children of Abraham, you would not, you could not, you durst not do so.

[3   OF CLOSE-HEARTED HYPOCRITES]

There are yet a third sort that come short of being the sons of Abraham, and they are the close-hearted hypocrites. These are a generation that are of a more refined kind than the last, but howsoever they carry the matter very covertly, yea, and are exceeding cunning, yet the truth will make them known. Many an hypocrite may come thus far, to be content to part with anything, and outwardly to suffer for the cause of God, to part with divers pleasures and lusts, and to perform many holy services. But here is the difference between Abraham and these men: Abraham forsook his goods and all, but your close-hearted hypocrites have always some God or other that they do homage to; their ease, or their wealth, or some secret lust, something or other they have set up as an idol within them; and so long as they may have and enjoy that, they will part with anything else. But thou must know, that if thou be one of Abraham's children, thou must come away from thy gods, thy god of pride, of self-love, of vain glory, and leave worshipping of these, and be content to be governed alone by God and his truth. This shall suffice for the first use; I cannot proceed further in the pressing thereof, because I would shut up all with the time.

[THE SECOND USE: INSTRUCTION ON THE ONE WAY]

The second use is a word of instruction, and it shall be but a word or two: that if all the saints of God must walk in the same way of life and salvation that Abraham did, then there is no byway to bring a man to happiness. Look what way Abraham went, you must go; there is no more ways; the same course that he took must be a copy for you to follow, a rule, as it were, for you to square your whole conversation by. There is no way but one to come to life and happiness. I speak it the rather to dash that idle device of many carnal men that think the Lord hath a new invention to bring them to life, and that they need not to go the ordinary way, but God hath made a shorter cut for them. Great men, and gentlemen, think God will spare them. What, must they be humbled, and fast, and pray? That is for poor men, and mean men: their places and estates will not suffer it; therefore surely God hath given a dispensation to them. And the poor men, they think it is for gentlemen, that have more leisure and time: alas, they live by their labor, and they must take pains for what they have, and therefore they cannot do what is required. But be not deceived: if there be any way besides that which Abraham went, then will I deny myself; but the case is clear, the Lord saith it, the Word saith it; the same way, the same footsteps that Abraham took, we must take, if ever we will come where Abraham is. You must not balk in this kind, whoever you are; God respecteth no man's person. If you would arrive at the same haven, you must sail through the same sea; you must walk the same way of grace, if you would come to the same kingdom of glory. It is a conceit that harboreth in the hearts of many men, nay, of most men in general, specially your great wise men, and your great rich men, that have better places and estates in the world than ordinary. What, think they, may not a man be saved without all this ado? What needs all this? Is there not another way besides this? Surely, my brethren, you must teach our Saviour Christ and the Apostle Paul another way; I am sure they never knew other. And he that dreameth of another way, must be content to go beside. There is no such matter as the Devil would persuade you; it is but his delusion to keep you under infidelity, and to shut you up to destruction under false and vain conceits. The truth is, here is the way, and the only way, and you must walk here if ever you come to life and happiness. Therefore be not deceived, suffer not your eyes to be blinded, but know what Abraham did; you must do the same, if not in action, yet in affection. If God say, forsake all, thou must do it, at least in affection; thou must still wait upon his power and providence, yield obedience to him in all things, be content to submit thyself to his will. This is the way you must walk in, if you ever come to heaven.

[THE THIRD USE: COMFORT TO THE SAINTS]

The last use shall be a use of comfort to all the saints and people of God, whose consciences can witness that they have labored to walk in the uprightness of their heart as Abraham did. I have two or three words to speak to these.

Be persuaded out of the Word of God that your course is good, and go on with comfort, and the God of Heaven be with you; and be sure of it, that you that walk with Abraham shall be at rest with Abraham, and it shall never repent you of all the pains that you have taken. Haply it may seem painful and tedious to you; yet, what Abigail said to David, let me say to you: Oh, saith she, let not my Lord do this: *when the Lord shall have done to my Lord according to all the good that he hath spoken concerning thee, and shall have appointed thee ruler over Israel, this shall be no grief unto thee, nor offence of heart, that thou hast shed blood causeless, or that my Lord hath avenged himself* (I Sam. 25:30, 31). My brethren, let me say so to you: you will find trouble and inconveniences, and hard measure at the hands of the wicked in this world; many Nabals and Cains will set themselves against you,[7] but go on, and bear it patiently; know it is a troublesome way, but a true way. It is grievous but yet good, and the end will be happy; it will never repent you,

---

[7] Nabal, a rich landholder, whose ungenerous treatment of David's men was balanced by the gifts and prayer of his wife, Abigail. I Samuel 25. On Cain see Genesis 4. [Ed.]

when the Lord hath performed all the good that he hath spoken concerning you. Oh! to see a man drawing his breath low and short, after he hath spent many hours and days in prayer to the Lord, grappling with his corruptions, and striving to pull down his base lusts, after he hath waited upon the Lord in a constant course of obedience. Take but such a man, and ask him, now his conscience is opened, whether the ways of holiness and sincerity be not irksome to him, whether he be not grieved with himself for undergoing so much needless trouble (as the world thinks it), and his soul will then clear this matter. It is true, he hath had a tedious course of it, but now his death will be blessed; he hath striven for a Crown, and now beholds a Crown; now he is beyond the waves; all the contempts, and imprisonments, and outrages of wicked men are now too short to reach him. He is so far from repenting, that he rejoyceth and triumpheth in reflecting back upon all the pains and care and labor of love, whereby he hath loved the Lord Jesus, in submitting his heart unto him. Take me another man, that hath lived here in pomp and jollity, hath had many livings, great preferments, much honor, abundance of pleasure, yet hath been ever careless of God and of his Word, profane in his course, loose in his conversation, and ask him upon his death-bed how it standeth with him. Oh! woe the time, that ever he spent it as he hath done. Now the soul begins to hate the man, and the very fight of him that hath been the instrument with it in the committing of sin. Now nothing but gall and wormwood remaineth; now the sweetness of the adulterer's lust is gone, and nothing but the sting of conscience remaineth. Now the covetous man must part with his goods, and the gall of asps must stick behind. Now the soul sinks within, and the heart is overwhelmed with sorrow. Take but these two men, I say, and judge by their ends, whether ever it will repent you that you have done well, that you have walked in the steps of the faith of Abraham.

My brethren, howsoever you have had many miseries, yet the Lord hath many mercies for you. God dealeth with his servants, as a father doth with his son, after he hath sent him on a great journey to do some business, and the weather falleth foul, and the way proveth dangerous, and many a storm, and great difficulties are to be gone through; oh how the heart of that father pitieth his son! How doth he resolve to requite him, if he ever live to come home again; what preparation doth he make to entertain and welcome him; and how doth he study to do good unto him! My brethren, so it is here. I beseech you, think of it, you that are the saints and people of God. You must find in your way many troubles and griefs (and we ought to find them), but be not discouraged; the more misery, the greater mercy. God the father seeth his servants; and if they suffer and endure for a good conscience, as his eye seeth them, so his soul pitieth them, his heart bleeds within him for them. That is, he hath a tender compassion of them, and he saith within himself, Well I will requite them if ever they come into my Kingdom; all their patience and care and conscience in walking in my ways, I will requite, and they shall receive a double reward from me, even a crown of eternal glory. Think of those things that are not seen; they are eternal. The things that are seen are temporal, and they will deceive us [II Cor. 4:18]. Let our hearts be carried after the other, and rest in them forever.

II

JONATHAN EDWARDS

Apostle to the Age of Reason

Jonathan Edwards (1703–1758)[1] lived when many landmarks of Puritanism had lost their guiding value. His life work represents an imposing effort to set the course anew—an intellectual achievement made especially significant by the way it blends the motifs of two great epochs in American history. To the end of his days he remained a grateful but never an uncritical or submissive legatee of the Puritan tradition; yet just as certainly his life can be seen as an appreciative apostolate to the Age of Reason. In an even more far-reaching perspective, he brought together in his great synthesis the perennial speculative quest of the Platonic tradition and the urgent demands of modern science. Probably no calumny sheds more discredit on its perpetrators than the representation of Edwards in anthologies—over and over again—with nothing more than his revival sermon, "Sinners in the Hands of an Angry God" (1741).

The external outlines of Edwards' life are very familiar and quickly told. Son of the minister in East Windsor, Connecticut, he showed at an early age a profound sensitivity in matters of religion, and after graduating from Yale College and serving a conventional apprenticeship as a college tutor and as a minister

---

[1] See Introduction, pp. 33–37.

in New York, he became in 1726 the junior colleague of his maternal grandfather, Solomon Stoddard (1643–1729), in the church at Northampton, Massachusetts. In the meantime his precocious interests in philosophy and theology had been deepened, as they would continue to be all his life, by his reading of Isaac Newton, John Locke, the Port Royal *Logic* of Antoine Arnould, and a wide range of other thinkers, ancient and modern. After 1734 his life was caught up in the religious turmoil and theological controversy of the great evangelical awakening that was sweeping through not only the colonial churches but also those of Great Britain and Protestant Europe. After his expulsion in 1750 from his Northampton church for his rigorous fencing of the communion table, he accepted a call to be an Indian missionary and parish minister in Stockbridge, Massachusetts. Despite the uncertainties of life on the frontier during the last great "French War," the years at Stockbridge were for him a time of most remarkable productivity. Four of his greatest treatises were published or written during these years. Then in 1757, with considerable reluctance, he accepted a call to be president of the newly-founded College of New Jersey (Princeton). He assumed his duties in the following January, only to die from a smallpox inoculation in March 1758.

The literary works of Jonathan Edwards are of vast extent and great diversity. The nearly thirty volumes projected in the new Yale Edition can be classified under several headings: sermons, exegetical studies, controversial works on Great Awakening issues, doctrinal treatises, essays in philosophical theology, and an immense body of unpublished notes. Additional obstacles are created for those who would understand the unifying elements of his thought by the way his ideas have been exposed—or left unexposed. Most of the sermons were heard by one limited group, the tracts and treatises reached another, while the posthumous works were read by still others during the ensuing two centuries. Only the present generation will have the benefit of his complete works, including the sermons, notebooks, and letters.

Yet we may better apprehend Edwards' inner spirit and appreciate his grand design if we remember the distinctive roles he played: (1) as an effective parish preacher in the New England Puritan tradition; (2) a defender of the Great Awakening against both its detractors and its overly enthusiastic proponents; (3) an apologist for classic Reformed doctrines in the Enlightenment's new world of thought; (4) a speculative theologian in the Platonic mold; and finally (5) an expositor of God's whole work of redemption as it is revealed in sacred history, world history, and even nature itself. When the full circle of Edwards' thought is grasped in both its unity and manifoldness, it will not be difficult to accept the claim that his work is the most impressive contribution to the Reformed theological tradition between John Calvin in the sixteenth century and Karl Barth in the twentieth.

Because no single selection, however brilliant or historic, could possibly exhibit the range of Edwards' theological work, and because the best brief works as well as his major treatises have been frequently republished, another method of presentation is attempted here. "The circle of Edwards' thought" is depicted by means of short passages drawn from nearly the full range of his writings, published and unpublished. Admittedly, the use of this method involves an interpretation of Edwards' total outlook; yet there is no other way of displaying in brief compass the boldness and grandeur of his design, the diversity of his interests, the richness of his mind, or the felicity of his style. The fact that these excerpts are drawn from every period of his life will also exhibit the remarkable unity of his vision. For reasons suggested in the first two excerpts, the reader is cautioned to proceed carefully and analytically, with his mind's eye on "the contexture and harmony of the whole." Indeed, to draw the best effect from these selections, the reader should turn to them after reading one or more secondary accounts of Edwards' thought.

Where applicable the text has been modernized in the manner employed in the Yale Edition. The ellipsis is used only within an excerpt, not at the beginning or end.

The Circle of Edwards' Thought:

Excerpts from His Published and Unpublished Writings

1. *The Names for Spiritual Things**

The reason why the names of spiritual things are all, or most of them, derived from the names of sensible or corporeal ones— as imagination, conception, apprehend, etc.—is because there was no other way of making others readily understand men's meaning, when they first signified these things by sound, than by giving of them the names of things sensible, to which they had an analogy. They could thus point it out with the finger and so explain themselves, as in sensible things. [*The Mind*, No. 23.]

2. *Language and Spiritual Things†*

The things of Christianity are so spiritual, so refined, so high and abstracted, and so much above the things we ordinarily

---

* From Sereno E. Dwight, ed., *The Works of President Edwards*, 10 vols. (New York: G. & C. & H. Carvill, 1830), I, Appendix H, 664–702.

† From the unpublished critical edition of the original manuscripts being prepared by Thomas A. Schafer. Used with his permission.

converse with and our common affairs, to which we adapt our words; and language not supplying of us with words completely adapted to those high and abstracted ideas, we are forced to use words which do [no] otherwise exhibit what we would than analogically. Which words in their ordinary use do not in everything, but only in some part, exhibit what we intend they should when used in divinity; and therefore [does] religion [abound] with so many paradoxes and seeming contradictions. And it is for want of distinguishing thus in the meaning of words in divinity, from what is intended by them in their ordinary use, that arise most of the jangles about religion in the world. And to one who is not much [used] to elevated thought, many things, that are in themselves as easy and natural as the things we every day converse with, seem like impossibility and confusion. 'Tis so in every case: the more abstracted the science is, and by how much the higher nature those things are of which that science treats; by so much the more [will] our way of thinking and speaking of the things of that science be beside our way of thinking and speaking of ordinary things, and by so much the more will that science abound with paradoxes and seeming contradictions. [*Miscellanies*, No. 83.]

3. *Nothing Can Not Be**

A state of absolute nothing is a state of absolute contradiction. Absolute nothing is the aggregate of all the contradictions in the world. . . . When we go to expel being out of our thoughts, we must be careful not to leave empty space in the room of it; and when we go to expel emptiness from our thoughts, we must not think to squeeze it out by anything close, hard, and solid;

---

*From Dwight, ed., *Works*, I, 44–48.

but we must think of the same that the sleeping rocks do dream of; and not till then shall we get a complete idea of nothing. When we go to inquire whether or no there can be absolutely nothing, we utter nonsense in so inquiring. [*Of Being.*]

4. *Space Is the Infinite Eternal God*

Space is the very thing that we can never remove, and conceive of its not being. We find that we can with ease conceive how all other beings should not be. We can remove them out of our minds, and place some other in the room of them; but space is the very thing that we can never remove and conceive of its not being. If a man would imagine space anywhere to be divided so as there should be nothing between the divided parts, there remains space between notwithstanding, and so man contradicts himself. And it is self-evident, I believe, to every man that space is necessary, eternal, infinite and omnipresent. But I had as good speak plain: I have already said as much as that space is God. And it is indeed clear to me that all the space there is, not proper to body, all the space there is without the bounds of Creation, all the space there was before the Creation, is God himself; and nobody would in the least pick at it, if it were not because of the gross conceptions that we have of space. [*Of Being.*]

5. *Only Things of the Mind Are Substantial*

Deprive the universe of light and motion and the case would stand thus with the universe: there would be neither white nor black, neither blue nor brown, neither bright nor shaded, pellucid nor opaque, no noise nor sound, neither heat nor cold, neither fluid nor solid, neither wet nor dry, neither hard nor soft, nor solidity, nor extension, nor figure, nor magnitude, nor proportion, nor body, nor spirit. What then is to become of the universe? Certainly it exists nowhere but in the divine mind. . . .

Corollary. It follows from hence that those beings which have knowledge and consciousness are the only proper and real and substantial beings, inasmuch as the being of other things is only by these. From hence we may see the gross mistake of those who think material things the most substantial beings and spirits more like a shadow, whereas spirits only are properly substance. [*Of Being.*]

6. *Of Truth in General*

Truth, in the general, may be defined after the most strict and metaphysical manner: the consistency and agreement of our ideas with the ideas of God. I confess this, in ordinary conversation, would not half so much tend to enlighten one in the meaning of the word as to say: the agreement of our ideas with the things as they are. But it should be enquired, What is it for our ideas to agree with things as they are—seeing that corporeal things exist no otherwise than mentally, and, as for most other things, they are only abstract ideas? Truth as to external things is the consistency of our ideas with those ideas or that train and series of ideas that are raised in our minds according to God's stated order and law. Truth as to abstract ideas is the consistency of our ideas with themselves—as when our idea of a circle, or a triangle, or any of their parts, is agreeable to the idea we have stated and agreed to call by the name of a circle, or a triangle. And it may still be said that truth is the consistency of our ideas with themselves. Those ideas are false that are not consistent with the series of ideas that are raised in our minds by, [i. e.,] according to, the order of nature.

Corollary 1. Hence we see in how strict a sense it may be said that God is truth itself.

Corollary 2. Hence it appears that truth consists in having perfect and adequate ideas of things. For instance, if I judge truly how far distant the moon is from the earth, we need not say that this truth consists in the perception of the relation between the two ideas of the moon and the earth, but in the [their?] adequateness.

Corollary 3. Hence, certainty is the clear perception of this perfection. Therefore, if we had perfect ideas of all things at once, that is, could have all in one view, we should know all truth at the same moment, and there would be no such thing as ratiocination, or finding out truth. And reasoning is only of use to us in the consequence of the paucity of our ideas and because we can have but very few in view at once. Hence it is evident that all things are self-evident to God. [*The Mind*, No. 10.]

〰 〰

7. *Of Truth and God*

After all that has been said and done, the only adequate definition of truth is the agreement of our ideas with existence. To explain what this existence is, is another thing. In abstract ideas it is nothing but the ideas themselves; so their truth is their consistency with themselves. In things that are supposed to be without us, it is the determination and fixed mode of God's exciting ideas in us. So that truth in these things is an agreement of our ideas with that series in God. It is existence, and that is all that we can say. It is impossible that we should explain a perfectly abstract and mere idea of existence; only we always find this, by running of it up, that God and real existence are the same.

Corollary. Hence we learn how properly it may be said that God is and that there is none else. And how proper are these names of the deity, Jehovah, and I am that I am! [Exodus 3:14.] [*The Mind*, No. 15.]

〜 〜

8. *Man's Knowledge of God: The Argument from Cause and Effect**

I will not affirm, that there is in the nature of things no foundation for the knowledge of the being of God without any evidence of it from his works. I do suppose there is a great absurdity, in the nature of things simply considered, in supposing that there should be no God, or in denying being in general, and supposing an eternal, absolute, universal nothing: and therefore that here would be foundation of intuitive evidence that it cannot be, and that eternal infinite most perfect Being must be; if we had strength and comprehension of mind sufficient, to have a clear idea of general and universal being, or, which is the same thing, of the infinite, eternal, most perfect divine Nature and Essence. But then we should not properly come to the knowledge of the being of God by arguing; but our evidence would be intuitive: we should see it, as we see other things that are necessary in themselves, the contraries of which are in their own nature absurd and contradictory; as we see that twice two is four; and as we see that a circle has no angles. If we had as clear an idea of universal infinite entity, as we have of these other things, I suppose we should most intuitively see the absurdity of supposing such being not to be; should immediately see there is no room for the question, whether it is possible that being, in the most general abstracted notion of it, should not be. But we have not that strength and extent of mind, to know this certainly in this intuitive independent manner: but the way that mankind come to the knowledge of the being of God, is that which the Apostle speaks of

*From Paul Ramsey, ed., *A Careful and Strict Enquiry into the Modern Prevailing Notions of the Freedom of the Will,* The Yale Edition (New Haven: Yale University Press, 1957). Reprinted with the permission of the publisher.

(Rom. 1:20), "The invisible things of Him, from the creation of the world, are clearly seen; being understood by the things that are made; even his eternal power and Godhead." We first ascend, and prove a posteriori, or from effects, that there must be an eternal cause; and then secondly, prove by argumentation, not intuition, that this being must be necessarily existent; and then thirdly, from the proved necessity of his existence, we may descend, and prove many of his perfections a priori.

But if once this grand principle of common sense be given up, that what is not necessary in itself, must have a cause; and we begin to maintain, that things may come into existence, and begin to be, which heretofore have not been, of themselves, without any cause; all our means of ascending in our arguing from the creature to the Creator, and all our evidence of the being of God, is cut off at one blow. In this case, we can't prove that there is a God, either from the being of the world, and the creatures in it, or from the manner of their being, their order, beauty and use. For if things may come into existence without any cause at all, then they doubtless may without any cause answerable to the effect. Our minds do alike naturally suppose and determine both these things; namely, that what begins to be has a cause, and also that it has a cause proportionable and agreeable to the effect. The same principle which leads us to determine, that there cannot be anything coming to pass without a cause, leads us to determine that there cannot be more in the effect than in the cause.

Yea, if once it should be allowed, that things may come to pass without a cause, we should not only have no proof of the being of God, but we should be without evidence of the existence of anything whatsoever, but our own immediately present ideas and consciousness. For we have no way to prove anything else, but by arguing from effects to causes: from the ideas now immediately in view, we argue other things not immediately in view: from sensations now excited in us, we infer the existence of things without us, as the causes of these sensations: and from the existence of these things, we argue other things, which they depend on, as effects on causes. We infer the past existence of ourselves, or anything else, by memory; only as we argue, that the ideas, which are now in our minds, are the consequences of past ideas and sensations. We immediately perceive nothing else but the ideas which are this moment extant in our minds. We perceive or know other things only by means of these, as necessarily connected with others, and dependent on them. But if things may be without causes, all this necessary connection and dependence is dissolved, and so all means of our knowledge is gone. If there be no absurdity or difficulty in supposing one thing to start out of nonexistence, into being, of itself without a cause; then there is no absurdity or difficulty in supposing the same of millions of millions. [*Freedom of the Will*, pp. 182–183.]

⤠ ⤟

9. *The Being of God and the Soul of Man*

That [the] first supreme and universal principle of things, from whence results the being, the nature, the powers and motions, and sweet order of the world, is properly an intelligent willing agent, such as our souls only without our imperfections, and not some inconceivable, unintelligent, necessary agent, seems most rational; because, of all the beings that we see or know anything of, man's soul only seems to be the image of that supreme universal principle.

These reasons may be given why we should suppose man's soul to be the image of that first principle. In the first place, it is evidently the most perfect and excellent of all the beings in the lower world. It's very plain that the other creatures are put in subjection to him and made to be subservient to him. 'Tis rational to conclude, that the most perfect of things that proceed from this principle should bear most of the image of itself. Secondly, 'tis only the soul of man that does as that supreme principle does. This is a principle of action, has a power of action in itself as that first principle has, and which no unperceiving being in this lower world has. Man's soul determines things in themselves indifferent (as motion and rest, the direction of motion, etc.), as the supreme cause does. Man's soul has an end in what it does, pursues some good that is the issue of its actions, as the first universal principle doth. Man's soul makes, forms, preserves, disposes and governs things within its sphere, as the first principle does the world. Man's soul influences the body, continues its nature and powers and constant regular motions and productions, and actuates it, as the supreme principle does the universe.

So that if there be anything amongst all the beings that flow from this first principle of all things, that bears any sort of resemblance to it or has anything of a shadow of likeness to it, spirits or minds, bid abundantly the fairest for it. [*Miscellanies,* No. 283.]

〰️

10. *The Being of God*

That is a gross and an unprofitable idea we have of God, as being something large and great as bodies are, and infinitely extended throughout the immense space. For God is neither little nor great with that sort of greatness, even as the soul of man—it is not at all extended, no more than an idea, and is not present anywhere as bodies are present. . . . So 'tis with respect to the increated Spirit. The greatness of a soul consists not in any extension, but [in] its comprehensiveness of idea and extendedness of operation. So the infiniteness of God consists in his perfect comprehension of all things, and the extendedness of his operation equally to all places. God is present nowhere any otherwise than the soul is in the body or brain; and he is present everywhere as the soul is in the body. We ought to conceive of God as being omnipotence, perfect knowledge, and perfect love; and not extended any otherwise than as power, knowledge and love are extended; and not as if it was a sort of unknown thing that we call substance, that is extended. [*Miscellanies*, No. 194.]

11. *Reason, Scriptures, and the Trinity*

There has been much cry of late against saying one word, particularly about the Trinity, but what the Scripture has said; judging it impossible but that if we did, we should err in a thing so much above us. But if they call that which necessarily results from the putting [together] of reason and Scripture, though it has not been said in Scripture in express words—I say, if they call this what is not said in the Scripture, I am not afraid to say twenty things about the Trinity which the Scripture never said. There may be deductions of reason from what has been said [in Scripture] of the most mysterious matters, besides what has been said (and safe and certain deductions too), as well as about the most obvious and easy matters.

I think that it is within the reach of naked reason to perceive certainly that there are three distinct in God, each of which is the same [God], three that must be distinct; and that there are not nor can be any more distinct, really and truly distinct, but three, either distinct persons or properties or anything else; and that of these three, one is (more properly than anything else) begotten of the other, and that the third proceeds alike from both, and that the first neither is begotten nor proceeds. . . . So that, if we turn it all the ways in the world, we shall never be able to make more than these three: God, the idea of God, and delight in God.

I think it really evident from the light of reason, that there are these three distinct in God. If God has an idea of himself, there is really a duplicity; because [if] there is no duplicity, it will follow that Jehovah thinks of himself no more than a stone. And if God loves himself and delights in himself, there is really a triplicity, three that cannot be confounded, each of which are the Deity substantially. And this is the only distinction that can be found or thought of in God. [*Miscellanies,* No. 94.]

⌒⌒ ⌒⌒

12. *The Creation an Emanation of God's Fulness**

As there is an infinite fulness of all possible good in God, a fulness of every perfection, of all excellency and beauty, and of infinite happiness; and as this fulness is capable of communication or emanation *ad extra;* so it seems a thing amiable and valuable in itself that it should be communicated or flow forth, that this infinite fountain of good should send forth abundant streams, that this infinite fountain of light should, diffusing its excellent fulness, pour forth light all around. And as this is in itself excellent, so a disposition to this in the Divine Being must be looked upon as a perfection or an excellent disposition. Such an emanation of good is, in some sense, a multiplication of it; so far as the communication or external stream may be looked upon as any thing besides the fountain, so far it may be looked on as an increase of good. And if the fulness of good that is in the fountain is in itself excellent and worthy to exist, then the emanation, or that which is as it were an increase, repetition or multiplication of it, is excellent and worthy to exist. Thus it is

---

*From *Dissertation on the End for Which God Created the World* in *The Works of President Edwards,* 4 vols. (New York: Leavitt & Trow, 1843), often called the New York Edition; it is a reprint of the Worcester Edition of 1808–1809, somewhat enlarged and slightly rearranged. Hereafter referred to as *The Works of President Edwards.*

fit, since there is an infinite fountain of light and knowledge, that this light should shine forth in beams of communicated knowledge and understanding; and as there is an infinite fountain of holiness, moral excellence and beauty, so it should flow out in communicated holiness. And that as there is an infinite fulness of joy and happiness, so these should have an emanation, and become a fountain flowing out in abundant streams, as beams from the sun.

From this view it appears another way to be a thing in itself valuable, that there should be such things as the knowledge of God's glory in other beings, and a high esteem of it, love to it, and delight and complacence in it;—this appears, I say, in another way, viz., as these things are but the emanations of God's own knowledge, holiness and joy.

Thus it appears reasonable to suppose, that it was what God had respect to as an ultimate end of his creating the world, to communicate of his own infinite fulness of good; or rather it was his last end, that there might be a glorious and abundant emanation of his infinite fulness of good *ad extra,* or without himself; and the disposition to communicate himself, or diffuse his own FULNESS, which we must conceive of as being originally in God as a perfection of his nature, was what moved him to create the world. [*God's End,* II, 206.]

⤙⤚

13. *God Upholds All Things*

The reason why it is so exceedingly natural to men to suppose that there is some latent *Substance,* or something that is altogether hid, that upholds the properties of bodies, is, because all see at first sight that the properties of bodies are such as need some cause that shall every moment have influence to their continuance, as well as a cause of their first existence. All therefore agree that there is something that is there, and upholds these properties. And it is most true, there undoubtedly is; but men are wont to content themselves in saying merely, that it is something; but that something is He, "by whom all things consist." [*The Mind*, No. 61.][1]

14. *The Dependence of All Creation**

Let us inquire . . . whether it be not evident that God does continually, by his immediate power *uphold* every created substance in being; and then let us see the *consequence*.

That God does, by his immediate power, *uphold* every created substance in being, will be manifest, if we consider that their present existence is a *dependent* existence, and therefore is an *effect*, and must have some *cause*; and the cause must be one of these two: either the *antecedent existence* of the same substance, or the *power* of the Creator. But it cannot be the *antecedent existence* of the same substance. For instance, the existence of the body of the *moon* at this present moment, cannot be the *effect* of its existence at the last foregoing moment. For not only was what existed the last moment no active cause, but wholly a passive thing; but this is also to be considered, that no cause can produce effects in a *time* and *place* in which itself is *not*. It is plain, nothing can exert itself, or operate, when and where it is not existing. But the moon's past existence was neither *where* nor *when* its present existence is. In point of time, what is *past* entirely ceases when *present* existence begins; otherwise it would not be *past*. The past moment is ceased and gone, when the present moment takes place; and does no more

---

*From *The Great Christian Doctrine of Original Sin Defended* in *The Works of President Edwards*.

---

[1] The final phrase is from Colossians 1:17: "And he is before all things, and by him all things consist." [Ed.]

coexist with it, than does any other moment that had ceased twenty years ago. Nor could the past existence of the particles of this *moving body* produce effects in any *other place* than where it then was. But its existence at the present moment, in every point of it, is in a different *place* from where its existence was at the last preceding moment. From these things I suppose it will certainly follow that the present existence, either of this, or any other created substance, cannot be an effect of its past existence. The existence (so to speak) of an effect, or thing dependent, in different parts of space or duration, though ever so *near* one to another, do not at all *coexist* one with the other; and therefore are as truly different effects, as if those parts of space and duration were ever so far asunder; and the prior existence can no more be the proper cause of the new existence, in the next moment, or next part of space, than if it had been in an age before, or at a thousand miles distance, without any existence to fill up the intermediate time or space. Therefore the existence of created substances, in each successive moment, must be the effect of the *immediate* agency, will, and power of God. . . .

   It will certainly follow from these things, that God's *preserving* created things in being is perfectly equivalent to a *continued creation*, or to his creating those things out of nothing at *each moment* of their existence. If the continued existence of created things be wholly dependent on God's preservation, then those things would drop into nothing, upon the ceasing of the present moment, without a new exertion of the divine power to cause them to exist in the following moment. If there be any who own that God preserves things in being, and yet hold that they would continue in being without any further help from him, after they once have existence; I think it is hard to know what they mean. To what purpose can it be to talk of God's *preserving* things in being, when there is no *need* of his preserving them? Or to talk of their being *dependent* on God for continued existence, when they would of themselves continue to exist without his help;

nay, though he should wholly withdraw his sustaining power and influence?

It will follow from what has been observed, that God's upholding created substance, or causing its existence in each successive moment, is altogether equivalent to an *immediate production out of nothing*, at each moment. Because its existence at this moment is not merely in part from *God*, but wholly from him, and not in any part or degree, from its *antecedent existence*. For the supposing that its antecedent existence *concurs* with God in *efficiency*, to produce some *part* of the effect, is attended with all the very same absurdities, which have been shown to attend the supposition of its producing it *wholly*. Therefore the antecedent existence is nothing, as to any proper influence or assistance in the affair; and consequently *God* produces the effect as much from *nothing*, as if there had been nothing *before*. So that this effect differs not at all from the first creation, but only *circumstantially;* as in *first* creation there had been no such act and effect of God's power *before;* whereas, his giving existence afterwards, *follows* preceding acts and effects of the same kind, in an established order.

Now, in the next place, let us see how the *consequence* of these things is to my present purpose. If the existence of created *substance*, in each successive moment, be wholly the effect of God's immediate power, in *that* moment, without any dependence on prior existence, as much as the first creation out of *nothing*, then what exists at this moment, by this power, is a *new effect*, and simply and absolutely considered, not the same with any past existence, though it be like it, and follows it according to a certain established method. And there is no identity or oneness in the case, but what depends on the *arbitrary* constitution of the Creator; who by his wise sovereign establishment so unites these successive new effects, that he *treats them as one*, by communicating to them like properties, relations and circumstances; and so leads *us* to regard and treat them as *one*. When I call this an *arbitrary constitution*, I mean, it is a constitution which depends on nothing but the *divine will;* which divine will depends on nothing but the *divine wisdom*. In this sense, the whole *course of nature*, with all that belongs to it, all its laws and methods, and constancy and regularity, continuance and proceeding, is an *arbitrary constitution*. In this sense, the continuance of the very being of the world and all its parts, as well as the manner of continued being, depends entirely on an *arbitrary constitution*. For it does not at all necessarily follow, that because there was sound, or light, or color, or resistance, or gravity, or thought, or consciousness, or any other dependent thing the last moment, that therefore there shall be the like at the next. All dependent existence whatsoever is in a constant flux, ever passing and returning; renewed every moment, as the colors of bodies are every moment renewed by the light that shines upon them; and all is constantly proceeding from *God*, as light from the sun. *In him we live, and move, and have our being.* [Acts 17:28.] [*Original Sin*, II, 488–490.]

᠆᠆᠆᠆᠆᠆

15. *The Dependence of Man**

It is by God's power . . . that we are preserved in a state of grace. I Pet. 1:5. "Who are kept by the power of God through faith unto salvation." As grace is at first from God, so it is continually from him, and is maintained by him, as much as light in the atmosphere is all day long from the sun, as well as at first dawning, or at sun-rising.

Men are dependent on the power of God for every exercise of grace, and for carrying on that work in the heart, for the subduing of sin and corruption, increasing holy principles, and enabling to bring forth fruit in good works, and at last bringing grace to its perfection, in making the soul completely amiable in Christ's glorious likeness, and filling of it with a satisfying joy and blessedness; and for the raising of the body to life, and

---

*From "God Glorified in Man's Dependence." A Sermon in *The Works of President Edwards*.

to such a perfect state, that it shall be suitable for a habitation and organ for a soul so perfected and blessed. These are the most glorious effects of the power of God, that are seen in the series of God's acts with respect to the creatures. [*God Glorified*, IV, 172–173.]

⌒⌒ ⌒⌒

16. *Of Free Will*

AXIOM. Let this be laid down first as a postulate before treating of those doctrines about free will: that whatever is, there is some cause or reason why it is—and prove it. [*Miscellanies*, No. 342.]

⌒⌒ ⌒⌒

17. *On Things Coming Into Existence Without Causes*

It is indeed as repugnant to reason, to suppose that an act of the will should come into existence without a cause, as to suppose the human soul, or an angel, or the globe of the earth, or the whole universe, should come into existence without a cause. And if once we allow, that such a sort of effect as a volition may come to pass without a cause, how do we know but that many other sorts of effects may do so too? [*Freedom of the Will*, p. 185.]

⌒⌒ ⌒⌒

18. *God's Foreknowledge and the Freedom of Man's Will*

If God did not foreknow the fall of man, nor the redemption by Jesus Christ, nor the volitions of man since the fall; then he did not foreknow the saints in any sense; neither as particular persons, nor as societies or nations; either by election, or mere foresight of their virtue or good works; or any foresight of anything about them relating to their salvation; or any benefit they have by Christ, or any manner of concern of theirs with a Redeemer. . . .

It will also follow from this notion, that as God is liable to be continually repenting what he has done; so he must be exposed to be constantly changing his mind and intentions, as to his future conduct; altering his measures, relinquishing his old designs, and forming new schemes and projections. For his purposes, even as to the main parts of his scheme, namely, such as belong to the state of his moral kingdom, must be always liable to be broken, through want of foresight, and he must be continually putting his system to rights, as it gets out of order, through the contingence of the actions of moral agents: he must be a being, who, instead of being absolutely immutable, must necessarily be the subject of infinitely the most numerous acts of repentance, and changes of intention, of any being whatsoever; for this plain reason, that his vastly extensive charge comprehends an infinitely greater number of those things which are to him contingent and uncertain. In such a situation, he must have little else to do, but to mend broken links as well as he can, and be rectifying his disjointed frame and disordered movements, in the best manner the case will allow. The supreme Lord of all things must needs be under great and miserable disadvantages, in governing the world which he has made, and has the care of, through his being utterly unable to find out things of chief importance, which hereafter shall befall his system; which if he did but know, he might make seasonable provision for.

According to the scheme I am endeavoring to confute, neither the fall of men nor angels, could be foreseen, and God must be greatly disappointed in these events; and so the grand scheme and contrivance for our redemption, and destroying the works of the devil, by the Messiah, and all the great things God has done in the prosecution of these designs, must be only the fruits of his own disappointment, and contrivances of his to mend and patch up, as well as he could, his system, which originally was all very good, and perfectly beautiful; but was marred, broken and confounded by the free will of angels and men. And still he must be liable to be totally disappointed a second time: he could not know, that he should have his desired success, in the incarnation, life, death, resurrection and exaltation of his only begotten Son, and other great works accomplished to restore the state of things: he could not know after all, whether there would actually be any tolerable measure of restoration; for this depended on the free will of man. [*Freedom of the Will*, pp. 253–256.]²

19. *God's Moral Excellency Necessary,*
Yet Virtuous and Praiseworthy

Dr. Whitby, in his *Discourse on the Five Points*, says, "If all human actions are necessary, virtue and vice must be empty names; we being capable of nothing that is blameworthy, or deserveth praise; for who can blame a person for doing only what he could not help, or judge that he deserveth praise only for what he could not avoid?"³ . . . And yet Dr. Whitby allows,

---

² This is one of the few passages where Edwards indulges his sense of humor. [Ed.]

³ Daniel Whitby (1638–1726) was an Anglican divine. In his *Discourse* of 1710 he took the Arminian position against the decrees of the Synod of Dort. Edwards cites pp. 14 and 300. See note, p. 25. [Ed.]

that God is without this freedom; and Arminians, so far as I have had opportunity to observe, generally acknowledge, that God is necessarily holy, and his will necessarily determined to that which is good.

So that, putting these things together, the infinitely holy God, who always used to be esteemed by God's people, not only virtuous, but a being in whom is all possible virtue, and every virtue in the most absolute purity and perfection, and in infinitely greater brightness and amiableness than in any creature; the most perfect pattern of virtue, and the fountain from whom all others' virtue is but as beams from the sun; and who has been supposed to be, on the account of his virtue and holiness, infinitely more worthy to be esteemed, loved, honored, admired, commended, extolled and praised, than any creature; and he who is thus everywhere represented in Scripture; I say, this being, according to this notion of Dr. Whitby, and other Arminians, has no virtue at all; virtue, when ascribed to him, is but "an empty name"; and he is deserving of no commendation or praise; because he is under necessity, he can't avoid being holy and good as he is; therefore no thanks to him for it. It seems, the holiness, justice, faithfulness, etc. of the most High, must not be accounted to be of the nature of that which is virtuous and praiseworthy. They will not deny that these things in God are good; but then we must understand them, that they are no more virtuous, or of the nature of anything commendable, than the good that is in any other being that is not a moral agent; as the brightness of the sun, and the fertility of the earth are good, but not virtuous, because these properties are necessary to these bodies, and not the fruit of self-determining power.

There needs no other confutation of this notion of God's not being virtuous or praiseworthy, to Christians acquainted with the Bible, but only stating and particularly representing of it. To bring texts of Scripture, wherein God is represented as in every respect, in the highest manner virtuous, and supremely praiseworthy, would be endless, and is altogether needless to such as have been brought up under the light of the gospel. [*Freedom of the Will*, p. 278.]

20. *Man's Nature, Self-Love, and Sin*

The best philosophy that I have met with of original sin and all sinful inclinations, habits and principles, undoubtedly is that of Mr. Stoddard's, of this town of Northampton: that is, that it is self-love in conjunction with the absence of the image and love of God; that natural and necessary inclination that man has to his own benefit, together with the absence of original righteousness; or in other words, the absence of that influence of God's Spirit, whereby love to God and to holiness is kept up to that degree, that this other inclination is always kept in its due subordination. But this being gone, his self-love governs alone; and having not this superior principle to regulate it, breaks out into all manner of exorbitancies, and becomes in unnumerable cases a vile and odious disposition, and causes thousands of unlovely and hateful actions. There is nothing new put into the nature that we call sin, but only the same self-love that necessarily belongs to the nature working and influencing, without regulation from that superior that primitively belongs to our nature, and that is necessary in order to the harmonious existing of it. This natural and necessary inclination to ourselves without that governor and guide, will certainly without anything else produce, or rather will become, all those sinful inclinations which are in the corrupted nature of man. [*Miscellanies*, No. 301.][4]

---

4 Solomon Stoddard (1643–1729) was Edwards' grandfather and from 1726 to 1729 his senior colleague in the Northampton ministry. See Stoddard's *Three Sermons* (Boston, 1717). The present tense in Edwards' first sentence may date this writing 1726–1729. [Ed.]

❦ ❧

21. *The Union of Adam and His Posterity*

That we may proceed with the greater clearness in considering the main objections against supposing the guilt of Adam's sin to be imputed to his posterity; I would premise some observations with a view to the right *stating* of the doctrine of the imputation of Adam's first sin, and then show the *reasonableness* of this doctrine, in opposition to the great clamor raised against it on this head.

I think it would go far towards directing us to the more clear and distinct conceiving and right stating of this affair, were we steadily to bear this in mind: that God, in each step of his proceeding with Adam, in relation to the covenant or constitution established with him, looked on his posterity as being *one with him*. . . . And though he dealt more immediately with Adam, yet it was as the *head* of the whole body, and the *root* of the whole tree; and in his proceedings with him, he dealt with all the branches, as if they had been then existing in their root.

From which it will follow, that both guilt, or exposedness to punishment, and also depravity of heart, came upon Adam's posterity just as they came upon him, as much as if he and they had all coexisted, like a tree with many branches; allowing only for the difference necessarily resulting from the place Adam stood in, as head or root of the whole, and being first and most immediately dealt with, and most immediately acting and suffering. Otherwise, it is as if, in every step of proceeding, every alteration in the root had been attended, at the same instant, with the same steps and alterations throughout the whole tree, in each individual branch. I think this will naturally follow on the supposition of there being a constituted *oneness* or *identity* of Adam and his posterity in this affair. . . .

From what has been observed it may appear, there is no sure ground to conclude, that it must be an absurd and impossible thing, for the race of mankind truly to partake of the *sin* of the first apostasy, so as that this, in reality and propriety, shall become *their* sin; by virtue of a *real* union between the root and branches of the world of mankind (truly and properly availing to such a consequence), established by the Author of the whole system of the universe; to whose establishments are owing all propriety and reality of *union*, in any part of that system; and by virtue of the full *consent* of the hearts of Adam's posterity to that first apostasy. And therefore the sin of the apostasy is not theirs, merely because God *imputes* it to them; but it is *truly* and *properly* theirs, and on that *ground*, God imputes it to them. [*Original Sin*, II, 481, 492–493.][5]

༺ঙ ৩༻

22. *Water a Type of Sin**

The water . . . is a type of sin or the corruption of man, and of the state of misery that is the consequence of it. It is like sin in its flattering appearance. How smooth and harmless does the water oftentimes appear, and as if it had paradise and heaven in its bosom. Thus when we stand on the banks of a lake or river, how flattering and pleasing does it oftentimes appear, as though under[neath] were pleasant and delightful groves and bowers and even heaven itself in its clearness, enough to tempt one unacquainted with its nature to descend thither. But indeed it is all a cheat: if we should descend into it, instead of finding pleasant, delightful groves and a garden of pleasure and heaven in its clearness, we should meet with nothing but death, a land of darkness, or darkness itself, etc. [*Images and Shadows*, No. 117.]

------

*From *Images and Shadows of Divine Things,* from the manuscript as edited by Thomas A. Schafer. Used with his permission.

------

[5] Preceding the final paragraph here given Edwards introduced the view of immediate and constant divine agency given as excerpt No. 14. [Ed.]

23. *Of Infinite Punishment and Infinite Grace*

It is no solid objection against God's aiming at an infinitely perfect union of the creature with himself, that the particular time
will never come when it can be said, the union is now infinitely
perfect. God aims at satisfying justice in the eternal damnation
of sinners; which will be satisfied by their damnation, considered no otherwise than with regard to its eternal duration. But
yet there never will come that particular moment, when it can
be said, that now justice is satisfied. But if this does not satisfy
our modern freethinkers, who do not like the talk about satisfying justice with an infinite punishment; I suppose it will not be
denied by any, that God, in glorifying the saints in heaven with
eternal felicity, aims to satisfy his infinite grace or benevolence, by the bestowment of a good infinitely valuable, because
eternal; and yet there never will come the moment, when it can
be said, that now this infinitely valuable good has been actually
bestowed. [*God's End,* II, 257.]

24. *On Man's Hardness of Heart**

It is probable that here are some, who hear me this day, who
at this very moment are unawakened, and are in a great degree
careless about their souls. I fear there are some among us who
are most fearfully hardened: their hearts are harder than the
very rocks. It is easier to make impressions upon an adamant
than upon their hearts. I suppose some of you have heard all
that I have said with ease and quietness: it appears to you as
great big sounding words, but doth not reach your hearts. You

---

*From "The Future Punishment of the Wicked Unavoidable and Intol-
erable." A Sermon in *The Works of President Edwards.*

have heard such things many times: you are old soldiers, and have been too much used to the roaring of heaven's cannon, to be frighted at it. It will therefore probably be in vain for me to say any thing further to you; I will only put you in mind that erelong God will deal with you. I cannot deal with you, you despise what I say; I have no power to make you sensible of your danger and misery, and of the dreadfulness of the wrath of God. The attempts of men in this way have often proved vain.

However, God hath undertaken to deal with such men as you are. It is his manner commonly first to let men try their utmost strength: particularly to let ministers try, that thus he may show ministers their own weakness and impotency; and when they have done what they can, and all fails, then God takes the matter into his own hands. [*Future Punishment,* IV, 264–265.]

༄ ༄

25. *On the Changing of Man's Heart: Conversion*

Hence we learn that the prime alteration that is made in conversion, that which is first and the foundation of all, is the alteration of the temper and disposition and spirit of the mind: for what is done in conversion, is nothing but conferring the Spirit of God, which dwells in the soul and becomes there a principle of life and action. 'Tis this is the new nature, and the divine nature; and the nature of the soul being thus changed, it admits divine light. Divine things now appear excellent, beautiful, glorious, which did not when the soul was of another spirit.

Indeed the first act of the Spirit of God, or the first that this divine temper exerts itself in, is in spiritual understanding, or in the sense of the mind, its perception of glory and excellency etc. in the ideas it has of divine things; and this is before any proper acts of the will. Indeed, the inclination of the soul is as immediately exercised in that sense of the mind which is called spiritual understanding, as the intellect. For it is not only the mere presence of ideas in the mind, but it is the mind's sense of their excellency, glory and delightfulness. By this sense or taste of the mind, especially if it be lively, the mind in many things distinguishes truth from falsehood. [*Miscellanies*, No. 397.]

26. God Stamps His Image on Men's Hearts

'Tis the manner of princes to instamp on their coin their image and their name. Thus Christ speaks of Caesar's image and superscription on their pieces of money; which is a type of what God doth to his saints that are his peculiar treasure, his jewels, and that are compared to pieces of money (Luke 15:8–10). He stamps his image on their hearts, and writes on them his name, as is often represented in Revelation. He owns them for his, he challenges them as his special propriety. [*Images and Shadows*, No. 138.]

27. Edwards' Experience of Divine Things[*]

Absolute sovereignty is what I love to ascribe to God. But my first conviction was not so.

The first instance that I remember of that sort of inward, sweet delight in God and divine things that I have lived much in since, was on reading those words, I Tim. 1:17. *Now unto the King eternal, immortal, invisible, the only wise God, be honor and glory for ever and ever, Amen. . . .*

---

[*]From *Some Account of His Conversion, Experience, and Religious Exercizes* in *The Works of President Edwards.*

From about that time, I began to have a new kind of apprehensions and ideas of Christ, and the work of redemption, and the glorious way of salvation by him. An inward, sweet sense of these things, at times, came into my heart; and my soul was led away in pleasant views and contemplations of them. And my mind was greatly engaged to spend my time in reading and meditating on Christ, on the beauty and excellency of his person, and the lovely way of salvation by free grace in him. I found no books so delightful to me, as those that treated of these subjects. Those words, Canticles 2:1, used to be abundantly with me, "I am the Rose of Sharon, and the Lily of the valleys.". . .

Not long after I first began to experience these things, I gave an account to my father of some things that had passed in my mind. I was pretty much affected by the discourse we had together; and when the discourse was ended, I walked abroad alone, in a solitary place in my father's pasture, for contemplation. And as I was walking there, and looking up on the sky and clouds, there came into my mind so sweet a sense of the glorious majesty and grace of God, that I know not how to express. I seemed to see them both in a sweet conjunction; majesty and meekness joined together; it was a sweet, and gentle, and holy majesty; and also a majestic meekness; an awful sweetness; a high, and great, and holy gentleness.

After this my sense of divine things gradually increased, and became more and more lively, and had more of that inward sweetness. The appearance of every thing was altered; there seemed to be, as it were, a calm, sweet cast, or appearance of divine glory, in almost every thing. God's excellency, his wisdom, his purity and love, seemed to appear in every thing; in the sun, moon, and stars; in the clouds, and blue sky; in the grass, flowers, trees; in the water, and all nature; which used greatly to fix my mind. I often used to sit and view the moon for continuance; and in the day, spent much time in viewing the clouds and sky, to behold the sweet glory of God in these things;

in the mean time, singing forth, with a low voice my contemplations of the Creator and Redeemer. [*Personal Narrative,* I, 15–17.][6]

୦୦ ୦୦

28. Of True Religion and Holy Affections*

I Peter 1:8. *Whom having not seen, ye love: in whom, though now ye see him not, yet believing, ye rejoice with joy unspeakable, and full of glory.*

The proposition or doctrine, that I would raise from these words is this,

DOCTRINE: True religion, in great part, consists in holy affections.

We see that the Apostle, in observing and remarking the operations and exercises of religion, in the Christians he wrote to, wherein their religion appeared to be true and of the right kind, when it had its greatest trial of what sort it was, being tried by persecution as gold is tried in the fire, and when their religion not only proved true, but was most pure, and cleansed from its dross and mixtures of that which was not true, and when religion appeared in them most in its genuine excellency and native beauty, and was found to praise, and honor, and glory; he singles out the religious affections of love and joy, that were then in exercise in them: these are the exercises of religion he takes notice of, wherein their religion did thus appear true and pure, and in its proper glory. [*Religious Affections,* p. 95.]

---

*From John E. Smith, ed., *A Treatise Concerning Religious Affections,* The Yale Edition (New Haven: Yale University Press, 1959), Reprinted with the permission of the publisher.

---

[6] Written when Edwards was about forty, remembering experiences of some twenty years before. [Ed.]

⌒ᶟ ᶟ⌒

29. *The Purpose of Mankind's Affections*

God has given to mankind affections, for the same purpose which he has given all the faculties and principles of the human soul for, viz. that they might be subservient to man's chief end, and the great business for which God has created him, that is the business of religion. And yet how common is it among mankind, that their affections are much more exercised and engaged in other matters, than in religion! In things which concern men's worldly interest, their outward delights, their honor and reputation, and their natural relations, they have their desires eager, their appetites vehement, their love warm and affectionate, their zeal ardent; in these things their hearts are tender and sensible, easily moved, deeply impressed, much concerned, very sensibly affected, and greatly engaged; much depressed with grief at worldly losses, and highly raised with joy at worldly successes and prosperity. But how insensible and unmoved are most men, about the great things of another world! How dull are their affections! How heavy and hard their hearts in these matters! Here their love is cold, their desires languid, their zeal low, and their gratitude small. How they can sit and hear of the infinite height and depth and length and breadth of the love of God in Christ Jesus, of his giving his infinitely dear Son, to be offered up a sacrifice for the sins of men, and of the unparalleled love of the innocent, holy and tender Lamb of God, manifested in his dying agonies, his bloody sweat, his loud and bitter cries, and bleeding heart, and all this for enemies, to redeem them from deserved, eternal burnings, and to bring to unspeakable and everlasting joy and glory; and yet be cold, and heavy, insensible, and regardless! Where are the exercises of our affections proper, if not here? . . .

But is there anything, which Christians can find in heaven or earth, so worthy to be the objects of their admiration and love, their earnest and longing desires, their hope, and their rejoicing, and their fervent zeal, as those things that are held forth to us in the gospel of Jesus Christ? In which, not only are things declared most worthy to affect us, but they are exhibited in the most affecting manner. The glory and beauty of the blessed Jehovah, which is most worthy in itself, to be the object of our admiration and love, is there exhibited in the most affecting manner that can be conceived of, as it appears shining in all its luster, in the face of an incarnate, infinitely loving, meek, compassionate, dying Redeemer. . . . So has God disposed things, in the affair of our redemption, and in his glorious dispensations, revealed to us in the gospel, as though everything were purposely contrived in such a manner, as to have the greatest, possible tendency to reach our hearts in the most tender part, and move our affections most sensibly and strongly. How great cause have we therefore to be humbled to the dust, that we are no more affected! [*Religious Affections,* pp. 122–124.]

◡◦ ◦◠

30. *The Divine and Supernatural Light**

A person . . . may have affecting views of the things of religion and yet be very destitute of spiritual light. Flesh and blood may be the author of this: one man may give another an affecting view of divine things with but common assistance: but God alone can give a spiritual discovery of them.

But I proceed to show . . . positively what this spiritual and divine light is.

And it may be thus described: a true sense of the divine excellency of the things revealed in the word of God, and a conviction of the truth and reality of them thence arising.

---

*From "A Divine and Supernatural Light, Immediately Imparted to the Soul by the Spirit of God, Shown to Be Both a Rational and Scriptural Doctrine." A Sermon in *The Works of President Edwards.*

This spiritual light primarily consists in . . . a real sense and apprehension of the divine excellency of things revealed in the word of God. A spiritual and saving conviction of the truth and reality of these things, arises from such a sight of their divine excellency and glory; so that this conviction of their truth is an effect and natural consequence of this sight of their divine glory.

There is therefore in this spiritual light a true sense of the divine and superlative excellency of the things of religion; a real sense of the **excellency of God and Jesus Christ**, and of the work of redemption, and the ways and works of God revealed in the gospel. There is a divine and superlative glory in these things; an excellency that is of a vastly higher kind, and more sublime nature than in other things; a glory greatly distinguishing them from all that is earthly and temporal. He that is spiritually enlightened truly apprehends and sees it, or has a sense of it. He does not merely rationally believe that God is glorious, but he has a sense of the gloriousness of God in his heart. There is not only a rational belief that God is holy, and that holiness is a good thing, but there is a sense of the loveliness of God's holiness. There is not only a speculatively judging that God is gracious, but a sense how amiable God is upon that account, or a sense of the beauty of this divine attribute. . . .

Thus there is a difference between having an opinion that God is holy and gracious, and having a sense of the loveliness and beauty of that holiness and grace. There is a difference between having a rational judgment that honey is sweet, and having a sense of its sweetness. A man may have the former, that knows not how honey tastes; but a man cannot have the latter unless he has an idea of the taste of honey in his mind. So there is a difference between believing that a person is beautiful, and having a sense of his beauty. The former may be obtained by hearsay, but the latter only by seeing the countenance. There is a wide difference between mere speculative rational judging any thing to be excellent, and having a sense of its

sweetness and beauty. The former rests only in the head, speculation only is concerned in it; but the heart is concerned in the
latter. When the heart is sensible of the beauty and amiableness
of a thing, it necessarily feels pleasure in the apprehension. It is
implied in a person's being heartily sensible of the loveliness of
a thing, that the idea of it is sweet and pleasant to his soul;
which is a far different thing from having a rational opinion that
it is excellent. [*Divine Light,* IV, 441–442.]

⸎ ⸎

31. *God Requires More Than Lifeless "Wouldings"*

That religion which God requires, and will accept, does not
consist in weak, dull and lifeless wouldings, raising us but a
little above a state of indifference: God, in his Word, greatly
insists upon it, that we be in good earnest, fervent in spirit, and
our hearts vigorously engaged in religion: "Be ye fervent in
spirit, serving the Lord" (Rom. 12:11). "And now Israel, what
doth the Lord thy God require of thee, but to fear the Lord thy
God, to walk in all his ways, and to love him, and to serve the
Lord thy God, with all thy heart, and with all thy soul?" (Deut.
10:12). And ch. 6:4–5: "Hear, O Israel; the Lord our God is one
Lord; and thou shalt love the Lord thy God, with all thy heart,
and with all thy soul, and with all thy might." 'Tis such a fervent, vigorous engagedness of the heart in religion, that is the
fruit of a real circumcision of the heart, or true regeneration,
and that has the promises of life; "And the Lord thy God will
circumcise thine heart, and the heart of thy seed, to love the
Lord thy God, with all thy heart, and with all thy soul, that
thou mayest live" (Deut. 30:6).

If we ben't in good earnest in religion, and our wills and inclinations be not strongly exercised, we are nothing. [*Religious
Affections,* p. 99.]

‿๏ ๏‿

32. *Of Excellence and Beauty*

There has nothing been more without a definition than excellency, although it be what we are more concerned with than any thing else whatsoever: yea, we are concerned with nothing else. But what is this excellency? Wherein is one thing excellent and another evil; one beautiful and another deformed? [*The Mind*, No. 1.][7]

‿๏ ๏‿

33. *Excellence is Consent to Being: Love*

Excellence in and among spirits is, in its prime and proper sense, being's consent to being. There is no other proper consent but that of minds, even of their will; which, when it is of minds towards minds, it is love, and when of minds towards other things, it is choice. Wherefore all the primary and original beauty or excellence, that is among minds, is love; and into this may all be resolved that is found among them.

As to that excellence that created spirits partake of, that it is all to be resolved into love, none will doubt that knows what is the sum of the Ten Commandments; or believes what the Apostle says, that love is the fulfilling of the law; or what Christ says, that on these two, loving God and our neighbor, hang all the law and the prophets. This doctrine is often repeated in the New Testament. We are told that the end of the commandment is love; that to love is to fulfill the royal law; and that all the law is fulfilled in this one word, love. [Romans 13:8; Matthew 22:37–40.] [*The Mind*, No. 45, pars. 1 and 10.]

---

[7] This writing probably dates from 1717–1720. [Ed.]

∽◈ ◈∾

34. *On the Nature of True Virtue**

Virtue is the beauty of the qualities and exercises of the heart, or those actions which proceed from them. So that when it is inquired, what is the nature of true virtue? this is the same as to inquire what that is, which renders any habit, disposition, or exercise of the heart truly beautiful?

I use the phrase true virtue, and speak of things truly beautiful, because I suppose it will generally be allowed, that there is a distinction to be made between some things which are truly virtuous, and others which only seem to be virtuous, through a partial and imperfect view of things: that some actions and dispositions appear beautiful, if considered partially and superficially, or with regard to some things belonging to them, and in some of their circumstances and tendencies, which would appear otherwise in a more extensive and comprehensive view, wherein they are seen clearly in their whole nature, and the extent of their connections in the universality of things.

There is a general and particular beauty. By a *particular* beauty, I mean that by which a thing appears beautiful when considered only with regard to its connection with, and tendency to, some particular things within a limited, and, as it were, a private sphere. And a *general* beauty is that by which a thing appears beautiful when viewed most perfectly, comprehensively and universally, with regard to all its tendencies, and its connections with every thing to which it stands related to. The former may be without and against the latter. As a few notes in a tune, taken only by themselves and in their relation to one another, may be harmonious, which, when considered

---

*From *Dissertation in the Nature of True Virtue* in *The Works of President Edwards*.

with respect to all the notes in the tune, or the entire series of sounds they are connected with, may be very discordant and disagreeable. . . . That only, therefore, is what I mean by true virtue, which is that belonging to the heart of an intelligent being, that is beautiful by a general beauty, or beautiful in a comprehensive view, as it is in itself, and as related to every thing that it stands in connection with. And therefore, when we are inquiring concerning the nature of true virtue, viz., wherein this true and general beauty of the heart does most essentially consist—this is my answer to the inquiry:

True virtue most essentially consists in benevolence to being in general. Or perhaps to speak more accurately, it is that consent, propensity and union of heart to being in general, that is immediately exercised in a general good will. . . .

And further, if being, simply considered, be the first object of a truly virtuous benevolence, then that being who has most of being, or has the greatest share of existence, other things being equal, so far as such a being is exhibited to our faculties, will have the greatest share of the propensity and benevolent affections of the heart. . . . Pure benevolence in its first exercise is nothing else but being's uniting consent, or propensity to being; appearing true and pure by its extending to being in general, and inclining to the general highest good, and to each being, whose welfare is consistent with the highest general good, in proportion to the degree of *existence* understood, other things being equal.

I say, "in proportion to the degree of existence," because one being may have more existence than another, as he may be greater than another. That which is great has more existence, and is further from nothing than that which is little. One being may have every thing positive belonging to it, or every thing which goes to its positive existence (in opposition to defect) in an higher degree than another; or a greater capacity and power, greater understanding, every faculty and every positive quality in a higher degree. An archangel must be supposed to have more existence, and to be every way further removed from nonentity, than a worm or a flea. [*True Virtue*, II, 261–265.][8]

35. The Emanation and Remanation
of the Divine Glory

The great and last end of God's works which is so variously expressed in Scripture, is indeed but *one;* and this *one* end is most properly and comprehensively called, THE GLORY OF GOD; by which name it is most commonly called in Scripture: and is fitly compared to an effulgence or emanation of light from a luminary, by which this glory of God is abundantly represented in Scripture. Light is the external expression, exhibition and manifestation of the excellency of the luminary, of the sun for instance: it is the abundant, extensive emanation and communication of the fulness of the sun to innumerable beings that partake of it. It is by this that the sun itself is seen, and his glory beheld, and all other things are discovered; it is by a participation of this communication from the sun, that surrounding objects receive all their lustre, beauty and brightness. It is by this that all nature is quickened and receives life, comfort, and joy. Light is abundantly used in Scripture to represent and signify these three things, knowledge, holiness and happiness. . . .

The emanation or communication of the divine fulness, consisting in the knowledge of God, love to God, and joy in God, has relation indeed both to God, and the creature; but it has relation to God as its fountain, as it is an emanation from God; and as the communication itself, or thing communicated, is

---

[8] The final paragraph here given was printed by Edwards as a footnote to the word "existence" in the preceding sentence. This work was written at Stockbridge, a quarter-century and more after the two preceding excerpts. [Ed.]

something divine, something of God, something of his internal
fulness, as the water in the stream is something of the fountain,
and as the beams of the sun, are something of the sun. And
again, they have relation to God, as they have respect to him
as their object; for the knowledge communicated is the knowledge of God; and so God is the object of the knowledge, and
the love communicated is the love of God; so God is the object
of that love, and the happiness communicated is joy in God;
and so he is the object of the joy communicated. In the creature's knowing, esteeming, loving, rejoicing in, and praising
God, the glory of God is both exhibited and acknowledged;
his fulness is received and returned. Here is both an *emanation*
and *remanation*. The refulgence shines upon and into the creature, and is reflected back to the luminary. The beams of glory
come from God, and are something of God, and are refunded
back again to their original. So that the whole is *of* God, and *in*
God, and *to* God, and God is the beginning, middle and end in
this affair. [*God's End*, II, 254–257.]

36. *The Great Design God is Pursuing*

There is doubtless some design that God is pursuing, and
scheme that he is carrying on, in the various changes and revolutions that from age to age happen in the world; there is some
certain great design, to which providence subordinates all the
successive changes that come to pass in the state of affairs of
mankind. All revolutions from the beginning of the world to
the end, are doubtless but various parts of one scheme, all con-
spiring for the bringing to pass the great event which is ultimately in view. And the scheme will not be finished, nor the
design fully accomplished, the great event fully brought to
pass, till the end of the world and the last revolution is brought
about. The world, it is most evident, is not an everlasting thing;
it will have an end: and God's end in making and governing
the world will not be fully obtained, nor his scheme be finished,

till the end of the world comes. If it were, he would put an end to it sooner; for God won't continue the world, won't continue to uphold it, and dispose and govern it, and cause changes and revolutions in it, after he has nothing further that he aims at by it.

God don't fully obtain his design in any one particular state that the world has been in at one time, but in the various successive states that the world is in, in different ages, connected in a scheme. 'Tis evident that he don't fully obtain his end, his design, in any one particular state that the world has ever been in; for if so, we should have no change. But God is continually causing revolutions; providence makes a continual progress, and continually is bringing forth things new in the state of the world, and very different from what ever were before; he removes one that he may establish another. And perfection will not be obtained till the last revolution, when God's design will be fully reached.

Nor yet are the past states of the world abolished by revolutions because they are in vain, or don't do anything towards promoting his design in creating the world; if so, providence would never have ordered them, the world never would have been in such a state. There remains therefore no other way, but that the various successive states of the world do in conjunction, or as connected in a scheme, together attain God's great design. [*Miscellanies*, No. 547.]

∽◦ ◦∾

37. *Retrospect and Prospect**

My method of study, from my first beginning the work of the ministry, has been very much by writing; applying myself, in this way, to improve every important hint; pursuing the clue to

---

*From *Letter to the Trustees of the College of New Jersey at Princeton* in *The Works of President Edwards.*

my utmost, when any thing in reading, meditation, or conversation, has been suggested to my mind, that seemed to promise light, in any weighty point; thus penning what appeared to me my best thoughts, on innumerable subjects, for my own benefit. The longer I prosecuted my studies, in this method, the more habitual it became, and the more pleasant and profitable I found it. The farther I travelled in this way, the more and wider the field opened, which has occasioned my laying out many things in my mind to do in this manner, if God should spare my life, which my heart hath been much upon; particularly many things against most of the prevailing errors of the present day, which I cannot with any patience see maintained (to the utter subverting of the gospel of Christ) with so high a hand, and so long continued a triumph, with so little control, when it appears so evident to me, that there is truly no foundation for any of this glorying and insult. I have already published something on one of the main points in dispute between the Arminians and Calvinists; and have it in view, God willing (as I have already signified to the public) in like manner to consider all the other controverted points, and have done much towards a preparation for it.

But beside these, I have had on my mind and heart (which I long ago began, not with any view to publication) a great work, which I call a History of the Work of Redemption, a body of divinity in an entire new method, being thrown into the form of a history; considering the affair of Christian theology, as the whole of it, in each part, stands in reference to the great work of redemption by Jesus Christ; which I suppose to be, of all others, the grand design of God, and the summum and ultimum of all the divine operations and decrees; particularly considering all parts of the grand scheme, in their historical order. The order of their existence, or their being brought forth to view, in the course of divine dispensations, or the wonderful series of successive acts and events; beginning from eternity, and descending from thence to the great work and successive dispensations of the infinitely wise God, in time, considering the chief events coming to pass in the church of God, and revolutions in the world of mankind, affecting the state of the church and the affair of redemption, which we have an account of in history or prophecy; till at last, we come to the general resurrection, last judgment, and consummation of all things; when it shall be said, It is done. I am Alpha and Omega, the Beginning and the End. Concluding my work, with the consideration of that perfect state of things, which shall be finally settled, to last for eternity. This history will be carried on with regard to all three worlds, heaven, earth and hell; considering the connected, successive events and alterations in each, so far as the Scriptures give any light; introducing all parts of divinity in that order which is most scriptural and most natural; a method which appears to me the most beautiful and entertaining, wherein every divine doctrine will appear to the greatest advantage, in the brightest light, in the most striking manner, showing the admirable contexture and harmony of the whole.

I have also, for my own profit and entertainment, done much towards another great work, which I call the Harmony of the Old and New Testament, in three parts. The first, considering the Prophecies of the Messiah, his redemption and kingdom; the evidences of their references to the Messiah, etc. comparing them all one with another, demonstrating their agreement, true scope, and sense; also considering all the various particulars wherein these prophecies have their exact fulfilment; showing the universal, precise, and admirable correspondence between predictions and events. The second part, considering the Types of the Old Testament, showing the evidence of their being intended as representations of the great things of the gospel of Christ; and the agreement of the type with the antitype. The third and great part, considering the Harmony of the Old and New Testament, as to doctrine and precept. In the course of this work, I find there will be occasion for an explanation of a very great part of the holy Scriptures; which may, in such a view, be explained in a method, which to me seems the most entertaining and profitable, best tending to lead the mind to a view of the true spirit, design, life and soul of the Scriptures, as well as their proper use and improvement.

I have also many other things in hand, in some of which I have made great progress, which I will not trouble you with an account of. Some of these things, if divine Providence favor, I should be willing to attempt a publication of. So far as I myself am able to judge of what talents I have, for benefiting my fellow creatures by word, I think I can write better than I can speak.

My heart is so much in these studies, that I cannot feel willing to put myself into an incapacity to pursue them any more in the future part of my life. [*Letter to the Princeton Trustees*, I, 48–49.] [9]

---

[9] This letter was dated October 19, 1757. The "future part" of Edwards' life was not to be long. He died five months later, at Princeton on March 22, 1758. [Ed.]

III

WILLIAM ELLERY CHANNING

Unitarian Patriarch

William Ellery Channing (1780–1842)[1] is properly remembered as the virtual personification of Unitarian Christianity in America. His life illustrates the intellectual process by which Unitarianism emerged. His ministry, in turn, had great shaping power on the new denomination, not least with respect to its powers of assimilation and change. The whole course of his life no less than the ideas that dominate his preaching makes him a figure of great symbolic value.

Channing was born at Newport, Rhode Island, and began his religious training at the Second Church under the stern ministry of Jonathan Edwards' most committed disciple, Samuel Hopkins (1721–1803). In retrospect he deeply valued this influence and his preaching always bore the marks of Hopkins' distinctive doctrine that "disinterested benevolence" (i.e., selflessness) was the essence of true virtue. While at Harvard College, Channing felt the beginnings of a conversion experience which took a deeper turn a few years later when he was serving as a private tutor in Virginia. To the end of his days these personal

---

[1] See Introduction, pp. 37–41.

disclosures would keep alive his interest in the religious affections and keep his faith far above "the pale negations of Boston Unitarianism" that Emerson found so repulsive. More immediately his conversion led to theological studies, and in 1803 he was ordained at the Federal Street Church in Boston where he ministered with ever-increasing influence until his death. When the Transcendentalist controversy erupted during the 1830's Channing took an even less active role than he had in the older conflict with orthodoxy. In the greatest of all American controversies, that on slavery, he overcame his inherent moderation with measured steps and proceeded to publish on the subject in 1835. Then in 1837, when the murder of Elijah Lovejoy also raised the issue of freedom of speech and the press, Channing took his stand in a way that gave great impetus to the antislavery cause in New England.

At the time of his death Channing was more than once referred to as America's most prominent religious leader; and the statement is not easily refuted. His explicit Unitarianism often made his own works suspect in evangelical circles, but New England's literary flowering in the early nineteenth century and a simultaneous surge of humanitarianism were often directly responsive to Channing's gently persuasive words. William Cullen Bryant, Henry Wadsworth Longfellow, Elizabeth Peabody, Dorthea Dix, Charles Sumner, Lydia Maria Child, Horace Mann, and many others testified to the force of his ideas in their lives and transmitted his thoughts to the nation. Emerson expressed a Transcendentalist consensus when he referred to Channing as "our bishop." From the 1840's to the present, moreover, there has been a party in the larger Unitarian movement which has explicitly placed itself in the "Channing tradition" and sought to preserve his commitment to biblical Christianity and his determination to keep the "liberal faith" in a living relationship with the Protestant churches. No other American gave such profound expression to rationalistic Christian liberalism as did he. He was in effect the theologian of the "Revolutionary generation" as well as a great religious liberator for the "Romantic generation" that followed.

The pastor-theologian, for three centuries, played a prominent role in American intellectual history, and Channing is one of the tradition's purest representatives. Except for a few essays written for periodicals, his published works consist entirely of sermons and addresses delivered during the four decades of his public ministry. Because he wished "to make the humblest his peers," he avoided the kinds of language and argument to which his readings and meditation might easily have led. Far from being an "advanced thinker," moreover, he was, if anything, somewhat old-fashioned. Unresponsive to the newer biblical and historical studies, tardy in his appreciation of romantic thought, he remained committed throughout his life to an idealistically shaded version of the Scottish Philosophy and remained deeply indebted to the rationalistic theologies that flourished in Great Britain during the eighteenth century. Yet he shows remarkable theological integrity and philosophic consistency. As Robert L. Patterson has suggested, Channing's emphasis on divine benevolence and "man's likeness to God" results in an impressive synthesis for which the term "perfectibilitarianism" is not inappropriate. There is no better summation of Channing's mature theological views than The Perfect Life, a series of twelve sermons that his nephew published in 1873. The selection that follows is tenth in that series, on a subject to which countless works would be devoted during the coming century. This sermon was preached in the winter of 1830–1831.

The Essence of

The Christian Religion

The Glorious Gospel of the Blessed God.–I Tim. 1:11.

These words express the excellence of the Christian religion. It is called the Gospel, that is, Good News. It is called the Glorious Gospel of the Blessed God, to denote the magnificence of the truths and blessings which it reveals. In this discourse I propose to set before you what it is in Christianity that gives it the chief claim to this high praise. I wish to exhibit to you its essential character, and to show what constitutes it worthy of all acceptation.

I [*The Central Principle*]

I begin with asking, What is Christianity? In answer to this question, it is not necessary that I should repeat the whole New Testament. This book contains the religion; but every verse is not a separate disconnected truth, so that each must be recited to give you an understanding of Christianity. There is a unity in the religion of Jesus.[1] And this may be summed up in narrow

From William Ellery Channing, *The Perfect Life,* in *Twelve Discourses* (Boston: Roberts Brothers, 1873), pp. 243–262.

[1] The emphasis on unity and "central principle" is a characteristic Unitarian critique of orthodox emphasis on proof-texts. See Channing's "Unitarian Christianity" (1819) in William Ellery Channing, *Unitarian Christianity and Other Essays,* Irving H. Bartlett, ed., The American Heritage Series (New York: The Liberal Arts Press, 1957), pp. 3–38. [Ed.]

compass. Through the various precepts of the New Testament you can trace One Spirit, of which they are all the forms. Its various doctrines may be reduced to a few great truths, perhaps to one single truth. Now to understand Christianity, the true method is to extract this ESSENCE, as it were, of the various teachings of our Lord; to rise to this Universal Spirit which pervades all his commands; to seize on this great central truth, around which all others gather, and from which all derive their glory. To understand Christianity, is not to view in succession every separate truth and precept, but to understand the relation of these various teachings to one another, and to the great end in which they all meet—just as to understand the human body, it is not enough to see the limbs singly and severed from each other, but to observe them in their combination, harmonious order and joint symmetry, as pervaded by one life, and all co-working to fulfil one destiny.

I believe that Christianity has ONE GREAT PRINCIPLE, which is *central*, around which all its truths gather, and which constitutes it the Glorious Gospel of the Blessed God. I believe that no truth is so worthy of acceptance and so quickening as this. In proportion as we penetrate into it, and are penetrated by it, we comprehend our religion, and attain to a living faith. This great principle can be briefly expressed. It is the doctrine, that "God purposes, in His unbounded fatherly love, to PERFECT THE HUMAN SOUL; to purify it from all sin; to create it after His own image; to fill it with His own spirit; to unfold it for ever; to raise it to life and immortality in heaven:—that is, to communicate to it from Himself a life of celestial power, virtue and joy." The elevation of men above the imperfections, temptations, sins, sufferings, of the present state, to a diviner being,—this is the great purpose of God, revealed and accomplished by Jesus Christ; this it is that constitutes the religion of Jesus Christ— glad tidings to all people: for it is a religion suited to fulfil the wants of every human being.

In the New Testament I learn that God regards the human soul with unutterable interest and love; that in an important sense it bears the impress of His own infinity, its powers being germs, which may expand without limit or end;[2] that He loves it, even when fallen, and desires its restoration; that He has sent His Son to redeem and cleanse it from all iniquity; that He forever seeks to communicate to it a divine virtue which shall spring up, by perennial bloom and fruitfulness, into everlasting life. In the New Testament I learn that what God wills is our PERFECTION; by which I understand the freest exercise and perpetual development of our highest powers—strength and brightness of intellect, unconquerable energy of moral principle, pure and fervent desire for truth, unbounded love of goodness and greatness, benevolence free from every selfish taint, the perpetual consciousness of God and of His immediate presence, co-operation and friendship with all enlightened and disinterested spirits, and radiant glory of benign will and beneficent influence, of which we have an emblem—a faint emblem only—in the sun that illuminates and warms so many worlds. Christianity reveals to me this moral perfection of man, as the great purpose of God.

When I look into man's nature, I see that moral perfection is his only true and enduring Good; and consequently the promise of this must be the highest truth which any religion can contain. The loftiest endowment of our nature is the moral power—the power of perceiving and practising virtue, of discerning and seeking goodness. Having this as our essential principle, we can have but one happiness as our end. There is a guide to felicity fixed by God in the very center of our being, and no other can take its place. Whoever obeys faithfully this principle of duty has peace with himself and with all beings. Whoever silences or withstands this is at war with himself and with all. And no

---

[2] See Channing's "Likeness to God" (1828) for an expansion of this theme. *Ibid.*, pp. 86–108. [Ed.]

hostility can be compared with this. It is not brute matter with which he is at war. He makes the principle of right in his heart, and in all other beings, that is, the highest principle in the universe, his reprover and foe. He must reconcile this sovereign power, and must make it his friend, or despair of happiness. To such a being as this, there is no sufficient good but moral perfection. If God do not purpose to raise man to this; if man may not look for this to the mercy, power and inspiration of the Almighty; then he has nothing to hope for worthy the name of happiness. Christianity is God's best gift, in so far as it proffers to us this only felicity, and places it within our reach; as it reveals this to be the great end of our creation. When Christianity is thus viewed, I understand why its revelations are called "unsearchable riches," and why it is said to express "a love which passeth knowledge."

By this language I do not mean to claim for Christianity the exclusive honour of discovering to us God's purpose of perfecting the human soul. The soul itself—in its powers and affections, in its unquenchable thirst and aspiration for unattained good—gives signs of a nature made for an interminable progress, such as cannot be now conceived. When, too, I contemplate the immensity and wonderful order of the material creation, and the beautiful structure of its minutest parts, I feel sure that mind, the yet nobler work of God, must be destined to a more enlarged and harmonious existence than I now experience or behold. Above all, conscience, in its secret monitions, its promises and forebodings, teaches that there is a futurity for men, where more is to be gained and more endured than is possible or imaginable on earth. But I need a more direct, immediate, explicit testimony to the purpose of God. And such a witness is Christianity. This religion is not a deduction of philosophy, resting on obscure truths, and intelligible but to a few. It is a solemn annunciation from heaven of human immortality, and of a diviner life than this. And it is sealed by miracles, that is, by divine interpositions, which are equally intelligible, striking and affecting to all.[3] I maintain that miracles are most appropriate proofs of a religion which announces the elevation of man to spiritual perfection. For what are miracles? They are the acts and manifestations of a spiritual power in the universe, superior to the powers and laws of matter. And on the existence of such a power, the triumph of our own spiritual nature over death and material influences must depend.

The miracles of Christianity, so far from shocking me, approve themselves at once to my intellect and my heart. They seem to me among the most reasonable as well as important events in human history. I prize them, not because they satisfy the passion for the wonderful—though this principle is one of the noble indications of our nature. But I prize them as discovering, in a way which all can comprehend, that there is some real being mightier than nature; that there is a mind which *can,* if it WILL, suspend or reverse the regular operations of the material world; that, of consequence, the power of death is not supreme, and that the mind may ascend to a perfection which nature cannot give. Christianity, in its miracles and doctrines, is the very charter and pledge which I need of this elevation of the human soul. And on this account I recognize it as the Glorious Gospel of the Blessed God, or as a religion making sure to its sincere disciples the most magnificent good which even Omnipotence can bestow.

I wish, my hearers, that I had power to give you some new conviction of the greatness of this good. How much to be deplored is it, that to so many men, the perfection of their nature never rises to view as a happiness which may be realized; that the consciousness of the capacity of reaching it, of being made for it, is well nigh stifled. The doctrine of that higher state of their powers and affections, of that purer life which Christianity

---

[3] Channing elaborates his lifelong position on miracles in "The Evidences of Revealed Religion" (1821), *Ibid.,* pp. 60–85. In the ensuing Transcendentalist controversy, Emerson's Divinity School Address (1838) was the classic counterstatement, see pp. 299–301. [Ed.]

sets before them, is assented to by vast multitudes with no thorough persuasion. And yet without this persuasion we know nothing of the purpose of our being. A darkness, thicker than night, without a star, hangs over our minds. We know neither ourselves nor our fellow-men. We have no explanation of life, of our sufferings, or of our enjoyments. We want that truth, which gives worth and grandeur to our whole existence; which alone inspires perfect trust in God; which alone teaches us respect for man; which is more than equal to the pressure of all trial; and which can carry us forward against the strength of passion, temptation and all forms of evil. How can this truth, without which we are so poor, be called into energetic life, and become a bright reality to us? It must become so, through our own resolute grasp—by effort, by reflection, by prayer, by resistance of the body, the senses and the outward world, by descending into our own minds, by listening to experience, as it daily teaches that there is no true good which has not its spring in the improvement of our highest nature.

II   [*The Perfection of Mind*]

The more I think of this central truth of Christianity, that is, of God's purpose to raise the soul to its PERFECTION, the more I feel the glory and excellence of this religion; the more I feel that, if it promised other goods, or promised happiness in other forms, it would cease to be glorious. No other heaven, than that which is found in our own perfection, would be a good worth living for. This truth I have often insisted on; but it seems to me so transcendent in worth as to merit frequent and earnest inculcation. On the understanding of it, our estimate of Christianity must entirely rest. Lay it down then as a primary, fundamental truth, that to a moral being there is but one essential enduring Good—and that is, the health, power and purity of his own soul. Hold this doctrine intelligently, and you hold the key that is gradually to unlock to you the mysteries of nature and providence, of duty, temptation and happiness, of this life and the life to come.[4]

This doctrine, that perfection of mind is our only happiness, by no means interferes with the great truth that God is our supreme good. God is indeed our eternal source of happiness. But how? Not by pouring profusely upon us gratifications which we may receive in a passive and inert condition, but by awakening our minds and hearts to action, that we may comprehend His character and thus derive from Him more and more of His own perfections. To enjoy God, we must bring Him near to ourselves, by concentrating the strength of our intellect in thought and meditation upon His goodness and perfections; and still more must his perfections be received into ourselves by esteem, veneration, sympathy and the adoption of His pure will as our own. I can enjoy God only so far as I receive the divine mind into my own. His wise and benevolent purposes must become mine own. I must inhale, if I may so speak, the SPIRIT that breathes through His works and His Word. I must approve and choose rectitude, as He chooses it; that is, love and cleave to it for its own sake. It is only by this diffusion of Himself through my spiritual nature, by the elevation which His perfect character imparts to my own, that God becomes to me the enduring and the highest Good.

The desire which I have to impress this great truth—that perfection of the soul is the only spring of happiness, and consequently that Christianity in revealing this as God's purpose is a glorious religion—induces me to offer a proof or illustration, which I hope will not be thought too refined for a popular address. It is a plain fact, then, that to a being endued with mind,

---

[4] The man-centered "key" of the foregoing passage—more than differing views on the Trinity—distinguished Unitarian Christianity from New England orthodoxy in general, and especially from the radical theocentricity of Edwards, cf. pp. 162–168. [Ed.]

or to an intelligent spiritual being, the highest objects of enjoyment are other minds or other spiritual beings. I find pleasure
in the knowledge and use of matter and of inferior animals.
But they cannot satisfy me. I long for intercourse with beings
who partake my own highest nature. And what is it in these
spiritual Beings which is fitted to give me the purest and most
enduring delight? I answer: their moral excellence.[5] Eclipse
this excellence in the supreme being; put out the light of His
wisdom, rectitude and omnipotent goodness; rob fellow-beings
of virtuous principle and the capacity of spiritual progress: and
what would remain in heaven or on earth to attract and move
us, to call forth attachment and trust, to inspire hope and joy?
The glory of the universe would be quenched. This excellence
of goodness is the one great object to be enjoyed, on earth or in
heaven. There is nothing else which can give enduring gratification. And how, I would ask, is this to be enjoyed, but by a corresponding excellence in our own spirits? To want this is to
want the organ by which to discern it in others. Who can fail to
recognize that by degrading his own character, he cuts himself
off from the enjoyment of pure and lofty souls; that the practice
of vice must seal his eyes to the beauty of virtue; that in narrow-
ing his intellect and heart, he unfits himself for communion with
great thoughts and noble purposes in others; and on the other
hand, that in proportion as he makes progress towards perfection, he strengthens the holy and happy bonds which unite
him with God and all excellent beings, and gains new power to
enjoy their excellence?

Mind is the great object to be enjoyed; and this is true to a
greater extent than we imagine.[6] Even outward, material na-

---

[5] Cf. Jonathan Edwards, pp. 185–187. [Ed.]

[6] Channing confessed that the "transcendental direction" of his thought,
and his "doctrine of ideas" were owed to the English Platonist, Richard
Price (1723–1791). "Price saved me from Locke's Philosophy." William
Henry Channing, *The Life of William Ellery Channing* (Boston: American
Unitarian Association, 1880), p. 34. [Ed.]

ture derives its chief power of contributing to our happiness, by being a manifestation of mental or spiritual excellence. No one truly enjoys the creation, but he who sees it everywhere as radiant with *Mind,* and as for ever showing forth the perfection of its author. We think, perhaps, that nature has a beauty of its own, in which we can delight, without reference to any reality above it. But natural beauty is an image or emblem of harmonious qualities of the mind. It is a type of spiritual beauty.[7] And he, to whom the last is not known by consciousness, by the dawning of beauty in his own soul, can know and feel but little of the former. Thus the perfection of our own minds makes us the heirs of all good, whether in the outward or the spiritual worlds. Let us, then, look to no other happiness. Let us feel that Christianity in revealing this, as God's purpose towards us, meets all our wants, and is the most glorious of God's provisions for His human family.

In this discourse I am aiming to set before you what I believe to be the central vital principle of Christianity. I conceive that we understand our religion, only so far as this great principle becomes pre-eminent to our view, and is seen to pervade and bind together the whole system. I have said that all the doctrines and precepts of the Gospel meet in this essential and all-comprehending truth. The purpose of God to raise the soul from the power of moral evil to perfection—this is the beginning and end of Christianity. To this all its teachings may be traced up; into this all may be resolved. Were there time, I might survey separately the particular doctrines of the Gospel, and show that they all may be referred to this. I shall now offer, however, one brief illustration only; but it is an all-sufficing one.

The first great doctrine of Christianity is the parental char-

---

[7] Cf. Edward's "Images and Shadows of Divine Things" (see pp. 152–153); Emerson's doctrine of correspondence (see p. 297); and Bushnell's view of "the whole universe of nature as a perfect analogon of the whole universe of thought or spirit" (see pp. 351, 325). [Ed.]

acter of God.[8] To us there is "one God even the Father." Christianity has no truth to teach more encouraging and inspiring than this. But what do we mean when we call God our FATHER. Does this term imply nothing more than that He created us? He created the stone: is He therefore its father? Do we mean that He gives us bodies and the pleasures of sensitive existence? These He gives to the bird and insect; but the Scriptures nowhere call Him their parent. No! It is clear that this word expresses a spiritual relation. It declares God's connexion with the human soul. God is the Father of those beings, and of those only, whom He has created in His own image, whom He has gifted with a Spirit like His own, whom He has framed for the end that they may approach Him in His highest attributes. To be a parent is to communicate a *kindred nature,* and to watch over, educate and guide this nature to perfect development. God loves us as a father, by loving supremely the soul in each of us, and by His intense concern to conform this soul to Himself. When you call God "Father," do not think of him as a fond indulgent being, anxious only for your enjoyment here and hereafter. This would be to degrade our Divine Benefactor. Think of this Father as looking upon the Spirit within you, with unutterable interest; as desiring for you no happiness but that of pure goodness; as purposing your perfection as His chief and crowning end in your creation. This is the only true view of God as our Father. And thus the doctrine of His parental character is one and the same with the great principle of communicating moral perfection, which I have so earnestly affirmed to be the essence and center of Christianity.

III [*History and Progress*]

My friends, the great purpose of God towards mankind, which I have this day set forth as the substance of Christianity,

---

[8] In his Divinity School Address Emerson attacked such conceptions; but Henry Ware, Jr., defended Channing's position on the "Personality of Deity," see pp. 299–303. [Ed.]

is one with which we cannot be too deeply impressed. We cannot too thoroughly understand and feel that the perfection of our nature, for which God made and redeemed us, is the highest good and the only true good. I consider the mind sound, wise, equal to its own happiness, only so far as it is possessed by this great truth. To expect happiness by any other process, than by cooperation with this purpose of God, is to insure disappointment, and to throw away our labour and our lives. All other purposes and all other means of felicity must come to naught. This great principle we cannot carry out too far. We may lay it down as universally and unerringly true, that nothing contributes to the enduring happiness of individuals, or of communities, but what contributes to this PERFECTION of human nature. Individuals and communities are perpetually seeking good in other ways, but only to reach disastrous failure and shame.

At this period, we see a mighty movement of the civilized world. Thrones are tottering, and the firmest establishments of former ages seem about to be swept away by the torrent of revolution.[9] In this movement I rejoice, though not without trembling joy. But I rejoice, only because I look at it in the light of the great truth which I have this day aimed to enforce; because I see, as I think, in the revolutionary spirit of our times, the promise of a freer and higher action of the human mind, the pledge of a state of society more fit to perfect human beings. I regard the present state of the world in this moral light altogether. The despotisms, which are to be prostrated, seem to be evils, chiefly as they have enslaved men's faculties, as they have bowed and weighed down the soul. The liberty, after which men aspire, is to prove a good only so far as it shall give force and enlargement to the mind; only so far as it shall conspire

---

[9] During the winter of 1830–1831, when this sermon was delivered, the revolutions of 1830 in half a dozen European countries were on everyone's mind, especially the fall of the restored Bourbon monarchy in France. In Britain events were moving toward the great Reform Bill of 1832. [Ed.]

with Christianity in advancing human nature. Men will gain little by escaping outward despotism, if the soul continues enthralled. Men must be subjected to some law; and unless the law in their own breast, the law of God, of duty, of perfection, be adopted by their free choice as the supreme rule, they will fall under the tyranny of selfish passion, which will bow their necks for an outward yoke.

I have hope in the present struggle of the world, because it seems to me more spiritual, more moral, in its origin and tendencies, than any which have preceded it. It differs much from the revolts of former times, when an oppressed populace or peasantry broke forth into frantic opposition to government, under the goading pressure of famine and misery. Men are now moved, not merely by physical wants and sufferings, but by ideas, by principles, by the conception of a BETTER STATE OF SOCIETY, under which the rights of human nature will be recognized, and greater justice be done to the mind in all classes of the community. There is then an element—spiritual, moral, and tending towards perfection—in the present movement; and this is my great hope. When I see, however, the tremendous strength of unsubdued passions, which mix with and often overpower this conception of a better order of society; when I consider the success with which the selfish, crafty and ambitious have turned to their own purposes the generous enthusiasm of the people; when I consider the darkness which hangs over the nations, the rashness with which they have rushed into infidelity and irreligion, as the only refuge from priestcraft and superstition; and when I consider how hard it is for men, in seasons of tumult and feverish excitement, to listen to the mild voice of wisdom teaching that moral perfection alone constitutes glory and happiness;—I fear. I fear not for the final results; not for the *ultimate* triumphs of truth, right, virtue, piety; not for the gradual melioration of men's lot: but for those nearer results, those immediate effects, which the men of this generation are to witness and to feel.

In such a state of the world, it seems to me of singular importance, that Christianity should be recognized and presented in its true character, as I have aimed to place it before you this day. The low views of our religion, which have prevailed too long, should give place to this highest one. They suited perhaps darker ages. But they have done their work, and should pass away. Christianity should now be disencumbered and set free from the unintelligible and irrational doctrines, and the uncouth and idolatrous forms and ceremonies, which terror, superstition, vanity, priestcraft and ambition have laboured to identify with it. It should come forth from the darkness and corruption of the past in its own celestial splendour, and in its divine simplicity. It should be comprehended as having but one purpose, the perfection of human nature, the elevation of men into nobler beings. I would have it so luminously displayed, that men should distinctly see how it tends, by all its influences and teachings, to the true freedom of the state, and to the honour and everlasting progress of the individual. Let Christianity be thus taught and viewed, and it will act as a new power on human affairs. And unless thus viewed, I despair of its triumphs. The time has gone by in which any religion is to take a strong and enduring hold on the world, except by offering itself in the high character ascribed to Christianity in this discourse. Men will yield their faith to no system which does not bear the plain marks of being adapted to the highest principles and powers of human nature, and which does not open to it a career of *endless improvement*. They are outgrowing unintelligible notions. They understand that the glory of a religion is to be measured by the moral glory, power, perfection, which it communicates to the mind. I know not, therefore, how a greater service can be rendered to Christianity, or how its power can be more extended, than by teaching it as a revelation of God's great purpose to perfect His human offspring, and as the great power or instrument by which this perfection is to be achieved.

My friends, I have been applying our subject to the actual state of the Christian and civilized world. Let me come nearer home. You have heard of God's purpose to purify and perfect the human soul, that He has sent His Son to redeem it from all evil, and to present it spotless before its Creator and Judge. Do you believe this? Have you faith in the human soul as formed for a higher life than it can now enjoy? Have you faith in your own souls, as capable of ascending to sinless purity? Has the perfection of your being risen before you as the one glorious good, for which existence was granted, for which its mingled joys and trials were measured out, for which the Father sent His Son from heaven? Do you believe that the blessedness of angels may be yours, and that to this bliss you are welcomed? You believe in God. But how? As the author of this outward universe? This is to pause at the threshold. Do you believe in Him yet more as the author of an inner universe, whose beauty, grandeur, harmony and exceeding excellence transcend immeasurably all that nature manifests of His infinite good-will? You speak of His love. Do you feel that this love is too lofty, too limitless, to content itself with any good that falls short of elevating His children into companionship with Himself? Have you learned to look through the body to the immortal spirit, and to feel that this is infinitely precious to the Father of spirits, and that it should be equally dear to you His child? This, and this alone, is Christian faith. Are we wanting in this faith in the destiny of the soul for perfection? Then we know Christianity only in the letter, and as a sound. Then the significance of the Glorious Gospel has never brightened on our view. Then the Light of Life has never risen within. Then our own souls are yet to be revealed to us. Then the all-illuminating truth, that gives unutterable interest to this infant stage of our existence, has never dawned on us. Then the Eternal Day, with its splendours of consolation, hope, peace and exhaustless power, has not beamed on us in blessing. But this truth may shine out, if our minds turn towards it. This day may dawn, and the infinite love of our Father for us rise like the morning. Let us aspire towards this living confidence, that it is the will of God to unfold and exalt without end the spirit that entrusts itself to Him in well-doing as to a faithful creator. And may the "God of all grace, who hath called us unto His eternal glory by Christ Jesus, after that ye have suffered awhile, make you perfect, stablish, strengthen, settle you. To Him be glory and dominion, for ever. Amen."[10]

------

[10] I Peter 5:10,11. [Ed.]

IV

NATHANIEL WILLIAM TAYLOR

Theologian of New School Protestantism

Nathaniel William Taylor (1786–1858)[1] died on the centenary
of Jonathan Edwards' death and thereby terminated what may
justifiably be considered an "Edwardsean era" in New England
theology. After the Civil War the theology of the Reformed
churches, whether liberal or conservative, would be in the custody
of men who looked elsewhere for inspiration and guidance. The
few surviving defenders of the old New England Theology, such
as Edwards Amasa Park of Andover (1808–1900), would lack an
opposition that cared to debate. When Taylor was at the height
of his powers, however, the New Divinity which had stemmed
from Northampton and Stockbridge still defined the major theological issues, just as the evangelical revivalism arising out of the
Great Awakening continued to shape the ethos of the Protestant
mainstream. All across the country, North and South, a whole
family of New School theologies were prospering with denominational variations. Taylor, therefore, could bring his ideas to
bear in a highly dynamic situation. He stands in a company and
not as a solitary figure. Even at the "home" of the New Haven
Theology a half-dozen professors made Yale a center of theological activity, while a legion of loyal graduates brought "Taylorism" to the grass roots and sent back a steady stream of students

---

[1] See Introduction, pp. 41–45.

to the University. Timothy Dwight himself could not have hoped for more.

Taylor was born in New Milford, Connecticut, the son of a well-to-do businessman and grandson of the town's minister, who had taken a conservative "Old Calvinist" stand in the turmoil created by the Great Awakening. In 1800 young Taylor left the family ambiance for Yale College and then, after a conversion experience, began theological training under President Dwight, whose protégé he became. In 1812 he was ordained as minister of the Center Church in New Haven, a lofty eminence for a young man. Here he developed a reputation as a person of great intellectual substance, yet he remained an effective revival preacher—a combination which led in 1822 to his appointment as Professor of Didactic Theology in the newly constituted theological faculty at Yale. For a quarter-century this faculty would be remarkably stable; morale was high, President Jeremiah Day added further luster to the institution's theological reputation, students were numerous, and the QUARTERLY CHRISTIAN SPECTATOR carried the New Haven Theology abroad.

Taylor flourished in this environment and seemed to relish the controversies that ensued—first, against the Unitarians, and later with orthodox Congregationalists and Presbyterians who thought that the theology expounded in New Haven conceded far too much to the Unitarians, to the Arminians, and to the "common sense" of the Common Man. Despite the charges, denials, and countercharges a few things are clear. Taylor (like his friend Lyman Beecher) believed that the kind of theology being shaped in the Andover anti-Unitarian polemics had set back the cause of orthodoxy by fifty years. He considered Princeton Seminary antediluvian. He thought that Edwards' doctrine of the will paralyzed revival preaching and scandalized the average person in democratic, freedom-loving America. Yet he prized the New England theological tradition and tried to formulate an acceptable compromise. God's moral government rather than his absolute sovereignty was his key concept; Scottish Common-Sense Realism was his major philosophical weapon. An ambiguous distinction between "inevitability" and "necessity" loomed large in his argument. In the revivalistic churches of ante-bellum America Taylorism proved itself eminently satisfactory, even though it ignored almost a century's development in Western philosophy and scholarship as well as many profoundly new currents of thought and feeling.

The New Haven men stated various aspects of their improved theology over and over again in many forms; but it was Taylor's address in 1828 to the annual assembly of Connecticut Congregational clergy that became his and the school's most celebrated—and controversial—manifesto. Except for some pruning of Taylor's heavy rhetorical punctuation, it is given in its entirety; and with good reason. For too long it has been read about rather than read. The doctrine of sin and human nature was the far-reaching question that most seriously divided the evangelical united front of that day. Moreover, Taylor's combination of finely spun argument and flamboyant eloquence reveals essential features of an important chapter in Protestant history.

Concio ad Clerum: A Sermon[1]

On Human Nature, Sin, and Freedom

Ephesians 2:3.

And were by nature the children of wrath, even as others.

The Bible is a plain book. It speaks, especially on the subject of sin, directly to human consciousness; and tells us beyond mis-

---

From Nathaniel William Taylor, *Concio ad Clerum. A Sermon Delivered in the Chapel of Yale College, September 10, 1828* (New Haven: Hezekiah Howe, 1828).

take, what sin is, and why we sin. In the text, the Apostle asserts the fact of the moral depravity of mankind, and assigns its cause. To be "the children of wrath" is to possess the character which deserves punishment; in other words, it is to be sinners, or to be entirely depraved in respect to moral character. The text then teaches; THAT THE ENTIRE MORAL DEPRAVITY OF MANKIND IS BY NATURE.

In illustrating this position, I shall attempt to show, First, In what the moral depravity of man consists; and Secondly, That this depravity is by nature.[2]

I   [*Moral Depravity Defined*]

By the moral depravity of mankind I intend generally, the entire sinfulness of their moral character—that state of the mind or heart to which guilt and the desert of wrath pertain. I may say then negatively,

---

[1] The published sermon was preceded by the following statement on a separate page:

"The author of this discourse has no reason to believe, that the views which it contains, are in any essential respect diverse from those of his brethren, who heard it. That the general proposition will meet with the approbation of all who hold the fundamental doctrines of the Gospel, he has no doubt. In regard to some of the more specific statements, he supposes that there is, in some limited degree, the semblance of controversy, rather than real diversity of opinion. It may be proper to remark, that he is not aware of any change in his own views on these points, since he entered the ministry; nor of any departure in any article of doctrinal belief, from his revered instructor in theology, the fomer President of the College [Timothy Dwight, 1752–1817]. Facts, however, which are extensively known, furnish, it is believed, a sufficient apology for the selection of the topic as well as for the publication of the discourse."

The sermon's title, *Concio ad Clerum* (*Advice to the Clergy*), was customary for the occasion. [Ed.]

[2] Section I contains the central theses of Taylorism and hence is specially defended from the charge of heresy in the "Remarks" that follow Section II. Section II serves chiefly to mollify his orthodox critics. [Ed.]

This depravity does not consist in any essential attribute or property of the soul—not in *any thing created* in man by his Maker. On this point, I need only ask—does God create in men a sinful nature, and damn them for the very nature he creates? Believe this, who can.

Nor does the moral depravity of men consist in a sinful nature, which they have corrupted by being *one* with Adam, and by *acting in his act.* To believe that I am one and the same being with another who existed thousands of years before I was born, and that by virtue of this identity I truly acted in his act, and am therefore as truly guilty of his sin as himself—to believe this, I must renounce the reason which my Maker has given me; I must believe it also, in face of the oath of God to its falsehood, entered upon the record.[3]

Nor does the moral depravity of men consist in any *constitutional propensities* of their nature. Whoever supposed himself or others to be guilty, for being hungry or thirsty after long abstinence from food or drink; or merely for desiring knowledge, or the esteem of his fellow-men, or any other good, abstractly from any choice to gratify such desires? Who does not know that a perfectly holy man must be subject to all these propensities? The man Christ Jesus was subject to every one of them, for he "was *in all points* tempted like as we are, yet without sin."[4]

Nor does any degree of *excitement* in these propensities or desires, not resulting in choice, constitute moral depravity. Suppose them then, in the providence of God, excited in any degree, and yet the man to prefer doing the will of God to their gratification; all will admit that it is the noblest act of obedience conceivable in a moral being. All will agree that the man who always triumphs over excited propensity, who duly subordinates

---

[3] Ezekiel 18:3,4. [Edwards *did* make this assertion in his characteristic way, see pp. 173–174. Ed.]

[4] Hebrews 4:15. [Ed.]

all his desires of inferior good to the will of God, is a perfect man. It is the uniform sentiment of inspired truth, that this ruling of the spirit, this government of himself, imparts unrivalled glory to his character. We add the express declaration of the Apostle: "*Blessed* is the man that *endureth* temptation."[5]

Nor does the moral depravity of men consist in *any disposition or tendency* to sin, which is *the cause of all sin*. It is important on this point to guard against error from the ambiguity of terms. There is an obvious distinction between a *disposition* or tendency to sin, which is prior to *all* sin, and a *sinful* disposition. I am not saying, then, that there is not what with entire propriety may be called a disposition or tendency to sin, which is the cause of *all* sin; nor that there is not, as *a consequence* of *this* disposition or tendency, what with equal propriety may be called a *sinful* disposition, which is the true cause of all *other* sin, itself excepted. But I say, that that which is the cause of *all* sin, is not itself sin. The cause of all sin itself sin! Whence then came the first sin? Do you say, from a previous sin as its cause? Then you say, there is a sin before the first sin. Our first parents and fallen angels were once holy. Tell us now, whence came *their* first sin? Do you still repeat, from a previous sin? And what sort of philosophy, reason, or common sense is this— a sin before the first sin—sin before all sin? Do you say there must be *difficulties* in theology? I ask must there be *nonsense* in theology?[6]

---

[5] James 1:12. [Ed.]

[6] The embarrassment which in some minds attends this part of the subject, seems to result from the different senses in which the word *disposition* is used. That this word, like most others, is used in different senses, is undeniable; sometimes denoting simply *tendency* or *bias*, and sometimes, the moral temper, the *governing affection* or *predominant inclination* of the mind. The manner of its use, however, if correct, always shews in which sense it is used. Thus if we speak of *a disposition* to sin, in the way of accounting for *all* sin, the case shews that we use the word simply in the sense of *tendency*; or as Edwards says, "a prevailing liableness or exposedness to such an event." For by the *very mode* of speaking, the *dispo-*

The question then still recurs, what is this moral depravity for which man deserves the wrath of God? I answer—*it is man's own act, consisting in a free choice of some object rather than God, as his chief good—or a free preference of the world and of worldly good, to the will and glory of God.*

In support of these views of the subject, I now appeal to the testimony of some of the ablest divines, of Apostles, and of common sense.

Says Calvin, speaking of our text, "our nature is there characterized, not as it was created by God, but as it was vitiated in Adam; *because* it would be unreasonable to make God the author of death."[7] Again, "natural depravity is not a substantial property originally innate, but can be imputed to none but man himself." He says of sin expressly, "it is voluntary." "If they are convicted of any fault, the Lord justly reproaches them with their own perverseness." "He who sins necessarily, sins no less voluntarily."[8]

The Westminster divines say, that "every sin both original and actual being a transgression of the righteous law of God &c."[9] I ask, is not transgression, action? is it not something done, and done knowingly and voluntarily?

---

sition and the *sin* are so distinguished as to show that we cannot mean, that the *disposition* is itself sin; it being spoken of as the cause of *all* sin. But if we speak of a *sinful* or *wicked disposition,* or *a worldly disposition,* or *an avaricious disposition,* or of *a disposition* as the cause of specific sinful acts, or if in any other way we imply *its sinfulness* by our mode of speaking, then the predicate shews that we intend a state of mind which includes *preference—a supreme or governing affection of the heart.* Such, it is supposed yond all question, is the *usus loquendi;* a due attention to which would have saved some theologians from no trivial amount of absurdity.

[7] John Calvin, *The Institutes of the Christian Religion,* I, 1, 6. [In this and succeeding quotations from Calvin, Bellamy, Edwards, and Emmons, Taylor has quoted somewhat inexactly. His interpretations can be and were contested but he has not distorted the statements of his authorities. His words, therefore, have been left uncorrected. Ed.]

[8] *Ibid.,* II, 5, 1. [See also II, 1, 11. Ed.]

[9] The Westminster Confession of Faith (1646), Chap. VI, Art. 6.

Dr. Bellamy, speaking of the *sinful* propensities of man, says "they are not created by God with the essence of the soul, but result from its native choice, or rather, more strictly, are themselves its native *choice.*—They are not natural in the same sense in which the *faculties* of our souls are; for they are not the workmanship of God but are our native *choice,* and the *voluntary, free, spontaneous* bent of our hearts."[10]

Says President Edwards, "The inferior principles of self-love and natural appetite which were given only to serve, (and which as he also says, 'were in man in innocence') being alone and left to themselves became reigning principles. Man did set up himself (which by the way was doing something) and the objects of his private affections and appetites as *supreme,* and so they took the place of God. Man's love to his own honour, private interest and pleasure which was before wholly subordinate unto love to God and regard to his glory (and while thus, he says also, 'all things were in excellent order and in their proper and perfect state') now disposes him to pursue those objects without regard to God's honour or law." Thus he adds, "it is easy to give an account, how total corruption of heart should follow—without God's putting *any evil* into his heart, or implanting any *bad principle,* or infusing any *corrupt taint,* and *so* becoming the author of depravity."[11] Again, he says, "If the essence of virtuousness or fault does not lie in the nature of the dispositions or *acts of the mind,* then it is certain, it lies no where at all." "That which makes vice hateful—is a certain deformity in that *evil will,* which is the soul of all vice." "If a thing be from us, and not

---

10 Joseph Bellamy, *True Religion Delineated,* Discourse I, Section V, Use I, Sub-section 3. Quoted from *Works* (New York Edition, 1808–1809), I, 201, 202. [Bellamy (1710–1790) was a major but not submissive Edwardsean. Edwards wrote a preface for this work when it appeared in 1750. Taylor was not a disciple of Bellamy, but their negative and affirmative theological relationships are important. Ed.]

11 Jonathan Edwards, *The Great Christian Doctrine of Original Sin Defended,* Part IV, Chap. II. Quoted from *Works* (Worcester Edition, 1808–1809), VI, 430, 431; see also pp. 427–436.

from our *choice,* it has not the nature of blame-worthiness or ill-desert."[12]

What says St. Paul? In the context he describes the nature of human depravity, and I request you to mark the agreement between his description and that of the last named author. He says "ye, who were dead in trespasses and sins, wherein ye *walked.*" You see it was a *walking—living* death. Dead as they were, they did something: "Wherein ye walked according to the course of this world."[13] And what is the course of this world? What is it, but as Edwards says, "Men setting up themselves and the objects of their private affections as supreme, so that these things take the place of God?" What is it, but a world loving the creature more than God the Creator, and acting accordingly. Again says this Apostle, "Among whom we all had our conversation"— our deportment and manner of life, "in the lusts of the flesh, fulfiling the desires of the flesh and the mind."[14] Now what is this, but freely and voluntarily yielding to propensities, which men ought to restrain and govern, and to subordinate to the will of God; what is it but propensities rising into a free preference of their objects, and going out into a free purpose of self-gratification? For how can men walk in the lusts of the flesh and fulfil the desires of the flesh and of the mind without preferring the gratification of these lusts and desires to other good? How live and act thus, without choosing to do it? You see then that the sin which the Apostle describes consists not merely in external action, nor merely in having propensities for natural good, but in acting freely, in yielding to these propensities as a matter of choice and preference.

What saith St. James?—"Let no man say when he is tempted,

---

[12] Jonathan Edwards, *Freedom of the Will,* Part IV, Section I. Quoted from *Works* (Worcester Edition), V, 220, 222. See also *Religious Affections,* Part I, Doctrine 1; *Works,* IV, 12–16.

[13] Ephesians 2:1, 2. [Ed.]

[14] Ephesians 2:3. [Ed.]

I am tempted of God," (and was there ever a more fatal tempter than God, if he creates sin in us?)—"for God is not tempted of evil neither tempteth he any man; but every man is tempted when he is drawn away of his own lust and enticed. *Then,* when lust, i. e. strong desire (the same word used by Paul when he says 'I have a *desire* to depart, &c.'—and by our Lord when he says 'with *desire* have I *desired* to eat this passover') *then* when lust hath conceived it bringeth forth sin."[15] Now when does lust or strong desire conceive and bring forth sin? When it rises into a preference of its object, and goes out in action to secure its own gratification.—Or, if you say the lust is itself the sin (though I think this is ascribing to the Apostle the absurdity of asserting sin before sin) yet be it so. What then is the lust which is sin, but *a preference of its object,* a *stronger* affection for it than for God? Interpret then the language of the Apostle either way, and you come to the same result—that all sin consists in freely preferring some inferior good to God. I might add to these many other passages. I only ask what is the import of the most common terms used by Apostles to describe sin in its true nature? I refer to such as these, *minding the flesh, walking in the flesh, living after the flesh, the flesh lusting against the Spirit,* what is this, but freely, voluntarily setting up the gratification of our natural propensities and appetites as our chief good, fixing our supreme affections upon it—setting the heart, when the living God claims it, upon some inferior good?

I now enquire, what says Common Sense? Take then any action which common sense in the common use of language calls a *sinful* action—what is the sin of it? As an example, take the act of murder. Now do we mean by this term in common usage, to denote simply the external act of killing? Clearly not. This may be by accident, or in obedience to a divine law. Do we mean simply the external act, together with the specific volition, to perform the act? Clearly not; for there must be such a

---

15 James 1:13,14. Philippians 1:23. Luke 22:15. [Ed.]

volition, though the act were performed in obedience to a divine command. It is only when the circumstances and manner of the action evince a selfish or malicious purpose, a state of mind in which the perpetrator of the deed shows a preference of some private selfish interest to the life of a fellow-being, and to the will of God, that we call it murder. So true is it, that we regard this state of mind as constituting the sin of the action, that could we ascertain independently of external action, the existence of such a preference, we should, as the Bible does, pronounce it murder. This preference then of some private interest, object or end, rather than God, common sense decides to be the sin of all that we call sinful action, and strictly speaking, the sum total of all sin.

But common sense decides the question in another form. And here we come to what I regard as the turning point of the whole controversy. So far as I know, the only argument in support of the opinion, that sin pertains to something which is not preference, is based in a supposed decision of common sense. The decision claimed is, that all particular or specific sins, as fraud, falsehood, injustice, unbelief, envy, pride, revenge, result from a *wicked heart,* from a *sinful disposition,* as the cause or source of such sinful acts. To this fact, I yield unqualified assent, as "the dictate of the universal sense & reason of mankind," and by this universal judgment, I wish the present question to be decided. Let us then look at the fact in its full force and just application. There is a man, then, whose course of life is wholly that of a worldling, his heart and hand shut against human woe, living without prayer, without gratitude, unmindful of God, and rejecting the Saviour of men, devising all, purposing all, doing all, for the sake of this world. Why is it? You say, and *all* say, and say *right,* it is owing to his love of the world—to his worldly disposition—to a heart set on the world. Now while all say this, and are right in saying it, we have one simple question to decide, viz. what do all *mean* by it? Every child can answer. Every child knows that the meaning is, that this man does freely and voluntarily fix his affection on worldly good, in preference to God; that the man has chosen the world as his chief good, his portion, his God. He knows that this is what is meant by *a worldly heart, a worldly disposition,* which leads to all *other* sins. So when we ascribe the sins of the miser to his *avaricious disposition,* we mean his supreme love of money; or the crimes of the hero or conqueror to his *ambitious disposition,* we mean his supreme love of fame, a state of mind which involves *preference* for its object. And whatever previous tendency, or if you will, previous disposition, there is to this state of mind; this state of mind itself and not any previous thing as the cause of it, is the *wicked heart*—the sinful disposition of men. They love the creature more than the Creator, when they can and ought to love the Creator most. This forbidden choice of worldly good, this preference of the low and sordid pleasures of the earth to God and his glory—this love of the world which excludes the love of the Father—*this*—*this* is man's depravity. This is that evil treasure of the heart, from which proceed evil things; this is the fountain, the source of all *other* abominations—man's free, voluntary preference of the world as his chief good, amid the revealed glories of a perfect God.

Having attempted to show in what the moral depravity of man consists, I now proceed to show that this depravity is by nature. This I understand the Apostle to assert when he says, "and were by nature the children of wrath."

II   [*Depravity is by Nature*]

What then are we to understand, when it is said that mankind are depraved *by nature?* I answer—*that such is their nature, that they will sin and only sin in all the appropriate circumstances of their being.*

To bring this part of the subject distinctly before the mind, it may be well to remark, that the question between the Calvinists and the Arminians on the point is this—whether the depravity or sinfulness of mankind is truly and properly ascribed to their *nature* or to their *circumstances of temptation?* And since, as it must be confessed, there can no more be sin without circumstances of temptation, than there can be sin without a nature to be tempted, why ascribe sin exclusively to nature? I answer, it is truly and properly ascribed to *nature,* and *not* to circumstances, because all mankind sin in all the appropriate circumstances of their being. For all the world ascribe an effect to the nature of a thing, when no possible change in its appropriate circumstances will change the effect; or when the effect is uniformly the same in all its appropriate circumstances. To illustrate this by an example: suppose a tree, which in one soil bears only bad fruit. Change its circumstances, transplant it to another soil, and it bears very good fruit. Now we say, and all would say, the fact that it bore bad fruit was owing to its situation, to its circumstances; for by changing its circumstances, you have changed its fruit. Suppose now another tree, which bears bad fruit place it where you will—change its situation from one soil to another, dig about it and dung it, cultivate it to perfection—do what you will, it still bears bad fruit only. Now every one says, the fact is owing to *the nature* of the tree—the cause is in the tree, in its nature and *not* in its circumstances. So of mankind, change their circumstances as you may; place them where you will within the limits of their being; do what you will to prevent the consequence, you have one uniform result, entire moral depravity. No change of condition, no increase of light nor of motives, no instructions nor warnings, no any thing, within the appropriate circumstances of their being, changes the result. Unless there be some interposition, which is not included in these circumstances, unless something be done which is above nature, the case is hopeless. Place a human being any where within the appropriate limits and scenes of his immortal existence, and such is his nature, that he will be a depraved sinner.

When therefore I say that mankind are entirely depraved *by nature,* I do not mean that their nature is *itself* sinful, nor that their nature is the *physical* or *efficient* cause of their sinning; but I mean that their nature is the occasion, or reason of their sinning—that *such is their nature, that in all the appropriate circumstances of their being, they will sin and only sin.*

Of this fact, I now proceed to offer some of the proofs.

1. I allege the text.[16] It is here to be remarked, that the Apostle does not say, nor can he mean, that the nature of man is itself sinful. He is assigning the cause of all sin, and says it is *by nature.* If you say that he teaches that the *nature* itself is *sinful,* then as the cause must precede its effect, you charge him with the absurdity of asserting that there is sin, before sin.

The Apostle doubtless conforms his phraseology to common usage, and must mean just what every plain man, using the same language in any similar case would mean. His language too, must be understood with such restrictions as the nature of the subject and correct usage require. How then do we understand one another when using such language? We say the lion by nature eats flesh; the ox by nature eats grass; the tree by nature bears bad fruit; and so in a thousand cases. Now we mean by this, that the *nature* of the thing is such, that uniformly in all its circumstances, it will be the cause or occasion of that which we assert—that the lion, for example, is of such a nature that he will eat flesh. So when the Apostle asserts, that mankind are by nature sinners, he must mean simply that such is their nature that uniformly in all the appropriate circumstances of their being, they will sin. He can no more mean that the nature itself is sinful, than we can mean in the example, that the nature of the lion is the same thing as the act of eating flesh, of which it is the cause. Still less can we suppose him to authorise the inference that the act of man in sinning, is not in some most

---

16 Ephesians 2:3; but this text should be read in the context of the classic passage of which it is a part, vv. 1–9. [Ed.]

important respects widely different from the act of a lion in eating flesh; so different that the one is sin, and the other not. This difference, the known nature of sin obliges us to suppose, it is intended not to deny, but to assume. The resemblance is simply in the *certainty* of the two things, and that which occasions this certainty; though in every other respect, especially in regard to the moral freedom and moral relations of man, the very nature of the acts spoken of, and the *mode* in which the certainty of them is occasioned, they are so diverse that the one is a moral act and has all the requisites of a moral act; the other cannot be a moral act.[17] The Apostle then, using language as all

---

[17] With respect to the difficulty in which the doctrine of depravity *by nature* has been supposed to involve the free-agency of man, it may be remarked, that it can result only from a misapprehension of the terms. When we speak of the depravity or sinfulness of man *by nature,* no one, who correctly interprets the language, can understand us to mean that *nature* is the *physical* or *efficient cause* of sin, operating by absolute and irresistible compulsion. All that can be properly understood is, that *nature* is the *occasion* of sin, as a free act. The very nature of the predicate, *sin,* requires the restriction of the phrase to this import. Who ever supposes when we speak of God as *by nature* holy, or of angels as *by nature* holy, that we intend that their nature is a *physical cause* of which holiness is a *physical effect?* or imagines that we intend to assert that which every one knows would annihilate the very nature of holiness? The known nature of the predicate and common sense of the speaker forbid such an interpretation. So in the present case, the Apostle cannot be understood to mean, nor can any one merely from using similar phraseology be properly or fairly understood to mean, that nature is a *physical cause* of which *sin* is a *physical effect.* The known nature of sin, the predicate, as a free act, is utterly at war with such a notion; we have a right to presume that no one can be so wanting in good sense as not to know this; or so uncandid as to suppose that we do not know it and assume it, or as to impute to us the opposite and palpably absurd view of sin. And as none ought ever to attribute flagrant absurdity to a writer or speaker whose language, according to correct usage, and just interpretation, expresses truth and good sense (they pervert his language if they do), they are obliged by the laws of interpretation, to understand *nature* in the present case, to denote simply the *occasion* of sin. But if *nature* is not a *physical cause* of sin, but simply the *occasion* of sin, then since nothing but *physical* influence or efficiency can be supposed in the present case to be inconsistent with moral freedom, the consistency between sinning *by nature* and sinning freely, is apparent. Let not an

other men use it, traces the universal depravity of men to *their nature*, and thus most explicitly teaches, contrary to the Arminian view, that it is *not* owing to circumstances. If this be not his meaning he uses language as no one else uses it, and the world, critics and all, may be safely challenged to tell what he does mean.

2. The Scriptures in many forms, teach the universal sinfulness of mankind in all the appropriate circumstances of their being.

First. They declare that "the imagination of man's heart is evil from his youth."[18] And I need not cite passages from the word of God to show in how many forms it declares, that there is none that doeth good, no not one; that all have gone out of the way; that all depart from God and yield themselves to sin from the first moment of accountable action—sinning so early, that in the figurative language of the Scriptures they are said to "go astray as soon as they be born speaking lies."[19] Thus God in his testimony, from the beginning to the end of it, asserts this appalling fact—the absolute uniformity of human sinfulness, throughout the world and throughout all ages. Not a solitary exception occurs. Even those who become holy through grace are not noted as exceptions, and doubtless, because the object is to describe the character which without grace, is common to all. One character then, if God's record be true, prevails with absolute unvarying uniformity, from the fall in Eden till time shall be no longer. Let the circumstances of men be what they may, the eye of God sees and the voice of God declares that "there is no difference; all are under sin."[20] Now I ask, why is not

---

objector ask, how can even this be consistent with the moral perfection of God? He starts *another* objection, and one, to answer which belongs to him as well as to me. One thing then at a time; and the question now is, if nature is simply the *occasion* of man's sinning, why may he not sin freely? Why not, as well as if *circumstances* or *motives* were the occasion? Why not, as well as God or angels be *holy by nature*, and yet be free?

18 Genesis 8:21. [Ed.]

19 Psalms 58:3. [Ed.]

20 Romans 3:22, 23. [Ed.]

the exception made—why, without intimating a single exempt case through favourable circumstances, or tracing sin in a single instance to adverse circumstances, why through all the tribes of men, is *all—all* sin—*all* depravity, in all the circumstances of their existence, according to God's testimony? If then the absolute uniformity of an event proves that it is *by nature*, then does this uniformity of human sinfulness prove that man is depraved by nature.

Secondly. The Scriptures teach the same thing, by asserting the universal necessity of regeneration by the Holy Spirit. "Except a man be born of water and of the Spirit, he cannot enter into the kingdom of God."[21] Now I ask, how can the interposition of this Divine Agent be necessary to produce holiness in man, if light and truth and motives will do it? God send the Holy Ghost to perform a work, and declare the necessity of his mission for the purpose, when it might as well be done, were there no Holy Ghost? No, Brethren. Without the transforming grace of this Divine Agent, we are all 'dead men' for eternity. It follows therefore that man is such a being, or has such a nature that he will sin in all circumstances of his being, if God does not interpose to save.

Thirdly. The *reason* assigned by our Lord for the necessity of the Spirit's agency, is equally decisive. "That which is born of the flesh is flesh."[22] If the phrase "is flesh" is equivalent to the expression, *is sinful*, then this passage is a decisive testimony on the point under consideration. Be this however as it may, one thing is undeniable from this conversation of our Lord with Nicodemus, viz. that the first birth of a human being is an event, which involves the necessity of another birth by the Divine Spirit. Say if you will, that what our Lord asserts in the passage cited is, that what is by natural birth is simply a man—a human being, thus intending to teach that none were the better for being born of Abraham; still our conclusion remains, viz. to be

---

[21] John 3:5. [Ed.]
[22] John 3:6. [Ed.]

born once—to become a human being, is to come under the necessity of being born again of the Spirit. As then we can be at no loss, concerning what it is to be born of the Spirit, it follows that to be born once, involves the certainty of sin—to become a human being is to become a sinner, unless there be a second birth of the Spirit.

Fourthly. I add but one more out of many other scriptural testimonies—the express declaration of the inefficiency of all truth and motives; or of all that is called *moral suasion.* Saith the Apostle "I have planted, Apollos watered, but God gave the increase; so then neither is he that planteth any thing, nor he that watereth, but God that giveth the increase."[23] But who are the men that can preach better than Paul and Apollos? Who can make the arrows of conviction thrill in the conscience, and bring the terrors of guilt and of God into the soul, as did the great Apostle of the Gentiles? Who by telling of a Saviour's love, or of heavenly glories can do more to charm sin out of the human heart, than Apollos that 'eloquent man and mighty in the Scriptures?'[24] And yet Paul was nothing, and Apollos nothing, without God. Let then human eloquence do its best (and it is not to be despised unless it be put in the place of the Holy Ghost)—let the powers of oratory to persuade, to allure, to awe be exhausted; such is the nature of man, that no accents of a Saviour's love, no lifting up of the everlasting doors, no rising smoke of torment, will save a human being from the character and the condemnation of a depraved sinner.

> The transformation of apostate man
> From fool to wise, from earthly to divine,
> Is work for Him that made him.[25]

---

23 I Corinthians 3:6, 7. [Ed.]

24 Acts 18:24. [Ed.]

25 William Cowper, *The Task*, Book V, line 695. Taylor changed the first word from "But" to "The." [Ed.]

3. I appeal to human consciousness. In making this appeal, I am aware that some may think I am not warranted. They seem to imagine that sin in its nature and its cause is something quite mysterious, and hidden from human discovery or comprehension. But, is this so?—God charge *sin* upon a world of accountable subjects—provide through the blood of his Son redemption from *sin*—summon all on pain of his wrath to repent of and to forsake *sin*—foretell a judgment of *sin*—award to some eternal salvation from *sin*, and to others eternal perdition for *sin*—in a word, give a law by which *is* the *knowledge of sin*, and not a soul of them be able to know or tell what *sin* is, or why he commits it! ! God surely charges sin upon the world as an intelligible reality. He charges it, in the matter and the cause of it upon human consciousness, and human consciousness must respond to the charge in a judgment going beforehand to condemnation. And if men do not know what that is, of which, if the charge of God be true, they are conscious, I beg leave to ask what do they know? What then are they conscious of? They are conscious that in all sin, they do freely and voluntarily set their hearts, their supreme affections on the world, rather than on God; they are conscious that this supreme love of the world is the fountain and source of all their *other* sins. They are also conscious, that they are led to set their hearts on the world by those propensities for worldly good, which belong to their *nature*. They know this as well as they know why they eat when they are hungry, or drink when they are thirsty. A man choose the world as his chief good, fix his whole heart upon it, and pursue it as if God were unworthy of a thought, and not know why he does so? He knows he does so, for the good there is in it—for the gratification of those natural propensities for this inferior good, which he ought to govern. He knows that it is not for want of knowledge; that it is not for want of motives to an opposite choice, that he thus makes light of God and everlasting glory. I say, he *knows* this, and I speak to the consciousness of all who hear me. All know, that propensities toward the good which the wealth or honour

or pleasure of the world affords—that desires of happiness from this world in some form, have led them to set their heart upon it, rather than on God. Yes, yes, we all know it, and not a man of us dares deny it.

4. I appeal to facts. And here the question is, making the proper exception in respect to those whose character has been changed by grace, what is the moral history of man since the first apostasy? It begins with a brother's imbruing his hands in a brother's blood—it terminates in the character that qualifies for companionship with the devil and his angels. What (the grace of God excepted) has ever been adequate to restrain man from sin? We pass by pagan nations, and merely glance at the utter inefficacy of even the miraculous interpositions of God to prevent sin and reclaim to duty. What was the character of men warned thus for a hundred and twenty years by Noah, God's commissioned servant? Its guilty millions swept to perdition by a deluge of waters, tell us. What the character of those under similar warnings, whom God destroyed by a storm of fire and brimstone on the cities of the plain? This emblem of the tempest of eternal fire, answers. On mount Sinai God descended amid thunderings and lightnings, and with his own voice promulged his law to the hosts of Israel; and yet as it were, in this very sanctuary of his awful presence, they made a molten calf and said 'these be thy Gods, O Israel.' In their future history, what a course of apostacies, rebellions, idolatries, amid the warnings of indignant prophets, and a series of miracles by which God shook heaven and earth, at almost every step of his providence? When all else was in vain, when prophets and holy men had been stoned and murdered for their faithfulness in reclaiming men to allegiance to their Maker, see God sending his own Son! Him, though speaking as never man spake, doing the works of God, and proving that in him dwelt all the fulness of the Godhead—him, they nailed to the cross. Look at the persecutions that followed. See how religion doomed to the rack and the fire, stands lifting her streaming eyes to heaven, with none but God to help —how kings and emperors like tigers, can feast as it were only

on Christian blood. See how every shrine is demolished where weakness can pray, and penitence can weep—how every thing is done, which human malice can invent, to blot out Christianity, name and memorial, from under heaven. And if you think that modern refinement and civilization have alleviated the picture, look at Paris in the French revolution—that city, the seat of art, of taste, of refinement, of every thing that can grace human nature short of religion, is converted as in a moment into a den of assassins, and her streets crowded with scaffolds raining blood on the gloomy processions of death, that pass beneath them. But we need not look to other ages or other countries.[26] In this land on which the Sun of Righteousness sheds his clearest, brightest day—here where the light of salvation, with all its motives, with all the love and grace of the Savior, with the glories of heaven and terrors of hell, is concentred and poured burning and blazing upon the human heart—here in this assembly, what do we find? Assassins and highwaymen, murderers of fathers and murderers of mothers? No. But we do find despisers of the Lord that bought them. We find every one whom grace has not made to differ, an enemy of God. And when the veil of eternity shall be drawn, and the light of eternity reveal the results—when the sinner's place in hell shall be fixed and the measure of his woe be full, then shall he know what that depravity is, which now tramples under foot the Son of God and does despite unto the Spirit of grace. These are the stubborn things, called facts; facts which show how dreadful is the depravity of man under the most perfect efforts of God to prevent it; facts which show into what depths of guilt and woe, the creature man will plunge, if the arm of grace does not hold him back; facts which show that he is depraved, not for want of light or motives, but depraved *by nature*. Especially, what other account can be given of the depravity which prevails, amid the splendours of Gospel day?

---

[26] Taylor's placing the United States in the procession of men and nations is worth noting. [Ed.]

Remarks

1. It is consistent with the doctrine of this discourse, that infants should be saved through the redemption of Christ. They belong to a race who by nature and in all the appropriate circumstances of their being, will sin.[27] The very birth of a human being is an event which involves the certainty of entire moral depravity, without the supernatural interposition of God to prevent it. Do you ask, when he will begin to sin? I answer, I *do not know* the precise instant. The Scriptures do not tell us— and I can see no possible use, in saying that we *do* know, what it is most palpably evident we do *not* know.[28] Is it then said, that we sin before we are born? But there is no such thing as sinning without acting; and an Apostle has told us of two infants, who, while "not yet born" had done "neither good nor

---

[27] Note that Taylor says "will" sin, not "must" or "will necessarily" sin. [Ed.]

[28] The ignorance of the writer on this point is not absolutely peculiar to himself. Says Dr. Emmons, "It is certainly supposable, that children may exist in this world, some space of time, before they become moral agents; but how long that space may be, whether an hour, a day, or a month or a year, or several years, as many suppose, *we do not presume to determine.* But during that space, whether longer or shorter, they are not moral agents, nor consequently accountable creatures in the sight of God or man." Nathanael Emmons, *Sermons on Various Subjects of Christian Doctrine and Duty* (Providence, 1825), p. 257. [Emmons (1745–1840) was perhaps the most interesting and daring of Edwards' successors in New England. Ed.]

President Edwards, speaking of the commencement of *actual sin* in men, expresses himself thus, they "commit sin immediately without any time intervening *after they are capable of understanding their obligation to God and reflecting on themselves;*"—"no *considerable time* passes *after men are capable of acting for themselves as the subjects of God's law,* before they are guilty of sin; because if the time were considerable, it would be great enough to deserve to be taken notice of." *Original Sin,* Part I, Chap. I, Sec. IV. Quoted from *Works* (Worcester Edition), VI, 161.

The reader will perceive that the views of the writer, respecting the point of time when men first commit sin, are to say the least not more *indefinite* than those of Dr. Emmons and President Edwards.

evil."[29] Do you say they begin to sin at their birth? But some knowledge of duty is requisite to sin, and we know, for the inspired historian has told us, of some children who had "no knowledge between good and evil."[30] Do you say it must be so, for they die and death among human beings proves sin. But children die before they are born, and perhaps also some children die who have no knowledge between good and evil. Do you say they are proper subjects of baptism, and this proves sin. How do you know that baptism is not administered to infants simply as a seal of the covenant, exhibiting and ratifying its promises of good respecting them? Do you say, the language of the Scriptures, is *universal,* that *all* have sinned. The language too is universal, that we are to "preach the Gospel to *every creature.*"[31] Of course, if your mode of interpretation is right, we are to preach the Gospel to infants—and to animals also!—to *every creature.*

Instead then of attempting to assign the precise instant in which men begin to sin, we choose to say they sin as soon as they become moral agents—they sin *as soon as they can;* and who will affirm that this is not soon enough? If it be asked how soon, can they sin? I answer very early; even *so early,* that they are justly represented as sinning from their youth—and in the figurative language of the scriptures, from their birth, and even before birth; *so early* that the literal interval, if there be such an interval, between birth and the commencement of sin is either so short or unimportant, that the Spirit of inspiration has not thought it worthy of particular notice.

If then you ask, what becomes of an infant if he dies, while yet an infant? I answer, he may be saved; in my belief he is saved, through the redemption that is in Christ Jesus. If you ask, how can this be? I reply, he belongs to a race who by nature, in

[29] Romans 9:11. [Taylor's quotation is not exact. Ed.]

[30] Deuteronomy 1:39. [Ed.]

[31] Mark 16:15. [Ed.]

all the circumstances of their immortal being without the grace of this redemption, will sin. Place an infant then from his birth under the influence of the most perfect example and instructions—yea place him amid heaven's purity and heaven's songs, and who shall say that he will not, without the supernatural grace of God's Spirit, be a depraved sinner and fall under condemnation? When made meet therefore for the celestial paradise and admitted there, *his* song may tell of the grace that brought him to its glories.

2. That sin or guilt pertains exclusively to voluntary action, is the true principle of orthodoxy. We have seen that the older orthodox divines assert this principle, and that they abundantly deny that God is the creator or author of sin. By some strange fatality however these writers are not believed by many, on these points; and we are told, as the ground for discrediting these unequivocal declarations, that they also constantly affirm that men are *born* with a corrupt and sinful nature, and with guilt upon them. True, very true. But now to the real question—how in the view of these writers, does this nature with which they are born become corrupt and sinful? By being so created? No such thing: for this they constantly and vehemently deny; and give as we have seen this reason for denying it—that it would make God the author of sin. How then is it, that in their view each has a corrupt and sinful nature when born, and yet that God does not create it? Why, by the *real act* of each—by each one's corrupting his nature, just as Adam did his. But how can this be? They tell us how; viz. that Adam and his posterity were in God's estimation and were thus truly constituted, ONE BEING, one MORAL WHOLE;—so that in Adam's act of sin, all his posterity *being* ONE *with him,* also acted as truly as Adam himself; and so, each and all corrupted their nature as freely and voluntarily as Adam corrupted his nature. The question is, not whether this is not very absurd, but what did these men believe and teach? And I say they *did* believe and *did* teach that all Adam's posterity *acted* in his act, 'sinned in *him* and fell with

him, and are considered truly and properly as sinning *in manner and form,* just as Adam sinned; and every one who has read his catechism or his primer must know it. This class of divines then never thought of predicating sin or guilt, except in cases of free voluntary action. So far as *they* are concerned therefore the doctrine of physical depravity is a theological novelty.

The history of this peculiarity, shows the same thing. The process has been this. The doctrine of imputation being rejected, as it has been in New England for many years, and with it *our personal identity with Adam,* there was no way left in which we could be viewed as the older divines viewed us: the criminal authors when born, of our own corrupt and sinful nature. Still the doctrine of a corrupt and sinful nature *as such* has been retained by *some,* and thus what the older divines made every man *as one in Adam* the author of, God must now answer for as its author by a creative act. Hence some have so professed and so preached, and have talked much of their own orthodoxy and of the heresy of others, and yet after all the outcry, not a theological writer of eminence has ventured to this hour to publish to the world such a doctrine. The entire annals of orthodoxy do not contain the doctrine that *God creates* a sinful nature in man. Those men who have fought the battles of orthodoxy from the reformation to the present day, and who have been esteemed its successful defenders, have held most firmly and asserted abundantly, that all sin or fault must belong *to the acts of the mind*—to the *evil will,* or belong to nothing at all. Brethren, were these men heretics for this? Is the man who believes and teaches the same thing, a heretic?[32]

---

[32] So far as the views of the Orthodox are understood, it would seem that we are reduced to the alternative of renouncing orthodoxy on this subject, in every *supposable* form of it, or of adopting some one of the following forms: either that Adam's posterity are ONE AND THE SAME BEING with Adam, and *so* guilty of his first sin by sinning *in him*—or that God *creates* in us a sinful nature or something else, which deserves his wrath— or that at the very moment of birth we sin with the knowledge of duty

3. The view of sin or moral depravity maintained in this discourse, cannot be justly ascribed to mental perversion, or to any sinister or selfish design. For, what possible motive or object, can be assigned as the cause of perverting truth and evidence in such a case? If popularity were the object, the charges of having departed from the true faith by renouncing former opinions, repeated from one end of the land to the other, show at least in respect to some of us, how ill-judged has been this expedient to gain popularity. Nor is this view of sin adopted for the sake of rejecting any one doctrine of orthodoxy, or of setting up any anti-orthodox peculiarity. For, they who adopt this view, as fully believe in the certainty of the universal and entire sinfulness of mankind—they as fully believe this sinfulness or depravity to be *by nature*—they as fully believe in the inefficacy of moral suasion and in the necessity of the Holy Spirit's agency in regeneration, as any other men. They no more deny that infants are sinners from their birth, that infants are saved through Christ, nor that they must become holy (if at all) by divine influence, than other men. And although they do deny that God creates the sin in them, and that sin pertains to any thing but voluntary action, yet the denial of either position is not an anti-orthodox peculiarity, for the ablest orthodox divines have ever denied both. The charge then of adopting this view of sin, for the purpose of opposing any doctrine of orthodoxy, is a slanderous charge.

---

and as voluntary transgressors of known law—or that we sin without the knowledge of right and wrong even in the lowest degree—or that as free moral agents, we sin knowingly and voluntarily when we become capable of thus sinning. Those who reject all these specific forms of the doctrine of depravity, must relinquish even the pretence to orthodoxy on this topic, and those who reject the last form of it, and adopt either of the preceding forms, will it is hoped favor the world with some better arguments on the subject than have hitherto been furnished.

[The first form listed is Edwards', see pp. 173–174. Taylor identifies his variation with the evolving post-Edwardsean New England Theology, rejecting both imputation and personal identity. Cf. works of H. Shelton Smith and Frank H. Foster in Bibliography. Ed.]

Can any cause then of mental perversion be fairly charged? The human mind pervert truth and evidence for the sake of believing that to be sin, which as it is agreed on all hands, imparts to sin its most malignant aspect, and reveals its fellest tendencies? Men believe that to be sin, which deserves the deepest damnation which any thing can deserve, merely because they wish to believe it! You may as well suppose that for a similar reason, a man should believe his doom already fixed in hell itself. If there be any view of sin which human selfishness will resist to the last, it is this which so embodies all its guilt and all its terrors; it is this which as we all know, makes the conscience of the wicked writhe in anguish, and an ungodly world hate the servant as it hated the Master whom it crucified. Such a view of sin, is not a device to obtain popularity, nor to corrupt the Gospel of God.

4. The universal depravity of mankind is not inconsistent with the moral perfection of God. It is not uncommon to ask (and I admit the facts on which the objection rests), how could a God of perfect sincerity and goodness bring a race of creatures into existence, and give them such *a nature* that they will all certainly sin and incur his wrath? It is also added, to increase the weight of the objection—why render this universal sinfulness of a race, the consequence of one man's act—why not give to each a fair trial for himself? I answer, God does give to each a fair trial for himself. Not a human being does or can become thus sinful or depraved but by his own choice. God does not compel him to sin by the *nature* he gives him. Nor is his sin, although a consequence of Adam's sin, in such a sense its consequence, as not to be a free voluntary act of his own. He sins freely, voluntarily. There is no other way of sinning. God (there is no irreverence in saying it) can make nothing else sin, but the sinner's act. Do you then say, that God gave man a nature, which He knew would lead him to sin? What if He did? Do you know that God could have done better, better on the whole or better, if he gave him existence at all, even for the individual

himself? The error lies in the gratuitous assumption that God could have adopted a moral system, and prevented all sin, or at least, the present degree of sin. For, no man knows this—no man can prove it. The assumption therefore is wholly unauthorised as the basis of the present objection, and the objection itself groundless. On the supposition that the evil which exists is in respect to divine prevention, incidental to the best possible system, and that notwithstanding the evil, God will secure the greatest good possible to him to secure, who can impeach either his wisdom or his goodness because evil exists? I say then that as ignorance is incompetent to make an objection, and as no one knows that this supposition is not a matter of fact, no one has a right to assert the contrary, or even to think it.[33] Suppose then God had adopted a different system, who is competent to foretell or to conjecture the results,—or even the results of one iota of change in the present system? Suppose God had made you just like Adam or even like Lucifer, and placed you in similar circumstances, do you know that you would not have sinned as he did? How do you know that had you commenced your immortal career with such aggravated guilt, God would not have found it necessary to send you to hell without an offer of mercy, and that you would not have sunk in deeper woe than that which now awaits you? How do you know that what might have been true respecting yourself, had not been true of any other possible system of accountable beings? How do you know, that had God ordered things otherwise than he has, this very world now cheered with the calls of mercy and brightened with the hopes of eternal life, yea that heaven itself would not now be trembling under the thunders of retributive vengeance? Man—man in his ignorance, alter the plan and procedure of his God! How

---

[33] Taylor here strung out a long footnote in which his general theological views are expounded. To facilitate reading, this excursus has now been placed at the end of the sermon. [Ed.]

dare he think of it? Beware, ye insects of a day, ye are judging HIM "whom the heaven of heavens cannot contain."

Now think of this, fellow sinner. God in adopting the present system with all the sin incidental to it, may have adopted the best possible. In giving to you the nature which he has, and in placing you in the circumstances in which he has, he may have done the best he could even for you. Say then is your existence a curse, for which your Maker is to be reproached? Is it a curse at all, unless *you* make it so? Does not his preference of holiness to sin on your part, evince toward you, perfect benevolence? Listen to his calls and entreaties and say if this is not the voice of sincerity and truth. Listen to his oath, 'that he has no pleasure at all in your death,' and say if he would regret your return to duty and to life? Look around you and see what proofs of love, what intimations of grace and glory provided for you, gladden every moment of your being. Think what God has done to save you; how he has laid his wrath on one for your sake, how he has cleared away the darkness and tempest around his throne and with smiles of mercy invites you to himself—how he bade angels sing in rapturous song "good will" to the guilty and the lost—how under his commission the swift messenger bears these tidings to you and to all—how mercy with tears points you to that crown of life—how God himself with the earnestness of a suppliant father—with the sincerity of a God entreats you to receive his great salvation. Say now, is he not good; is he not sincere? What 'child of wrath,' will not trust in such a God to save him?

5. We see the importance of this view of man's depravity, compared with any other, in its bearing on the preaching of the Gospel. To what purpose do we preach the Gospel to men, if we cannot reach the conscience with *its charge of guilt* and *obligations to duty?* And how I ask can this be done, unless sin and duty be shown to consist simply and wholly in acts and doings which are their own? Can this be done if we tell them and they

believe us, that their sin is something which God creates in them; or something done by Adam thousands of years before they existed? I care not what you call it, taste, disposition, volition, exercise, if it be that which *cannot* be unless God creates it, and cannot but be if he exerts his power to produce it, can we fasten the arrows of conviction in the conscience, and settle on the spirit the forebodings of a *merited* damnation? Can men be induced to make an effort to avoid sin which is thus produced in them, or to perform duties which must with the same passivity on their part, be produced in them? Does God charge on men, as that which deserves his endless indignation, what [He] Himself does? Does God summon men to repentance with commands and entreaties, and at the same time tell them, that all efforts at compliance are as useless, as the muscular motions of a corpse to get life again? Does this book of God's inspiration, shock and appal the world, with the revelation of such things, respecting God and respecting man? Will the charge of *such sin* on man, touch the secret place of tears? Will the exhibition of such a God, allure the guilty to confide in his mercy. If so, preach it out—preach it consistently—preach nothing to contradict it—dwell on your message, that God creates men sinners and damns them for being so. Tell them such is *their* nature and such the *mode* of his interposition, that there is no more hope from acting on the part of the sinner than from not acting; tell them they may as well sleep on, and sleep away these hours of mercy, as attempt anything in the work of their salvation; that all is as hopeless with effort as without it. Spread over this world such a curtain of sackcloth, such a midnight of terror, and how as the appropriate effect, would each accountable immortal, either sit down in the sullenness of inaction, or take his solitary way to hell in the frenzy of despair!

But such is not the message of wrath and of mercy, by which a revolted world is to be awed and allured back to its Maker. The message we are to deliver to men is a message of wrath, because they are the perpetrators of the deed that deserves wrath. It is a message of mercy to men who by acting, are to comply with the terms of it, and who can never hope to comply even through God's agency, without putting themselves to the doing of *the very thing* commanded of God. And it is only by delivering such a message, that we, Brethren, can be "workers together with God." Let us then go forth with it; and clearing God, throw all the guilt of sin with its desert of wrath, upon the sinner's single self. Let us make him see and feel that he can go to hell only as a self-destroyer—that it is this fact, that will give those chains their strength to hold him, and those fires the anguish of their burning. Let us if we can, make this conviction take hold of his spirit, and ring in his conscience like the note of the second death. If he trembles at the sound in his ears, then let us point him to that mercy which a dying Jesus feels for him, and tell him with the sympathies of men who have been in the same condemnation, that he need but to love and trust Him, and heaven is his inheritance. Without derogating from the work of God's Spirit let us urge him to his duty—*to his duty*—to *his duty*, as a point-blank direction to business now on hand and now to be done. With the authorised assurance that 'peradventure God may give him repentance,' let us make known to him the high command of God, "*strive* to enter in at the strait gate," and make him hear every voice of truth and mercy in heaven and on earth, echoing the mandate.

Then shall the ministers of reconciliation be clad with truth as with a garment, and delivering their message not only in its substance but in its true manner and form, shall commend themselves to every man's conscience in the sight of God. Having his strength perfected in their weakness, they shall go forth 'as archangels strong,' and bidding the wide earth receive God's salvation, the bands of hell shall break, and a redeemed world return to the dominion of its God.

Finally, I cannot conclude without remarking, how fearful are the condition and prospects of the sinner. His sin is his own. He yields himself by his own free act, by his own choice, to those propensities of his nature, which under the weight of God's authority he *ought to govern.* The gratification of these he makes his chief good, immortal as he is. For this he lives and acts—this he puts in the place of God—and for this, and for nothing better he tramples on God's authority and incurs his wrath. Glad would he be, to escape the guilt of it. Oh—could he persuade himself that the fault is not his own—this would wake up peace in his guilty bosom. Could he believe that God is bound to convert and save him; or even that he could make it certain that God will do it, this would allay his fears, this would stamp a bow on the cloud that thickens, and darkens, and thunders damnation on his guilty path. But his guilt is all his own, and a just God may leave him to his choice. He is going on to a wretched eternity, the self-made victim of its woes. Amid sabbaths and bibles, the intercessions of saints, the songs of angels, the intreaties of God's ambassadors, the accents of redeeming love, and the blood that speaketh peace, he presses on to death. God beseeching with tenderness and terror—Jesus telling him he died once and could die again to save him—mercy weeping over him day and night—heaven lifting up its everlasting gates —hell burning, and sending up its smoke of torment, and the weeping and the wailing and the gnashing of teeth, within his hearing—and onward still he goes. See the infatuated immortal! Fellow sinner,—IT IS YOU.

Bowels of divine compassion—length, breadth, height, depth of Jesus' love—Spirit of all grace, save him—Oh save him—or he dies forever.

[*Excursus on Sin, Human Freedom, and*
God's Moral Government]

The difficulties on this difficult subject as it is extensively regarded, result in the view of the writer from two very common but groundless assumptions—assumptions which so long as they are admitted and reasoned upon, *must* leave the subject involved in insuperable difficulties. [See note, p. 238.]

The assumptions are these; First, *that sin is the necessary means of the greatest good and as such, so far as it exists, is preferable on the whole to holiness in its stead.* Secondly, *that God could in a moral system have prevented all sin or at least the present degree of sin.*

In further explanation of the ground taken in answering the above objection, the following enquiries are submitted to the consideration of the candid.

Is not the assumption that the degree of sin which exists, or even any degree of sin, is on the whole preferable to holiness in its stead, inconsistent alike with the benevolence and the sincerity of God? With his benevolence. If such be the nature of God, of man, of holiness, of sin, of all things, that sin is the necessary means of the greatest good, ought it not to be made the subject of precept—would it not be, by a benevolent moral Governor? For how can it be consistent with the benevolence of a moral governor, to require of his subjects that moral conduct which is not on the whole for the best?

If it be said that it is on the whole for the best that *he* should *require* it, but not on the whole for the best that *they* should *perform* it—what is this but to say that it is on the whole for the best that he should practice deception on his subjects? And what then becomes of his *sincerity?* Let us take an example or two. Who would regard the command of a parent as *sincere*, it being known that he prefers on the whole the disobedience of the child to his obedience? Who would regard the invitation of a friend as *sincere*, being fully apprised that he prefers on the whole its rejection to its acceptance? If it be said that no subjects of God have such knowledge of God's preference of sin to holiness in their own case, then the question is whether their ignorance alters *the fact;* and whether he is truly *sincere*, when he would be justly pronounced *insincere* if *the real fact were known?* Besides, after the commission of sin, the fact of such a preference, if there be one, is known. How then does the *sincerity* of God appear when it is placed beyond a doubt by the event, that he did prefer on the whole, the sin committed by the subject to the holiness required in his law? Is it then possible that God should be sincere in his commands and invitations, unless holiness in man be on the whole preferable to sin in its stead?

Further, it is extensively maintained that virtue is founded in utility, i. e. that such is the nature, relations and tendencies of things, that greater happiness will result from virtue or holiness than from vice or sin. How then can sin in the nature of things be the necessary means of the greatest good?

Again, if sin be *the necessary means* of the greatest good, who can reasonably regard the commission of it with sorrow or even regret? What benevolent being duly informed, can ingenuously regret that by sin he has put it in the power of God to produce greater good, than God could otherwise produce? Ought it not rather to be matter of grateful praise that he has sinned, and thus furnished, by what he has done, the necessary means of the greatest possible good? Surely the act considered simply in the relation of the necessary means of such an end, is not a matter for regret; this being the very reason, why God himself is supposed to prefer it.

Is it then said, that *the intention* is selfish and sinful? Be it so. Had the subject however been fully apprised of the utility of the deed and the real preference of God (as in the case of the destruction of the Canaanites), his own interest and his duty would have been coincident; and how does it appear that in this case he had not performed the act from a *benevolent* intention? And how great is the guilt of a selfish intention which, for aught that appears, is occasioned by deception on the part of the lawgiver? Is it said that the selfish intention is necessary to the action as the means of good? But where is an instance in which the good educed from a sinful action is dependent on the selfish intention of the agent? Is it said, that otherwise God could not

shew mercy in its forgiveness? Does God then deceive his subjects in regard to the true nature and tendency of moral acts,
and thus occasion their sin that he may have the glory of for-
giving it? Is this the glory of his mercy? Besides, how does it
appear that the subject did not really *intend* good? The law of
God, according to the assumption, is no proof that transgression
is not on the whole for the best; indeed the subject knows that
all sin will prove to be the necessary means of the greatest good;
how then does it appear that with this knowledge he was not
truly benevolent in performing the deed? What reason then for
sorrow or regret remains?

The second assumption now claims our notice; viz. *that God
could have prevented all sin, or at least the present degree of
sin, in a moral system.*

If holiness in a moral system be preferable on the whole to
sin in its stead, why did not a benevolent God, were it possible
to him, prevent all sin and secure the prevalence of universal
holiness? Would not a moral universe of perfect holiness, and of
course of perfect happiness, be happier and better than one com-
prising sin and its miseries? And must not infinite benevolence
accomplish all the good it can? Would not a benevolent God
then, *had it been possible to him in the nature of things,* have
secured the existence of universal holiness in his moral kingdom?

Is the reader startled by an enquiry which seems to limit the
power of God? But does not *he* equally limit the power of God
by supposing, or rather affirming, that God COULD NOT secure
the greatest good without the existence of sin? On either supposition there is what may be called a limitation of the power of
God by *the nature of things.* In one case, the limitation is supposed to result from *the nature of sin;* in the other, from *the
nature of moral agency.* If then one of these suppositions *must*
be made, which is the most honourable to God?

Further, does not he who is startled by this supposition, limit
the goodness of God? Undeniably he does, if it be conceded that
holiness is on the whole preferable to sin in its stead. For he

who admits this, and maintains that God *could* have secured the existence of holiness instead of sin, must also admit that God is not good enough to accomplish all the good in his power; not good enough to prevent the worst of evils. And who does most reverence to God, he who supposes that God *would* have prevented all sin in his moral universe, but *could* not, or he who affirms that he *could* have prevented it, but *would* not? Or is it more honourable to God to suppose that such is the nature of sin, that he *could not* accomplish the highest good without it, than to suppose that such is the nature of *free agency* that God *could not* wholly prevent its perversion?

But the main enquiry on this point remains—does the supposition that God could not prevent sin in a moral system, limit his power at all? To suppose or affirm that God cannot perform what is *impossible in the nature of things,* is not properly to limit his power. Is there then the least particle of evidence, that the entire prevention of sin in moral beings is possible to God in the nature of things? If not, then what becomes of the very common assumption of such possibility?

All evidence of the truth of this assumption must be derived either from *the nature of the subject,* or from *known facts.* Is there such evidence from *the nature of the subject?* It is here to be remarked, that the prevention of sin by any influence that destroys the *power to sin,* destroys moral agency. Moral agents then must possess the *power to sin.* Who then can prove *a priori* or from the nature of the subject, *that a being who* CAN *sin, will* NOT *sin?* How can it be proved *a priori* or from the nature of the subject, that a thing *will not be,* when for aught that appears, it *may* be? On this point, is it presumptuous to bid defiance to the powers of human reason?

Is there any evidence from *facts?* Facts, so far as they are known to us, furnish no support to the assumption, that God could in a moral system prevent all sin, or even the present degree of sin. For we know of no creature of God, whose holiness is secured without that influence which results either directly or indirectly, from the existence of sin and its punishment. How then can it be shown *from facts,* that God could secure any of his moral creatures in holiness, without this influence; or to what purpose is it to allege instances of the prevention of sin *under* this influence, to prove that God could prevent it *without* this influence? Rather, do not all known facts furnish a strong presumption to the contrary? If God could prevent all sin without this influence, why has he not done it? Be this however as it may, since God has not, so far as we know, prevented sin in a single instance without this influence, how can it be proved *from facts,* that he could have prevented all sin, or even the present degree of sin in a moral system? Had his creatures done what *they* could, then indeed there had been more holiness and less sin. But the question is, what could *God* have done to secure such a result? Had he prevented the sins of one human being to the present time, or had he brought to repentance one sinner more than he has, who can prove that the requisite interposition for the purpose, would not result in a vast increase of sin in the system, including even the apostacy and augmented guilt of that individual? In a word, who is competent to foretell, or authorised even to *surmise* the consequences of the least iota of change in the present system of influence to produce holiness and prevent sin? If no one, then all assumptions on the subject, like that under consideration, are wholly unwarranted. It may be true, that God will secure under the present system of things, the greatest degree of holiness and the least degre of sin, which *it is possible to him in the nature of things* to secure. Neither the *nature of the subject,* nor *known facts,* furnish a particle of evidence to the contrary. The assumption therefore, that God could in a moral system have prevented all sin or the present degree of sin, is wholly gratuitous and unauthorised, and *ought never to be made the basis of an objection or an argument.*

As an apology for this note, the writer would say that the objection alluded to in the discourse, so commonly rises in the mind in connexion with the subject, that it was thought proper to notice it; and while he knows of no refutation except the one given, he was desirous of attempting still further to free the subject from distressing and groundless perplexity. This is done in his own view, simply by dismissing from the mind the two assumptions which have been examined. The mode in which the mind will in this way, be led to view the character and government of God may, it is believed, to be shown to be free from embarrassment by an example.

Suppose then the father of several sons to have foreknown with minute accuracy the various propensities and tendencies of their nature, and *all the possible* conditions or circumstances in which he might place them, with all the results of each condition. Suppose him also to foresee with absolute certainty, that to place them at a public seminary, although he knows it will be, unavoidably to himself, attended with a temporary course of vice on their part, will nevertheless result in greater good than he can secure by placing them in any *other* condition or circumstances. Suppose it to be true, and known to him, that their uniform good conduct at the seminary would be far better on the whole or in every respect than their misconduct. Suppose him now to send them at the proper age, to the place of their education with solemn and unqualified injunctions of uniform good conduct; and all the results to be as foreseen. Now can the procedure of this father be impeached in any respect whatever? Does he not evince wisdom and benevolence in every part of it? Does he not evince the most absolute and perfect sincerity in his injunctions of right conduct? Does he not at the same time furnish by what *he* does, adequate and decisive ground for acquiescence in view of the incidental evil; and is there not equally decisive ground for repentance to his disobedient children in what *they* do? If these things are so in the procedure of this father, why are they not so in the procedure of God?

The writer hopes he shall not be charged *without proof*, with denying what he fully believes—that the providential purposes or decrees of God extend to all actual events, sin not excepted.

God may really purpose the existence of sin, whether he purpose it for one reason or for another; he may, as the example shows, as really purpose sin though wholly an evil, considered as *incidental*, so far as his power of prevention is concerned, to the best moral system, as purpose it considered as so excellent in its nature and relations as to be the necessary means of the greatest good. And while the theory now proposed exhibits the providential government of God as the basis of submission, confidence, and joy, under all the evils that befall his dependent creatures; it also presents, as no other theory in the view of the writer does present, the Moral Government of God in its unimpaired perfection and glory, to deter from sin and allure to holiness his accountable subjects.[34]

---

[34] Taylor's views on these subjects are vastly expanded in his *Lectures on the Moral Government of God,* 2 vols. (New York: Clark, Austin & Smith, 1859), posthumously edited by Noah Porter.

V

CHARLES HODGE

Architect of Princeton Orthodoxy

Charles Hodge (1797–1878)[1] became a professor in the Presbyterian seminary at Princeton in 1822, the same year Taylor received his appointment at Yale; and each was soon pronouncing the other a major menace to the well-being of the American churches. Aside from these formal circumstances, few similarities remain. The New Haven men forced a gap in New England's orthodox tradition, and in due course liberals moved through that breach to capture both the Andover and Hartford seminaries. The Princeton Seminary, however, shaped a new conservatism and created a fortress that held its ground for a century. Regarding the free-ranging intellect of Edwards with suspicion and viewing revivalism as insubstantial, it chose biblical inerrancy and strict confessionalism as its means of defense. To support this strategy Princeton marshaled great dialectical skill, massive theological efforts, and much impressive erudition. It provided a shelter whither revivalists and Fundamentalists could flee when the ideas of Darwin or Wellhausen endangered their tents and tabernacles. They taught theological responsibility to anti-intellectuals in many denominations where learning had been held in disrepute.

---

[1] See Introduction, pp. 45–48.

Charles Hodge was not precisely the founder of the Princeton Theology, and a long line of distinguished men came after him, but he and his works are the most indispensable element in any historical account of the tradition. "No man has ever been so completely the embodiment of the school." He was born in Philadelphia, baptized in the Presbyterian church founded by George Whitefield and Gilbert Tennent, and educated at the college, and then at the seminary in Princeton, and finally in Germany. His intellectual hero was Archibald Alexander, the seminary's first professor. His career was externally the simple one of a busy professor with many admiring students and alumni. He was also the "beast of burden" on the editorial staff of the influential PRINCETON REVIEW. In the turbulent politics of Presbyterianism he became a defender of the "Old School" against every type of "neologian" who would moderate or mitigate the Westminster tradition—or introduce a new idea at Princeton. In polemics he turned on New School men in his own church as well as the theologians of Yale, Mercersburg, and Andover. When fears were put aside that publication of his lectures in SYSTEMATIC THEOLOGY would not reduce the flow of students to Princeton, they were finally published (1871–1873). It is widely believed that Charles Hodge lies buried in those three heavy volumes. The republication of the famous work in 1952 suggests, however, that stories of his death have been exaggerated. THE WAY OF LIFE (1841), a popular version of his views widely distributed by American and British tract societies, was also reprinted in England in 1959. Nonrecognition of Hodge's continuing role in American Protestantism betokens a serious misunderstanding of the contemporary scene.

The selection that follows is drawn from the Introduction to Hodge's SYSTEMATIC THEOLOGY. The first part is from Chapter I "On Method"; and the second is from Chapter VI, "The Protestant Rule of Faith." In the latter Hodge treats the nature, authority and proper use of the Bible. The views so firmly propounded here are characteristic of his entire outlook, central to his system, and the primary ground for his place in the conservative tradition of American Reformed theology. The section on inspiration may seem wearisome, but its relentless pinning down of the doctrine is the essential and most fateful feature of the Princetonian legacy. As had Taylor (Selection IV), Hodge here provides an excellent example of the approach to theology which, later, Bushnell attacked (Selection VII).

SYSTEMATIC THEOLOGY

Introduction

On Theological Method

THEOLOGY A SCIENCE

In every science there are two factors: facts and ideas; or, facts and the mind. Science is more than knowledge. Knowledge is the persuasion of what is true on adequate evidence. But the facts of astronomy, chemistry, or history do not constitute the science of those departments of knowledge. Nor does the mere orderly arrangement of facts amount to science. Historical facts arranged in chronological order, are mere annals. The philosophy of history supposes those facts to be understood in their causal relations. In every department the man of science is assumed to understand the laws by which the facts of experience are determined; so that he not only knows the past, but can predict the future. The astronomer can foretell the relative position of the heavenly bodies for centuries to come. The chemist can tell with certainty what will be the effect of certain chemi-

From Charles Hodge, *Systematic Theology,* 3 vols. (New York: Charles Scribner's Sons, 1872), I, 1–17; 151–188.

cal combinations. If, therefore, theology be a science, it must include something more than a mere knowledge of facts. It must embrace an exhibition of the internal relation of those facts, one to another, and each to all. It must be able to show that if one be admitted, others cannot be denied.

The Bible is no more a system of theology, than nature is a system of chemistry or of mechanics. We find in nature the facts which the chemist or the mechanical philosopher has to examine, and from them to ascertain the laws by which they are determined. So the Bible contains the truths which the theologian has to collect, authenticate, arrange, and exhibit in their internal relation to each other. This constitutes the difference between biblical and systematic theology. The office of the former is to ascertain and state the facts of Scripture. The office of the latter is to take those facts, determine their relation to each other and to other cognate truths, as well as to vindicate them and show their harmony and consistency. This is not an easy task, or one of slight importance.

It may naturally be asked, why not take the truths as God has seen fit to reveal them, and thus save ourselves the trouble of showing their relation and harmony?

The answer to this question is, in the first place, that it cannot be done. Such is the constitution of the human mind that it cannot help endeavoring to systematize and reconcile the facts which it admits to be true. . . .

Second, A much higher kind of knowledge is thus obtained, than by the mere accumulation of isolated facts. . . . We cannot know what God has revealed in his Word unless we understand, at least in some good measure, the relation in which the separate truths therein contained stand to each other. It cost the Church centuries of study and controversy to solve the problem concerning the person of Christ; that is, to adjust and bring into harmonious arrangement all the facts which the Bible teaches on that subject.

Third, We have no choice in this matter. If we would discharge our duty as teachers and defenders of the truth, we must endeavor to bring all the facts of revelation into systematic order and mutual relation. It is only thus that we can satisfactorily exhibit their truth, vindicate them from objections, or bring them to bear in their full force on the minds of men.

Fourth, Such is evidently the will of God. . . . And as He wills that men should study his works and discover their wonderful organic relation and harmonious combination, so it is his will that we should study his Word, and learn that, like the stars, its truths are not isolated points, but systems, cycles, and epicycles, in unending harmony and grandeur. Besides all this, although the Scriptures do not contain a system of theology as a whole, we have in the Epistles of the New Testament, portions of that system wrought out to our hands. These are our authority and guide.

THEOLOGICAL METHOD

Every science has its own method, determined by its peculiar nature. This is a matter of so much importance that it has been erected into a distinct department. Modern literature abounds in works on Methodology, *i. e.*, on the science of method. They are designed to determine the principles which should control scientific investigations. If a man adopts a false method, he is like one who takes a wrong road which will never lead him to his destination. The two great comprehensive methods are the *à priori* and the *à posteriori*. The one argues from cause to effect, the other from effect to cause. The former was for ages applied even to the investigation of nature. Men sought to determine what the facts of nature must be from the laws of mind or assumed necessary laws. Even in our own day we have had Rational Cosmogonies, which undertake to construct a theory of the universe from the nature of absolute being and its necessary modes of development. Every one knows how much it cost to establish the method of induction on a firm basis, and to secure a general recognition of its authority. According to this method, we begin with collecting well-established facts, and from them infer the general laws which determine their occurrence. From the fact that bodies fall toward the centre of the earth, has been inferred the general law of gravitation, which we are authorized to apply far beyond the limits of actual experience. This inductive method is founded upon two principles: First, That there are laws of nature (forces) which are the proximate causes of natural phenomena. Secondly, That those laws are uniform; so that we are certain that the same causes, under the same circumstances, will produce the same effects. There may be diversity of opinion as to the nature of these laws. They may be assumed to be forces inherent in matter; or, they may be regarded as uniform modes of divine operation; but in any event there must be some cause for the phenomena which we perceive around us, and that cause must be uniform and permanent. On these principles all the inductive sciences are founded; and by them the investigations of natural philosophers are guided.

The same principle applies to metaphysics as to physics; to psychology as well as to natural science. Mind has its laws as well as matter, and those laws, although of a different kind, are as permanent as those of the external world.

The methods which have been applied to the study of theology are too numerous to be separately considered. They may, perhaps, be reduced to three general classes: First, The Speculative; Second, The Mystical; Third, The Inductive. . . . [Hodge then discusses these competing methods. Under the first head he dismisses (1) Deists and Rationalists, (2) Rationalistic Supernaturalists in the school of Leibnitz and Wolff, and before them the mediaeval Scholastics, and (3) Transcendentalists and the German idealistic theologians. Under the second head he dismisses not only the perennial mystical tradition but also those who would ground theology in private illumination, the feelings or intuition. He proceeds then to describe the third and proper method. Ed.]

THE INDUCTIVE METHOD AS APPLIED TO THEOLOGY

The Bible is to the theologian what nature is to the man of science. It is his store-house of facts; and his method of ascertaining what the Bible teaches, is the same as that which the natural philosopher adopts to ascertain what nature teaches.

In the first place, he comes to his task with all the assumptions above mentioned. He must assume the validity of those laws of belief which God has impressed upon our nature. In these laws are included some which have no direct application to the natural sciences. Such, for example, as the essential distinction between right and wrong; that nothing contrary to virtue can be enjoined by God; that it cannot be right to do evil that good may come; that sin deserves punishment, and other similar first truths, which God has implanted in the constitution of all moral beings, and which no objective revelation can possibly contradict. These first principles, however, are not to be arbitrarily assumed. No man has a right to lay down his own opinions, however firmly held, and call them "first truths of reason," and make them the source or test of Christian doctrines. Nothing can rightfully be included under the category of first truths, or laws of belief, which cannot stand the tests of universality and necessity, to which many add self-evidence. But self-evidence is included in universality and necessity, in so far, that nothing which is not self-evident can be universally believed, and what is self-evident forces itself on the mind of every intelligent creature.[1]

FACTS TO BE COLLECTED

In the second place, the duty of the Christian theologian is to ascertain, collect, and combine all the facts which God has

---

[1] Philosophically Hodge, like Channing and Taylor, stands with the British post-Lockean tradition, especially as it was shaped by Scottish "Common-Sense" Realism. [Ed.]

revealed concerning himself and our relation to Him. These facts are all in the Bible.[2] This is true, because everything revealed in nature, and in the constitution of man concerning God and our relation to Him, is contained and authenticated in Scripture. It is in this sense that "the Bible, and the Bible alone, is the religion of Protestants."[3] It may be admitted that the truths which the theologian has to reduce to a science, or, to speak more humbly, which he has to arrange and harmonize, are revealed partly in the external works of God, partly in the constitution of our nature, and partly in the religious experience of believers; yet lest we should err in our inferences from the works of God, we have a clearer revelation of all that nature reveals, in his word; and lest we should misinterpret our own consciousness and the laws of our nature, everything that can be legitimately learned from that source will be found recognized and authenticated in the Scriptures; and lest we should attribute to the teaching of the Spirit the operations of our own natural affections, we find in the Bible the norm and standard of all genuine religious experience. The Scriptures teach not only the truth, but what are the effects of the truth on the heart and conscience, when applied with saving power by the Holy Ghost.

In the third place, the theologian must be guided by the same rules in the collection of facts, as govern the man of science.

1. This collection must be made with diligence and care. It is not an easy work. There is in every department of investigation great liability to error. Almost all false theories in science and false doctrines in theology are due in a great degree to mistakes as to matters of fact. . . .

2. This collection of facts must not only be carefully con-

---

2 Here Hodge begins an exposition of Scriptural hermeneutics (interpretive method) that became the hallmark of the Princeton Theology. [Ed.]

3 The famous slogan of William Chillingworth, see note 13, p. 290. [Ed.]

ducted, but also comprehensive, and if possible, exhaustive. An imperfect induction of facts led men for ages to believe that the sun moved round the earth, and that the earth was an extended plain. In theology a partial induction of particulars has led to like serious errors. It is a fact that the Scriptures attribute omniscience to Christ. From this it was inferred that He could not have had a finite intelligence, but that the Logos was clothed in Him with a human body with its animal life. But it is also a Scriptural fact that ignorance and intellectual progress, as well as omniscience, are ascribed to our Lord. Both facts, therefore, must be included in our doctrine of his person. We must admit that He had a human, as well as a divine intelligence. . . .

PRINCIPLES TO BE DEDUCED FROM FACTS

In the fourth place, in theology as in natural science, principles are derived from facts, and not impressed upon them. The properties of matter, the laws of motion, of magnetism, of light, etc., are not framed by the mind. They are not laws of thought. They are deductions from facts. The investigator sees, or ascertains by observation, what are the laws which determine material phenomena; he does not invent those laws. His speculations on matters of science unless sustained by facts, are worthless. It is no less unscientific for the theologian to assume a theory as to the nature of virtue, of sin, of liberty, of moral obligation, and then explain the facts of Scripture in accordance with his theories. His only proper course is to derive his theory of virtue, of sin, of liberty, of obligation, from the facts of the Bible. He should remember that his business is not to set forth his system of truth (that is of no account), but to ascertain and exhibit what is God's system, which is a matter of the greatest moment. If he cannot believe what the facts of the Bible assume to be true, let him say so. Let the sacred writers have their doctrine, while he has his own.[4] To this ground a large class of

---

[4] Echoes of many theological controversies of the day can be heard in the passages that follow. The deviations of New England theologians and especially the errors of Taylor are directly attacked. [Ed.]

modern exegetes and theologians, after a long struggle, have actually come. They give what they regard as the doctrines of the Old Testament; then those of the Evangelists; then those of the Apostles; and then their own. This is fair. So long, however, as the binding authority of Scripture is acknowledged, the temptation is very strong to press the facts of the Bible into accordance with our preconceived theories. If a man be persuaded that certainty in acting is inconsistent with liberty of action; that a free agent can always act contrary to any amount of influence (not destructive of his liberty) brought to bear upon him, he will inevitably deny that the Scriptures teach the contrary, and thus be forced to explain away all facts which prove the absolute control of God over the will and volitions of men. If he hold that sinfulness can be predicated only of intelligent, voluntary action in contravention of law, he must deny that men are born in sin, let the Bible teach what it may. If he believes that ability limits obligation, he must believe independently of the Scriptures, or in opposition to them, it matters not which, that men are able to repent, believe, love God perfectly, to live without sin, at any, and all times, without the least assistance from the Spirit of God. If he deny that the innocent may justly suffer penal evil for the guilty, he must deny that Christ bore our sins. If he deny that the merit of one man can be the judicial ground of the pardon and salvation of other men, he must reject the Scriptural doctrine of justification. It is plain that complete havoc must be made of the whole system of revealed truth, unless we consent to derive our philosophy from the Bible, instead of explaining the Bible by our philosophy. If the Scriptures teach that sin is hereditary, we must adopt a theory of sin suited to that fact. If they teach that men cannot repent, believe, or do anything spiritually good, without the supernatural aid of the Holy Spirit, we must make our theory of moral obligation accord with that fact. If the Bible teaches that we bear the guilt of Adam's first sin, that Christ bore our guilt, and endured the penalty of the law in our stead, these are facts with which we must make our principles agree. It would be easy to show that in every department of theology—in regard to the nature of God, his relation to the world, the plan of salvation, the person and work of Christ, the nature of sin, the operations of divine grace, men, instead of taking the facts of the Bible, and seeing what principles they imply, what philosophy underlies them, have adopted their philosophy independently of the Bible, to which the facts of the Bible are made to bend. This is utterly unphilosophical. It is the fundamental principle of all sciences, and of theology among the rest, that theory is to be determined by facts, and not facts by theory. As natural science was a chaos until the principle of induction was admitted and faithfully carried out, so theology is a jumble of human speculations, not worth a straw, when men refuse to apply the same principle to the study of the Word of God.

THE SCRIPTURES CONTAIN
ALL THE FACTS OF THEOLOGY

This is perfectly consistent, on the one hand, with the admission of intuitive truths, both intellectual and moral, due to our constitution as rational and moral beings; and, on the other hand, with the controlling power over our beliefs exercised by the inward teachings of the Spirit, or, in other words, by our religious experience. And that for two reasons: First, All truth must be consistent. God cannot contradict himself. He cannot force us by the constitution of the nature which He has given us to believe one thing, and in his Word commanded us to believe the opposite. And, second, All the truths taught by the constitution of our nature or by religious experience, are recognized and authenticated in the Scriptures. This is a safeguard and a limit. We cannot assume this or that principle to be intuitively true, or this or that conclusion to be demonstrably certain, and make them a standard to which the Bible must conform. What is self-evidently true, must be proved to be so, and is always recognized in the Bible as true. Whole systems of theologies are founded upon intuitions, so called, and if every man is at liberty to exalt his own intuitions, as men are accustomed to call their strong convictions, we should have as many theologies in the world as there are thinkers. The same remark is applicable to religious experience. There is no form of conviction more intimate and irresistible than that which arises from the inward teaching of the Spirit. All saving faith rests on his testimony or demonstrations (I Cor. 2:4). Believers have an unction from the Holy One, and they know the truth, and that no lie (or false doctrine) is of the truth. This inward teaching produces a conviction which no sophistries can obscure, and no arguments can shake. It is founded on consciousness, and you might as well argue a man out of a belief of his existence, as out of confidence that what he is thus taught of God is true. Two things, however, are to be borne in mind. First, That this inward teaching or demonstration of the Spirit is confined to truths objectively revealed in the Scriptures. It is given, says the Apostle, in order that we may know things gratuitously given, *i. e.*, revealed to us by God in his Word (I Cor. 2:10–16). It is not, therefore, a revelation of new truths, but an illumination of the mind, so that it apprehends the truth, excellence, and glory of things already revealed. And second, This experience is depicted in the Word of God. The Bible gives us not only the facts concerning God, and Christ, ourselves, and our relations to our Maker and Redeemer, but also records the legitimate effects of those truths on the minds of believers. So that we cannot appeal to our own feelings or inward experience, as a ground or guide, unless we can show that it agrees with the experience of holy men as recorded in the Scriptures.

THE TEACHING OF THE SPIRIT

Although the inward teaching of the Spirit, or religious experience, is no substitute for an external revelation, and is no part of the rule of faith, it is, nevertheless, an invaluable guide in determining what the rule of faith teaches. The distin-

guishing feature of Augustinianism as taught by Augustine himself, and by the purer theologians of the Latin Church throughout the Middle Ages, which was set forth by the Reformers, and
especially by Calvin and the Geneva divines, is that the inward
teaching of the Spirit is allowed its proper place in determining
our theology. The question is not first and mainly, What is true
to the understanding, but what is true to the renewed heart?
The effort is not to make the assertions of the Bible harmonize
with the speculative reason, but to subject our feeble reason to
the mind of God as revealed in his Word, and by his Spirit in
our inner life. It might be easy to lead men to the conclusion
that they are responsible only for their voluntary acts, if the
appeal is made solely to the understanding. But if the appeal be
made to every man's, and especially to every Christian's inward
experience, the opposite conclusion is reached. We are convinced of the sinfulness of states of mind as well as of voluntary
acts, even when those states are not the effect of our own agency,
and are not subject to the power of the will. We are conscious
of being sold under sin; of being its slaves; of being possessed
by it as a power or law, immanent, innate, and beyond our control. Such is the doctrine of the Bible, and such is the teaching
of our religious consciousness when under the influence of the
Spirit of God. The true method in theology requires that the
facts of religious experience should be accepted as facts, and
when duly authenticated by Scripture, be allowed to interpret
the doctrinal statements of the Word of God.[5] So legitimate and
powerful is this inward teaching of the Spirit, that it is no uncommon thing to find men having two theologies—one of the
intellect, and another of the heart. The one may find expression
in creeds and systems of divinity, the other in their prayers and
hymns. It would be safe for a man to resolve to admit into his

---

[5] On this issue of the "internal testimony" Hodge reveals certain New
School affinities. He feared subjectivism less than some of his successors.
See Bernard Ramm, *Witness of the Spirit* (Grand Rapids: Wm. B. Eerd-
mans Publishing Company, 1959). [Ed.]

theology nothing which is not sustained by the devotional writings of true Christians of every denomination. It would be easy to construct from such writings, received and sanctioned by Romanists, Lutherans, Reformed, and Remonstrants, a system of Pauline or Augustinian theology, such as would satisfy any intelligent and devout Calvinist in the world.

The true method of theology is, therefore, the inductive, which assumes that the Bible contains all the facts or truths which form the contents of theology, just as the facts of nature are the contents of the natural sciences. It is also assumed that the relation of these Biblical facts to each other, the principles involved in them, the laws which determine them, are in the facts themselves, and are to be deduced from them, just as the laws of nature are deduced from the facts of nature. In neither case are the principles derived from the mind and imposed upon the facts, but equally in both departments, the principles or laws are deduced from the facts and recognized by the mind....

The Protestant Rule of Faith

STATEMENT OF THE DOCTRINE

All Protestants agree in teaching that "the word of God, as contained in the Scriptures of the Old and New Testaments, is the only infallible rule of faith and practice."[6] ... The Westminster Confession teaches: "Under the name of Holy Scripture, or the Word of God written, are now contained all the books of the Old and New Testament, which are these: etc. ... All which are given by inspiration of God, to be the rule of faith and life. The whole counsel of God concerning all things necessary for his own glory, man's salvation, faith, and life, is either expressly set down in Scripture, or by good and necessary consequence

---

[6] Omitted are Hodge's long supportive quotations from Lutheran, Swiss, French, and English confessions. [Ed.]

may be deduced from Scripture; unto which nothing at any time is to be added whether by new revelations of the Spirit or traditions of men. All things in Scripture are not alike plain in themselves, nor alike clear unto all; yet those things which are necessary to be known, believed, and observed, for salvation, are so clearly propounded and opened in some place of Scripture or other, that not only the learned, but the unlearned, in a due use of the ordinary means, may attain unto a sufficient understanding of them."[7]

From these statements it appears that Protestants hold, (1) That the Scriptures of the Old and New Testaments are the Word of God, written under the inspiration of the Holy Spirit, and are therefore infallible, and of divine authority in all things pertaining to faith and practice, and consequently free from all error whether of doctrine, fact, or precept. (2) That they contain all the extant supernatural revelations of God designed to be a rule of faith and practice to his Church. (3) That they are sufficiently perspicuous to be understood by the people, in the use of ordinary means and by the aid of the Holy Spirit, in all things necessary to faith or practice, without the need of any infallible interpreter.

THE CANON

Before entering on the consideration of these points, it is necessary to answer the question, What books are entitled to a place in the canon, or rule of faith and practice? Romanists answer this question by saying, that all those which the Church has decided to be divine in their origin, and none others, are to be thus received. Protestants answer it by saying, so far as the Old Testament is concerned, that those books, and those only, which Christ and his Apostles recognized as the written Word of God, are entitled to be regarded as canonical. This recogni-

---

[7] Chap. I, Art. 2. [Ed.]

tion was afforded in a twofold manner: First, many of the books of the Old Testament are quoted as the Word of God, as being given by the Spirit; or the Spirit is said to have uttered what is therein recorded. Secondly, Christ and his Apostles refer to the sacred writings of the Jews—the volume which they regarded as divine—as being what it claimed to be, the Word of God. When we refer to the Bible as of divine authority, we refer to it as a volume and recognize all the writings which it contains as given by the inspiration of the Spirit. In like manner when Christ or his Apostles quote the "Scriptures," or the "law and the prophets," and speak of the volume then so called, they give their sanction to the divine authority of all the books which that volume contained. All, therefore, that is necessary to determine for Christians the canon of the Old Testament, is to ascertain what books were included in the "Scriptures" recognized by the Jews of that period. This is a point about which there is no reasonable doubt. The Jewish canon of the Old Testament included all the books and no others, which Protestants now recognize as constituting the Old Testament Scriptures. On this ground Protestants reject the so-called apocryphal books. They were not written in Hebrew and were not included in the canon of the Jews. They were, therefore, not recognized by Christ as the Word of God. This reason is of itself sufficient. It is however confirmed by considerations drawn from the character of the books themselves. They abound in errors, and in statements contrary to those found in the undoubtedly canonical books.

The principle on which the canon of the New Testament is determined is equally simple. Those books, and those only which can be proved to have been written by the Apostles, or to have received their sanction, are to be recognized as of divine authority. The reason of this rule is obvious. The Apostles were the duly authenticated messengers of Christ, of whom He said, "He that heareth you, heareth me." [Luke 10:16.]

THE SCRIPTURES ARE INFALLIBLE, I. E., GIVEN BY INSPIRATION OF GOD

The infallibility and divine authority of the Scriptures are due to the fact that they are the word of God; and they are the word of God because they were given by the inspiration of the Holy Ghost.

A. THE NATURE OF INSPIRATION. DEFINITION

The nature of inspiration is to be learnt from the Scriptures; from their didactic statements, and from their phenomena. There are certain general facts or principles which underlie the Bible, which are assumed in all its teachings, and which therefore must be assumed in its interpretation. We must, for example, assume, (1) That God is not the unconscious ground of all things; nor an unintelligent force; nor a name for the moral order of the universe; nor mere causality; but a Spirit, a self-conscious, intelligent, voluntary agent, possessing all the attributes of our spirits without limitation, and to an infinite degree. (2) That He is the creator of the world, and extra-mundane, existing before, and independently of it; not its soul, life, or animating principle; but its maker, preserver, and ruler. (3) That as a spirit He is everywhere present, and everywhere active, preserving and governing all his creatures and all their actions. (4) That while both in the external world and in the world of mind He generally acts according to fixed laws and through secondary causes, He is free to act, and often does act immediately, or without the intervention of such causes, as in creation, regeneration, and miracles. (5) That the Bible contains a divine, or supernatural revelation. The present question is not, Whether the Bible is what it claims to be; but, What does it teach as to the nature and effects of the influence under which it was written?

On this subject the common doctrine of the Church is, and

ever has been, that inspiration was an influence of the Holy Spirit on the minds of certain select men, which rendered them the organs of God for the infallible communication of his mind and will. They were in such a sense the organs of God, that what they said God said.

B. INSPIRATION SUPERNATURAL

This definition includes several distinct points. *First.* Inspiration is a supernatural influence. It is thus distinguished, on the one hand, from the providential agency of God, which is everywhere and always in operation; and on the other hand, from the gracious operations of the Spirit on the hearts of his people. According to the Scriptures, and the common views of men, a marked distinction is to be made between those effects which are due to the efficiency of God operating regularly through second causes, and those which are produced by his immediate efficiency without the intervention of such causes. The one class of effects is natural; the other, supernatural. Inspiration belongs to the latter class. It is not a natural effect due to the inward state of its subject, or to the influence of external circumstances.

No less obvious is the distinction which the Bible makes between the gracious operations of the Spirit and those by which extraordinary gifts are bestowed upon particular persons. Inspiration, therefore, is not to be confounded with spiritual illumination. They differ, first, as to their subjects. The subjects of inspiration are a few selected persons; the subjects of spiritual illumination are all true believers. And, secondly, they differ as to their design. The design of the former is to render certain men infallible as teachers; the design of the latter is to render men holy; and of course they differ as to their effects. Inspiration in itself has no sanctifying influence. Balaam was inspired. Saul was among the prophets. Caiaphas uttered a prediction which "he spake not of himself." (John 11:51.) In the last day many will be able to say to Christ, "Lord, Lord, have we not prophesied in thy name? and in thy name have cast out devils? and in thy name done many wonderful works?" To whom he will say: "I never knew you; depart from me, ye that work iniquity." (Matt. 7:22, 23.)

C. DISTINCTION BETWEEN REVELATION AND INSPIRATION

Second. The above definition assumes a difference between revelation and inspiration. They differ, first, as to their object. The object of revelation is the communication of knowledge. The object or design of inspiration is to secure infallibility in teaching. Consequently they differ, secondly, in their effects. The effect of revelation was to render its recipient wiser. The effect of inspiration was to preserve him from error in teaching. These two gifts were often enjoyed by the same person at the same time. That is, the Spirit often imparted knowledge, and controlled in its communication orally or in writing to others. This was no doubt the case with the Psalmists, and often with the Prophets and Apostles. Often, however, the revelations were made at one time, and were subsequently, under the guidance of the Spirit, committed to writing. Thus the Apostle Paul tells us that he received his knowledge of the gospel not from man, but by revelation from Jesus Christ; and this knowledge he communicated from time to time in his discourses and epistles. In many cases these gifts were separated. Many of the sacred writers, although inspired, received no revelations. This was probably the fact with the authors of the historical books of the Old Testament. The evangelist Luke does not refer his knowledge of the events which he records to revelation, but says he derived it from those "which from the beginning were eyewitnesses, and ministers of the Word." (Luke 1:2.) It is immaterial to us where Moses obtained his knowledge of the events recorded in the book of Genesis; whether from early documents, from tradition, or from direct revelation. No more causes are to be assumed for any effect than are necessary. If the sacred writers had sufficient sources of knowledge in themselves, or in those about them, there is no need to assume any direct revelation. It is enough for us that they were rendered infallible as teachers. . . .

D. INSPIRED MEN THE ORGANS OF GOD

A *third* point included in the Church doctrine of inspiration is, that the sacred writers were the organs of God, so that what they taught, God taught. It is to be remembered, however, that when God uses any of his creatures as his instruments, He uses them according to their nature. He uses angels as angels, men as men, the elements as elements. Men are intelligent voluntary agents; and as such were made the organs of God. The sacred writers were not made unconscious or irrational. The spirits of the prophets were subject to the prophets. (I Cor. 14:32.) They were not like calculating machines which grind out logarithms with infallible correctness. The ancients, indeed, were accustomed to say, as some theologians have also said, that the sacred writers were as pens in the hand of the Spirit; or as harps, from which He drew what sounds He pleased. These representations were, however, intended simply to illustrate one point, namely, that the words uttered or recorded by inspired men were the words of God. The Church has never held what has been stigmatized as the mechanical theory of inspiration. The sacred writers were not machines. Their self-consciousness was not suspended; nor were their intellectual powers superseded. Holy men spake as they were moved by the Holy Ghost. It was men, not machines; not unconscious instruments, but living, thinking, willing minds, whom the Spirit used as his organs. Moreover, as inspiration did not involve the suspension or suppression of the human faculties, so neither did it interfere with the free exercise of the distinctive mental characteristics of the individual. If a Hebrew was inspired, he spake Hebrew; if a Greek, he spake Greek; if an educated man, he spoke as a man of culture; if uneducated, he spoke as such a man is wont to speak. If his mind was logical, he reasoned, as Paul did; if emotional and contemplative, he wrote as John wrote. All this is involved in the fact that God uses his instruments according to their nature. The sacred writers impressed their peculiarities on their several productions as plainly as though they were the subjects of no extraordinary influence. This is one of the phenomena of the Bible patent to the most cursory reader. It lies in the very nature of inspiration that God spake in the language of men; that He uses men as his organs, each according to his peculiar gifts and endowments. When He ordains praise out of the mouth of babes, they must speak as babes, or the whole power and beauty of the tribute will be lost. There is no reason to believe that the operation of the Spirit in inspiration revealed itself any more in the consciousness of the sacred writers, than his operations in sanctification reveal themselves in the consciousness of the Christian. As the believer seems to himself to act, and in fact does act out of his own nature; so the inspired penmen wrote out of the fulness of their own thoughts and feelings, and employed the language and modes of expression which to them were the most natural and appropriate. Nevertheless, and none the less, they spoke as they were moved by the Holy Ghost, and their words were his words.

E. PROOF OF THE DOCTRINE

That this is the Scriptural view of inspiration; that inspired men were the organs of God in such a sense that their words are to be received not as the words of men, but as they are in truth, as the words of God (I Thess. 2:13), is proved,—

1. From the signification and usage of the word. It is, of course, admitted that words are to be understood in their historical sense. If it can be shown what idea the men living in the apostolic age attached to the word *theopneustos* and its equivalents, that is the idea which the Apostles intended to express by them. All nations have entertained the belief not only that God

has access to the human mind and can control its operations, but that He at times did take such possession of particular persons as to make them the organs of his communications. . . . The idea of inspiration is therefore fixed. It is not to be arbitrarily determined. We must not interpret the word or the fact, according to our theories of the relation of God to the world, but according to the usage of antiquity, sacred and profane, and according to the doctrine which the sacred writers and the men of their generation are known to have entertained on the subject. According to all antiquity, an inspired man was one who was the organ of God in what he said, so that his words were the words of the god of which he was the organ. When, therefore, the sacred writers use the same words and forms of expression which the ancients used to convey that idea, they must in all honesty be assumed to mean the same thing.

ARGUMENT FROM THE MEANING OF THE WORD PROPHET

2. That this is the Scriptural idea of inspiration is further proved from the meaning of the word prophet. The sacred writers divide the Scriptures into the "law and the prophets." As the law was written by Moses, and as Moses was the greatest of the prophets, it follows that all the Old Testament was written by prophets. If, therefore, we can determine the Scriptural idea of a prophet, we shall thereby determine the character of their writings and the authority due to them. A prophet, then, in the Scriptural sense of the term, is a spokesman, one who speaks for another, in his name, and by his authority; so that it is not the spokesman but the person for whom he acts, who is responsible for the truth of what is said. In Exodus 7:1, it is said, "See, I have made thee a god to Pharaoh; and Aaron thy brother shall be thy prophet," *i. e.*, thy spokesman. This is explained by what is said in Exodus 4:14–16, "Is not Aaron the Levite thy brother? I know that he can speak well. . . . Thou shalt speak unto him, and put words into his mouth; and I will

be with thy mouth, and with his mouth, and will teach you what ye shall do. And he shall be thy spokesman unto the people; and he shall be, even he shall be, to thee instead of a mouth, and thou shalt be to him instead of God." (See Jer. 36:17, 18.) . . .

This is precisely what the Apostle Peter teaches when he says (II Peter 1:20, 21) "No prophecy of the Scripture is of any private interpretation. For the prophecy came not in old time by the will of man: but holy men spake as they were moved (*pheromenoi, borne along* as a ship by the wind) by the Holy Ghost." Prophecy, *i. e.*, what a prophet said, was not human, but divine. It was not the prophet's own interpretation of the mind and will of God. He spoke as the organ of the Holy Ghost.

WHAT THE PROPHETS SAID GOD SAID

3. It is another decisive proof that the sacred writers were the organs of God in the sense above stated, that whatever they said the Spirit is declared to have said. Christ himself said that David by the Spirit called the Messiah Lord. (Matt. 22:43) David in the 95th Psalm said, "To-day if ye will hear his voice, harden not your heart;" but the Apostle (Heb. 3:7) says that these were the words of the Holy Ghost. Again, in ch. 10:15, the same Apostle says, "Whereof the Holy Ghost also is a witness to us: for after that he had said before, This is the covenant that I will make with them after those days, saith the Lord." Thus quoting the language of Jeremiah (31:33) as the language of the Holy Ghost. In Acts 4:25, the assembled Apostles said, "with one accord," "Lord thou art God. . . . Who by the mouth of thy servant David hast said, Why did the heathen rage?" In Acts 28:25, Paul said to the Jews, "Well spake the Holy Ghost by Esaias the prophet unto our fathers." It is in this way that Christ and his Apostles constantly refer to the Scriptures, showing beyond doubt that they believed and taught, that what the sacred writers said the Holy Ghost said.

INSPIRATION OF THE NEW TESTAMENT WRITERS

This proof bears specially, it is true, only on the writings of the Old Testament. But no Christian puts the inspiration of the Old Testament above that of the New. The tendency, and we may even say the evidence, is directly the other way. If the Scriptures of the old economy were given by inspiration of God, much more were those writings which were penned under the dispensation of the Spirit. Besides, the inspiration of the Apostles is proved, (1) From the fact that Christ promised them the Holy Spirit, who should bring all things to their remembrance, and render them infallible in teaching. It is not you, He said, that speak, but the Spirit of my Father speaketh in you. He that heareth you heareth me. He forbade them to enter upon their office as teachers until they were endued with power from on high. (2) This promise was fulfilled on the day of Pentecost, when the Spirit descended upon the Apostles as a mighty rushing wind, and they were filled with the Holy Ghost, and began to speak as the Spirit gave them utterance (*dabat eloqui,* as the Vulgate more literally renders the words). From this moment they were new men, with new views, with new spirit, and with new power and authority. The change was sudden. It was not a development. It was something altogether supernatural; as when God said, Let there be light, and there was light. Nothing can be more unreasonable than to ascribe this sudden transformation of the Apostles from narrow-minded, bigoted Jews, into enlightened, large-minded, catholic Christians, to mere natural causes. Their Jewish prejudices had resisted all the instructions and influence of Christ for three years, but gave way in a moment when the Spirit came upon them from on high. (3) After the day of Pentecost the Apostles claimed to be the infallible organs of God in all their teachings. They required men to receive what they taught not as the word of man but as the word of God (I Thess. 2:13); they declared, as Paul does (I Cor. 14:37), that the things which they wrote were the commandments of the Lord. They made the salvation of men to depend on faith in the doctrines which they taught. Paul pronounces anathema even an angel from heaven who should preach any other gospel than that which he had taught. (Gal. 1: 8.) John says that whoever did not receive the testimony which he bore concerning Christ, made God a liar, because John's testimony was God's testimony. (I John 5:10.) "He that knoweth God, heareth us; he that is not of God, heareth not us." (4:6.) This assertion of infallibility, this claim for the divine authority of their teaching, is characteristic of the whole Bible. The sacred writers all, and everywhere, disclaim personal authority; they never rest the obligation to faith in their teachings, on their own knowledge or wisdom; they never rest it on the truth of what they taught as manifest to reason or as capable of being proved by argument. They speak as messengers, as witnesses, as organs. They declare that what they said God said, and, therefore, on his authority it was to be received and obeyed.

THE TESTIMONY OF PAUL

The Corinthians objected to Paul's preaching that he did not attempt any rational or philosophical proof of the doctrines which he propounded; that his language and whole manner of discourse were not in accordance with rhetorical rules. He answers these objections—first, by saying that the doctrines which he taught were not the truths of reason, were not derived from the wisdom of men, but were matters of divine revelation; that he simply taught what God declared to be true; and secondly, that as to the manner of presenting these truths, he was the mere organ of the Spirit of God. In I Cor. 2:7–13, he sets forth this whole subject in the clearest and most concise manner. The things which he taught, which he calls "the wisdom of God," "the things of the Spirit," *i. e.*, the gospel, the system of doctrine taught in the Bible, he says, had never entered into the mind of man. God had revealed those truths by his Spirit; for the

Spirit is the only competent source of such knowledge. "For
what man knoweth the things of a man, save the spirit of man
which is in him? even so, the things of God knoweth no man,
but the Spirit of God." So much for the source of knowledge,
and the ground on which the doctrines he taught were to be
received. As to the second objection, which concerned his language and mode of presentation, he says, These things of the
Spirit, thus revealed, we teach "not in the words which man's
wisdom teacheth; but which the Holy Ghost teacheth, . . . *combining spiritual with spiritual, i. e.,* clothing the truths of the
Spirit in the words of the Spirit. There is neither in the Bible
nor in the writings of men, a simpler or clearer statement of the
doctrines of revelation and inspiration. Revelation is the act of
communicating divine knowledge by the Spirit to the mind. Inspiration is the act of the same Spirit, controlling those who
make the truth known to others. The thoughts, the truths made
known, and the words in which they are recorded, are declared
to be equally from the Spirit. This, from first to last, has been
the doctrine of the Church, notwithstanding the endless diversity of speculations in which theologians have indulged on the
subject. This then is the ground on which the sacred writers
rested their claims. They were the mere organs of God. They
were his messengers. Those who heard them, heard God; and
those who refused to hear them, refused to hear God. (Matt. 10:
40; John 13:20.)

4. This claim to infallibility on the part of the Apostles was
duly authenticated, not only by the nature of the truths which
they communicated, and by the power which those truths have
ever exerted over the minds and hearts of men, but also by the
inward witness of the Spirit of which St. John speaks, when he
says, "He that believeth on the Son of God hath the witness in
himself" (I John 5:10); "an unction from the Holy One." (I John
2:20.) It was confirmed also by miraculous gifts. As soon as the
Apostles were endued with power from on high, they spake in

"other tongues;" they healed the sick, restored the lame and the blind. "God also," as the Apostle says (Heb. 2:4), "bearing them witness, both with signs, and wonders, and with divers miracles, and gifts of the Holy Ghost, according to his own will." And Paul tells the Corinthians that the signs of an Apostle had been wrought among them "in all patience, in signs, and wonders, and mighty deeds." (II Cor. 12:12.) The mere working of miracles was not an evidence of a divine commission as a teacher. But when a man claims to be the organ of God, when he says that God speaks through him, then his working of miracles is the testimony of God to the validity of his claims. And such testimony God gave to the infallibility of the Apostles.

The above considerations are sufficient to show, that according to the Scriptures, inspired men were the organs, or mouth of God, in the sense that what they said and taught has the sanction and authority of God.

F. INSPIRATION EXTENDS EQUALLY TO ALL PARTS OF SCRIPTURE

This is the *fourth* element of the Church doctrine on this subject. This means, first, that all the books of Scripture are equally inspired. All alike are infallible in what they teach. And secondly, that inspiration extends to all the contents of these several books. It is not confined to moral and religious truths, but extends to the statements of facts, whether scientific, historical, or geographical. It is not confined to those facts the importance of which is obvious, or which are involved in matters of doctrine. It extends to everything which any sacred writer asserts to be true.

This is proved, (1) Because it is involved in, or follows as a necessary consequence from, the proposition that the sacred writers were the organs of God. If what they assert, God asserts, which, as has been shown, is the Scriptural idea of inspiration, their assertions must be free from error. (2) Because our Lord expressly says, "The Scripture cannot be broken" (John 10:35), *i. e.*, they cannot err. (3) Because Christ and his Apostles refer to all parts of the Scriptures, or to the whole volume, as the word of God. They make no distinction as to the authority of the Law, the Prophets, or the Hagiographa. They quote the Pentateuch, the historical books, the Psalms, and the Prophets, as all and equally the word of God. (4) Because Christ and the writers of the New Testament refer to all classes of facts recorded in the Old Testament as infallibly true. Not only doctrinal facts, such as those of the creation and probation of man; his apostasy; the covenant with Abraham; the giving the law upon Mount Sinai; not only great historical facts, as the deluge, the deliverance of the people out of Egypt, the passage of the Red Sea, and the like; but incidental circumstances, or facts of apparently minor importance, as *e. g.* that Satan tempted our first parents in the form of a serpent; that Moses lifted up a serpent in the wilderness; that Elijah healed Naaman, the Syrian, and was sent to the widow in Sarepta; that David ate the shew-bread in the temple; and even that great stumbling-block, that Jonah was three days in the whale's belly, are all referred to by our Lord and his Apostles with the sublime simplicity and confidence with which they are received by little children. (5) It lies in the very idea of the Bible, that God chose some men to write history; some to indite psalms; some to unfold the future; some to teach doctrines. All were equally his organs, and each was infallible in his own sphere. As the principle of vegetable life pervades the whole plant, the root, stem, and flower; as the life of the body belongs as much to the feet as to the head, so the Spirit of God pervades the whole Scripture, and is not more in one part than in another. Some members of the body are more important than others; and some books of the Bible could be far better spared than others. There may be as great a difference between St. John's Gospel and the Book of Chronicles as between a man's brain and the hair of his head; nevertheless the life of the body is as truly in the hair as in the brain.

G. THE INSPIRATION OF THE SCRIPTURES EXTENDS TO THE WORDS

1. This again is included in the infallibility which our Lord ascribes to the Scriptures. A mere human report or record of a divine revelation must of necessity be not only fallible, but more or less erroneous.

2. The thoughts are in the words. The two are inseparable. If the words, priest, sacrifice, ransom, expiation, propitiation, purification by blood, and the like, have no divine authority, then the doctrine which they embody has no such authority.[8]

3. Christ and his Apostles argue from the very words of Scripture. Our Lord says that David by the Spirit called the Messiah Lord, *i. e.*, David used that word. It was in the use of a particular word, that Christ said (John 10:35), that the Scriptures cannot be broken. "If he call them gods unto whom the word of God came, and the Scripture cannot be broken," etc. The use of that word, therefore, according to Christ's view of the Scripture, was determined by the Spirit of God. Paul, in Gal. 3:16, lays stress on the fact, that in the promise made to Abraham, a word used is singular and not plural, "seed," "as of one," and not "seeds as of many." Constantly it is the very words of Scripture which are quoted as of divine authority.

4. The very form in which the doctrine of inspiration is taught in the Bible, assumes that the organs of God in the communication of his will were controlled by Him in the words which they used. "I have put my words in thy mouth." (Jer. 1:9.) "It is not ye that speak, but the Spirit of your Father which speaketh in you." (Matt. 10:20.) They spake "as the Spirit gave them utterance." (Acts 2:4.) "Holy men of God spake as they were moved by the Holy Ghost." (II Pet. 1:21.) All these, and similar modes of expression with which the Scriptures abound, imply that the

---

[8] Hodge probably had Bushnell in mind here; and Bushnell certainly was attacking the view of scriptural and doctrinal language which Hodge is propounding. See pp. 328–342. [Ed.]

words uttered were the words of God. This, moreover, is the
very idea of inspiration as understood by the ancient world. The
words of the oracle were assumed to be the words of the divinity, and not those selected by the organ of communication. And
this, too, as has been shown, was the idea attached to the gift
of prophecy. The words of the prophet were the words of God,
or he could not be God's spokesman and mouth. It has also been
shown that in the most formally didactic passage in the whole
Bible on this subject (I Cor. 2:10–13), the Apostle expressly
asserts that the truths revealed by the Spirit, he communicated
in words taught by the Spirit.

PLENARY INSPIRATION

The view presented above is known as the doctrine of plenary
inspiration. Plenary is opposed to partial. The Church doctrine
denies that inspiration is confined to parts of the Bible; and
affirms that it applies to all the books of the sacred canon. It denies that the sacred writers were merely partially inspired; it
asserts that they were fully inspired as to all that they teach,
whether of doctrine or fact. This of course does not imply that
the sacred writers were infallible except for the special purpose
for which they were employed.[9] They were not imbued with
plenary knowledge. As to all matters of science, philosophy, and
history, they stood on the same level with their contemporaries.
They were infallible only as teachers, and when acting as the
spokesmen of God. Their inspiration no more made them astronomers than it made them agriculturists. Isaiah was infallible
in his predictions, although he shared with his countrymen the
views then prevalent as to the mechanism of the universe. Paul
could not err in anything he taught, although he could not recol-

---

[9] The relatively liberal but ambiguous statement made here as a matter
"of course" would entail millions of angry, polemical words during the
succeeding century's great Fundamentalist Controversy. [Ed.]

lect how many persons he had baptized in Corinth. The sacred writers also, doubtless, differed as to insight into the truths which they taught. The Apostle Peter intimates that the prophets searched diligently into the meaning of their own predictions. When David said God had put "all things" under the feet of man, he probably little thought that "all things" meant the whole universe. (Heb. 2:8.) And Moses, when he recorded the promise that childless Abraham was to be the father "of many nations," little thought that it meant the whole world. (Rom. 4:13). Nor does the Scriptural doctrine on this subject imply that the sacred writers were free from errors in conduct. Their infallibility did not arise from their holiness, nor did inspiration render them holy. Balaam was inspired, and Saul was among the prophets. David committed many crimes, although inspired to write psalms. Peter erred in conduct at Antioch; but this does not prove that he erred in teaching. The influence which preserved him from mistakes in teaching was not designed to preserve him from mistakes in conduct.

H. GENERAL CONSIDERATIONS IN SUPPORT OF THE DOCTRINE

On this point little need be said. If the questions, What is the Scriptural doctrine concerning inspiration? and, What is the true doctrine? be considered different, then after showing what the Scriptures teach on the subject, it would be necessary to prove that what they teach is true. This, however, is not the position of the Christian theologian. It is his business to set forth what the Bible teaches. If the sacred writers assert that they are the organs of God; that what they taught He taught through them; that they spoke as they were moved by the Holy Ghost, so that what they said the Holy Spirit said, then, if we believe their divine mission, we must believe what they teach as to the nature of the influence under which they spoke and wrote. This is the reason why in the earlier period of the Church there was no separate discussion of the doctrine of inspiration.[10] That was regarded as involved in the divine origin of the Scriptures. If they are a revelation from God, they must be received and obeyed; but they cannot be thus received without attributing to them divine authority, and they cannot have such authority without being infallible in all they teach.

The organic unity of the Scriptures proves them to be the product of one mind. They are not only so united that we cannot believe one part without believing the whole; we cannot believe the New Testament without believing the Old; we cannot believe the Prophets without believing the Law; we cannot believe Christ without believing his Apostles; but besides all this they present the regular development, carried on through centuries and millenniums, of the great original promise, "The seed of the woman shall bruise the serpent's head."[11] This development was conducted by some forty independent writers, many of whom understood very little of the plan they were unfolding, but each contributed his part to the progress and completion of the whole.

If the Bible be the work of one mind, that mind must be the mind of God. He only knows the end from the beginning. He only could know what the Bible reveals. No one, says the Apostle, knows the things of God but the Spirit of God. He only could reveal the nature, the thoughts, and purposes of God. He only could tell whether sin can be pardoned. No one knows the Son but the Father. The revelation of the person and work of Christ is as clearly the work of God as are the heavens in all their majesty and glory.

Besides, we have the witness in ourselves. We find that the

---

10 The decisive emergence of *inspiration* as a major doctrinal question came about rather late, and in two main stages: first in the post-Reformation period in Protestant controversy with the Roman Church's view of infallibility and tradition; then progressively as modern science and critical scholarship raised new problems. Hodge belongs to the latter stage but for argumentation draws heavily on the former. [Ed.]

11 See Genesis 3:15; Romans 16:20; Revelation 12:17. [Ed.]

truths revealed in the Bible have the same adaptation to our souls that the atmosphere has to our bodies. The body cannot live without air, which it receives and appropriates instinctively, with full confidence in its adaptation to the end designed. In like manner the soul receives and appropriates the truths of Scripture as the atmosphere in which alone it can breathe and live. Thus in receiving the Bible as true, we necessarily receive it as divine. In believing it as a supernatural revelation, we believe its plenary inspiration.

This doctrine involves nothing out of analogy with the ordinary operations of God. We believe that He is everywhere present in the material world, and controls the operations of natural causes. We know that He causes the grass to grow, and gives rain and fruitful seasons. We believe that He exercises a like control over the minds of men, turning them as the rivers of water are turned. All religion, natural and revealed, is founded on the assumption of this providential government of God. Besides this, we believe in the gracious operations of his Spirit, by which He works in the hearts of his people to will and to do; we believe that faith, repentance, and holy living are due to the ever-present influence of the Holy Spirit. If, then, this wonder-working God everywhere operates in nature and in grace, why should it be deemed incredible that holy men should speak as they were moved by the Holy Ghost, so that they should say just what He would have them say, so that their words should be his words.

After all Christ is the great object of the Christian's faith. We believe him and we believe everything else on his authority. He hands us the Old Testament and tells us that it is the Word of God; that its authors spoke by the Spirit; that the Scriptures cannot be broken. And we believe on his testimony. His testimony to his Apostles is no less explicit, although given in a different way. He promised to give them a mouth and a wisdom which their adversaries could not gainsay or resist. He told them to take no thought what they should say, "For the Holy Ghost shall teach you in the same hour what ye ought to say." (Luke 12:12.) "It is not ye that speak but the Spirit of your Father which speaketh in you." He said to them "he that receiveth you receiveth me"; and He prayed for those who should believe on Him through their word. We believe the Scriptures, therefore, because Christ declares them to be the Word of God. Heaven and earth may pass away, but his word cannot pass away. . . .

I. OBJECTIONS

A large class of the objections to the doctrine of inspiration, which for many minds are the most effective, arise from the rejection of one or other of the presumptions specified on a preceding page. . . . But although the theologian may rightfully dismiss all objections founded on the denial of the common principles of natural and revealed religion, there are others which cannot be thus summarily disposed of. The most obvious of these is, that the sacred writers contradict each other, and that they teach error. . . . The objection under consideration, namely, that the Bible contains errors, divides itself into two. The first, that the sacred writers contradict themselves, or one the other. The second, that the Bible teaches what is inconsistent with the facts of history or science.

As to the former of these objections, it would require, not a volume, but volumes to discuss all the cases of alleged discrepancies. All that can be expected here is a few general remarks: (1) These apparent discrepancies, although numerous, are for the most part trivial; relating in most cases to numbers or dates. (2) The great majority of them are only apparent, and yield to careful examination. (3) Many of them may fairly be ascribed to errors of transcribers. (4) The marvel and the miracle is that there are so few of any real importance. . . .

The second great objection to the plenary inspiration of the Scripture is that it teaches what is inconsistent with historical and scientific truth. Here again it is to be remarked, (1) That we must distinguish between what the sacred writers themselves thought or believed, and what they teach. They may have believed that the sun moves round the earth, but they do not so teach. (2) The language of the Bible is the language of common life; and the language of common life is founded on apparent, and not upon scientific truth. It would be ridiculous to refuse to speak of the sun rising and setting, because we know that it is not a satellite of our planet. (3) There is a great distinction between theories and facts. Theories are of men. Facts are of God. The Bible often contradicts the former, never the latter. (4) There is also a distinction to be made between the Bible and our interpretation. The latter may come into competition with settled facts; and then it must yield. Science has in many things taught the Church how to understand the Scriptures. The Bible was for ages understood and explained according to the Ptolemaic system of the universe; it is now explained without doing the least violence to its language, according to the Copernican system. Christians have commonly believed that the earth has existed only a few thousands of years. If geologists finally prove that it has existed for myriads of ages, it will be found that the first chapter of Genesis is in full accord with the facts, and that the last results of science are embodied on the first page of the Bible. It may cost the Church a severe struggle to give up one interpretation and adopt another, as it did in the seventeenth century, but no real evil need be apprehended. The Bible has stood, and still stands in the presence of the whole scientific world with its claims unshaken.[12] Men hostile or indifferent to

---

[12] Hodge would yield in astronomy and geology what he would not yield in biology. See his *What Is Darwinism?* (1874). The relation of Hodge's emphasis on the precise *words* of Scripture and the distinctions here made, especially (1) and (3), would force his son, A. A. Hodge, and Benjamin Warfield to a more rigidly defined theory. Recognizing the possibility for errors of transcription, they would demand historical critics to prove that the "original autographs" had been in error. See Loetscher, *The Broadening Church*, pp. 29–31. [Ed.]

its truths may, on insufficient grounds, or because of their personal opinions, reject its authority; but, even in the judgment of the greatest authorities in science, its teachings cannot fairly be impeached. . . .

Maimonides, the greatest of the Jewish doctors since the time of Christ, taught as early as the twelfth century that the sacred writers of the Old Testament enjoyed different degrees of divine guidance. He placed the inspiration of the Law much above that of the Prophets; and that of the Prophets higher than that of the Hagiographa. This idea of different degrees of inspiration was adopted by many theologians, and in England for a long time it was the common mode of representation. The idea was that the writers of Kings and Chronicles needed less, and that they received less of the divine assistance than Isaiah or St. John.

In attempting to prove the doctrine of plenary inspiration the arguments which bear against all these forms of partial inspiration were given or suggested. The question is not an open one. It is not what theory is in itself most reasonable or plausible, but simply, What does the Bible teach on the subject? If our Lord and his Apostles declare the Old Testament to be the Word of God; that its authors spake as they were moved by the Holy Ghost; that what they said, the Spirit said; if they refer to the facts and to the very words of Scripture as of divine authority; and if the same infallible divine guidance was promised to the writers of the New Testament, and claimed by themselves; and if their claim was authenticated by God himself; then there is no room for, as there is no need of, these theories of partial inspiration. The whole Bible was written under such an influence as preserved its human authors from all error, and makes it for the Church the infallible rule of faith and practice.

THE COMPLETENESS OF THE SCRIPTURES

By the completeness of the Scriptures is meant that they contain all the extant revelations of God designed to be a rule of faith and practice to the Church. It is not denied that God reveals himself, even his eternal power and Godhead, by his works, and has done so from the beginning of the world. But all the truths thus revealed are clearly made known in his written Word. Nor is it denied that there may have been, and probably were, books written by inspired men, which are no longer in existence. Much less is it denied that Christ and his Apostles delivered many discourses which were not recorded, and which, could they now be known and authenticated, would be of equal authority with the books now regarded as canonical. All that Protestants insist upon is, that the Bible contains all the extant revelations of God, which He designed to be the rule of faith and practice for his Church; so that nothing can rightfully be imposed on the consciences of men as truth or duty which is not taught directly or by necessary implication in the Holy Scriptures. This excludes all unwritten traditions, not only; but also all decrees of the visible Church; all resolutions of conventions, or other public bodies, declaring this or that to be right or wrong, true or false. The people of God are bound by nothing but the Word of God. On this subject little need be said. The completeness of Scripture, as a rule of faith, is a corollary of the Protestant doctrine concerning tradition. If that be true, the former must also be true. . . . If we would stand fast in the liberty wherewith Christ has made us free, we must adhere to the principle that in matters of religion and morals the Scriptures alone have authority to bind the conscience.

PERSPICUITY OF THE SCRIPTURES. THE RIGHT OF PRIVATE JUDGMENT

The Bible is a plain book. It is intelligible by the people. And they have the right, and are bound to read and interpret it for themselves; so that their faith may rest on the testimony of the Scriptures, and not on that of the Church. Such is the doctrine of Protestants on this subject.

It is not denied that the Scriptures contain many things hard to be understood; that they require diligent study; that all men need the guidance of the Holy Spirit in order to right knowledge and true faith. But it is maintained that in all things necessary to salvation they are sufficiently plain to be understood even by the unlearned.

It is not denied that the people, learned and unlearned, in order to the proper understanding of the Scriptures, should not only compare Scripture with Scripture, and avail themselves of all the means in their power to aid them in their search after the truth, but they should also pay the greatest deference to the faith of the Church. If the Scriptures be a plain book, and the Spirit performs the functions of a teacher to all the children of God, it follows inevitably that they must agree in all essential matters in their interpretation of the Bible. And from that fact it follows that for an individual Christian to dissent from the faith of the universal Church (*i. e.*, the body of true believers), is tantamount to dissenting from the Scriptures themselves.

What Protestants deny on this subject is, that Christ has appointed any officer, or class of officers, in his Church to whose interpretation of the Scriptures the people are bound to submit as of final authority. What they affirm is that He has made it obligatory upon every man to search the Scriptures for himself, and determine on his own discretion what they require him to believe and to do. . . .

THE PEOPLE COMMANDED
TO SEARCH THE SCRIPTURES

The Scriptures are not only addressed to the people, but the people were called upon to study them, and to teach them unto their children. It was one of the most frequently recurring injunctions to parents under the old dispensation, to teach the Law unto their children, that they again might teach it unto theirs. The "holy oracles" were committed to the people, to be taught by the people; and taught immediately out of the Scriptures, that the truth might be retained in its purity. Thus our Lord commanded the people to search the Scriptures, saying,

"They are they which testify of me." (John 5:39.) He assumed that they were able to understand what the Old Testament said of the Messiah, although its teachings had been misunderstood by the scribes and elders, and by the whole Sanhedrin. Paul rejoiced that Timothy had from his youth known the Holy Scriptures, which were able to make him wise unto salvation. He said to the Galatians (1:8, 9), "Though we, or an angel from heaven, . . . if any *man* preach any other gospel unto you than that ye have received, let him be accursed." This implies two things: first, that the Galatian Christians, the people, had a right to sit in judgment on the teaching of an Apostle, or of an angel from heaven; and secondly, that they had an infallible rule by which that judgment was to be determined, namely, a previous authenticated revelation of God. If, then, the Bible recognizes the right of the people to judge of the teaching of Apostles and angels, they are not to be denied the right of judging of the doctrines of bishops and priests. The principle laid down by the Apostle is precisely that long before given by Moses (Deut. 8:1–3), who tells the people that if a prophet should arise, although he worked wonders, they were not to believe or obey him, if he taught them anything contrary to the Word of God. This again assumes that the people had the ability and the right to judge, and that they had an infallible rule of judgment. It implies, moreover, that their salvation depended upon their judging rightly. For if they allowed these false teachers, robed in sacred vestments and surrounded by the insignia of authority, to lead them from the truth, they would inevitably perish.

4. It need hardly be remarked that this right of private judgment is the great safeguard of civil and religious liberty. If the Bible be admitted to be the infallible rule of faith and practice in accordance with which men are bound on the peril of their souls, to frame their creed and conduct; and if there be a set of men who have the exclusive right of interpreting the Scripture, and who are authorized to impose their interpretations on the people as of divine authority, then they may impose on them

what conditions of salvation they see fit. And the men who have the salvation of the people in their hands are their absolute masters. Both reason and experience fully sustain the dictum of Chillingworth, when he says, "He that would usurp an absolute lordship and tyranny over any people, need not put himself to the trouble and difficulty of abrogating and disannulling the laws made to maintain the common liberty; for he may frustrate their intent, and compass his own design as well, if he can get the power and authority to interpret them as he pleases, and add to them what he pleases, and to have his interpretations and additions stand for laws; if he can rule his people by his laws, and his laws by his lawyers."[13] This is precisely what the Church of Rome has done, and thereby established a tyranny for which there is no parallel in the history of the world. . . . This cannot be the foundation of the faith of God's elect. That foundation is the testimony of God himself speaking his word, and authenticated as divine by the testimony of the Spirit with and by the truth in the heart of the believer.

RULES OF INTERPRETATION

If every man has the right, and is bound to read the Scriptures, and to judge for himself what they teach, he must have certain rules to guide him in the exercise of this privilege and duty. These rules are not arbitrary. They are not imposed by human authority. They have no binding force which does not flow from their own intrinsic truth and propriety. They are few and simple.

1. The words of Scripture are to be taken in their plain historical sense. That is, they must be taken in the sense attached

---

[13] William Chillingworth, *The Religion of Protestants, A Safe Way to Salvation* (1637), Answer II, Par. 1. Quoted from *Works* (Philadelphia: Hooker & Agnew, 1841), p. 105. Chillingworth (1602–1644), a sometime convert to Rome who returned to Anglicanism, was a renowned apologist for Protestantism, though a latitudinarian liberal and not a precursor of Hodge. [Ed.]

to them in the age and by the people to whom they were addressed. This only assumes that the sacred writers were honest, and meant to be understood.

2. If the Scriptures be what they claim to be, the word of God, they are the work of one mind, and that mind divine. From this it follows that Scripture cannot contradict Scripture. God cannot teach in one place anything which is inconsistent with what He teaches in another. Hence Scripture must explain Scripture. If a passage admits of different interpretations, that only can be the true one which agrees with what the Bible teaches elsewhere on the same subject. If the Scriptures teach that the Son is the same in substance and equal in power and glory with the Father, then when the Son says, "The Father is greater than I," the superiority must be understood in a manner consistent with this equality. It must refer either to subordination as to the mode of subsistence and operation, or it must be official. A king's son may say, "My father is greater than I," although personally his father's equal. This rule of interpretation is sometimes called the analogy of Scripture, and sometimes the analogy of faith. There is no material difference in the meaning of the two expressions.

3. The Scriptures are to be interpreted under the guidance of the Holy Spirit, which guidance is to be humbly and earnestly sought. The ground of this rule is twofold: First, the Spirit is promised as a guide and teacher. He was to come to lead the people of God into the knowledge of the truth. And secondly, the Scriptures teach, that "the natural man receiveth not the things of the Spirit of God: for they are foolishness unto him; neither can he know them, because they are spiritually discerned." (I Cor. 2: 14.) The unrenewed mind is naturally blind to spiritual truth. His heart is in opposition to the things of God. Congeniality of mind is necessary to the proper apprehension of divine things. As only those who have a moral nature can discern moral truth, so those only who are spiritually minded can truly receive the things of the Spirit.

The fact that all the true people of God in every age and in every part of the Church, in the exercise of their private judgment, in accordance with the simple rules above stated, agree as to the meaning of Scripture in all things necessary either in faith or practice, is a decisive proof of the perspicuity of the Bible, and of the safety of allowing the people the enjoyment of the divine right of private judgment.

VI

RALPH WALDO EMERSON

Transcendentalist Prophet

Ralph Waldo Emerson (1803–1882)[1] is less in need of an introduction than any person represented in this volume, possibly less
in need than any American thinker or writer. Indeed, Emerson
is so taken for granted as a household possession that many would
doubt the propriety of including him in a volume of theology.
Yet he was, as George E. Woodberry long ago insisted, "exclusively a man of religion" whose every thought is corollary to his
religious premises. He left the churches behind in the 1830's, but
he never, in effect, left the pulpit; and if the Transcendental
movement was primarily a "religious demonstration," Emerson
above all made it so. Moreover, he was able to transmit his concern for "religious affections" and the claims of the soul to those
who were alienated from the evangelical churches. While guardi-
ans of orthodoxy fulminated, he, in due course, infiltrated the
textbooks, the schoolrooms, and the parlors of the nation. Maurice Maeterlinck beautifully put it: "Behold Emerson, the good
morning shepherd of pale meadows, green with a new optimism,
both natural and plausible. . . . He came for many just when he
should have come, and just when they had extreme need of explanations." By the same token, however, Emerson and his co-

---

[1] See Introduction, pp. 48–50; 58–62.

horts are more responsible than Eleanor Porter for Pollyanna's prominence in the American pantheon, and for this reason, too, he needs to be reread in a theological context.

Quite aside from his broad influence on American attitudes, Emerson had a direct impact on theology. With an evocativeness none of his contemporaries could equal, he conveyed a profound new sense of religion's nature and role. His point of view resembled Schleiermacher's great romantic answer to the Enlightenment. Emerson, too, castigated the "pale negations" of rationalistic religion. He dwelt on man's religious feeling and drew out the idealistic and pantheistic implications of this primary intuition. Proclaiming "the identity of the law of gravitation with purity of heart," he proclaimed "that Duty . . . is one thing with Science, with Beauty, and with Joy." If St. Paul's preaching to the Athenians of him "in whom we live, and move, and have our being" (Acts 17:28) became a favorite nineteenth-century sermon text, Emerson was in part accountable. He also awakened men to the religions of the East and forced into view a new set of questions about Christianity and its mission. Though others brought far more erudition and systematic reasoning to the subject, he is the great native source of American liberal theology.

Emerson was the son of the urbane minister of Boston's First Church. After receiving his college and divinity education at Harvard he became the minister of the Second Church. He resigned from this position in 1832, chiefly because of reservations concerning the Lord's Supper, and retired to Concord where he lived until his death, except for many travels as an itinerant lecturer, a tour of Europe, and a few other journeys. The chief incidents in his life are readings, meditations, conversations, and publications. He fulfilled the usual duties of a townsman, preached on Sunday in the early years, took a stand on slavery, met with the informal "Transcendental Club" occasionally, and

edited THE DIAL (a Transcendental quarterly) for two years—but
never became a crusader, an organizer, or the self-conscious leader
of a "school of thought."

The sources of Emerson's thought, like the influences it had,
are difficult to trace. Yet the similarity of his message to the
British and German romantics is anything but coincidental. In
"The American Scholar" (1837) he pays tribute to Carlyle, Coleridge, and Wordsworth, and behind them were Schleiermacher,
Herder, Schelling, and Goethe. But Emerson's reading ranged
widely: Plato, Plotinus, the religious scriptures of Asia, and Swedenborg. There was also Channing and his heritage. And all of
this he shaped in his own deeply personal way and in response to
his own needs. The synthetic result can only be called Emersonian, and nowhere does its theological import attain more
characteristic or forthright expression than in the Divinity School
Address in July 1838, delivered at Harvard. For that reason,
no doubt, this became the most controversial, the most clearly
event-making utterance of his entire career.

The form of the Address varies little from a classic ordination
sermon. It is, in fact, a charge to a whole class of future ministers.
As a Unitarian manifesto it ranks with those of Channing in 1819
and Parker in 1841. Much of its content derives from his own
experience of the Church—his notebooks as usual providing both
general and particular ideas—with some of the generalizations
stemming from very particular post-mortems (there is no better
word!) on the sermons of Concord's minister, Barzillai Frost.
Though his summons brought down the wrath of orthodox Unitarians and rocked that denomination to its roots, he never replied to his critics or returned directly to the subject, except in
the sense that almost all that he ever wrote involved this theme.
The Address, therefore, merits a fresh and deliberate reading.
Those who regard it as familiar should be sure they penetrate

Emerson's dicta on Reason and the Understanding, the Law of laws and the moral sentiment, intuition and the religious sentiment. None of us, moreover, should forget Jonathan Bishop's warning that Emerson was ever "entrusting the essence of his meanings to the qualities of his language." He is not easily paraphrased. The text used here is precisely that which Emerson himself saw through the press in 1849.

The Divinity School Address

Delivered before the Senior Class at the Harvard Divinity School,
Cambridge on July 15, 1838

In this refulgent summer, it has been a luxury to draw the breath of life. The grass grows, the buds burst, the meadow is spotted with fire and gold in the tint of flowers. The air is full of birds, and sweet with the breath of the pine, the balm-of-Gilead, and the new hay. Night brings no gloom to the heart with its welcome shade. Through the transparent darkness the stars pour their almost spiritual rays. Man under them seems a young child, and his huge globe a toy. The cool night bathes the world as with a river, and prepares his eyes again for the crimson dawn. The mystery of nature was never displayed more happily. The corn and the wine have been freely dealt to all creatures, and the never-broken silence with which the old bounty goes forward, has not yielded yet one word of explanation. One is constrained to respect the perfection of this world, in which our senses converse. How wide; how rich; what invitation from every property it gives to every faculty of man! In its fruitful soils; in its navigable sea; in its mountains of metal and stone; in its forests of all woods; in its animals; in its chemical ingredients;

From Ralph Waldo Emerson, *Nature; Addresses, and Lectures* (Boston and Cambridge: James Munroe and Company, 1849), pp. 113–146.

in the powers and path of light, heat, attraction, and life, it is well worth the pith and heart of great men to subdue and enjoy it. The planters, the mechanics, the inventors, the astronomers, the builders of cities, and the captains, history delights to honor.

But when the mind opens, and reveals the laws which traverse the universe, and make things what they are, then shrinks the great world at once into a mere illustration and fable of this mind.[1] What am I? and What is? asks the human spirit with a curiosity new-kindled, but never to be quenched. Behold these out-running laws, which our imperfect apprehension can see tend this way and that, but not come full circle. Behold these infinite relations, so like, so unlike; many, yet one. I would study, I would know, I would admire forever. These works of thought have been the entertainments of the human spirit in all ages.

A more secret, sweet, and overpowering beauty appears to man when his heart and mind open to the sentiment of virtue. Then he is instructed in what is above him. He learns that his being is without bound; that, to the good, to the perfect, he is born, low as he now lies in evil and weakness. That which he venerates is still his own, though he has not realized it yet. *He ought.* He knows the sense of that grand word, though his analysis fails entirely to render account of it. When in innocency, or when by intellectual perception, he attains to say,—'I love the Right; Truth is beautiful within and without, forevermore. Virtue, I am thine: save me: use me: thee will I serve, day and night, in great, in small, that I may be not virtuous, but virtue;' —then is the end of the creation answered, and God is well pleased.

The sentiment of virtue is a reverence and delight in the presence of certain divine laws. It perceives that this homely game

---

[1] In *Nature* Emerson had said, "Every natural fact is a symbol of some spiritual fact . . . . Parts of speech are metaphors, because the whole of nature is a metaphor of the human mind. The laws of moral nature answer to those of matter as face to face in a glass." *Nature; Addresses, and Lectures,* pp. 24, 30. See also Bushnell on language, pp. 319–370. [Ed.]

of life we play, covers, under what seem foolish details, principles that astonish. The child amidst his baubles, is learning the action of light, motion, gravity, muscular force; and in the game of human life, love, fear, justice, appetite, man, and God, interact. These laws refuse to be adequately stated. They will not be written out on paper, or spoken by the tongue. They elude our persevering thought; yet we read them hourly in each other's faces, in each other's actions, in our own remorse. The moral traits which are all globed into every virtuous act and thought, —in speech, we must sever, and describe or suggest by painful enumeration of many particulars. Yet, as this sentiment is the essence of all religion, let me guide your eye to the precise objects of the sentiment, by an enumeration of some of those classes of facts in which this element is conspicuous.

The intuition of the moral sentiment is an insight of the perfection of the laws of the soul. These laws execute themselves. They are out of time, out of space, and not subject to circumstance. Thus; in the soul of man there is a justice whose retributions are instant and entire. He who does a good deed, is instantly ennobled. He who does a mean deed, is by the action itself contracted. He who puts off impurity, thereby puts on purity. If a man is at heart just, then in so far is he God; the safety of God, the immortality of God, the majesty of God do enter into that man with justice. If a man dissemble, deceive, he deceives himself, and goes out of acquaintance with his own being. A man in the view of absolute goodness, adores, with total humility. Every step so downward, is a step upward. The man who renounces himself, comes to himself.

See how this rapid intrinsic energy worketh everywhere, righting wrongs, correcting appearances, and bringing up facts to a harmony with thoughts. Its operation in life, though slow to the senses, is, at last, as sure as in the soul. By it, a man is made the Providence to himself, dispensing good to his goodness, and evil to his sin. Character is always known. Thefts never enrich; alms never impoverish; murder will speak out of stone walls. The least admixture of a lie,—for example, the taint of vanity, the least attempt to make a good impression, a favorable appearance,—will instantly vitiate the effect. But speak the truth, and all nature and all spirits help you with unexpected furtherance. Speak the truth, and all things alive or brute are vouchers, and the very roots of the grass underground there, do seem to stir and move to bear you witness. See again the perfection of the Law as it applies itself to the affections, and becomes the law of society. As we are, so we associate. The good, by affinity, seek the good; the vile, by affinity, the vile. Thus of their own volition, souls proceed into heaven, into hell.

These facts have always suggested to man the sublime creed, that the world is not the product of manifold power, but of one will, of one mind; and that one mind is everywhere active, in each ray of the star, in each wavelet of the pool; and whatever opposes that will, is everywhere balked and baffled, because things are made so, and not otherwise. Good is positive. Evil is merely privative, not absolute: it is like cold, which is the privation of heat. All evil is so much death or nonentity. Benevolence is absolute and real. So much benevolence as a man hath, so much life hath he. For all things proceed out of this same spirit, which is differently named love, justice, temperance, in its different applications, just as the ocean receives different names on the several shores which it washes. All things proceed out of the same spirit, and all things conspire with it. Whilst a man seeks good ends, he is strong by the whole strength of nature. In so far as he roves from these ends, he bereaves himself of power, of auxiliaries; his being shrinks out of all remote channels, he becomes less and less, a mote, a point, until absolute badness is absolute death.

The perception of this law of laws awakens in the mind a sentiment which we call the religious sentiment, and which makes our highest happiness. Wonderful is its power to charm and to command. It is a mountain air. It is the embalmer of the world. It is myrrh and storax, and chlorine and rosemary. It makes the sky and the hills sublime, and the silent song of the stars is it. By it, is the universe made safe and habitable, not by science or power. Thought may work cold and intransitive in things, and find no end or unity; but the dawn of the sentiment of virtue on the heart, gives and is the assurance that Law is sovereign over all natures; and the worlds, time, space, eternity, do seem to break out into joy.

This sentiment is divine and deifying. It is the beatitude of man. It makes him illimitable. Through it, the soul first knows itself. It corrects the capital mistake of the infant man, who seeks to be great by following the great, and hopes to derive advantages *from another*,—by showing the fountain of all good to be in himself, and that he, equally with every man, is an inlet into the deeps of Reason. When he says, "I ought;" when love warms him; when he chooses, warned from on high, the good and great deed; then, deep melodies wander through his soul from Supreme Wisdom. Then he can worship, and be enlarged by his worship; for he can never go behind this sentiment. In the sublimest flights of the soul, rectitude is never surmounted, love is never outgrown.

This sentiment lies at the foundation of society, and successively creates all forms of worship. The principle of veneration never dies out. Man fallen into superstition, into sensuality, is never quite without the visions of the moral sentiment. In like manner, all the expressions of this sentiment are sacred and permanent in proportion to their purity. The expressions of this sentiment affect us more than all other compositions. The sentences of the oldest time, which ejaculate this piety, are still fresh and fragrant. This thought dwelled always deepest in the minds of men in the devout and contemplative East; not alone in Palestine, where it reached its purest expression, but in Egypt, in Persia, in India, in China. Europe has always owed to oriental genius, its divine impulses. What these holy bards said, all sane men found agreeable and true. And the unique impression of Jesus upon mankind, whose name is not so much written as ploughed into the history of this world, is proof of the subtle virtue of this infusion.

Meantime, whilst the doors of the temple stand open, night and day, before every man, and the oracles of this truth cease never, it is guarded by one stern condition; this, namely; it is an intuition. It cannot be received at second hand. Truly speaking, it is not instruction, but provocation, that I can receive from another soul. What he announces, I must find true in me, or wholly reject; and on his word, or as his second, be he who he may, I can accept nothing. On the contrary, the absence of this primary faith is the presence of degradation. As is the flood so is the ebb. Let this faith depart, and the very words it spake, and the things it made, become false and hurtful. Then falls the church, the state, art, letters, life. The doctrine of the divine nature being forgotten, a sickness infects and dwarfs the constitution. Once man was all; now he is an appendage, a nuisance. And because the indwelling Supreme Spirit cannot wholly be got rid of, the doctrine of it suffers this perversion, that the divine nature is attributed to one or two persons, and denied to all the rest, and denied with fury. The doctrine of inspiration is lost; the base doctrine of the majority of voices, usurps the place of the doctrine of the soul. Miracles, prophecy, poetry; the ideal life, the holy life, exist as ancient history merely; they are not in the belief, nor in the aspiration of society; but, when suggested, seem ridiculous. Life is comic or pitiful, as soon as the high ends of being fade out of sight, and man becomes nearsighted, and can only attend to what addresses the senses.

These general views, which, whilst they are general, none will contest, find abundant illustration in the history of religion, and especially in the history of the Christian church. In that, all of us have had our birth and nurture. The truth contained in that, you, my young friends, are now setting forth to teach. As the Cultus, or established worship of the civilized world, it has great historical interest for us. Of its blessed words, which have been the consolation of humanity, you need not that I should speak. I shall endeavor to discharge my duty to you, on this occasion, by pointing out two errors in its administration, which daily appear more gross from the point of view we have just now taken.

Jesus Christ belonged to the true race of prophets. He saw with open eye the mystery of the soul. Drawn by its severe harmony, ravished with its beauty, he lived in it, and had his being there. Alone in all history, he estimated the greatness of man. One man was true to what is in you and me. He saw that God incarnates himself in man, and evermore goes forth anew to take possession of his world. He said, in this jubilee of sublime emotion, 'I am divine. Through me, God acts; through me, speaks. Would you see God, see me; or, see thee, when thou also thinkest as I now think.' But what a distortion did his doctrine and memory suffer in the same, in the next, and the following ages! There is no doctrine of the Reason which will bear to be taught by the Understanding.[2] The understanding caught this high chant from the poet's lips, and said, in the next age, 'This was Jehovah come down out of heaven. I will kill you, if you say he was a man.' The idioms of his language, and the figures of his rhetoric, have usurped the place of his truth; and churches are not built on his principles, but on his tropes. Christianity became a Mythus, as the poetic teaching of Greece and of Egypt, before.[3] He spoke of miracles; for he felt that man's life was a miracle, and all that man doth, and he knew that this daily miracle shines, as the character ascends. But the word Miracle, as pronounced by Christian churches, gives a false im-

---

[2] The chief source of Transcendentalist distinctions between the Reason and the Understanding was Samuel Taylor Coleridge. See his *Aids to Reflection,* especially the discussion of No. VIII among the "Aphorisms on That Which Is Indeed Spiritual Religion." The Reason unlike the Understanding transcended sense-derived knowledge. [Ed.]

[3] Compare Emerson's doctrine with the Neo-Platonic writings attributed to the so-called Egyptian Hermes; Walter Scott, *Hermetica* (Oxford: Clarendon Press, 1924). [Ed.]

pression; it is Monster.[4] It is not one with the blowing clover and the falling rain.

He felt respect for Moses and the prophets; but no unfit tenderness at postponing their initial revelations, to the hour and the man that now is; to the eternal revelation in the heart. Thus was he a true man. Having seen that the law in us is commanding, he would not suffer it to be commanded. Boldly, with hand, and heart, and life, he declared it was God. Thus is he, as I think, the only soul in history who has appreciated the worth of a man.

1. In this point of view we become very sensible of the first defect of historical Christianity. Historical Christianity has fallen into the error that corrupts all attempts to communicate religion. As it appears to us, and as it has appeared for ages, it is not the doctrine of the soul, but an exaggeration of the personal, the positive, the ritual. It has dwelt, it dwells, with noxious exaggeration about the *person* of Jesus. The soul knows no persons. It invites every man to expand to the full circle of the universe, and will have no preferences but those of spontaneous love. But by this eastern monarchy of a Christianity, which indolence and fear have built, the friend of man is made the injurer of man. The manner in which his name is surrounded with expressions, which were once sallies of admiration and love, but are now petrified into official titles, kills all generous sympathy and liking. All who hear me, feel, that the language that describes Christ to Europe and America, is not the style of friendship and enthusiasm to a good and noble heart, but is appropriated and formal,—paints a demigod, as the Orientals or the Greeks would describe Osiris or Apollo.[5] Accept the in-

---

[4] Cf. Channing on miracles, p. 200. [Ed.]

[5] These pages are the *locus classicus* in American literature of a major liberal interpretation of Jesus. Later in the century the religious-historical school would seek to document this relationship of early Christianity and the mystery religions. See Rudolf Bultmann, *Primitive Christianity in Its Contemporary Setting* (New York: Meridian Books, 1956), pp. 135–179. [Ed.]

jurious impositions of our early catechetical instruction, and even honesty and self-denial were but splendid sins, if they did not wear the Christian name. One would rather be

'A pagan, suckled in a creed outworn,'[6]

than to be defrauded of his manly right in coming into nature, and finding not names and places, not land and professions, but even virtue and truth foreclosed and monopolized. You shall not be a man even. You shall not own the world; you shall not dare, and live after the infinite Law that is in you, and in company with the infinite Beauty which heaven and earth reflect to you in all lovely forms; but you must subordinate your nature to Christ's nature; you must accept our interpretations; and take his portrait as the vulgar draw it.

That is always best which gives me to myself. The sublime is excited in me by the great stoical doctrine, Obey thyself. That which shows God in me, fortifies me. That which shows God out of me, makes me a wart and a wen. There is no longer a necessary reason for my being. Already the long shadows of untimely oblivion creep over me, and I shall decease forever.

The divine bards are the friends of my virtue, of my intellect, of my strength. They admonish me, that the gleams which flash across my mind, are not mine, but God's; that they had the like, and were not disobedient to the heavenly vision. So I love them. Noble provocations go out from them, inviting me to resist evil; to subdue the world; and to Be. And thus by his holy thoughts, Jesus serves us, and thus only. To aim to convert a man by miracles, is a profanation of the soul. A true conversion, a true Christ, is now, as always, to be made, by the reception of beautiful sentiments. It is true that a great and rich soul, like his, falling among the simple, does so preponderate, that, as his did, it names the world. The world seems to them to exist for him, and they have not yet drunk so deeply of his sense, as to see that

---

6 William Wordsworth, "The World is too much with us." [Ed.]

only by coming again to themselves, or to God in themselves, can they grow forevermore. It is a low benefit to give me something; it is a high benefit to enable me to do somewhat of myself. The time is coming when all men will see, that the gift of God to the soul is not a vaunting, overpowering, excluding sanctity, but a sweet, natural goodness, a goodness like thine and mine, and that so invites thine and mine to be and to grow.

The injustice of the vulgar tone of preaching is not less flagrant to Jesus, than to the souls which it profanes. The preachers do not see that they make his gospel not glad, and shear him of the locks of beauty and the attributes of heaven. When I see a majestic Epaminondas, or Washington; when I see among my contemporaries, a true orator, an upright judge, a dear friend; when I vibrate to the melody and fancy of a poem; I see beauty that is to be desired. And so lovely, and with yet more entire consent of my human being, sounds in my ear the severe music of the bards that have sung of the true God in all ages. Now do not degrade the life and dialogues of Christ out of the circle of this charm, by insulation and peculiarity. Let them lie as they befel, alive and warm, part of human life, and of the landscape, and of the cheerful day.

2. The second defect of the traditionary and limited way of using the mind of Christ is a consequence of the first; this, namely; that the Moral Nature, that Law of laws, whose revelations introduce greatness,—yea, God himself, into the open soul, is not explored as the fountain of the established teaching in society. Men have come to speak of the revelation as somewhat long ago given and done, as if God were dead. The injury to faith throttles the preacher; and the goodliest of institutions becomes an uncertain and inarticulate voice.

It is very certain that it is the effect of conversation with the beauty of the soul, to beget a desire and need to impart to others the same knowledge and love. If utterance is denied, the thought lies like a burden on the man. Always the seer is a sayer. Somehow his dream is told: somehow he publishes it with solemn joy: sometimes with pencil on canvas; sometimes with chisel on stone; sometimes in towers and aisles of granite, his soul's worship is builded; sometimes in anthems of indefinite music; but clearest and most permanent, in words.

The man enamored of this excellency, becomes its priest or poet. The office is coeval with the world. But observe the condition, the spiritual limitation of the office. The spirit only can teach. Not any profane man, not any sensual, not any liar, not any slave can teach, but only he can give, who has; he only can create, who is. The man on whom the soul descends, through whom the soul speaks, alone can teach. Courage, piety, love, wisdom, can teach; and every man can open his door to these angels, and they shall bring him the gift of tongues. But the man who aims to speak as books enable, as synods use, as the fashion guides, and as interest commands, babbles. Let him hush.

To this holy office, you propose to devote yourselves. I wish you may feel your call in throbs of desire and hope. The office is the first in the world. It is of that reality, that it cannot suffer the deduction of any falsehood. And it is my duty to say to you, that the need was never greater of new revelation than now. From the views I have already expressed, you will infer the sad conviction, which I share, I believe, with numbers, of the universal decay and now almost death of faith in society. The soul is not preached. The Church seems to totter to its fall, almost all life extinct.[7] On this occasion, any complaisance would be criminal, which told you, whose hope and commission it is to preach the faith of Christ, that the faith of Christ is preached.

It is time that this ill-suppressed murmur of all thoughtful men against the famine of our churches; this moaning of the

---

[7] The 1830's were one of the great evangelical revival times in American history; and, for that reason perhaps, the time of turning in the antislavery movement. Emerson's statement on *intellectual* "famine in the churches" would be hard to deny, however, unless one accent the newer impulses which he in part represented. [Ed.]

heart because it is bereaved of the consolation, the hope, the grandeur, that come alone out of the culture of the moral nature; should be heard through the sleep of indolence, and over the din of routine. This great and perpetual office of the preacher is not discharged. Preaching is the expression of the moral sentiment in application to the duties of life. In how many churches, by how many prophets, tell me, is man made sensible that he is an infinite Soul; that the earth and heavens are passing into his mind; that he is drinking forever the soul of God? Where now sounds the persuasion, that by its very melody imparadises my heart, and so affirms its own origin in heaven? Where shall I hear words such as in elder ages drew men to leave all and follow,—father and mother, house and land, wife and child? Where shall I hear these august laws of moral being so pronounced, as to fill my ear, and I feel ennobled by the offer of my uttermost action and passion? The test of the true faith, certainly, should be its power to charm and command the soul, as the laws of nature control the activity of the hands,— so commanding that we find pleasure and honor in obeying. The faith should blend with the light of rising and of setting suns, with the flying cloud, the singing bird, and the breath of flowers. But now the priest's Sabbath has lost the splendor of nature; it is unlovely; we are glad when it is done; we can make, we do make, even sitting in our pews, a far better, holier, sweeter, for ourselves.

Whenever the pupit is usurped by a formalist, then is the worshipper defrauded and disconsolate. We shrink as soon as the prayers begin, which do not uplift, but smite and offend us. We are fain to wrap our cloaks about us, and secure, as best we can, a solitude that hears not. I once heard a preacher who sorely tempted me to say, I would go to church no more. Men go, thought I, where they are wont to go, else had no soul entered the temple in the afternoon. A snow storm was falling around us. The snow storm was real; the preacher merely spectral; and the eye felt the sad contrast in looking at him, and then out of the window behind him, into the beautiful meteor of the snow. He had lived in vain. He had no one word intimating that he had laughed or wept, was married or in love, had been commended, or cheated, or chagrined. If he had ever lived and acted, we were none the wiser for it. The capital secret of his profession, namely, to convert life into truth, he had not learned. Not one fact in all his experience, had he yet imported into his doctrine. This man had ploughed, and planted, and talked, and bought, and sold; he had read books; he had eaten and drunken; his head aches; his heart throbs; he smiles and suffers; yet was there not a surmise, a hint, in all the discourse, that he had ever lived at all. Not a line did he draw out of real history. The true preacher can be known by this, that he deals out to the people his life,—life passed through the fire of thought. But of the bad preacher, it could not be told from his sermon, what age of the world he fell in; whether he had a father or a child; whether he was a freeholder or a pauper; whether he was a citizen or a countryman; or any other fact of his biography. It seemed strange that the people should come to church. It seemed as if their houses were very unentertaining, that they should prefer this thoughtless clamor. It shows that there is a commanding attraction in the moral sentiment, that can lend a faint tint of light to dulness and ignorance, coming in its name and place. The good hearer is sure he has been touched sometimes; is sure there is somewhat to be reached, and some word that can reach it. When he listens to these vain words, he comforts himself by their relation to his remembrance of better hours, and so they clatter and echo unchallenged.

I am not ignorant that when we preach unworthily, it is not always quite in vain. There is a good ear, in some men, that draws supplies to virtue out of very indifferent nutriment. There is poetic truth concealed in all the common-places of prayer and of sermons, and though foolishly spoken, they may be wisely heard; for, each is some select expression that broke out in a moment of piety from some stricken or jubilant soul, and its excellency made it remembered. The prayers and even the dogmas of our church, are like the zodiac of Denderah, and the astronomical monuments of the Hindoos, wholly insulated from anything now extant in the life and business of the people. They mark the height to which the waters once rose. But this docility is a check upon the mischief from the good and devout. In a large portion of the community, the religious service gives rise to quite other thoughts and emotions. We need not chide the negligent servant. We are struck with pity, rather, at the swift retribution of his sloth. Alas for the unhappy man that is called to stand in the pulpit, and *not* give bread of life. Everything that befalls, accuses him. Would he ask contributions for the missions, foreign or domestic? Instantly his face is suffused with shame, to propose to his parish, that they should send money a hundred or a thousand miles, to furnish such poor fare as they have at home, and would do well to go the hundred or the thousand miles to escape. Would he urge people to a godly way of living;—and can he ask a fellow-creature to come to Sabbath meetings, when he and they all know what is the poor uttermost they can hope for therein? Will he invite them privately to the Lord's Supper? He dares not. If no heart warm this rite, the hollow, dry, creaking formality is too plain, than that he can face a man of wit and energy, and put the invitation without terror. In the street, what has he to say to the bold village blasphemer? The village blasphemer sees fear in the face, form, and gait of the minister.[8]

Let me not taint the sincerity of this plea by any oversight of the claims of good men. I know and honor the purity and strict conscience of numbers of the clergy. What life the public worship retains, it owes to the scattered company of pious men, who minister here and there in the churches, and who, sometimes

---

[8] Much of this diatribe on the preacher is based on Emerson's notebooks; it is, in part, an apology for his own resignation from the Second Church, in which incident both public prayer and the Lord's Supper were issues. [Ed.]

accepting with too great tenderness the tenet of the elders, have
not accepted from others, but from their own heart, the genuine
impulses of virtue, and so still command our love and awe, to
the sanctity of character. Moreover, the exceptions are not so
much to be found in a few eminent preachers, as in the better
hours, the truer inspirations of all,—nay, in the sincere moments of every man. But with whatever exception, it is still true,
that tradition characterizes the preaching of this country; that it
comes out of the memory, and not out of the soul; that it aims
at what is usual, and not at what is necessary and eternal; that
thus, historical Christianity destroys the power of preaching,
by withdrawing it from the exploration of the moral nature of
man, where the sublime is, where are the resources of astonish-
ment and power. What a cruel injustice it is to that Law, the
joy of the whole earth, which alone can make thought dear and
rich; that Law whose fatal sureness the astronomical orbits
poorly emulate, that it is travestied and depreciated, that it is
behooted and behowled, and not a trait, not a word of it ar-
ticulated. The pulpit in losing sight of this Law, loses its reason,
and gropes after it knows not what. And for want of this culture, the soul of the community is sick and faithless. It wants
nothing so much as a stern, high, stoical, Christian discipline,
to make it know itself and the divinity that speaks through it.
Now man is ashamed of himself; he skulks and sneaks through
the world, to be tolerated, to be pitied, and scarcely in a thousand years does any man dare to be wise and good, and so draw
after him the tears and blessings of his kind.

Certainly there have been periods when, from the inactivity
of the intellect on certain truths, a greater faith was possible in
names and persons. The Puritans in England and America,
found in the Christ of the Catholic Church, and in the dogmas
inherited from Rome, scope for their austere piety, and their
longings for civil freedom. But their creed is passing away, and
none arises in its room. I think no man can go with his thoughts
about him, into one of our churches, without feeling, that what

hold the public worship had on men is gone, or going. It has lost its grasp on the affection of the good, and the fear of the bad. In the country, neighborhoods, half parishes are *signing off,*—to use the local term. It is already beginning to indicate character and religion to withdraw from the religious meetings. I have heard a devout person, who prized the Sabbath, say in bitterness of heart, "On Sundays, it seems wicked to go to church." And the motive, that holds the best there, is now only a hope and a waiting. What was once a mere circumstance, that the best and the worst men in the parish, the poor and the rich, the learned and the ignorant, young and old, should meet one day as fellows in one house, in sign of an equal right in the soul,—has come to be a paramount motive for going thither.

My friends, in these two errors, I think, I find the causes of a decaying church and a wasting unbelief. And what greater calamity can fall upon a nation, than the loss of worship? Then all things go to decay. Genius leaves the temple, to haunt the senate, or the market. Literature becomes frivolous. Science is cold. The eye of youth is not lighted by the hope of other worlds, and age is without honor. Society lives to trifles, and when men die, we do not mention them.

And now, my brothers, you will ask, What in these desponding days can be done by us? The remedy is already declared in the ground of our complaint of the Church. We have contrasted the Church with the Soul. In the soul, then, let the redemption be sought. Wherever a man comes, there comes revolution. The old is for slaves. When a man comes, all books are legible, all things transparent, all religions are forms. He is religious. Man is the wonderworker. He is seen amid miracles. All men bless and curse. He saith yea and nay, only. The stationariness of religion; the assumption that the age of inspiration is past, that the Bible is closed; the fear of degrading the character of Jesus by representing him as a man; indicate with sufficient clearness the falsehood of our theology. It is the office of a true teacher to show us that God is, not was; that He speaketh, not spake. The true Christianity,—a faith like Christ's in the infinitude of man,—is lost. None believeth in the soul of man, but only in some man or person old and departed. Ah me! no man goeth alone. All men go in flocks to this saint or that poet, avoiding the God who seeth in secret. They cannot see in secret; they love to be blind in public. They think society wiser than their soul, and know not that one soul, and their soul, is wiser than the whole world. See how nations and races flit by on the sea of time, and leave no ripple to tell where they floated or sunk, and one good soul shall make the name of Moses, or of Zeno, or of Zoroaster, reverend forever. None assayeth the stern ambition to be the Self of the nation, and of nature, but each would be an easy secondary to some Christian scheme, or sectarian connection, or some eminent man. Once leave your own knowledge of God, your own sentiment, and take secondary knowledge, as St. Paul's, or George Fox's, or Swedenborg's, and you get wide from God with every year this secondary form lasts, and if, as now, for centuries,—the chasm yawns to that breadth, that men can scarcely be convinced there is in them anything divine.

Let me admonish you, first of all, to go alone; to refuse the good models, even those which are sacred in the imagination of men, and dare to love God without mediator or veil. Friends enough you shall find who will hold up to your emulation Wesleys and Oberlins, Saints and Prophets. Thank God for these good men, but say, 'I also am a man.' Imitation cannot go above its model. The imitator dooms himself to hopeless mediocrity. The inventor did it, because it was natural to him, and so in him it has a charm. In the imitator, something else is natural, and he bereaves himself of his own beauty, to come short of another man's.

Yourself a newborn bard of the Holy Ghost,—cast behind you all conformity, and acquaint men at first hand with Deity. Look to it first and only, that fashion, custom, authority, pleasure, and money, are nothing to you,—are not bandages over your eyes, that you cannot see,—but live with the privilege of the immeasurable mind. Not too anxious to visit periodically all families and each family in your parish connection,—when you meet one of these men or women, be to them a divine man; be to them thought and virtue; let their timid aspirations find in you a friend; let their trampled instincts be genially tempted out in your atmosphere; let their doubts know that you have doubted, and their wonder feel that you have wondered. By trusting your own heart, you shall gain more confidence in other men. For all our penny-wisdom, for all our soul-destroying slavery to habit, it is not to be doubted, that all men have sublime thoughts; that all men value the few real hours of life; they love to be heard; they love to be caught up into the vision of principles. We mark with light in the memory the few interviews we have had, in the dreary years of routine and of sin, with souls that made our souls wiser; that spoke what we thought; that told us what we knew; that gave us leave to be what we inly were. Discharge to men the priestly office, and, present or absent, you shall be followed with their love as by an angel.

And, to this end, let us not aim at common degrees of merit. Can we not leave, to such as love it, the virtue that glitters for the commendation of society, and ourselves pierce the deep solitudes of absolute ability and worth? We easily come up to the standard of goodness in society. Society's praise can be cheaply secured, and almost all men are content with those easy merits; but the instant effect of conversing with God, will be, to put them away. There are persons who are not actors, not speakers, but influences; persons too great for fame, for display; who disdain eloquence; to whom all we call art and artist, seems too nearly allied to show and by-ends, to the exaggeration of the finite and selfish, and loss of the universal. The orators, the poets, the commanders encroach on us only as fair women do, by our allowance and homage. Slight them by preoccupation of mind, slight them, as you can well afford to do, by high and universal aims, and they instantly feel that you have right, and that it is in lower places that they must shine. They also feel your right; for they with you are open to the influx of the all-knowing Spirit, which annihilates before its broad noon the little shades and gradations of intelligence in the compositions we call wiser and wisest.

In such high communion, let us study the grand strokes of rectitude: a bold benevolence, an independence of friends, so that not the unjust wishes of those who love us, shall impair our freedom, but we shall resist for truth's sake the freest flow of kindness, and appeal to sympathies far in advance; and,—what is the highest form in which we know this beautiful element,—a certain solidity of merit, that has nothing to do with opinion, and which is so essentially and manifestly virtue, that it is taken for granted, that the right, the brave, the generous step will be taken by it, and nobody thinks of commending it. You would compliment a coxcomb doing a good act, but you would not praise an angel. The silence that accepts merit as the most natural thing in the world, is the highest applause. Such souls, when they appear, are the Imperial Guard of Virtue, the perpetual reserve, the dictators of fortune. One needs not praise their courage,—they are the heart and soul of nature. O my friends, there are resources in us on which we have not drawn. There are men who rise refreshed on hearing a threat; men to whom a crisis which intimidates and paralyzes the majority,—demanding not the faculties of prudence and thrift, but comprehension, immovableness, the readiness of sacrifice,—comes graceful and beloved as a bride. Napoleon said of Massena, that he was not himself until the battle began to go against him; then, when the dead began to fall in ranks around him, awoke his powers of combination, and he put on terror and victory as a robe. So it is in rugged crises, in unweariable endurance, and in aims which put sympathy out of question, that the angel is shown. But these are heights that we can scarce remember and

look up to, without contrition and shame. Let us thank God
that such things exist.

And now let us do what we can to rekindle the smouldering,
nigh quenched fire on the altar. The evils of the church that now
is are manifest. The question returns, What shall we do? I confess, all attempts to project and establish a Cultus with new
rites and forms, seem to me vain. Faith makes us, and not we it,
and faith makes its own forms. All attempts to contrive a system
are as cold as the new worship introduced by the French to the
goddess of Reason,—to-day, pasteboard and fillagree, and ending tomorrow in madness and murder. Rather let the breath of
new life be breathed by you through the forms already existing.
For, if once you are alive, you shall find they shall become
plastic and new. The remedy to their deformity is, first, soul,
and second, soul, and evermore, soul. A whole popedom of
forms, one pulsation of virtue can uplift and vivify. Two ines-
timable advantages Christianity has given us; first; the Sabbath, the jubilee of the whole world; whose light dawns welcome alike into the closet of the philosopher, into the garret of
toil, and into prison cells, and everywhere suggests, even to the
vile, the dignity of spiritual being. Let it stand forevermore, a
temple, which new love, new faith, new sight shall restore to
more than its first splendor to mankind. And secondly, the institution of preaching,—the speech of man to men,—essentially
the most flexible of all organs, of all forms. What hinders that
now, everywhere, in pulpits, in lecture-rooms, in houses, in
fields, wherever the invitation of men or your own occasions
lead you, you speak the very truth, as your life and conscience
teach it, and cheer the waiting, fainting hearts of men with new
hope and new revelation?

I look for the hour when that supreme Beauty, which ravished
the souls of those eastern men, and chiefly of those Hebrews,
and through their lips spoke oracles to all time, shall speak in
the West also. The Hebrew and Greek Scriptures contain im-

mortal sentences, that have been bread of life to millions. But they have no epical integrity; are fragmentary; are not shown in their order to the intellect. I look for the new Teacher, that shall follow so far those shining laws, that he shall see them come full circle; shall see their rounding complete grace; shall see the world to be the mirror of the soul; shall see the identity of the law of gravitation with purity of heart; and shall show that the Ought, that Duty, is one thing with Science, with Beauty, and with Joy.

VII

HORACE BUSHNELL

Father of Progressive Orthodoxy

Horace Bushnell (1802–1876)[1] spent his entire career in a single long pastorate in Hartford, and through his work there and his reflections upon it he became the great prototype of the modern American urban-surburban minister. He was in many respects a pioneer. He broke paths for the church into the new "child oriented" culture for which the United States would later be internationally known. He did his best to find a mode of preserving the values of his Puritan heritage and defending the essentials of Christian doctrine in the new intellectual climate heralded by Schleiermacher, Coleridge, and Emerson. In a time of growing "rugged individualism" and "states-rights" he sought to moderate the pain of institutional transition by stressing the organic nature of human relationships in the family, church, and nation. Finally and supremely, he wrestled all his life with the question of vicarious sacrifice and atonement, focusing his results not only on the Church's central doctrinal question (the meaning of Christ's work) but also on the nation's great political question: for whom and to what end was the blood shed in the American Civil War? Bushnell turned to these problems of propitiation and expiation three times with major publications and in many sermons and

---

[1] See Introduction, pp. 58–64.

addresses. To have all men reconciled with God and with each other was the hope that united his major writings. And the course of his life, not surprisingly, fitted him for his task.

Born in Bantam, Connecticut, of a Methodist father and an Episcopalian mother both of whom had entered the covenanted life of Congregationalism, Bushnell grew up in a rural town in the western part of that state during the "Age of Homespun." He went to Yale College, made a try at journalism, studied law, and then after a conversion that owed much to his reading of Coleridge's AIDS TO REFLECTION, he entered the Yale Divinity School. On graduation he accepted a call to the new North Church in Hartford (1833) which he served actively until 1859, becoming another in the long line of American pastor-theologians.

In a church situation torn by controversy over Taylorism and the revival question, Bushnell's role as a reconciler began immediately. But with the years, he carried these issues to new intellectual ground and moved on to other problems. In CHRISTIAN NURTURE (1847) he underlined the organic nature of family and church, stressed Baptism as the beginning of a person's religious life and, against the revivalists, argued that a properly nurtured person need experience no conversion—and might never remember being other than a child of God. In his book, GOD IN CHRIST (1849), and his defense of that work, CHRIST IN THEOLOGY (1851), Bushnell furthered his revolution, most memorably with his "Dissertation on Language," which is a milestone in American thought. For Bushnell, as for Edwards and Emerson before him, a theory of language had ontological implications. As it would for Royce, it also deepened his argument for the corporate nature of human existence. Above all, his conception of religious language altered traditional views of creeds, and opened the way for the understanding and reinterpretation of the Scriptures and of Christian doctrine. Much of his subsequent writing documents his continuing labors toward that end.

The importance of the essay on language in Bushnell's own theological career and in the history of American theology, combined with the new relevance which twentieth-century philosophers and theologians have assigned to the subject, make it the obvious selection to represent Bushnell's work. Because of its great length, however, some abridgment has been necessary; but deletions have been limited to some opening references to other essays in the original volume, to Bushnell's confessedly tentative account of the origins of language, and to repetitious illustrative material. The argument is left entirely intact; indeed, certain important extensions of the argument that he made in CHRIST IN THEOLOGY have been added as editorial footnotes. Taken together, these two works reveal with remarkable clarity Bushnell's involvement with the new ideas, fears, and enthusiasms of his age.

PRELIMINARY DISSERTATION ON

THE NATURE OF LANGUAGE

AS RELATED TO THOUGHT AND SPIRIT

When views of religious truth are advanced, which either really or apparently differ from such as are commonly accepted, the difference will often be referable to causes that lie back of the arguments by which they are maintained—some peculiarity of temperament, some struggle of personal history, unknown to the public, the assumption or settlement of some supposed law or principle of judgment, which affects, of course, all subordinate decisions.

From Horace Bushnell, *God in Christ* (Hartford: Brown and Parsons, 1849), pp. 9–97; with additions from "Language and Doctrine," *Christ in Theology* (Hartford: Brown and Parsons, 1851), pp. 15–89.

Thus, if Hume or Blanco White[1] had come, at last, into a settled belief in what is commonly called orthodox or evangelical truth, any man, who understands at all the philosophy of opinions, will see that he would have held all his points or articles of belief under forms and relations that had some reference, more or less palpable, to his own spiritual history, and the struggles through which he had passed. It must be so; it lies not in his choice to have it otherwise. This, too, most likely is, in the estimation of Providence, the real value of the man; that for which he exists, and for which his mental struggles have been appointed—which, if it were known, ought surely to secure him a degree of patience, or even a respectful hearing. . . .

In offering these suggestions, [however,] it is not my design to lay open to the public, even by implication, facts of personal history. . . . The subject of which I speak, is language; a very different instrument, certainly, from what most men think it to be, and one, which if they are understood more exactly, they would use it more wisely. In the misuse or abuse of this instrument, a great part of our religious difficulties have their spring. We have misconceived, as it seems to me, both its nature and its capacities, and our moral reasonings are, to just the same extent, infected with error. Indeed, it is such an instrument, that I see not how any one, who rightly conceives its nature, can hope any longer to produce in it a real and proper system of dogmatic truth. He will doubt the capacity of language to serve any such purpose. He will also suspect that our logical or deductive processes under it, are more likely, in general, to be false than true. And yet, in the matter of Christian doctrine, or Christian theology, we are found committing ourselves most unsuspectingly to language and logic, as if the instrument were sufficient, and the method infallible. . . .

---

[1] David Hume (1711–1776) was an English philosopher. Joseph Blanco White (1775–1841) was a Spanish-born Roman Catholic priest who became a prominent Anglican, then later, finding Protestant dogmatism oppressive, became a Unitarian. [Ed.]

It is undoubtedly true, as many have asserted, that human language is a gift of God to the race, though not, I think, in the sense often contended for. It is by no means asserted, in the scriptures to which they refer, that God himself pronounced the sounds, or vocal names, by which the objects of the world were represented, nor that He framed these names into a grammar. It is only implied in what is said that He first called into action the instinct of language in our father, by directing his mind to the objects round him, "to see what *he* would call them." He was, Himself, in this view, the occasional cause of the naming process; and, considering the nature of the first man to have been originally framed for language, he was the creative cause; still the man himself, in his own freedom, is the immediate, operative cause; the language produced is as truly a human, as a divine product. It is not only *for* the race, but it is also *of* the race—a human development, as truly as knowledge, or virtue, or the forms of the social state.

But, if we believe the scriptures, there is far less depending on this particular history than many seem to suppose. For, in whatever manner the first language came into being, it is expressly declared, afterwards, to be in existence no longer. Thus when it is affirmed in the history of Babel and the dispersion, that God there confounded the language of the race, that they might "not understand" each other and might be "scattered abroad over the earth," it is plainly testified, howsoever the first language came into being, that it exists no longer.[2] Accordingly, the attempt so eagerly prosecuted, in former times, to ascertain what living language is descended from the first language, is really an attempt, under countenance of the Bible, to prove the Bible untrue. And so, when our modern ethnologists undertake, as they say, in behalf of the scriptures, to establish the unity of the human race, by tracing all human languages to some com-

---

[2] Genesis 11:1–9. Bushnell's conservative interpretation is worth noting. [Ed.]

mon source, through a comparison of terms, or names, found in them all, they would seem to controvert the authority of the scriptures by their argument, quite as effectually as they sustain it. No fair construction can be given to the history of the dispersion, as recorded by Moses, without understanding him to affirm the virtual destruction of the one language of the race by a miracle. According to the representation given, they are here thrown back once more, on their linguistic instincts; and we are to look for the development of new languages, radically distinct from each other, such as the free movement of small families or circles, instigated each by peculiar circumstances and causes, may produce. Nor have our ethnologists been able, as yet, with all their supposed discoveries, to disprove, at all, the original distinctness of many of the existing languages. Within certain circles of language, they seem to have a degree of success; but when they pass to certain larger circles—from the Indo-Germanic languages, for example, to the American or the Chinese—they find the matter offered to their theories wholly intractable and unreducible. So, I will even dare to prophecy, it always will be. . . .

At the same time, it cannot be pretended, by those who are most sanguine in the hope of sometime reducing all existing languages to a common origin or parentage, that the investigations hitherto made have yielded any definite token of success, except within certain acknowledged limits of affinity. The fact that there are living languages, between which no real affinity can be discovered, still exists in its integrity. And therefore we must either admit the existence of races originally distinct, or else we must refer these languages to the scripture solution of a miracle. . . .[3]

---

[3] Bushnell's interest in linguistics, philology, and related disciplines had led him to intensive study of the works of Johann C. Adelung (1732–1806), Wilhelm von Humboldt (1767–1835), Heinrich J. Klaproth (1783–1835), Friedrich Schlegel (1772–1829), Alexander B. Johnson (1786–1867), and others. His now somewhat dated arguments from these authorities are here omitted. [Ed.]

As probably no one will imagine that God has, at any time, pronounced to the different families of the race so many languages, we fall back, most naturally, upon the view just given of the formation of the first language, and take up the belief that all these different languages are so many free developments of the race; though all from God, in the sense that he has created in all human beings a certain free power of self-representation or expression, which is itself a distinct capacity for language, and, in one view, language itself.

Nor is there any so great impossibility or mystery in this matter of originating a language, as many seem to suppose. I hope it will not offend the romantic or marvelling propensity of my readers, if I affirm that a new language has been created and has perished, in Connecticut, within the present century. A very distinguished citizen, whose name is familiar to the country at large, himself a scholar and a keen philosophic observer, had a pair of twin boys, who were drawn to each other with such a mysterious and truly congenital fondness as to be totally occupied with each other, and thus to make little or no progress in learning the language of the family. Meantime, they were constantly talking with each other in a language constructed between them, which no one but themselves could understand. In this language they conversed at their plays as freely as men at their business, and in a manner that indicated the most perfect intelligence between them. At an early age one of them died; and with him died, never to be spoken again, what, beyond any reason for doubt, was the root of a new original diversity of human speech—a new tongue. Nor is there any reason to doubt that incipient and rudimental efforts of nature, in this direction, are often made, though in cases and modes that escape attention. Indeed, to believe that any two human beings, shut up wholly to each other, to live together until they are of a mature age, would not construct a language, is equivalent, in my estimation, to a denial of their proper humanity. . . .

[Here omitted is a ten-page imaginary account as to how a "small circle. . . . of unlanguaged men" may have invented nouns for things and actions, then nouns to designate spiritual or intellectual beings, and finally verbs used in a grammatical context. The crux of Bushnell's entire theory is his account of the transition from the "language of things" to a "language of intelligence" which will "serve the uses of mind." Ed.]

How, then, shall our experimenters proceed? Obviously they cannot advance at all, save through the mediation of things; that is, of objects and acts in the sensible world, which may come in to their aid as signs of thought, or interpreters between them. It is only as there is a Logos in the outward world, answering to the logos or internal reason of the parties, that they can come into a mutual understanding in regard to any thought or spiritual state whatever. To use a more familiar expression, there is a vast analogy in things, which prepares them, as forms, to be signs or figures of thoughts, and thus, bases or types of words. Our bodily mechanism and the sensible world we live in are, in fact, made up of words, to represent our thoughts and internal states. They only want naming, and then, passing into sound, to be re-produced or have their images called up by sounds, they drop out, so to speak, their gross material quality, and become words of spirit, or what the poet calls "winged words"—cursitating forms of life, that fly out in sound upon the air, as interpreters and messengers of thought between the minds of men. . . .

We find, then, that every language contains two distinct departments: the physical department, that which provides names for things; and the intellectual department, that which provides names for thought and spirit. In the former, names are simple representatives of things, which even the animals may learn. In the latter, the names of things are used as representatives of thought, and cannot, therefore, be learned, save by beings of intelligence—*(intus lego)*—that is, beings who can read the inner sense, or receive the inner contents of words; beings in whom the Logos of the creation finds a correspondent logos, or reason, to receive and employ the types it offers, in their true power. . . .

In this view, which it is not rash to believe will sometime be fully established, the outer world is seen to be a vast menstruum of thought or intelligence. There is a logos in the forms of things, by which they are prepared to serve as types or images of what is inmost in our souls; and then there is a logos also of construction in the relations of space, the position, qualities, connections, and predicates of things, by which they are framed into grammar. In one word, the outer world, which envelops our being, is itself language, the power of all language. Day unto day uttereth speech, and night unto night showeth knowledge; there is no speech nor language where their voice is not heard—their line is gone out through all the earth, and their words to the end of the world.[4]

And if the outer world is the vast dictionary and grammar of thought we speak of, then it is also itself an organ throughout of Intelligence. Whose intelligence? By this question we are set directly confronting God, the universal Author, no more to hunt for Him by curious arguments and subtle deductions, if haply we may find Him; but He stands EXPRESSED every where, so that, turn whichsoever way we please, we behold the outlooking of His intelligence. No series of Bridgewater treatises, piled even to the moon, could give a proof of God so immediate, complete, and conclusive.[5]

In such a view of the world, too, and its objects, there is an amazing fund of inspiration elsewhere not to be found. The holding of such a view is, in fact, sufficient of itself, to change a man's intellectual capacities and destiny; for it sets him always in the presence of Divine thoughts and meanings; makes even the words he utters luminous of Divinity, and to the same extent, subjects of love and reverence. . . .

---

[4] Psalm 19:2–4. Cf. Jonathan Edwards' interesting anticipation of Bushnell, pp. 152–153. [Ed.]

[5] Francis Henry Egerton, Earl of Bridgewater (1756–1829), bequeathed funds to the Royal Society to foster publications on "the Power, Wisdom, and Goodness of God as manifested in the Creation." Eight special studies were published before 1840. [Ed.]

[Here follows an eight-page section wherein Bushnell marshals support for his language theory, especially from Friedrich Schlegel, John Locke, and Friedrich Rauch. He begins by quoting a "truly eloquent paragraph" by Josiah Willard Gibbs: "There can be no exercise, in the whole business of instruction, more useful to the mind, than the analysis of sentences, in the concentrated light of grammar and logic. It brings one into the sanctuary of human thought. All else is but standing in the outer court. He who is without, may, indeed, offer incense; but he who penetrates within, worships and adores. It is here that the man of science, trained to close thought and clear vision, surveys the various objects of his study with a more expanded view, and a more discriminative mind. It is here that the interpreter, accustomed to the force and freshness of natural language, is prepared to explain God's revealed Word with more power and accuracy. It is here that the orator learns to wield, with a heavier arm, the weapons of his warfare. It is here that every one, who loves to think, beholds the deep things of the human spirit, and learns to regard with holy reverence the sacred symbols of human thought." Ed.[6]]

We pass now to the application of these views of language, or the power they are entitled to have, in matters of moral and religious inquiry and especially in Christian theology.

There are, as we discover, two languages, in fact, in every language. Or perhaps I shall be understood more exactly, if I say that there are, in every human tongue, two distinct departments. First, there is a literal department, in which sounds are provided as names for physical objects and appearances. Secondly, there is a department of analogy or figure, where physical objects and appearances are named as images of thought or

---

[6] "Historical and Critical View of Cases in the Indo-European Languages," *Quarterly Christian Spectator*, IX, 1837, 120. Gibbs (1790–1861) was professor of sacred languages at the Yale Divinity School. Bushnell owed more to him than to any other of his seminary professors. [Ed.]

spirit, and the words get their power, as words of thought, through the physical images received into them. Thus, if I speak of my *pen*, I use a word in the first department of language, uttering a sound which stands for the instrument with which I write. But if I speak of the *spirit* of a man, or the *sincerity* of a Christian, I use words that belong to the second department of language, where the sounds do not stand for the mental ideas as being names directly applied to *them*, but represent, rather, certain images in the physical state, which are the natural figures or analogies of those mental ideas. How it was necessary, in the genesis of language, that it should fall into this twofold distribution, has been shown already. The man who knows his tongue only by vernacular usage, is aware of no such distribution. Many, who are considered to be educated persons, and are truly so, are but half aware of it. At least, they notice only now and then, when speaking of matters pertaining to thought and spirit, that a word brought into use has a physical image in it. For example, when speaking of a good man's *heart*, they observe that the word has a physical image connected with it, or that it names also a vital organ of the body. Then they either say, that the word has two meanings, a physical and a spiritual, not observing any law of order or connection by which the physical becomes the basis or type of the spiritual; or, they raise a distinction between what they call the *literal* and *figurative* uses of the word. But this distinction of literal and figurative, it does not appear to be noticed, even by philologists, runs through the very body of the language itself, making two departments; one that comprises the terms of sensation, and the other the terms of thought. They notice, in the historical investigation of words, that they are turning up all the while, a subsoil of physical bases; and, though they cannot find in every particular case, the physical term on which the word is built, they attain to a conviction that every word has a physical root, if only it could be found; and still the natural necessity, that all words relating to thought and spirit should be figures, and as such, get their significance, they do not state. They still retain the impression that some of the terms of thought are literal, and some figurative.

This is the manner of the theologians. They assume that there is a literal terminology in religion as well as a figurative (as doubtless there is, in reference to matters of outward fact and history, but nowhere else) and then it is only a part of the same mistake to accept words, not as signs or images, but as absolute measures and equivalents of truth; and so to run themselves, by their argumentations, with a perfectly unsuspecting confidence, into whatever conclusions the *logical forms* of the words will carry them. Hence, in great part, the distractions, the infinite multiplications of opinion, the errors and sects and strifes of the Christian world. We can never come into a settled consent in the truth, until we better understand the nature, capacities and incapacities of language, as a vehicle of truth.

In order, now, that I may excite our younger theologians especially to a new investigation of this subject, as being fundamental, in fact, to the right understanding of religious truth, I will dismiss the free form of dissertation, and set forth under numerical indications a series of points or positions, inviting each their attention, and likely, though with some modifications, perhaps, to be finally verified.

1. Words of thought and spirit are possible in language only in virtue of the fact that there are forms provided in the world of sense, which are cognate to the mind, and fitted, by reason of some hidden analogy, to represent or express its interior sentiments and thoughts.

2. Words of thought and spirit are, in fact, names of such forms or images existing in the outward or physical state.

3. When we investigate the relation of the form, or etymological base, in any word of thought or spirit, to the idea ex-

pressed, we are able to say (negatively) that the idea or thought has no such form, or shape, or sensible quality, as the word has. If I speak of *right (straight, rectus)* it is not because the internal law of the conscience, named by this word, has any straightness or lineal quality whatever. Or if I speak of *sin, peccatum, hamartia,* where, in so many languages, as I might also show in a great variety of others, the image at the root of the word is one of lineal divarication (as when an arrow is shot at the mark, and misses or turns aside) it is not because sin, as a moral state of being, or a moral act, has any lineal form in the mind. Thoughts, ideas, mental states, we cannot suppose have any geometric form, any color, dimensions, or sensible qualities whatever.

4. We can also say (positively) in reference to the same subject, that there is always some reason in every form or image made use of, why it should be used; some analogic property or quality which we feel instinctively, but which wholly transcends speculative inquiry. If there is no lineal straightness in rectitude, no linear crookedness or divarication in sin, taken as an internal state, still it is the instinct of our nature to feel some sense of correspondence between these images and the states they represent. . . .

5. There are no words, in the physical department of language, that are exact representatives of particular physical things. For whether we take the theory of the Nominalists or the Realists, the words are, in fact, and practically, names only of genera, not of individuals or species. To be even still more exact, they represent only certain sensations of sight, touch, taste, smell, hearing—one or all. Hence the opportunity in language, for endless mistakes and false reasonings, in reference to matters purely physical. . . .

6. It follows, that as physical terms are never exact, being only names of genera, much less have we any terms in the spiri-

tual department of language that are exact representatives of
thought. For, first, the word here used will be the name only of
a genus of physical images. Then, secondly, it will have been
applied over to signify a genus of thoughts or sentiments. And
now, thirdly, in a particular case, it is drawn out to signify a
specific thought or sentiment which, of course, will have qualities or incidents peculiar to itself. What, now, can steer a word
through so many ambiguities and complications, and give it an
exact and determinate meaning in the particular use it is applied
to serve? Suppose, for example, one desires to speak of the
bitterness displayed by another, on some given occasion. In the
first place, this word *bitterness,* taken physically, describes not
a particular sensation common to all men, but a genus of sensations; and as some persons have even a taste for bitter things,
it is impossible that the word, taken physically, should not have
an endless variety of significations, ranging between disgust and
a positive relish of pleasure. . . .

And the same is true of the great mass of words employed in
moral and spiritual uses, such as love, gentleness, contentment,
patience, wisdom, justice, order, pride, charity. We think we
have the same ideas in them, or rather (which is more likely)
we think nothing about it; but we find continually that, when
we come to particular uses, we fall into disagreements, often
into protracted and serious controversies; and whether it be said
that the controversy is about words or things, it is always a controversy about the real applicability of words.

What, then, it may be asked, is the real and legitimate use of
words, when applied to moral subjects? for we cannot dispense
with them, and it is uncomfortable to hold them in universal
scepticism, as being only instruments of error. Words, then, I
answer, are legitimately used as the signs of thoughts to be expressed. They do not literally convey, or pass over a thought out
of one mind into another, as we commonly speak of doing. They
are only hints, or images, held up before the mind of another, to
put *him* on generating or reproducing the same thought; which

he can do only as he has the same personal contents, or the generative power out of which to bring the thought required. Hence, there will be different measures of understanding or misunderstanding, according to the capacity or incapacity, the ingenuousness or moral obliquity of the receiving party—even if the communicating party offers only truth, in the best and freshest forms of expression the language provides.

There is only a single class of intellectual words that can be said to have a perfectly determinate significance, viz., those which relate to what are called necessary ideas. They are such as time, space, cause, truth, right, arithmetical numbers, and geometrical figures. Here the names applied, are settled into a perfectly determinate meaning, not by any peculiar virtue in *them*, but by reason of the absolute exactness of the ideas themselves. Time cannot be anything more or less than time; truth cannot, in its idea, be anything different from truth; the numerals suffer no ambiguity of count or measure; a circle must be a circle; a square, a square. As far as language, therefore, has to do with these, it is a perfectly exact algebra of thought, but no farther.

It will, perhaps, be imagined by some, indeed, it is an assumption continually made, that words of thought, though based on mere figures or analogies in their original adoption, gradually lose their indeterminate character, and settle down under the law of use, into a sense so perfectly unambiguous, that they are to be regarded as literal names, and real equivalents of the thoughts they signify. There could not be a greater mistake. For, though the original type, or historic base of the word may pass out of view, so that nothing physical or figurative is any longer suggested by it, still it will be impossible that mere use should have given it an exact meaning, or made it the literal name of any moral or intellectual state. The word *sin* is of this description, and most persons seem to imagine that it names a given act or state, about which there is no diversity of understanding.

Contrary to this, no two minds ever had the same impression

of it. The whole personal history of every man, his acts, temptations, wants, and repentances; his opinions of God, of law, and
of personal freedom; his theory of virtue, his decisions of the
question, whether sin is an act, or a state; of the will, or of the
heart: in fact, his whole theology and life will enter into his
impression of this word *sin*, to change the quality, and modify
the relations of that which it signifies. It will also be found, as a
matter of fact, that the interminable disputes of the theologians
on this particular subject, originate in fundamental differences
of view concerning the nature of sin, and are themselves incon-
testible proofs that, simple as the word is, and on the lips of
everybody (as we know it to be), there is yet no virtual agreement of meaning connected with the word.* The same, as just
now intimated, is true of *hope, fear, love,* and other like familiar
terms, which we fancy have a meaning so well settled. They
have a dictionary meaning that is settled; but yet, hope, fear,
love, is to every man what his own life-experience, and his theories, and mental struggles have made it, and he sees it, of necessity, under a color quite peculiar to himself; so peculiar, that he
will even advance concerning it, what another cannot find the
truth of, or receive. And this is true of all the intellectual terms
in language, with the exception of a class just named, relating to
necessary and absolute truths. Besides these, there is no word
of thought, or spirit, that exactly measures its ideas, or does any
thing more than offer some proximate notion, or shadow of the
thought intended. . . .

7. Words of thought or spirit are not only inexact in their
significance, never measuring the truth or giving its precise
equivalent, but they always affirm something which is false, or
contrary to the truth intended. They impute *form* to that which

---

* This entire volume could have been designed to illustrate Bushnell's
contention, by making every Selection lead toward or away from Taylor's
Concio ad Clerum; but this would have narrowed the scope of the survey
unpardonably. [Ed.]

really is out of form. They are related to the truth, only as form to spirit—earthen vessels in which the truth is borne, yet always offering their mere pottery as being the truth itself. Bunyan beautifully represents their insufficiency and earthiness when he says—

> My dark and cloudy words, they do but hold
> The truth, as cabinets inclose the gold.[7]

—only it needs to be added, that they palm off upon us, too often, their "dark and cloudy" qualities as belonging inherently to the golden truths they are used to express. Therefore, we need always to have it in mind, or in present recollection, that they are but signs, in fact, or images of that which has no shape or sensible quality whatever; a kind of painting, in which the speaker, or the writer, leads on through a gallery of pictures or forms, while we attend him, catching at the thoughts suggested by his forms. In one view, they are all false; for there are no shapes in the truths they represent, and therefore we are to separate continually, and by a most delicate process of art, between the husks of the forms and the pure truths of thought presented in them. We do this insensibly, to a certain extent, and yet we do it imperfectly, often. A very great share of our theological questions, or disputes, originate in the incapacity of the parties to separate truths from their forms, or to see how the same essential truth may clothe itself under forms that are repugnant. There wants to be a large digestion, so to speak, of form in the teacher of theology or mental philosophy, that he may always be aware how the mind and truth, obliged to clothe themselves under the laws of space and sensation, are taking, continually, new shapes or dresses—coming forth poetically, mystically, allegorically, dialectically, fluxing through definitions, symbols, changes of subject and object, yet remaining still

---

[7] John Bunyan, *The Pilgrim's Progress* (1678–1685), "The Author's Apology for His Book," lines 127–128. [Ed.]

the same; for if he is wanting in this, if he is a mere logicker, fastening on a word as the sole expression and exact equivalent of a truth, to go on spinning his deductions out of the form of the word (which yet have nothing to do with the idea) then he becomes a one-word professor, quarreling, as for truth itself, with all who chance to go out of his word; and, since words are given, not to imprison souls, but to express them, the variations continually indulged by others are sure to render him as miserable in his anxieties, as he is meagre in his contents, and busy in his quarrels. . . .

8. But if we are liable thus to be carried away by the forms contained in our words, into conclusions or impressions that do not belong to the truths they are used to signify, we are also to peruse their forms with great industry, as being, at the same time, a very important key to their meaning. The original type or etymology of words is a most fruitful study. Even when they pass into meanings that seem to be contrary one to another, it will yet be found, in almost every case, that the repugnant meanings are natural growths, so to speak, of the same vital root; as some kinds of trees are seen to throw out leaves having several different shapes. The etymologists have been hard pressed, often, by ridicule, and it is not to be denied that they have sometimes produced fancies in place of facts. As little is it to be denied that words do, now and then, present no aspect of agreement in their senses, with the types out of which they spring. They appear to have suffered some kind of violence—to have fallen among thieves, and been left, half dead, from the injury they have suffered. And yet there is a wonderful light shed upon words, in most cases, by the simple opening of their etymologies. Distinctions are very often drawn at a stroke, in this way, which whole chapters of dissertation would not exhibit as well. Sometimes a dark subject is made luminous, at once, by the simple reference to an etymology; and then we are even amazed to see what depths of wisdom, or spiritual insight, have been hid, as it were, in our language, even from ourselves. . . .

9. Since all words, but such as relate to necessary truths, are inexact representations of thought, mere types or analogies, or, where the types are lost beyond recovery, only proximate expressions of the thoughts named; it follows that language will be ever trying to mend its own deficiencies, by multiplying its forms of representation. As, too, the words made use of generally carry something false with them, as well as something true, associating form with the truths represented, when really there is no form; it will also be necessary, on this account, to multiply words or figures, and thus to present the subject on opposite sides or many sides. Thus, as form battles form, and one form neutralizes another, all the insufficiencies of words are filled out, the contrarieties liquidated, and the mind settles into a full and just apprehension of the pure spiritual truth. Accordingly we never come so near to a truly well rounded view of any truth, as when it is offered paradoxically; that is, under contradictions; that is, under two or more dictions, which, taken as dictions, are contrary one to the other.

Hence the marvelous vivacity and power of that famous representation of Pascal: "What a chimera, then, is man! What a novelty! What a chaos! What a subject of contradiction! A judge of every thing, and yet a feeble worm of the earth; the depositary of truth, and yet a mere heap of uncertainty; the glory and the outcast of the universe. If he boasts, I humble him; if he humbles himself, I boast of him; and always contradict him, till he is brought to comprehend that he is an incomprehensible monster."[8]

Scarcely inferior in vivacity and power is the familiar passage of Paul: "as deceivers, and yet true; as unknown, and yet well known; as dying, and behold, we live; as chastened, and not

---

[8] Blaise Pascal, *Thoughts on Religion and Other Important Subjects* (London: Samuel Bagster, 1803), p. 158. The anonymous translator singles out precisely this passage for discussion in his introductory memoir, pp. 70, 71. Texts and translations of the *Pensées* vary widely but all contain this passage in some form or other. [Ed.]

killed; as sorrowful, yet always rejoicing; as poor, yet making many rich; as having nothing, yet possessing all things."[9]

So, also, it will be found, that the poets often express their most inexpressible, or evanescent thoughts, by means of repugnant or somewhat paradoxical epithets; as, for example, Coleridge, when he says,—

> The stilly murmur of the distant sea
> Tells us of silence.[10]

Precisely here, too, I suppose, we come upon what is really the true conception of the Incarnation and the Trinity. These great Christian mysteries or paradoxes, come to pass under the same conditions or laws which pertain to language. All words are, in fact, only incarnations, or insensings of thought. If we investigate the relations of their forms to the truths signified, we have the same mystery before us; if we set the different, but related forms in comparison, we have the same aspect of repugnance or inconsistency. And then we have only to use the repugnant forms as vehicles of pure thought, dismissing the contradictory matter of the forms, and both words and the Word are understood without distraction,—all by the same process.

Probably, the most contradictory book in the world is the Gospel of John; and that, for the very reason that it contains more and loftier truths than any other. No good writer, who is

---

[9] II Corinthians 6:8–10. [Ed.]

[10] Samuel Taylor Coleridge, "Lines Written in the Album at Elbingerode, in the Hartz Forest." Coleridge's conceptions also lay behind Bushnell's return to these themes in *Christ in Theology*, p. 33: "The principle difficulty we have with language now is, that it will not put into the theoretic understanding what the imagination only can receive, and will not open to the head what the heart only can interpret. It is a great trouble with us that we can not put the whole scheme of redemption, which God could execute only by the volume of expression contained in the life and death of his incarnate Son, into a theologic formula or article of ten words. It is as if, being unable to compress the whole tragic force of Lear into some one sentence of Edgar's gibberish, we lose our patience, and cry out upon the poverty of language and conception in the poem." [Ed.]

occupied in simply expressing truth, is ever afraid of inconsist-
encies or self-contradictions in his language. It is nothing to him
that a quirk of logic can bring him into absurdity. If at any time
he offers definitions, it is not to get a footing for the play of his
logic, but it is simply as multiplying forms or figures of that
which he seeks to communicate—just as one will take his friend
to different points of a landscape, and show him cross views, in
order that he may get a perfect conception of the outline. Having nothing but words in which to give definitions, he understands the impossibility of definitions as determinate measures
of thought, and gives them only as being *other forms* of the truth
in question, by aid of which it may be more adequately conceived. On the other hand, a writer without either truth or
genius, a mere uninspired, unfructifying logicker, is just the
man to live in definitions. He has never a doubt of their possibility. He lays them down as absolute measures, then draws
along his deductions, with cautious consistency, and works out,
thus, what he considers to be the exact infallible truth. But his
definitions will be found to hang, of necessity, on some word or
symbol, that symbol to have drawn every thing to itself, or into
its own form, and then, when his work is done, it will be both
consistent and false—false, because of its consistency.[11]

10. It is part of the same view, that logic itself is a defective,
and often deceitful instrument. I speak not here of logic as a

----

[11] Cf. Bushnell's discussion of definitions in *Christ and Theology*, p. 51:
"What are called definitions in theology and metaphysics are generally
nothing better than preparations for a plentiful harvest of errors—not because definitions may not be useful and are not a natural resort of the intelligence, but that being commonly drawn in the most abstract language
possible, they are supposed to have absolute meanings clear of form and
figure; when yet they are just as truly under form and figure as the wildest
rhapsodies, only that the figure has been staled by time, and is therefore
less palpable. And then, after the definitions have been accepted as absolute, how many deductions, spun out of the mere forms of the words or
sentences, will be taken as the veritable sons and daughters of the truth
defined." [Ed.]

science, but of that deductive, proving, spinning method of practical investigation, commonly denoted by the term *logical*. It is very obvious, that no turn of logical deduction can prove anything, by itself, not previously known by inspection or insight. And yet, there is always a busy-minded class of sophists or speculators, who, having neither a large observation, nor a power of poetic insight, occupy themselves as workers in words and propositions, managing to persuade themselves and others that they are great investigators, and even discoverers of truth. . . .

It seems to be supposed, or rather assumed, by the class of investigators commonly called logical, that after the subject matter of truth has been gotten into propositions, and cleared, perhaps, by definitions, the faculty of intuition, or insight, may be suspended, and we may go on safely, to reason upon the forms of the words themselves, or the "analogy the words bear to each other." And so, by the mere handling of words and propositions, they undertake to evolve, or, as they commonly speak, to *prove* important truths. They reason, not by or through formulas, but upon them. After the formulas are got ready, they shut their eyes to all interior inspection of their terms, as in algebra, and commit themselves to the mere grammatic laws or predications of their words—expecting, under these, by inversion, evolution, equation, *reductio ad absurdum,* and the like, to work out important results. And this is popularly called *reasoning.* . . .[12]

Observe, in a single proposition—the simplest affirmation that

---

[12] Bushnell granted, however, that "in the pure alegebraic process the result is wholly different." Cf. *Christ in Theology,* p. 16: "It was not my design to make an assault upon logic itself as a science. I was not ignorant that all the sublime results of the calculus are fruits of genuine logic. I only meant that, as soon as we carry this method into moral and religious philosophy, and subject our mind to it as a dominant influence there, we are sure to be enveloped in sophistries without end or limit; for words, in this case, have a wholly different relation to their truths—a relation of form or symbol, and not of mere notation." [Ed.]

can be invented, I might almost say, pertaining to the intellectual life—how indefinite any mere formula must be. I assert that "*man thinks.*" Here the subject is man, of whom is predicated some causative agency, and some form of result. As regards the agency, it may be understood (1.) that the man thinks under a law of mechanical necessity, as a machine works; or (2.) that he thinks under a law of plastic self-determinating necessity, as a tree grows; or (3.) that he thinks under a law of mental suggestion, which he can only interrupt by his will; or (4.) that he wills to think; or (5.) that he thinks spontaneously. And then as to the product, *thought,* nothing is so difficult as to settle any definite conception of that; but we will suppose only five more ambiguities here—combining which, in as many pairs as they will make, with the five preceding, we have twenty-five distinct meanings.

If, now, going back to the subject, *man,* it be asked whether the formula intends (1.) man as created in his natural freedom and innocence; or (2.) man as under the power and bondage of evil; or (3.) man as illuminated and suggestively directed or swayed by the supernatural grace of God; or (4.) man as regenerated in good, and contesting with currents of evil thought still running in his nature—all of which are important distinctions— we have then just a hundred different meanings in our simple formula—*man thinks.* Or, dismissing arithmetic as inappropriate, we may better say that the language is only tropical, and the meanings, of course, indefinitely variable. For all these, language provides only a single form of predicate—a single grammatic formula. And yet it seems to be imagined that we can saddle mere forms of words, and ride them into necessary unambiguous conclusions! . . .

As great mischief and perplexity is often wrought by raising the question of before and after, under the laws of time. The speculative, would-be philosopher wants to be able always to say which is first in the soul's action—this or that. What endless debates have we had in theology concerning questions of pri-

ority—whether faith is before repentance, or repentance before
faith; whether one or the other is before love, or love before
them both; whether justification is before sanctification, and the
like. We seem to suppose that a soul can be taken to pieces, or
have its exercises parted and put under laws of time, so that we
can see them go, in regular clock-work order. Whereas, being
alive in God when it is truly united to Him, its right exercises,
being functions of life, are of course mutual conditions one of
another. Passing out of mechanism, or the empire of dead atoms,
into the plastic realm of life, all questions of before and after we
leave behind us. We do not ask whether the heart causes the
heaving of the lungs, or whether the lungs have priority, and
keep up the beating of the heart; or whether the digestive faculty is first in time, or the assimilative, or the nervous. We look
at the whole body as a vital nature, and finding every function
alive, every fibre active, we perceive that all the parts, even the
minutest, exist and act as mutual conditions one of another. And
so it is in spiritual life. Every grace supposes every other as its
condition, and time is wholly out of the question. But, the moment any one of our atomizing and mechanising speculators
comes into the field, the question of priority is immediately
raised. Perceiving that love seems to imply or involve faith, he
declares that faith is first. Then, as another is equally sure that
faith implies love, he maintains that love is first. A third, in the
same way, that repentance is before both; a fourth, that both are
before repentance. And now we have a general debate on hand,
in which the formulas will be heard ringing as flails, for a dozen
years, or a century. Meantime, it will happen that all the several
schools of wisdom are at fault, inasmuch as none of the priorities
are first, or rather all are first; being all conditions mutually of
one another. Might it not have been better, at the first, to clear
ourselves of time and the law it weaves into words and predicates—to perceive, as by a little insight we may, that, in all vital
and plastic natures, the functions have a mutual play?

In the speculative logicking use of formulas, it sometimes

happens, also, that the argument contains a law of degrees, and thus constructs, when fairly carried out, an infinite series. Thus, in the argument for a God, "an effect," we are told, "infers a cause; a design, a designer." The doubter assents: "but," he adds, "the supposed designer is one who is adapted, in his nature, to the making of designs, and therefore, I perceive, in this adaptation of means to ends in him, that following the same law, there is a designer back of him. Go with me, then, up an infinite series, as the argument legitimately requires, or else excuse me from the first step, as you excuse yourself from the second." By just this kind of process it was that Shelley, immersed in the logic of Oxford, became an atheist; as also all the scholars of that great university might properly be, and would, if they yielded implicitly to the drill under which they are placed, and forgot all the simpler wisdom of nature, in the learned wisdom that is taught them.

But if we can think it any thing to *see* God—all formulas, inferences, degrees, out of the question—if we can say "God is expressed to us here on every side, shining out as a Form of Intelligence in every object round us," it will not be difficult to find the God our logic denies us. This, in fact, is the real virtue of Paley's argument; only, to give it a more imposing logical form, he has run it into a suicidal series by the statement.[13]

In offering these illustrations of the value of the logical method in religious and moral reasonings, I have only hinted at some of the important issues involved. To set the subject forth in all its momentous relations would require a volume; and such a volume the world intensely needs.

11. In the reading or interpretation of an author, writing on

---

[13] William Paley (1743–1805), English apologist and utilitarian moral philosopher, is especially remembered for his ingenious summary of "arguments from design." In Bushnell's day Paley's *A View of the Evidences of Christianity* (1794) and *Natural Theology* (1802) were still popular college and seminary texts and were disseminated by the American Tract Society. Cf. William James on such theologians, pp. 503, 513. [Ed.]

intellectual and moral subjects, we are to observe, first of all, whether he takes up some given word or figure, and makes it a law to his thinking. If some symbol that he uses to-day stands by him also to-morrow, rules his doctrine, shapes his argument, drawing every thing into formal consistency with it, then we are to take up the presumption that he is out of the truth, and set ourselves to find where his mistake is. . . .

12. If we find the writer, in hand, moving with a free motion, and tied to no one symbol, unless in some popular effort, or for some single occasion; if we find him multiplying antagonisms, offering cross views, and bringing us round the field to show us how it looks from different points, then we are to presume that he has some truth in hand which it becomes us to know. We are to pass round accordingly with him, take up all his symbols, catch a view of him here, and another there, use one thing to qualify and interpret another, and the other to shed light upon that, and, by a process of this kind, endeavor to comprehend his antagonisms, and settle into a complete view of his meaning.

What Goethe says of himself is true of all efficient writers: "I have always regarded all I have done, as solely symbolical, and, at bottom, it does not signify whether I make pots or dishes." And then, what Eckermann says of him in his preface, follows of course: "Goethe's detached remarks upon poetry often have an appearance of . . . contradiction. Sometimes he lays all the stress on the material which the outward world affords, sometimes upon that which is given to the inward world of the poet; sometimes the greatest importance is attached to the subject, sometimes to the mode of treating it; sometimes all is made to depend on perfection of form, sometimes form is to be neglected, and all the attention paid to the spirit. But all these seeming contradictions are, in fact, only successive presentations of single sides of a truth, which, by their union, manifest completely to us its existence, and guide us to a perception of its nature. . . . I confide in the insight and comprehensive power of the cultivated reader not to look at any one part, as seen by itself, but to keep his eye on the significance of the whole, and by that means, to bring each particular truth into its proper place and relations."[14]

Is it a fault of Goethe that he must be handled in this manner? Rather is it one of the highest proofs of his genius and the real greatness of his mind. Had he been willing to stay under some one figure, and draw himself out into formal consistency, throwing off none of these bold antagonisms, he must have been a very different character—not Goethe, but some dull proser or male spinster of logic, never heard of by us.

What, then, shall we say of Christ and the Gospel of John? If it requires such an array of antagonisms to set forth the true idea of poetry, what does it require to set forth God and redemption? What should we expect, in such a work, but a vast compilation of symbols and of forms, which to the mere wordsman, are contrary to each other? And then what shall we do?—what, for example, with the trinity, the atonement, the bondage and freedom of sin? Shall we say, with the infidel, this is all a medley of contradiction—mere nonsense, fit only to be rejected? Shall we take up these bold antagonisms, as many orthodox believers have done, seize upon some one symbol as the real form of the truth, and compel all the others to submit to it; making, thus, as many sects as there are symbols, and as many petty wars about each truth as it has sides or inches of surface? Or shall we endeavor, with the Unitarians, to decoct the whole mass of symbol, and draw off the extract into pitchers of our own; fine, consistent, nicely-rounded pitchers, which, so far from setting out any where towards infinity, we can carry at pleasure by the handle, and definitely measure by the eye? What critic has ever thought of handling Goethe in the methods just named? We

---

14 S. M. Fuller [Margaret Fuller d'Ossoli], *Conversations with Goethe in the Last Years of His Life, Translated from the German of* [*Johann*] *Eckermann* (Boston: Hilliard, Gray, and Company, 1839), p. 6. [Ed.]

neither scout his inconsistency, nor drill him into some one of his forms, not decoct him into forms of our own. But we call him the many-sided great man; we let him stand in his own chosen symbols, whether they be "pots or dishes," and do him the greater honor because of the complexity and the magnificent profusion of his creations.

There is no book in the world that contains so many repugnances, or antagonistic forms of assertion, as the Bible. Therefore, if any man please to play off his constructive logic upon it, he can easily show it up as the absurdest book in the world. But whosoever wants, on the other hand, really to behold and receive all truth, and would have the truth-world overhang him as an empyrean of stars, complex, multitudinous, striving antagonistically, yet comprehended, height above height, and deep under deep, in a boundless score of harmony; what man soever, content with no small rote of logic and catechism, reaches with true hunger after this, and will offer himself to the many-sided forms of the scripture with a perfectly ingenuous and receptive spirit; he shall find his nature flooded with senses, vastnesses, and powers of truth, such as it is even greatness to feel. God's own lawgivers, heroes, poets, historians, prophets, and preachers and doers of righteousness, will bring him their company, and representing each his own age, character, and mode of thought, shine upon him as so many cross lights on his field of knowledge, to give him the most complete and manifold view possible of every truth. He has not only the words of Christ, the most manifold of all teachers, but he has gospels which present him in his different words and attitudes; and then, besides, he has four, some say five, distinct writers of epistles, who follow, giving each his own view of the doctrine of salvation and the Christian life, views so unlike or antagonistical that many have regarded them as being quite irreconcileable: Paul, the dialectic, commonly so called; John, the mystic; James, the moralizer; Peter, the homilectic; and perhaps a fifth in the epistle to the Hebrews, who is a Christian templar and He-braizer. The Old Testament corresponds. Never was there a book uniting so many contrarious aspects of one and the same truth. The more complete, therefore, because of its manifold-ness; nay, the more really harmonious, for its apparent want of harmony.

How, then, are we to receive it and come into its truth? Only in the comprehensive manner just now suggested; not by de-stroying the repugnances, but by allowing them to stand, offer-ing our mind to their impressions, and allowing it to gravitate inwardly, towards that whole of truth, in which they coalesce. And when we are in that whole, we shall have no dozen propo-sitions of our own in which to give it forth; neither will it be a whole which we can set before the world, standing on one leg, in a perfectly definite shape, clear of all mystery; but it will be such a whole as requires a whole universe of rite, symbol, incar-nation, historic breathings, and poetic fires, to give it expression in a word, just what it now has.

Finding it not a Goethe, but as much greater than he as God is greater than a genius of our own human race, when we think of ourselves trying to give out the substantial import of the vol-ume in a few scant formulas, it will probably occur to us just to ask what figure we should make, in a similar attempt upon one who is no more than a German poet? And then, it will not be strange if we drop our feeble, bloodless sentences and dogmas, whether of belief or denial, and return, duly mortified, into the faith of those august and magnificent forms of scripture—incar-nation; Father, Son, and Holy Ghost; atonement as blood, life, sacrifice, propitiation, ransom, liberty, regeneration, wisdom, righteousness, sanctification, and redemption—the great mys-tery of godliness.

13. The views of language and interpretation I have here offered, suggest the very great difficulty, if not impossibility of

mental science and religious dogmatism. In all such uses or attempted uses, the effort is to make language answer a purpose that is against its nature. The "winged words" are required to serve as beasts of burden; or, what is no better, to forget their poetic life, as messengers of the air, and stand still, fixed upon the ground, as wooden statues of truths. Which, if they seem to do; if, to comfort our studies of dogma, they assume the inert faces we desire, and suffer us to arrange the fixed attitudes of their bodies, yet, as little Memnons touched and made vocal by the light, they will be discoursing still of the free empyrean, disturbing, and scattering, by their voices, all the exact meanings we had thought to hold them to, in the nice corporeal order of our science.

In algebra and geometry, the ideas themselves being absolute, the terms or names also may be; but in mental science and religion, no such exactness is possible, because our apprehensions of truth are here only proximate and relative. I see not, therefore, how the subject matter of mental science and religion can ever be included under the fixed forms of dogma. Definitions cannot bring us over the difficulty; for definitions are, in fact, only changes of symbol, and, if we take them to be more, will infallibly lead us into error. In fact, no man is more certain to run himself into mischievous error, than he who places implicit confidence in definitions. After all, definitions will be words, and science will be words, and words, place them in whatever shapes we may, will be only shadows of truth. . . . Probably it will be found, after all, that the only way to make up a real man is to put the whole dictionary into him; and then, most likely, some spaces will be found vacant, some members wanting. . . .

And then, if our complete dictionary man should be finally produced, alive, mysterious, acting diseasedly, in what shape would the now completed science be as likely to emerge, as in those forms of life which a Shakspeare, or some great universal poet of humanity might set before us? Poets, then, are the true metaphysicians, and if there be any complete science of man to come, they must bring it.[15]

Is it to be otherwise in religion? Can there be produced, in human language, a complete and proper Christian theology; can the Christian truth be offered in the molds of any dogmatic statement? What is the Christian truth? Pre-eminently and principally, it is the expression of God—God coming into expression, through histories and rites, through an incarnation, and through language—in one syllable, by the WORD. The endeavor is, by means of expression, and under the laws of expression, to set forth God—His providence, and His government, and, what is more and higher than all, God's own feeling, His truth, love, justice, compassion. Well, if it be something for a poet to express man, it is doubtless somewhat more for a book to be constructed that will express God, and open His eternity to man. And if it would be somewhat difficult to put the poet of humanity into a few short formulas, that will communicate all he expresses, with his manifold, wondrous art, will it probably be easier to transfer the grand poem of salvation, that which expresses God, even the feeling of God, into a few dull propositions; which, when they are produced, we may call the sum total of the Christian truth? Let me freely confess that, when I see the human teacher elaborating a phrase of speech, or mere dialectic proposition, that is going to tell what God could only show me by the history of ages, and the mystic life and death of Jesus our Lord, I should be deeply shocked by his irreverence, if I were not rather occupied with pity for his infirmity.

---

[15] Bushnell underlines the kinship of poetry and religion in *Christ in Theology*, p. 87: "The poetic forms of utterance are closer to the fires of religion within us, more adequate revelations of consciousness, because they reveal it in flame. Parable, symbol, description, illustration, emphasis and tone, the look of divine charity and the conduct of a soul in the divine beauty—these, I hope you will agree, are better and more adequate revelations of truth than theology, in its best form, can be." [Ed.]

It ought not to be necessary to remind any reader of the bible, that religion has a natural and profound alliance with poetry. Hence, a very large share of the bible is composed of poetic contributions. Another share, equally large, is that which comes to us in a form of history and fact; that is, of actual life, which is equally remote from all abstractions, and, in one view, equally poetic; for history is nothing but an evolution or expression of God and man in their own nature and character. The teachings of Christ are mere utterances of truth, not argumentations over it. He gives it forth in living symbols, without definition, without *proving* it, ever, as the logicians speak, well understanding that truth is that which shines in its own evidence, that which *finds* us, to use an admirable expression of Coleridge, and thus enters into us.

But Paul,—was not Paul a dialectician? *the* dialectician, some say; for, confessedly, there is no other among all the scripture writers. Did Paul, then, it will be asked, set himself to an impossible task, when he undertook to reason out and frame into logical order, a scheme of Christian theology? To this, I answer, that I find no such Paul in the scripture, as this method of speaking supposes. Paul undertakes no theologic system, in any case. He only speaks to some actual want, to remove some error, rectify some hurtful mistake. There is nothing of the system-maker about him. Neither is he to be called a dogmatizer, or a dialectic writer, in any proper sense of the term. True, there is a form of reasoning, or argumentation about him, and he abounds in illatives; piling "For" upon "For" in constant succession. But, if he is narrowly watched, it will be seen that this is only a dialectic form that had settled on his language, under his old theologic discipline, previous to his conversion; for every man gets a language constructed early in life, which nothing can change afterwards. Notwithstanding his deductive manner, it will be plain to any one who reads him with a true insight, that, under the form of ratiocination, he is not so much theologizing, as flaming in the holy inspirations of truth; speaking not as a logician, but as a seer. Under so many illatives and deductive propositions, he is emitting fire, not formulas for the mere speculative understanding; rolling on, in the vehement power of a soul possessed with Christ, to declare the mystery that hath been hid for ages; conceiving nowhere that he is the first professor of Christian dogmatics; nowhere thinking, as a Christian Rabbi, to prepare a Targum on the Gospels.[16]

Besides, it will be clear, on examination, that his illatives often miscarry, when taken as mere instruments, or terms of logic, while, if we conceive him rushing on through so many "Fors" and parentheses, which belong to his old Pharisaic culture, and serve as a continuous warp of connectives to his speech—now become the vehicle or channel, not for the modes of Rabbi Gamaliel, but for a stream of Christian fire—what before seemed to wear a look of inconsequence, assumes a port of amazing energy, and he becomes the fullest, heartiest, and most irresistible of all the inspired writers of the Christian scriptures. But, in order to this his true attitude, we must make him a seer, and not a system maker; we must read his epistle as a prophesying of the spirit, not as a Socratic lecture.[17]

---

[16] Targum, in Aramaic, means "translation." The Targums were Aramaic paraphrases of Old Testament writings, used after Hebrew was no longer the current language. [Ed.]

[17] Bushnell could go further, using a famously ambiguous text (Romans 1:20) to make St. Paul a theorist of language, and following this interpretation with an appeal to the Hermetic and Platonic traditions. *Christ in Theology*, pp. 36–38: "Thus Paul, taking notice of this same analogy, says: 'For the invisible things of Him, from the creation of the world, are clearly seen, being understood by the things that are made, even His eternal power and Godhead;' in which, as I understand him, he not only expresses his conviction that the forms of the world do, in fact, represent the nature and power of God, but he also argues *to* that fact from the manifest necessity that, if the creation of the world be issued from God, it must represent the mind by which it is conceived, and must, in all its particular forms or objects, reveal those archetypes of thought in God which shaped them in their birth. . . .

"Nor is it only the extreme mystic interpreters, such as Swedenborg and Origen, that discover this correspondence or analogy, and who bring

We find little, therefore, in the scriptures, to encourage the hope of a complete and sufficient Christian dogmatism, or of a satisfactory and truly adequate system of scientific theology. Language, under the laws of logic or speculation, does not seem to be adequate to any such use or purpose. The scriptures of God, in providing a clothing for religious truth, have little to do with mere dialectics, much to do with the freer creations of poetry; and that for reasons, evidently, which ought to waken a salutary scepticism in us, in regard to the possibility of that, which so many great minds have been attempting with so great confidence for so many hundreds of years. With due respect, also, I will venture to ask, whether the actual results of this immense engineering process, which we call dogmatic and po-

---

it into discredit, by asserting a precisely threefold meaning in the words of Scripture, and other like fancies. It is apprehended, also, by the insight of poets and philosophic observers, not only as pertaining to the Scripture forms, but to every thing in the outward state. 'The severe schools,' says Sir Thomas Browne, 'shall never laugh me out of the philosophy of Hermes, that this visible world is but a picture of the invisible, wherein, as in a portrait, things are seen, not truly, but in equivocal shapes, and as they counterfeit some more real substance in that invisible fabric.' And it is remarkable that this Egyptian Hermes, to whom he refers, and who is computed to have lived even twenty centuries before Christ, was able, in the depths of nature, and apart from the aids of revelation, to verify it as a truth, that 'all things which are in heaven are in the earth, after an earthly manner; and all which are in the earth are in heaven, [the world of thought and spirit,] after a celestial manner.' The same general truth, under a different form, was maintained by Plato, when he represented that all visible things are the outward birth of intellectual types or thoughts represented in them." [Bushnell's brackets.]

Thomas Browne (1604–1682), *Religio Medici* (1642), Part I, Section 12, "Of the Holy Trinity." Coleridge also uses this passage in his *Aids to Reflection.* Hermes Trismegistus was the reputed author of supposedly ancient Egyptian books of wisdom. Bushnell accepts the traditional dating. The Hermetic writings actually show heavy Neo-Platonic influence and date from the early centuries A.D. but show little or no Christian influence. The substance of Bushnell's quotation is often expressed in Hermetic writings. See Walter Scott, *Hermetica* (Oxford: Clarendon Press, 1924). [Ed.]

lemic theology—as surely polemic as dogmatic—does not give some countenance to the doubt I am suggesting? . . .

It accords, also, with this, that while natural science is advancing with so great rapidity and certainty of movement, the advances of mental science and theology are so irregular and obscure, and are wrought out by a process so conflicting and tortuous. They seem, in fact, to have no advance, save what may be called a cultivation of symbol, produced by the multifarious industry of debate and system-making. There is, however, one hope for mental and religious truth, and their final settlement, which I confess I see but dimly, and can but faintly express, or indicate. It is, that physical science, leading the way, setting outward things in their true proportions, opening up their true contents, revealing their genesis and final causes and laws, and weaving all into the unity of a real universe, will so perfect our knowledges and conceptions of them, that we can use them, in the second department of language, with more exactness. There is, we have also seen, in what we call nature, that is, in its objects, an outward grammar of relations, which constructs the grammar of language; or what is not far different, the logic of propositions. In the laws of nature, I suppose, there is, in like manner, an internal grammar, which is certain, as it is evolved, to pass into language, and be an internal grammar in that, systematizing and steadying its uses. And then language will be as much more full and intelligent, as it has more of God's intelligence, in the system of nature, imparted to its symbols. For, undoubtedly, the whole universe of nature is a perfect analogon of the whole universe of thought or spirit. Therefore, as nature becomes truly a universe only through science revealing its universal laws, the true universe of thought and spirit cannot sooner be conceived. It would be easy to show, in this connection, the immense force already exerted over the empire of spiritual truth, by astronomy, chemistry, geology, the revelations of light and electricity, and especially of the mysterious and plastic workings of life, in the animal and vegetable kingdoms. We are accustomed to say, that this is not the same world to live in that it was fifty years ago. Just as true is it, that it is not the same world to *think* in, that it then was—of which, also, we shall, by and by, take notice.

If, then, it please any one to believe, notwithstanding the present incapacities of dogmatism, that when, through science, we are able to see things physical in their true force and relations, having, also, within us, inbreathed by the spirit of God, a comprehensive heart and feelings sufficiently cleared of prejudice, to behold, in the universal mirror of God, His universal truth—if, I say, any one please to believe, that now the Christian world may arrive at some final and determinate apprehensions of Christian doctrine, I will not object. But, if they do, observe, it will only be that they have settled, at last, into a comprehensive reception of the universal symbolism, and not that they have invented a few propositions, so intensely significant and true, as to dispense with all besides.

14. It is important to notice, as connected with the subject of language, that dogmatical propositions, such as are commonly woven into creeds and catechisms of doctrine, have not the certainty they are commonly supposed to have. They only give us the seeing of the authors, at the precise stand-point occupied by them, at the time, and they are true only as seen from that point—not even there, save in a proximate sense. Passing on, descending the current of time, we will say, for two centuries, we are brought to a different point, as when we change positions in a landscape, and then we are doomed to see things in a different light, in spite of ourselves. It is not that the truth changes, but that we change. Our eye changes color, and then the color of our eye affects our seeing. We are different men, living as parts in a different system of things and thinkings, denyings, and affirmings; and, as our contents and our antagonisms are different, we cannot see the same truths in the same forms. It may

even be necessary to change the forms, to hold us in the same truths.[18]

I could name phrases that have been brought into the creeds of many of our New England churches, within the present half century, which are already waxing old, and are doomed, within the next half century, to ask a re-modification.

Besides, in the original formation of any creed, catechism, or system of divinity, there is always a latent element of figure, which, probably, the authors know not of, but without which, it is neither true to them, nor to anybody. But in a long course of repetition, the figure dies out, and the formula settles into a literality, and then, if the repetition goes on, it is really an assent to what is not true; for that which was true, at the beginning, has now become untrue—and that, however paradoxical it may seem, by being assented to. What I here speak of, might be

---

[18] Bushnell published very little historical writing but his reading was extensive and his outlook is pervaded by a rather radical historicism. He was more outspoken in *Christ in Theology*, pp. 72–73: "Purely theologic systems are structures raised by the logical understanding, when it undertakes to be the architect, in the forms and measures of words, of the Divine System—articulations of symbols, organized by one or another, to represent his universe and be the infinite he proposes to men. And as there is no limit to the possible systems that may be framed or composted in this manner, one system is continually rising up, and will be, to chase another and claim, in turn, the assent of the world. On one hand, are God and eternity as an infinite material, out of form. On the other, is the formal understanding working at or upon this material, or professing to do so; trying new resolutions of the conceptions or figures by which it is represented, taking one figure instead of another and repaying what is scant in that by what is fuller in another; and so, having gotten a few forms of words mortised together by the carpentry of logic, it offers them to the world as another and better account of the Infinite Material—that is, of God and divine government. And so it comes to pass that, while there is but one truth, we have many theologies—little finite universes all, soap-bubble worlds rising by their own levity, whirled away by all cross winds of philosophy and Providential history, bursting in tiny collisions, or without collision, by the mere thinness of their films, and not leaving moisture enough at the point where they vanish to show where they were." [Ed.]

easily illustrated by a reference to the dogmatic history of opinions, concerning sin and free will. The will is under no mechanical laws.[19] Hence, in all the reasonings, affirmations, and denials relating to the will and its modes of responsible activity, language, being mostly derived from the mechanical world, must somehow be divorced, in the use, from all its mechanical laws, else it imports a falsity. But the difficulty is, to keep the language up to that self-active unmechanical sense in which, only, it was true in the original use; for a dull, unthinking repetition lets it down very soon under the old mechanical laws, and then the same, or closely similar, forms of reasoning and assertion are false. Hence, in part, the necessity, I suppose, that this particular class of subjects should be reinvestigated every fifty years. Considering the infirmities of language, therefore, all formulas of doctrine should be held in a certain spirit of accommodation. They cannot be pressed to the letter, for the very sufficient reason that the letter is never true. They can be regarded only as proximate representations, and should therefore be accepted not as laws over belief, or opinion, but more as badges of consent and good understanding. The moment we begin to speak of them as guards and tests of purity, we confess that we have lost the sense of purity, and, with about equal certainty, the virtue itself.

At the same time, it is remarkable with what ease a man, who is sensible of the fluxing nature and significance of words, may assent to almost any creed, and that, with a perfectly sincere doubt, whether he does not receive it in its most interior and real meaning; that is, whether going back to the men who made it, taking their stand point, and abating what belongs to the form of a truth, in distinction from the truth itself, he does not come into the real senses or interior beliefs they clothed in these

---

[19] Here as in other ways Bushnell absorbed the teachings of Nathaniel William Taylor and the Scottish Philosophy's argument for human agency, see pp. 43–45, 211–249. But Bushnell greatly enlarged the conception in his major work on *Nature and the Supernatural* (1858). [Ed.]

forms. Perhaps it is on this account that I have never been able to sympathise, at all, with the abundant protesting of the New England Unitarians, against creeds. So far from suffering even the least consciousness of constraint, or oppression, under any creed, I have been readier to accept as great a number as fell in my way; for when they are subjected to the deepest chemistry of thought, that which descends to the point of relationship between the form of the truth and its interior formless nature, they become, thereupon, so elastic, and run so freely into each other, that one seldom need have any difficulty in accepting as many as are offered him. He may regard them as only a kind of battle-dooring of words, blow answering to blow, while the reality of the play, viz. *exercise,* is the same, whichever side of the room is taken, and whether the stroke is given by the right hand or the left.

The greatest objection that I know, to creeds—that is, to creeds of a theoretic or dogmatic character—is that they make so many appearances of division, where there really is none, till the appearances make it. They are likely, also, unless some debate or controversy sharpens the mind to them, and keeps them alive, to die out of meaning, and be assented to, at last, as a mere jingle of words. Thus we have, in many of our orthodox formulas of trinity, the phrase, "the same in substance," and yet, how many are there, even of our theologians, to whom it will now seem a heresy, to say this with a meaning. And the clause following, "equal in power and glory," will be scarcely less supportable, when a view of trinity is offered which gives the terms an earnest and real significance.[20]

On these accounts, the best creed is that which stays by the

---

[20] Ever since Edwards, New England theologians had been wrestling with the Trinitarian issues; and the Unitarian controversy sharpened these discussions, leading to various modifications and restatements. Throughout his life Bushnell strove for a viable doctrine of the Trinity and a correlated Christology. He began this work in the volume to which this Dissertation was the Introduction. [Ed.]

concrete most faithfully, and carries its doctrine, as far as possible, in a vehicle of fact and of real life. This is the peculiar excellence and beauty of what is called the "Apostle's Creed." If, however, creeds of theory, or systematic dogma, must be retained, the next best arrangement would be to allow assent to a great number of such creeds at once; letting them qualify, assist, and mitigate each other. And a virtual allowance of this is, in fact, one of the best points in our Saybrook Platform, which accepts the acknowledgment, either of its own Articles, or of the "Doctrinal Articles of the Church of England," or of the "Westminster Confession," or of the "Confession agreed on at the Savoy;" and if it be indifferent which of the four is received, there can be no objection, certainly, if all are received.[21] And it is in just this way that the scripture has its meaning filled out, qualified, fortified, secured against subsiding into falsity, or becoming a mere jingle of sounds. We have so many writers set before us, each in his own habit, and giving his own form of the truth; offering the truth, some at one pole, and some at the other, that, when we receive and entertain them all, making, in fact, a creed of them all, they act as complementary forces, and, by their joint effect, keep us ever in the fullest, liveliest, and most many-sided apprehension of the Christian truth.

15. I have said nothing of the manner in which the user of language imparts himself to it. Undoubtedly every human language has, in its words and forms, indelible marks of the personal character and habit of the men by whom it was originally produced. Nay, it may, even, be said that every language carries in its bosom some flavor of meaning or import, derived from all the past generations that have lived in it. Not more truly does it represent the forms of nature, than it does within, or under these forms, the contents, also, of history. And, therefore, what is

---

[21] Since 1708–1709 the Saybrook Platform had been the official standard of Connecticut Congregationalism. See pp. 36–42 and also Williston Walker, *The Creeds and Platforms of Congregationalism*, pp. 463–523. [Ed.]

called usage, has a certain importance, when we seek the import or right use of words. But not any such importance as the lexicographers, and the Blairizing critics, have given it.[22] Usage is a guide to use, but never a limit upon use. We have our freedom, as our fathers had, and as good a right to use words with new meanings, certainly, as to have new thoughts.

And just here, it is, that we come upon a matter, which, if it be too mysterious to be investigated, is yet too important to be overlooked. In every writer, distinguished by mental life, words have a significance and power breathed into them, which is wholly peculiar—whether it be in the rhythm, the collocations, the cadences, or the internal ideas, it may be impossible to guess. But his language is his own, and there is some chemistry of life in it that belongs only to him, as does the vital chemistry of his body. This holds of every writer, who can properly be called a living soul. If he be a dead soul, or one that is coffined in mere logic and uses, then his language, being dead, will be like all other dead language; for death is always like itself. In what manner it is, that words, in common, ordinary use—words that have been staled in their significance, as raisins are preserved in their own sugar—receive a new inbreathing of life and power, it is impossible, I have said, to explain. Pascal cites, for illustration, the different games that may be played with the same tennis balls, which, in fact, is only appealing to death and chance for the illustration of life. Better, is it, to conceive the spirit of the author, as living in his words, in the same manner as Coleridge conceives the spirit of his country living in its outward sceneries and objects:

> I had found
> That outward forms, the loftiest, still receive
> Their finer influence from the Life within.[23]

---

[22] Hugh Blair (1718–1800) of Edinburgh, though a preromantic of sorts, exerted a strong conservative influence on English usage and literary taste, especially through his *Lectures on Rhetoric and Belles Lettres* (1783). He would have discountenanced a word like "Blairizing." [Ed.]

[23] Samuel Taylor Coleridge, "The Eolian Harp." [Ed.]

Accordingly, it is the right of every author, who deserves attention at all, to claim a certain liberty, and even to have it for a merit that he cannot be judged exactly by old uses and formulas. Life is organic; and if there be life in his work, it will be found not in some noun or verb that he uses, but in the organic whole of his creations.[24] Hence, it is clear that he must be apprehended in some sense, as a whole, before his full import can be received in paragraphs and sentences. Until then, he will, of necessity, appear to be obscure, enigmatical, extravagant, or even absurd. He cannot be tested by the jingle of his words, or by auscultation applied to the breathing of his sentences. No decree of condemnation must be passed upon him, because he does not make himself understood, sentence by sentence; for, if he infuses into words a life-power of his own, or does more than simply to recombine old impressions, he cannot make himself intelligible, fully, save through a kind of general acquaintance. It may, even, be to his praise, that he is not too easily understood. For, in this matter of understanding, two things are requisite; first, a matter which is understandable; and, second, a power that is capable of understanding; and if there be some things offered, hard to be understood, then there must be a power of digestion strong enough to master them; and if, in fault of that, some crude, and over-confident sophister dangerously wrests the words, the blame is with him. Nor is it enough, in such a case, that the reading man, or public, be of a naturally sound mind, or even that they bring to the subject, capacities of a very high order; for words, as we have seen, never carry, or transfer a thought; they only offer hints or symbols, to put others on generating the same thought, which, in many cases, they are not likely to do, unless they have been long enough practiced in the subject discussed, to know where it lies; and not even

---

[24] Organicism was a vital feature of Bushnell's thought, whether with reference to selfhood, family, church, nation, human society as a whole or, indeed, the message and meaning of Christianity. See the Postscript to this selection, p. 369. [Ed.]

then, if the writer is at all out of the system of his day, without such a degree of exercise in his forms of thought as will begat a certain general insight of his method and symbol.

They cannot run to a dictionary, and draw out the shroud of an old meaning from that, by which to conceive, or in which to clothe words and phrases that have their vital force, in no small part, from the man himself; and which, therefore, can be fully understood only by reference to the total organism of which they are members. The reading man, therefore, before he thinks to judge the writing man, must first endeavor to generate the writing man. And this, without supposing any defect of capacity in himself, will sometimes be difficult. He may be too young, or too old; having too little breadth, or too little flexibility, to make a sufficient realization of the truth presented. It costs me no mortification, to confess that the most fructifying writer I ever read, was one in whom I was, at first, able only to see glimpses, or gleams of truth; one whom it required years of study and reflection, of patient suspension and laborious self-questioning, to be able fully to understand; and, indeed, whom I never since have read, at all, save in a chapter or two, which I glanced over, just to see how obvious and clear, what before was impossible, had now become.

Shall I dare to go further? Shall I say that of all the "clear" writers and speakers I have ever met with—those, I mean, who are praised by the multitude for their transparency—I have never yet found one that was able to send me forward an inch; or one that was really true, save in a certain superficial, or pedagogical sense, as being an accurate distributor of that which is known. The roots of the known are always in the unknown; and, if a man will never show the root of any thing, if he will treat of the known as *separate* from the unknown, and as having a complete knowledge of it, which he has not—pretending, still, to be an investigator, and to exert an obstetric force, when he is only handling over old knowledges and impressions—he may easily enough be clear. Nothing, in fact, is easier, if one is either able to be shallow, or willing to be false. He is clear, because he stands out *before* the infinite and the unknown; separated, bounded off [de-finite]²⁵ so that you see the whole compass of his head, just so many inches in diameter. But the writer, who is to help us on, by some real advance or higher revelation, will, for that reason, be less comprehensible, and offer more things hard to be understood. He will be, as it were, a face, setting *out from* a back ground of mystery; a symbolism, through which the infinite and the unknown are looking out upon us, and by kind significances, tempting us to struggle into that holy, but dark profound, which they are opening. Of course, we are not to make a merit of obscurity; for nothing is more to be admired than the wondrous art by which some men are able to propitiate and assist the generative understanding of others, so as to draw them readily into higher realizations of truth. But there is a limit, we must acknowledge, even to this highest power of genius; it cannot quite create a soul under the ribs of death.

Whatever may be thought of these suggestions, for some, I suppose, will give them little weight, it is obvious that, since language is rather an instrument of suggestion than of absolute conveyance for thought, since it acts suggestively, through symbols held up in the words, which symbols and words are never exact measures of any truth (always imputing somewhat of form to the truth which does not belong to it, always somewhat contrary to each other)—this being true, it is obvious that a very little of perverse effort expended on his words, can subject a writer to almost any degree of apparent absurdity. And, what is specially to be noticed, there is no other human work, in which so much of applause can be gotten at so cheap a rate and with so small a modicum of talent. The work, indeed, is always half done beforehand. The words are ready to quarrel, as soon as any one will see them, and nothing is necessary, in fact, but to play off a little of constructive ingenuity on their forms, to

---

²⁵ Bushnell's brackets. This praise in the preceding paragraph is probably for Coleridge. [Ed.]

set them at war with one another and the whole universe besides. And, when it is done, many will be sure to admire and praise what they call the profound and searching logic displayed. Now, the truth is, that no many-sided writer, no one who embraces all the complementary forces of truth, is ever able to stand in harmony before himself (such is the nature of language) save by an act of internal construction favorable to himself, and preservative of his mental unity. It follows, of necessity, that without this favorable act of construction extended to his words, no true teacher can be saved from contradiction and confusion—no one, especially, who presents more than a half, or tenth part of a truth. Therefore, every writer, not manifestly actuated by a malignant or evil spirit, is entitled to this indulgence. The mind must be offered up to him, for the time, with a certain degree of sympathy. It must draw itself into the same position; take his constructions; feel out, so to speak, his meanings, and keep him, as far as may be, in a form of general consistency. Then, having endeavored thus, and for a sufficient length of time, to reproduce him or his thought, that is, to make a realization of him, some proper judgment may be formed in regard to the soundness of his doctrine.[26]

I need not say how different is the method ordinarily pursued. The decision is an off-hand decision. No time is allowed to cross-question the writer's representations, and see how one symbol interprets, qualifies, and corrects another. First impressions are sufficient and infallible. It is found that a very little pressure against the harmony of words and phrases, produces woeful discords and absurdities, which it will be a pleasant proof of superior acumen to exhibit. And then, as a vulture lighting upon a lamb, tears out some member, and bears it off, screaming over the prey, as if he were saying—See how absurdly that lamb was put together!—so we are to see a member torn out here or there,

---

[26] Bushnell's thoughts on "understanding" and "sympathy" suggest the theory of *Verstehen* formed and employed by Wilhelm Dilthey (1833–1911). Cf. Dilthey, *Pattern and Meaning in History,* H. P. Rickman, ed. (New York: Harper Torchbooks, 1961). [Ed.]

separated from all the vital connections of reason, turned about in the screws of constructive logic, properly so called, and held up as a foolish thing, to pity or derision! May we not believe, that when the nature of language, as an instrument of thought, is properly understood, this vulture talent, which has so long violated the delicate integrity of opinions, and the sacred rights of truth, will be estimated according to its dignity?

It needs also to be remarked, in this connection, that a writer is not, of course, to be blamed because he is variously interpreted by his readers, or because the public masses have a degree of difficulty in conceiving his precise meaning. It should be so, and will be, if he has any thing of real moment to say. There has always been most of controversy, for this reason, about the meaning of the greatest authors and teachers. Plato, for example, and Aristotle; Bacon, Shakspeare, and Goethe; Job, Paul, John, and especially CHRIST HIMSELF. What, in fact, do we see, in the endless debate, kept up for these eighteen hundred years, over the words of Jesus, but an illustration of the truth, that infinitesimals, though there be many of them, are not the best judges of infinites. And something of the same principle pertains, in the judgment or inspection of merely human teachers. They may be obscure, not from weakness only, which, certainly, is most frequent, but quite as truly by reason of their exceeding breadth, and the piercing vigor of their insight. And when this latter is true, as it sometimes may be, then to invoke a sentence of popular condemnation, because the writer has not made himself perfectly intelligible, or clear to the whole public, is, in fact, to assist or instigate the multitude in practicing a fraud against themselves. And, what is worse, if possible, it encourages an ill-natured and really unchristian spirit in them, excusing their impatience with every form of teaching that requires an effort of candor, or an ingenuous spirit.

16. That I may not seem to be offering to the public, doctrines, the real import of which I have not considered myself,

something must be said of the consequences likely to result to religion, from the admission of views such as I have here presented. Only, be it observed, that their truth depends, in no degree, on any expectations of good, or any vaticinations of evil, which the faith of one, or the panic of another may raise.

Unquestionably, the view of language here presented must produce, if received, a decided mitigation of our dogmatic tendencies in religion. It throws a heavy shade of discouragement on our efforts in this direction. It shows that language is, probably, incapable of any such definite and determinate use as we have supposed it to be in our theological speculations; that, for this reason, dogma has failed hitherto, and about as certainly will hereafter. Taking away, thus, the confidence of the speculative theologer, it will limit, proportionally, his eagerness. It will, also, reduce the very excessive eminence he has, at present, in the public estimation, requiring a readjustment of the scale that now pertains between this and the historical, literary, and practical departments of Christian study. Or, better still, showing that the advancement and the real amount of true theology depends, not on logical deductions and systematic solutions, but principally on the more cultivated and nicer apprehension of symbol, it may turn the industry of our teachers more in this direction, giving a more esthetic character to their studies and theories, and drawing them as much closer to the practical life of religion.[27]

---

[27] Bushnell expounds more positive views on theology, creeds, and the philosophy of religion in *Christ and Theology,* pp. 64–65, 78–79, 84–87: "But the question will now be raised, what place have we left for Christian theology, or for any reliable conception of the Christian scheme of salvation? That I have little respect for pure dogmatism, or for merely speculative theology, is sufficiently apparent . . . . And yet I have a certain conviction, whether I can show the reasons or not, that we must have something, somehow held and exercised, that may be called theology. We must define, distinguish, arrange and frame into order the matter of our knowledge. System is the instinct of intelligence, and to crucify the instinct of system is, in one view, to crucify intelligence. . . .

"If all human language is found to be under conditions of form, while truth itself, being spiritual, is out of form, or has no form, it does not follow that Christian doctrine is to be despaired of, or treated with indifference. It is only to be sought with greater patience, a more delicate candor, and a more ingenuous love. And for just this reason, Christian doctrine may be worth a great deal more to the world than it would be, if it could be bolted into the mind by terms of absolute notation, apart from all conditions of candor, justice and sympathy with God or man.

"If we ask for the best and healthiest and least uncertain forms of truth, . . . I would say that we ought to adhere as closely as possible, in all catechisms and confessions, to the simple historic matter of the gospel. This is the real substructure, the pillar and ground of all truth—it is the gospel as God shapes it. . . . At the same time there is no harm in articles more theologic, if rightly employed. . . . If we comfort ourselves in a general sense of agreement under them, they must be held for comfort, not for judgment. Still, the crystal will not shape itself by the book of mineralogy, but by its own secret laws; and the Church of God will not any more shape itself in church articles, but in the incarnate mystery of the Life. The soundest doctrine for this purpose, that *we* can furnish, will, in God's opinion, be the doctrine of the heart; 'For it is a good thing [an excellent cure for strange doctrine] that the heart be established with grace.' [Heb. 13:9.]

"The ablest exposition I have seen of this subject is that of Dr. Rothe, translated in the Postscript to Mr. Morell's *Philosophy of Religion*. His object is to find a place, or show a true ground for speculative theology. And, though he does not intimate, what I believe to be just, that the true line of direction in all fruitful study, is that which proposes rather divinity than theology, he yet lays down the distinction under other terms, and makes it the center of his exposition. And he brings his exposition thus to the true conclusion, that Christian theology is the speculative or logical exposition of the Christian consciousness, considered as containing the divine; just as philosophy is of the natural and personal self-consciousness; and that one has the same *kind* of validity and verity as the other. . . .

"If it is so blended with that experience, as to have its light therein, and be corrected and amplified thereby as an open system; if it is catholic in the same, as acknowledging all other systems based in the same divine, evangelical experience, and built upon the same Scripture foundation; in a word, if it is saturated with divinity, so as to be divinity according to the true force of that word, formerly so current, but latterly so far displaced, then it is the true wisdom of God. Not all wisdom, but true; for still there is a livelier and more competent medium of truth than any that classes in the modes of speculation; I mean the medium of simple expression. The poetic forms of utterance are closer to the fires of religion within us, more adequate revelations of consciousness, because they reveal it in flame. Parable, symbol, description, illustration, emphasis and tone, the look of a divine charity and the conduct of a soul in the divine

Without being at all aware of the fact, as it would seem, our theologic method in New England has been essentially rationalistic; though not exactly in the German sense.[28] The possibility of reasoning out religion, though denied in words, has yet been tacitly assumed. Not allowing ourselves to be rationalists *over* the scriptures, we have yet been as active and confident rationalists *under* them, as it was possible to be—assuming, always, that they address their contents to the systematic, speculative reason of men, into which they are to be received, and by which they are to be digested into formulas—when they are ready for use. We have had a certain negative way of declaring against the competence of the natural man to understand spiritual things, but it has been done principally in that way only, and as a convenient method of cutting off speculative arguments that could not be speculatively answered. It has not been held, as a practical, positive, and earnest Christian truth, that there is a PERCEPTIVE POWER in spiritual life, an unction of the Holy One, which is itself a kind of inspiration—an immediate, experimental knowledge of God, by virtue of which, and partly in the degree of which, Christian theology is possible. No real doubt has been held of the perfect sufficiency of formulas or of natural logic, handled by the natural understanding, to settle them.

The views of language here offered lead to a different method.

---

beauty—these, I hope you will agree, are better and more adequate revelations of truth than theology, in its best form, can be."

Brackets and italics *within* the above quotations are Bushnell's. Richard Rothe (1799–1867), a brilliant philosophic theologian of Heidelberg, conservative and deeply religious in spirit, and profoundly responsive to Schleiermacher, Schelling, and Hegel, answered very directly to Bushnell's need. John Daniel Morell (1816–1891), an Englishman with unusually large interests in Continental thought, clinched his own position on *The Philosophy of Religion* (New York: D. Appleton & Co., 1849) with a twenty-page extract from Rothe's *Theologische Ethik*. [Ed.]

[28] In Bushnell's day the term *rationalism* in the "German sense" ordinarily referred to historico-critical studies of the Bible. The New England tradition from Edwards to Taylor, on the other hand, was rationalistic in its theological method. [Ed.]

The scriptures will be more studied than they have been, and in a different manner—not as a magazine of propositions and mere dialectic entities, but as inspirations and poetic forms of life, requiring, also, divine inbreathings and exaltations in us, that we may ascend into their meaning. Our opinions will be less catechetical and definite, using the word as our definers do, but they will be as much broader as they are more divine; as much truer, as they are more vital and closer to the plastic, undefinable mystery of spiritual life. We shall seem to understand less, and shall actually receive more. No false *pre-cision,* which the nature and conditions of spiritual truth forbid, will, by cutting up the body of truth into definite and dead morsels, throw us into states of excision and division, equally manifold. We shall receive the truth of God in a more entire organic and organific manner, as being itself an essentially vital power. It will not be our endeavor to pull the truth into analytic distinctions, as if theology were a kind of inorganic chemistry, and the last end of discovery, an atomic theory; but we shall delight in truth, more as a concrete, vital nature, incarnated in all fact and symbol round us—a vast, mysterious, incomprehensible power, which best we know, when most we love.

Striving ever outward, towards the infinite, and not inward or downward, upon speculative minima or atoms, we shall be kept in a humbler, and far less positive state of mind. Our judgments of others will be less peremptory, and, as we are more modest, we shall be as much more patient and charitable. And our views of language, as an instrument wholly inadequate to the exact representation of thought, will operate, immediately, to favor the same result.

If any should be apprehensive that the views here offered may bring in an age of mysticism, and so of interminable confusion, they will greatly misconceive their import, and also the nature of mysticism itself. A mystic is one who finds a secret meaning, both in words and in things, back of their common or accepted meaning—some agency of LIFE, or LIVING THOUGHT, hid under the forms of words and institutions, and historical events. Hence, all religious writers and teachers, who dwell on the representative character of words and things, or hold the truths of religion, not in mechanical measures and relations, but as forms of life, are so far mystics. Thus Neander gives it, as a characteristic of the apostle John

> that a reference to communion with the Redeemer, in the inward life, and in the present, predominates over the reference to the future, and to outward facts; he dwells upon the elements of the inner life, the facts of Christian consciousness, and only slightly adverts to outward matters of fact and ecclesiastical arrangements. In accordance with this spirit, he exhibits all the particular incidents in the outward history of Christ, only as a manifestation of his indwelling glory, by which this may be brought home to the heart; he always avails himself of these narratives, to introduce what the Redeemer declared, respecting his relation to mankind, as the source of life. John is the representative of the truth which lies at the basis of that tendency of the Christian spirit, which sets itself in opposition to a one-sided intellectualism, and ecclesiastical formality—and is distinguished by the name of mysticism.[29]

I make no disavowal, then, of the fact, that there is a mystic element, as there should be, in what I have represented as the source of meaning in language, and also in the views of Christian life and doctrine that follow. Man is designed in his very nature to be a partially mystic being; the world to be looked

---

[29] John Augustus William Neander, *History of the Planting and Training of the Christian Church*, J. E. Ryland, trans. (Philadelphia: J. M. Campbell & Co., 1844), pp. 317–318. One of the founders of modern church history, Neander was an admirer of Schleiermacher and entertained a warm sympathy for piety and religious feeling. He and Bushnell use the term "mysticism" more inclusively than most expositors of *the* "mystical tradition." [Ed.]

upon as a mystic world. Christ himself revealed a decidedly
mystic element in his teachings. There is something of a mystic
quality in almost every writing of the New Testament. In John,
it is a character. In "the dialectic" Paul, there are very many
passages quite as mystical as any in John.

Now, the very cautious and salutary scepticism I have maintained, concerning the insufficiency and the partially repugnant
character of words, leaves as little room as possible to apprehend any danger of wildness, or confusion from the entrance of
a mystic element, thus qualified and guarded. There is nothing,
in fact, that we so much need, as an apostle John among our
other apostles; and I fervently hope that God will sometime
send us such a gift. The very last thing to be feared is, that our
loss-and-gain style of religion, the stern, ironlimbed speculative
logic of our New England theology, will receive some fatal dam-
age from a trace of the mystic element. It will produce no over-
turnings, sap no foundations, dissolve no formulas, run to no
license or extravagance. It will enter only as life came into the
bones; which, though they rose up into a limbered and active
state, and were hidden somewhat from the eye, by an envelope
of muscle and skin, were yet as good bones as before; probably
as much better and more systematic, as there was more of the
life-order in them and about them.

The two principal results, then, which I suppose may follow,
should these views of language be allowed to have their effect
in our theology, are a more comprehensive, friendly, and fraternal state than now exists between different families of Christians; and, as the confidence of dogma is mitigated, a more present, powerful, and universal conviction entering into the Christian body, that truth, in its highest and freest forms, is not of
the natural understanding, but is, rather, as Christ himself declared—spirit and life. We shall have more of union, therefore,
and more of true piety enlightened by the spirit of God—neither of which involves any harm or danger.

[*Postscript on the Instituted Church*][30]

Now, if it seem to any of you that in such an estimate of theology as I have given all organization is likely to perish, let me
suggest for your comfort that when God organizes, he will do
it, not by a part, but by all—not by theology alone, but by all the
outgoings, aims, actions, instrumentalities, and functions of the
spiritual body. He does not organize the solar system by gravity
alone, but by all the other powers acting with it—nay, by each
and every dead particle and living atom acting with it. I can
not, therefore, see that he will call on the theologians to organize
and keep up the church for him. But he will be the organizing
principle and Head of the body Himself. And being the head,
he will have many sorts of members, all various functions under
him. He will have theologies (probably more than one), confessions, offices, sacraments, days and rites of worship, sermons,
and homilies, and living voices, holy charities and Christly aims,
drawing all the faithful together; and with all these martyred
men and women, who, being dead will yet live in the times
following; and by all these he will organize the church. And
this will be an organization solid and true. I can trust it without
a particle of anxiety; though, if I were obliged to join some
theologic council or chair in preparing the scheme of speculative doctrine that should keep all safe and be the containing law
of the future church, I think I should never sleep again. Let
God organize all by all. Nothing is more clear, at this moment,
than that this is the only hope; for the reign of dogma, and state
power, and ceremony, and priestly orders—every thing that has
held the organizing power in past ages, is now breaking down
into impotence and passing away. And what shall we see in this,

[30] The "Postscript" that follows is taken from the final section of "Language and Doctrine" in *Christ and Theology*, pp. 87–89. [Ed.]

but a preparation for the reign of the Spirit as just now suggested; which, if it comes into this valley of bones lying apart, and breathes into them, as the Life itself of God, will they not come together and live? This, it seems to me, is the sound method of organization; and if this will not make a strong compact of growth and unity in the truth, I see not that more can be hoped from theologic articles. Either Christ will organize the body for all time in his own Incarnate Person, or else it never can be organized.

VIII

JOHN WILLIAMSON NEVIN

Romantic Church Reformer

John Williamson Nevin (1803–1886)[1] was twice converted. His first conversion came during a revival when he was a college student. He was converted a second time when he was a Presbyterian seminary professor, whereupon he entered the German Reform Church and shortly afterward began publishing what was in effect his apologia pro vita sua, a work on THE HISTORY AND GENIUS OF THE HEIDELBERG CATECHISM (1840–1842). In Nevin's second career as a professor in the seminary at Mercersburg he participated in one of the most significant movements of theological renewal and church reform in nineteenth-century America.

Nevin's life down to 1840 is an almost perfect illustration of the religious and ecclesiastical patterns which he was to weigh and find wanting in his later writings. Born in a pious Scot-Irish home in Pennsylvania, he received his college education and his personal experience of regeneration in the fervently evangelical atmosphere maintained by President Eliphalet Nott at Union College, Schenectady, New York. In 1823 he entered

---

[1] See Introduction, pp. 48–52.

Princeton Seminary, and on graduation filled in for two years as an instructor while Charles Hodge went abroad to study. In 1829 he joined the faculty of the Presbyterian seminary in Pittsburgh. Here he became active as a religious journalist and participated in a wide variety of causes dear to the "evangelical united front" of that day, including the antislavery movement. He was opposed to the "party spirit" that threatened his own denomination in those years, and the Schism of 1837–1838 hastened his second conversion. In later years he would name the "Sect Spirit" as the Anti-Christ.

The presence at Mercersburg of two young German scholar-theologians, Friedrich Rauch (1806–1841) and Philip Schaff (1819–1893), transformed Nevin's move to that seminary from a minor personal event into an important episode in church history. In these men Nevin found an animated embodiment of the very stream of contemporary thought that had been changing his own mind in recent years. Rauch had become a convinced Hegelian during his years at Heidelberg, and his PSYCHOLOGY (1841) was one of the very earliest knowledgable expressions of Hegelian views in America. (Nevin saw its second edition through the press after Rauch's untimely death.) Nevin began an enormously fruitful collaboration with Schaff after his arrival in 1844. A movement of renewal took form, and within it several distinct elements could be discerned: a deepened historical consciousness owing much to Hegel and to the church historian, Augustus Neander; an appropriation of idealistic philosophy and with it an intensely organismic view of the Church; a bold critique of "Modern Puritanism" and its individualistic waywardness from the original catholicity of the Reformed tradition; and a concrete program of doctrinal and liturgical reform.

Schaff's scholarship and writing ranged over the whole of

church history, and the Inaugural Discourse with which he began his career at Mercersburg was fittingly called THE PRINCIPLE OF PROTESTANTISM. When translated by Nevin and published with his own sermon on Catholic Unity (1845), the book became for them a joint manifesto. It called for a larger, more dialectical understanding of the Church's history—one in which the Lutheran and Reformed elements of Protestantism would be taken up into a larger view and this ultimately into a fuller yet thoroughly evangelical Catholicism. Nevin's contributions to the movement—theological, historical, and practical—continued to show equal, if not possibly greater versatility, especially in his learned articles in the MERCERSBURG REVIEW. Like Schaff, Nevin's scope of interests was wide whether he was engaged in polemics or in positive theological construction. Beside his work on the Heidelberg Catechism, two other works illustrate his abiding concerns. THE ANXIOUS BENCH (1843) was an attack on the methods and theology of Charles G. Finney's high-pressure revivalism, and THE MYSTICAL PRESENCE (1846) was an historical and theological work on the Eucharist, calling the Reformed churches (including Charles Hodge and the Presbyterians) back to Calvin and the great Reformation confessions, and through them to the great tradition of the Church.

The selection that follows is taken from THE MYSTICAL PRESENCE. It includes the Preface (a forceful justification of the book), Chapter I on the "Reformed or Calvinistic Doctrine of the Lord's Supper," major portions of Chapter II, "The Modern Puritan Theory," and the core of the final Chapter wherein Nevin presents his own "Biblical Argument." These sections display Nevin's keen historical judgments, his theological method, and above all his central diagnosis and prescription for the Church.

THE MYSTICAL PRESENCE

The Reformed or Calvinistic Doctrine of

the Lord's Supper

INTRODUCTORY REMARKS

The *Question of the Eucharist* is one of the most important belonging to the history of religion. It may be regarded indeed as in some sense central to the whole Christian system. For Christianity is grounded in the living union of the believer with the person of Christ; and this great fact is emphatically concentrated in the mystery of the Lord's Supper; which has always been clothed on this very account, to the consciousness of the Church, with a character of sanctity and solemnity, surpassing that of any other Christian institution.

The sacramental controversy of the sixteenth century then was no mere war of words; much less the offspring of mere prejudice, passion or blind self-will, as many in their fanatical superiority to the vast problem involved in it are ready to imagine. It belonged to the inmost sanctuary of theology, and was intertwined particularly with all the arteries of the Christian life. This was *felt* by the spiritual heroes of the Reformation. They had no right to overlook the question which was here thrown in their way, or to treat it as a question of small importance, whose claims might safely be postponed in favour of other interests, that might appear to be brought into jeopardy by its agitation. That this should seem so easy to much of our modern Protestantism, serves only to show, what is shown also by many other facts, that much of our modern Protestantism

From John Williamson Nevin, *The Mystical Presence. A Vindication of the Reformed or Calvinistic Doctrine of the Holy Eucharist* (Philadelphia: J. B. Lippincott & Co., 1846), pp. 51–62, 105, 117–126, 138–154, 199–247.

has fallen away sadly from the theological earnestness and depth of the period to which we now refer. With the revival of a deeper theology, there cannot fail to be a revival of interest also, on the part of the Church, in the sacramental question; as on the other hand there can be no surer sign than the want of such interest, in the case of any section of the Church at any given time, that its theology is without power and its piety infected with disease.

On this question, it is well known, the Protestant world split, from the very beginning, into two great divisions, which have never come since to a true and full inward reconciliation. Strangely enough however both [of these] sections of the Church have seriously receded, to no inconsiderable extent, from the ground on which they stood in the sixteenth century. This fact is most broadly and palpably apparent in the modern posture of the *Lutheran* Church, especially as known on this side of the Atlantic. All who have any knowledge whatever of history, are aware that the American Lutheran Church, in its reigning character, has entirely forsaken at this point the position originally occupied by the same communion in the old world.[1] Not only indeed has the proper Lutheran position been surrendered in favour of the Reformed doctrine; but even this doctrine itself, as it stood in the beginning, has come to be looked upon as altogether too high toned in the same direction; so that the very view which was denounced in the days of *Joachim Westphal* and *Tilemann Hesshuss,* as foul sacramentarian heresy, by which cities and nations were exposed to the fierce judgments of heaven, is now counted an extreme on precisely the opposite side, little better than the popish error of transubstantiation itself.[2] But this falling away from the ortho-

---

[1] On the American Lutheran situation, see pp. 52–57 and 427–460. [Ed.]

[2] Joachim Westphal (1510–1574) and Tilemann Hesshuss (1527–1588) were leaders of the strictly orthodox party in the intra-Lutheran Eucharistic controversy during the 1560's and after. [Ed.]

doxy of the sixteenth century is not confined to the Lutheran Church. The view of the Eucharist now generally predominant in the *Reformed* Church also, involves a similar departure, not so broad indeed but equally material, from its proper original creed, as exhibited in its symbolical books. An unchurchly, rationalistic tendency, has been allowed to carry the Church gradually more and more off from the ground it occupied in the beginning, till its position is found to be at length, to a large extent, a new one altogether.

In the nature of the case, this change must involve much more than the simple substitution of one theory of the Lord's Supper for another. The doctrine of the eucharist is intimately connected with all that is most deep and central in the Christian system as a whole; and it is not possible for it to undergo any material modification in any direction, without a corresponding modification at the same time of the theory and life of religion at other points. If it be true then, that such a falling away from the eucharistic view of the sixteenth century, as is now asserted, has taken place in the Reformed Church, it is very certain that the revolution is not confined to this point. It must affect necessarily the whole view, that is entertained of Christ's person, the idea of the Church, and the doctrine of salvation throughout. Not that the change in the theory of the Lord's Supper may be considered the origin and cause, properly speaking, of any such general theological revolution; but because it could not occur, except as accompanied by this general revolution, of which it may be taken as the most significant exponent and measure.

Under this view, the subject presents itself to us, as one of great interest and importance. The question involved in it, is not one of historical curiosity simply, the bearings of which in a religious view may be regarded as indifferent or of only slight account. It is a question of the utmost moment for theology and religion, which at this time particularly no friend of our evangelical Protestant faith should consider himself at liberty to overlook.[3]

To see and feel the truth of the assertion, that the modern popular view of the Lord's Supper is chargeable with a serious defection from the original Protestant orthodoxy at this point, it is only necessary to have some correct apprehension of what was actually believed and taught on the subject, by the Reformed Church as well as by the Lutheran, in the age of the Reformation. This cannot fail of itself to reveal, in the way of contrast, the true posture of the Church at the present time.

It is of course with the doctrine of the *Reformed* Church only, in the view now mentioned, as distinguished from the Lutheran, that the present inquiry is concerned. Our object is, to bring into view the theory of the Lord's Supper, as it stood in the general creed of this section of the Church in the sixteenth century. . . .

To obtain a proper view of the original doctrine of the Reformed Church on the subject of the eucharist, we must have recourse particularly to Calvin. Not that he is to be considered the creator, properly speaking, of the doctrine. It grew evidently out of the general religious life of the church itself, in its antagonism to the Lutheran dogma on the one hand, and the low Socinian extreme on the other.[4] Calvin however was the theological organ, by which it first came to that clear expression, under which it continued to be uttered subsequently in the symbolical books. His profound, far-reaching, and deeply penetrating mind drew forth the doctrine from the heart of the Church, exhibited it in its proper relations, proportions and distinctions,

---

[3] Nevin supported his position with an extended quotation from Frederick D. Maurice, *The Kingdom of Christ* (New York: Appleton, 1843), p. 308. [Ed.]

[4] Faustus Socinus (1539–1604), an Italian antitrinitarian reformer, organized the Polish Brethren. The Racovian Catechism (published in Rakow, 1605) expresses their beliefs. Nevin uses the term Socinian vaguely to designate the "sacramentarian" or Zwinglian view. [Ed.]

gave it form in this way for the understanding, and clothed it with authority as a settled article of faith in the general creed. He may be regarded then as the accredited interpreter and expounder of the article, for all later times. A better interpreter in the case, we could not possibly possess. Happily, too, his instructions and explanations here are very full and explicit. He comes upon the subject from all sides, and handles it under all forms, didactically and controversially; so that we are left in no uncertainty whatever, with regard to his meaning, at a single point.

Any theory of the eucharist will be found to accord closely with the view that is taken, at the same time of the nature of the union generally between Christ and his people. Whatever the life of the believer may be as a whole in this relation, it must determine the form of his communion with the Saviour in the sacrament of the Supper, as the central representation of its significance and power. Thus, the sacramental doctrine of the primitive Reformed Church stands inseparably connected with the idea of an inward living union between believers and Christ, in virtue of which they are incorporated into his very nature, and made to subsist with him by the power of a common life.[5] In full correspondence with this conception of the Christian salvation, as a process by which the believer is mystically inserted more and more into the person of Christ, till he becomes thus at last fully transformed into his image, it was held that nothing less than such a real participation of his living person is involved always in the right use of the Lord's Supper. The following distinctions may serve to define and explain more fully, the nature of the communion which holds between Christ and his people, in the whole view now mentioned, as taught by Calvin and the Reformed Church generally, in the sixteenth century.

1. The union of *believers* with Christ is not simply that of a

---

[5] Nevin footnotes this entire section with extensive quotations from the works of John Calvin. [Ed.]

common humanity, as derived from *Adam*. In this view, all men partake of one and the same nature, and each may be said to be in relation to his neighbour bone of his bone and flesh of his flesh. So Christ took not on him the nature of angels, but of men. He was born of a woman, and appeared among us in the likeness and fashion of our own life, only without sin. But plainly our relation to his nature, and through this to his mediatorial work, as Christians, is something quite different from this general consanguinity of the human race. Where we are said to be of the same life with him, "members of his body, of his flesh and of his bones," it is not on the ground merely of a joint participation with him in the nature of Adam, but on the ground of our participation in his own nature as a higher order of life. Our relation to him is not circuitous and collateral only; it holds in a direct connection with his person.

2. In this view, the relation is more again than a simply *moral* union. Such a union we have, where two or more persons are bound together by inward agreement, sympathy, and correspondence. Every common friendship is of this sort. It is the relation of the disciple to the master, whom he loves and reveres. It is the relation of the devout Jew to Moses, his venerated lawgiver and prophet. It holds also undoubtedly between the believer and Christ. The Saviour lives much in his thoughts and affections. He looks to him with an eye of faith, embraces him in his heart, commits himself to his guidance, walks in his steps, and endeavours to become clothed more and more with his very mind itself. In the end the correspondence will be found complete. We shall be like him in all respects, one with him morally, in the fullest sense. But Christianity includes more than such a moral union, separately considered. This union itself is only the result here of a relation more inward and deep. It has its ground in the force of a common life, in virtue of which Christ and his people are one even before they become thus assimilated to his character. So in the sacrament of the Lord's Supper; it is not simply a moral approach that the true worshipper is permitted

to make to the glorious object of his worship. His communion with Christ does not consist merely in the good exercises of his own mind, the actings of faith, and contrition, and hope, and love, the solemn recollections, the devotional feelings, the pious resolutions, of which he may be himself the subject, during the sacramental service. Nor is the sacrament a sign only, by which the memory and heart may be assisted in calling up what is past or absent, for the purposes of devotion; as the picture of a friend is suited to recall his image and revive our interest in his person, when he is no longer in our sight. Nor is it a pledge simply of our own consecration to the service of Christ, or of the faithfulness of God as engaged to make good to us in a general way the grace of the new covenant; as the rainbow serves still to ratify and confirm the promise given to Noah after the flood. All this would bring with it in the end nothing more than a moral communication with Christ, so far as the sacrament itself might be concerned. It could carry with it no virtue or force, more than might be put into it in every case by the spirit of the worshipper himself. Such however is not the nature of the ordinance. It is not simply an occasion, by which the soul of the believer may be excited to pious feelings and desires; but it embodies the actual presence of the grace it represents in its own constitution; and this grace is not simply the promise of God on which we are encouraged to rely, but the very life of the Lord Jesus Christ himself. We communicate, in the Lord's supper, not with the divine promise merely, not with the thought of Christ only, not with the recollection simply of what he has done and suffered for us, not with the lively present sense alone of his all-sufficient, all-glorious salvation; but with the living Saviour himself, in the fulness of his glorified person, made present to us for the purpose by the power of the Holy Ghost.

3. The relation of believers to Christ, then, is more again than that of a simply *legal* union. He is indeed the representative of his people, and what he has done and suffered on their behalf is counted to their benefit, as though it had been done by them-

selves. They have an interest in his merits, a title to all the advantages secured by his life and death. But this external imputation rests at last on an inward, real unity of life, without which it could have no reason or force. Our interest in Christ's merits and benefits can be based only upon a previous interest in his person; so in the Lord's Supper, we are made to participate, not merely in the advantages secured by his mediatorial work, the rewards of his obedience, the fruits of his bitter passion, the virtue of his atonement, and the power of his priestly intercession, but also in his true and proper life itself. We partake of his merits and benefits only so far as we partake of his substance.

4. Of course, once more, the communion in question is not simply with Christ in his *divine nature* separately taken, or with the *Holy Ghost* as the representative of his presence in the world. It does not hold in the influence of the Spirit merely, enlightening the soul and moving it to holy affections and purposes. It is by the Spirit indeed we are united to Christ. Our new life is comprehended in the Spirit as its element and medium. But it is always bound in this element to the person of the Lord Jesus Christ himself. Our fellowship is with the Father and with his son Jesus Christ, *through* the Holy Ghost. As such it is a real communion with the Word made flesh; not simply with the divinity of Christ, but with his humanity also; since both are inseparably joined together in his person, and a living union with him in the one view, implies necessarily a living union with him in the other view likewise. In the Lord's Supper, accordingly, the believer communicates not only with the Spirit of Christ, or with his divine nature, but with Christ himself in his whole living person; so that he may be said to be fed and nourished by his very flesh and blood. The communion is truly and fully with the *Man* Christ Jesus, and not simply with Jesus as the Son of God.

These distinctions may serve to bound and define the Reformed doctrine of the Eucharist on the side towards *Rationalism*. All pains were taken to guard it from the false tendency to which it stood exposed in this direction. The several conceptions of the believer's union and communion with Christ which have now been mentioned, were explicitly and earnestly rejected, as being too low and poor altogether for the majesty of this great mystery. In opposition to all such representations, it was constantly affirmed that Christ's people are inserted by faith into his very life; and that the Lord's Supper, forming as it does an epitome of the whole mystery, involves to the worthy communicant an actual participation in the substance of his person under this view. The participation is not simply in his Spirit, but in his flesh also and blood. It is not figurative merely and moral, but *real, substantial* and *essential*.

But it is not enough to settle the boundaries of the doctrine on the side of Rationalism. To be understood properly, it must be limited and defined, in like manner, on the side of *Romanism*.

1. In the first place then it excludes entirely the figment of *transubstantiation*. According to the Church of Rome, the elements of bread and wine in the sacrament are literally transmuted into the actual flesh and blood of Christ. The accidents, outward properties, sensible qualities only, remain the same; while the original substance is converted supernaturally into the true body of the glorified Saviour, which is thus exhibited and received in an outward way in the sacramental mystery. This transmutation too is not limited to the actual solemnity of the sacramental act itself, but is held to be of permanent force; so that the elements continue afterwards to be the true body of Christ, and are proper objects of veneration and worship accordingly. This theory was rejected as a gross superstition, even by the Lutheran Church, and of course found still less favor in the other section of the Protestant communion. The Reformed doctrine admits no change whatever in the elements. Bread remains bread, and wine remains wine.

2. The doctrine excludes, in the second place, the proper Lutheran hypothesis of the sacrament, technically distinguished by the title *consubstantiation*. According to this view, the body and

blood of Christ are not actually substituted supernaturally for the elements; the bread and wine remain unchanged, in their essence as well as in their properties. But still the body and blood of Christ are in their very substance *present,* where the supper is administered. The presence is not indeed bound to the elements, apart from their sacramental use. It holds only in the moment and form of this use as such; a mystery in this respect, transcending all the common laws of reason and nature. It is however a true, corporal presence of the blessed Saviour. Hence his body is received by the worshipper *orally,* though not in the form and under the quality of common food; and so not by believers simply, but by unbelievers also, to their own condemnation. The dogma was allowed in the end to involve also, by necessary consequence, the ubiquity of Christ's glorified body. Bread and wine retain their own nature, but Christ, who is in virtue of the *communicatio idiomatum* present in his human nature in all places where he may please to be, imparts his true flesh and blood, *in, with* and *under* the outward signs to all communicants, whether with or without faith, by the inherent power of the ordinance itself.[6]

In opposition to this view, the Reformed Church taught that the participation of Christ's flesh and blood in the Lord's Supper is *spiritual* only, and in no sense corporal. The idea of a local presence in the case, was utterly rejected. The elements cannot be said to comprehend or include the body of the Saviour in any sense. It is not *there,* but remains constantly in heaven, according to the scriptures. It is not handled by the minister and taken into the mouth of the communicant. The manducation of it is not oral, but only by faith. It is present in fruition accordingly to believers only in the exercise of faith; the impenitent and un-

---

[6] Lutherans generally considered the term "consubstantiation" to misrepresent their doctrine of the Real Presence. The doctrine of the *communicatio idiomatum* deals with the relation of the divine and human in Jesus Christ. [Ed.]

believing receive only the naked symbols, bread and wine, without any spiritual advantage to their own souls.

Thus we have the doctrine defined and circumscribed on both sides; with proper distinction from all that may be considered a tendency to Rationalism in one direction, and from all that may be counted a tendency to Romanism in the other. It allows the *presence* of Christ's person in the sacrament, including even his flesh and blood, so far as the actual participation of the believer is concerned. Even the term *real presence*, Calvin tells us he was willing to employ, if it were to be understood as synonymous with *true* presence; by which he means a presence that brings Christ truly into communion with the believer in his human nature, as well as in his divine nature. The word *real*, however, was understood ordinarily to denote a local, corporal presence, and on this account was not approved. To guard against this, it may be qualified by the word *spiritual;* and the expression will then be quite suitable to the nature of the doctrine, as it has been now explained. A *real* presence, in opposition to the notion that Christ's flesh and blood are not made present to the communicant in *any* way. A *spiritual* real presence, in opposition to the idea that Christ's body is in the elements in a local or corporal manner. Not real simply, and not spiritual simply; but real, and yet spiritual at the same time. The body of Christ is in heaven, the believer on earth; but by the power of the Holy Ghost, nevertheless, the obstacle of such vast local distance is fully overcome, so that in the sacramental act, while the outward symbols are received in an outward way, the very body and blood of Christ are at the same time inwardly and supernaturally communicated to the worthy receiver, for the real nourishment of his new life. Not that the material particles of Christ's body are supposed to be carried over, by this supernatural process, into the believer's person. The communion is spiritual, not material. It is a participation of the Saviour's life. Of his life, however, as human, subsisting in a true bodily form. The living energy, the vivific virtue, as Calvin styles it, of

Christ's flesh, is made to flow over into the communicant, making him more and more one with Christ himself, and thus more and more an heir of the same immortality that is brought to light in his person.

Two points in particular, in the theory now exhibited, require to be held clearly in view.

The first is, that the sacrament is made to carry with it an *objective* force, so far as its principal design is concerned. It is not simply suggestive, commemorative, or representational. It is not a sign, a picture, deriving its significance from the mind of the beholder. The virtue which it possesses is not put into it by the faith of the worshipper in the first place, to be taken out of it again by the same faith, in the same form. It is not imagined of course in the case that the ordinance can have any virtue *without* faith, that it can confer grace in a purely mechanical way. All thought of the *opus operatum*, in this sense, is utterly repudiated. Still faith does not properly clothe the sacrament with its power. It is the condition of its efficacy for the communicant, but not the principle of the power itself. This belongs to the institution in its own nature. The signs are bound to what they represent, not subjectively simply in the thought of the worshipper, but objectively, by the force of a divine appointment. The union indeed is not natural but sacramental. The grace is not comprehended *in* the elements, as its depository and vehicle outwardly considered. But the union is none the less real and firm, on this account. The grace goes inseparably along with the signs, and is truly present for all who are prepared to make it their own. The signs in this view are also *seals;* not simply as they attest the truth and reality of the grace in a general way, but as they authenticate also its presence under the sacramental exhibition itself. This is what we mean by the objective force of the institution; and this, we say, is one point that must always be kept in view, in looking at the doctrine that is now the subject of our attention.

The other point to be steadily kept in sight is, that the invisible grace of the sacrament, according to the doctrine, is the substantial life of the Saviour himself, particularly in his human nature. He became flesh for the life of the world, and our communion with him, involves a real participation in him as the principle of life *under this form.* Hence in the mystery of the Supper, his flesh and blood are really exhibited always in their essential force and power, and really received by every worthy communicant.

Such is the proper sacramental doctrine of the Reformed Church as it stood in the sixteenth century. It is easy to show that it labours under serious difficulties. With these however at present, we have no concern. They can have no bearing one way or another, upon the simply historical inquiry in which we are now engaged. My object has been thus far only to describe and define the doctrine itself. . . .

The Modern Puritan Theory

It cannot be denied that the view generally entertained of the Lord's Supper at the present time, in the Protestant Church, involves a wide departure from the faith of the sixteenth century with regard to the same subject. The fact must be at once clear to every one at all familiar with the religious world as it now exists, as soon as he is made to understand in any measure the actual form in which the sacramental doctrine was held in the period just mentioned.

This falling away from the creed of the Reformation is not confined to any particular country or religious confession. It has been most broadly displayed among the continental churches of Europe, in the form of that open, rampant rationalism, which has there to so great an extent triumphed over the old orthodoxy at so many other points. But it is found widely prevalent also in Great Britain and in this country. It is especially striking, of course, as has been already remarked, in the case of the Lutheran Church, which was distinguished from the other Protestant confession, in the beginning, mainly by its high view of the Lord's Supper, and the zeal it showed in opposition to what it stigmatized reproachfully as sacramentarian error. In this respect, it can hardly be recognized indeed as the same communion. The original name remains, but the original distinctive character is gone. Particularly is this the case, with a large part at least, of the Lutheran Church in our own country. . . .

Now the first point that claims attention in the case, is the fact of such a difference between the view here exhibited and the Reformed doctrine of the sixteenth century, as has been already affirmed. So far as this goes, it is not necessary to decide absolutely on the nature of the difference. We may call it a change for the worse or a change for the better, as it may happen to strike our judgment. But the *fact* of the difference itself all must allow. The theology of New England, in the case before us, is not the theology of the Reformed Church of the sixteenth century. This Puritan theory of the power and virtue of the sacraments, is not the theory that was held by Calvin and that appears in the symbolical books of the first Calvinistic Churches.

We need only to make ourselves at home in the first place among the opinions of the sixteenth century, as presented for instance in Hospinian or Planck, and then pass over suddenly to the thinking of our own time . . . in order to *feel* the full force of the difference.[7] It is a transition into another spiritual element entirely. The difference is not simply in words and forms of expression. It extends to thoughts themselves. A different view prevails, in the two cases, of the nature of the sacraments, and of their relation to the ends for which they have been instituted; and along with this, the fact cannot be disguised, a different view also of the nature of the Christian salvation itself, in its

---

[7] Rodolphus Hospinianus (1547–1626) and Gottlieb Jakob Planck (1751–1833) were eminent historians of doctrine, Reformed and Lutheran respectively. Both dealt extensively with Protestant Eucharistic controversy. [Ed.]

relation to the person of the glorious Redeemer. Calvin could
not possibly have approved what appears to have been the sacramental doctrine of Edwards. Ursinus must have openly condemned the style in which the subject is presented by Ridgely.
Dr. Dick virtually pronounces himself at variance with all the
early Reformed symbols. Even Owen himself could hardly have
endured with patience, the language of Dr. Dwight. The difference is real and serious. The doctrine that runs through these
extracts, is not the doctrine of the Reformed Church as it stood
in the beginning.

To make the case more plain, let the following particulars be
noticed, as characterizing in general the departure of the modern Puritan from the old Reformed view. They will show that
it is a question of something more than mere words.

1. In the old Reformed view, the communion of the believer
with Christ in the Supper is taken to be *specific* in its nature,
and *different* from all that has place in the common exercises of
worship. The sacrament, not the elements of course separately
considered, but the ordinance as the union of element and word,
is held to be such an exhibition of saving grace, as is presented
to the faith of the Church under no other form. It is not simply
the word brought to mind in its ordinary force. The outward is
not merely the occasion by which the inward, in the case, is
made present to the soul as a separate existence; but inward and
outward, by the energy of the Spirit, are made to flow together
in the way of a common life; and come thus to exert a peculiar,
and altogether extraordinary power, in this form, to the benefit
of the believer. "There is a peculiar communion with Christ,"
says Dr. Owen, "which we have in no other ordinance;" and this,
he adds, has been the faith of the whole Church in all ages. "A
way of receiving Christ by eating and drinking; something
peculiar, that is not in prayer, that is not in the hearing of the
word, nor in any other part of divine worship whatever; a pecu-

liar participation of Christ, a peculiar acting of faith towards Christ."[8]

In the modern Puritan view, on the contrary, this specific peculiar virtue of the sacraments is not recognized. Christ is present, we are told by Dr. Dick, in all ordinances; "and he is present in the same manner in them all, namely by his Spirit, who renders them effectual means of salvation." So with Dr. Dwight the entire force of the institution, is made to consist in the occasion it affords, for the affections and exercises of common religious worship. The idea of a peculiar sacramental power, belonging to this form of worship as such, seems to have no place at all in his system.

2. In the old Reformed view, the sacramental transaction is a *mystery;* nay, in some sense an actual *miracle.* The Spirit works here in a way that transcends, not only the human understand-

---

[8] In the contrasting of the classic Reformed and the Modern Puritan views that follow, Nevin did not give titles or page numbers for his quotations. Because such references do not seem necessary here, Nevin's method of quoting his sources and separating them with a long dash is retained. Precise citations are given in the new edition of *The Mystical Presence,* Bard Thompson and George H. Bricker, eds., Lancaster Series on the Mercersburg Theology (Philadelphia & Boston: United Church Press, 1966).

On the Reformed view Nevin refers to the confessions of France (Gallic, 1559), the Netherlands (Belgic, 1566), Scotland (Old Scotch, 1560), Germany (Heidelburg Catechism, 1563), and Great Britain (Westminster, 1647); the Genevan reformers, William Farel (1489–1565), John Calvin (1509–1640), and Theodore Beza (1519–1605); the Puritan John Owen (1616–1683), the Anglican Richard Hooker (1553–1600), the Italian refugee theologian, Peter Martyr Vermigli (1500–1562), and Zacharias Ursinus (1534–1583), coauthor of and commentator upon the Heidelberg Catechism. As Modern Puritans he exhibits Jonathan Edwards and three of his famed successors, Samuel Hopkins (1721–1803), Joseph Bellamy (1719–1790), and Timothy Dwight (1752–1817); three Presbyterians, Albert Barnes (1798–1870), a prominent New School minister and writer; Ashbel Green (1762–1848), a president of Princeton College; and John Dick (1764–1833), a theologian of the Scottish Secession Church widely read in America and recipient of a Princeton D.D. in 1815. [Ed.]

ing, but the ordinary course of the world also in every other view. There is a form of action in the sacraments, which now belongs indeed to the regular order of the life that is comprehended in the Church, but which as thus established still involves a character that may be denominated *supernatural,* as compared with the ordinary constitution, not only of nature, but even of the Christian life itself. "Not without reason," says Calvin, "is the communication, which makes us flesh of Christ's flesh and bone of his bones denominated by Paul *a great mystery.* In the sacred Supper, therefore, we acknowledge it a *miracle,* transcending both nature and our own understanding, that Christ's life is made common to us with himself and his flesh given to us as aliment." "This *mystery* of our coalition with Christ," says the Gallic Confession, "is so sublime, that it transcends all our senses and also the whole course of nature." "The mode is such," according to the Belgic Confession, "as to surpass the apprehension of our mind, and cannot be understood by any." "The *mysteriousness,*" we are told by Dr. Owen, "is beyond expression; the *mysterious* reception of Christ in this peculiar way of exhibition."

Contrast with this now the style in which the ordinance is represented, from the proper Puritan stand-point, in the extracts already quoted. We find it spoken of, it is true, with great respect, as full of interest, significance and power. But it is no mystery; much less a miracle. As little so, it would seem, in the view of Dr. Dwight, as a common fourth of July celebration. The ends contemplated in the one case are religious, in the other patriotic; but the institutions as related to these ends are in all material respects of one and the same order. The ends proposed in the Supper "the enlargement and rectification of our *views*—the purification of our *affections*—the amendment of our *lives.* The means are efficacious and desirable; at the same time simple; *intelligible to the humblest capacity;* in no respect burdensome; lying within the reach of all men; incapable of being misconstrued without violence; and therefore not easily susceptible of *mystical* or superstitious perversion. In their own proper, undiguised nature, they appeal powerfully to the *senses,* the *imagination,* and the *heart;* and at the same time enlighten in the happiest manner, the *understanding.*" All this is said to show "the *wisdom* of this institution." "There seems to have been a disposition in that age," says Dr. Dick, with reference to the sixteenth century, "to believe that there was a presence of Christ in the eucharist *different* from his presence in the other ordinances of the gospel; an undefined something, which corresponded to the strong language used at the institution of the Supper: *This is my body,—this is my blood.* Acknowledging it to be figurative, many still thought that a *mystery* was couched under it." Dr. Dick himself of course finds no mystery in the case. Calvin's doctrine accordingly is rejected, as *incomprehensible;* not understood by himself (as the great theologian indeed humbly admits) and beyond the understanding also of his readers. "Plain, literal language is best, especially on spiritual subjects, and should have been employed by Protestant Churches with the utmost care, as the figurative terms of Scripture have been so grossly mistaken." To this we may add, that the very reason why *such* plain, simple language as might have suited Dr. Dick has *not* been employed by the Protestant Churches in their symbolical books, is to be found in the fact that these Protestant Churches believed and intended to assert the presence of a mystery in the sacrament, for the idea of which no place is allowed in *his* creed, and that could not be properly represented therefore by any language which this creed might supply.

3. The old Reformed doctrine includes always the idea of an *objective force* in the sacraments. The sacramental union between the sign and the thing signified is real, and holds in virtue of the constitution of the ordinance itself, not in the faith simply or inward frame of the communicant. Without faith indeed this force which belongs to the sacrament cannot avail to the benefit of the communicant; faith forms the indispensable condition, by

whose presence only the potential in this case can become actual, the life that is present be brought to take effect in the
interior man. But the condition here, as in all other cases, is
something different from the thing itself, for which it makes
room. The grace of the sacrament comes from God; but it comes
as such under the sacrament as its true and proper form; not
inhering in the elements indeed, outwardly considered; but still
mysteriously lodged, by the power of the Holy Ghost, in the
sacramental transaction as a whole. The grace is truly present,
according to Calvin, even where it is excluded from the soul by
unbelief; as much so as the fertilizing qualities of the rain, that
falls fruitless on the barren rock. Unbelief may make it of no
effect; but the intrinsic virtue of the sacrament itself still remains the same. The bread and wine are the sure pledge still of
the presence of what they represent, and "a true exhibition of it
on the part of God." "The symbols," say Beza and Farel, "are by
no means naked; but so far as God is concerned, who makes the
promise and offer, they always have the thing itself truly and certainly joined with them, whether proposed to believers or unbelievers."— —"We do utterly condemn the vanity of those who
affirm, that the sacraments are nothing else but mere naked
signs." *Old Scotch Confession.*— —"Those signs then are by no
means vain or void." *Belgic Confessions.*— —"We teach that the
things signified are together with the signs in the right use exhibited and communicated." *Ursinus.* The sacrament in this view,
not only signifies, but *seals* to believers, the grace it carries in its
constitution. It is not simply a pledge that the blessings it represents are sure to them, in a general way, apart from this particular engagement itself; as when a man by some outward stipula-
tion binds himself to fulfil the terms of a contract in another
place and at another time. The sacramental transaction certifies
and makes good the grace it represents, as actually communicated at the time. So it is said to *exhibit* also the thing signified.
The thing is *there;* not the name of the thing only, and not its
sign or shadow; but the actual substance itself. "The sacrament

is no picture," says Calvin, "but the true, veritable pledge of our union with Christ." To say that the body of Christ is adumbrated by the symbol of bread, only as a dead statue is made to represent Hercules or Mercury, he pronounces profane. The signs, Owen tells us, "*exhibit* that which they do not contain. It is no empty, painted feast. Here is something really exhibited by Jesus Christ unto us, to receive, besides the outward pledges of bread and wine."

How different from all this again, the light in which the subject is presented in our modern Puritan theology. Here too the sacraments are indeed said to seal, and also to exhibit, the grace they represent. But plainly the old, proper sense of these terms, in the case, is changed. The *seal* ratifies simply a covenant, in virtue of which certain blessings are made sure to the believer, on certain conditions, under a wholly different form. Two parties in the transaction, Christ and his people, stipulate to be faithful to each other in fulfilling the engagements of a mutual contract; and in doing so, they both affix their seal to the sacramental bond. Such is the view presented very distinctly by Edwards, Hopkins, and Bellamy. The contract of salvation according to this last, is in the Lord's Supper, "externally and visibly sealed, ratified, and confirmed, on both sides, with as much formality as any written instrument is mutually sealed by the parties, in any covenant among men. And now if both parties are sincere in the covenant thus sealed, and if both abide by and act according to it, the communicant will be saved." So the sacrament is allowed to be exhibitional; not however of any actual present substance, as the old doctrine always held; but only in the way of figure, shadow or sign. A picture or statue may be said to exhibit their original, to the same extent. The sacramental elements are Christ's *proxy.* "Or the matter may be more fitly represented by *this* similitude: it is as if a prince should send an ambassador to a woman in a foreign land, proposing marriage, and by his ambassador should send her his picture, &c." *Edwards.*——With Dr. Dwight the sacrament is reduced fully to the character of a mere occasion, by which religious affections are excited and supported in the breast of the worshipper. He seems to have no idea at all of an objective force, belonging to the institution in its own nature. All is subjective, and subjective only. All turns on the adaptation of the rite to instruct and affect. He measures its wisdom and power, wholly by this standard. It is admirably *contrived* to work upon "the senses, the imagination, and the heart," as well as to "enlighten the understanding." Its whole force, when all is done, is the amount simply of the good thoughts, good feelings, and good purposes, that are brought to it, and made to go along with it, on the part of the worshippers themselves.

4. According to the old Reformed doctrine the invisible grace of the sacrament, includes a real participation in his *person*. That which is made present to the believer, is the very life of Christ himself in its true power and substance. The doctrine proceeds on the assumption that the Christian salvation stands in an actual union between Christ and his people, mystical but in the highest sense real, in virtue of which they are as closely joined to him, as the limbs are to the head in the natural body. They are in Him, and He is in them, not figuratively but truly; in the way of a growing process that will become complete finally in the resurrection. The power of this fact is mysteriously concentrated in the Holy Supper. Here Christ communicates *himself* to his Church; not simply a right to the grace that resides in his person, or an interest by outward grant in the benefits of his life and death; but his person itself, as the ground and fountain, from which all these other blessings may be expected to flow.

This idea is exhibited under all forms in which it could well be presented, and in terms the most clear and explicit. Christ first, and *then* his benefits. Calvin will hear of no other order but this. The same view runs through all the Calvinistic symbols. Not a title to Christ *in* his benefits, the efficacy of his atonement, the work of his spirit; but a true property in his life itself, out of which only that other title can legitimately spring. "We are quickened by a real participation of him, which he designates by the terms *eating* and *drinking* that no person might suppose the life which we receive from him to consist in simple knowledge." *Calvin*. We communicate with Christ's *substance*. "A substantial communication is affirmed by me everywhere." *Id*— —"He nourishes and vivifies us by the substance of his body and blood." *Gallic Confession*.— —"It is *not only* to embrace with a believing heart all the sufferings and death of Christ, and thereby to obtain the pardon of sin and life eternal; but also *besides* that to become more and more united to his sacred body, by the Holy Ghost, &c." *Heidelberg Catechism*. — —"We teach that he is present and united with us by the Holy Ghost, albeit his body be far absent from us." *Ursinus*.— — "In the Supper we are made partakers, not only of the Spirit of Christ, and his satisfaction, justice, virtue, and operation; but also of the very substance and essence of his true body and blood, &c." *Id*.— —"*Christ* crucified, *and* all benefits of his death." *Westminster Confession*.— —"It is on all sides plainly confessed, that this sacrament is a true and a real participation of Christ, who thereby imparteth himself, even his whole entire person, as a mystical head, unto every soul that receiveth him, and that every such receiver doth incorporate or unite himself unto Christ as a mystical member of him." *Hooker*.— —A peculiar exhibition of Christ under outward signs, "and a mysterious reception of him in them really, so as to come to a real substantial incorporation in our souls." *Owen*.

As the modern Puritan theory eviscerates the institution of all objective force, under any view, it must of course still more decidedly refuse to admit the idea of any such virtue belonging to it as that now mentioned. The union of the believer with Christ it makes to be moral only; or at least a figurative incorporation with his Spirit! The sacred Supper forms an occasion, by which the graces of the pious communicant are called into favourable exercise; and his faith in particular is assisted in apprehending and appropriating the precious contents of the Christian salvation, as wrought out by the Redeemer's life and death! He participates in this way in the fruits of Christ's love, the benefits of his mediatorial work, his imputed righteousness, his heavenly intercession, the influences of his Spirit, &c.; but in the substantial life of Christ himself he has no part whatever. "A mutual solemn profession of the two parties transacting the convenant of grace, and visibly united in that covenant." *Edwards.* So also *Hopkins* and *Bellamy.*— —"Sensible impressions are much more powerful than those which are made on the understanding, &c." *Dwight.*— —"The ends proposed in the institution of the Lord's Supper are, the enlargement and rectification of our views concerning the noblest of all subjects, the purification of our affections and the amendment of our lives." *Id.*— —"Stript of all metaphorical terms, the action must mean that in the believing and grateful commemoration of his death, we enjoy the blessings which were purchased by it, in the same manner in which we enjoy them when we exercise faith in hearing the Gospel." *Dick.*— —"No man who admits that the bread and wine are only signs and figures, can consistently suppose the words, I Cor.10:16, to have any other meaning, than that we have communion with Christ in the fruits of his sufferings and death; or that receiving the symbols we receive by faith the benefits procured by the pains of his body and the effusion of his blood." *Id.*— —Christ's "*doctrine* is truly that which will give life to the soul." *Barnes.*— —"To dwell or abide in him, is to remain in the belief of his doctrine and in the participation of all the benefits of his death." *Id.*— —"The whole design of the sacramental bread, is by a striking emblem to call to *remembrance,* in a vivid manner, the dying sufferings of our Lord." *Id.*

5. In the old Reformed view of the Lord's Supper, the communion of the believer in the true person of Christ, in the form now stated, is supposed to hold with him especially as the Word

made *flesh*. His humanity forms the medium of his union with the Church. The life of which he is the fountain, flows forth from him only as he is the Son of Man. To have part in it at all, we must have part in it as a real human life; we must eat his flesh and drink his blood; take into us the substance of what he was as man; so as to become flesh of his flesh and bone of his bones. "The very flesh in which he dwells is made to be vivific for us, that we may be nourished by it to immortality." *Calvin.*— —"This sacred communication of his flesh and blood, in which Christ transfuses his life into us, just as if he penetrated our bones and marrow, he testifies and seals also in the Holy Supper." *Id.*— —"I do not teach that Christ dwells in us simply by his Spirit, but that he so raises us to himself as to transfuse into us the vivific vigor of his flesh." *Id.*— —"The very substance itself of the Son of Man." *Beza and Farel.*— —"That same substance which he took in the womb of the Virgin, and which he carried up into heaven." *Beza and Peter Martyr.*— —"As the eternal deity has imparted life and immortality to the flesh of Jesus Christ, so likewise his flesh and blood, when eaten and drunk by us, confer upon us the same prerogatives." *Old Scotch Confession.*— —"That which is eaten is the very, natural body of Christ, and what is drunk his true blood." *Belgic Confession.* — —"Flesh of his flesh and bone of his bone. . . . We are as *really* partakers of his true body and blood, as we receive these holy signs." *Heidelberg Catechism.*— —"We are in such sort coupled, knit, and incorporated into his true, essential human body, by his Spirit dwelling both in him and us, that we are flesh of his flesh and bone of his bones." *Ursinus.*— —"They that worthily communicate in the sacrament of the Lord's Supper, do therein feed upon the body and blood of Christ—truly and really." *Westminster Catechism.*

All this the modern Puritan view utterly repudiates, as semi-popish mysticism. It will allow no real participation of Christ's person in the Lord's Supper, under any form: but least of all under the form of his humanity. Such communion as it is willing to admit, it limits to the presence of Christ in his divine nature, or to the energy he puts forth by his Spirit. As for all that is said about his body and blood, it is taken to be mere figure, intended to express the value of his sufferings and death. With his body in the strict sense, his life as incarnate, formerly on earth and now in heaven, we can have no communion at all, except in the way of remembering what was endured in it for our salvation. The *flesh* in any other view profiteth nothing; it is only the Spirit that quickeneth. The language of the Calvinistic confessions on this subject, is resolved into bold, violent metaphor, that comes in the end to mean almost nothing. "If he (Calvin) meant that there is some mysterious communication with his human nature, we must be permitted to say the notion was as incomprehensible to himself as it is to his readers." *Dick.*— —"There is an absurdity in the notion that there is any communion with the body and blood of Christ, considered in themselves." *Id.* — —"Justly does our Confession of Faith declare, that the body and blood of Christ are as *really,* but spiritually present to the faith of believers, &c. . . . What blessed visions of faith are those, in which this precious grace creates an *ideal* presence of the suffering, bleeding, dying, atoning Saviour! Then Gethsemane, and Pilate's hall, and the cross, the thorny crown, the nails, the spear, the hill of Calvary, are in present view!" *Green.*— —"This broken bread shows the manner in which my body will be broken; or this will serve to call my dying sufferings to your *remembrance.*" *Barnes.*

Let this suffice in the way of comparison. The two theories, it is clear, are different throughout. Nor is the difference such as may be considered of small account. It is not simply formal or accidental. The modern Puritan view evidently involves a material falling away, not merely from the form of the old Calvinistic doctrine, but from its inward life and force. It makes a great difference surely, whether the union of the believer with Christ be regarded as the power of one and the same life, or as holding only in a correspondence of thought and feeling; whether the Lord's Supper be a sign and seal only of God's grace in general, or the pledge also of a special invisible grace present in the transaction itself; and whether we are united by means of it to the person of Christ, or only to his merits; and whether finally we communicate in the ordinance with the whole Christ, in a real way, or only with his divinity. Such, however, is the difference that stares us in the face, from the comparison now made. All must see and feel that it exists, and that it is serious.

Under this view then simply the subject is entitled to earnest attention. Apart from all judgment upon the character of the change which has taken place, the fact itself is one that may well challenge consideration. We have no right to overlook it, or to treat it as though it did not exist. We have no right to hold it unimportant, or to take it for granted with unreflecting presumption that the truth is all on the modern side. The mere fact is serious. For the doctrine of the eucharist lies at the very heart of Christianity itself; and the chasm that divides the two systems here is wide and deep. For churches that claim to represent, by true and legitimate succession, the life of the Reformation under its best form, the subject is worthy of being laid to heart. Only ignorance or frivolity can allow themselves to make light of it.

A strong presumption is furnished *against* the modern Puritan doctrine, as compared with the Calvinistic or Reformed, in the fact that the first may be said to be of yesterday only in the history of the Church, while the last, so far as the difference in question is concerned, has been the faith of nearly the whole Christian world from the beginning. It included indeed a protest against the errors with which the truth had been overlaid in the church of Rome. It rejected transubstantiation and the sacrifice of the mass; and refused to go with Luther in his dogma of a local presence. But in all this it formed no rupture with the original doctrine of the Church. That which had constituted the central idea of this doctrine from the first, and which appears even under the perversions that have just been named, it still continued to hold with a firm grasp. It is this central idea, the true and proper substance of the ancient church faith precisely, that created the difference between the Reformed doctrine and the modern Puritan. In the Reformed system it is present in all its force; in the other it is wanting. The voice of antiquity is all on the side of the sixteenth century, in its high view of the sacrament. To the low view which has since come to prevail, it lends no support whatever. [Omitted here is Nevin's section on "The Faith of the Early Church" in which he seeks to show that the Reformers properly rejected mediaeval errors but preserved the early Church's witness. In the concluding paragraph that follows he relates his findings to the contemporary scene. Ed.]

To clear ourselves of transubstantiation and the mass, is it necessary that we should strip the sacrament of *all* mystery, and refuse to allow it any objective force whatever? So thought not the Reformers, as we have already seen. Not only Luther and Melancthon, but Calvin also, and Beza and Ursinus, and the fathers of the *Reformed* Church generally, discovered a proper anxiety here to save the substance of the primitive faith, while they endeavoured to rescue it from the errors with which it had become overlaid in the Church of Rome. They honoured, in this case as in other cases also, the authority of the ancient fathers, and the life of the early Church; and they took pains accordingly to show, as far as they could, that this testimony, rightly interpreted and understood, was on *their* side, and not on the side of Rome. It was reserved for a later time, and for a theology of different spirit from that which generally prevailed in the sixteenth century, to treat this whole appeal with contempt, by charging the Church with corruption and superstition from the very start, and pretending to construct the entire scheme of Christianity *de novo* from the scriptures, without any regard to the primitive faith whatever.

[RATIONALISM AND SUBJECTIVISM]

The modern Puritan theory of the Lord's Supper, as it involves a falling away from the general faith of the Reformation, finds at the same time no sanction whatever in the faith of the primitive Church. This of itself constitutes certainly a powerful presumption against it. What right, we may ask, has Puritanism had to depart thus from the creed of the sixteenth century, and the creed of whole ancient Christianity, at the same time? The right of private judgment, it may be replied, against the authority of tradition. But is not tradition itself in this case the judgment merely, which has been entertained of the sense of the Bible by the Reformers and the early Church? Why then should the particular judgment of Puritanism, as such, be allowed to carry with it any such weight as is needed to bear down the judgment of the universal Church besides from the beginning? In the very nature of the case, strong grounds and solid arguments should be exhibited, to justify this modern particularity of faith, in its palpable defection from the general creed of Christendom, with regard to an article so momentous as the one now under contemplation. The presumption here, I repeat it, is *against* modern Puritanism. The simple statement of the case, is adapted *prima facie*, when fairly understood, to create an impression unfavourable to its claims.

But this is not all. A still farther presumption against the same view, is created by the fact that in departing from the faith of the Reformation, it is found to be in full harmony with the false Pelagian tendency, by which the truth under other forms, as originally held by the Reformers, has been so widely subverted in different Protestant lands. The modern Puritan view of the Lord's Supper, is constitutionally rationalistic.

As a matter of course, the Socinians of the sixteenth century sunk the conception of the sacraments to the general level of their false theological system. As they denied the divinity of the Saviour, and reduced the whole Christian salvation to a mere system of morality, they could see in the sacraments naturally nothing more than external, simply human ceremonies. Their idea was, that Christianity, as a *spiritual* religion, had no dependence on forms and rites as such; and hence in this case, they made no account whatever of any virtue or force, that might be supposed to belong to the sacraments themselves, considered as divine institutions. To attribute to them any objective value, they counted mere Jewish ritualism. . . . With the rise of Arminianism in the following century, in the bosom of the Reformed Church, we find a similar undervaluation of the sacraments, reducing them in the end again to mere signs. . . .

The triumph of Rationalism, during the eighteenth century, in Germany and throughout Europe generally, brought with it of course a still more extensive degradation of religious views. It is not necessary here to trace the rise of this apostacy and its connection with the previous state of Protestantism. Enough to say, that it grew out of a tendency involved in the very nature of Protestantism from the beginning; the opposite exactly of that by which the Catholic Church previously had been carried into an equally false extreme, on the other side. As Romanism had sacrificed the rights of the individual to the authority of the general—the claims of the subjective to the overwhelming weight of the objective; so the tendency of Protestantism may be said to have been from the very start, to assert these same rights and claims in the way of violent reaction, at the cost of the opposite interest.[9] In the age of the Reformation itself, deeply imbued as it was with the positive life of truth and faith,

---

[9] A deeply pondered dialectical view of church history, with an obvious debt to Hegel, is a fundamental feature of the Mercersburg analysis. To emphasize this view Nevin added a Preliminary Essay to *The Mystical Presence,* an historical essay on changing conceptions of the Church by Karl Ullmann (1796–1865), famous for his history of *Reformers before the Reformation* (1841–1842). See also Nevin's Introduction to Schaff's *The Principle of Protestantism.* [Ed.]

this tendency was powerfully held within limits. With Luther, and Calvin, and the Reformers generally, the principle of freedom was still held in check by the principle of authority, and the reason of the individual was required to bend to the idea of a divine revelation as something broader and more sure than itself. It came not however in all this, it must be confessed, to a true inward reconciliation of these polar forces. The old orthodoxy, it is now generally allowed, particularly under the form it carried in the Lutheran Church, involved in itself accordingly the necessity of such a process of inward conflict and dissolution, as it has since been called to pass through; in order that the contradiction which was lodged in its bosom, might come fairly into view, and the way be opened thus for its reconstruction, under a form at once more perfect and more true to its own nature.

The characteristic tendency of Protestantism already mentioned, burst finally through all the counteracting force, with which it had been restrained in the beginning. Religion ran out into sheer subjectivity; first in the form of Pietism, and afterwards in the overflowing desolation of Rationalism, reducing all to the character of the most flat natural morality. The eighteenth century was characteristically infidel. As an age, it seemed to have no organ for the supernatural. All was made to shrink to the dimensions of the mere human spirit, in its isolated character. Theology of course was robbed of all its higher life. Even the supernaturalism of the period was rationalistic; and occupying as it did in fact a false position with regard to the truth, by which a measure of right was given to the rival interest, it proved altogether incompetent to maintain its ground against the reigning spirit. The views of Rationalism may be said to infect the whole theology of this period, and also of the first part of the present century, openly heretical and professedly orthodox alike.

In the nature of the case, this may be expected to show itself in low views of the sacraments, Baptism and the Lord's Supper.

Rationalism is too *spiritual,* to make much account of outward forms and services of any sort in religion. All must be resolved into the exercises of the worshipper's own mind. The subjective is every thing; the objective next to nothing. Hence the supernatural itself is made to sink into the form of the simply moral. The sacraments of course become signs, and signs *only.* Any power they may have is not to be found in *them,* but altogether in such use merely as a pious soul may be able to make of them, as *occasions* for quickening its own devout thoughts and feelings. . . .

[THE SPIRIT OF SECT]

Parallel to a great extent with the development of the subjective principle in the false form now noticed, runs the revelation also of the same tendency in the equally false form of sectarism and schism. No one can study attentively the character of either, without being led to see that the two tendencies are but different phases of one and the same spiritual obliquity. No one, in reading the history of the Church, can well fail to be struck with the many points of correspondence, which are found universally to hold between the two forms of life, in spite of the broad difference by which they might seem to be separated, in many cases, on a superficial view. The spirit of sect is characteristically full of religious pretension; and professing to make supreme account of religion as something personal and experimental, it assumes always a more than ordinarily spiritual character, and moves in the element of restless excitement and action. Hence it is often, generally indeed at the start, fanatical and wild; especially in the way of opposition to outward forms and the existing order of the Church generally. And yet how invariably it falls in with the rationalistic way of thinking, as far as it may *think* at all, from the very beginning; and how certainly its principles and views, when carried out subsequently to their legitimate results, are found to involve in the end the worst errors of Rationalism itself. Both systems are antagonistic to the idea of the *Church.* Both are disposed to trample under foot the authority of *history*. Both make the *objective* to be nothing, and the *subjective* to be all in all. Both undervalue the *outward*, in favour of what they conceive to be the *inward*. Both despise *forms*, under pretence of exalting the *spirit*. Both of course sink the *sacraments* to the character of mere outward rites; or possibly deny their necessity altogether. Both affect to make much of the *Bible*; at least in the beginning; though sometimes indeed it is made to yield, with sectarism, to the imagination of some superior inward light more directly from God; and in all cases, it is forced to submit, to the tyranny of mere private interpretation, as the only proper measure of its sense. With both forms of thinking, the idea of Christianity as a permanent order of life, a real supernatural constitution unfolding itself historically in the world, is we may say wanting altogether. All at last is flesh, the natural life of man as such; exalted it may be in its own order, but never of course transcending itself so as to become *spirit*. The sect principle may indeed affect to move in the highest sphere of the heavenly and divine; carrying it possibly to an absolute rupture even with all that belongs to the present world. But in this case it begins in the spirit, only to end the more certainly in the flesh. Hyper-spiritualism is ever fleshly pseudo-spiritualism; that is sure to fall back sooner or later impotent and self-exhausted, into the low element from which it has vainly pretended to make its escape. Anabaptism finds its legitimate, natural end in the excesses of Münster; as Mormonism in the like excesses of Nauvoo. What a difference apparently between the inspiration of George Fox, and the cold infidelity of Elias Hicks.[10] And yet the last is the true spiritual descendant of the first. The inward light of the one, and the light of reason as

---

[10] In 1534 Anabaptist dominance in the city of Münster led to violence and gross excesses—an isolated instance however. In 1844 when Nauvoo, Illinois, was the main Mormon settlement, factionalism within and hostility without led to violence and the lynching of the Smith brothers. George Fox (1624–1691) was the founder of the Quakers; Elias Hicks (1748–1830) was a liberal leader who precipitated a division among American Friends in 1827. [Ed.]

held by the other, come to the same thing at last. Both contradict the true concept of religion. Both are supremely subjective, and in this view supremely rationalistic at the same time.

It is by no fortuitous coincidence then, that we find the spirit of *sect* since the Reformation (as indeed before it also) in close affinity with the spirit of theoretic rationalism, in its low estimate of the Christian sacraments. The relationship of the two systems, in the case, is inward and real. The Anabaptists and Socinians of the sixteenth century, go here hand in hand together; as do also the Mennonites and Arminians of Holland, in the century following. All hold the sacraments to be signs only for the understanding and heart of the pious communicant, without any objective value or force in their own nature. All alike reduce them to the character of something outward and accidental only to the true Christian life. The Quakers, more consistently true than all sects besides to the spiritualistic theory out of which the sect life springs, agree with infidelity itself, in rejecting the sacraments altogether. Not from the Christ without, the objective historical Christ, as revealing himself in the Church and exhibited in the sacramental symbols, but only from the Christ within, the interior spiritual life of the believer himself, is any true salvation to be expected. "Whenever the soul is turned towards the light of the Lord within, and is thus made to participate of the celestial life that nourishes the interior man, (the privilege of the believer at any time), it may be said to enjoy the Lord's Supper, and to partake of his flesh and blood." To insist upon the outward sacraments is to fall back to Judaism, and to magnify rites and forms at the cost of that spiritual worship, which alone is worthy of our own nature, or suitable to the character of God.

The anti-sacramental tendency of the sect spirit is strikingly revealed under its true rationalistic nature, in the disposition so commonly shown by it to reject infant baptism. If the sacraments are regarded as in themselves outward rites only, that can have no value or force except as the grace they represent is made to be present by the subjective exercises of the worshipper, it is hard to see on what ground infants, who are still without knowledge or faith, should be admitted to any privilege of the sort. If there be no objective reality in the life of the Church, as something more deep and comprehensive than the life of the individual believer separately taken, infant baptism becomes necessarily an unmeaning contradiction. Hence invariably (as already remarked in the first part of the present chapter) where the true church consciousness is brought to yield to the spirit of sect, the tendency to depreciate the ordinance in this form is found to prevail to the same extent; and so on the other hand, there is no more sure criterion and measure of the presence of the sect spirit, as distinguished from the true spirit of the Church, than the tendency now mentioned, wherever it may be exhibited. The baptistic principle, whether carried out fully in practice or not, constitutes the certain mark of sectarianism all the world over. It may be controlled in many cases by outward influences, or by some remnant possibly of church feeling still preserved, so as not to come openly into view; but it will be found then as a worm at least at the root of the institution here in view, consuming all its vigor, and turning it in fact into the powerless form for which it is unbelievingly and rationalistically taken. Where it comes, however, to a full triumph of the sect character, the baptistic principle, for the most part, asserts its authority in a more open way. Infant baptism is discarded as a relic of Roman superstition. Here again the Anabaptists and Mennonites appear in close connection with Socinians and Arminians; whose judgment at least with regard to the point in hand, though not their practice, has ever been substantially the same. According to the Racovian Catechism, the baptism of infants is without authority and without reason, and to be tolerated only as a harmless inveterate prejudice.[11] The Remonstrants of Holland (Arminians) much in the same

---

[11] On Rocovian Catechism, see note 4, p. 377. [Ed.]

way declare the rite worthy of being continued to avoid scandal, but hold it to be of no binding authority in its own nature. In our own country, as was remarked before, we have, at the present time, an exemplification of the sect feeling at this point, on a large scale. The Baptists, as they are called, including all the sects that reject the baptism of infants, form, it is said, the most numerous religious profession in the United States: and the baptistic principle, it is plain, prevails still more widely, where the practice, through the force of denominational tradition, remains of an opposite character.

It appears then that the spirit of heresy, and the spirit of *schism*, in the case before us, are substantially one and the same. Both are unchurchly and anti-sacramental, to the same extent. It is not an accidental resemblance simply, that connects them together in this view; but the inward power of a common life. It belongs to the very genius of sect to be rationalistic.

[THE PURITAN LEGACY]

And now it cannot be denied, that the modern Puritan theory of the Lord's Supper, as it has been presented to us in contrast with the old Calvinistic doctrine, is strikingly in harmony with the whole style of thinking here offered to our view. This must be apparent at once to any one, who will only take the trouble to refer again to the illustrations of the Puritan theory that have been already quoted, and to compare them with the modes of thought and language employed by the rationalistic school on the same subject. The ground on which much of our American theology is here standing at the present time, is palpably the same with that occupied by the old rationalistic supernaturalism of Germany. . . .

It is not necessary that we should be able to trace any outward connection between the two forms of theology thus compared, to establish their actual affinity. It is enough that they are inwardly connected, and that they belong to the same general development of a false tendency comprehended in Protestantism itself. This tendency has shown its power from the beginning, as a spirit of heresy in one direction, and a spirit of schism in another; but it may be said to have come to the fullest revelation of its bad life, during the last century and the first part of the present. That the modern Puritan theology should be deeply affected by its influence, might seem to be in the circumstances precisely what was to be expected. Puritanism, as all know, involves in its original constitution a large measure of the tendency which has just been mentioned. It formed from the start, a marked advance, in this direction, upon the character of the Reformed Church, as it stood in the beginning; showing itself more decidedly independent of all objective authority, and more favourable by far to a mere abstract spiritualism in religion.

The danger to which the Reformed Church might be said to have been most liable, in its very nature, from the first, came here to be something more than danger; it appeared as actual ultra-protestantism itself, hostile to the proper idea of the Church, and irreverent towards all history at the same time. Nor has the history of this system of thinking since furnished any reason to suppose in its case a change of character, in the respect here noticed. On the contrary, it is clear that the wrong element which was embodied in it at the beginning, has been only confirmed and consolidated since, under the same character; for to this very influence must be referred, to a great extent, more or less directly, the curse of sectarism, as it has now become so widely established both in Great Britain and in this country. That some leaven of rationalism then should enter into its theology, in these circumstances, must appear, after what has already been said, a matter of course. This may be, notwithstanding the presence of a large amount of religious life in connection with the same system.

Be all this as it may, however, it must at all events be regarded as a presumption against the modern Puritan view of the Lord's

Supper, that, in departing from the doctrine of the Reformation, it is found to fall in so strikingly with what may be styled the apostacy of Rationalism in the same direction. It might seem sufficiently startling to be sundered, in such a case, from the general faith of Christendom as it has stood from the beginning. But still more startling, certainly, is the thought of such separation in *such* company. This much is clear. The Reformation included in its original and proper constitution, two different elements or tendencies; and it was felt that it could be true to itself, only by acknowledging the authority of both, as mutually necessary each for the perfection and proper support of the other. In the nature of the case, however, there was a powerful liability in the movement to become ultraistic and extreme, on that side which seemed to carry the most direct *protest* against the errors of the Church, as it stood before. In the course of time, undeniably, this became, as we have already seen, its general character. The simply Protestant tendency was gradually sundered, in a great measure, from its true Catholic complement and counterpoise; and in this abstract character it has run out into theoretical and practical rationalism, to a fearful extent, in all parts of the Church. The low view of the sacraments, which we have now under consideration, came in with this unfortunate obliquity. It belongs historically and constitutionally to the bastard form, under which the original life of Protestantism has become so widely caricatured in the way of heresy and schism. Its inward affinity with the spirit of Rationalism, in one direction, and the spirit of Sect in another (two different phases only of the same modern Antichrist) is too clear to be for one moment called in question.[12] In this character, it forms most certainly, like the whole system with which it is associated, a departure from the faith, not only of the Lutheran, but of the Reformed Church also, as it stood in the sixteenth century. It

---

12 Nevin expanded on this ultimate accusation in his *Antichrist, or the Spirit of Sect and Schism* (1848). [Ed.]

involves in this respect, what would have been counted, at that time, not only a perversion, but a very serious perversion of the true Protestant doctrine.

Now, with this neological and sectarian view, we find the modern Puritan theory of the Lord's Supper to be in full agreement. Both sink its objective virtue wholly out of sight. Both do this, on the principle of making the service spiritual and rational, instead of simply *ritual*. Both, in this way, wrong the claims of Christianity as a supernatural *life*, in favour of its claims as a divine doctrine. Both proceed on the same false abstraction, by which soul and body, outward and inward, are made to be absolutely different, and in some sense really antagonistic, spheres of existence. Both show the same utter disregard to the authority of all previous history, and affect to construct the whole theory of the Church, doctrine, sacraments, and all, in the way of independent private judgment, from the Bible and common sense. Both, in all this, involve a like defection, and substantially to the same extent, from the creed of the Reformation; and would have been regarded accordingly, not only by Luther, but by Calvin also, and Beza, and Ursinus, and the fathers of the Reformed Church generally, as alike treasonable to the interest, which has become identified with their great names.

This much, we say, is clear. Let it carry with it such weight as may of right belong to it; and no more. The question is not to be decided, we all know, by church authority and mere blind tradition. The primitive Church may have gone astray from the very start. The fathers of the Reformation were not infallible; and it must be allowed, that the life of the Reformation, in its *first* form, was the product or birth spiritually of the Catholic Church as it stood before, and not of the sects that broke away from it in the middle ages. If the Reformers had sprung from this line of witnesses on the outside, it is quite likely their Protestantism would have been something vastly different from the gigantic new creation we find it to be in fact. The birth, it may be taken for granted, *did* partake largely of the character of the womb, in which it had been carried for so many centuries before. These *Catholic* Reformers *may* have been wrong, in the case now before us, as in many other points. Whole Christendom *may* have been wrong, not only in the form, but in the very substance of its faith, with regard to the sacraments, for more than fifteen hundred years; till this modern view began to reveal itself in the Protestant world, partly in the form of infidelity, and partly in the form of a claim to superior evangelical piety. The coincidence in this case too *may* be accidental only, and not natural or necessary. With regard to all this, we utter here no positive judgment. We wish simply to exhibit facts as they stand. But in this character, they have their solemn weight. They create a powerful presumption, as I before said, *against* the modern Puritan view, and impose upon all an *à priori* obligation of great force, not to acquiesce in it without examination.

[The mode of the foregoing sections is almost purely historical and their purpose largely critical. The chief significance of *The Mystical Presence* undoubtedly derives from this forceful and profound comparative analysis. Yet Nevin often insists that deviation on the sacrament always symbolizes a deeper, more general "disease." Hence he devoted a considerable portion of his career to the formulation of a theology that would place the "Eucharistic Presence" in its proper context. The concluding two sections of this book provide an exciting anticipation of that creative enterprise. He by no means sought to repristinate the sixteenth-century doctrine. In Chapter III he cleared Calvin's theory of certain admitted difficulties, then set forth his own "scientific statement" in twenty-seven carefully defended "theses." In Chapter IV, "The Biblical Argument," he presented his own interpretation, basing it on the doctrine of the Incarnation and drawing significantly from the renaissance of philosophical theology and biblical study then proceeding on the Continent. A few passages drawn from this final chapter reveal its essential spirit. Ed.]

Biblical Argument

THE INCARNATION

"The Word became flesh!"[13] In this simple, but sublime enunciation, we have the whole gospel comprehended in a word. From the glorious orb of light which is here made to burst upon our view, all that would else be dark and chaotic becomes at once irradiated with the bright majesty and everlasting harmony of truth itself. The incarnation is the key that unlocks the sense of all God's revelations.

It is the key that unlocks the sense of all God's works, and brings to light the true meaning of the universe. The world, and especially Man, who may be said to gather into his person at last all lower forms of existence, himself the summit of the vast organic pyramid, is a mystery that is solved and interpreted finally only in this fact. Nature and Revelation, the world and Christianity, as springing from the same divine Mind, are not two different systems joined together in a merely outward way. They form a single whole, harmonious with itself in all its parts. The sense of the one then is necessarily included and comprehended in the sense of the other. The mystery of the new creation, must involve in the end the mystery of the old; and the key that serves to unlock the meaning of the first, must serve to unlock at the same time the inmost secret of the last.

The incarnation forms thus the great central FACT of the world. It is a magnificent thought on which *Heinrich Steffens* bases his system of anthropology, that Man is to be viewed, "as the end of a boundless Past, the centre of a boundless Present, and the beginning of a boundless Future."[14] In the most emi-

---

[13] John 1:14; I John 1:1–3. [Ed.]

[14] Heinrich (or Henrik) Steffens (1773–1845), a Norwegian-born natural scientist and philosopher, was part of the romantic circle that included Schelling and Schleiermacher. [Ed.]

nent sense may we say this, of Him who is the centre of Humanity itself, the Son of Man, as revealed in the person of Jesus Christ. All nature and all previous history unite, to form one grand, universal prophecy of his presence. All becomes significant and complete at last, only in his person.

Nature, through all lower forms of existence, looks upwards continually to the idea of man. The inorganic struggles towards the organic; the plant towards the animal; and the animal nature, improving upon itself from one order of life to another, rests not till it is superseded finally by the human. Thus all converge towards the same end; each inferior nature foreshadowing that which is to follow, till the vast system becomes symmetrical and full, in a form of perfection which may be said to include at last and mirror the true sense of the whole.[15]

---

[15] It is hardly necessary to say, that the idea here presented implies no possibility whatever of a regular development, on the part of any lower form of existence, upwards to the sphere of that which stands above it. This thought, which has been exhibited with no small measure of plausibility by the author of the little volume entitled *Vestiges of Creation*, has been justly repudiated by the Christian world as contrary to all revelation and religion. It contradicts, besides, all sound philosophy. The process of growth and historical development can never, as such, evolve from any form of existence more than was actually involved in it from the beginning. But who can imagine at all, that the life of the animal is ever potentially present in the life of the plant. To say that the law of existence in the one case, is made to include at a certain point *more* than was comprehended in it before, is only to play with words; for the *more* which appears in that case must be considered in all respects a new creation, and in no intelligible sense whatever the product or birth of what existed previously. The difference between the animal and man, is just as broad as that between the animal and the plant. There is an impassable gulf between the two forms of existence, which nothing short of a new creation can ever surmount in the case of the lower. But all this has nothing to do with the view presented in the text. It is affirmed here, simply, that the lower forms of existence look prophetically towards those which are above them. They cannot be said to carry these in their womb, in any sense; but they foreshadow their presence, and in this way find their own full meaning always in something beyond themselves. The evidence of this is so plain, that the fact will not be called in question by any who have even the most general

Without man the entire world would be shorn of its meaning. It is by the medium of his personality only, that it becomes transparent with thought and is made to utter any intelligible sound. The world finds itself, comes to the knowledge of itself, in man. All is dark till it has made its way up to the sphere of human consciousness. There all becomes light. Man is the centre of nature; the key to all its mysteries; the idea, which binds its manifold parts into one, and makes them complete as a single organic whole.

But what man is to nature in this way, Christ may be said to be in some sense to man. Humanity itself is never complete, till it reaches his person. It includes in its very constitution a struggle towards the form in which it is here exhibited, which can never rest till this end is attained. Our nature reaches after a true and real union with the nature of God, as the necessary complement and consummation of its own life. The *idea* which it embodies can never be fully actualized, under any other form. The incarnation then is the proper completion of humanity. Christ is the true ideal Man. Here is reached ultimately the highest summit of human life, which is at the same time of course the crowning sense of the world, or that in which it finds its last and full signification. Here the human consciousness itself, the medium of order and light for the sphere of mere nature, is raised into a higher sphere, from which a new life is made to pour itself forth again over the whole world. Man finds himself in God, and wakes to the full sense of his own being, in being enabled thus to fall back, in a full, free way, on the absolute ground of his life. The one only medium of such inward, living communication with the divine nature, is the mystery of

---

acquaintance with the actual constitution of the world. [Robert Chambers (1802–1871) published *Vestiges of the Natural History of Creation* anonymously in 1844. It expounded evolution in very positive, but pre-Darwinian, terms. Nevin is unprepared to accept the idea of organic evolution. Yet even the need to utter this disclaimer reveals the developmentalism latent in his outlook. Ed.]

the incarnation, as exhibited in the man Christ Jesus. This forms accordingly, without a figure, the inmost and last sense of all God's works. The world, from its extreme circumference, looks inward to this fact as its true and proper centre, and presses towards it continually, from every side, as the end of its entire constitution. All is one vast prophecy of the coming of Christ.

History too converges, from the beginning, always towards the same point. Not only here and there, have we solitary annunciations, more or less obscure, of the glorious advent of the Messiah. History, like nature, is one vast prophecy of the incarnation, from beginning to end. How could it be otherwise, if the idea of humanity, as we have seen, required from the first such a union with the divine nature, in order that it might be complete? What is history, but the process by which this idea is carried forward, according to the immanent law of its own nature, in the way of a regular development towards its appointed end? The introduction of *sin*—itself a world-fact, inseparably incorporated with this process almost from its start, and turning all violently into a false direction—only served to add a deeper emphasis to the meaning of life, in the view now noticed. The necessity of a real union with the divine nature, became a necessity at the same time of redemption, the loud cry of suffering humanity after an atonement for sin. The development of this want might be said to form thus the great burden of history, onward from the fall. All of course, in this view, had a reference prophetically to the coming of Christ. The whole creation groaned and travailed in pain together, reaching forward, as it were, with earnest expectation, to the hour of this deliverance. Not only Judaism, but Paganism too, preached beforehand the great event. Both looked, from different sides, in the same direction and towards the same end. Both found their inmost meaning verified at last and explained in Christ.

Paganism must ever be of course essentially false, under all its forms. But all falsehood involves some truth, of which it is the caricature, but from which at the same time it draws its life. The time has been, when a superficial infidelity sought to bring the mysteries of Christianity into discredit, by comparing them with the mythological dreams and speculations of the heathen world. But that time, it may be trusted, has come to an end. Christianity as the absolute religion, *must* in the nature of the case, take up into itself, and exhibit in a perfect form, the fragments and rudiments of truth contained in all relative religions. It is not a doctrine, but a divine *fact*, into which all previous religious tendencies and developments are ultimately gathered as their proper end. As in Nature, all lower developments of life, however defective or seemingly monstrous, find their true meaning and value, only as analogies and relative approximations to the nature of man—whose perfection and dignity in this way they serve, not to disparage, but to authenticate and magnify. So do the ancient religions, both of the Orient and West, conspire to bear testimony in favour of Christ, falling down as it were before him, and presenting unto him gifts, "gold and frankincense and myrrh." Brahmanism, Buddhism, Parsism, the religion of Egypt and the religion of Greece, each in its own way, look ever in the same direction, and are heard to utter in the end the same voice. All prophesy of Christ; for all proclaim the inmost want of humanity to be a true union with God, and their character is determined simply by the form in which it is attempted in each case to bring this great life problem to its proper resolution. . . .

Judaism, we all know, had respect to the coming of Christ, from the beginning. The preparation which in the case of the heathen world was negative only, assumed here a *positive* character. The religion of the Old Testament, from the time of Adam down to the time of John the Baptist, stood throughout on the ground of a supernatural revelation that might be said not only to foreshadow the great fact of the incarnation, but directly to open the way also for its manifestation. It is not simply the necessity of a union with God on the part of man, the cry for redemption and salvation, which it is felt can be reached only in this way, that is here made to reveal itself in the world's history. A real approximation to men on the part of God, in the way of a movement to meet this want, is exhibited at the same time. Heathenism might be said to run out in a helpless attempt violently to deify humanity itself; a process that must ever fall back, with new despair, to the point from which it started. In the religion of the Old Testament, God descends towards man, and holds out to his view in this way the promise of a real union of the divine nature with the human, as the end of the gracious economy thus introduced.

To such a *real* union it is true, the dispensation itself never came. . . . Towards this ultimate point however the whole process of condescension constantly tended, as its necessary consummation. The meaning of the entire system lay in its reference to Christianity. Not only did it contain particular types and particular prophecies of the incarnation; it was all one vast type, and throughout one continuous prophecy, in this direction. We may say of the Old Testament as a whole, what is said of its last and greatest representative in particular. It was the voice of one crying in the wilderness, prepare ye the way of the Lord, make straight in the desert a highway for our God! It might be said in some sense to carry the Gospel in its womb. All the great truths which were afterwards brought to light by Christ, lay more or less undisclosed in its revelations, growing and ripening gradually for the full birth towards which they struggled, and to which they attained finally in his person. Without Christianity, Judaism would have no meaning, no proper reality. It becomes real, only by losing itself, and finding itself at the same time, in the new dispensation. The law, as such, made nothing perfect. All served only to harbinger the advent of the Messiah, and to proclaim his presence when he came. All foreshadowed and foretokened the mystery of the incarnation.

Here then, as before said, we reach the central FACT, at once ultimate and primal, in the constitution of the world. All nature and all history flow towards it, as their true and proper end, or spring from it as their principle and ground. The incarnation, by which divinity and humanity are joined together, and made one, in a real, inward and abiding way, is found to be the scope of all God's counsels and dispensations in the world. The mystery of the universe is interpreted in the person of Jesus Christ. . . .

It is by no mere figure of speech, that Christ is represented to be the author of a new creation. Nor may we say of this creation, that it is moral simply, consisting in a new order of thought and character on the part of men. It is no revolution of the old, no historical advance upon the past merely, that is here brought into view; but the introduction, literally and strictly, of a new element, a new divine force, into the very organism of the world itself. The incarnation, in this view, is fully parallel with the work, by which in the beginning "the worlds were framed by the word of God;" and in the case of which, we are told "things which are seen were not made of things which do appear." [Heb. 11:3.] As the formation of man on the sixth day was necessary to perfect in a higher sphere the organization already called into being in a lower, of which at the same time it could not be said to be, in any sense, the product or result; so in the end, to crown all with a still higher perfection, the Word itself, by which the heavens and the earth were created before, became permanently joined with humanity in the person of Jesus Christ, as the principle of a new earth and new heavens—the continuation and necessary complement of the previous organization, but in no sense again its historical product or birth. . . .

The great argument for the truth of Christianity, is the person of Jesus himself, as exhibited to us in the faith of the Church. The incarnation is the FACT of all facts that may be said itself to authenticate all truth in the world besides. The first miracle, and the only miracle, we may say, of Christianity, is the new creation in which it starts. All else is but the natural product and expression of the life thus introduced into the world. Nothing *so* natural, as the supernatural itself in the Saviour's person. Jesus Christ authenticates himself. All foreign, external credentials here can have, in the very nature of the case, only a subordinate and secondary value. He is himself the principle and ground, the alpha and omega of all truth.

Christ is the principle of a new creation. To be so in truth, he must be incorporated, under this character, with the inmost life of humanity. For, as we have seen, the world centres in man; and out to its extreme physical circumference, all takes its form and complexion from the nature which thus constitutes its living, spiritual heart. To descend into the world at all then, so as to become united to its constitution as a principle of organic renovation, it was necessary that the Word should become *flesh*. The new creation reveals itself in man. Christ is the second ADAM.

His manhood was real. The incarnation was no mere theophany; no transient wonder; no illusion exhibited to the senses. "Christ, the Son of God, became man, by taking to himself a true body and a reasonable soul, being conceived by the power of the Holy Ghost, in the womb of the Virgin Mary, of her substance, and born of her, yet without sin." John makes it the mark of Antichrist to call this in question. (I John 4:1–3; II John 7.) The nature which he took upon him was truly and fully the nature of Adam; and it was not joined to him in the way of an outward accident or appendage merely. The union was inward and complete; two natures, but one single undivided person.

Christ, however, was not simply a descendant of Adam, and a brother thus of the human family, as standing in the same relation. To his natural birth must be joined his supernatural conception. He took our nature upon him; but, in doing so, he raised it into a higher sphere, by uniting it with the nature of God, and became thus the root of a new life for the race. His assumption of humanity was something general, and not merely particular. The Word became flesh; not a single man only, as one among many; but *flesh,* or humanity in its universal conception. How else could he be the principle of a general life, the origin of a new order of existence for the human world as such? How else could the value of his mediatorial work be made over to us in a real way, by a true imputation, and not a legal fiction only? The entire scheme of the Christian salvation requires and assumes throughout, this view of the incarnation and no other. To make it a merely individual case, a fact of no wider force than the abstract person of Jesus himself, thus resolving his relationship to his people into their common relationship to Adam, is to turn all at last into an unreal theophany, and thus to overthrow the doctrine altogether. . . .

Christ then was not the founder simply of a religious school; of vastly greater eminence, it might be, than Pythagoras, Plato, or Moses, but still a teacher of truth only in the same general sense. Christianity is not a *Doctrine,* to be taught or learned like a system of philosophy or a rule of moral conduct. Rationalism is always prone to look upon the gospel in this way. . . . In opposition to all this, we say of Christianity that it is a LIFE. Not a rule or mode of life simply; not something that in its own nature requires to be reduced to practice; for that is the character of all morality. But life in its very nature and constitution, and as such the actual substance of truth itself. This is its grand distinction. Here it is broadly separated from all other forms of religion, that ever have claimed, or ever can claim, the attention of the world. "The law came by Moses, but GRACE and TRUTH by Jesus Christ" [John 1:17]. . . . Christ does not exhibit himself accordingly as the medium only, by which the truth is brought nigh to men. He claims always to *be* himself, all that the idea of salvation claims. He does not simply point men to heaven. He does not merely profess to give right instruction. He does not present to them only the promise of life, as secure to them from God on certain conditions. But he says, "I AM the *Way,* and the *Truth,* and the LIFE; no man cometh unto the Father but by ME" (John 14:6). . . .

"I am the Resurrection and the Life! He that believeth in me, though he were dead, yet shall he live. And whosoever liveth and believeth in me, shall never die" (John 11:25, 26). The *resurrection* and *life* here named, are only different aspects of the same idea. The first is the form simply in which the last reveals itself, in its victorious struggle with death. Both reveal themselves together in Christ. It is in him personally, as the bearer of our fallen humanity, that death is swallowed up in victory, by the power of that divine life of which he was the incarnation. From him, the same life flows over to his people in the way of real communication. He does not merely preach the resurrection. It is comprehended in his person. He hath in himself abolished death, and thus brought life and immortality to light through the gospel. (II Tim. 1:10.) The revelation does not consist in this, that he has removed all doubt from the doctrine of a future state, and made it certain that men will live hereafter. It is not the doctrine, but the fact itself, that is brought to light. Immortality, in its true sense, has been introduced into the world only by Christ. . . .

Parallel exactly with this relation to the natural creation, only in a far higher order of life, the apostle now declares his relation to be also to the supernatural constitution revealed in the Church. . . . Christianity then is a Life, not only as revealed at first in Christ, but as continued also in the Church. It flows over from Christ to his people, always in this form. They do not simply bear his name, and acknowledge his doctrine. They are so united with him as to have part in the substance of his life itself. Their conversion is a new *birth;* "not of blood, nor of the will of the flesh, nor of the will of man, but of God" (John 1:12, 13). "That which is born of the flesh, is flesh." As such, it can never rise above its own nature. No cultivation, no outward aid, no simply moral appliances, can ever lift it into a higher sphere. This requires a new *life*. "That which is born of the Spirit, is spirit;" all else necessarily comes short of the distinction. All else accordingly is something lower than Christianity. (John 3:1–8.) . . .

The whole morality of the gospel is made to root itself in the presence and power of the new life, thus derived from Christ. This forms its grand characteristic distinction, as compared with the so called virtue of the common world. All duties are enforced on the ground of what the Christian has become by his heavenly birth, as the subject of the Christian salvation. All relations hold *in Christ Jesus.* The motives to every virtue are drawn from the grace of the gospel itself, as already constituting the actual state of those on whom they are urged. . . . Such is the tenor throughout of the Christian morality. Its superiority to other ethical systems does not consist in its being simply a more full and accurate statement of the duties God requires of man than can be found elsewhere; but in this rather, that it reveals the true ground of all moral relations in Christ, and refers every duty in this way to a principle which it could not have in any other form, and which infuses into it accordingly a new character altogether. The whole structure of life, ethically viewed, becomes a new creation in Christ Jesus.

Christ is the principle of the whole Christian salvation. From him it flows over, as the power of a divine life, into the persons of his people. This implies of course the most close and intimate connection. The union however which exists in this case, is more than that of simple derivation. . . . No more apt or beautiful illustration of this union between Christ and the Church can be imagined than that which he has himself furnished, in the allegory of the vine and its branches. "I am the vine, ye are the branches; he that abideth in me, and I in him, the same bringeth forth much fruit; for without me ye can do nothing." (John 15:1–8.) . . . Nature finds its divine archetype or *Urbild* at last, only in the sphere of the Spirit. Thus the connection which holds between the vine and its branches is not so much a figure of the life union that has place between Christ and believers, as the very reflex of this mystery itself. He is accordingly the TRUE vine, in whom is revealed, in this case, the full reality, of which only an adumbration is present in all lower forms of life. The union between the vine and its branches is organic. They are not placed together in an outward and merely mechanical way. The vine reveals itself in the branches; and the branches have no vitality apart from the vine. All form one and the same life. The nature of the stock is reproduced continually, with all its qualities, in every shoot that springs from its growth, no matter how far removed from the root. And all this is only the symbol of Christ's relation to his people. Here, in a far higher sphere, the region of the Spirit as distinguished from that of mere nature, it is one and the same life again that reigns in the root and all its branches. The union is organic. The parts exist not separately from the whole, but grow out of it, and stand in it continually, as their own true and proper life. Christ dwells in his people by the Holy Ghost, and is formed in them the hope of glory. They grow up into him in all things; and are transformed into the same image, from glory to glory, as by the Spirit of the Lord. The life of Christ is reproduced in them, under the same true human character that belongs to it in his own person. . . .

[THE INCARNATION AND THE EUCHARIST]

The Lord's Supper can never be understood, except as viewed in its relations to the whole system of truth, which has been brought to light by the bible. The view we have already taken then, of the new creation in Christ Jesus and his mystical relation to the Church, has all served only to open the way for placing the ordinance in its true and proper light.

The great difficulty here is in rising to a full, abiding sense of the truth and reality of Christianity itself, as a supernatural constitution permanently established *under this character* in the world. We are too prone to restrict the idea of supernatural interposition in this case to the single historical person of Jesus Christ himself, an error that tends directly to throw a certain magical, docetic character, over the whole fact of the incarnation, and to sink Christianity at the same time to the form of a mere abstract spiritualism in the sphere of the flesh. For it is one thing to be spiritualistic in the flesh, and quite another thing to be divinely real in the Spirit. We must not sunder the supernatural in Christ, from the life of his body which is the Church. Christianity is strictly and truly a new creation in Christ Jesus; a supernatural order of life, revealed and made constant and abiding, in the midst of the course of nature as it stood before. As such, it includes resources, powers, divine realities, not only peculiar to itself, but altogether transcending the common natural constitution of human life. All this, at the same time, under a true historical form. The supernatural has become itself natural, not in the way however of putting off its own distinction, as compared with what nature had been before, and still is under any other view; but by falling into the regular process of the world's history, so as to form to the end of time indeed its true central stream. To question the presence of such supernatural resources and powers in Christianity, when we look at it properly, is to question in fact the revelation of the supernatural in Christ himself. Either we must fall back at best to the old Ebionitic stand-point of Christian Judaism,[16] or we must allow that the power of a truly divine life, the constitution of the Spirit as distinguished from the constitution of mere nature, is in the Church, not transiently and sporadically as under the old Testament, but with real immanent constancy, as forming the inmost character of the Church itself.

The supernatural, as thus made permanent and historical in the Church, must, in the nature of the case, correspond with the form of the supernatural, as it appeared originally in Christ himself. For it is all one and the same life or constitution. The Church must have a true theanthropic character throughout. The union of the divine and human in her constitution must be inward and real, a continuous revelation of God in the flesh, exalting this last continuously into the sphere of the Spirit.

---

[16] On the Ebionites, see note 70, p. 570. [Ed.]

Let all this be properly apprehended and felt, and it cannot fail at once to exert a powerful influence over our judgment with regard to the Lord's Supper. For it is plain, that this ordinance holds a central place in the general system of Christian worship. The solemn circumstances under which it was originally instituted, the light in which it has always been regarded in the Church, and the very instinct, we may say, of our religious nature itself, which no rationalism can effectually suppress, all conspire to show that it forms in truth the inmost sanctuary of religion, and the most direct and close approach we are ever called to make into the divine presence. The mystery of Christianity is here concentrated into a single visible transaction, by which it is made as it were transparent to the senses, and caused to pass before us in immediate living representation. No matter how poor may be the general view entertained of the gospel, even for the lowest rationalistic spiritualism itself, the Lord's Supper (if it be not discarded entirely, as with the unhappy Quaker) constitutes the most significant and impressive exhibition of the grace of the New Testament; the most graphic *picture*, at least, if nothing more, of the salvation which has been procured for us by the Saviour's sufferings and death. All that is wanted, then, to make it a true sacrament to our view—the *seal* as well as the *sign* of the invisible grace it represents—is that we should have a true and full persuasion of the supernatural character of Christianity itself, as a permanent and not simply transient fact in the history of the world.

IX

CHARLES PORTERFIELD KRAUTH

Lutheran Confessionalist

Charles Porterfield Krauth (1823–1883)[1] represents two vital phases in American church history. As a third generation American, he reveals the speed with which an adjustment to American ways was being accomplished in many parts of the older Lutheranism of the eastern United States. At the same time he personifies both a rejection of revivalistic evangelicalism and a return to the major motifs of the Lutheran Reformation. His views, however, were anticipated by his father, Charles Philip Krauth (1797–1867), who after serving as pastor of the first English Lutheran church in Philadelphia became the first president of the college at Gettysburg (1834–1850) and then concluded his career at the seminary in Gettysburg, where he became a moderate but effective counterweight to the "American" Lutheranism of Professor Samuel S. Schmucker. In 1850 the elder Krauth made a convention address the occasion for stating that Americanization was not in itself a sufficient goal and defined the Lutheran Church as a "conservative influence," a via media "between Roman Catholic and Protestant extremes." In that same year he began a

---

[1] See Introduction, pp. 52–57.

decade's editorship of the new EVANGELICAL REVIEW, a scholarly journal which became a kind of Lutheran parallel to the MERCERSBURG REVIEW.

Charles Porterfield Krauth was born in Virginia and educated in the school, college, and seminary at Gettysburg. In 1841 he began his own ministry in a series of Maryland and Virginia parishes, pursuing all along an extremely rigorous program of linguistic and scholarly training, and also experiencing a gradual disenchantment with the puritanic churchmanship he had been practicing. As early as 1844 he began to resist the prevailing American Lutheran or Modern Puritan view of the sacraments; by 1849 when the EVANGELICAL REVIEW published his translation of a section from Heinrich Schmid's DOCTRINAL THEOLOGY OF THE LUTHERAN CHURCH, the change was virtually complete. Thereafter, for over three decades his influence continually widened—in his own church, in Lutheranism, and in the country. He left Winchester, Virginia, in 1855 for a church in Pittsburgh; then in 1859 he moved to a Philadelphia parish where he also served as editor of THE LUTHERAN AND MISSIONARY during the critical years of controversy with American Lutheranism (1860–1867). He was also professor of theology in the new seminary founded at Philadelphia in 1864. At the University of Pennsylvania he became concurrently professor of philosophy in 1868 and Vice Provost in 1873.

Despite these many duties his scholarly activity was prodigious. It consisted of a steady stream of essays and books, nearly always related to historical, doctrinal, or liturgical issues; energetic efforts to rally and unite all of the confessional Lutheran synods of America to the General Council which was organized in 1869; articles on Lutheran subjects for encyclopedias and other reference works; translations of F. A. G. Tholuck's COMMENTARY

ON THE GOSPEL OF JOHN (1859), Hermann Ulrici's REVIEW OF STRAUSS'S LIFE OF CHRIST (1874), and many other essays and documents; and also American editions of such philosophical and apologetical works as would support the idealistic modification of Scottish Realism which he expounded in his philosophy courses. Needless to say, many of Krauth's works were ephemeral and many others have long since been superseded. Yet he remains an historic figure, important for his part in the immense labor of making Lutheranism conscious of its own tradition and aware of its American responsibilities. For a decade he was the dominant intellectual force in the General Council and his influence was long lasting.

The chief literary monument of Krauth's career is his immense tome, THE CONSERVATIVE REFORMATION AND ITS THEOLOGY (1871), in which nearly all of his leading views are presented. In it one may discern the revolutionary impact of historical research and historicism on all efforts to maintain an orthodox doctrinal witness. This volume, like Krauth's whole oeuvre, also displays the radical differences, both spiritual and methodological, between Lutheran "Confessionalism" of the nineteenth century and Lutheran "Orthodoxy" of the seventeenth. The selection that follows is drawn from this book. It includes the portion of his Preface where he delineates the issues of Catholicism and Protestantism in the existing church situation, an historical section on the Lutheran Reformation, a section on the confessional principle in general and the Augsburg Confession in particular, and, finally, the core of his theological statement on the Eucharist, an issue which had riven the Reformation cause at the outset and which Krauth, like the Mercersburg theologians, considered still to be the crux of all efforts for church renewal or ecclesiastical reconciliation.

THE CONSERVATIVE REFORMATION

AND ITS THEOLOGY

Preface

That some form of Christianity is to be the religion of the world, is not only an assured fact to the believer in Revelation, but must be regarded as probable, even in the judgment which is formed on purely natural evidence. Next in transcendent importance to that fact, and beyond it in present interest, as a question relatively undecided, is the question, *What* form of Christianity is to conquer the world? Shall it be the form in which Christianity now exists, the form of intermingling and of division, of internal separation and warfare? Is the territory of Christendom forever to be divided between antagonistic communions, or occupied by them conjointly? Shall there be to the end of time the Greek, the Roman, the Protestant churches, the sects, and the heretical bodies? Or shall one or other of these specific forms lift itself above the tangled mass, and impose order on chaos? Or shall a form yet unrevealed prove the church of the future? To this the answer seems to be, that the logic of the question, supported by eighteen centuries of history, renders it probable that some principle, or some combination of principles now existent, will assuredly, however slowly, determine the ultimate, world-dominating type of Christianity. Unless there be an exact balance of force in the different tendencies, the internally strongest of them will ultimately prevail over

From Charles Porterfield Krauth, *The Conservative Reformation and Its Theology, As Represented in the Augsburg Confession, and in the History and Literature of the Evangelical Lutheran Church* (Philadelphia: J. B. Lippincott & Co., 1871), pp. vii–xv, 1–17, 201–216, 585–587, 619, 629, 652–657, 829–830.

the others, and, unless a new force superior to it comes in, will be permanent.

The history of Christianity, in common with all genuine history, moves under the influence of two generic ideas: the conservative, which desires to secure the present by fidelity to the results of the past; the progressive, which looks out, in hope, to a better future. Reformation is the great harmonizer of the two principles. Corresponding with Conservatism, Reformation, and Progress are three generic types of Christianity; and under these *genera* all the species are but shades, modifications, or combinations, as all hues arise from three primary colors. Conservatism without Progress produces the Romish and Greek type of the Church. Progress without Conservatism runs into Revolution, Radicalism, and Sectarianism. Reformation is antithetical both to passive persistence in wrong or passive endurance of it, and to Revolution as a mode of relieving wrong. Conservatism is opposed to Radicalism both in the estimate of wrong and the mode of getting rid of it. Radicalism errs in two respects: in its precipitance it often mistakes wheat for tares, and its eradication is so hasty and violent that even when it plucks up tares it brings the wheat with them. Sober judgment and sober means characterize Conservatism. Reformation and Conservatism really involve each other. That which claims to be Reformatory, yet is not Conservative, is Sectarian; that which claims to be Conservative, and is not Reformatory, is Stagnation and Corruption. True Catholicity is Conservatism, but Protestantism is Reformatory; and these two are complementary, not antagonistic. The Church problem is to attain a Protestant Catholicity or Catholic Protestantism. This is the end and aim of Conservative Reformation.

Reformation is the means by which Conservatism of the good that is, and progress to the good yet to be won, is secured. Over against the stagnation of an isolated Conservatism, the Church is to hold Reformation as the instrument of progress. Over against the abuses of a separatistic and one-sided progressiveness, she is to see to it that her Reformation maintains that due reverence for history, that sobriety of tone, that patience of spirit, and that moderation of manner, which are involved in Conservatism. The good that has been is necessary to the safety of the good that is to be. There are to be no absolutely fresh starts. If the foundation were removed, the true course would not be to make a new one, but to find the old one, and lay it again. But the foundation never was wholly lost, nor was there, in the worst time of the accumulation of wood, hay, and stubble, an utter ceasing of the building of gold, silver, and precious stones upon it. The Reformation, as Christian, accepted the old foundation; as reformatory, it removed the wood, hay, and stubble; as conservative, it carefully separated, guarded, and retained the gold, silver, and precious stones, the additions of pious human hands, befitting the foundation and the temple which was to be reared upon it. Rome had accumulated greatly and given up nothing, till the foundation upheld little but perishing human traditions, and the precious things were lost in the heaps of rubbish. The revolutionary spirit of the radical Reform proposed to leave nothing but the foundation, to sweep from it everything which had been built upon it. The Conservative, equally accepting the foundation which has been laid once for all, proposed to leave on it everything precious, pure, and beautiful which had risen in the ages. The one proposed to pull down the temple; the other, to purify it, and to replace its weak and decayed portions with solid rock. The great work of the sixteenth century, which bears the generic title of the Reformation, was divided between these tendencies; not, indeed, absolutely to the last extreme, but yet really divided. The whole Protestant movement in the Church of the West was reformatory as over against papal Rome, and was so far a unit; but it was divided within itself, between the conservative and radical tendencies. The conservative tendency embodied itself in the Reformation in which Luther was the leader; the radical, in Zwingle and his school. Calvin came in to occupy a relatively mediating position,—conservative as compared with the ultra-ism of Zwinglianism, and of the heretical tendencies which Zwinglianism at once nurtured, yet, relatively to Lutheranism, largely radical.

The Church of England is that part of the Reformed Church for which most affinity with the conservatism of Lutheranism is usually claimed. That Church occupies a position in some respects unique. First, under Henry VIII., ceasing to be Popish without ceasing to be Romish; then passing under the influences of genuine reformation into the positively Lutheran type; then influenced by the mediating position of the school of Bucer, and of the later era of Melanchthon, a school which claimed the ability practically to co-ordinate the Lutheran and Calvinistic positions; and finally settling into a system of compromise, in which is revealed the influence of the Roman Catholic views of Orders in the ministry, and, to some extent, of the Ritual; of the Lutheran tone of reformatory conservatism, in the general structure of the Liturgy, in the larger part of the Articles, and especially in the doctrine of Baptism; of the mediating theology in the doctrine of predestination; and of Calvinism in particular changes in the Book of Common Prayer, and, most of all, in the doctrine of the Lord's Supper. . . .

The Eclectic Reformation is like the Eclectic Philosophy—it accepts the common affirmation of the different systems, and refuses their negations.[1] Like the English language, the English Church is a miracle of compositeness. In the wonderful tessellation of their structure is the strength of both, and their weakness. The English language is two languages inseparably conjoined. It has the strength and affluence of the two, and something of the awkwardness necessitated by their union. The Church of England has two great elements; but they are not

---

[1] Eclecticism was the name given to the system of the French philosopher Victor Cousin (1792–1867) and his many disciples. At first committed to the Scottish Philosophy so popular in America, Cousin later incorporated other tendencies, notably German romantic idealism. [Ed.]

perfectly preserved in their distinctive character, but, to some extent, are confounded in the union. With more uniformity than any other great Protestant body, it has less unity than any. Partly in virtue of its doctrinal indeterminateness, it has been the home of men of the most opposite opinions: no Calvinism is intenser, no Arminianism lower, than the Calvinism and Arminianism which have been found in the Church of England. It has furnished able defenders of Augustine, and no less able defenders of Pelagius. Its Articles, Homilies, and Liturgy have been a great bulwark of Protestantism; and yet, seemingly, out of the very stones of that bulwark has been framed, in our day, a bridge on which many have passed over into Rome. It has a long array of names dear to our common Christendom as the masterly vindicators of her common faith, and yet has given high place to men who denied the fundamental verities confessed in the general creeds. It harbors a skepticism which takes infidelity by the hand, and a revised mediævalism which longs to throw itself, with tears, on the neck of the Pope and the Patriarch, to beseech them to be gentle, and not to make the terms of restored fellowship too difficult. The doctrinal indeterminateness which has won has also repelled, and made it an object of suspicion not only to great men of the most opposite opinions, but also to great bodies of Christians. It has a doctrinal laxity which excuses, and, indeed, invites, innovation, conjoined with an organic fixedness which prevents the free play of the novelty. Hence the Church of England has been more depleted than any other, by secessions. Either the Anglican Church must come to more fixedness in doctrine or to more pliableness in form, or it will go on, through cycle after cycle of disintegration, toward ruin. . . .

These present difficulties in the Anglican Churches proceed not from contradiction of its principles, but from development of them. These two classes of seeds were sown by the husbandmen themselves—that was the compromise. The tares may grow till the harvest, side by side with the wheat, with which they mingle, but which they do not destroy, but the thorns which choke the seed must be plucked up, or the seed will perish. Tares are men; thorns are moral forces of doctrine or of life. The agitation in the Anglican Churches can end only in the victory of the one tendency and the silencing of the other, or in the sundering of the two. In Protestantism nothing is harder than to silence, nothing easier than to sunder. If the past history of the Anglican Church, hitherto unvaried in the ultimate result, repeat itself here, the new movement will end in a formal division, as it already has in a moral one. The trials of a Church which has taken a part in our modern civilization and Christianity which entitles it to the veneration and gratitude of mankind, can be regarded with indifference only by the sluggish and selfish, and with malicious joy only by the radically bad.[2]

The classification of Churches by tendencies is, of course, relative. No great organization moves so absolutely along the line of a single tendency as to have nothing in it beyond that tendency, or contradictory to it. The wilfulness of some, the feeble-mindedness of others, the power of surrounding influences, modify all systems in their actual working. There was some conservatism in the Swiss reformation, and there has been and is something of the reformatory tendency in the Church of Rome. The Reformation took out a very large part of the best material influenced by this tendency in Rome, but not all of it.

The object of this book is not to delineate the spirit and doctrines of the Reformation as a general movement over against the doctrinal and practical errors of the Roman Church, but to state and vindicate the faith and spirit of that part of the movement which was conservative, as over against the part which was radical. It is the Lutheran Reformation in those features which distinguish it from the Zwinglian and Calvinistic Ref-

---

[2] Krauth's prediction of Protestant Episcopal schism was not entirely unfulfilled. In 1873 a small group of seceders did found the Reformed Episcopal Church. [Ed.]

ormations, which forms the topic of this book. Wherever Calvin abandoned Zwinglianism he approximated Lutheranism. Hence, on important points, this book, in defending Lutheranism over against Zwinglianism, defends Calvinism over against Zwinglianism also. It even defends Zwinglianism, so far as, in contrast with Anabaptism, it was relatively conservative. The Pelagianism of the Zwinglian theology was corrected by Calvin, who is the true father of the Reformed Church, as distinguished from the Lutheran. The theoretical tendencies of Zwingle developed into Arminianism and Rationalism; his practical tendencies into the superstitious anti-ritualism of ultra-Puritanism: and both the theoretical and practical found their harmony and consummation in Unitarianism.

The positions taken in this book are largely counter, in some respects, to the prevailing theology of our time and our land. No man can be more fixed in his prejudice against the views here defended than the author himself once was; no man can be more decided in his opinion that those views are false than the author is now decided in his faith that they are the truth. They have been formed in the face of all the influences of education and of bitter hatred or of contemptuous disregard on the part of nearly all who were most intimately associated with him in the period of struggle.[3] Formed under such circumstances, under what he believes to have been the influence of the Divine Word, the author is persuaded that they rest upon grounds which cannot easily be moved. In its own nature his work is, in some degree, polemical; but its conflict is purely with opinions, never with persons. The theme itself, as it involves questions within our common Protestantism, renders the controversy principally one with defects or errors in systems least remote in the main from the faith vindicated in this vol-

---

[3] On Krauth's theological development, see Adolph Spaeth, *Charles Porterfield Krauth*, 2 vols. (Philadelphia: General Council Publication House, 1898, 1909), I, chaps. 3–6. [Ed.]

ume. It is most needful that those nearest each other should calmly argue the questions which still divide them, as there is most hope that those already so largely in affinity may come to a yet more perfect understanding. . . .

A true unity in Protestantism would be the death of Popery; but Popery will live until those who assail it are one in their answer to the question: What shall take its place?[4] This book is a statement and a defence of the answer given to that question by the communion under whose banner the battle with Rome was first fought,—under whose leaders the greatest victories over Rome were won. If this Church has been a failure, it can hardly be claimed that the Reformation was a success; and if Protestantism cannot come to harmony with the principles by which it was created, as those principles were understood by the greatest masters in the reformatory work, it must remain divided until division reaches its natural end—absorption and annihilation.

The Reformation: Its Occasion and Cause

The immediate occasion of the Reformation seemed insignificant enough. Three hundred and fifty-three years ago, on the 31st of October, immense crowds were pouring into an ancient city of Germany, bearing in its name, Wittenberg, the memorial of its founder, Wittekind the Younger. The weather-beaten and dingy little edifices of Wittenberg forbade the idea that the beauty of the city or its commercial importance drew the masses to it. Within that city was an old church, very miserable and battered, and very venerable and holy, which attracted these crowds. It was the "Church of all Saints," in which were shown,

---

[4] Popery, Romanism, and Catholicism are distinct terms in Krauth's understanding, as will be clear to the careful reader of this Preface. Protestant Catholicity or Catholic Protestantism was his goal. [Ed.]

to the inexpressible delight of the faithful, a fragment of Noah's Ark, some soot from the furnace into which the three young Hebrews were cast, a piece of wood from the crib of the infant Saviour, some of St. Christopher's beard, and nineteen thousand other relics equally genuine and interesting. But over and above all these allurements, so well adapted to the taste of the time, His Holiness, the Pope, had granted indulgence to all who should visit the church on the first of November. Against the door of that church of dubious saints, and dubious relics, and dubious indulgences, was found fastened, on that memorable morning, a scroll unrolled. The writing on it was firm; the nails which held it were well driven in; the sentiments it conveyed were moderate, yet very decided. The material, parchment, was the same which long ago had held words of redemption above the head of the Redeemer. The contents were an amplification of the old theme of glory—Christ on the cross, the only King. The Magna Charta, which had been buried beneath the Pope's throne, reappeared on the church door. The keynote of the Reformation was struck full and clear at the beginning, Salvation through Christ alone.

It is from the nailing up of these Theses the Reformation takes its date. That act became, in the providence of God, the starting-point of the work which still goes on, and shall forever go on, that glorious work in which the truth was raised to its original purity, and civil and religious liberty were restored to men. That the Reformation is the spring of modern freedom, is no wild assertion of its friends. One of the greatest Roman Catholic writers of recent times, Michelet, in the Introduction to his Life of Luther, says: "It is not incorrect to say, that Luther has been the restorer of liberty in modern times. If he did not create, he at least courageously affixed his signature to that great revolution which rendered the right of examination lawful in Europe. And, if we exercise, in all its plenitude at this day, this first and highest privilege of human intelligence, it is to him we are most indebted for it; nor can we think, speak, or write, without being made conscious, at every step, of the immense benefit of this intellectual enfranchisement;" and he concludes with the remark: "To whom do I owe the power of publishing what I am now inditing, except to this liberator of modern thought?"...[5]

The occasions and cause of so wonderful and important an event as the Reformation have naturally occupied very largely the thoughts of both its friends and its foes. On the part of its enemies the solution of its rapid rise, its gigantic growth, its overwhelming march, has been found by some in the rancor of monkish malice—the thing arose in a squabble between two sets of friars, about the farming of the indulgences—a solution as sapient and as completely in harmony with the facts as would be the statement that the American Revolution was gotten up by one George Washington, who, angry that the British Government refused to make him a collector of the tax on tea, stirred up a happy people to rebellion against a mild and just rule.

The solution has been found by others in the lust of the human heart for change—it was begotten in the mere love of novelty; men went into the Reformation as they go into a menagerie, or adopt the new mode, or buy up some "novelist's last." Another class, among whom the brilliant French Jesuit, Audin, is conspicuous, attribute the movement mainly to the personal genius and fascinating audacity of the great leader in the movement.[6] Luther so charmed the millions with his marvellous speech and magic style, that they were led at his will. On the part of some, its nominal friends, reasons hardly more adequate have often been assigned. Confounding the mere aids, or at

---

[5] Jules Michelet, *The Life of Luther* (London: David Bogue, 1846), p. xii. First French edition published, 1835. [Ed.]

[6] Jean Marie Vincent Audin (1793–1851) was not a Jesuit but a romantic Roman Catholic layman who wrote voluminously on historical subjects including the age of the Reformation. He had to defend himself from accusations of being pro-Protestant. His scholarship was shoddy. See his *History of the Life, Writings and Doctrines of Luther,* 2 vols. (London, 1854). [Ed.]

most, the mere occasions of the Reformation with its real causes, an undue importance has been attributed in the production of it to the progress of the arts and sciences after the revival of letters. Much stress has been laid upon the invention of printing, and the discovery of America, which tended to rouse the minds of men to a new life. Much has been said of the fermenting political discontents of the day, the influence of the great Councils in diminishing the authority of the Pope, and much has been made, in general, of the causes whose root is either wholly or in part in the earth. The Rationalist represents the Reformation as a triumph of reason over authority. The Infidel says, that its power was purely negative; it was a grand subversion; it was mightier than Rome, because it believed less than Rome; it prevailed, not by what it taught, but by what it denied; and it failed of universal triumph simply because it did not deny everything. The insect-minded sectarian allows the Reformation very little merit except as it prepared the way for the putting forth, in due time, of the particular twig of Protestantism on which he crawls, and which he imagines bears all the fruit, and gives all the value to the tree. . . . The Reformation, as they take it, originated in the divine plan for furnishing a nursery for sectarian Aphides.

But we must have causes which, however feeble, are adapted to the effects. A little fire indeed kindleth a great matter, but however little, it must be genuine fire. Frost will not do, and a painting of flame will not do, though the pencil of Raphael produced it. . . . The Word of God kindled the fire of the Reformation. That Word lay smouldering under the ashes of centuries; it broke forth into flame, in Luther and the other Reformers; it rendered them lights which shone and burnt inextinguishably; through them it imparted itself to the nations; and from the nations it purged away the dross which had gathered for ages. "The Word of God," says St. Paul, "is not bound."[7] Through the centuries which followed the corruption of Christianity, the

---

[7] II Timothy 2:9. [Ed.]

Word of God was still in being. In lonely cloisters it was laboriously copied. Years were sometimes spent in finishing a single copy of it, in the elaborate but half barbaric beauty which suited the taste of those times. Gold and jewels, on the massive covers, decorated the rich workmanship; costly pictures were painted as ornaments on its margin; the choicest vellum was used for the copies; the rarest records of heathen antiquity were sometimes erased to make way for the nobler treasures of the Oracles of the Most High. There are single copies of the Word, from that mid-world of history, which are a store of art, and the possession of one of which gives a bibliographical renown to the city in whose library it is preserved.

No interdict was yet laid upon the reading of the Word, for none was necessary. The scarcity and costliness of books formed in themselves a barrier more effectual than the interdict of popes and councils. Many of the great teachers in the Church of Rome were devoted students of the Bible. From the earliest writings of the Fathers, down to the Reformation, there is an unbroken line of witnesses for the right of all believers freely to read the Holy Scriptures. No man thought of putting an artificial limitation on its perusal; on the contrary, there are expressions of regret in the mediæval Catholic writers that, in the nature of the case, so few could have access to these precious records. . . .

The Church of Rome did not apprehend the danger which lay in that Book. Previous to the Reformation there were not only editions of the Scripture in the originals, but the old Church translation into Latin (the Vulgate) and versions from it into the living languages were printed. In Spain, whose dark opposition to the Word of God has since become her reproach and her curse, and in which no such book as the one of which we are about to speak has come forth for centuries, in Spain, more than a hundred years before there was enough Hebrew type in all England to print three consecutive lines, the first great POLYGLOT BIBLE, in Hebrew, Chaldee, Greek, and Latin, was issued at Complutum under the direction of Ximenes, her renowned cardinal and chief minister of state. It came forth in a form which, in splendor and value, far surpassed all that the world had yet seen. We may consider the Complutensian Polyglot, the crown of glory to the labors of the Middle Ages. It links itself clearly in historical connection with the GRAND BIBLICAL ERA, the Reformation itself, for though the printing of it was begun in 1502, and finished in 1517, it was not published till 1522, and in 1522, the FIRST EDITION OF THE NEW TESTAMENT, in German, came from the hand of Luther, fixing the cornerstone of the grand edifice, whose foundation had been laid in the Ninety-five Theses of 1517.

This, then, is the historical result of the facts we have presented, that the Middle Ages became, in the wonderful providence of God, the conservators of the Word which they are charged with suppressing; and were unconsciously tending toward the sunrise of the truth, which was to melt away their mists forever. . . .[8]

That Book was to Luther, henceforth, the thing of beauty of his life, the joy of his soul forever. He read and re-read, and prayed over its sacred teachings, till the place of each passage, and all memorable passages in their places fixed themselves in his memory. To the study of it, all other study seemed tame. A single passage of it would ofttimes lie in his thoughts days and nights together. The Bible seemed to fuse itself into his being, to become a part of his nature. Often in his writings he does not so much remark upon it, as catch its very pulse and clothe his own mind in its very garb. He is lifted to the glory of the reproducer—and himself becomes a secondary prophet and apostle. His soul ceased to be a mere vessel to hold a little of the living water, and became a fountain through which it sprang to re-

---

[8] Unusual for an American, Krauth appropriates the rediscovery of the Middle Ages pioneered by Michelet and others; and, even more unusual, joins the Mercersburg and Oxford movements in judging them providential. Unlike the latter, he does the same for the Reformation. [Ed.]

fresh and gladden others. As with Luther, so was it with Melanchthon, his noble coworker, with Zwingle in Switzerland, at a later period with Calvin in France, with Tyndale and Cranmer in England, with Knox in Scotland. The Word of God was the fire in their souls which purified them into Christians—and the man who became a Christian was already unconsciously a Reformer. . . .

When the great princes and free cities of our Church at Augsburg, in 1530, laid their Confession before the Emperor and potentates, civil and ecclesiastical, of the realm, they said: "We offer the Confession of the faith held by the pastors and preachers in our several estates, and the Confession of our own faith, *as drawn from the Holy Scriptures, the pure Word of God.*" That Confession repeatedly expresses, and in every line implies that the Word of God is the sole rule of faith and of life. The same is true of the Apology or Defence of the Confession by Melanchthon, which appeared in the following year, and which was adopted by the larger part of our Church as expressing correctly her views. Seven years later, the articles of Smalcald were prepared by Luther, for presentation at a general council, as an expression of the views of our Church. In this he says: "Not from the works or words of the Fathers are articles of faith to be made. We have another rule, to wit: that God's Word shall determine articles of faith—and, beside it, none other—no, not an angel even."[9]

Half a century after the Augsburg Confession had gone forth on its sanctifying mission, our Church in Germany, in order that her children might not mistake her voice amid the bewildering conflicts of theological strife, which necessarily followed such a breaking up of the old modes of human thought as was brought about by the Reformation, set forth her latest and amplest Con-

---

[9] Krauth gives his own translation from the Preface to the Augsburg Confession, 8; The Apology, Art. XXVII, 60; and the Smalcald Articles, Part Two, Art. II, 15. Cf. Theodore Tappert, ed., *The Book of Concord* (Philadelphia: Muhlenberg Press, 1959). [Ed.]

fession. This Confession, with reference to the harmony it was designed to subserve, and under God did largely subserve, was called the Formula of Concord. That document opens with these words: "We believe, teach, and confess that the only rule and law, by which all teachings and all teachers are to be estimated and judged, *is none other whatsoever* than the writings of the prophets and the apostles, alike of the Old and of the New Testament, as it is written: 'Thy word is a lamp unto my feet, and a light unto my path;' and St. Paul saith (Gal. 1:8): 'Though we, or an angel from heaven, preach any other Gospel unto you, than that which we have preached unto you, let him be accursed.'"

"All other writings," it continues, "whether of the Fathers, or of recent authors, be their name what they may, are by no means whatsoever to be likened to Holy Scripture; but are, in such sense, to be subjected to it, as to be received in none other way than as witnesses, which show how and where, after the apostles' times, the doctrines of the apostles and prophets were preserved." "We embrace," say our confessors, "the Augsburg Confession, not because it was written by our theologians, but because it was taken from God's Word, and solidly built on the foundation of Holy Scripture."

With equal clearness do the other Churches of the Reformation express themselves on this point.

If, then, the Reformers knew the movements of their own minds, it was God's Word, and it alone, which made them confessors of the truth. And it is a fundamental principle of the Reformation, that God's word is the sole and absolute authority, and rule of faith, and of life, a principle without accepting which, no man can be truly Evangelical, Protestant, or Lutheran. . . .

Three hundred and fifty-three years ago, the first thrill of the earthquake of the Reformation was felt in Europe. Men knew so little of its nature, that they imagined it could be suppressed. They threw their weight upon the heaving earth, and hoped to make it lie still. They knew not that they had a power to deal with, which was made more terrible in its outburst by the attempt to confine it. As the result of the opposition to the Reformation, Europe was made desolate. After the final struggle of the Thirty Years' War, Europe seemed ruined; its fields had been drenched with blood, its cities laid in ashes, hardly a family remained undivided, and the fiercest passions had been so aroused, that it seemed as if they could never be allayed.

Yet the establishment of the work of the Reformation has richly repaid Europe for all it endured. The earthquake has gone, the streams of desolation have been chilled, and the nations make a jubilee over the glorious anniversary of that grand movement which, by the depravity of men, was made the occasion of so much disturbance and misery. The evils of which the Reformation was the occasion, have passed away. We must go to the page of history to know what they were. The blessings of which the Reformation was the cause, abide; we feel them in our homes, in the Church, in the State; they are inwoven with the life of our life. Once feeling them, we know that this would be no world to live in without them. . . .

The Primary Confession: The Confession of Augsburg

It is with a solemn and holy delight we have learned to traverse the venerable edifice, which the hands of our fathers erected in the sixteenth century. There is none of the glitter which catches and fascinates the childish eye, but all possesses that solid grandeur which fills the soul. Every part harmonizes with the whole, and conspires in the proof that their work was not to pull down, but to erect. The spirit of the Reformation was no destroying angel, who sat and scowled with a malignant joy over the desolation which spread around. It was overshadowed by the wings of that Spirit who brooded indeed on the waste of waters and the wilderness of chaos, but only that he might unfold the germs of life that lay hidden there, and bring forth light and order from the darkness of the yet formless and void creation. It is vastly more important, then, to know what the Reformation retained than what it overthrew; for the overthrow of error, though often an indispensable prerequisite to the establishment of truth, is not truth itself; it may clear the foundation, simply to substitute one error for another, perhaps a greater for a less. Profoundly important, indeed, is the history of that which the Reformation accomplished against the errors of Romanism, yet it is as nothing to the history of that which it accomplished for itself. The overthrow of Romanism was not its primary object; in a certain sense it was not its object at all. Its object was to establish truth, no matter what might rise or fall in the effort. Had the Reformation assumed the form which some who have since borne the name of Protestants would have given it, it would not even have been a splendid failure; the movement which has shaken and regenerated a world would have ended in few miserable squabbles, a few *autos da fe;* and the record of a history, which daily makes the hearts of thousands burn within them, would have been exchanged for some such brief notice as this: that an irascible monk, named Luder, or Luther, and a few insane coadjutors, having foolishly attempted to overthrow the holy Roman See, and remaining obstinate in their pernicious and detestable heresies, were burned alive, to the glory of God and the Virgin Mary, and to the inexpressible satisfaction of all the faithful. The mightiest weapon which the Reformation employed against Rome was, not Rome's errors, but Rome's truths. It professed to make no discoveries, to find no unheard-of interpretations; but taking the Scriptures in that very sense to which the greatest of her writers had assented, uncovering the law and the gospel of God which she retained, applying them as her most distinguished and most honored teachers had applied them, though she had made them of none effect by her traditions, the Reformation took into its heart the life-stream of sixteen centuries, and came forth in the stature and strength of a Christianity, grown from the infancy of primitive ages, to the ripened manhood of that maturer period. There was no fear of truth, simply because Rome held it, and no disposition to embrace error, because it might be employed with advantage to Rome's injury. While it established broadly and deeply the right of private judgment, it did not make that abuse of it which has since been so common. From the position, that the essential truths of the word of God are clear to any Christian mind that examines them properly, it did not leap to the conclusion, that a thousand generations or a thousand examiners were as likely, or more likely, to be wrong than one. They allowed no *authority* save to the word of God, but they listened respectfully to the witness of believers of all time.

The tone which is imparted to the mind and heart, by the theology of the Reformation, is just what we now most need. But where are we to commence, it may be asked, in the infinite variety of works that have been written about the Reformation and its theology? "Art is long and life is fleeting." And how is the clergyman to find the books, or buy them when found, or read them when bought, destitute, as he is too wont to be, alike of money and time? We reply, that an immense treasure lies in a narrow compass, and within the reach of every minister in our land. By a careful study of the symbolical books of our Church, commencing with the Augsburg Confession and its Apology, a more thorough understanding of the history, difficulties, true genius, and triumphs of the Reformation will be attained, than by reading everything that can be got, or that has ever been written *about* that memorable movement. It is, indeed, too much the fashion now to read *about* things, to the neglect of the great original sources themselves. In general literature much is written and read about Homer and Shakspeare, until these great poets attract less attention than their critics. In theology it is the prevailing practice to have students read introductions to the Bible, and essays on various features of it, to such a degree that the Bible itself, except in an indirect form, is hardly studied at all, and the student, though often introduced to it, never fairly makes its acquaintance. All these illustrative works, if well executed, have their value; but that value presupposes such a general acquaintance with the books to which they serve as a guide, as is formed by every man for himself who carefully examines them. The greatest value of every work of the human mind, after all, generally lies in that which needs no guide, no critic, no commentator. . . .

And this principle it is easy to apply as regards its bearings on those great masterly treatises which form our Symbolical books. *They are parts of the Reformation itself:* not merely witnesses in the loose sense in which histories are, but the actual results, the quintessence of the excited theological and moral elements of the time. In them you are brought into immediate contact with that sublime convulsion itself. Its strength and its weakness, its fears and its hopes, the truths it exalted, the errors and abuses it threw down, are here presented in the most solemn and strongly authenticated form in which they gave them to posterity. They are nerves running from the central seat of thought of that ancient, glorious, and immortal time, to us, who form the extremities. To see the force of every word, the power of every allusion, requires an intimate acquaintance with the era and the men, in forming which the student will be led delightfully into a thorough communion and profound sympathy with that second greatest period in human history. . . .

But are those Confessions, after all, of any value to the *American* Lutheran preacher? it may be asked. We cannot conceal our sorrow, that that term, "American," should be made so emphatic, dear and hallowed though it be to our heart. Why should we break or weaken the golden chain which unites us to the high and holy associations of our history as a Church, by thrusting into a false position a word which makes a national appeal? Is there a conflict between the two, when carried to their very farthest limits? Must Lutheranism be shorn of its glory to adapt it to our times or our land? No! Our land is great,

and wide, and glorious, and destined, we trust, under the sunlight of her free institutions, long to endure; but our faith is
wider, and greater, and is eternal. The world owes more to the
Reformation than to America; America owes more to it than to
herself. The names of our Country and of our Church should
excite no conflict, but blend harmoniously together. We are
placed here in the midst of sectarianism, and it becomes us, not
lightly to consent to swell that destructive torrent of separatism
which threatens the welfare of pure Christianity on our shores
more than all other causes combined. We are surrounded by the
children of those Churches, which claim an origin in the Reformation. We sincerely respect and love them; we fervently pray
that they may be increased in every labor of love, and may be
won more and more to add to that precious truth, which they
set forth with such power, those no less precious doctrines
which, in the midst of so wide an abandonment of the faith
once delivered to the saints, God has, in our Confession, preserved to us. But how shall we make ourselves worthy of their
respect, and lift ourselves out of the sphere of that pitiful little
sectarianism which is crawling continually over all that is
churchly and stable? We must begin by knowing ourselves, and
being true to that knowledge. . . .

Let our ministry enter upon a profound study of the history
and of the principles of our Church, and if the result of a ripe
judgment shall be any other than an increased devotion to the
first, and an ardent embracing of the second, we shall feel ourselves bound to re-examine the grounds on which such an examination has led us to repose with the confidence of a child on
that maternal bosom, where so many, whose names are bright
on earth and in heaven, have rested their dying heads, and have
experienced that what she taught them was sufficient, not only
to overcome every trial of life, but every terror of the grave. . . .

[In the remainder of this chapter and in that which followed
Krauth recounted the history of Augsburg Confession, stressing
its own insistence that it asserts "nothing which departs from the

Church Catholic, the Universal Christian Church." He then
dealt with the several secondary confessions and the controversies leading up to the formulation and acceptance of the Formula of Concord in 1580. The substance of Chapter VIII is a
critique of the sections on Lutheran theology in William G. T.
Shedd's two-volume *History of Christian Doctrine* (New York:
Charles Scribner & Co., 1863). The final section of the book consisted of six chapters on the "Specific Theology of the Conservative Reformation," with the final three being devoted to the
question of the Eucharist. The selection as it continues is taken
from the first of these three except for the final paragraph which
is the final paragraph of the book. Ed.]

The Doctrine of the Lord's Supper

In approaching one of the highest, if not the very highest, of the
mysteries of our faith, it becomes us to prepare ourselves for a
most earnest, patient, and candid investigation of the Scriptural
grounds on which that faith rests. The Lord's Supper has been
looked at too much as if it were an isolated thing, with no ante-
cedents, no presuppositions, no sequences; as if there were nothing before it, nothing after it, helping to determine its true character; while, in fact, it links itself with the whole system of
Revelation, with the most vital parts of the Old and New Testament, so that it cannot be torn from its true connections without
logically bringing with it the whole system. There is no process
by which the doctrine of the Lutheran Church, in regard to the
Lord's Supper, can be overthrown, which does not overthrow
the entire fabric of the Atonement. No man can deem our distinctive doctrine of the Lord's Supper non-fundamental who
thoroughly understands it in all its relations.

The first thing worthy of note in regard to the sacramental
mystery is its antiquity. It meets us at the threshold of the divine
history of our race. In Eden we see already the idea of natural

and supernatural eating. We have there the natural eating terminating in the natural, in the words: "Of every tree of the Garden thou mayest freely eat." Closely following upon this we have the idea of supernatural eating, with the natural bodily organ: "Of the tree of the knowledge of good and evil thou shalt not eat; for in the day thou eatest thereof thou shalt surely die." Man did eat of it, and found it a sacrament of death. In, with, and under that food, as a divine means judicially appointed, was communicated death. That

> mortal taste
> Brought death into the world and all our woe.[10]

The great loss of Paradise Lost was that of the Sacrament of Life, of that food, in, with, and under which was given immortality, so objectively, positively, and really that even fallen man would have been made deathless by it: "Now lest he put forth his hand, and take also of the tree of life, and eat, and live forever," Gen. 3:22. The great gain of Paradise Regained is that of the Sacrament of Life. Christ says: "I am the life;" "The bread that I will give is My flesh, which I will give for the life of the world." The cross of Christ is the tree of life, and He the precious fruit borne by heavenly grace upon it. The cross is the centre of Paradise Regained, as the tree of life was the centre of the first Paradise. Christ's body is the organ of the life purchased by His obedience and death. The Holy Supper is the sacrament of that body, and, through the body, the sacrament of the life which that body brings. But that same body is also a sacrament of death to the unworthy recipient. The whole sacrament on its two sides of death and life is in it united: salvation to the believer, judgment to the unworthy. After the creation of man, God's first provision was for the generation and birth of the race, the foreshadowing of regeneration and of the new birth, for

---

[10] John Milton, *Paradise Lost,* Book I, lines 2–3. The quotations which precede are from Genesis 2:16–17. [Ed.]

which, in Holy Baptism, the first provision is made in the new creation of the New Testament. The next provision made for man was that of sustenance for the life given, or yet to be given. In the Garden of Eden was a moral miniature of the universe; and with the act of eating were associated the two great realms of the natural and the supernatural; and with this was connected the idea of the one as a means of entering the other, of the natural as the means of entering into the supernatural. There were natural trees, with purely natural properties, whose fruit was eaten naturally, and whose benefits were simply natural; bodily eating, terminating in a bodily sustenance. But there was also the natural terminating in the supernatural. There were two trees, striking their roots into the same soil, lifting their branches in the same air—natural trees—but bearing, by Heaven's ordinance, in, with, and under their fruitage, supernatural properties. One was the sacramental tree of good. We call it a *sacramental* tree, because it did not merely symbolize life, or signify it; but, by God's appointment, so gave life—in, with, and under its fruit—that to receive its fruit was to receive life. The fruit which men there would have eaten was the communion of life. On Gen. 3:22, the sound old Puritan commentator, Poole, thus paraphrases: "Lest he take also of the tree of life, as he did take of the tree of knowledge, and thereby profane that *sacrament of eternal life.*"[11]

With this tree of life was found the tree which was the sacrament of judgment and of death, and by man's relations to that tree would be tested whether he were good or evil, and by it he would continue to enjoy good or plunge himself into evil. By an eating, whose organs were natural, but whose relations were

---

[11] Matthew Poole (1624–1679), a great Puritan biblical scholar and commentator, a polemicist against Unitarians and Roman Catholics, ejected from the Church of England in 1662, is best remembered for his monumental *Synopsis Criticorum* (5 vols., 1669) and his *Annotations upon the Holy Bible* (2 vols., 1685). Krauth quotes from the modern three-volume edition of the latter (London: S. Holdsworth, 1840–1841), I, 10. [Ed.]

supernatural, man fell and died. This whole mystery of evil, these pains and sorrows which overwhelm the race, the past, the present, and the future of sin, revolve around a single natural eating, forbidden by God, bringing the offender into the realm of the supernatural for judgment. We learn here what fearful grandeur may be associated in the moral government of God, with a thing in itself so simple as the act of eating. The first record of Revelation is a warning against the plausible superficiality of rationalism. It was the rationalistic insinuation of Satan, as to the meaning of God's Word, which led to the Fall. Abandon faith in the letter of God's Word, said the Devil. Our first parents obeyed the seductive insinuation and died. . . .

Well might Luther write upon the table at Marburg: "This is My body;" simple words, framed by infinite wisdom so as to resist the violence and all the ingenuity of men.[12] Rationalism in vain essays to remove them with its cunning, its learning, and its philosophy. Fanaticism gnashes its teeth at them in vain. They are an immovable foundation for faith in the sacramental mystery, and the gates of hell cannot shake the faith of the Church, that our Lord Jesus with the true body and true blood which He gave for our redemption on the Cross, is truly present in the Holy Supper, to *apply* the redemption through the very organs by which it was *wrought out*. The sacrifice was made once for all—its application goes on to the end of time. The offence of the Master's Cross now rests upon His table, and thither the triumph of the Cross shall follow it. On the Cross and at the table the saints discern the body of the Lord, and in simple faith are determined to know in both nothing but Jesus Christ and Him crucified. . . .

In the doctrine of Transubstantiation, nevertheless, as in almost all of her corruptions, the Church of Rome has not so much

---

[12] He refers to an incident in the Marburg Colloquy of 1528 at which Luther, Melanchthon, Zwingli, Butzer, *et al.* sought unsuccessfully to compose their doctrinal differences. [Ed.]

absolutely removed the foundation, as hidden it by the wood, hay, and stubble of human device. Truth can sometimes be reached by running the corruptions of it back to the trunk on which they were grafted. Such an error as that of Transubstantiation could never have been grafted on an original faith like that of Zwingli in regard to the Lord's Supper. The tendency of the Zwinglian view, if it be corrupted, is to laxer, not to higher, views of the sacramental mystery. Such an error as the doctrine of the immaculate conception of the Virgin Mary never could have been grafted on a faith originally Socinian. It is a corruption which presupposes as a truth, to be corrupted in its inference, the divinity and sinlessness of our Lord Jesus Christ; and just as the comparatively modern corruption of the worship of the Virgin is a proof that faith in the Godhead of Jesus Christ was part of the primitive faith, so does the comparatively modern corruption of Transubstantiation prove that faith in the objective supernatural presence of the body and blood of our Lord was part of the primitive faith. A rotten apple always presupposes a sound apple. However corrupt a fig may be, we know that it grew on a fig-tree, and not on a thistle. . . .

The current view of un-Lutheran Protestantism practically is, that all we need for our redemption is a *dead Christ*. We are to look back to Calvary to find peace in thinking of what was there done, and at the Lord's Supper we are to look back to the sacrifice once made for our sins. The current view excludes the necessity of a living Saviour in our redemption. According to it, we redeem ourselves, or the Spirit of God redeems us, by what Christ once did, and without any personal work on His part now. To the theology of a large part of the Church it would be no disturbing element if the divine nature of Christ had been separated from the human after the resurrection. Instead of a robust and mighty faith which hangs upon a living Saviour, and lives by His life, we have a religion of sentiment verging away into sentimentality; a religion which lives by its own thoughts about a Saviour of bygone times. We have had in our hands a

book on the Lord's Supper, by an American preacher, the fron-
tispiece of which represents a lonely tombstone, and on it the
words: "To the memory of my Saviour." Nothing could more
sadly, yet vigorously, epitomize the tendency of which we
speak—the graveyard tendency, which turns the great festival
of the redemption into a time of mourning, and coldly furnishes
forth the marriage tables with the baked meats of the funeral.
The glory of the Lutheran system in all its parts, and especially
in its doctrine of the Lord's Supper, is, that it accepts, in all its
fulness, the Apostle's argument, "If, when we were enemies, we
were reconciled to God by the death of His Son, MUCH MORE,
being reconciled, we shall be saved by His LIFE." Never, indeed,
has the human heart been so taught as by our system in its purity to turn to the death of Christ for hope; but our Church has
been led by the Holy Spirit too deeply into all the fulness of
truth to make an antagonism between the death of her Saviour
and His life.

If Christ must die to make our redemption, He must live
to apply it. If the Lord's Supper is a sacrament of the redemption made by His death, it is also a sacrament of the same redemption applied by His life. If it tells us that His body and
blood were necessary to make our redemption, it tells us also
that they are still necessary to apply the redemption they then
made. He made the sacrifice once for all—He applies it constantly. We live by Him, we must hang on Him—the vine does
not send up one gush of its noble sap and then remain inert. It
receives the totality of life, once for all, but the sap which sustains it must flow on—its one, unchanging and abiding life puts
itself forth into the new offshoots, and by constant application
of itself maintains the old branches. If the sap-life ceases, the
seed-life cannot save. Cut the branch off, and the memory of the
life will not keep it from withering; it must have the life itself—
and this it must derive successively from the vine. It could not
exist without the original life of the vine, nor can it exist without
the present life of the vine, be its past what it may. Faith cannot

feed on itself, as many seem to imagine it can—it must have its object. The ordinances, the Word, and the sacraments give to it that by which it lives. Faith in the nutritious power of bread does not nourish—the bread itself is necessary.

The man who feels a moral repugnance to the Scripture doctrine of the Eucharist, will find, if he analyzes his feelings thoroughly, that they take their root in a repugnance to the doctrine of the atonement by Christ's body and blood. The man who asks what use is there in a sacramental application of them in the Lord's Supper, really asks, what use was there in a redemptory offering of them on Calvary. He may be using the terms of Scripture, but if He takes his inmost thoughts before his God, he will probably find that he has been denying the true vicarious character of the sacrifice of our Lord—that he has fallen into that conception of the sacrifice on Calvary which is essentially Socinian, for everything which brings down the oblation of the Son of God into the sphere of the natural *is* essentially Socinian.[13] He will find that in his view his Lord is only a glorious martyr, or that the power of His sacrifice is only a moral power; that the cross is but a mighty sermon, and that those awful words, which, in their natural import unbare, as it is nowhere else unbared, the heart of Deity in the struggle of its unspeakable love and fathomless purpose; that all these are oriental poesy—figures of speech—graces of language. The theory of the atonement, which pretends to *explain* it, is rotten at the core. The atonement, in its whole conception, belongs to a world which man cannot now enter. The blessings and adaptations of it we can comprehend in some measure. We can approach them with tender hearts full of gratitude; but the *essence* of the atonement we can understand as little as we understand the essence of God.

If Christ, through His body broken, made remission of sins, why do we ask to what end is the doctrine that the same body

---

13 On Socinianism, see note 4, p. 377. [Ed.]

through which He made the remission is that through which He applies it? His body *as such* could make no remission of sins, but, through the Eternal Spirit, with which it was conjoined in personal unity, it made redemption—His body, *as such,* may have no power to apply the redemption or to be with the redeemed, but, through the same relation by which it entered into the sphere of the supernatural to make redemption, it reveals itself now in that same sphere to apply it. All theology, without exception, has had views of the atonement which were lower or higher, as its views of the Lord's Supper were low or high. Men have talked and written as if the doctrine of our Church, on this point, were a stupid blunder, forced upon it by the self-will and obstinacy of one man. The truth is, that this doctrine, clearly revealed in the New Testament, clearly confessed by the early Church, lies at the very heart of the Evangelical system— Christ is the centre of the system, and in the Supper is the centre of Christ's revelation of Himself. The glory and mystery of the incarnation combine there as they combine nowhere else. Communion with Christ is that by which we live, and the Supper is *"the* Communion." Had Luther abandoned this vital doctrine, the Evangelical Protestant Church would have abandoned him. He did not make this doctrine—next in its immeasurable importance to that of justification by faith, with which it indissolubly coheres—the doctrine made him. The doctrine of the Lord's Supper is the most vital and practical in the whole range of the profoundest Christian life—the doctrine which, beyond all others, conditions and vitalizes that life, for in it the character of faith is determined, invigorated, and purified as it is nowhere else. It is not only a fundamental doctrine, but is among the most fundamental of fundamentals.[14]

We know what we have written. We know, that to take our Saviour at His word here, to receive the teachings of the New

---

[14] Cf. Selection No. VIII, pp. 374–378, where Nevin formulates the same thesis. [Ed.]

Testament in their obvious intent, is to incur with the current religionism a reproach little less bitter than if we had taken up arms against the holiest truths of our faith. We are willing to endure it. Our fathers were willing to shed their blood for the truth, and shall we refuse to incur a little obloquy? The fact that we bear the name of a Church which stood firm when rationalizing tendencies directed themselves with all their fury against this doctrine of the Word of God, increases our responsibility. When, at a later and sadder period, she yielded to subtlety what she had maintained successfully against force, and let her doctrine fall, she fell with it. When God lifted her from the dust, He lifted her banner with it, and on that banner, as before, the star of a pure Eucharistic faith shone out amid the lurid clouds of her new warfare, and there it shall shine forever. Our Saviour has spoken; His Church has spoken. His testimony is explicit, as is hers. The Lutheran Church has suffered more for her adherence to this doctrine than from all other causes, but the doctrine itself repays her for all her suffering. To her it is a very small thing that she should be judged of man's judgment; but there is one judgment she will not, she dare not hazard, the judgment of her God, which they eat and drink to themselves who will not discern the Lord's body in the Supper of the Lord.

We do not wish to be misunderstood in what we have said as to the *moral* repugnance to our doctrine of the Supper. We distinguish between a mere intellectual difficulty and an aversion of the affections. How New Testament-like, how Lutheran have sounded the sacramental hymns and devotional breathings of men whose theory of the Lord's Supper embodied little of its divine glory. The glow of their hearts melted the frostwork of their heads. When they treat of sacramental communion, and of the mystical union, they give evidence, that, with their deep faith in the atonement, there is connected, in spite of the rationalizing tendency which inheres in their system, a hearty acknowledgment of the supernatural and incomprehensible character of the Lord's Supper. On the other hand, the evidence is overwhelming, that as low views of the Lord's Supper prevail, in that proportion the doctrine of the atonement exhibits a rationalizing tendency. We repeat the proposition, confirmed by the whole history of the Church, that a moral repugnance to the doctrine that the body and blood of Christ are the medium through which redemption is *applied,* has its root in a moral repugnance to the doctrine that His precious body and blood are the medium through which redemption was *wrought....*

We have dwelt at what may seem disproportioned length upon the doctrine of the Lord's Supper; but we have done so not in the interests of division, but of peace. At this point the division opened, and at this point the restoration of peace must begin. Well-set bones knit precisely where they broke; and well knit, the point of breaking becomes the strongest in the bone. The Reformation opened with a prevailingly conservative character. There lay before it not merely a glorious possibility, but an almost rapturous certainty, waiting upon the energy of Reform guided by the judgment of Conservatism. The Reformation received its first appalling check in the invasion of its unity in faith, by the crudities of Carlstadt, soon to be followed by the colder, and therefore yet more mischievous, sophistries of Zwingle. The effort at reformation, in some shape, was beyond recall. Henceforth the question was between conservative reformation and revolutionary radicalism. Rome and the world-wide errors which stand or fall with her, owe their continued baleful life, not so much to the arts of her intrigue, the terror of her arms, the wily skill and intense devotion of Jesuitism and the orders, as they owe it to the division and diversion created by the radicalism which enabled them to make a plausible appeal to the fears of the weak and the caution of the wise. But for this, it looks as if the great ideal of the conservative reformation might have been consummated; the whole Church of the West might have been purified. All those mighty resources which Rome now spends against the truth, all those mighty agencies by which one form of Protestantism tears down another, might have been hallowed to one service—Christ enthroned in His renovated Church, and sanctifying to pure uses all that is beautiful in her outward order. The Oriental Church could not have resisted the pressure.[15] The Church Catholic, transfigured by her faith, with robes to which snow has no whiteness and the sun no splendor, would have risen in a grandeur before which the world would have stood in wonder and awe. But such yearnings as these wait long on time. Their consummation was not then to be, but it shall be yet.

---

15 By "Oriental Church" Krauth refers, of course, to the Eastern Orthodox Church and possibly the other ancient eastern churches. He obviously would have relished the resumption of dialogue during the age of Pope John XXIII and the Second Vatican Council. [Ed.]

X

JOSIAH ROYCE

Idealist Philosopher of Religion

Josiah Royce (1855–1916)[1] is America's most outstanding exponent of idealistic philosophy, or if subcategories are used, America's most eminent absolute idealist. He played a leading role in the great triumph that idealistic ways of thinking enjoyed in American academic circles during the later nineteenth century. Nostalgic writers also dwell fondly on his name and memory in connection with the "golden age" in American philosophy—when in the Harvard ambiance alone one could imagine in daily conversation Royce, James, Santayana, Peirce, Palmer, Münsterberg, and several lesser lights. No other American, moreover, so effectively turned the resources of philosophic idealism to the problems of religion and the church. Nor was Royce's dealing with theological questions sporadic. His bachelor's thesis, written at the University of California, was on the theology of Aeschylus' PROMETHEUS; his first book, THE RELIGIOUS ASPECT OF PHILOSOPHY, appeared in 1885. This was followed by THE CONCEPTION OF GOD (1897), and STUDIES OF GOOD AND EVIL (1902) in which he published further essays on the aspects of religion and philosophy. THE SOURCES OF RELIGIOUS INSIGHT (1911) and his final major

---

[1] See Introduction, pp. 64–73.

work, THE PROBLEM OF CHRISTIANITY (1913), are works of philosophical theology. Looking backward, furthermore, we may see these last two works as completing and filling out the social implications of his two great series of Gifford Lectures, THE WORLD AND THE INDIVIDUAL (1900–1901).

Royce's parents were English-born Forty-Niners who, after an arduous crossing of the American continent and several moves within California, finally came to rest in Grass Valley, a mining town in Nevada County. Royce finished high school in San Francisco, received his B.A. from the University of California, studied in Germany for two years, and then after further teaching and study in the United States, came in 1882 to Harvard, where he remained for the rest of his life as a professor of philosophy. These decades were enormously productive, not least because of his close friendship and continuous dialogue with William James.

From his days in Grass Valley to the writing of his last book Royce turned again and again to the idea and the problem of community. True community, he was convinced, was divine; it was also the condition of human happiness and goodness. He devoted a great portion of his philosophical labor, therefore, either to clarifying the social dimensions of the human situation or to prescriptions for broadening and purifying the communities of men—and the Great Community of man. Only in this context could he believe in the universal significance of the Church.

In THE SOURCES OF RELIGIOUS INSIGHT and in THE PROBLEM OF CHRISTIANITY Royce dealt directly with the corporate nature of selfhood, atonement, and salvation. In this sense these two works constitute a profound contribution to the Social Gospel. It is worth noting, however, that unlike most other preachers of social Christianity in his day (Walter Rauschenbusch, for example), Royce does not make the social teachings of Jesus his point of departure and the churches so many agencies for their propagation. He turns rather to the Letters of St. Paul and the Pauline doctrine of the Church as the body of Christ. In this context he can show the social nature of language, thought, and selfhood and express his convictions on the nature of community and the organic unity of reality. He also clarifies his idea of loyalty, "the heart of all the virtues, the central duty amongst all duties."

The selection that follows is the last of Royce's Bross Lectures on THE SOURCES OF RELIGIOUS INSIGHT. It is both a résumé of the entire lecture series (if not his whole life work) and an anticipation of his last great treatise, THE PROBLEM OF CHRISTIANITY. Yet the selection stands by itself as a complete essay. Only a few nonsubstantive references to earlier lectures in the second and third paragraphs are omitted.

THE SOURCES OF RELIGIOUS INSIGHT

The Unity of the Spirit and the

Invisible Church

My present and concluding lecture must begin with some explanations of what I mean by the term "The Unity of the Spirit." Then I shall have to define my use of the term "The Invisible Church." Thereafter, we shall be free to devote ourselves to the consideration of a source of religious insight as omnipresent as it is variously interpreted by those who, throughout all the religious world, daily appeal to its guidance. The outcome of

From Josiah Royce, *The Sources of Religious Insight,* The Bross Lectures, 1911; Lectures Delivered before Lake Forest College on the Foundation of the Late William Bross (New York: Charles Scribner's Sons, 1912), pp. 257–297. Reprinted with the permission of Charles Scribner's Sons. Copyright 1912 The Trustees of Lake Forest University; renewal copyright 1940.

our discussion may help some of you, as I hope, to turn your attention more toward the region where the greatest help is to be found in the cultivation of that true loyalty which, if I am right, is the heart and core of every higher religion.

In these lectures I have repeatedly called the religious objects, that is, the objects whereof the knowledge tends to the salvation of man, "superhuman" and "supernatural" objects. I have more or less fully explained, as I went, the sense in which I hold these objects to be both superhuman and supernatural. But every use of familiar traditional terms is likely to arouse misunderstandings. I have perfectly definite reasons for my choice of the traditional words in question as adjectives wherewith to characterise the religious objects. But I do not want to leave in your minds any doubts as to what my usage is deliberately intended to imply. I do not want to seem to make any wrong use of the vaguer associations which will be in your minds when something human is compared with something superhuman, and when the natural and the supernatural are contrasted. This closing lecture, in which I am to deal with an aspect of spiritual life which we have everywhere in our discourse tacitly presupposed, but which now is to take its definitive place on our list of sources of religious insight, gives me my best opportunity to forestall useless misunderstandings by putting myself upon record as to the precise sense in which both the new source itself and everything else superhuman and supernatural to which religion has a rational right to appeal is, to my mind, a reality, and is a source or an object of human insight. I shall therefore explain the two adjectives just emphasised by giving you a somewhat fuller account of their sense than I have heretofore stated. . . .

I   THE SUPERHUMAN AND THE SUPERNATURAL

In my general sketch of the characteristics of human nature which awaken in us the sense of our need for salvation, I laid stress . . . upon our narrowness of outlook as one principal and

pervasive defect of man as he naturally is constituted. . . . Now
man's narrowness of natural outlook upon life is first of all due
to something which I have to call the "form" of human consciousness. . . . But technical clearness as to such topics is hard
to attain. Allow me, then, to insist with some care upon matters which are as influential in moulding our whole destiny as
they are commonly neglected in our discussions of the problems
of life and of reality.

*Man can attend to but a very narrow range of facts at any one
instant.* Common-sense observation shows you this. Psychological experiment emphasises it in manifold ways. Listen to a
rhythmic series of beats—drum beats—or the strokes of an en-
gine, or the feet of horses passing by in the street. You cannot
directly grasp with entire clearness more than a very brief se-
quence of these beats, or other sounds, or of rhythmic phrases
of any kind. If the rhythm of a regularly repeated set of sounds
is too long, or too complex, it becomes confused for you. You
cannot make out by your direct attention what it is at least until
it has by repetition grown familiar. Let several objects be
brought before you at once. You can attend to one and then to
another at pleasure if only they stay there to be attended to.
But only a very few distinct objects can be suddenly seen at
once, and at a single glance, and recognised, through that one
instantaneous presentation, for what they are. If the objects are
revealed to you in the darkness by an electric spark, or are seen
through a single slit in a screen that rapidly moves before your
eyes—so that the objects are exposed to your observation only
during the extremely brief time when the slit passes directly
between them and your eyes—this limit of your power to grasp
several distinct objects at once, upon a single inspection, can be
experimentally tested. The results of such experiments concern
us here only in the most general way. Enough—as such tests
show—what one may call the *span* of our consciousness, its
power to grasp many facts in any one individual moment of our
lives, is extremely limited. It is limited as to the number of simultaneously presented facts that we can grasp at one view,

can distinguish, and recognise, and hold clearly before us. It is also limited with regard to the number and the duration of the successive facts that we can so face as directly to grasp the character of their succession, rhythmic or otherwise.

Now this limitation of the span of our consciousness is, I repeat, an ever-present defect of our human type of conscious life. That is why I call it a defect in the "form" of our conscious life. It is not a defect limited to the use of any one of our senses. It is not a failure of eyes or of ears to furnish to us a sufficient variety of facts to observe. On the contrary, both our eyes and our ears almost constantly rain in upon us, especially during our more desultory waking life, an overwealth of impressions. If we want to know facts, and to attain clearness, we have to pick out a few of these impressions, from instant to instant, for more careful direct inspection. In any case, then, this limitation is not due to the defects of our senses. It is our whole conscious make-up, our characteristic way of becoming aware of things, which is expressed by this limitation of our conscious span. On this plan our human consciousness is formed. Thus our type of awareness is constituted. In this way we are all doomed to live. It is our human fate to grasp clearly only a few facts or ideas at any one instant. And so, being what we are, we have to make the best of our human nature.

Meanwhile, it is of our very essence as reasonable beings that we are always contending with the consequences of this our natural narrowness of span. We are always actively rebelling at our own form of consciousness, so long as we are trying to know or to do anything significant. We want to grasp many things at once, not merely a few. We want to survey life in long stretches, not merely in instantaneous glimpses. We are always like beings who have to see our universe through the cracks that our successive instants open before us, and as quickly close again. And we want to see things, *not* through these instantaneous cracks, but without intervening walls, with wide outlook, and in all their true variety and unity. Nor is this rebellion of ours against the mere form of consciousness any merely idle curiosity or peevish seeking for a barren wealth of varieties. Salvation itself is at stake in this struggle for a wider clearness of outlook. The wisest souls, as we have throughout seen, agree with common-sense prudence in the desire to see at any one instant greater varieties of ideas and of objects than our form of consciousness permits us to grasp. To escape from the limitations imposed upon us by the natural narrowness of our span of consciousness—by the form of consciousness in which we live—this is the common interest of science and of religion, of the more contemplative and of the more active aspects of our higher nature. *Our form of consciousness is one of our chief human sorrows.*

By devices such as the rhythmic presentation of facts to our attention we can do something—not very much—to enlarge our span of consciousness. But for most purposes we can make only an *indirect,* not a *direct,* escape from our limitations of span. Our salvation depends upon the winning of such indirect successes. Indirectly we escape, in so far as we use our powers of habit-forming, of memory, and of abstraction, to prepare for us objects of momentary experience such as have come to acquire for us a wide range of meaning, so that, when we get before our momentary attention but a few of these objects at once, we still are able to comprehend, after our human fashion, ranges and connections and unities of fact which the narrow form of our span of consciousness forbids us to grasp with directness. Thus, the repetition of similar experiences forms habits such that each element of some new instant of passing experience comes to us saturated with the meaning that, as we look back upon our past life, we suppose to have resulted from the whole course of what has happened. And through such endlessly varied processes of habit-forming, we come to reach stages of insight in which the instantaneous presentation of a few facts gets for us, at a given moment, the value of an indirect appreciation of what we never directly grasp—that is, the value of a wide survey of life. All that we usually call knowledge is due to such indirect grasping of what the instant can only hint to us, although we usually feel as if this indirect presentation were itself a direct insight. Let me exemplify: The odour of a flower may come to us burdened with a meaning that we regard as the total result of a whole summer of our life. The wrinkled face of an old man reveals to us, in its momentarily presented traces, the signs of what we take to have been his lifetime's experience and slowly won personal character. And, in very much the same way, almost any passing experience may seem to us to speak with the voice of years, or even of ages, of human life. To take yet another instance: a single musical chord epitomises the result of all our former hearings of the musical composition which it introduces.

In this way we live, despite our narrowness, *as if* we saw widely; and we constantly view *as if it were* our actual experience, a sense and connection of things which actually never gets fully translated in any moment of our lives, but is always simply presupposed as the interpretation which a wider view of life *would* verify. Thus bounded in the nutshell of the passing instant, we count ourselves (in one way or another, and whatever our opinions), kings of the infinite realm of experience, or would do so were it not that, like Hamlet, we have so many "bad dreams," which make us doubt the correctness of our interpretations, and feel our need of an escape from this stubborn natural prison of our own form of consciousness. We therefore appeal, in all our truth-seeking, to a wider view than our own present view.

Our most systematic mode of indirect escape from the consequences of our narrow span of consciousness, is the mode which our thinking processes, that is, our dealings with abstract and general ideas exemplify.

Such abstract and general ideas, as we earlier saw, are means to ends—never ends in themselves. By means of generalisation or abstraction we can gradually come to choose signs which we can more or less successfully substitute for long series of presented objects of experience; and we can also train ourselves into active ways of estimating or of describing things—ways such, that by reminding ourselves of these our active attitudes toward the business of life, we can seem to ourselves to epitomise in an instant the sense of years or even of ages of human experience. Such signs and symbols and attitudes constitute our store of general and abstract ideas. Our more or less systematic and voluntary thinking is a process of observing, at one or another instant, the connections and the meanings of a very few of these our signs and attitudes at once. We actively put together these ideas of ours, and watch, at the instant, the little connections that then and there are able to appear, despite the narrowness of our span of consciousness. That, for instance, is what happens when we add up columns of figures, or think out a problem, or plan our practical lives. But because each of the ideas used, each of these signs or symbols or attitudes, can be more or less safely substituted for some vast body of facts of experience, what we observe only in and through our narrow span can indirectly help us to appreciate something whose real meaning only a very wide range of experience, a consciousness whose span is enormously vaster than ours, could possibly present directly.

Thus, confined to our own form and span of consciousness as we are, we spend our lives in acquiring or devising ways to accomplish indirectly what we are forbidden directly to attain, namely, the discovery of truth and of meaning such as only a consciousness of another form than ours can realise. Now, as I maintained in our third and fourth lectures, *the whole validity and value of this indirect procedure of ours depends upon the principle that such a wider view of things, such a larger unity of consciousness, such a direct grasp of the meanings at which we indirectly but ceaselessly aim is a reality in the universe.* As I there maintained, *the whole reality of the universe itself must be defined, in terms of the reality of such an inclusive and direct grasp of the whole sense of things.* I can here only repeat my opinion that this thesis is one which nobody can deny without self-contradiction.

Now the difference between the narrow form of consciousness that we human beings possess and the wider and widest forms of consciousness whose reality every common-sense effort to give sense to life, and every scientific effort to discover the total verdict of experience presupposes—the difference, I say, between these two forms of consciousness is *literally* expressed by calling the one form (the form that we all possess) *human,* and by calling the other form (the form of a wider consciousness which views experience as it is) *superhuman.* The wider conscious view of things that we share only indirectly, through the devices just pointed out, is certainly not human; for no mortal man ever directly possesses it. It is real; for, as we saw in our study of the reason, if you deny this assertion in one shape, you reaffirm it in another. For you can define the truth and falsity of your opinions only by presupposing a wider view that sees as a whole what you see in fragments. That unity of consciousness which we presuppose in all our indirect efforts to get into touch with its direct view of truth is above our level. It includes what we actually get before us in our form of consciousness. It also includes all that we are trying to grasp indirectly. Now what is not human, and is above our level, and includes all of our insight, but transcends and corrects our indirect efforts by its direct grasp of facts as they are, can best be called superhuman. *The thesis that such a superhuman consciousness is a reality is a thesis precisely equivalent to the assertion that our experience has any real sense or connection whatever* beyond the mere fragment of connectedness that, at any one instant, we directly grasp.

Furthermore, to call such a larger consciousness—inclusive of our own, but differing from ours, in form, by the vastness of its span and the variety and completeness of the connections that it surveys—to call it, I say, a *supernatural* consciousness is to use a phraseology that can be very deliberately and, if you choose, technically defended. By "natural" we mean simply: Subject to the laws which hold for the sorts of beings whose character and behaviour our empirical sciences can study. If you suddenly found that you could personally and individually and clearly grasp, by an act of direct attention, the sense and connection of thousands of experiences at once, instead of the three or four presented facts of experience whose relations you can now directly observe in any one of your moments of consciousness, you would indeed say that you had been miraculously transformed into another type of being whose insight had acquired an angelic sort of wealth and clearness. But whenever you assert (as every scientific theory, and every common-sense opinion, regarding the real connections of the facts of human experience requires you to assert), that not only thousands, but a countless collection of data of human experience actually possess a perfectly coherent total sense and meaning, such as no individual man ever directly observes, this your assertion, which undertakes to be a report of facts, and which explicitly relates to facts of experience, implies the assertion that there exists such a superhuman survey of the real nature and connection of our own natural realm of conscious life. We ourselves are strictly limited by the natural conditions that determine our own form of consciousness. And no conditions can be regarded by us as more characteristically natural than are these. For us human beings to transcend those conditions, by surveying countless data at once, would require an uttermost exception to the natural laws which are found to govern our human type of consciousness. To believe that any man ever had accomplished the direct survey of the whole range of the physical connections of the solar and stellar systems at once—in other words, had grasped the whole range of astronomical experience in a single act of attention—would be to believe that a most incredible miracle had at some time taken place—an incredible miracle so far as any knowledge that we now possess enables us to foresee what the natural conditions under which man lives, and is, in human form, conscious, permit. But, on the other hand, to accept, as we all do, the validity of that scientific interpretation of the data of human experience which astronomy reports is to acknowledge that such an interpretation more or less completely records a system of facts which are nothing if they are not in some definite sense empirical, although, in their wholeness, they are experienced by no man. That is, the acceptance of the substantial truth of astronomy involves the acknowledgment that some such, to us simply superhuman, consciousness is precisely as real as the stars are real, and as their courses, and as all their relations are real. Yet, of course, we cannot undertake to investigate any process such as would enable us to define the natural conditions under which any such superhuman survey of astronomical facts would become psychologically possible.

The acceptance of our natural sciences, as valid interpretations of connections of experience which our form of consciousness forbids us directly to verify, logically presupposes, at every step, that such superhuman forms and unities of consciousness are real. For the facts of science are indefinable except as facts in and for a real experience. But, on the other hand, we can hope for no advance in physical or in psychological knowledge which would enable us to bring these higher forms of consciousness under what we call natural laws. So the superhuman forms of consciousness remain for us also supernatural. *That* they are, we must acknowledge, if any assertion whatever about our world is to be either true or false. For all assertions are made about experience, and about its real connections, and about its systems. But *what* conditions, *what* natural causes, bring such superhuman forms of consciousness into existence we are unable to investigate. For every assertion about nature or about natural laws presupposes that natural facts and laws are real only in so far as they are the objects known to such higher unities of consciousness. The unities in question are themselves no natural objects; while all natural facts are objects for them and are expressions of their meaning.

Thus definite are my reasons for asserting that forms of consciousness superior to our own are real, and that they are all finally united in a single, world-embracing insight, which has also the character of expressing a world-will. Thus definite are also my grounds for calling such higher unities of consciousness both superhuman and supernatural. By the term "The unity of the spirit" I name simply *the unity of meaning which belongs to these superhuman forms of consciousness.* We ourselves partake of this unity, and share it, in so far as, in our lives also, we discover and express, in whatever way our own form of consciousness permits, truth and life that bring us into touch and into harmony with the higher forms of consciousness, that is, with the spirit which, in its wholeness, knows and estimates the world, and which expresses itself in the life of the world.

Thus near are we, in every exercise of our reasonable life, to the superhuman and to the supernatural. Upon the other hand, there is positively no need of magic, or of miracle, or of mysterious promptings from the subconscious, to prove to us the reality of the human and of the supernatural, or to define our reasonable relations with it. And the essential difference between our own type of consciousness and this higher life is a difference of form, and is also a difference of content precisely in so far as its wider and widest span of conscious insight implies that the superhuman type of consciousness possesses a depth of meaning, a completeness of expression, a wealth of facts, a clearness of vision, a successful embodiment of purpose which, in view of the narrowness of our form of consciousness, do not belong to us.

Man needs no miracles to show him the supernatural and the superhuman. You need no signs and wonders, and no psychical research, to prove that the unity of the spirit is a fact in the world. Common-sense tacitly presupposes the reality of the unity of the spirit. Science studies the ways in which its life is expressed in the laws which govern the order of experience. Reason gives us insight into its real being. Loyalty serves it, and repents not of the service. Salvation means our positive harmony with its purpose and with its manifestation.

II   THE UNITY OF THE SPIRIT

Amongst the sources of insight which bring us into definite and practical relations with that spiritual world whose nature has now been again defined, one of the most effective is the life and the word of other men who are minded to be loyal to genuine causes, and who are already, through the service of their common causes, brought together in some form of spiritual brotherhood. The real unity of the life of such fellow-servants of the Spirit is itself an instance of a superhuman conscious reality; and its members are devoted to bringing themselves into harmony with the purposes of the universe. Any brotherhood of men who thus loyally live in the Spirit is, from my point of view, a brotherhood essentially religious in its nature, precisely in proportion as it is practically moved by an effort to serve—not merely the special cause to which its members, because of their training and their traditions, happen to be devoted, but also the common cause of all the loyal. Such a brotherhood, so far as it is indeed human, and, therefore narrow, may not very expressly define what this common cause of all the loyal is, for its members may not be thoughtfully reflective people. But if, while rejoicing in their own prefectly real fraternal unity, they are also practically guided by the love of furthering brotherhood amongst men in general; if they respect the loyalty of other men so far as they understand that loyalty; if they seek, not to sow discord amongst the brethren of our communities, but to be a city set on a hill, that not only cannot be hid, but is also a model for other cities—a centre for the spreading of the spirit of loyalty —then the members of such an essentially fruitful brotherhood are actually loyal to the cause of causes. They are a source of insight to all who know of their life, and who rightly appreciate its meaning. And of such is the kingdom of loyalty. And the communities which such men form and serve are essentially religious communities. Each one is an example of the unity of the Spirit. Each one stands for a reality that belongs to the super-human world.

Since the variety of social forms which appear under human conditions is an unpredictably vast variety, and since the motives which guide men are endlessly complex, different communities of loyal people may possess such a religious character and value in the most various degrees. For it results from the narrowness of the human form of consciousness that men, at any one moment, know not the whole of what they mean. No sharp line can be drawn sundering the brotherhoods and partnerships, and other social organisations which men devise, into those which for the men concerned are consciously religious, and those which, by virtue of their absence of interest in the larger and deeper loyalties are secular. The test whereby such a distinction should be made is in principle a definite test. But to apply the test to every possible case requires a searching of human hearts and a just estimate of deeds and motives whereto, in our ignorance, we are very generally inadequate.

A business firm would seem to be, in general, no model of a religious organisation. Yet it justly demands loyalty from its members and its servants. If it lives and acts merely for gain, it is secular indeed. But if its business is socially beneficent, if its cause is honourable, if its dealings are honest, if its treatment of its allies and rivals is such as makes for the confidence, the cordiality, and the stability of the whole commercial life of its community and (when its influence extends so far) of the world, if public spirit and true patriotism inspire its doings, if it is always ready on occasion to sacrifice gain for honour's sake—then there is no reason why it may not become and be a genuinely and fervently religious brotherhood. Certainly a family can become a religious organisation; and some of the most ancient traditions of mankind have demanded that it should be one. There is also, and justly, a religion of patriotism, which regards the country as a divine institution. Such a religion serves the unity of the spirit in a perfectly genuine way. Some of the most momentous religious movements in the world's history have grown out of such an idealised patriotism. Christianity, in transferring local names from Judea to a heavenly world, has borne witness to the sacredness that patriotism, upon its higher levels, acquires.

In brief, the question whether a given human brotherhood is a religious institution or not is a question for that brotherhood to decide for itself, subject only to the truth about its real motives. Has its cause the characters that mark a fitting cause of loyalty? Does it so serve its cause as thereby to further the expression of the divine unity of the spirit in the form of devoted human lives, not only within its own brotherhood, but as widely as its influence extends? Then it is an essentially religious organisation. Nor does the extent of its worldly influence enable you to decide how far it meets these requirements. Nor yet does the number of persons in its membership form any essential criterion. Wherever two or three are gathered together, and are living as they can in the Spirit that the divine will (which wills the loyal union of all mankind) requires of them—there, indeed, the work of the Spirit is done; and the organisation in question is a religious brotherhood. It needs no human sanction to make it such. Though it dwell on a desert island, and though all its members soon die and are forgotten of men, its loyal deeds are irrevocable facts of the eternal world; and the universal life knows that here at least the divine will is expressed in human acts.

But so far as such communities both exist and are distinctly recognisable as religious in their life and intent, they form a source of religious insight to all who come under their influence. Such a source acts as a means whereby any or all of our previous sources may be opened to us, may become effective, may bear fruit. *Hence, in this new source, we find the crowning source of religious insight.*

This last statement is one which is accepted by many who would nevertheless limit its application to certain religious communities, and to those only; or who, in some cases, would limit its application to some one religious community. There are, for instance, many who say, for various special reasons, that the crowning source of religious insight is the visible church. By this term those who use it in any of its traditional senses, mean one religious institution only, or at most only a certain group of religious organisations. The visible church is a religious organisation, or group of such organisations, which is characterized by certain traditions, by a certain real or supposed history, by a more or less well-defined creed, and by further assertions concerning the divine revelation to which it owes its origin and authority. With the doctrinal questions involved in the understanding of this definition, these lectures, as you now well know, have no direct concern. It is enough for our present purpose to say that the visible church thus defined is indeed, and explicitly, and in our present sense, a religious organisation. In all those historical forms which here concern us, the visible church has undertaken to show men the way to salvation. It has carried out its task by uniting its members in a spiritual brotherhood. It has in ideal extended its interest to all mankind. It has aimed at universal brotherhood. It has defined and called out loyalty. It has conceived this loyalty as a service of God and as a loyalty to the cause of all mankind. Its traditions, the lives of its servants, its services, its teachings, have been and are an inexhaustible source of religious insight to the vast multitudes whom it has influenced and, in its various forms and embodiments, still influences. Not unnaturally, therefore, those who accept its own doctrines regarding its origin and history view such a visible church not only as by far the most important source of religious insight, but also as a source occupying an entirely unique position.

The deliberate limitations of the undertaking of these lectures forbid me, as I have just reminded you, to consider in any detail this supposed uniqueness of the position which so many of you will assign to some form of the historical Christian church. After what I have said as to the nature and the variety of the forms which the spiritual life has taken, and still takes, amongst men, you will nevertheless not be surprised if, without attempting to judge the correctness of the traditions of the visible church, I forthwith point out that, to the higher religious life of mankind the life of the visible church stands related as part to whole; and that very vast ranges of the higher religious life of mankind have grown and flourished outside of the influence of Christianity. And when the religious life of mankind is viewed in its historical connections, truth requires us to insist that Christianity itself has been dependent for its insight and its power upon many different sources, some of which assumed human form not only long before Christianity came into being, but in nations and in civilisations which were not dependent for their own spiritual wealth upon the Jewish religious traditions that Christianity itself undertook to transform and to assimilate. Christianity is, in its origins, not only Jewish but Hellenic, both as to its doctrines and as to its type of spirituality. It is a synthesis of religious motives which had their sources widely spread throughout the pre-Christian world of Hellenism. Its own insight is partly due to the non-Christian world.

As a fact, then, the unity of the Spirit, the religious life which has been and is embodied in the form of human fraternities, is the peculiar possession of no one time, or nation, and belongs to no unique and visible church. Yet such an unity is a source of religious insight. We have a right to use it wherever we find it and however it becomes accessible to us. As a fact, we all use such insight without following any one principle as to the selection of the historical sources. Socrates and Plato and Sophocles are religious teachers from whom we have all directly or indirectly learned, whether we know it or not. Our own Germanic ancestors, and the traditions of the Roman Empire, have influenced our type of loyalty and have taught us spiritual truth that we should not otherwise know.

Moreover, that which I have called the cause of all the loyal, the real unity of the whole spiritual world, is not merely a moral ideal. It is a religious reality. Its servants and ministers are present wherever religious brotherhood finds sincere and hearty manifestation. In the sight of a perfectly real but superhuman knowledge of the real purposes and effective deeds of mankind, *all the loyal, whether they individually know the fact or not, are, and in all times have been, one genuine and religious brotherhood.* Human narrowness and the vicissitudes of the world of time have hidden, and still hide, the knowledge of this community of the loyal from human eyes. But indirectly it comes to light whenever the loyalty of one visible spiritual community comes, through any sort of tradition, or custom, or song or story, or wise word or noble deed, to awaken new manifestations of the loyal life in faithful souls anywhere amongst men.

I call the community of all who have sought for salvation through loyalty the Invisible Church. What makes it invisible to us is our ignorance of the facts of human history and, still more, our narrowness in our appreciation of spiritual truth. And I merely report the genuine facts, human and superhuman, when I say that *whatever any form of the visible church has done or will do for the religious life of mankind, the crowning source of religious insight is, for us all, the actual loyalty, service, devotion, suffering, accomplishment, traditions, example, teaching, and triumphs of the invisible church of all the faithful.* And by the invisible church I mean the brotherhood consisting of all who, in any clime or land, live in the Spirit.

Our terms have now been, so far as my time permits, sharply defined. I am here not appealing to vague sentiments about human brotherhood, or to merely moral ideals about what we merely hope that man may yet come to be. And I am not for a moment committing myself to any mere worship of humanity, so long as one conceives humanity as the mere collection of those who are subject to the natural laws that govern our present physical and mental existence. Humanity, viewed as a mere product of nature, is narrow-minded and degraded enough. Its life is full of uncomprehended evils and of mutual misunderstandings. It is not a fitting object of any religious reverence. But it needs salvation. It has been finding salvation through loyalty. And the true cause, the genuine community, the real spiritual brotherhood of the loyal is a superhuman and not merely a human reality. It expresses itself in the lives of the loyal. In so far as these expressions directly or indirectly inspire our own genuine loyalty, they give us insight. Of such insight, whatever you may learn from communion with any form of the visible church, is an instance—a special embodiment. The invisible church, then, is no merely human and secular institution. It is a real and superhuman organisation. It includes and transcends every form of the visible church. It is the actual subject to which belong all the spiritual gifts which we can hope to enjoy. If your spiritual eyes were open, no diversity of human tongues, no strangeness of rites or of customs or of other forms of service, no accidental quaintnesses of tradition or of symbols or of creeds, would hide from your vision its perfections. It believes everywhere in the unity of the Spirit, and aims to save men through winning them over to the conscious service of its own unity. And it grants you the free grace of whatever religious insight you can acquire from outside yourself. If you are truly religious, you live in it and for it. You conceive its life in your own way and, no doubt, under the limitations of your own time and creed. But you cannot flee from its presence. And your salvation lies in its reality, in your service, and in your communion with its endlessly varied company of those who suffer and who in the might of the spirit overcome.

Let me tell you something of this life of the invisible church.

III   THE INVISIBLE CHURCH

And first let me speak of its membership. We have now repeatedly defined the test of such membership. The invisible church is the spiritual brotherhood of the loyal. Only a searcher of hearts can quite certainly know who are the really loyal. We can be sure regarding the nature of loyalty. That loyalty itself should come to men's consciousness in the most various forms and degrees, and clouded by the most tragic misunderstandings, the narrow form of human consciousness, and the blindness and variety of human passion, make necessary.

If one is loyal to a narrow and evil cause, as the robber or the pirate may be loyal to his band or to his ship, a conscious effort to serve the unity of the whole spiritual world may seem at first sight to be excluded by the nature of the loyalty in question. But what makes a cause evil, and unworthy of loyal service, is the fact that its service is destructive of the causes of other men, so that the evil cause preys upon the loyalty of the spiritual brethren of those who serve it, and so that thereby the servants of this cause do actual wrong to mankind. But this very fact may not be understood by the individual robber or pirate. He may be devoted with all his heart and soul and mind and strength to the best cause that he knows. He may therefore sincerely conceive that the master of life authorises his cause. In that case, and so far as this belief is sincere, the robber or pirate may be a genuinely religious man.

Does this statement seem to you an absurd quibble? Then look over the past history of mankind. Some at least of the Crusaders were genuinely religious. That we all readily admit. But they were obviously, for the most part, robbers and murderers, and sometimes pirates, of what we should now think the least religious type if they were to-day sailing the Mediterranean or devastating the lands. Read in *Hakluyt's Voyages* the accounts of the spirit in which the English explorers and warriors of the Elizabethan age accomplished their great work.[1] In these accounts a genuinely religious type of patriotism and of Christi-

---

[1] Richard Hakluyt, *The Principall Navigations, Voiages And Discoveries Of The English nation, made by Sea or ouer Land* (1589). Louis B. Wright expands on Royce's theme in *Religion and Empire: The Alliance between Piety and Commerce in English Expansion, 1558–1625* (Chapel Hill: The University of North Carolina Press, 1943). [Ed.]

anity often expresses itself side by side with a reckless hatred of the Spaniard and a ferocity which tolerates the most obvious expressions of mere natural greed. These heroes of the beginnings of the British Empire often hardly knew whether they were rather the adventurous merchants, or the loyal warriors for England, or the defenders of the Christian faith, or simply pirates. In fact they were all these things at once. Consider the Scottish clans as they were up to the eighteenth century. The spirit that they fostered has since found magnificent expression in the loyalty of the Scottish people and in its later and far-reaching service of some of the noblest causes that men know. Yet these clans loved cattle-thieving and tortured their enemies. When did they *begin* to be really patriots and servants of mankind? When did they begin to be truly and heartily religious? Who of us can tell?

Greed and blindness are natural to man. His form of consciousness renders him unable, in many cases, to realise their unreasonableness, even when he has already come into sincerely spiritual relations with the cause of all the loyal. What we *can* know is that greed and blindness are never of themselves religious, and that the way of salvation is the way of loyalty. But I know not what degrees of greedy blindness are consistent with an actual membership in the invisible church, as I have just defined its membership. When I meet, however, with the manifestations of the spirit of universal loyalty, whether in clansman, or in crusader, or in Elizabethan and piratical English defender of his country's faith, or in the Spaniard whom he hated, I hope that I may be able to use, not the greed or the passions of these people, but their religious prowess, their free surrender of themselves to their cause, as a source of insight.

Membership in the invisible church is therefore not to be determined by mere conventions, but by the inward spirit of the faithful, as expressed in their loyal life according to their lights. Yet of those who seem to us most clearly to belong to the service of the spirit, it is easy to enumerate certain very potent groups, to whose devotion we all owe an unspeakably great debt. The sages, the poets, the prophets, whose insight we consulted in our opening lecture, and have used throughout these discourses, form such groups. It is indifferent to us to what clime or land or tongue or visible religious body they belonged or to-day belong. They have sincerely served the cause of the spirit. They are to us constant sources of religious insight. Even the cynics and the rebels, whom we cited in our opening lecture, have been, in many individual cases, devoutly religious souls who simply could not see the light as they consciously needed to see it, and who loyally refused to lie for convention's sake. Such have often served the cause of the spirit with a fervour that you ill understand so long as their words merely shock you. They often seem as if they were hostile to the unity of the spirit. But, in many cases, it is the narrowness of our nature, the chaos of our unspiritual passions, the barren formalism of our conventions that they assail. And such assaults turn our eyes upward to the unity of the spirit from whence alone consolation and escape may come. Indirectly, therefore, such souls are often the misunderstood prophets of new ways of salvation for men. When they are loyal, when their very hardness is due to their resolute truthfulness, they are often amongst the most effective friends of a deeper religious life.

A notable criterion whereby, quite apart from mere conventions, you may try the spirits that pretend or appear to be religious, and may discern the members of the invisible church from those who are not members, is the criterion of the prophet Amos: "Woe unto them that are at ease in Zion."[2] This, as I said earlier, is one of the favourite tests applied by moralists for distinguishing those who serve from those who merely enjoy. That it is also a religious test, and *why* it is a religious test, our acquaintance with the spirit of loyalty has shown us. Religion, when triumphant, includes, indeed, the experience of inward

---

[2] Amos 6:1. [Ed.]

peace; but the peace which is not won through strenuous loyal service is deceitful and corrupting.[3] It is the conquest over and through tribulation which saves. Whoever conceives religion merely as a comfortable release from sorrows, as an agreeable banishment of cares, as a simple escape from pain, knows not what evil is, or what our human nature is, or what our need of salvation means, or what the will of the master of life demands. Therefore, a visible church that appears simply in the form of a cure for worry, or a preventive of trouble, seems to me to be lacking in a full sense of what loyalty is. Worry is indeed, in itself, not a religious exercise. But it is often an effective pre-liminary, and is sometimes, according to the vicissitudes of natural temper, a relatively harmless accompaniment, to a deeply religious life. Certainly the mere absence of worry, the mere attainment of a sensuous tranquility, is no criterion of membership in the invisible church. Better a cynic or a rebel against conventional religious forms, or a pessimist, or a worry-ing soul, if only such a being is strenuously loyal according to his lights, than one to whom religion means simply a tranquil adoration without loyalty. But, of course, many of the tranquil are also loyal. When this is true we can only rejoice in their attainments.

If we look for other examples still of types of spirituality which seem to imply membership in the invisible church, I my-self know of few better instances of the genuinely religious spirit than those which are presented to us, in recent times, by the more devoted servants of the cause of any one of the advancing natural sciences. And such instances are peculiarly instructive, because many great men of science, as a result of their personal temperament and training, are little interested in the forms of the visible church, and very frequently are loath to admit that their calling has religious bearings. But when the matter is rightly viewed, one sees that the great scientific investigator is

---

[3] See Rauschenbusch's emphasis, and his tribute to Royce, p. 851. [Ed.]

not only profoundly loyal, but serves a cause which, at the present time, probably does more to unify every sort of wholesome human activity, to bind in one all the higher interests of humanity, to bring men of various lands and races close together in spirit than does any other one special cause that modern men serve. The cause of any serious scientific investigator is, from my point of view, a superhuman cause, for precisely the reasons which I have already explained to you.

The individual scientific worker, uninterested as he usually is in metaphysics, and unconcerned as he often is about the relation of his task to the interests of the visible church, knows indeed that with all his heart, and soul, and mind, and strength he serves a cause that he conceives to be worthy. He knows, also, that this cause is beneficent, and that it plays a great part in the directing of human activities, whether because his science already has practical applications, or because the knowledge of nature is in itself an elevating and enlarging influence for mankind. The scientific investigator knows also that, while his individual experience is the source to which he personally looks for new observations of facts, his private observations contribute to science only in so far as other investigators can verify his results. Hence his whole scientific life consists in submitting all his most prized discoveries to the rigid test of an estimate that belongs to no individual human experience, but that is, or that through loyal efforts tends to become, the common possession of the organised experience of all the workers in his field. So far the devoted investigator goes in his own consciousness as to his work.

Beyond this point, in estimating his ideals and his value, he sometimes seems not to wish to go, either because he is unreflective or because he is modest. But when we remember that the unity of human experience, in the light of which scientific results are tested, and to whose growth and enrichment the scientific worker is devoted, is indeed a superhuman reality of the type that we have now discussed; when we also recall the profound values which the scientific ideal has for all departments of human life in our day; when, further, we see how resolutely the true investigator gives his all to contribute to what is really the unity of the spirit, we may well wonder who is in essence more heartily religious than the completely devoted scientific investigator—such a man, for instance, as was Faraday.

When I have the fortune to hear of really great scientific workers who are as ready to die for their science (if an experiment or an observation requires risk) as to live for it through years of worldly privation and of rigid surrender of private interests to truth, and when I then by chance also hear that some of them were called, or perhaps even called themselves, irreligious men, I confess that I think of the little girl who walked by Wordsworth's side on the beach at Calais. The poet estimated her variety of religious experience in words that I feel moved to apply to the ardently loyal hero of science:

> Thou dwellest in Abraham's bosom all the year,
> And worship'st at the temple's inmost shrine,
> God being with thee when we know it not.

There also exists a somewhat threadbare verse of the poet Young which tells us how "the undevout astronomer is mad."[4] I should prefer to say that the really loyal scientific man who imagines himself undevout is not indeed mad at all, but, like Wordsworth's young companion at Calais, unobservant of himself and of the wondrous and beautiful love that inspires him. For he is, indeed, inspired by a love for something much more divine than is that august assemblage of mechanical and physical phenomena called the starry heavens. The soul of his work is the service of the unity of the spirit in one of its most exalted forms.

---

[4] William Wordsworth, *Sonnet Composed upon the Beach near Calais, 1802:* "It is a beauteous Evening, calm and free." Edward Young, *Night Thoughts on Life, Death and Immortality,* Night IX, line 771. [Ed.]

That all who, belonging to any body of the visible church, are seriously loyal to the divine according to their lights, are members also of the invisible church, needs, after what I have said, no further explanation.

But if, surveying this multitude that no man can number from every kindred, and tribe, and nation, and tongue, you say that entrance to the invisible church is guarded by barriers that seem to you not high enough or strong enough, I reply that this membership is indeed tested by the severest of rules. Do you serve with all your heart, and soul, and mind, and strength a cause that is superhuman and that is indeed divine? This is the question which all have to answer who are to enter this the most spiritual of all human brotherhoods.

IV   COMMUNION WITH THE FAITHFUL

The invisible church is to be to us a source of insight. This means that we must enter into some sort of communion with the faithful if we are to enjoy the fruits of their insight. And, apart from one's own life of loyal service itself, the principal means of grace—that is, the principal means of attaining instruction in the spirit of loyalty, encouragement in its toils, solace in its sorrows, and power to endure and to triumph—the principal means of grace, I say, which is open to any man lies in such communion with the faithful and with the unity of the spirit which they express in their lives. It is natural that we should begin this process of communion through direct personal relations with the fellow-servants of our own special cause. Hence whatever is usually said by those who belong to any section of the visible church regarding the spiritual advantages which follow from entering the communion of their own body may be accepted, from our present point of view, as having whatever truth the devotion and the religious life of any one body of faithful servants of the unity of the spirit may give to such statements when applied precisely to their own members. But to us all alike the voice of the invisible church speaks—it sustains us all alike by its counsels, not merely in so far as our own personal cause and our brethren of that service are known to us, but in so far as we are ready to understand the loyal life, and to be inspired by it, even when those who exemplify its intents and its values are far from us in their type of experience and in the manner of their service.

You remember the rule of loyalty: "So serve your cause that if possible through your service everybody whom you influence shall be rendered a more devoted servant of his own cause, and thereby of the cause of causes—the unity of all the loyal." Now the rule for using the invisible church as a source of insight is this: "So be prepared to interpret, and sympathetically to comprehend, the causes and the service of other men, that whoever serves the cause of causes, the unity of all the loyal, may even thereby tend to help you in your personal service of your own special cause." To cultivate the comprehension and the reverence for loyalty, however, and wherever loyalty may be found, is to prepare yourself for a fitting communion with the invisible church.

And in such communion I find the crowning source of religious insight. What I say is wholly consistent then with the recognition of the preciousness of the visible church to its members. Once more, however, I point out the fact that the visible church is as precious as it is because it is indeed devoted to the unity of the spirit, that is, because it is a part and an organ of the invisible church.

V   CHARITY AND LOYALTY

I cannot close this extremely imperfect sketch of our crowning source of insight without applying to our present doctrine of the invisible church, the eternally true teaching of St. Paul regarding spiritual gifts.[5]

---

[5] I Corinthians 12. [Ed.]

As Paul's Corinthians, in their little community, faced the problem of the diversity of the gifts and powers whereby their various members undertook to serve the common cause—as this diversity of gifts tended from the outset to doctrinal differences of opinion, as the differences threatened to confuse loyalty by bringing brethren into conflict—even so, but with immeasurably vaster complications, the whole religious world, the invisible community of the loyal, has always faced, and still faces, a diversity of powers and of forms of insight, a diversity due to the endlessly various temperaments, capacities and sorts and conditions of men. The Corinthian church, as Paul sketched its situation, was a miniature of religious humanity. All the ways that the loyal follow lead upward to the realm of the spirit, where reason is at once the overarching heaven and the all-vitalising devotion which binds every loyal individual to the master of life. But in our universe the one demands the many. The infinite becomes incarnate through the finite. The paths that lead the loyal to the knowledge of the eternal pass for our vision, with manifold crossings and with perplexing wanderings, through the wilderness of this present world. The divine life is won through suffering. And religious history is a tale of suffering—of mutual misunderstanding amongst brethren who have from moment to moment been able to remember God only by narrowly misreading the hearts of their brethren. The diversity of spiritual gifts has developed, in religious history, an endless war of factions. The invisible church has frequently come to consciousness in the form of sects that say: "Ours alone is the true spiritual gift. Through our triumph alone is the world to be saved. Man will reach salvation only when our own Jerusalem is the universally recognised holy city."

Now it is useless to reduce the many to the one merely by wiping out the many. It is useless to make some new sect whose creed shall be that there are to be no sects. *The unity of the visible church, under any one creed, or with any one settled system of religious practices, is an unattainable and undesirable ideal.*

The varieties of religious experience in James's sense of that term are endless.[6] The diversity of gifts is as great as is the diversity of strong and loyal personalities. What St. Paul saw, in the miniature case presented to him by the Corinthian church, was that all the real gifts, and all the consequently inevitable differences of approach to the religious problems, and all the differences of individual religious insight were necessary to a wealthy religious life, and might serve the unity of the spirit, if only they were conceived and used subject to the spiritual gift which he defined as Charity.

Now the Pauline Charity is simply *that* form of loyalty which should characterise a company of brethren who already have recognised their brotherhood, who consciously know that their cause is one and that the spirit which they serve is one. For such brethren, loyalty naturally takes the form of a self-surrender that need not seek its own, or assert itself vehemently, because the visible unity of the community in question is already acknowledged by all the faithful present, so that each intends to edify, not himself alone, but his brethren, and also intends not to convert his brother to a new faith, but to establish him in a faith already recognised by the community. Yet since the Corinthians, warring over their diversity of gifts, had come to lose sight of the common spirit, Paul simply recalls them to their flag, by his poem of charity, which is also a technically true statement of how the principle of loyalty applies to a brotherhood fully conscious of its common aim.[7]

But the very intimacy of the Pauline picture of charity makes it hard to apply this account of the loyalty that should reign within a religious family to the problems of a world where faith does not understand faith, where the contrasts of opinion seem to the men in question to exclude community of the spirit, where the fighting blood even of saintly souls is stirred by persecutions

---

[6] See Selection XI. [Ed.]

[7] I Corinthians 13. [Ed.]

or heated by a hatred of seemingly false creeds. And Paul himself could not speak in the language of charity, either when he referred to those whom he called "false brethren" or characterised the Hellenic-Roman spiritual world to whose thought and spirit he owed so much.[8] As the Corinthians, warring over the spiritual gifts, were a miniature representation of the motives that have led to religious wars, so St. Paul's own failure to speak with charity as soon as certain matters of controversy arose in his mind, shows in miniature the difficulty that the visible church, in all its forms, has had to unite loyal strenuousness of devotion to the truth that one sees with tolerance for the faiths whose meaning one cannot understand.

And yet, what Paul said about charity must be universalised if it is true. When we universalise the Pauline Charity, it becomes once more the loyalty that, as a fact, is now justified in seeking her loyal own; but that still, like charity, rejoices in the truth. Such loyalty loves loyalty even when race or creed distinctions make it hard or impossible for us to feel fond of the persons and practices and opinions whereby our more distant brethren embody their spiritual gifts. Such loyalty is tolerant. Tolerance is what charity becomes when we have to deal with those whose special cause we just now cannot understand. Loyalty is tolerant, *not* as if truth were indifferent, or as if there were no contrast between worldliness and spirituality, but is tolerant precisely in so far as the best service of loyalty and of religion and of the unity of the spirit consists in helping our brethren not to our own, but to *their* own. *Such loyalty implies genuine faith in the abiding and supreme unity of the spirit.*

Only by thus universalising the doctrine which Paul preached to the Corinthians can we be prepared to use to the full this crowning source of insight—the doctrine, the example, the life, the inspiration, which is embodied in the countless forms and expressions of the invisible church.

---

[8] See II Corinthians 11:26, Colossians 2:8, *et al.* [Ed.]

The work of the invisible church—it is just that work to which all these lectures have been directing your attention. The sources of insight are themselves the working of its spirit in our spirits.

If I have done anything (however unworthy) to open the minds of any of you to these workings, my fragmentary efforts will not have been in vain. I have no authority to determine your own insight. Seek insight where it is to be found.

XI

WILLIAM JAMES

Philosopher of Religious Experience

William James (1842–1910)[1] is universally known as a founder of Pragmatism and as a great psychologist who came to that interest through medicine and physiology and only later moved on to philosophy. He is remembered as the philosophic voice for practical, down-to-earth activism and the "cash-value" of ideas, a scientifically trained enemy of useless metaphysical speculation, an evolutionary theorist who pondered the "survival-power" of beliefs. None of these qualifications, however, nor all of them together, would seem to make him a likely candidate for a theological anthology. Yet he remains a monumental figure in American religious thought. Like his friend and colleague, Josiah Royce, he turned constantly to the subject of religion—and not only in his astonishingly wide range of reading nor simply as a psychological observer, but in his major philosophical works. Religion is the concern not only of his great classic, THE VARIETIES OF RELIGIOUS EXPERIENCE but also of A PLURALISTIC UNIVERSE, THE WILL TO BELIEVE, and many other important essays. "We may view his ideas about God and the religious aspect of life," writes John E. Smith, "as the culmination of his philosophy." Motivating the

---

[1] See Introduction, pp. 64–73.

greater part of his work was an intense inner conflict raised by the opposing claims of Science and Religion, of positivistic material-ism and his conviction that "all is not vanity."

James was born in New York. His father, Henry James, Sr., was a fugitive from Calvinism and the Princeton Seminary who be-came a dedicated and highly original apostle of a nonauthoritarian religious synthesis that rested chiefly on the ideas of Swedenborg, Emerson, and Fourier. As he was well-to-do, he provided his son with an excellent but highly unconventional education, mostly in Europe. The son continued these associations all his life, often returned to Europe, and maintained a vast correspondence with friends abroad. That William James was probably the most genu-inely cosmopolitan of all major American philosophers may ex-plain the large corpus of European commentary on his works. His early vocational indecision, however, was almost his undoing; and at one time he was on the verge of suicide. He studied painting, went on Agassiz's zoological expedition to Brazil, studied at the Lawrence Scientific School, and not until 1869, after long inter-ruptions, did he receive his M.D. In 1872 he began his long career on the Harvard faculty.

James's place in the history of thought has always been difficult to assign and a headnote is no place for an extended argument; but a caveat may be permissible. One probably should not inter-pret James' thought as a "growing out of" the mainline tradition of British empiricism that runs from Locke to Mill but as "out-growing" it. Though always intensely empirical and "close to life" in his thinking, James chose his most decisive influences else-where. His pluralistic fideism, his arguments for human freedom, his definition of reality as "pure experience," his convictions as to the actuality of God and the reality of the unseen—all relate him to the romantic tradition. An early letter to his brother Henry (June 1, 1869) illustrates this intellectual kinship: "Reading of the revival, or rather of the birth of German literature, Kant, Schiller, Goethe, Jacobi, Fichte, Schelling, [the] Schlegels, Tieck, Richter, Herder, Steffens, W. Humboldt, and a number of others, puts one into a real classical period. These men were all interesting as men, each standing as a type or representative of a certain way of taking life, and beginning at the bottom—taking nothing for granted. In England the only parallel I can think of is Coleridge, and in France Rousseau and Diderot."

On April 30, 1870, when in the depths of his most severe spiritual crisis, he was rescued by a philosophical conversion experience—the occasion being his acceptance of Charles Renouvier's definition of freewill as "the sustaining of a thought because I choose to when I might have other thoughts." This definition might be taken as a key to all of James' published work, from his PSYCHOLOGY to his WILL TO BELIEVE. Ralph Barton Perry considers it beyond doubt that "Renouvier's was the greatest individual influence upon the development of James's thought." After the death of this great French thinker, James' "most important philosophical and personal attachment" was to Henri Bergson, whose CREATIVE EVOLUTION he greeted as "perfectly glorious." Even James' deep respect for the pioneer experimental psychologist, Gustav Theodor Fechner (1801–1867), sprang from the "gorgeous extravagances" of Fechner's speculation and his philosophic effort to bring religious feeling and scientific method into meaningful relation.

In retrospect, therefore, we may think of James's continuing Auseinandersetzung with Royce as an extremely creative replication of the great debate that went on in Berlin between the idealisms of Schleiermacher and Hegel—however, at a century's remove and in another intellectual milieu. For James as for Schleiermacher religious experience was the proper point of departure for discussing matters of religion. His lectures on THE VARIETIES

OF RELIGIOUS EXPERIENCE *can be understood as a twentieth-century version of Schleiermacher's* DISCOURSES ON RELIGION TO ITS CULTURED DESPISERS. *There is also an existential strain in James' persistent attention to selfhood, anxiety, decision, and human effort. One can imagine Kierkegaard from beyond the grave applauding James' famous "Damn the Absolute."*

Among James's works there are many candidates for inclusion in a collection of theological writings, but his Gifford Lectures of 1901–1902 on THE VARIETIES OF RELIGIOUS EXPERIENCE *contain ideas that flash from so many facets of his mind, belong in so rich a vein of theological discourse, and have remained so relevant in the succeeding half-century that they could not be left aside. The selection that follows consists of the greater part of his lecture "The Reality of the Unseen," and his final "Conclusions." Cut off from the larger book though they are, these chapters convey the main substance of an important theological contribution to religious thought and reveal James' theological concerns with remarkable clarity.*

THE VARIETIES OF RELIGIOUS EXPERIENCE

The Reality of the Unseen

Were one asked to characterize the life of religion in the broadest and most general terms possible, one might say that it consists of the belief that there is an unseen order, and that our supreme good lies in harmoniously adjusting ourselves thereto. This belief and their adjustment are the religious attitude in the

From William James, *The Varieties of Religious Experience. A Study in Human Nature, Being the Gifford Lectures on Natural Religion Delivered at Edinburgh in 1901–1902* (London: Longmans, Green, and Co., 1902), pp. 53–58, 72–77, 485–519.

soul. I wish during this hour to call your attention to some of the psychological peculiarities of such an attitude as this, of belief in an object which we cannot see. All our attitudes, moral, practical, or emotional, as well as religious, are due to the 'objects' of our consciousness, the things which we believe to exist, whether really or ideally, along with ourselves. Such objects may be present to our senses, or they may be present only to our thought. In either case they elicit from us a *reaction;* and the reaction due to things of thought is notoriously in many cases as strong as that due to sensible presences. It may be even stronger. The memory of an insult may make us angrier than the insult did when we received it. We are frequently more ashamed of our blunders afterwards than we were at the moment of making them; and in general our whole higher prudential and moral life is based on the fact that material sensations actually present may have a weaker influence on our action than ideas of remoter facts.

The more concrete objects of most men's religion, the deities whom they worship, are known to them only in idea. It has been vouchsafed, for example, to very few Christian believers to have had a sensible vision of their Saviour; though enough appearances of this sort are on record, by way of miraculous exception, to merit our attention later. The whole force of the Christian religion, therefore, so far as belief in the divine personages determines the prevalent attitude of the believer, is in general exerted by the instrumentality of pure ideas, of which nothing in the individual's past experience directly serves as a model.

But in addition to these ideas of the more concrete religious objects, religion is full of abstract objects which prove to have an equal power. God's attributes as such, his holiness, his justice, his mercy, his absoluteness, his infinity, his omniscience, his tri-unity, the various mysteries of the redemptive process, the operation of the sacraments, etc., have proved fertile wells of inspiring meditation for Christian believers. We shall see later that the absence of definite sensible images is positively insisted on by the mystical authorities in all religions as the *sine qua non* of a successful orison, or contemplation of the higher divine truths. Such contemplations are expected (and abundantly verify the expectation, as we shall also see) to influence the believer's subsequent attitude very powerfully for good.

Immanuel Kant held a curious doctrine about such objects of belief as God, the design of creation, the soul, its freedom, and the life hereafter. These things, he said, are properly not objects of knowledge at all. Our conceptions always require a sense-content to work with, and as the words 'soul,' 'God,' 'immortality,' cover no distinctive sense-content whatever, it follows that theoretically speaking they are words devoid of any significance. Yet strangely enough they have a definite meaning *for our practice*. We can act *as if* there were a God; feel *as if* we were free; consider Nature *as if* she were full of special designs; lay plans *as if* we were to be immortal; and we find then that these words do make a genuine difference in our moral life. Our faith *that* these unintelligible objects actually exist proves thus to be a full equivalent in *praktischer Hinsicht*, as Kant calls it, or from the point of view of our action, for a knowledge of *what* they might be, in case we were permitted positively to conceive them. So we have the strange phenomenon, as Kant assures us, of a mind believing with all its strength in the real presence of a set of things of no one of which it can form any notion whatsoever.

My object in thus recalling Kant's doctrine to your mind is not to express any opinion as to the accuracy of this particularly uncouth part of his philosophy, but only to illustrate the characteristic of human nature which we are considering, by an example so classical in its exaggeration.[1] The sentiment of reality

---

1 James's reference to Kant's doctrine as "curious" and "uncouth" is itself curious—and slightly uncouth. James's own doctrine is clearly post-Kantian; and the neo-Kantians figured significantly in his own thought. [Ed.]

can indeed attach itself so strongly to our object of belief that our whole life is polarized through and through, so to speak, by its sense of the existence of the thing believed in, and yet that thing, for purpose of definite description, can hardly be said to be present to our mind at all. It is as if a bar of iron, without touch or sight, with no representative faculty whatever, might nevertheless be strongly endowed with an inner capacity for magnetic feeling; and as if, through the various arousals of its magnetism by magnets coming and going in its neighborhood, it might be consciously determined to different attitudes and tendencies. Such a bar of iron could never give you an outward description of the agencies that had the power of stirring it so strongly; yet of their presence, and of their significance for its life, it would be intensely aware through every fibre of its being.

It is not only the Ideas of pure Reason, as Kant styled them, that have this power of making us vitally feel presences that we are impotent articulately to describe. All sorts of higher abstractions bring with them the same kind of impalpable appeal. Remember those passages from Emerson which I read at my last lecture.[2] The whole universe of concrete objects, as we know them, swims, not only for such a transcendentalist writer, but for all of us, in a wider and higher universe of abstract ideas, that lend it its significance. As time, space, and the ether soak through all things, so (we feel) do abstract and essential goodness, beauty, strength, significance, justice, soak through all things good, strong, significant, and just.

Such ideas, and others equally abstract, form the background for all our facts, the fountain-head of all the possibilities we

---

[2] He had quoted a long passage from Emerson's Divinity School Address, beginning "These laws" and ending "this infusion." See pp. 298–301. His observation was that "Emersonianism . . . seems to let God evaporate into abstract Ideality," a worship of "mere abstract laws." "The universe has a divine soul of order, which soul is moral, being also soul within the soul of man." *Varieties,* pp. 32–33. [Ed.]

conceive of. They give its 'nature,' as we call it, to every special thing. Everything we know is 'what' it is by sharing in the nature of one of these abstractions. We can never look directly at them, for they are bodiless and featureless and footless, but we grasp all other things by their means, and in handling the real world we should be stricken with helplessness in just so far forth as we might lose these mental objects, these adjectives and adverbs and predicates and heads of classification and conception.

This absolute determinability of our mind by abstractions is one of the cardinal facts in our human constitution. Polarizing and magnetizing us as they do, we turn towards them and from them, we seek them, hold them, hate them, bless them, just as if they were so many concrete beings. And beings they are, beings as real in the realm which they inhabit as the changing things of sense are in the realm of space.

Plato gave so brilliant and impressive a defense of this common human feeling, that the doctrine of the reality of abstract objects has been known as the platonic theory of ideas ever since. Abstract Beauty, for example, is for Plato a perfectly definite individual being, of which the intellect is aware as of something additional to all the perishing beauties of the earth. "The true order of going," he says, in the often quoted passage in his 'Banquet,' "is to use the beauties of earth as steps along which one mounts upwards for the sake of that other Beauty, going from one to two, and from two to all fair forms, and from fair forms to fair actions, and from fair actions to fair notions, until from fair notions he arrives at the notion of absolute Beauty, and at last knows what the essence of Beauty is."[3] In our last lecture we had a glimpse of the way in which a platonizing writer like Emerson may treat the abstract divineness of things, the moral structure of the universe, as a fact worthy of

---

[3] Plato, *Symposium*, 211–212. Quoted from *The Dialogues of Plato*, Jowett trans., 4 vols. (Oxford: Clarendon Press, 1871), I, 527.

worship. In those various churches without a God which to-day are spreading through the world under the name of ethical societies, we have a similar worship of the abstract divine, the moral law believed in as an ultimate object. 'Science' in many minds is genuinely taking the place of a religion. Where this is so, the scientist treats the 'Laws of Nature' as objective facts to be revered. A brilliant school of interpretation of Greek mythology would have it that in their origin the Greek gods were only half-metaphoric personifications of those great spheres of abstract law and order into which the natural world falls apart—the sky-sphere, the ocean-sphere, the earth-sphere, and the like; just as even now we may speak of the smile of the morning, the kiss of the breeze, or the bite of the cold, without really meaning that these phenomena of nature actually wear a human face.

As regards the origin of the Greek gods, we need not at present seek an opinion. But the whole array of our instances leads to a conclusion something like this: It is as if there were in the human consciousness a *sense of reality, a feeling of objective presence, a perception* of what we may call *'something there,'* more deep and more general than any of the special and particular 'senses' by which the current psychology supposes existent realities to be originally revealed. If this were so, we might suppose the senses to waken our attitudes and conduct as they so habitually do, by first exciting this sense of reality; but anything else, any idea, for example, that might similarly excite it, would have that same prerogative of appearing real which objects of sense normally possess. So far as religious conceptions were able to touch this reality-feeling, they would be believed in in spite of criticism, even though they might be so vague and remote as to be almost unimaginable, even though they might be such non-entities in point of *whatness,* as Kant makes the objects of his moral theology to be. . . .

Such is the human ontological imagination, and such is the convincingness of what it brings to birth. Unpicturable beings are realized, and realized with an intensity almost like that of an hallucination. They determine our vital attitude as decisively as the vital attitude of lovers is determined by the habitual sense, by which each is haunted, of the other being in the world. A lover has notoriously this sense of the continuous being of his idol, even when his attention is addressed to other matters and he no longer represents her features. He cannot forget her; she uninterruptedly affects him through and through.

I spoke of the convincingness of these feelings of reality, and I must dwell a moment longer on that point. They are as convincing to those who have them as any direct sensible experiences can be, and they are, as a rule, much more convincing than results established by mere logic ever are. One may indeed be entirely without them; probably more than one of you here present is without them in any marked degree; but if you do have them, and have them at all strongly, the probability is that you cannot help regarding them as genuine perceptions of truth, as revelations of a kind of reality which no adverse argument, however unanswerable by you in words, can expel from your belief. The opinion opposed to mysticism in philosophy is sometimes spoken of as *rationalism*. Rationalism insists that all our beliefs ought ultimately to find for themselves articulate grounds. Such grounds, for rationalism, must consist of four things: (1) definitely statable abstract principles; (2) definite facts of sensation; (3) definite hypotheses based on such facts; and (4) definite inferences logically drawn. Vague impressions of something indefinable have no place in the rationalistic system, which on its positive side is surely a splendid intellectual tendency, for not only are all our philosophies fruits of it, but physical science (amongst other good things) is its result.

Nevertheless, if we look on man's whole mental life as it exists, on the life of men that lies in them apart from their learning and science, and that they inwardly and privately follow, we have to confess that the part of it of which rationalism can give an account is relatively superficial. It is the part that has the *prestige* undoubtedly, for it has the loquacity, it can challenge you for proofs, and chop logic, and put you down with words. But it will fail to convince or convert you all the same, if your dumb intuitions are opposed to its conclusions. If you have intuitions at all, they come from a deeper level of your nature than the loquacious level which rationalism inhabits. Your whole subconscious life, your impulses, your faiths, your needs, your divinations, have prepared the premises, of which your consciousness now feels the weight of the result; and something in you absolutely *knows* that that result must be truer than any logic-chopping rationalistic talk, however clever, that may contradict it. This inferiority of the rationalistic level in founding belief is just as manifest when rationalism argues for religion as when it argues against it. That vast literature of proofs of God's existence drawn from the order of nature, which a century ago seemed so overwhelmingly convincing, to-day does little more than gather dust in libraries, for the simple reason that our generation has ceased to believe in the kind of God it argued for. Whatever sort of a being God may be, we *know* to-day that he is nevermore that mere external inventor of 'contrivances' intended to make manifest his 'glory' in which our great-grandfathers took such satisfaction, though just how we know this we cannot possibly make clear by words either to others or to ourselves. I defy any of you here fully to account for your persuasion that if a God exist he must be a more cosmic and tragic personage than that Being.[4]

The truth is that in the metaphysical and religious sphere, articulate reasons are cogent for us only when our inarticulate feelings of reality have already been impressed in favor of the same conclusion. Then, indeed, our intuitions and our reason work together, and great world-ruling systems, like that of the Buddhist or of the Catholic philosophy, may grow up. Our im-

---

[4] See the related observations of Edwards and Bushnell, pp. 179, 325. [Ed.]

pulsive belief is here always what sets up the original body of truth, and our articulately verbalized philosophy is but its showy translation into formulas. The unreasoned and immediate assurance is the deep thing in us, the reasoned argument is but a surface exhibition. Instinct leads, intelligence does but follow. If a person feels the presence of a living God after the fashion shown by my quotations, your critical arguments, be they never so superior, will vainly set themselves to change his faith.[5]

Please observe, however, that I do not yet say that it is *better* that the subconscious and non-rational should thus hold primacy in the religious realm. I confine myself to simply pointing out that they do so hold it as a matter of fact.

So much for our sense of the reality of the religious objects. Let me now say a brief word more about the attitudes they characteristically awaken.

We have already agreed that they are *solemn;* and we have seen reason to think that the most distinctive of them is the sort of joy which may result in extreme cases from absolute self-surrender. The sense of the kind of object to which the surrender is made has much to do with determining the precise complexion of the joy; and the whole phenomenon is more complex than any simple formula allows. In the literature of the subject, sadness and gladness have each been emphasized in turn. The ancient saying that the first maker of the Gods was fear receives voluminous corroboration from every age of religious history; but none the less does religious history show the part which joy has evermore tended to play. Sometimes the joy has been primary; sometimes secondary, being the gladness of deliverance from the fear. This latter state of things, being the more complex, is also the more complete; and as we proceed, I think we shall have abundant reason for refusing to leave out either the

---

5 See James's "The Sentiment of Rationality," in *The Will to Believe and Other Essays* (New York: Longmans, Green, and Co., 1897), pp. 63–110. [Ed.]

sadness or the gladness, if we look at religion with the breadth of view which it demands.[6] Stated in the completest possible terms, a man's religion involves both moods of contraction and moods of expansion of his being. But the quantitative mixture and order of these moods vary so much from one age of the world, from one system of thought, and from one individual to another, that you may insist either on the dread and the submission, or on the peace and the freedom as the essence of the matter, and still remain materially within the limits of the truth. The constitutionally sombre and the constitutionally sanguine onlooker are bound to emphasize opposite aspects of what lies before their eyes.

The constitutionally sombre religious person makes even of his religious peace a very sober thing. Danger still hovers in the air about it. Flexion and contraction are not wholly checked. It were sparrowlike and childish after our deliverance to explode into twittering laughter and caper-cutting, and utterly to forget the imminent hawk on bough. Lie low, rather, lie low; for you are in the hands of a living God. In the Book of Job, for example, the impotence of man and the omnipotence of God is the exclusive burden of its author's mind. "It is as high as heaven; what canst thou do?—deeper than hell; what canst thou know?"[7] There is an astringent relish about the truth of this conviction which some men can feel, and which for them is as near an approach as can be made to the feeling of religious joy.

In Job [says that coldly truthful writer, the author of Mark Rutherford] God reminds us that man is not the measure of his creation. The world is immense, constructed on no plan or theory which the intellect of man can grasp. It is *transcendent* everywhere. This is the burden of every verse, and is the secret, if there be one, of the poem. Sufficient or insufficient, there is nothing more.... God is great, we know not his ways. He takes

---

[6] See Edwards' testimony, pp. 177–179. [Ed.]

[7] Job 11:8.

from us all we have, but yet if we possess our souls in patience, we *may* pass the valley of the shadow, and come out in sunlight again. We may or we may not! . . . What more have we to say now than God said from the whirlwind over two thousand five hundred years ago?[8]

If we turn to the sanguine onlooker, on the other hand, we find that deliverance is felt as incomplete unless the burden be altogether overcome and the danger forgotten. Such onlookers give us definitions that seem to the sombre minds of whom we have just been speaking to leave out all the solemnity that makes religious peace so different from merely animal joys. In the opinion of some writers an attitude might be called religious, though no touch were left in it of sacrifice or submission, no tendency to flexion, no bowing of the head. Any "habitual and regulated admiration," says Professor J. R. Seeley,[9] "is worthy to be called a religion"; and accordingly he thinks that our Music, our Science, and our so-called 'Civilization,' as these things are now organized and admiringly believed in, form the more genuine religions of our time. Certainly the unhesitating and unreasoning way in which we feel that we must inflict our civilization upon 'lower' races, by means of Hotchkiss guns, etc., reminds one of nothing so much as of the early spirit of Islam spreading its religion by the sword. . . .[10]

---

[8] William Hale White, *Mark Rutherford's Deliverance* (London: Trübner & Co., 1885), pp. 196, 198.

[9] In his book (too little read, I fear), *Natural Religion*, 3rd ed. (Boston: Roberts Brothers, 1886), pp. 91, 122. [John R. Seeley (1834–1895) had published a provocative, rather naturalistic life of Jesus *(Ecce Homo)* in 1866. His *Natural Religion* (1882), drawing on Wordsworth and Goethe, held true religion not to be dependent on miracle or radical supernaturalism. James' quotation is composite but fair. Ed.]

[10] The Boer War and Spanish-American War had recently heightened James' anti-imperialism. [The final paragraph of Lecture III follows but, being largely procedural, is here omitted. In succeeding lectures James considers Healthy-mindedness, the Sick Soul, the Divided Self, Conversion, Saintliness, Mysticism, Philosophy, and other topics. Our Selection is resumed with his Conclusions.] [Ed.]

Conclusions

The material of our study of human nature is now spread before us; and in this parting hour, set free from the duty of description, we can draw our theoretical and practical conclusions. In my first lecture, defending the empirical method, I foretold that whatever conclusions we might come to could be reached by spiritual judgments only, appreciations of the significance for life of religion, taken 'on the whole.' Our conclusions cannot be as sharp as dogmatic conclusions would be, but I will formulate them, when the time comes, as sharply as I can.

Summing up in the broadest possible way the characteristics of the religious life, as we have found them, it includes the following beliefs:—

1. That the visible world is part of a more spiritual universe from which it draws its chief significance;

2. That union or harmonious relation with that higher universe is our true end;

3. That prayer or inner communion with the spirit thereof—be that spirit 'God' or 'law'—is a process wherein work is really done, and spiritual energy flows in and produces effects, psychological or material, within the phenomenal world.

Religion includes also the following psychological characteristics:—

4. A new zest which adds itself like a gift to life, and takes the form either of lyrical enchantment or of appeal to earnestness and heroism.

5. An assurance of safety and a temper of peace, and, in relation to others, a preponderance of loving affections.

In illustrating these characteristics by documents, we have been literally bathed in sentiment. In re-reading my manuscript, I am almost appalled at the amount of emotionality which I find in it. After so much of this, we can afford to be dryer and less sympathetic in the rest of the work that lies before us.

The sentimentality of many of my documents is a consequence of the fact that I sought them among the extravagances of the subject. If any of you are enemies of what our ancestors used to brand as enthusiasm, and are, nevertheless, still listening to me now, you have probably felt my selection to have been sometimes almost perverse, and have wished I might have stuck to soberer examples. I reply that I took these extremer examples as yielding the profounder information. To learn the secrets of any science, we go to expert specialists, even though they may be eccentric persons, and not to commonplace pupils. We combine what they tell us with the rest of our wisdom, and form our final judgment independently. Even so with religion. We who have pursued such radical expressions of it may now be sure that we know its secrets as authentically as any one can know them who learns them from another; and we have next to answer, each of us for himself, the practical question: what are the dangers in this element of life? and in what proportion may it need to be restrained by other elements, to give the proper balance?

But this question suggests another one which I will answer immediately and get it out of the way, for it has more than once already vexed us. Ought it to be assumed that in all men the mixture of religion with other elements should be identical? Ought it, indeed, to be assumed that the lives of all men should show identical religious elements? In other words, is the existence of so many religious types and sects and creeds regrettable?

To these questions I answer 'No' emphatically. And my reason is that I do not see how it is possible that creatures in such different positions and with such different powers as human individuals are, should have exactly the same functions and the same duties. No two of us have identical difficulties, nor should we be expected to work out identical solutions. Each, from his peculiar angle of observation, takes in a certain sphere of fact and trouble, which each must deal with in a unique manner. One of us must soften himself, another must harden himself; one must yield a point, another must stand firm,—in order the better to defend the position assigned him. If an Emerson were forced to be a Wesley, or a Moody forced to be a Whitman, the total human consciousness of the divine would suffer. The divine can mean no single quality, it must mean a group of qualities, by being champions of which in alternation, different men may all find worthy missions. Each attitude being a syllable in human nature's total message, it takes the whole of us to spell the meaning out completely. So a 'god of battles' must be allowed to be the god for one kind of person, a god of peace and heaven and home, the god for another. We must frankly recognize the fact that we live in partial systems, and that parts are not interchangeable in the spiritual life. If we are peevish and jealous, destruction of the self must be an element of our religion; why need it be one if we are good and sympathetic from the outset? If we are sick souls, we require a religion of deliverance; but why think so much of deliverance, if we are healthy-minded? Unquestionably, some men have the completer experience and the higher vocation, here just as in the social world; but for each man to stay in his own experience, whate'er it be, and for others to tolerate him there, is surely best.

But, you may now ask, would not this one-sidedness be cured if we should all espouse the science of religions as our own religion? In answering this question I must open again the general relations of the theoretic to the active life.

Knowledge about a thing is not the thing itself. You remember what Al-Ghazzali told us in the Lecture on Mysticism,— that to understand the causes of drunkenness, as a physician understands them, is not to be drunk.[11] A science might come to

---

[11] Cf. Edwards, pp. 182–183. [Ed.]

understand everything about the causes and elements of religion, and might even decide which elements were qualified, by their general harmony with other branches of knowledge, to be considered true; and yet the best man at this science might be the man who found it hardest to be personally devout. *Tout savoir c'est tout pardonner.*[12] The name of Renan would doubtless occur to many persons as an example of the way in which breadth of knowledge may make one only a dilettante in possibilities, and blunt the acuteness of one's living faith.[13] If religion be a function by which either God's cause or man's cause is to be really advanced, then he who lives the life of it, however narrowly, is a better servant than he who merely knows about it, however much. Knowledge about life is one thing; effective occupation of a place in life, with its dynamic currents passing through your being, is another.

For this reason, the science of religions may not be an equivalent for living religion; and if we turn to the inner difficulties of such a science, we see that a point comes when she must drop the purely theoretic attitude, and either let her knots remain uncut, or have them cut by active faith. To see this, suppose that we have our science of religions constituted as a matter of fact. Suppose that she has assimilated all the necessary historical material and distilled out of it as its essence the same conclusions which I myself a few moments ago pronounced. Suppose that she agrees that religion, wherever it is an active

---

12 "To know all is to pardon all." [Ed.]

13 In Lecture II, p. 37 James had quoted a passage from Ernst Renan (1823–1892), the French scholar and religious philosopher, to exemplify a nonreligious outlook. The quotation closed with these words: "St. Augustine's phrase: *Lord, if we are deceived, it is by thee!* remains a fine one, well suited to our modern feeling. Only we wish the Eternal to know that if we accept the fraud, we accept it knowingly and willingly. We are resigned in advance to losing the interest on our investments of virtue, but we wish not to appear ridiculous by having counted on them too securely." *Feuilles detachées* (Paris: Calmann Lévy, Editeur, 1892), pp. 394–398. [Ed.]

thing, involves a belief in ideal presences, and a belief that in our prayerful communion with them, work is done, and something real comes to pass. She has now to exert her critical activity, and to decide how far, in the light of other sciences and in that of general philosophy, such beliefs can be considered *true*.

Dogmatically to decide this is an impossible task. Not only are the other sciences and the philosophy still far from being completed, but in their present state we find them full of conflicts. The sciences of nature know nothing of spiritual presences, and on the whole hold no practical commerce whatever with the idealistic conceptions towards which general philosophy inclines. The scientist, so-called, is, during his scientific hours at least, so materialistic that one may well say that on the whole the influence of science goes against the notion that religion should be recognized at all. And this antipathy to religion finds an echo within the very science of religions itself. The cultivator of this science has to become acquainted with so many groveling and horrible superstitions that a presumption easily arises in his mind that any belief that is religious probably is false. In the 'prayerful communion' of savages with such mumbo-jumbos of deities as they acknowledge, it is hard for us to see what genuine spiritual work—even though it were work relative only to their dark savage obligations—can possibly be done.

The consequence is that the conclusions of the science of religions are as likely to be adverse as they are to be favorable to the claim that the essence of religion is true. There is a notion in the air about us that religion is probably only an anachronism, a case of 'survival,' an atavistic relapse into a mode of thought which humanity in its more enlightened examples has outgrown; and this notion our religious anthropologists at present do little to counteract.

This view is so widespread at the present day that I must consider it with some explicitness before I pass to my own conclusions. Let me call it the 'Survival theory,' for brevity's sake.

The pivot round which the religious life, as we have traced it, revolves, is the interest of the individual in his private personal destiny. Religion, in short, is a monumental chapter in the history of human egotism. The gods believed in—whether by crude savages or by men disciplined intellectually—agree with each other in recognizing personal calls. Religious thought is carried on in terms of personality, this being, in the world of religion, the one fundamental fact. To-day, quite as much as at any previous age, the religious individual tells you that the divine meets him on the basis of his personal concerns.

Science, on the other hand, has ended by utterly repudiating the personal point of view. She catalogues her elements and records her laws indifferent as to what purpose may be shown forth by them, and constructs her theories quite careless of their bearing on human anxieties and fates. Though the scientist may individually nourish a religion, and be a theist in his irresponsible hours, the days are over when it could be said that for Science herself the heavens declare the glory of God and the firmament showeth his handiwork. Our solar system, with its harmonies, is seen now as but one passing case of a certain sort of moving equilibrium in the heavens, realized by a local accident in an appalling wilderness of worlds where no life can exist. In a span of time which as a cosmic interval will count but as an hour, it will have ceased to be. The Darwinian notion of chance production, and subsequent destruction, speedy or deferred, applies to the largest as well as to the smallest facts. It is impossible, in the present temper of the scientific imagination, to find in the driftings of the cosmic atoms, whether they work on the universal or on the particular scale, anything but a kind of aimless weather, doing and undoing, achieving no proper history, and leaving no result. Nature has no one distinguishable ultimate tendency with which it is possible to feel a sympathy. In the vast rhythm of her processes, as the scientific mind now follows them, she appears to cancel herself. The books of natural theology which satisfied the intellects of our grandfathers seem to us quite grotesque, representing, as they did, a God who conformed the largest things of nature to the paltriest of our private wants.[14] The God whom science recognizes must be a God of universal laws exclusively, a God who does a wholesale, not a retail business. He cannot accommodate his processes to the convenience of individuals. The bubbles on the foam which coats a stormy sea are floating episodes, made and unmade by the forces of the wind and water. Our private selves are like those bubbles,—epiphenomena, as Clifford, I believe, ingeniously called them; their destinies weigh nothing and determine nothing in the world's irremediable currents of events.[15]

You see how natural it is, from this point of view, to treat religion as a mere survival, for religion does in fact perpetuate the traditions of the most primeval thought. To coerce the spiritual powers, or to square them and get them on our side, was, during enormous tracts of time, the one great object in our dealings with the natural world. For our ancestors, dreams, hallucinations, revelations, and cock-and-bull stories were inextricably mixed with facts. Up to a comparatively recent date such distinctions as those between what has been verified and what is only conjectured, between the impersonal and the personal aspects of existence, were hardly suspected or conceived. Whatever you imagined in a lively manner, whatever you thought fit to be true, you affirmed confidently; and whatever you affirmed, your comrades believed. Truth was what had not yet been contradicted, most things were taken into the mind from the point of view of their human suggestiveness, and the

---

[14] In a long footnote James exhibited "arguments from design" by the rationalistic philosopher-theologians Christian Wolff (1679–1754) and William Derham (1675–1735). [Ed.]

[15] Though a friend of the British mathematician and philosopher William K. Clifford (1845–1879), James found his theories of mind too mechanistic. [Ed.]

attention confined itself exclusively to the æsthetic and dramatic aspects of events.

How indeed could it be otherwise? The extraordinary value, for explanation and prevision, of those mathematical and mechanical modes of conception which science uses, was a result that could not possibly have been expected in advance. Weight, movement, velocity, direction, position, what thin, pallid, uninteresting ideas! How could the richer animistic aspects of Nature, the peculiarities and oddities that make phenomena picturesquely striking or expressive, fail to have been first singled out and followed by philosophy as the more promising avenue to the knowledge of Nature's life? Well, it is still in these richer animistic and dramatic aspects that religion delights to dwell. It is the terror and beauty of phenomena, the 'promise' of the dawn and of the rainbow, the 'voice' of the thunder, the 'gentleness' of the summer rain, the 'sublimity' of the stars, and not the physical laws which these things follow, by which the religious mind still continues to be most impressed; and just as of yore, the devout man tells you that in the solitude of his room or of the fields he still feels the divine presence, that inflowings of help come in reply to his prayers, and that sacrifices to this unseen reality fill him with security and peace.

Pure anachronism! says the survival-theory;—anachronism for which deanthropomorphization of the imagination is the remedy required. The less we mix the private with the cosmic, the more we dwell in universal and impersonal terms, the truer heirs of Science we become.

In spite of the appeal which this impersonality of the scientific attitude makes to a certain magnanimity of temper, I believe it to be shallow, and I can now state my reason in comparatively few words. That reason is that, so long as we deal with the cosmic and the general, we deal only with the symbols of reality, but *as soon as we deal with private and personal phenomena as such, we deal with realities in the completest sense of the term.* I think I can easily make clear what I mean by these words.

The world of our experience consists at all times of two parts, an objective and a subjective part, of which the former may be incalculably more extensive than the latter, and yet the latter can never be omitted or suppressed. The objective part is the sum total of whatsoever at any given time we may be thinking of, the subjective part is the inner 'state' in which the thinking comes to pass. What we think of may be enormous,—the cosmic times and spaces, for example,—whereas the inner state may be the most fugitive and paltry activity of mind. Yet the cosmic objects, so far as the experience yields them, are but ideal pictures of something whose existence we do not inwardly possess but only point at outwardly, while the inner state is our very experience itself; its reality and that of our experience are one. A conscious field *plus* its object as felt or thought of *plus* an attitude towards the object *plus* the sense of a self to whom the attitude belongs—such a concrete bit of personal experience may be a small bit, but it is a solid bit as long as it lasts; not hollow, not a mere abstract element of experience, such as the 'object' is when taken all alone. It is a *full* fact, even though it be an insignificant fact; it is of the *kind* to which all realities whatsoever must belong; the motor currents of the world run through the like of it; it is on the line connecting real events with real events. That unsharable feeling which each one of us has of the pinch of his individual destiny as he privately feels it rolling out on fortune's wheel may be disparaged for its egotism, may be sneered at as unscientific, but it is the one thing that fills up the measure of our concrete actuality, and any would-be existent that should lack such a feeling, or its analogue, would be a piece of reality only half made up.

If this be true, it is absurd for science to say that the egotistic elements of experience should be suppressed. The axis of reality runs solely through the egotistic places,—they are strung upon it like so many beads. To describe the world with all the various feelings of the individual pinch of destiny, all the various spiritual attitudes, left out from the description—they being as describable as anything else—would be something like offering a printed bill of fare as the equivalent for a solid meal. Religion makes no such blunder. The individual's religion may be egotistic, and those private realities which it keeps in touch with may be narrow enough; but at any rate it always remains infinitely less hollow and abstract, as far as it goes, than a science which prides itself on taking no account of anything private at all.

A bill of fare with one real raisin on it instead of the word 'raisin,' with one real egg instead of the word 'egg,' might be an inadequate meal, but it would at least be a commencement of reality. The contention of the survival-theory that we ought to stick to non-personal elements exclusively seems like saying that we ought to be satisfied forever with reading the naked bill of fare. I think, therefore, that however particular questions connected with our individual destinies may be answered, it is only by acknowledging them as genuine questions, and living in the sphere of thought which they open up, that we become profound. But to live thus is to be religious; so I unhesitatingly repudiate the survival-theory of religion, as being founded on an egregious mistake. It does not follow, because our ancestors made so many errors of fact and mixed them with their religion, that we should therefore leave off being religious at all.[16] By being religious we establish ourselves in possession of ultimate reality at the only points at which reality is given us to guard. Our responsible concern is with our private destiny, after all.

------

16 Even the errors of fact may possibly turn out not to be as wholesale as the scientist assumes. . . . Thus the divorce between scientist facts and religious facts may not necessarily be as eternal as it at first sight seems, nor the personalism and romanticism of the world, as they appeared to primitive thinking, be matters so irrevocably outgrown. The final human opinion may, in short, in some manner now impossible to foresee, revert to the more personal style, just as any path of progress may follow a spiral rather than a straight line. If this were so, the rigorously impersonal view of science might one day appear as having been a temporarily useful eccentricity rather than the definitively triumphant position which the sectarian scientist at present so confidently announces it to be.

You see now why I have been so individualistic throughout these lectures, and why I have seemed so bent on rehabilitating the element of feeling in religion and subordinating its intellectual part. Individuality is founded in feeling; and the recesses of feeling, the darker, blinder strata of character, are the only places in the world in which we catch real fact in the making, and directly perceive how events happen, and how work is actually done. Compared with this world of living individualized feelings, the world of generalized objects which the intellect contemplates is without solidity or life. As in stereoscopic or kinetoscopic pictures seen outside the instrument, the third dimension, the movement, the vital element, are not there. We get a beautiful picture of an express train supposed to be moving, but where in the picture, as I have heard a friend say, is the energy or the fifty miles an hour?[17]

Let us agree, then, that Religion, occupying herself with personal destinies and keeping thus in contact with the only absolute realities which we know, must necessarily play an eternal part in human history. The next thing to decide is what she reveals about those destinies, or whether indeed she reveals anything distinct enough to be considered a general message to mankind. We have done as you see, with our preliminaries, and our final summing up can now begin.

I am well aware that after all the palpitating documents

---

[17] When I read in a religious paper words like these: "Perhaps the best thing we can say of God is that he is *the Inevitable Inference*," I recognize the tendency to let religion evaporate in intellectual terms. Would martyrs have sung in the flames for a mere inference, however inevitable it might be? Original religious men, like Saint Francis, Luther, Behmen, have usually been enemies of the intellect's pretension to meddle with religious things. Yet the intellect, everywhere invasive, shows everywhere its shallowing effect. See how the ancient spirit of Methodism evaporates under those wonderfully able rationalistic booklets (which every one should read) of a philosopher like Professor Bowne. . . . [James cites three doctrinal works of Borden Parker Bowne (1847–1910), a philosopher-theologian of Boston University whose "personalistic idealism" had vast influence in American Methodism. Ed.]

which I have quoted, and all the perspectives of emotion-in-spiring institution and belief that my previous lectures have opened, the dry analysis to which I now advance may appear to many of you like an anticlimax, a tapering-off and flattening out of the subject, instead of a crescendo of interest and result. I said awhile ago that the religious attitude of Protestants appears poverty-stricken to the Catholic imagination. Still more poverty-stricken, I fear, may my final summing up of the subject appear at first to some of you. On which account I pray you now to bear this point in mind, that in the present part of it I am expressly trying to reduce religion to its lowest admissible terms, to that minimum, free from individualistic excrescences, which all religions contain as their nucleus, and on which it may be hoped that all religious persons may agree. That established, we should have a result which might be small, but would at least be solid; and on it and round it the ruddier additional beliefs on which the different individuals make their venture might be grafted, and flourish as richly as you please. I shall add my own over-belief (which will be, I confess, of a somewhat pallid kind, as befits a critical philosopher), and you will, I hope, also add your over-beliefs, and we shall soon be in the varied world of concrete religious constructions once more. For the moment, let me dryly pursue the analytic part of the task.

Both thought and feeling are determinants of conduct, and the same conduct may be determined either by feeling or by thought. When we survey the whole field of religion, we find a great variety in the thoughts that have prevailed there; but the feelings on the one hand and the conduct on the other are almost always the same, for Stoic, Christian, and Buddhist saints are practically indistinguishable in their lives. The theories which Religion generates, being thus variable, are secondary; and if you wish to grasp her essence, you must look to the feelings and the conduct as being the more constant elements. It is between these two elements that the short circuit exists on which she carries on her principal business, while the ideas and symbols and other institutions form loop-lines which may be perfections and improvements, and may even some day all be united into one harmonious system, but which are not to be regarded as organs with an indispensable function, necessary at all times for religious life to go on. This seems to me the first conclusion which we are entitled to draw from the phenomena we have passed in review.

The next step is to characterize the feelings. To what psychological order do they belong?

The resultant outcome of them is in any case what Kant calls a 'sthenic' affection, an excitement of the cheerful, expansive, 'dynamogenic' order which, like any tonic, freshens our vital powers. In almost every lecture, but especially in the lectures on Conversion and on Saintliness, we have seen how this emotion overcomes temperamental melancholy and imparts endurance to the Subject, or a zest, or a meaning, or an enchantment and glory to the common objects of life. The name of 'faith-state,' by which **Professor Leuba** designates it, is a good one. It is a biological as well as a psychological condition, and Tolstoy is absolutely accurate in classing faith among the forces *by which men live.* The total absence of it, anhedonia, means collapse.

The faith-state may hold a very minimum of intellectual content. . . . It may be a mere vague enthusiasm, half spiritual, half vital, a courage, and a feeling that great and wondrous things are in the air. When, however, a positive intellectual content is associated with a faith-state, it gets invincibly stamped in upon belief, and this explains the passionate loyalty of religious persons everywhere to the minutest details of their so widely differing creeds. Taking creeds and faith-state together, as forming 'religions,' and treating these as purely subjective phenomena, without regard to the question of their 'truth,' we are obliged, on account of their extraordinary influence upon action and endurance, to class them amongst the most important biological functions of mankind. Their stimulant and anæsthetic effect is so great that Professor Leuba, in a recent article, goes so far as to say that so long as men can *use* their God, they care very little who he is, or even whether he is at all. "The truth of the matter can be put," says Leuba, "in this way: *God is not known, he is not understood; he is used*—sometimes as meat-purveyor, sometimes as moral support, sometimes as friend, sometimes as an object of love. If he proves himself useful, the religious consciousness asks for no more than that. Does God really exist? How does he exist? What is he? are so many irrelevant questions. Not God, but life, more life, a larger, richer, more satisfying life, is, in the last analysis, the end of religion. The love of life, at any and every level of development, is the religious impulse."[18]

At this purely subjective rating, therefore, Religion must be considered vindicated in a certain way from the attacks of her critics. It would seem that she cannot be a mere anachronism and survival, but must exert a permanent function, whether she be with or without intellectual content, and whether, if she have any, it be true or false.

We must next pass beyond the point of view of merely subjective utility, and make inquiry into the intellectual content itself.

First, is there, under all the discrepancies of the creeds, a common nucleus to which they bear their testimony unanimously?

And second, ought we to consider the testimony true?

I will take up the first question first, and answer it immediately in the affirmative. The warring gods and formulas of the various religions do indeed cancel each other, but there is a

---

[18] James H. Leuba, "A Study in the Psychology of Religious Phenomena," *American Journal of Psychology*, VII (April, 1896), 345-349; "The Contents of Religious Consciousness," *The Monist*, XI (July, 1901), 536, 571, 572, abridged. [Citations of Leuba consolidated. Ed.]

certain uniform deliverance in which religions all appear to meet. It consists of two parts:—

1. An uneasiness; and

2. Its solution.

1. The uneasiness, reduced to its simplest terms, is a sense that there is *something wrong about us* as we naturally stand.

2. The solution is a sense that *we are saved from the wrongness* by making proper connection with the higher powers.

In those more developed minds which alone we are studying, the wrongness takes a moral character, and the salvation takes a mystical tinge. I think we shall keep well within the limits of what is common to all such minds if we formulate the essence of their religious experience in terms like these:—

The individual, so far as he suffers from his wrongness and criticises it, is to that extent consciously beyond it, and in at least possible touch with something higher, if anything higher exist. Along with the wrong part there is thus a better part of him, even though it may be but a most helpless germ. With which part he should identify his real being is by no means obvious at this stage; but when stage 2 (the stage of solution or salvation) arrives, the man identifies his real being with the germinal higher part of himself; and does so in the following way. *He becomes conscious that this higher part is conterminous and continuous with a* MORE *of the same quality, which is operative in the universe outside of him, and which he can keep in working touch with, and in a fashion get on board of and save himself when all his lower being has gone to pieces in the wreck.*

It seems to me that all the phenomena are accurately describable in these very simple general terms.[19] They allow for the divided self and the struggle; they involve the change of personal centre and the surrender of the lower self; they express

---

[19] The practical difficulties are: 1, to 'realize the reality' of one's higher part; 2, to identify one's self with it exclusively; and 3, to identify it with all the rest of ideal being.

the appearance of exteriority of the helping power and yet account for our sense of union with it; and they fully justify our feelings of security and joy. There is probably no autobiographic document, among all those which I have quoted, to which the description will not well apply. One need only add such specific details as will adapt it to various theologies and various personal temperaments, and one will then have the various experiences reconstructed in their individual forms.

So far, however, as this analysis goes, the experiences are only psychological phenomena. They possess, it is true, enormous biological worth. Spiritual strength really increases in the subject when he has them, a new life opens for him, and they seem to him a place of conflux where the forces of two universes meet; and yet this may be nothing but his subjective way of feeling things, a mood of his own fancy, in spite of the effects produced. I now turn to my second question: What is the objective 'truth' of their content?[20]

The part of the content concerning which the question of truth most pertinently arises is that 'MORE of the same quality' with which our own higher self appears in the experience to come into harmonious working relation. Is such a 'more' merely our own notion, or does it really exist? If so, in what shape does it exist? Does it act, as well as exist? And in what form should we conceive of that 'union' with it of which religious geniuses are so convinced?

It is in answering these questions that the various theologies perform their theoretic work, and that their divergencies most come to light. They all agree that the 'more' really exists; though some of them hold it to exist in the shape of a personal god or gods, while others are satisfied to conceive it as a stream of ideal

---

20 The word 'truth' is here taken to mean something additional to bare value for life, although the natural propensity of man is to believe that whatever has great value for life is thereby certified as true. [James's doctrine of truth was evolving. See his *Pragmatism* (1907) and *The Meaning of Truth* (1909). Ed.]

tendency embedded in the eternal structure of the world. They all agree, moreover, that it acts as well as exists, and that something really is effected for the better when you throw your life into its hands. It is when they treat of the experience of 'union' with it that their speculative differences appear most clearly. Over this point pantheism and theism, nature and second birth, works and grace and karma, immortality and reincarnation, rationalism and mysticism, carry on inveterate disputes.

At the end of my lecture on Philosophy[21] I held out the notion that an impartial science of religions might sift out from the midst of their discrepancies a common body of doctrine which she might also formulate in terms to which physical science need not object. This, I said, she might adopt as her own reconciling hypothesis, and recommend it for general belief. I also said that in my last lecture I should have to try my own hand at framing such an hypothesis.

The time has now come for this attempt. Who says 'hypothesis' renounces the ambition to be coercive in his arguments. The most I can do is, accordingly, to offer something that may fit the facts so easily that your scientific logic will find no plausible pretext for vetoing your impulse to welcome it as true.

The 'more,' as we called it, and the meaning of our 'union' with it, form the nucleus of our inquiry. Into what definite description can these words be translated, and for what definite facts do they stand? It would never do for us to place ourselves offhand at the position of a particular theology, the Christian theology, for example, and proceed immediately to define the 'more' as Jehovah, and the 'union' as his imputation to us of the righteousness of Christ. That would be unfair to other religions, and, from our present standpoint at least, would be an over-belief.

---

[21] *Varieties*, Lecture XVIII, p. 455. [Ed.]

We must begin by using less particularized terms; and, since one of the duties of the science of religions is to keep religion in connection with the rest of science, we shall do well to seek first of all a way of describing the 'more,' which psychologists may also recognize as real. The *subconscious self* is nowadays a well-accredited psychological entity; and I believe that in it we have exactly the mediating term required. Apart from all religious considerations, there is actually and literally more life in our total soul than we are at any time aware of. The exploration of the transmarginal field has hardly yet been seriously undertaken, but what Mr. Myers said in 1892 in his essay on the Subliminal Consciousness is as true as when it was first written: "Each of us is in reality an abiding psychical entity far more extensive than he knows—an individuality which can never express itself completely through any corporeal manifestation. The Self manifests through the organism; but there is always some part of the Self unmanifested; and always, as it seems, some power of organic expression in abeyance or reserve."[22] Much of the content of this larger background against which our conscious being stands out in relief is insignificant. Imperfect memories, silly jingles, inhibitive timidities, 'dissolutive' phenomena of various sorts, as Myers calls them, enter into it for a large part. But in it many of the performances of genius seem also to have their origin; and in our study of conversion, of mystical experiences, and of prayer, we have seen how striking a part invasions from this region play in the religious life.

Let me then propose, as an hypothesis, that whatever it may be on its *farther* side, the 'more' with which in religious experience we feel ourselves connected is on its *hither* side the sub-

---

22 Frederic W. H. Myers, "The Subliminal Consciousness," *Proceedings of the Society for Psychical Research*, VII (1891–1892), 305. [Myers' essay continues in VIII (1892). See also James' eulogy of Myers (1843–1901), *Proceedings*, XVII (1901–1903), 13–23; and Myers' posthumous magnum opus, *Human Personality*, 2 vols. (New York: Longmans, Green and Co., 1903). James' interest in 'psychical research' was strong and persistent. Ed.]

conscious continuation of our conscious life. Starting thus with a recognized psychological fact as our basis, we seem to preserve a contact with 'science' which the ordinary theologian lacks. At the same time the theologian's contention that the religious man is moved by an external power is vindicated, for it is one of the peculiarities of invasions from the subconscious region to take on objective appearances, and to suggest to the Subject an external control. In the religious life the control is felt as 'higher'; but since on our hypothesis it is primarily the higher faculties of our own hidden mind which are controlling, the sense of union with the power beyond us is a sense of something, not merely apparently, but literally true.

This doorway into the subject seems to me the best one for a science of religions, for it mediates between a number of different points of view. Yet it is only a doorway, and difficulties present themselves as soon as we step through it, and ask how far our transmarginal consciousness carries us if we follow it on its remoter side. Here the over-beliefs begin: here mysticism and the conversion-rapture and Vedantism and transcendental idealism bring in their monistic interpretations and tell us that the finite self rejoins the absolute self, for it was always one with God and identical with the soul of the world. Here the prophets of all the different religions come with their visions, voices, raptures, and other openings, supposed by each to authenticate his own peculiar faith.

Those of us who are not personally favored with such specific revelations must stand outside of them altogether and, for the present at least, decide that, since they corroborate incompatible theological doctrines, they neutralize one another and leave no fixed result. If we follow any one of them, or if we follow philosophical theory and embrace monistic pantheism on non-mystical grounds, we do so in the exercise of our individual freedom, and build out our religion in the way most congruous with our personal susceptibilities. Among these susceptibilities intellectual ones play a decisive part. Although the religious question is primarily a question of life, of living or not living in the higher union which opens itself to us as a gift, yet the spiritual excitement in which the gift appears a real one will often fail to be aroused in an individual until certain particular intellectual beliefs or ideas which, as we say, come home to him, are touched. These ideas will thus be essential to that individual's religion;—which is as much as to say that over-beliefs in various directions are absolutely indispensable, and that we should treat them with tenderness and tolerance so long as they are not intolerant themselves. As I have elsewhere written, the most interesting and valuable things about a man are usually his over-beliefs.

Disregarding the over-beliefs, and confining ourselves to what is common and generic, we have in *the fact that the conscious person is continuous with a wider self through which saving experiences come,* a positive content of religious experience which, it seems to me, *is literally and objectively true as far as it goes.* If I now proceed to state my own hypothesis about the farther limits of this extension of our personality, I shall be offering my own over-belief—though I know it will appear a sorry under-belief to some of you—for which I can only bespeak the same indulgence which in a converse case I should accord to yours.

The further limits of our being plunge, it seems to me, into an altogether other dimension of existence from the sensible and merely 'understandable' world. Name it the mystical region, or the supernatural region, whichever you choose. So far as our ideal impulses originate in this region (and most of them do originate in it, for we find them possessing us in a way for which we cannot articulately account), we belong to it in a more intimate sense than that in which we belong to the visible world, for we belong in the most intimate sense wherever our ideals belong. Yet the unseen region in question is not merely ideal, for it produces effects in this world. When we commune with it, work is actually done upon our finite personality, for we are turned into new men, and consequences in the way of conduct follow in the natural world upon our regenerative change. But that which produces effects within another reality must be termed a reality itself, so I feel as if we had no philosophic excuse for calling the unseen or mystical world unreal.

God is the natural appellation, for us Christians at least, for the supreme reality, so I will call this higher part of the universe by the name of God. We and God have business with each other; and in opening ourselves to his influence our deepest destiny is fulfilled. The universe, at those parts of it which our personal being constitutes, takes a turn genuinely for the worse or for the better in proportion as each one of us fulfills or evades God's demands. As far as this goes I probably have you with me, for I only translate into schematic language what I may call the instinctive belief of mankind: God is real since he produces real effects.

The real effects in question, so far as I have as yet admitted them, are exerted on the personal centres of energy of the various subjects, but the spontaneous faith of most of the subjects is that they embrace a wider sphere than this. Most religious men believe (or 'know,' if they be mystical) that not only they themselves, but the whole universe of beings to whom the God is present, are secure in his parental hands. There is a sense, a dimension, they are sure, in which we are *all* saved, in spite of the gates of hell and all adverse terrestrial appearances. God's existence is the guarantee of an ideal order that shall be permanently preserved. This world may indeed, as science assures us, some day burn up or freeze; but if it is part of his order, the old ideals are sure to be brought elsewhere to fruition, so that where God is, tragedy is only provisional and partial, and shipwreck and dissolution are not the absolutely final things. Only when this farther step of faith concerning God is taken, and remote objective consequences are predicted, does religion, as it seems to me, get wholly free from the first immediate subjective experience, and bring a *real hypothesis* into play. A good hypothesis in science must have other properties than those of the phenomenon it is immediately invoked to explain, otherwise it is not prolific enough. God, meaning only what enters into the religious man's experience of union, falls short of being an hypothesis of this more useful order. He needs to enter into wider cosmic relations in order to justify the subject's absolute confidence and peace.

That the God with whom, starting from the hither side of our own extra-marginal self, we come at its remoter margin into commerce should be the absolute world-ruler, is of course a very considerable over-belief. Over-belief as it is, though, it is an article of almost every one's religion. Most of us pretend in some way to prop it upon our philosophy, but the philosophy itself is really propped upon this faith. What is this but to say that Religion, in her fullest exercise of function, is not a mere illumination of facts already elsewhere given, not a mere passion, like love, which views things in a rosier light. It is indeed that, as we have seen abundantly. But it is something more, namely, a postulator of new *facts* as well. The world interpreted religiously is not the materialistic world over again, with an altered expression; it must have, over and above the altered expression, *a natural constitution* different at some point from that which a materialistic world would have. It must be such that different events can be expected in it, different conduct must be required.

This thoroughly 'pragmatic' view of religion has usually been taken as a matter of course by common men. They have interpolated divine miracles into the field of nature, they have built a heaven out beyond the grave. It is only transcendentalist metaphysicians who think that, without adding any concrete details to Nature, or subtracting any, but by simply calling it the expression of absolute spirit, you make it more divine just as it stands. I believe the pragmatic way of taking religion to be the deeper way. It gives it body as well as soul, it makes it claim, as everything real must claim, some characteristic realm of fact as its very own. What the more characteristically divine facts are, apart from the actual inflow of energy in the faith-state and the prayer-state, I know not. But the over-belief on which I am ready to make my personal venture is that they exist. The whole drift of my education goes to persuade me that the world of our present consciousness is only one out of many worlds of consciousness that exist, and that those other worlds must contain experiences which have a meaning for our life also; and that although in the main their experiences and those of this world keep discrete, yet the two become continuous at certain points, and higher energies filter in. By being faithful in my poor measure to this over-belief, I seem to myself to keep more sane and true. I *can*, of course, put myself into the sectarian scientist's attitude, and imagine vividly that the world of sensations and of scientific laws and objects may be all. But whenever I do this, I hear that inward monitor of which W. K. Clifford once wrote, whispering the word 'bosh!' Humbug is humbug, even though it bear the scientific name, and the total expression of human experience, as I view it objectively, invincibly urges me beyond the narrow 'scientific' bounds. Assuredly, the real world is of a different temperament,—more intricately built than physical science allows. So my objective and my subjective conscience both hold me to the over-belief which I express. Who knows whether the faithfulness of individuals here below to their own poor over-beliefs may not actually help God in turn to be more effectively faithful to his own greater tasks?

XII

WALTER RAUSCHENBUSCH

Champion of the Social Gospel

Walter Rauschenbusch (1861–1918)[1] is generally regarded as the personification of the Social Gospel in America. H. Shelton Smith goes further to assert that he was "the foremost molder of American Christian thought in his generation." Winthrop H. Hudson, on the other hand, depicts him as a "lonely prophet" whose thought "ran counter to the prevailing tendencies of the time." These statements may perhaps be harmonized with the observation that Rauschenbusch moved from relative obscurity to national prominence during the very years when a pervasive social awakening occurred in the Protestant churches; and that his combination of liberal theology and ethical theory won extremely widespread acceptance among those who made the Social Gospel a powerful force in American life. His outrage and compassion, moreover, aroused the social conscience of many who could not share his views of the Church, the Kingdom, or the Christian faith.

The significance of Rauschenbusch, therefore, is very great. He was an exceptionally forceful expositor of the Ritschlian theology, which during his lifetime was at the height of its influence throughout the Protestant world. He is thus a major example of religious liberalism. But he was also a hard-headed, creative, and undoctrinaire social theorist, who went beyond outrage and com-

---

[1] See Introduction, pp. 73–77.

passion, beyond generalities and truisms, to penetrating criticism of the social order. Finally, and especially in his last years, he revised his earlier confidence in human progress, and with his doctrine of a "Kingdom of Evil" made clear that he discerned an intrenched adversary to his gospel. If this awareness had been more widely appropriated during the 1920's, the Social Gospel movement might have been better prepared for the cataclysms that awaited it "just around the corner."

Rauschenbusch was born in Rochester, New York, where his father was a professor in the "German Department" of the Baptist Theological Seminary. He received his preparatory education at a gymnasium in Germany, but returned to Rochester for his college and divinity degrees. From 1886 until 1897, when he joined the faculty of the Rochester Seminary, he served as pastor of a German Baptist Church on New York's West Side. Here, in the proximity of Hell's Kitchen, he learned the meaning of urban woe, and this experience soon had deep spiritual and institutional consequences. In 1892 he and a few Baptist minister-friends organized the Brotherhood of the Kingdom, which, with the passing years, grew in both size and influence. He also played an active role in awakening his own denomination to the social problems of the day. By 1907, when the publication of CHRISTIANITY AND THE SOCIAL CRISIS brought him nationwide recognition, Rauschenbusch became convinced that the pietism of his early years had little bearing on what was most urgent in the world. He insisted that "religion and ethics are inseparable, and that ethical conduct is the supreme and sufficient religious act." The Church, he believed, was an instrument for the propagation of the teachings of Jesus. The doctrine of the "Kingdom of God on earth" had become his principal basis for making Christianity essentially a social ethic. The years that followed led to further publication and widening influence, despite the difficulties and sorrow that the war with Germany *occasioned.* In 1910 his PRAYERS OF THE SOCIAL AWAKENING appeared; his CHRISTIANIZING THE SOCIAL ORDER (1912) was devoted largely to social analysis. In 1916 he published an interchurch study-text for the laity, THE SOCIAL PRINCIPLES OF JESUS, which was probably read by more people than any of his other books; and finally in the year before his death, his Taylor Lectures, A THEOLOGY OF THE SOCIAL GOSPEL (1917), were delivered at Yale.

Rauschenbusch's place in the history of American theology is secured chiefly by his first book. It appeared at a most propitious moment, attained great influence, and best expressed the genius of its author. It was crucially augmented, however, by his last book, which both by its nature and content has stood the test of time much more effectively. The selections that follow, therefore, are taken from these two books. In the Introduction to CHRISTIANITY AND THE SOCIAL CRISIS he explains his own motivation and outlines the argument of the book. In Chapter II he expounds the "gospel" of the Social Gospel, the animating basis for everything he felt Christians ought to be doing about the social order and the central biblical argument for his entire position. In Chapter VIII of A THEOLOGY OF THE SOCIAL GOSPEL he explains his concept of the "Super-personal forces of evil" on which his theological reputation as a social realist chiefly rests.

CHRISTIANITY AND THE SOCIAL CRISIS

Introduction

Western civilization is passing through a social revolution unparalleled in history for scope and power. Its coming was inevi-

---

From Walter Rauschenbusch, *Christianity and the Social Crisis* (New York: The Macmillan Company, 1907), pp. xi–xv, 44–92. Reprinted with the permission of the publisher.

table. The religious, political, and intellectual revolutions of the past five centuries, which together created the modern world, necessarily had to culminate in an economic and social revolution such as is now upon us.

By universal consent, this social crisis is the overshadowing problem of our generation. The industrial and commercial life of the advanced nations are in the throes of it. In politics all issues and methods are undergoing upheaval and re-alignment as the social movement advances. In the world of thought all the young and serious minds are absorbed in the solution of the social problems. Even literature and art point like compass-needles to this magnetic pole of all our thought.

The social revolution has been slow in reaching our country. We have been exempt, not because we had solved the problems, but because we had not yet confronted them. We have now arrived, and all the characteristic conditions of American life will henceforth combine to make the social struggle here more intense than anywhere else. The vastness and the free sweep of our concentrated wealth on the one side, the independence, intelligence, moral vigor, and political power of the common people on the other side, promise a long-drawn grapple of contesting forces which may well make the heart of every American patriot sink within him.

It is realized by friend and foe that religion can play, and must play, a momentous part in this irrepressible conflict.

The Church, the organized expression of the religious life of the past, is one of the most potent institutions and forces in Western civilization. Its favor and moral influence are wooed by all parties. It cannot help throwing its immense weight on one side or the other. If it tries not to act, it thereby acts; and in any case its choice will be decisive for its own future.

Apart from the organized Church, the religious spirit is a factor of incalculable power in the making of history. In the idealistic spirits that lead and in the masses that follow, the religious spirit always intensifies thought, enlarges hope, un-fetters daring, evokes the willingness to sacrifice, and gives coherence in the fight. Under the warm breath of religious faith, all social institutions become plastic. The religious spirit re-moves mountains and tramples on impossibilities. Unless the economic and intellectual factors are strongly reënforced by religious enthusiasm, the whole social movement may prove abortive, and the New Era may die before it comes to birth.

It follows that the relation between Christianity and the social crisis is one of the most pressing questions for all intelligent men who realize the power of religion, and most of all for the reli-gious leaders of the people who give direction to the forces of religion.

The question has, in fact, been discussed frequently and ear-nestly, but it is plain to any thoughtful observer that the com-mon mind of the Christian Church in America has not begun to arrive at any solid convictions or any permanent basis of action. The conscience of Christendom is halting and groping, per-plexed by contradicting voices, still poorly informed on essen-tial questions, justly reluctant to part with the treasured maxims of the past, and yet conscious of the imperious call of the future.

This book is to serve as a contribution to this discussion. Its first chapters are historical, for nothing is more needed than a true comprehension of past history if we are to forecast the future correctly and act wisely in the present. I have tried to set forth the religious development of the prophets of Israel, the life and teachings of Jesus, and the dominant tendencies of primitive Christianity, in order to ascertain what was the origi-nal and fundamental purpose of the great Christian movement in history. Every discussion of the question which appeals to history has to cover this ground, but usually only detached frag-ments of the material are handled at all, and often without in-sight adequate to give their true meaning even to these frag-ments. I am in hopes that these chapters will contribute some facts and points of view that have not yet become common property.[1]

The outcome of these first historical chapters is that the essential purpose of Christianity was to transform human society into the kingdom of God by regenerating all human relations and reconstituting them in accordance with the will of God. The fourth chapter raises the question why the Christian Church has never undertaken to carry out this fundamental purpose of its existence. I have never met with any previous attempt to give a satisfactory historical explanation of this failure, and I regard this chapter as one of the most important in the book.

The fifth chapter sets forth the conditions which constitute the present social crisis and which imperatively demand of Christianity that contribution of moral and religious power which it was destined to furnish.

The sixth chapter points out that the Church, as such, has a stake in the social movement. The Church owns property, needs income, employs men, works on human material, and banks on its moral prestige. Its present efficiency and future standing are bound up for weal or woe with the social welfare of the people and with the outcome of the present struggle.

The last chapter suggests what contributions Christianity can make and in what main directions the religious spirit should exert its force.

In covering so vast a field of history and in touching on such a multitude of questions, error and incompleteness are certain, and the writer can claim only that he has tried to do honest

---

[1] Chapter I stated its thesis in the title: "The Historical Roots of Christianity: The Hebrew Prophets." The background for the prophetic demands of Jesus is provided. For his interpretation Rauschenbusch expressed deep indebtedness to the Scottish scholar, George Adam Smith (1856–1942), especially his two-volume contribution to The Expositors Bible, *The Book of the Twelve Prophets* (New York: A. C. Armstrong & Son, 1896–1898). See also by Smith, *Modern Criticism and the Preaching of the Old Testament* (New York: A. C. Armstrong & Son, 1901). [Ed.]

work. Moreover, it is impossible to handle questions so vital to the economic, the social, and the moral standing of great and antagonistic classes of men, without jarring precious interests and convictions, and without giving men the choice between the bitterness of social repentance and the bitterness of moral resentment. I can frankly affirm that I have written with malice toward none and with charity for all. Even where I judge men to have done wrong, I find it easy to sympathize with them in the temptations which made the wrong almost inevitable, and in the points of view in which they intrench themselves to save their self-respect. I have tried—so far as erring human judgment permits—to lift the issues out of the plane of personal selfishness and hate, and to put them where the white light of the just and pitying spirit of Jesus can play upon them. If I have failed in that effort, it is my sin. If others in reading fail to respond in the same spirit, it is their sin. In a few years all our restless and angry hearts will be quiet in death, but those who come after us will live in the world which our sins have blighted or which our love of right has redeemed. Let us do our thinking on these great questions, not with our eyes fixed on our bank account, but with a wise outlook on the fields of the future and with the consciousness that the spirit of the Eternal is seeking to distil from our lives some essence of righteousness before they pass away.

I have written this book to discharge a debt. For eleven years I was pastor among the working people on the West Side of New York City. I shared their life as well as I then knew, and used up the early strength of my life in their service. In recent years my work has been turned into other channels, but I have never ceased to feel that I owe help to the plain people who were my friends. If this book in some far-off way helps to ease the pressure that bears them down and increases the forces that bear them up, I shall meet the Master of my life with better confidence.

The Social Aims of Jesus

THE NEW SOCIAL INSIGHT INTO THE GOSPEL[2]

A man was walking through the woods in springtime. The air was thrilling and throbbing with the passion of little hearts, with the love-wooing, the parent pride, and the deadly fear of the birds. But the man never noticed that there was a bird in the woods. He was a botanist and was looking for plants.

A man was walking through the streets of a city, pondering the problems of wealth and national well-being. He saw a child sitting on the curbstone and crying. He met children at play. He saw a young mother with her child and an old man with his grandchild. But it never occurred to him that little children are the foundation of society, a chief motive power in economic effort, the most influential teachers, the source of the purest pleasures, the embodiment of form and color and grace. The man had never had a child and his eyes were not opened.

A man read through the New Testament. He felt no vibration of social hope in the preaching of John the Baptist and in the shouts of the crowd when Jesus entered Jerusalem. He caught no revolutionary note in the Book of Revelation. The social movement had not yet reached him. Jesus knew human nature when he reiterated: "He that hath ears to hear, let him hear."

We see in the Bible what we have been taught to see there. We drop out great sets of facts from our field of vision. We read other things into the Bible which are not there. During the Middle Ages men thought they saw their abstruse scholastic

---

2 Those who read only English are fortunate in having at their command two excellent books on the subject of this chapter: *Jesus Christ and the Social Question* by Professor Francis G. Peabody of Harvard (New York: The Macmillan Company, 1900) and *The Social Teaching of Jesus* by Professor Shailer Mathews of the University of Chicago (New York: The Macmillan Company, 1897). The former is very sympathetic in its treatment; the latter perhaps more incisive in its methods.

philosophy and theology amid the simplicity of the gospels. They found in the epistles the priests and bishops whom they knew, with robe and tonsure, living a celibate life and obeying the pope. When the Revival of Learning taught men to read all books with literary appreciation and historic insight, many things disappeared from the Bible for their eyes, and new things appeared. A new language was abroad and the Bible began to speak that language. If the Bible was not a living power before the Reformation, it was not because the Bible was chained up and forbidden, as we are told, but because their minds were chained by preconceived ideas, and when they read, they failed to read.

We are to-day in the midst of a revolutionary epoch fully as thorough as that of the Renaissance and Reformation. It is accompanied by a reinterpretation of nature and of history. The social movement has helped to create the modern study of history. Where we used to see a panorama of wars and strutting kings and court harlots, we now see the struggle of the people to wrest a living from nature and to shake off their oppressors. The new present has created a new past.[3] The French Revolution was the birth of modern democracy, and also of the modern school of history.

The Bible shares in that new social reinterpretation. The stories of the patriarchs have a new lifelikeness when they are read in the setting of primitive social life. There are texts and allusions in the New Testament which had been passed by as of slight significance; now they are like windows through which we see miles of landscape. But it is a slow process. The men who write commentaries are usually of ripe age and their lines of interest were fixed before the social movement awoke men. They follow the traditions of their craft and deal with the same

---

[3] Rauschenbusch was professionally a church historian and the historical outlook was a vital element of his thought. See his essay "The Influence of Historical Studies on Theology," *American Journal of Theology*, XI (1907), 111–127. [Ed.]

questions that engaged their predecessors. Eminent theologians, like other eminent thinkers, live in the social environment of wealth and to that extent are slow to see. The individualistic conception of religion is so strongly fortified in theological literature and ecclesiastical institutions that its monopoly cannot be broken in a hurry. It will take a generation or two for the new social comprehension of religion to become common property.

The first scientific life of Christ was written in 1829 by Karl Hase.[4] Christians had always bowed in worship before their Master, but they had never undertaken to understand his life in its own historical environment and his teachings in the sense in which Jesus meant them to be understood by his hearers. He had stood like one of his pictures in Byzantine art, splendid against its background of gold, but unreal and unhuman. Slowly, and still with many uncertainties in detail, his figure is coming out of the past to meet us. He has begun to talk to us as he did to his Galilean friends, and the better we know Jesus, the more social do his thoughts and aims become.

JESUS NOT A SOCIAL REFORMER

Under the influence of this new historical study of Christ, and under the pressure of the intense new social interest in contemporary life, the pendulum is now swinging the other way. Men are seizing on Jesus as the exponent of their own social convictions. They all claim him. "He was the first socialist." "Nay, he was a Tolstoian anarchist." "Not at all; he was an upholder of law and order, a fundamental opponent of the closed shop." It is a great tribute to his power over men and to the many-sidedness of his thought that all seek shelter in his great shadow.

But in truth Jesus was not a social reformer of the modern type. Sociology and political economy were just as far outside of his range of thought as organic chemistry or the geography

---

[4] Karl Hase (1800–1890) is mentioned here only as a pioneer. His long-popular handbook on Jesus was of small aid to Rauschenbusch. [Ed.]

of America. He saw the evil in the life of men and their sufferings, but he approached these facts purely from the moral, and not from the economic or historical point of view. He wanted men to live a right life in common, and only in so far as the social questions are moral questions did he deal with them as they confronted him.

And he was more than a teacher of morality. Jesus had learned the greatest and deepest and rarest secret of all—how to live a religious life.[5] When the question of economic wants is solved for the individual and all his outward adjustments are as comfortable as possible, he may still be haunted by the horrible emptiness of his life and feel that existence is a meaningless riddle and delusion. If the question of the distribution of wealth were solved for all society and all lived in average comfort and without urgent anxiety, the question would still be how many would be at peace with their own souls and have that enduring joy and contentment which alone can make the outward things fair and sweet and rise victorious over change. Universal prosperity would not be incompatible with universal *ennui* and *Weltschmerz.* Beyond the question of economic distribution lies the question of moral relations; and beyond the moral relations to men lies the question of the religious communion with that spiritual reality in which we live and move and have our deepest being—with God, the Father of our spirits. Jesus had realized the life of God in the soul of man and the life of man in the love of God. That was the real secret of his life, the well-spring of his purity, his compassion, his unwearied courage, his unquenchable idealism: he knew the Father. But if he had that greatest of all possessions, the real key to the secret of life, it was his highest social duty to share it and help others to gain what he had. He had to teach men to live as children in the pres-

---

[5] German Baptist Pietism influenced Rauschenbusch greatly, and here as elsewhere he conceded the importance of the religious life, yet he remained ambivalent and uncertain as to the nature of true religion. His judgments of traditional piety became increasingly adverse. [Ed.]

ence of their Father, and no longer as slaves cringing before a despot. He had to show them that the ordinary life of selfishness and hate and anxiety and chafing ambition and covetousness is no life at all, and that they must enter into a new world of love and solidarity and inward contentment. There was no service that he could render to men which would equal that. All other help lay in concentric circles about that redemption of the spirit and flowed out from it.

No comprehension of Jesus is even approximately true which fails to understand that the heart of his heart was religion. No man is a follower of Jesus in the full sense who has not through him entered into the same life with God. But on the other hand no man shares his life with God whose religion does not flow out, naturally and without effort, into all relations of his life and reconstructs everything that it touches. Whoever uncouples the religious and the social life has not understood Jesus. Whoever sets any bounds for the reconstructive power of the religious life over the social relations and institutions of men, to that extent denies the faith of the Master.

HIS RELATION TO CONTEMPORARY MOVEMENTS

If we want to understand the real aims of Jesus, we must watch him in his relation to his own times. He was not a timeless religious teacher, philosophizing vaguely on human generalities. He spoke for his own age, about concrete conditions, responding to the stirrings of the life that surged about him. We must follow him in his adjustment to the tendencies of the time, in his affinity for some men and his repulsion of others. That is the method by which we classify and locate a modern thinker or statesman.

The Christian movement began with John the Baptist. All the evangelists so understood it.[6] John himself accepted Jesus as the one who was to continue and consummate his own work. Jesus

---

[6] Mark 1; Matthew 3; Luke 3; John 1.

linked John closely to himself. He paid tribute to the rugged bravery and power of the man, and asserted that the new religious era had begun with John as an era of strenuous movement and stir. "The Law and the prophets were until John; from that time the gospel of the kingdom of God is preached, and every man entereth violently into it."[7]

Both Jesus and the people generally felt that in John they had an incarnation of the spirit of the ancient prophets. He wore their austere garb; he shared their utter fearlessness, their ringing directness of speech, their consciousness of speaking an inward message of God. The substance of his message was also the same. It was the old prophetic demand for ethical obedience. He and his disciples fasted[8] and he taught them certain forms of prayer,[9] but in his recorded teaching to the people there is not a word about the customary ritual of religion, about increased Sabbath observance, about stricter washings and sacrifices, or the ordinary exercises of piety. He spoke only of repentance, of ceasing from wrongdoing. He hailed the professional exponents of religion who came to hear him, as a brood of snakes wriggling away from the flames of the judgment. He demolished the self-confidence of the Jew and his pride of descent and religious monopoly, just as Amos or Jeremiah did. If God wanted children of Abraham, they were cheap and easy to get; God could turn the pebbles of the Jordan valley into children of Abraham by the million. But what God wanted, and found hard to get, was men who would quit evil. Yet God was bound to get such and would destroy all others. Now was the time to repent and by the badge of baptism to enroll with the purified remnant.[10]

The people asked for details. What would repentance in-

---

[7] Luke 16:16; 7:18–35; Matthew 11:2–19.

[8] Matthew 11:18, 9:14.

[9] Luke 11:1.

[10] Matthew 3:5–12.

volve? "What then must we do?" He replied: "He that hath
two coats, let him share with him that hath none; and he that
hath food, let him do likewise."[11] The way to prepare for the
Messianic era and to escape the wrath of the Messiah was to
institute a brotherly life and to equalize social inequalities. If
John thus conceived of the proper preparation for the Messianic
salvation, how did he conceive of the Messianic era itself? Luke
records his advice to two special classes of men, the tax-gatherers and the soldiers. The tax-gatherers had used their legal
powers for grafting and lining their pockets with the excess ex-
torted from the people. The soldiers had used their physical
force for the same ends, like a New York policeman taking a
banana from the push-cart while the Italian tries to look pleasant. John told them to stop being parasites and to live on their
honest earnings.[12]

Would any preacher have defined repentance in these terms
if his eyes had not been open to the social inequality about him
and to the exploitation of the people by the representatives of
organized society? Luke characterized John's purpose by quoting the call of Isaiah to make ready the way of the Lord by
levelling down the hills and levelling up the valleys and making the crooked things straight.[13] John would not have been so
silent about the ordinary requirements of piety, and so terribly
emphatic in demanding the abolition of social wrongs, if he had
not felt that here were the real obstacles to the coming of the
kingdom of God. From this preaching, coupled with our general knowledge of the times, we can infer what his points of
view and his hopes and expectations were, and also what the
real spring of the remarkable popular movement was which he
initiated. It was the national hope of Israel that carried the multitudes into the desert to hear John. The judgment which he

---

[11] Luke 3:11.

[12] Luke 3:10–14.

[13] Isaiah 40:3–4; Luke 3:4–5. [Ed.]

proclaimed was not the individual judgment of later Christian theology, but the sifting of the Jewish people preparatory to establishing the renewed Jewish theocracy. The kingdom of God which he announced as close at hand was the old hope of the people, and that embraced the restoration of the Davidic kingdom, the reign of social justice, and the triumph of the true religion. John was a true descendant of the prophets in denying that Jewish descent constituted a claim to share in the good time coming. He put the kingdom on an ethical basis. But it was still a social hope and it required social morality. According to our evangelists the work of John came to an end because he had attacked Herod Antipas for his marriage with Herodias.[14] According to Josephus[15] it was because Herod feared the great influence of John over the people and wanted to forestall a revolutionary rising under his impulse. The two explanations are not incompatible. Josephus had very direct lines of information about John[16] and his intimation deserves the more weight because his book was written for a Roman audience and his general tendency was to pass with discreet silence the revolutionary tendencies in his people.

Now Jesus accepted John as the forerunner of his own work. It was the popular movement created by John which brought Jesus out of the seclusion of Nazareth. He received John's baptism as the badge of the new Messianic hope and repentance. His contact with John and the events at the Jordan were evidently of decisive importance in the progress of his own inner life and his Messianic consciousness. When he left the Jordan the power of his own mission was upon him. He took up the formula of John: "The kingdom of God has come nigh; repent!" He continued the same baptism. He drew his earliest and choic-

---

[14] Matthew 14:3–5.

[15] Josephus, *Antiquities* XVIII. 5, 2.

[16] Ernest Renan, *The Life of Jesus* (New York: Carleton, Publisher, 1864), pp. 152–153.

est disciples from the followers of John. When John was dead, some thought Jesus was John risen from the dead. He realized clearly the difference between the stern ascetic spirit of the Baptist and his own sunny trust and simple human love,[17] but to the end of his life he championed John and dared the Pharisees to deny his divine mission.[18] It seems impossible to assume that his own fundamental purpose, at least in the beginning of his ministry, was wholly divergent from that of John. In the main he shared John's national and social hope. His aim too was the realization of the theocracy.[19]

Moreover, in joining hands with John, Jesus clasped hands with the entire succession of the prophets with whom he classed John. Their words were his favorite quotations. Like them he disregarded or opposed the ceremonial elements of religion and insisted on the ethical. Like them he sided with the poor and oppressed. As Amos and Jeremiah foresaw the conflict of their people with the Assyrians and the Chaldeans, so Jesus foresaw his nation drifting toward the conflict with Rome, and like them he foretold disaster, the fall of the temple and of the holy city. That prophetic type of religion which we have tried to set forth in the previous chapter, and which constituted the chief religious heritage of his nation, had laid hold on Jesus and he had laid hold of it and had appropriated its essential spirit. In the poise and calm of his mind and manner, and in the love of his heart, he was infinitely above them all.[20] But the greatest of all prophets was still one of the prophets, and that large interest in the national and social life which had been inseparable from the religion of the prophets was part of his life too. The pre-

---

[17] Matthew 11:16–19; Mark 2:18–22.

[18] Mark 11:27–33.

[19] Theocracy is here used in its literal sense to mean the rule or the kingdom of God, not rule by ecclesiastical authorities. [Ed.]

[20] This superiority is beautifully expressed in Julius Wellhausen, *Israelitische und Jüdische Geschichte* (Berlin: Georg Reimer Verlag, 1901), chap. XXIV, "Das Evangelium."

sumption is that Jesus shared the fundamental religious purpose of the prophets. If any one asserts that he abandoned the collective hope and gave his faith solely to religious individualism, he will have to furnish express statements in which Jesus disavows the religious past of his people.

THE PURPOSE OF JESUS: THE KINGDOM OF GOD

The historical background which we have just sketched must ever be kept in mind in understanding the life and purpose of Jesus. He was not merely an initiator, but a consummator. Like all great minds that do not merely imagine Utopias, but actually advance humanity to a new epoch, he took the situation and material furnished to him by the past and moulded that into a fuller approximation to the divine conception within him. He embodied the prophetic stream of faith and hope. He linked his work to that of John the Baptist as the one contemporary fact to which he felt most inward affinity.

Jesus began his preaching with the call: "The time is fulfilled; the kingdom of God is now close at hand; repent and believe in the glad news."[21] The kingdom of God continued to be the centre of all his teaching as recorded by the synoptic gospels. His parables, his moral instructions, and his prophetic predictions all bear on that.

We have no definition of what he meant by the phrase. His audience needed no definition. It was then a familiar conception and phrase. The new thing was simply that this kingdom was at last on the point of coming.

We are not at all in that situation to-day. Any one who has tried to grasp the idea will have realized how vague and elusive it seems. It stands to-day for quite a catalogue of ideas.[22] To the ordinary reader of the Bible, "inheriting the kingdom of

---

[21] Mark 1:15.

[22] See the list of definitions in Shailer Mathews, *The Social Teaching of Jesus*, p. 53, note 1.

heaven" simply means being saved and going to heaven. For others it means the millennium. For some the organized Church; for others "the invisible Church." For the mystic it means the hidden life with God. The truth is that the idea in the sense in which Jesus and his audiences understood it almost completely passed out of Christian thought as soon as Christianity passed from the Jewish people and found its spiritual home within the great Graeco-Roman world. The historical basis for the idea was wanting there. The phrase was taken along, just as an emigrant will carry a water-jar with him; but the water from the well of Bethlehem evaporated and it was now used to dip water from the wells of Ephesus or from the Nile and Tiber. The Greek world cherished no such national religious hope as the prophets had ingrained in Jewish thought; on the other hand it was intensely interested in the future life for the individual, and in the ascetic triumph over flesh and matter. Thus the idea which had been the centre of Christ's thought was not at all the centre of the Church's thought, and even the comprehension of his meaning was lost and overlaid. Only some remnants of it persisted in the millennial hope and in the organic conception of the Church.

The historical study of our own day has made the first thorough attempt to understand this fundamental thought of Jesus in the sense in which he used it, but the results of this investigation are not at all completed. There are a hundred critical difficulties in the way of a sure and consistent interpretation that would be acceptable to all investigators. The limits of space and the purpose of this book will not permit me to do justice to the conflicting views.[23] I shall have to set down my own re-

---

23 Albert Schweitzer (1875–1965) had posed a wide array of these problems in 1906 with his epoch-making *Von Reimarus zu Wrede*, published in English as *The Quest of the Historical Jesus* (London: A. & C. Black, 1910; reprinted in paperback, New York: The Macmillan Company, 1961). Surveying a century of New Testament research, he challenged almost every image, concept, and conclusion expressed by Rauschenbusch, Pea-

sults with only an occasional reference to the difficulties that beset them.

We saw in the previous chapter that the hope of the Jewish people underwent changes in the course of its history.[24] It took a wider and more universal outlook as the political horizon of the people widened. It became more individual in its blessings. It grew more transcendent, more purely future, more apocalyptic and detached from present events, as the people were deprived of their political autonomy and health. Moreover it was variously understood by the different classes and persons that held it. Because this hope was so comprehensive and all-embracing, every man could select and emphasize that aspect which appealed to him. Some thought chiefly of the expulsion of the Roman power with its despotic officials, its tax-extorters, and its hated symbols. Others dwelt on the complete obedience to the Law which would prevail when all the apostates were cast out and all true Israelites gathered to their own. And some quiet religious souls hoped for a great outflow of grace from God and a revival of true piety; as the hymn of Zacharias expresses it: "that we, being delivered out of the hand of our enemies, should serve him without fear, in holiness and right-

---

body, and Mathews. After half a century the prospects for their type of interpretation has scarcely improved. See James M. Robinson, *A New Quest of the Historical Jesus* (Naperville, Ill.: Alec R. Allenson, Inc., 1959); Günther Bornkamm, *Jesus of Nazareth* (New York: Harper & Brothers, 1960); Carl E. Braaten and Roy A. Harrisville, eds., *The Historical Jesus and the Kerygmatic Christ* (Nashville, Tenn.: Abingdon Press, 1964), especially chapter 8 by Harrisville, "Representative American Lives of Jesus;" and Reginald H. Fuller, *Foundations of New Testament Christology* (New York: Charles Scribner's Sons, 1965). For over twenty years, however, Rauschenbusch's rendering was a basic element in the American Social Gospel. [Ed.]

[24] On the later Messianic hope of the Jewish people, see Shailer Mathews, *The Messianic Hope in the New Testament* (Chicago: University of Chicago Press, 1905); Emil Schürer, *A History of the Jewish People in the Time of Jesus Christ,* 5 vols. (New York: Charles Scribner's Sons, 1891), IV, Sect. 29; also V, Sect. 32, v.

eousness before him all our days."[25] But even in this spiritual
ideal the deliverance from the national enemies was a condition of a holy life for the nation. Whatever aspect any man
emphasized, it was still a national and collective idea. It involved the restoration of Israel as a nation to outward independence, security, and power, such as it had under the Davidic
kings. It involved that social justice, prosperity, and happiness
for which the Law and the prophets called, and for which the
common people always long. It involved that religious purity
and holiness of which the nation had always fallen short. And
all this was to come in an ideal degree, such as God alone by
direct intervention could bestow.

When Jesus used the phrase "the kingdom of God," it inevitably evoked that whole sphere of thought in the minds of
his hearers. If he did not mean by it the substance of what they
meant by it, it was a mistake to use the term. If he did not mean
the consummation of the theocratic hope, but merely an internal
blessedness for individuals with the hope of getting to heaven,
why did he use the words around which all the collective hopes
clustered? In that case it was not only a misleading but a dangerous phrase. It unfettered the political hopes of the crowd; it
drew down on him the suspicion of the government; it actually
led to his death.

Unless we have clear proof to the contrary, we must assume
that in the main the words meant the same thing to him and to
his audiences. But it is very possible that he seriously modified
and corrected the popular conception. That is in fact the process
with every great, creative religious mind: the connection with
the past is maintained and the old terms are used, but they are
set in new connections and filled with new qualities. In the
teaching of Jesus we find that he consciously opposed some
features of the popular hope and sought to make it truer.

For one thing he would have nothing to do with bloodshed

---

[25] Luke 1:74–75.

and violence. When the crowds that were on their way to the Passover gathered around him in the solitude on the Eastern shore of the lake and wanted to make him king and march on the capital, he eluded them by sending his inflammable disciples away in the boat, and himself going up among the rocks to pray till the darkness dispersed the crowd.[26] Alliance with the Messianic force-revolution was one of the temptations which he confronted at the outset and repudiated;[27] he would not set up God's kingdom by using the devil's means of hatred and blood. With the glorious idealism of faith and love Jesus threw away the sword and advanced on the intrenchments of wrong with hand outstretched and heart exposed.

He repudiated not only human violence, he even put aside the force which the common hope expected from heaven. He refused to summon the twelve legions of angels either to save his life or to set up the kingdom by slaying the wicked. John the Baptist had expected the activity of the Messiah to begin with the judgment. The fruitless tree would be hewn down; the chaff would be winnowed out and burned; and there was barely time to escape this.[28] Jesus felt no call to that sort of Messiahship. He reversed the programme; the judgment would come at the end and not at the beginning. First the blade, then the ear, and then the full corn in the ear, and at the very last the harvest. Only at the end would the tares be collected; only when the net got to shore would the good fish be separated from the useless creatures of the sea. Thus the divine *finale* of the judgment was relegated to the distance; the only task calling for present action was to sow the seed.[29]

The popular hope was all for a divine catastrophe. The kingdom of God was to come by a beneficent earthquake. Some day

---

[26] Matthew 14:22–23; John 6:14–15.

[27] Matthew 4:8–10.

[28] Matthew 3:10–12.

[29] The parables of Matthew 13; also Mark 4:26–29.

it would come like the blaze of a meteor, "with outward observation," and they could say: "Lo, there it is!"[30] We have
seen that the prophetic hope had become catastrophic and
apocalyptic when the capacity for political self-help was paralyzed. When the nation was pinned down helplessly by the
crushing weight of the oppressors, it had to believe in a divine
catastrophe that bore no causal relation to human action. The
higher spiritual insight of Jesus reverted to the earlier and nobler prophetic view that the future was to grow out of the present by divine help. While they were waiting for the Messianic
cataclysm that would bring the kingdom of God ready-made
from heaven, he saw it growing up among them. He took his illustrations of its coming from organic life. It was like the seed
scattered by the peasant, growing slowly and silently, night and
day, by its own germinating force and the food furnished by
the earth. The people had the impatience of the uneducated
mind which does not see processes, but clamors for results, big,
thunderous, miraculous results. Jesus had the scientific insight
which comes to most men only by training, but to the elect few
by divine gift. He grasped the substance of that law of organic
development in nature and history which our own day at last
has begun to elaborate systematically. His parables of the
sower, the tares, the net, the mustard-seed, and the leaven are
all polemical in character. He was seeking to displace the crude
and misleading catastrophic conceptions by a saner theory
about the coming of the kingdom. This conception of growth
demanded not only a finer insight, but a higher faith. It takes
more faith to see God in the little beginnings than in the completed results; more faith to say that God is now working than
to say that he will some day work.

Because Jesus believed in the organic growth of the new
society, he patiently fostered its growth, cell by cell. Every
human life brought under control of the new spirit which he

---

[30] Luke 17:20–21.

himself embodied and revealed was an advance of the kingdom of God. Every time the new thought of the Father and of the right life among men gained firmer hold of a human mind and brought it to the point of action, it meant progress. It is just as when human tissues have been broken down by disease or external force, and new tissue is silently forming under the old and weaving a new web of life. Jesus incarnated a new type of human life and he was conscious of that. By living with men and thinking and feeling in their presence, he reproduced his own life in others and they gained faith to risk this new way of living. This process of assimilation went on by the natural capacities inherent in the social organism, just as fresh blood will flow along the established arteries and capillaries. When a nucleus of like-minded men was gathered about him, the assimilating power was greatly reënforced. Jesus joyously felt that the most insignificant man in his company who shared in this new social spirit was superior to the grandest exemplification of the old era, John the Baptist.[31] Thus Jesus worked on individuals and through individuals, but his real end was not individualistic, but social, and in his method he employed strong social forces. He knew that a new view of life would have to be implanted before the new life could be lived and that the new society would have to nucleate around personal centres of renewal. But his end was not the new soul, but the new society; not man, but Man.

The popular hope was a Jewish national hope. Under the hands of Jesus it became human and therefore universal. John the Baptist had contradicted the idea that a Jew was entitled to participation in the good time coming by virtue of his national descent. Every time Jesus met a Gentile, we can see the Jewish prejudices melt away and he gladly discovered the human brotherhood and spiritual capacity in the alien. "Verily I say unto you, I have not found so great faith, no, not in Israel," and

---

[31] Matthew 11:11.

he immediately makes room at the Messianic table-round for those who shall come from the east and the west to sit down with the patriarchs, while the sons of the kingdom, the Jews who were properly entitled to it, would be cast out.[32] He reminded the indignant audience at Nazareth that the great Elijah had found his refuge with a heathen Phœnician and Elisha had healed only a Syrian leper.[33] When one leper out of ten thanked him, he took pains to point out that this one was a Samaritan foreigner,[34] and when he wanted to hold up a model of human neighborliness, he went out of his way to make him a Samaritan, an alien, and a heretic.[35] Thus the old division of humanity into Jews and Gentiles began to fade out in his mind, and a new dividing line ran between the good and the evil, between those who opened their heart to the new life and those who closed it. He approached the bold cosmopolitanism of Paul, that "in Christ Jesus there is neither Jew nor Greek."[36] But as soon as religion was thus based, not on national prerogatives, but on human needs and capacities, the kingdom of God became universal in scope, an affair of all humanity. This was a modification of immense importance.

Another subtle and significant change in the conception of the kingdom came through the combination of all these changes. If the kingdom was not dependent on human force nor on divine catastrophes, but could quietly grow by organic processes; if it was not dependent on national reconstruction, but could work along from man to man, from group to group, creating a new life as it went along; then the kingdom in one sense was already here. Its consummation, of course, was in the future, but its fundamental realities were already present.

---

[32] Matthew 8:10–12.

[33] Luke 4:23–30.

[34] Luke 17:11–19.

[35] Luke 10:25–37.

[36] Galatians 3:28.

This is the point on which scholars are most at odds. Was the kingdom in Christ's conception something eschatological, all in the future, to be inaugurated only by a heavenly catastrophe? Or was it a present reality? There is material for both views in his sayings. It is important here to remember that the sayings of Jesus were handed down by oral repetition among Christians for thirty or forty years before they were recorded in our gospels. But any one can test for himself the fact that with the best intentions of veracity, a message or story changes a little when it passes from one mind to another, or even when it is repeated often by the same man. Something of his tastes and presuppositions flows into it. Unless we assume an absolute divine prevention of any such change, we must allow that it is wholly probable that the Church which told and retold the sayings of Jesus insensibly moulded them by its own ideas and hopes. And if that is true, then no part of the sayings of Christ would be so sure to be affected as his sayings about his return and the final consummation of the kingdom. That was the hottest part of the faith of the primitive Church and anything coming in contact with it would run fluid. But any modifications on this question would all be likely to be in the direction of the catastrophic hope. That was the form of the Jewish hope before Christ touched it; he certainly did not succeed in weaning his disciples from it; it was the form most congenial to cruder minds; it chimed best with the fervid impatience of the earliest days; its prevalence is attested by the wide circulation of the Jewish apocalyptic literature among Christians. It is thus exceedingly probable that the Church spilled a little of the lurid colors of its own apocalypticism over the loftier conceptions of its Master, and when we read his sayings to-day, we must allow for that and be on the watch against it.

Like the old prophets, Jesus believed that God was the real creator of the kingdom; it was not to be set up by manmade evolution. It is one of the axioms of religious faith to believe that. He certainly believed in a divine consummation at the close. But the more he believed in the supreme value of its spiritual and moral blessings, and in the power of spiritual forces to mould human life, the more would the final act of consummation recede in importance and the present facts and processes grow more concrete and important to his mind. It was an act of religious faith for John the Baptist to assert that the long-desired kingdom was almost here. It was a vastly higher act of faith for Jesus to say that it was actually here. Others were scanning the horizon with the telescope to see it come; he said, "It is already here, right in the midst of you."[37] Any one who reversed the direction of his life and became as a child could enter into it.[38] Any one who saw that love to God and man was more than the whole sacrificial ritual was not far from the kingdom.[39] The healing power going out to the demonized was proof that a stronger one had come upon the lord of this world and was stripping him of his property, and that the kingdom was already come upon them.[40] Thus the future tense was changing to the present tense under the power of faith and insight into spiritual realities. In the gospel and epistle of John we have a confirmation of this translation of the future tense into the present. The expected antichrist is already here; the judgment is now quietly going on; the most important part of the resurrection is taking place now. The discourse about the future coming of the Lord in the Synoptists is replaced in John by the discourse about the immediate coming of the Comforter.[41]

This, then, is our interpretation of the situation. Jesus, like all the prophets and like all his spiritually minded countrymen, lived in the hope of a great transformation of the national, so-

---

37 Luke 17:21.

38 Matthew 18:1–4.

39 Mark 12:28–34.

40 Matthew 12:28.

41 I John 2:18; John 3:16–21, 5:19–29.

cial, and religious life about him. He shared the substance of
that hope with his people, but by his profounder insight and his
loftier faith he elevated and transformed the common hope. He
rejected all violent means and thereby transferred the inevitable
conflict from the field of battle to the antagonism of mind
against mind, and of heart against lack of heart. He postponed
the divine catastrophe of judgment to the dim distance and put
the emphasis on the growth of the new life that was now going
on. He thought less of changes made *en masse*, and more of the
immediate transformation of single centres of influence and of
social nuclei. The Jewish hope became a human hope with universal scope. The old intent gaze into the future was turned
to faith in present realities and beginnings, and found its task
here and now.

Luke says that the boy Jesus "advanced in wisdom and stature, and in favor with God and men"; that is, he grew in his
intellectual, physical, religious, and social capacities. It is contrary to faith in the real humanity of our Lord to believe that he
ever stopped growing. The story of his temptation is an account
of a forward leap in his spiritual insight when he faced the
problems of his Messianic task. When a growing and daring
mind puts his hand to a great work, his experiences in that
work are bound to enlarge and correct his conception of the
purpose and methods of the work. It is wholly in harmony with
any true conception of the life of Jesus to believe that his conception of the kingdom became vaster and truer as he worked
for the kingdom, and that he moved away from the inherited
conceptions along the lines which our study has suggested.

But after all this has been said, it still remained a social hope.
The kingdom of God is still a collective conception, involving
the whole social life of man. It is not a matter of saving human
atoms, but of saving the social organism. It is not a matter of
getting individuals to heaven, but of transforming the life on
earth into the harmony of heaven. If he put his trust in spiritual
forces for the founding of a righteous society, it only proved

his sagacity as a society-builder. If he began his work with the smallest social nuclei, it proved his patience and skill. But Jesus never fell into the fundamental heresy of later theology; he never viewed the human individual apart from human society; he never forgot the gregarious nature of man. His first appeal was to his nation. When they flocked about him and followed him in the early Galilean days, it looked as if by the sheer power of his spirit he would swing the national soul around to obey him, and he was happy. There must have been at least a possibility of that in his mind, for he counted it as guilt that the people failed to yield to him. He did not merely go through the motions of summoning the nation to fealty, knowing all the while that such a thing lay outside of his real plan. No one will understand the life of Jesus truly unless he has asked himself the question, What would have happened if the people as a whole had accepted the spiritual leadership of Jesus? The rejection of his reign involved the political doom of the Galilean cities and of Jerusalem;[42] would the acceptance of his reign have involved no political consequences? The tone of sadness in his later ministry was not due simply to the approach of his personal death, but to the consciousness that his purpose for his nation had failed. He began then to draw his disciples more closely about him and to create the nucleus of a new nation within the old; it was the best thing that remained for him to do, but he had hoped to do better. He also rose then to the conviction that he would return and accomplish in the future what he had hoped to accomplish during his earthly life. The hope of the Coming and the organization of the Church together enshrine the social element of Christianity; the one postpones it, the other partly realizes it. Both are the results of a faith that rose triumphant over death, and laid the foundations of a new commonwealth of God even before the old had been shaken to ruins.

---

[42] Matthew 11:20–24; Luke 19:41–44.

THE KINGDOM OF GOD AND THE ETHICS OF JESUS

All the teaching of Jesus and all his thinking centered about the hope of the kingdom of God. His moral teachings get their real meaning only when viewed from that centre. He was not a Greek philosopher or Hindu pundit teaching the individual the way of emancipation from the world and its passions, but a Hebrew prophet preparing men for the righteous social order. The goodness which he sought to create in men was always the goodness that would enable them to live rightly with their fellow-men and to constitute a true social life.

All human goodness must be social goodness. Man is fundamentally gregarious and his morality consists in being a good member of his community. A man is moral when he is social; he is immoral when he is anti-social. The highest type of goodness is that which puts freely at the service of the community all that a man is and can. The highest type of badness is that which uses up the wealth and happiness and virtue of the community to please self. All this ought to go without saying, but in fact religious ethics in the past has largely spent its force in detaching men from their community, from marriage and property, from interest in political and social tasks.

The fundamental virtue in the ethics of Jesus was love, because love is the society-making quality. Human life originates in love. It is love that holds together the basal human organization, the family. The physical expression of all love and friendship is the desire to get together and be together. Love creates fellowship. In the measure in which love increases in any social organism, it will hold together without coercion. If physical coercion is constantly necessary, it is proof that the social organization has not evoked the power of human affection and fraternity.

Hence when Jesus prepared men for the nobler social order of the kingdom of God, he tried to energize the faculty and habits of love and to stimulate the dormant faculty of devotion to the common good. Love with Jesus was not a flickering and wayward emotion, but the highest and most steadfast energy of a will bent on creating fellowship.

The force of that unitive will is best seen where fellowship is in danger of disruption. If a man has offended us, that fact is not to break up our fraternity, but we must forgive and forgive and forgive, and always stand ready to repair the torn tissues of fellowship.[43] If we remember that we have offended and our brother is now alienated from us, we are to drop everything, though it be the sacrifice we are just offering in the temple, and go and re-create fellowship.[44] If a man hates us or persecutes and reviles us, we must refuse to let fraternity be ruined, and must woo him back with love and blessings.[45] If he smites us in the face, we must turn the other cheek instead of doubling the barrier by returning the blow.[46] These are not hard and fast laws or detached rules of conduct. If they are used as such, they become unworkable and ridiculous. They are simply the most emphatic expressions of the determination that the fraternal relation which binds men together must not be ruptured. If a child can be saved from its unsocial self-will only by spanking it, parental love will have to apply that medicine. If a rough young fellow will be a happier member of society for being knocked down, we must knock him down and then sit down beside him and make a social man of him. The law of love transcends all other laws. It does not stop where they stop, and occasionally it may cut right across their beaten tracks. When Mary of Bethany broke the alabaster jar of ointment, the disciples voiced the ordinary law of conduct: it was wasteful luxury; the money might have fed the poor. Jesus took her side. While the disciples were thinking of the positions they were to get when their master became king, her feminine intui-

---

43 Matthew 18:21–22.

44 Matthew 5:23–24.

45 Matthew 5:43–48.

46 Matthew 5:38–42.

tion had seen the storm-cloud lowering over his head and had heard the mute cry for sympathy in his soul, and had given him the best she had in the abandonment of love. "This is a beautiful deed that she has done." The instinct of love had been a truer guide of conduct than all machine-made rules of charity.[47]

Jesus was very sociable. He was always falling into conversation with people, sometimes in calm disregard of the laws of propriety. When his disciples returned to him at the well of Samaria, they were surprised to find him talking with a woman![48] Society had agreed to ostracize certain classes, for instance the tax-collectors. Jesus refused to recognize such a partial negation of human society. He accepted their invitations to dinner and invited himself to their houses, thereby incurring the sneer of the respectable as a friend of publicans and a glutton and wine-drinker.[49] He wanted men to live as neighbors and brothers and he set the example. Social meals are often referred to in the gospels and furnished him the illustrations for much of his teaching.[50] His meals with his disciples had been so important a matter in their life that they continued them after his death. His manner in breaking the bread for them all had been so characteristic that they recognized him by it after his resurrection.[51] One of the two great ritual acts in the Church grew out of his last social meal with his friends. If we have ever felt how it brings men together to put their feet under the same table, we shall realize that in these elements of Christ's life a new communal sociability was working its way and creating a happy human society, and Jesus refused to surrender so great an attainment to the ordinary laws of fasting.[52]

Pride disrupts society. Love equalizes. Humility freely takes its place as a simple member of the community. When Jesus

---

[47] Mark 14:3–9.
[48] John 4:27.
[49] Matthew 11:19.
[50] Luke 14.
[51] Luke 24:30–31.
[52] Mark 2:18–19.

found the disciples disputing about their rank in the kingdom, he rebuked their divisive spirit of pride by setting a little child among them as their model;[53] for an unspoiled child is the most social creature, swift to make friends, happy in play with others, lonely without human love. When Jesus overheard the disciples quarrelling about the chief places at the last meal, he gave them a striking object lesson in the subordination of self to the service of the community, by washing their dusty sandalled feet.[54]

All these acts and sayings receive their real meaning when we think of them in connection with the kingdom of God, the ideal human society to be established. Instead of a society resting on coercion, exploitation, and inequality, Jesus desired to found a society resting on love, service, and equality. These new principles were so much the essence of his character and of his view of life, that he lived them out spontaneously and taught them in everything that he touched in his conversations or public addresses. God is a father; men are neighbors and brothers; let them act accordingly. Let them love, and then life will be true and good. Let them seek the kingdom, and all things would follow. Under no circumstance let them suffer fellowship to be permanently disrupted. If an individual or a class was outside of fraternal relations, he set himself to heal the breach. The kingdom of God is the true human society; the ethics of Jesus taught the true social conduct which would create the true society. This would be Christ's test for any custom, law, or institution: does it draw men together or divide them?

INSISTENCE ON CONDUCT
AND INDIFFERENCE TO RITUAL

In our study of the Old Testament prophets, we saw that indifference or hostility to ritual religion was a characteristic of

---

[53] Mark 9:33–37.
[54] Luke 22:24–30; John 13:1–20.

prophetic religion, and that this turned the full power of the religious impulse into the sluice of ethical conduct. Jesus was a successor of the prophets in this regard.

He used the temple as a place to meet men. He valued the temple as a house of prayer and fiercely resented the intrusion of the money-making spirit within it.[55] But otherwise it was of no religious importance to him. According to the Gospel of John he foretold a stage of religion in which the old burning issue of the true place of worship would be antiquated and dead.[56] Stephen, who understood Jesus better than most of the apostles, had scant reverence for the temple.[57] The temple sacrifices are mentioned by Jesus only to say that the duty of fraternal reconciliation takes precedence of the duty of proceeding with sacrificial ritual.[58] . . .

This revolutionary attitude to inherited religion, which so jarred the earnest and painstaking representatives of traditional piety, is explained by Christ's conception of the kingdom of God. They thought it was a Jewish affair and would rest on careful religious observances. He thought it was a human affair and would rest on right human relations. He would tolerate nothing that hallowed wrong, not even religion. He had no patience with religious thought which hampered the attainment of a right social life. To them the written Law inherited from the past was the supreme thing; to Jesus the better human life to be established in the future was the supreme thing.

HIS TEACHING ON WEALTH

Like all the greatest spiritual teachers of mankind, Jesus realized a profound danger to the better self in the pursuit of wealth. Whoever will watch the development of a soul that has

---

[55] Mark 11:15–19.

[56] John 4:19–24.

[57] Acts 6:14; 7:44–50.

[58] Matthew 5:23–24.

bent its energies to the task of becoming rich, can see how perilous the process is to the finer sense of justice, to the instinct of mercy and kindness and equality, and to the singleness of devotion to higher ends; in short, to all the higher humanity in us. It is a simple fact: "Ye cannot serve God and mammon;" each requires the best of a man. "The cares of this life and the deceitfulness of riches"—note that quality of deceitfulness— will choke the good seed like rank weeds which appropriate soil and sunshine for their own growth.[59] When a man lays up treasure, his heart almost inevitably is with his treasure. Then gradually the inner light in him is darkened; the eye of his conscience is filmed and blurred.[60] Wealth is apt to grow stronger than the man who owns it. It owns him and he loses his moral and spiritual freedom. The spirit of the world is always deluding men into thinking that "a man's life consisteth in the abundance of things that he possesseth,"[61] but when he builds his life on that theory, he is lost to the kingdom of God. And the worst of it is that he does not know it. The harlot and the drunkard have their hours of remorse and self-abasement; the covetous man does not even know that he is on the downward way. Saint Francis Xavier, the noble Jesuit missionary, said that in the confessional men had confessed to him all sins that he knew and some that he had never imagined, but none had ever of his own accord confessed that he was covetous.

But Jesus did not fear riches merely as a narcotic soul-poison. In his desire to create a true human society he encountered riches as a prime divisive force in actual life. It wedges society apart in horizontal strata between which real fellow-feeling is paralyzed. It lifts individuals out of the wholesome dependence on their fellows and equally out of the full sense of responsibility to them. That is the charm of riches and their curse.

---

[59] Matthew 13:22.

[60] Matthew 6:19–34.

[61] Luke 12:15.

This is the key to the conversation of Jesus with the rich young man, who was so honestly and lovably anxious to have a share in the Messianic salvation.[62] He could truthfully say that he had lived a good life. Jesus accepted his statement, but if he would be perfect, he bade him get rid of his wealth and join the company of the disciples. This demand has been understood either as a test or as a cure. Some think that it was merely a test; if he had consented to give up his wealth, it would not have been necessary to give it up. Some think it was a cure for the love of money which was really needed in this exceptional case. On either supposition the advice concerned merely this young man's soul; it was medicine to be swallowed by him for his own good alone. But Jesus immediately rises from this concrete case to the general assertion that it is hard for any rich man to enter the kingdom of God, harder than for a camel to wedge through the eye of a needle. The young man who was departing with clouded face was simply a demonstration of a general fact. Clearly here was a case where the heart was anchored to its treasure.

The solution for this "hard saying" has been sought in the remark quoted only in Mark: "How hard it is for them that *trust* in riches to enter the kingdom." A man may have riches safely, if only he will not trust in them for salvation. It is easy to satisfy that requirement. But unfortunately the best manuscripts do not contain the phrase about trusting. The critical editions of the Greek text drop it or place it in the margin.[63] Some early copyist probably felt as anxious to dull the sharpness of the saying as some modern preachers.

The solution lies in another direction. We think of the salvation of the individual in the life to come, and find it hard that so fine a young fellow should be barred out of heaven because

---

[62] Mark 10:17–31.

[63] Mark 10:24. The Revised Standard Version omits the phrase, "for them that trust in riches," from the text proper. [Ed.]

he was rich. Jesus was thinking of the righteous society on earth which he was initiating and of the young man's fitness for that. Suppose the young man had kept his property and had thus joined the discipleship. How would that have affected the spirit of the group? Would not the others have felt jealously that he was in a class by himself? If Jesus had shown him favor, would not even the Master's motives have been suspected? If he had replenished the common purse from his private wealth, it would have given them a more opulent living; it would have attracted selfish men and would have paralyzed the influence of Jesus on the poor. Then the crowds would have been at his heels, not merely for healing, but for the loaves and fishes—with dessert added. Judas would have been deeply pleased with such a reënforcement of the apostolate, but Jesus would have gone through the same sorrow which came upon Francis of Assisi when property was forced upon his Order and its early spirit was corrupted. It is all very well to say that rich and poor are alike in Christ, but in fact only exceptional characters, like Jesus himself, can sit at a rich man's table and be indifferent to the fact that he is rich. Others can forget it for a while under the pressure of a great common danger or sorrow or joy, but in general the sense of equality will prevail only where substantial equality exists. The presence of the rich young man would have been ruinous to the spirit of the discipleship and would have put a debased interpretation on the hope of the kingdom. Jesus did not ask him to hand over his property for the common purse, as the Church in later times did constantly, but simply to turn it back to social usefulness and come down to the common level.

The meeting of Jesus and the rich young man has often been painted, but always as a private affair between the man and Jesus. At the St. Louis Exposition there was a painting representing Jesus sitting in a barnlike building with a group of plain people about him, women, old men, and the disciples. Before him stands the young man richly dressed, a bird of very different feather. Jesus by his gesture is evidently drawing in the listening group. It was not a matter between the man and God, but between the man and God and the people. The theological interpretations of the passage, like the artistic, have failed to take account of this third factor in the moral situation. If the kingdom of God is the true human society, it is a fellowship of justice, equality, and love. But it is hard to get riches with justice, to keep them with equality, and to spend them with love. The kingdom of God means normal and wholesome human relations, and it is exceedingly hard for a rich man to be in normal human relations to others, as many a man has discovered who has honestly tried. It can be done only by an act of renunciation in some form.

It gives a touch of cheerful enjoyment to exegetical studies to watch the athletic exercises of interpreters when they confront these sayings of Jesus about wealth. They find it almost as hard to get around the needle's eye as the camel would find it to get through. The resources of philology have been ransacked to turn the "camel" into an anchor-rope, and Oriental antiquarian lore has been summoned to prove that the "needle's eye" was a little rear-gate of the Oriental house through which the camel, by judiciously going down on its knees, could work its way. There is a manifest solicitude to help the rich man through. There has not been a like fraternal anxiety for the Pharisee; he is allowed to swallow his camel whole.[64] In the case of the parable of the unjust steward, there are something like thirty-six different interpretations on record.[65] They differ so widely in their allegorical explanations that we are left in doubt if the lord of the steward is God or the devil. Yet the parable seems simple if one is not afraid of breaking crockery by handling it as Jesus did.

A rich man had farmed out his lands to various tenants on

---

[64] Matthew 23:24.

[65] Luke 16:1–9. [Rauschenbusch's "social gospel explanation" should be noted carefully. Ed.]

shares. A steward managed the whole and collected the rents. His master became suspicious of him and gave him notice of dismissal. It would take effect as soon as his accounts were made up. The steward confronted a painful situation. He looked at his white hands and concluded that manual labor was not in his line. His social pride would not permit him to beg. So he concluded, as others have done, to "graft." He used the brief term of authority still left him to get on the right side of the tenant farmers by reducing on paper the amount of their harvests and consequently of the shares due to the proprietor. He could hope to enjoy their comfortable hospitality for some time in return for the substantial present he made them out of his master's pocket. In fact they would have to "stand in" with their confederate to keep him silent. When his master learned of it, he could not help admiring the cleverness of the rascal, even though it was at his expense.

Jesus too admired the shrewdness and foresight which the men of the present social order exhibit within their plane of life. If only the children of light would be as wise in theirs! His application is that the men who hold the dishonest money of the present era will do well to use the brief term of power left to them before the Messianic era begins. Let them do kindness to the children of the kingdom, and they may hope by their gratitude to get some sort of borrowed shelter when the situation is reversed and the pious poor are on top.

The story shows a very keen insight into the contemporary methods of grafting and into the state of mind of the grafter. No one could have told the story who had not thought incisively about social conditions. Interpreters have found it necessary to defend Jesus because he holds up an immoral transaction for admiration and imitation. Probably Jesus never imagined that a teacher of his well-known bent of mind would be supposed to approve of financial trickery. It is precisely because he was so completely outside of and above this whole realm of dealing that he could play with the material as he did, just as a confirmed socialist might use the watering of stock or the "promotion" of a mining company as an illustration of the beauties of socialism. It is hard to imagine Jesus without a smile of sovereign humor in advising these great men to get a plank ready for the coming deluge.

The parable of the steward has often been so allegorized and spiritualized that the application to the rich has almost evaporated. His contemporary hearers saw the point. "The Pharisees, who were lovers of money, heard all these things and they scoffed at him." The Greek verb means literally: "they turned up their nose at him."[66] Jesus replied to their scoff by telling the story of Dives and Lazarus.[67] It was not intended to give information about the future life. Its sting is in the reference to the five brothers of Dives, who were living as he had lived and were in imminent peril of faring as he fared. They were the men who refused to do what the parable of the steward advised them to do.

There is a notable difference between our gospels in regard to the amount of teaching on wealth which they report, and in regard to the sharpness of edge which it bears. The Gospel of John is at one extreme; we should hardly know that Jesus had any interest in questions of property if we had only the fourth gospel. There the centre of his teaching is not the kingdom of God, but the eternal life; his interests are religious and theological. The divine figure of the Son of God moves through the doubts and discussions of men like the silver moon sailing serene through the clouds. Luke is at the other extreme.[68] He alone

---

[66] Luke 16:14.

[67] Luke 16:19–21.

[68] Few biblical scholars before or since have seen Luke's undeniable interest in the poor as warrant for considering him a "socialist" as Rauschenbusch does in these several paragraphs. He is apparently much indebted to the works of Peabody (pp. 191–202) and Mathews (pp. 140–157) cited in note 2, p. 538. Cf. Ernest F. Scott, *The Literature of the New Testament* (New York: Columbia University Press, 1932), pp. 84–87. [Ed.]

570 Theology In America

reports the parables of the rich fool, the unjust steward, and Dives and Lazarus. He also gives a sharper social turn to sayings reported by the other gospels. For instance, in the beatitudes of Matthew, Jesus blesses the poor in spirit, those who hunger and thirst after righteousness, the meek and the pure in heart. In Luke he cheers the socially poor, the physically hungry, and puts his meaning beyond question by following up his blessings on the poor with corresponding woes to the rich, the satiated, and the frivolous.[69]

Many critics doubt that Jesus taught as Luke reports him. They think that Luke drew this class of material from a Jewish-Christian source which was tainted with Ebionitic tendencies. I fail to be convinced by their arguments. The other evangelists report so much of a similar nature that the sections reported by Luke alone seem quite in keeping with the mind of Jesus. The material in question seems to bear the literary and artistic coinage of Christ's intellect as much as any other material in the gospels. The "Ebionitic sections" run all through the narrative of Luke, so that they were not drawn from some brief document covering a small portion of Christ's life. The critical suspicions seem to rest on a moral dislike for the radical attitude toward wealth taken by Jesus according to Luke, rather than on sound critical principles. But if it is a question of moral insight, we may fairly doubt who saw more truly, Jesus or the modern middle-class critics.[70]

An ascetic distrust of property and the property instinct very early affected the Christian Church after its transition to the Greek world, and it is important to be on the watch against any influence of this alien tendency on those who reported the say-

---

69 Cf. Matthew 5:1–12 with Luke 6:20–26.

70 The Ebionites constituted a small movement or sect of extreme Judaizing Christians who during the early centuries of the Church emphasized strict obedience to the Jewish Law, the virtue of poverty, and also the simple humanity of Jesus. Most subsequent scholarship confirms Rauschenbusch's doubts as to an Ebionite source for Luke. [Ed.]

ings of Christ. But the radical teachings of Jesus are not ascetic, but revolutionary, and that distinction is fundamental. What is called Ebionitic is simply the strong democratic and social feeling which pervaded later Judaism. The probability is rather that the later reporters softened this social radicalism and spiritualized his thought, than that some Ebionitic followers of Jesus imported their social unrest into his spiritual teaching.

In any case, Luke put his indorsement on this conception of Christ's thought. He was the only writer in the New Testament, so far as we know, who was of Greek descent and character. He had a singular affinity for all that was humane, generous, heroic, and humanly stirring and touching, and he tells his stories with a distinct artistic note. Men like Stephen, Barnabas, and Paul were his heroes. To him alone we owe the parable of the good Samaritan, of the prodigal son, of the Pharisee and publican, and the story of the great sinner and the penitent thief. The socialist among the evangelists was also the one who has given us the richest expressions of the free grace of God to sinful men, without which our evangel would be immeasurably poorer. If he was tainted with Ebionitic and Jewish spirit in reporting the teachings on wealth, how did he escape being tainted with the legal and narrow spirit of Jewish Christianity which must have saturated his supposed Ebionitic sources?

THE SOCIAL AFFINITIES OF JESUS

As with the Old Testament prophets, the fundamental sympathies of Jesus were with the poor and oppressed. In the glad opening days of his preaching in Galilee, when he wanted to unfold his programme, he turned to the passage of Isaiah where the prophet proclaimed good tidings to the poor, release to the captives, liberty to the bruised, and the acceptable year of the Lord for all. Now, said Jesus, that is to be fulfilled.[71] To John in

---

[71] Luke 4:16–22.

prison he offered as proof that the Messiah had really come, that the helpless were receiving help, and the poor were listening to glad news.[72] The Church has used the miracles of Jesus for theological purposes as evidences of his divine mission. According to the Synoptic gospels, Jesus himself flatly refused to furnish them for such a purpose to the contemporary theologians.[73] His healing power was for social help, for the alleviation of human suffering. It was at the service of any wretched leper, but not of the doubting scribes. To get the setting of his life we must remember the vast poverty and misery of Oriental countries. It threatened to ingulf him entirely and to turn him into a travelling medical dispensary. . . .

Jesus proceeded from the common people. He had worked as a carpenter for years, and there was nothing in his thinking to neutralize the sense of class solidarity which grows up under such circumstances. The common people heard him gladly because he said what was in their hearts.[74] His triumphal entry into Jerusalem was a poor man's procession; the coats from their backs were his tapestry, their throats his brass band, and a donkey was his steed. During the last days in Jerusalem he was constantly walking into the lion's cage and brushing the sleeve of death. It was the fear of the people which protected him while he bearded the powers that be. His midnight arrest, his hasty trial, the anxious efforts to work on the feelings of the crowd against him, were all a tribute to his standing with the common people.

Dr. W. M. Thomson, in his *The Land and the Book,* beautifully says: "With uncontrolled power to possess all, he owned nothing. He had no place to be born in but another man's stable, no closet to pray in but the wilderness, no place to die but on the

---

[72] Matthew 11:2–5.

[73] Matthew 12:38–39, 16:1–4.

[74] Mark 12:37.

cross of an enemy, and no grave but one lent by a friend."[75] That, perhaps, overstates his poverty. But it is fair to say that by birth and training, by moral insight and conviction, by his sympathy for those who were down, and by his success in winning them to his side, Jesus was a man of the common people, and he never deserted their cause as so many others have done. Whenever the people have caught a glimpse of him as he really was, their hearts have hailed Jesus of Nazareth as one of them.

THE REVOLUTIONARY CONSCIOUSNESS OF JESUS

There was a revolutionary consciousness in Jesus; not, of course, in the common use of the word "revolutionary," which connects it with violence and bloodshed. But Jesus knew that he had come to kindle a fire on earth. Much as he loved peace, he knew that the actual result of his work would be not peace but the sword. His mother in her song had recognized in her own experience the settled custom of God to "put down the proud and exalt them of low degree," to "fill the hungry with good things and to send the rich empty away."[76] King Robert of Sicily recognized the revolutionary ring in those phrases, and thought it well that the Magnificat was sung only in Latin. The son of Mary expected a great reversal of values. The first would be last and the last would be first.[77] He saw that what was exalted among man was an abomination before God,[78] and therefore these exalted things had no glamour for his eye. This revolution-

---

[75] William McClure Thomson, *The Land and the Book* (London: T. Nelson and Sons, 1866) p. 407. [Thomson (1843–1894) was a veteran missionary in Syria and Palestine. His book was a colorful, informative, and very widely read account of sites and peoples in the Holy Land; it was published in Britain and America in many one- two- and three-volume editions for a half-century after 1859. Ed.]

[76] Luke 1:52–53.

[77] Mark 10:31.

[78] Luke 16:15.

ary note runs even through the beatitudes where we should least expect it. The point of them is that henceforth those were to be blessed whom the world had not blessed, for the kingdom of God would reverse their relative standing. Now the poor and the hungry and sad were to be satisfied and comforted; the meek who had been shouldered aside by the ruthless would get their chance to inherit the earth, and conflict and persecution would be inevitable in the process.[79]

We are apt to forget that his attack on the religious leaders and authorities of his day was of revolutionary boldness and thoroughness. He called the ecclesiastical leaders hypocrites, blind leaders who fumbled in their casuistry, and everywhere missed the decisive facts in teaching right and wrong. Their piety was no piety; their law was inadequate; they harmed the men whom they wanted to convert.[80] Even the publicans and harlots had a truer piety than theirs.[81] If we remember that religion was still the foundation of the Jewish State, and that the religious authorities were the pillars of existing society, much as in mediæval Catholic Europe, we shall realize how revolutionary were his invectives. It was like Luther anathematizing the Catholic hierarchy.

His mind was similarly liberated from spiritual subjection to the existing civil powers. He called Herod, his own liege sovereign, "that fox."[82] When the mother of James and John tried to steal a march on the others and secure for her sons a pledge of the highest places in the Messianic kingdom,[83] Jesus felt that this was a backsliding into the scrambling methods of the present social order, in which each tries to make the others serve him, and he is greatest who can compel service from most. In the new

---

[79] Matthew 5:1–12.
[80] See the whole of Matthew 23.
[81] Matthew 21:23–32.
[82] Luke 13:32.
[83] Matthew 20:20–28.

social order, which was expressed in his own life, each must seek to give the maximum of service, and he would be greatest who would serve utterly. In that connection he sketched with a few strokes the pseudo-greatness of the present aristocracy: "Ye know that they which are supposed to rule over the nations lord it over them, and their great ones tyrannize over them. Thus shall it not be among you."[84] The monarchies and aristocracies have always lived on the fiction that they exist for the good of the people, and yet it is an appalling fact how few kings have loved their people and have lived to serve. Usually the great ones have regarded the people as their oyster. In a similar saying reported by Luke, Jesus wittily adds that these selfish exploiters of the people graciously allow themselves to be called "benefactors."[85] His eyes were open to the unintentional irony of the titles in which the "majesties," "excellencies," and "holinesses" of the world have always decked themselves. Every time the inbred instinct to seek precedence cropped up among his disciples he sternly suppressed it. They must not allow themselves to be called Rabbi or Father or Master, "for all ye are brothers."[86] Christ's ideal of society involved the abolition of rank and the extinction of those badges of rank in which former inequality was incrusted. The only title to greatness was to be distinguished service at cost to self.[87] All this shows the keenest insight into the masked selfishness of those who hold power, and involves a revolutionary consciousness, emancipated from reverence for things as they are.

The text, "Give to Cæsar what is Cæsar's" seems to mark off a definite sphere of power for the emperor, coördinate with God's

---

[84] In the last phrase of Mark 10:42 Rauschenbusch reads "tyrannize" in lieu of "exercise authority" which is given in the King James, American Standard, and Revised Standard versions. He is supported by some modern translations. Cf. Matthew 20:24. [Ed.]

[85] Luke 22:25. [Cf. passages in preceding note. Ed.]

[86] Matthew 23:1–12.

[87] Matthew 20:26–28.

sphere.[88] It implies passive obedience to constituted authority and above all guarantees Cæsar's right to levy taxes. Consequently it has been very dear to all who were anxious to secure the sanctions of religion for the existing political order. During the Middle Ages that text was one of the spiritual pillars that supported the Holy Roman Empire.[89] But in fact we misread it if we take it as a solemn decision, fixing two coördinate spheres of life, the religious and the political. His opponents were trying to corner Jesus. If he said "pay the Roman tax," he disgusted the people. If he said "do not pay," Rome would seize him, for its patience was short when its taxes were touched. Jesus wittily cut the Gordian knot by calling for one of the coins. It bore the hated Roman face and stamp on it—clear evidence whence it issued and to whom it belonged. If they filled their pockets with Cæsar's money, let them pay Cæsar's tax. The significant fact to us is that Jesus spoke from an inward plane which rose superior to the entire question. It was a vital question for Jewish religion; it did not even touch the religion of Jesus. Moreover, it was not purely a religious question with them; matters that concern money somehow never are purely religious. In paying tribute to Cæsar, they seemed to deny the sovereignty of Jehovah, Israel's only king; that was, indeed, one point for grief. But another point was that they had to pay, pay, pay; and money is such a dear thing! Jesus felt none of their fond reverence for cash. Hence he could say, Give to Cæsar the stuff that belongs to him, and give to God what he claims.

We have another incident in which his inward attitude to taxation comes out.[90] The Jews annually paid a poll-tax of half a shekel for the support of the temple worship, which sufficed to maintain it in splendor. The collector met Peter and asked if his master did not intend to pay. Peter, probably knowing his

---

[88] Matthew 22:15–22.

[89] James Bryce, *The Holy Roman Empire* (New York: The Macmillan Company, 1904), pp. 112–113.

[90] Matthew 17:24–27.

custom hitherto, said, "Certainly." When he came into the house, Jesus, who seems to have overheard the conversation, asked him from whom the kings of the earth usually exacted taxes, from their subjects or their sons. Peter rightly judged that the subjects usually did the paying, and the members of the royal family were exempt. "Then," said Jesus, "as we are sons of God and princes of the blood-royal, we are exempt from God's temple-tax. But lest we give offence, go catch a fish and pay the tax." We all know by experience that the expression of the face and eye are often quite essential for understanding the spirit of a conversation. We must think of Jesus with a smile on his lips during this conversation with his friend Peter. Yet something of his most fundamental attitude to existing institutions found expression in this gentle raillery. He was inwardly free. He paid because he wanted to, and not because he had to.

Camille Desmoulins, one of the spiritual leaders of the French Revolution, called Jesus *"le bon sans-culotte."* Emile de Laveleye, the eminent Belgian economist, who had the deepest reverence for Christianity as a social force, said, "If Christianity were taught and understood conformably to the spirit of its founder, the existing social organism could not last a day."[91] James Russell Lowell said, "There is dynamite enough in the New Testament, if illegitimately applied, to blow all our existing institutions to atoms."[92]

These men have not seen amiss. Jesus was not a child of this world. He did not revere the men it called great; he did not accept its customs and social usages as final; his moral conceptions did not run along the grooves marked out by it. He nour-

---

[91] Emile Louis Victor de Laveleye, *Primitive Property* (London: Macmillan Co., 1878), p. xxxi. [Rauschenbusch took the quotation from Mathews, *Social Teaching*, p. 149n. Ed.]

[92] James Russell Lowell, "The Progress of the World" 1886, *The Complete Works*, Fireside Edition, 11 vols. (Boston and New York, 1891–1892), VII, 181. [In this passage Lowell is opposing both socialistic tendencies and universal suffrage, hence the word "illegitimately." Ed.]

ished within his soul the ideal of a common life so radically different from the present that it involved a reversal of values, a
revolutionary displacement of existing relations. This ideal was
not merely a beautiful dream to solace his soul. He lived it out
in his own daily life. He urged others to live that way. He held
that it was the only true life, and that the ordinary way was
misery and folly. He dared to believe that it would triumph.
When he saw that the people were turning from him, and that
his nation had chosen the evil way and was drifting toward the
rocks that would destroy it, unutterable sadness filled his soul,
but he never abandoned his faith in the final triumph of that
kingdom of God for which he had lived. For the present, the
cross; but beyond the cross, the kingdom of God. If he was not
to achieve it now, he would return and do it then.

That was the faith of Jesus. Have his followers shared it? We
shall see later what changes and limitations the original purpose
and spirit of Christianity suffered in the course of history. But
the Church has never been able to get entirely away from the
revolutionary spirit of Jesus. It is an essential doctrine of Christianity that the world is fundamentally good and practically
bad, for it was made by God, but is now controlled by sin. If a
man wants to be a Christian, he must stand over against things
as they are and condemn them in the name of that higher conception of life which Jesus revealed. If a man is satisfied with
things as they are, he belongs to the other side. For many centuries the Church felt so deeply that the Christian conception
of life and the actual social life are incompatible, that any one
who wanted to live the genuine Christian life, had to leave the
world and live in a monastic community. Protestantism has
abandoned the monastic life and settled down to live in the
world. If that implies that it accepts the present condition as
good and final, it means a silencing of its Christian protest and
its surrender to "the world." There is another alternative. Ascetic
Christianity called the world evil and left it. Humanity is waiting for a revolutionary Christianity which will call the world

evil and change it. We do not want "to blow all our existing institutions to atoms," but we do want to remould every one of them. A tank of gasoline can blow a car sky-high in a single explosion, or push it to the top of a hill in a perpetual succession of little explosions. We need a combination between the faith of Jesus in the need and the possibility of the kingdom of God, and the modern comprehension of the organic development of human society.

We saw at the outset of our discussion that Jesus was not a mere social reformer. Religion was the heart of his life, and all that he said on social relations was said from the religious point of view. He has been called the first socialist. He was more; he was the first real man, the inaugurator of a new humanity. But as such he bore within him the germs of a new social and political order. He was too great to be the Saviour of a fractional part of human life. His redemption extends to all human needs and powers and relations. Theologians have felt no hesitation in founding a system of speculative thought on the teachings of Jesus, and yet Jesus was never an inhabitant of the realm of speculative thought. He has been made the founder and organizer of a great ecclesiastical machine, which derives authority for its offices and institutions from him, and yet "hardly any problem of exegesis is more difficult than to discover in the gospels an administrative or organizing or ecclesiastical Christ."[93] There is at least as much justification in invoking his name today as the champion of a great movement for a more righteous social life. He was neither a theologian, nor an ecclesiastic, nor a socialist. But if we were forced to classify him either with the great theologians who elaborated the fine distinctions of scholasticism; or with the mighty popes and princes of the Church who built up their power in his name; or with the men who are giving their heart and life to the propaganda of a new social system—where should we place him?

---

[93] Francis G. Peabody, *Jesus Christ and the Social Question*, p. 89.

A THEOLOGY FOR THE SOCIAL GOSPEL

The Super-Personal Forces of Evil

Individualistic theology has not trained the spiritual intelligence of Christian men and women to recognize and observe spiritual entities beyond the individual. Our religious interest has been so focused on the soul of the individual and its struggles that we have remained uneducated as to the more complex units of spiritual life.

The chief exception to this statement is our religious insight into the history of Israel and Judah, into the nature of the family, and the qualities of the Church. The first of these we owe to the solidaristic vision of the Old Testament prophets who saw their nation as a gigantic personality which sinned, suffered, and repented. The second we owe to the deep interest which the Church from the beginning has taken in the purity of family life and the Christian nurture of the young. The third we owe to the high valuation the Church has always put on itself. It has claimed a continuous and enduring life of its own which enfolds all its members and distinguishes it from every other organization and from the totality of the worldly life outside of it. It is hard to deny this. Not only the Church as a whole, but distinctive groups and organizations within the Church, such as the Friends or the Jesuit Order, have maintained their own character and principles tenaciously against all influences. This is the noblest view that we can take of the Church, that the spirit of her Lord has always been an informing principle of life within her, and that, though faltering, sinning, and defiled, she has kept her own collective personality intact. Paul's discussion of the

From Walter Rauschenbusch, *A Theology for the Social Gospel* (New York: The Macmillan Company, 1917), pp. 69–76. Reprinted with the permission of The Macmillan Company. Copyright 1917, renewed 1945 by Pauline E. Rauschenbusch.

Church as the body of Christ (I Cor: xii) is the first and classical discussion in Christian thought of the nature and functioning of a composite spiritual organism.

The Church is not the only organism of that kind, though pre-eminent among them all. Others are less permanent, less distinctive, less attractive, and less selfassertive, but the spiritual self-consciousness of the Church is built up on the social self-consciousness which it shares with other social organisms.

Josiah Royce, one of the ablest philosophical thinkers our nation has produced, has given us, in *The Problem of Christianity*, his mature reflections on the subject of the Christian religion. The book is a great fragment, poorly balanced, confined in the main to a modern discussion of three great Pauline conceptions, sin, atonement, and the Church. The discussion of the Church is the ablest part of it; I shall return to that later. Following the lead of Wundt's Völkerpsychologie,[1] Professor Royce was deeply impressed with the reality of super-personal forces in human life. He regards the comprehension of that fact as one of the most important advances in knowledge yet made.

There are in the human world two profoundly different grades, or levels, of mental beings,—namely, the beings that we usually call human individuals, and the beings that we call communities. Any highly organized community is as truly a human being as you and I are individually human. Only a community is not what we usually call an individual human being because it has no one separate and internally well-knit physical organism of its own; and because its mind, if you attribute to it any one mind, is therefore not manifested through the expressive movements of such a single separate human organism. Yet there are reasons for attributing to a

---

[1] Wilhelm Wundt (1832–1920) was a founder of modern experimental psychology. He also had systematic philosophical interests and was a pioneer investigator of the psychological dimension of cultural and linguistic phenomena, including the psychological characteristics of groups and peoples (*Völkerpsychologie:* folk-psychology). [Ed.]

community a mind of its own.—The communities are vastly more complex, and, in many ways, are also immeasurably more potent and enduring than are the individuals. Their mental life possesses, as Wundt has pointed out, a psychology of its own, which can be systematically studied. Their mental existence is no mere creation of abstract thinking or of metaphor; and is no more a topic for mystical insight, or for phantastic speculation, than is the mental existence of an individual man.[2]

This conception is of great importance for the doctrine of sin. I have spoken in the last chapter about the authority of the group over the individual within it, and its power to impose its own moral standard on its members, by virtue of which it educates them upward, if its standard is high, and debases them, if it is low. We need only mention some of the groups in our own national social life to realize how they vary in moral quality and how potent they are by virtue of their collective life: high school fraternities; any college community; a trade union; the I. W. W.; the Socialist party; Tammany Hall; any military organization; an officers' corps; the police force; the inside group of a local political party; the Free Masons; the Grange; the legal profession; a conspiracy like the Black Hand.

These super-personal forces count in the moral world not only through their authority over their members, but through their influence in the general social life. They front the world outside of them. Their real object usually lies outside. The assimilative power they exert over their members is only their form of discipline by which they bring their collective body into smooth and efficient working order. They are the most powerful ethical forces in our communities.

Evil collective forces have usually fallen from a better estate

---

[2] *The Problem of Christianity*, 2 vols. (New York: The Macmillan Company, 1913), I, 164–167. [Rauschenbusch has consolidated several short passages into a single paragraph, but without distorting the meaning. On Royce, see pp. 72–73, 461–492. Ed.]

Organizations are rarely formed for avowedly evil ends. They drift into evil under sinister leadership, or under the pressure of need or temptation. For instance, a small corrupt group in a city council, in order to secure control, tempts the weak, conciliates and serves good men, and turns the council itself into a force of evil in the city; an inside ring in the police force grafts on the vice trade, and draws a part of the force into protecting crime and brow-beating decent citizens; a trade union fights for the right to organize a shop, but resorts to violence and terrorizing; a trust, desiring to steady prices and to get away from anti-quated competition, undersells the independents and evades or purchases legislation. This tendency to deterioration shows the soundness of the social instincts, but also the ease with which they go astray, and the need of righteous social institutions to prevent temptation.[3]

In the previous chapter it was pointed out that the love of gain is one of the most unlimited desires and the most inviting outlet for sinful selfishness. The power of combination lends itself to extortion. Predatory profit or graft, when once its sources are opened up and developed, constitutes an almost overwhelming temptation to combinations of men. Its pursuit gives them cohesion and unity of mind, capacity to resist common dangers, and an outfit of moral and political principles which will justify their anti-social activities. The aggressive and defensive doings of such combinations are written all over history. History should be re-written to explain the nature of human parasitism. It would be a revelation. The Roman publicani, who collected the taxes from conquered provinces on a contract basis; the upper class in all slave-holding communities; the landlord class in all ages and countries, such as East Prussia, Ireland, Italy, and Russia; the great trading companies in the

---

[3] Reinhold Niebuhr's immensely influential *Moral Man and Immoral Society* (New York: Charles Scribner's Sons, 1932) was, in effect, a realistic reopening of this theory of collective evil. See pp. 76–77, 80–81. [Ed.]

early history of commerce;—these are instances of social groups consolidated by extortionate gain. Such groups necessarily resist efforts to gain political liberty or social justice, for liberty and justice do away with unearned incomes. Their malign influence on the development of humanity has been beyond telling.

The higher the institution, the worse it is when it goes wrong. The most disastrous backsliding in history was the deterioration of the Church. Long before the Reformation the condition of the Church had become the most serious social question of the age. It weighed on all good men. The Church, which was founded on democracy and brotherhood, had, in its higher levels, become an organization controlled by the upper classes for parasitic ends, a religious duplicate of the coercive State, and a chief check on the advance of democracy and brotherhood. Its duty was to bring love, unity and freedom to mankind; instead it created division, fomented hatred, and stifled intellectual and social liberty. It is proof of the high valuation men put on the Church that its corruption seems to have weighed more heavily on the conscience of Christendom than the corresponding corruption of the State. At least the religious Revolution antedated the political Revolution by several centuries. To-day the Church is practically free from graft and exploitation; its sins are mainly sins of omission; yet the contrast between the idea of the Church and its reality, between the force for good which it might exert and the force which it does exert in public life, produces profounder feelings than the shortcomings of the State.

While these pages are being written, our nation is arming itself to invade another continent for the purpose of overthrowing the German government, on the ground that the existence of autocratic governments is a menace to the peace of the world and the freedom of its peoples. This momentous declaration of President Wilson recognizes the fact that the Governments of

Great States too may be super-personal powers of sin; that they may in reality be only groups of men using their fellow-men as pawns and tools; that such governments have in the past waged war for dynastic and class interests without consulting the people; and that in their diplomacy they have cunningly contrived plans of deception and aggression, working them out through generations behind the guarded confidences of a narrow and privileged class.

There is no doubt that these charges justly characterize the German government. There is no doubt that they characterize all governments of past history with few exceptions, and that even the democratic governments of to-day are not able to show clean hands on these points. The governments even of free States like the Dutch Republic, the city republics of Italy, and the British Empire have been based on a relatively narrow group who determined the real policies and decisions of the nation. How often have we been told that in our own country we have one government on paper and another in fact? Genuine political democracy will evidence its existence by the social, economic, and educational condition of the people. Generally speaking, city slums, a spiritless and drunken peasantry, and a large emigration are corollaries of class government. If the people were free, they would stop exploitation. If they can not stop exploitation, the parasitic interests are presumably in control of legislation, the courts, and the powers of coercion. Parasitic government is sin on a high scale. If this war leads to the downfall or regeneration of all governments which support the exploitation of the masses by powerful groups, it will be worth its cost.[4]

The social gospel realizes the importance and power of the super-personal forces in the community. It has succeeded in

---

[4] Recognizing the catastrophic character of World War I more clearly than most Americans, Rauschenbusch's social expectations had become more somber. He did not see evil exclusively in the enemy camp. [Ed.]

awakening the social conscience of the nation to the danger of allowing such forces to become parasitic and oppressive. A realization of the spiritual power and value of these composite personalities must get into theology, otherwise theology will not deal adequately with the problem of sin and of redemption, and will be unrelated to some of the most important work of salvation which the coming generations will have to do.

XIII

H. RICHARD NIEBUHR

Neo-Orthodox Theologian

Helmut Richard Niebuhr (1894–1962),[1] his brother Reinhold Niebuhr (1892–   ), and Paul Tillich (1886–1965), the German theologian who in 1933 began his long and influential American career at Union Theological Seminary, personify neo-orthodoxy to most Americans. And this is appropriate. Though each has shown distinctive interests and tendencies, they illustrate nearly all of the movement's dominant characteristics. If H. Richard Niebuhr is selected for consideration here, it is chiefly because he (unlike Tillich) was a life-long American and because his deeply lamented death makes historical remarks more fitting.

One remarkable characteristic of the theologians whose teaching and writing made the 1930's a time of dramatic change in the prevailing temper of American theology—and aside from those already mentioned, one thinks of Walter Lowrie, Douglas Horton, Edwin Lewis, Walter Marshall Horton, and George Richards, among others—was that so many of them individually had experienced a profound change of mind (some frankly called it a conversion) during the years between 1925 and 1935. Their published works can often be divided into those written Before

---

[1] See Introduction, pp. 77–84.

and After such an experience. Nor was Richard Niebuhr an exception in this respect.

Until 1932, when he came to Yale as a professor of Christian ethics, most of Niebuhr's life was lived within the institutions of the German Evangelical Church. Born in Missouri as a minister's son, ordained in 1916 after graduation from a denominational college and seminary, he later served both as professor and college president in these same institutions, Eden Theological Seminary (Missouri) and Elmhurst College (Illinois). His warmth of piety and churchly concern certainly owed much to that heritage. A great deal of his future work was forecast, however, in his unpublished Ph.D. dissertation, submitted at Yale in 1924 on "The Religious Philosophy of Ernst Troeltsch," the German historian and theologian. Almost all of his later thought in one way or another testified to his deep respect for Troeltsch's grappling with historicism and its problems. THE SOCIAL SOURCES OF DENOMINATIONALISM (1929) was primarily a study in historical sociology, but it also served as an unmasking operation directed at the unedifying Protestant scene of the Twenties. In its day it was a rather bold critique of the churches' unreflective commitment to middle-class ideology. The book's theological and ethical teaching was a fairly direct version of the Social Gospel's characteristic liberalism, showing considerable indebtedness to Adolf von Harnack's WHAT IS CHRISTIANITY?

Shortly after 1929 Niebuhr began to modify his theological position. In later years he would remember this change of mind as occasioned by a combination of personal, national, and international factors. His translation of Tillich's THE RELIGIOUS SITUATION in 1932 begins to document his movement toward a more positive dealing with the church's confessional stand in a world of historical flux. Five years later the same change is evidenced in his book, THE KINGDOM OF GOD IN AMERICA, a major reevaluation of the entire American Protestant tradition from its Puritan origins to his own day. During the last three decades of his career his teaching and writing continued to be in movement, being always related dialectically to whatever he considered to be the theological fashion of the day, even when neo-orthodoxy was the fashion. Yet his last book, RADICAL MONOTHEISM (1960), which is more radical than is often supposed, develops a theme expounded in THE KINGDOM OF GOD IN AMERICA (1937). His posthumously published ethical lectures echo his concern for "the responsible self" announced in 1935 in THE CHURCH AGAINST THE WORLD.

This last-mentioned volume, from which the selection is taken, testified to Niebuhr's personal development amidst the world turmoil and economic distress of the Thirties. It also comes about as close as any single book to being a manifesto of the neo-orthodox theological movement. The book was appropriately a collaborative labor of three like-minded friends: an Introduction and concluding chapter by Niebuhr and other chapters by Francis Miller (1895–) of the World Student Christian Federation (then as now an organization that attracted provocative thinkers) and Wilhelm Pauck (1901–) who had come from Germany in 1925 and recently published in English an important exposition of Karl Barth's theology. Their book was, as the jacket copy declared, a "stern summons." Niebuhr's contribution drew out all the critical implications of his earlier SOCIAL SOURCES; they were now rooted, however, in a conception of the Church and its traditional message that put a new face on the matter. He does not repudiate Rauschenbusch's insistence upon Christian social concern—if anything he materially deepens it. Yet he addresses the Church in an entirely different—perhaps one may say in a "characteristically neo-orthodox"—way. Niebuhr does not merely admonish the churches, along with other public agencies, to do something; the Church is questioned from within and summoned to be truly itself. This demand that the Church explore its own historical inner meaning, its long "lived-experience" (erlebnis), would be deepened in Niebuhr's THE MEANING OF REVELATION (1941). This concern for the church-world relationship would, in turn, find further expression in CHRIST AND CULTURE (1951). Already implicit, however, are other themes that became progressively more explicit in his later writings: an insistence on the historicity of all things human, a view of the organic nature of church and society in which resonate the ideas of Bushnell and Royce, and a moral philosophy that reflects his lifelong admiration for Jonathan Edwards' vision of Being.

The selection that follows consists of Niebuhr's two contributions to THE CHURCH AGAINST THE WORLD, complete except for a few passages dealing with editorial or other distinctly peripheral matters.

THE CHURCH AGAINST THE WORLD

The Question of the Church

The title of our book is not so much the enunciation of a theme as it is the declaration of a position. We are seeking not to expound a thesis but to represent a point of view and to raise a question. The point of view is from within the church, is that of churchmen who, having been born into the Christian community, having been nurtured in it and having been convinced of the truth of its gospel, know no life apart from it. It is, moreover, the point of view of those who find themselves within a

---

From H. Richard Niebuhr, *The Church Against the World* (Chicago: Willett, Clark & Company, 1935), pp. 1–13. Reprinted with the permission of Harper and Row, Publishers.

threatened church. The world has always been against the church, but there have been times when the world has been partially converted, and when the church has lived with it in some measure of peace; there have been other times when the world was more or less openly hostile, seeking to convert the church. We live, it is evident, in a time of hostility when the church is imperiled not only by an external worldliness but by one that has established itself within the Christian camp. Our position is inside a church which has been on the retreat and which has made compromises with the enemy in thought, in organization, and in discipline. Finally, our position is in the midst of that increasing group in the church which has heard the command to halt, to remind itself of its mission, and to await further orders.

The question which we raise in this situation may best be stated in the gospel phrase, "What must we do to be saved?" The "we" in this question does not refer to our individual selves, as though we were isolated persons who could have a life apart from the church or apart from the nation and the race. It denotes rather the collective self, the Christian community. In an earlier, individualistic time evangelical Christians raised the question of their salvation one by one, and we cannot quarrel with them; they realized the nature of their problem as it appeared to them in their own day. Today, however, we are more aware of the threat against our collective selves than of that against our separate souls. We are asking: "What must we the nation, or we the class, or we the race do to be saved?" It is in this sense that we ask, "What must we the church do to be saved?" It is true that the authors of these brief essays have no commission to ask the question for others, nor to raise it as though they conceived themselves as spokesmen of the church. Yet they can and must ask it, as responsible members of the body of Christ, who believe that many of their fellow members are asking it also, and that the time has come for an active awareness of and discussion of its meaning.

The point of view represented and the question raised are to be distinguished, we believe, from those of many of our contemporaries who look at the church from the outside. Though some of these are members, yet they do not seem to be committed to the church, and they appear to direct their questions to it rather than to raise them as members of the community. They seem to criticize the church by reference to some standard which is not the church's but that of civilization or of the world. Apparently they require the church to engage in a program of salvation which is not of a piece with the church's gospel. They demand that it become a savior, while the church has always known that it is not a savior but the company of those who have found a savior. These critics have a right to be heard. A church which knows that it is not self-sufficient nor secure in righteousness but dependent on God for judgment and renewal as well as for life will expect him to use as instruments of his judgment the opponents and critics of Christianity. Yet the judgment of the outsider is not the final judgment of God, and his standard is not the divine standard for the church. An individual can profit greatly by the criticism of his fellows yet he will realize that they are judging him by standards which are neither his own nor God's, that he is both a worse and a better man than their judgments indicate, and that the greatest service they can render him is to call him back to his own best self. He will realize that he is not under any obligation to conform to the ideals which his friends or his critics set up for him, but that he is indeed obligated to be true to his own ideal. It is so with the church. Much as it may profit by the criticisms of those outside, it must not forget that they are asking it to conform to principles not its own, and endeavoring to use it for ends foreign to its nature. The question of the church, seen from the inside, is not how it can measure up to the expectations of society nor what it must do to become a savior of civilization, but rather how it can be true to itself: that is, to its Head. What must it do to be saved?

This question is not a selfish one; it is only the question of a responsible self.[1] Critics of the gospel of salvation, who characterize it as self-centered and intent upon self-satisfaction, thoroughly misunderstand the sources and the bearing of the cry for salvation. In the period of individualism, persons sought redemption not because they desired pleasures in "the by-and-by" but because they found themselves on the road to futility, demoralization, and destructiveness. Because they were concerned with their own impotence in good works and with the harm they were doing to others, they were not less altruistic than those who were concerned only with doing good, and inattentive to the evil consequences of many good works. The avowed altruists were not less selfish than seekers after salvation just because they wished to be saviors rather than saved. Nor is it true that the desire for salvation is unsocial. It arises—for the church today as for individuals in all times—not in solitariness but within the social nexus. The church has seen all mankind involved in crisis and has sought to offer help—only to discover the utter insufficiency of its resources. Confronting the poverty, the warfare, the demoralization of human life, it has sought within itself for the wisdom and the power with which to give aid, and has discovered its impotence. Therefore it must cry, "What must I do to be saved?" It has made pronouncements against war, promoted schemes for peace, leagues of nations, pacts for the outlawry of war, associations for international friendship, organizations of war resisters; but the march of Mars is halted not for a moment by the petty impediments placed in its way. The church has set up programs of social justice, preached utopian ideals, adopted resolutions, urged charity, proclaimed good will among men; but neither the progressive impoverishment of the life of the many nor the growth of the

---

[1] The title of Niebuhr's posthumously published Robertson Lectures, delivered at the University of Glasgow in 1960, was *The Responsible Self* (New York: Harper & Row, Publishers, 1963), with a valuable Introduction by James M. Gustafson. [Ed.]

privileges of the few has been stayed by its efforts. It has set up schemes of moral and religious education, seeking to inculcate brotherly love, to draw forth sympathetic good will, to teach self-discipline; but the progress of individual and social disintegration goes on. The church knows that the meaning of its life lies in the service it can give to God's creatures. It cannot abandon its efforts to help. Yet, looking upon the inadequacy and the frequent futility of its works, how can it help but cry, "What must I do to be saved?"

The question has another and more positive source. The church has been made to realize not only the ineffectiveness but the harmfulness of much of its labor. The individual raises the question of his salvation, rather than that of his saviorhood, when he faces the fact that he is not only not a Messiah but actually a sinner; that he is profiting by, consenting to, and sharing in man's inhumanity to man; that he is not the man upon the cross but one of the crowd beneath. So, the church has discovered that it belongs to the crucifiers rather than to the crucified; that all talk of becoming a martyr in the cause of good will, some time in the future, is but wishful thinking with little relevance to present reality. Its outside critics have taxed the church with giving opium to the people, and with securing its own position as well as that of its allies by preaching contentment to the poor. Had it been poor as Jesus was poor, had it identified itself with those to whom it preached contentment, had it not profited by the system of distribution which brings poverty, its conscience would have been clear. It would have been able to respond that it had preached nothing which it had not practiced. But being what it is, the church has been unable to refute the charge with a wholly good conscience. It knows that it has often been an obstruction in the path of social change and that it has tried to maintain systems of life which men and God had condemned to death. Its outside critics have held the church responsible for the increase of nationalism. They have pointed to the role of Protestantism, Pietism, and even of Catholicism in

fostering the sense of national destiny, in giving religious sanction to the imperialist programs of kings and democracies, in
justifying nationalist wars and in blessing armies bound on conquest. The church stands convicted of this sin without being at
all confident that it has found out how to resist similar temptations in the future. At all events, it knows that it has been on the
side of the slayers rather than of the slain. The critics have reminded the church of its part in the development of that economic system which, whatever its virtues, has revealed its vices
so clearly to our times that none can take pride in having assisted it to success, in however innocent a role. The harm which
the church has done and is doing in these and other areas of
human life may be greatly exaggerated in its adversaries' indict-
ments. But no section of the church can plead "not guilty" to
all the counts. Convicted by its conscience more than by its foes,
it joins the penitents at its own altars, asking, "What must we do
to be saved?"

In the crisis of the world the church becomes aware of its
own crisis: not that merely of a weak and responsible institution
but of one which is threatened with destruction. It is true, as
Francis Miller points out in his essay, that the church will probably survive in some form in any circumstances, and that the
real question is whether it will survive as a reliable witness to
the Christian faith.[2] Yet it is also true that the larger question
receives part of its urgency from the threat of extinction. It was
when Israel's life as a nation was in danger that the prophets
came to understand the more dire peril to Israel as a people of
God. The knowledge of death played a part in the conversions of
Augustine and Luther. So the church is being awakened to its
inner crisis by the external one in which it is involved. It has
seen enough of the indifference or hostility of the world, and
of the defeats of some of its component parts, to realize that its

---

[2] Chapter II in the same volume, "American Protestantism and the
Christian Faith." [Ed.]

continuance in the world is by no means a certainty. It knows the ways of God too well not to understand that he can and will raise up another people to carry out the mission entrusted to it if the Christian community fail him. It cannot look to the future with assurance that it carries a guarantee of immortality. The knowledge of the external crisis—in which as an institution it must become increasingly involved—may lead it to inquire first into the conditions of physical survival. Yet a society based, as the church has been, upon the conviction that to seek life is to lose it, must discover the fallacy in any attempt merely to live for the sake of living. Like any Christian individual faced with death, the church then realizes that the important question is not how to save its life but rather how to keep its soul, how to face loss, impoverishment, and even death without surrendering its self, its work, and its service.

From the point of view of civilization the question of the church seems often to be regarded as that of an institution which has failed to adjust itself to the world and which is making desperate efforts to overcome its maladjustments. The problem it presents is that of a conservative organization which has not kept abreast of the times, which has remained medieval while the world was growing modern, dogmatic while civilization was becoming scientific; which is individualistic in a collectivist period and theological in a time of humanism. The answer, it is thought, must come from science, politics, history, civilization. If the church is intent on being saved, then, from this point of view, it must direct its question to civilization. But within the church the problem has a different aspect. There is a sense, to be sure, in which the church must adjust itself to the world in which it lives and become all things to all men in order that it may win some. It is true also, within certain limits, that failure to adjust results in decay as is evident in all mere traditionalism. But the desire to become all things to all men still presupposes a faith which does not change and a gospel to which they are to be won. The failure of traditionalism, moreover, is less in its lack of adjustment to changing conditions than in the confusion of the spirit with the letter and in blindness to the actual shift of attention from meaning to symbol that has taken place within the church.

In the faith of the church, the problem is not one of adjustment to the changing, relative, and temporal elements in civilization but rather one of constant adjustment, amid these changing things, to the eternal. The crisis of the church from this point of view is not the crisis of the church in the world, but of the world in the church. What is endangered in the church is the secular element: its prestige as a social institution, its power as a political agency, its endowment as a foster-child of nation or of class. And this very peril indicates that the church has adjusted itself too much rather than too little to the world in which it lives. It has identified itself too intimately with capitalism, with the philosophy of individualism, and with the imperialism of the West. Looking to the future, the danger of the church lies more in a readiness to adjust itself to new classes, races, or national civilizations than in refusal to accept them. This moment of crisis, between a worldliness that is passing and a worldliness that is coming, is the moment of the church's opportunity to turn away from its temporal toward its eternal relations and so to become fit again for its work in time.

From the point of view of the church, moreover, the threat against it is being made not by a changing world but by an unchanging God. The "cracks in time" which now appear are fissures too deep for human contriving, and reveal a justice too profound to be the product of chance. The God who appears in this judgment of the world is neither the amiable parent of the soft faith we recently avowed nor the miracle worker of a superstitious supernaturalism; he is rather the eternal God, Creator, Judge, and Redeemer, whom prophets and apostles heard, and saw at work, casting down and raising up. He uses all things temporal as his instruments, but resigns his sovereignty to none.

Hence the fear of the church is not inspired by men but by the living God, and it directs its question not to the changing world with its self-appointed messiahs but to its sovereign Lord.

Because this is true the church can raise the question of the church but cannot answer it. It knows where to go to hear the answer; it cannot specify at what time or in what way that answer will come: so that it will be compelled to obedience by the authority of the word and the conviction in its heart. It knows that it must go to the place of penitence. It knows that it must go into silence and quiet. It knows that it must go to the Scriptures, not in worship of the letter, but because this is the place where it is most likely to hear the reverberations of that commandment and that promise which sent it on its way. . . .[3]

Toward the Independence of the Church

The relation of the church to civilization is necessarily a varying one since each of these entities is continually changing and each is subject to corruption and to conversion. The history of the relationship is marked by periods of conflict, of alliance, and of identification. A converted church in a corrupt civilization withdraws to its upper rooms, into monasteries and conventicles; it issues forth from these in the aggressive evangelism of apostles, monks and friars, circuit riders and missionaries; it relaxes its rigorism as it discerns signs of repentance and faith; it enters into inevitable alliance with converted emperors and governors, philosophers and artists, merchants and entrepreneurs, and begins to live at peace in the culture they produce

---

From H. Richard Niebuhr, *The Church Against the World* (Chicago: Willett, Clark & Company, 1935), pp. 123–156. Reprinted with the permission of Harper and Row, Publishers.

---

[3] The final paragraph (here omitted) merely comments on the book's joint authorship. [Ed.]

under the stimulus of their faith; when faith loses its force, as generation follows generation, discipline is relaxed, repentance grows formal, corruption enters with idolatry, and the church, tied to the culture which it sponsored, suffers corruption with it. Only a new withdrawal followed by a new aggression can then save the church and restore to it the salt with which to savor society. This general pattern has been repeated three times in the past: in the ancient world, in the medieval, and in the modern. It may be repeated many times in the future. Yet the interest of any generation of Christians lies less in the pattern as a whole than in its own particular relation to the prevailing civilization. The character of that relation is defined not only by the peculiar character of the contemporary church and the contemporary culture but even more by the demand which the abiding gospel makes upon Christianity. The task of the present generation appears to lie in the liberation of the church from its bondage to a corrupt civilization. It would not need to be said that such an emancipation can be undertaken only for the sake of a new aggression and a new participation in constructive work, were there not so many loyal churchmen who shy away at every mention of withdrawal as though it meant surrender and flight rather than renewal and reorganization prior to battle. Their strategy calls for immediate attack, as though the church were unfettered, sure of its strength and of its plan of campaign.

In speaking of the church's emancipation from the world we do not imply, as the romantic perversion of Christianity implies, that civilization as such is worldly, in the apostolic meaning of that term. Nor do we identify the world with nature as spiritualist asceticism does. The essence of worldliness is neither civilization nor nature, but idolatry and lust. Idolatry is the worship of images instead of that which they image; it is the worship of man, the image of God, or of man's works, images of the image of God. It appears wherever finite and relative things or powers are regarded as ends-in-themselves, where man is treated as existing for his own sake, where civilization is valued for civilization's sake, where art is practiced for art's sake, where life is lived for life's sake or nation adored for nation's sake. It issues in a false morality, which sets up ideals that do not correspond to the nature of human life and promulgates laws that are not the laws of reality but the decrees of finite, self-aggrandizing and vanishing power. Worldliness may be defined in New Testament terms as the lust of the flesh, the lust of the eyes, and the pride of life. As idolatry is the perversion of worship so lust is the perversion of love. It is desire desiring itself, or desire stopping short of its true object, seeking satisfaction in that which is merely the symbol of the satisfactory. It is pride, the perversion of faith, since it is faith in self instead of the faith of a self in that which gives meaning to selfhood. Such worldliness is far more dangerous to man in civilization than in primitive life because of the interdependence of developed society and the power of its units. The temptation to idolatry and lust is the greater the more man is surrounded by the works of his own hands. Moreover, every civilization is conditioned in all its forms by its faith, be it idolatrous or divine, so that it is difficult to draw a precise line between culture and religion. Nevertheless, Christianity regards worldliness rather than civilization as the foe of the gospel and of men; it rejects the ascetic and romantic efforts to solve life's problems by flight from civilization.

Idolatry and lust can be directed to many things. Worldliness is protean; understood and conquered in one form it assumes another and yet another. In contemporary civilization it appears as a humanism which regards man as existing for his own sake and which makes him the object of his own worship. It appears also as a nationalism in which man is taught to live and die for his own race or country as the ultimate worthful reality, and which requires the promotion of national power and glory at the expense of other nations as well as of the individuals with their own direct relation to the eternal. It has exhibited itself in the guise of a capitalism for which wealth is the great creative and redemptive power, and as an industrialism which worships the tawdry products of human hands as the sources of life's meaning. Humanity, nation, wealth, industry—these are all but finite entities, neither good nor bad in themselves; in their rightful place they become ministers to the best; regarded and treated as self-sufficient and self-justifying they become destructive to self and others. In the modern world they have become ends-in-themselves. A culture which was made possible only by the liberation of men from ancient idolatries and lusts has succumbed to its own success. It is not merely a secular culture, as though it had simply eliminated religion from its government, business, art and education. It has not eliminated faith but substituted a worldly for a divine faith. It has a religion which, like most religion, is bad—an idolatrous faith which brings with it a train of moral consequences, destructive of the lives of its devotees and damning them to a hell of dissatisfaction, inner conflict, war and barbarism as lurid as any nether region which the imagination of the past conceived.

The church allied with the civilization in which this idolatry prevails has become entangled not only in its culture but also in its worldliness. This captivity of the church is the first fact with which we need to deal in our time.

I THE CAPTIVE CHURCH

The church is in bondage to capitalism. Capitalism in its contemporary form is more than a system of ownership and distribution of economic goods. It is a faith and a way of life. It is faith in wealth as the source of all life's blessings and as the savior of man from his deepest misery. It is the doctrine that man's most important activity is the production of economic goods and that all other things are dependent upon this. On the basis of this initial idolatry it develops a morality in which economic worth becomes the standard by which to measure all other values and the economic virtues take precedence over courage, temperance, wisdom and justice, over charity, humility and fidelity. Hence nature, love, life, truth, beauty and justice are exploited or made the servants of the high economic good. Everything, including the lives of workers, is made a utility, is desecrated and ultimately destroyed. Capitalism develops a discipline of its own but in the long run makes for the overthrow of all discipline since the service of its god demands the encouragement of unlimited desire for that which promises—but must fail—to satisfy the lust of the flesh and the pride of life.

The capitalist faith is not a disembodied spirit. It expresses itself in laws and social habits and transforms the whole of civilization. It fashions society into an economic organization in which production for profit becomes the central enterprise, in which the economic relations of men are regarded as their fundamental relations, in which economic privileges are most highly prized, and in which the resultant classes of men are set to struggle with one another for the economic goods. Education and government are brought under the sway of the faith. The family itself is modified by it. The structure of cities and their very architecture is influenced by the religion. So intimate is the relation between the civilization and the faith, that it is difficult to participate in the former without consenting to the latter and becoming entangled in its destructive morality. It was possible for Paul's converts to eat meat which had been offered to idols without compromising with paganism. But the products which come from the altars of this modern idolatry— the dividends, the privileges, the status, the struggle—are of such a sort that it is difficult to partake of them without becoming involved in the whole system of misplaced faith and perverted morality.[1]

---

[1] The theory that modern capitalism is a system with a religious foundation and a cultural superstructure obviously runs counter to the widely accepted Marxian doctrine. It is not our intention to deny many elements in the Marxian analysis: the reality of the class struggle, the destructive self-contradiction in modern capitalism, the effect of capitalism upon gov-

No antithesis could be greater than that which obtains between the gospel and capitalist faith. The church has known
from the beginning that the love of money is the root of evil,
that it is impossible to serve God and Mammon, that they that
have riches shall hardly enter into life, that life does not consist in the abundance of things possessed, that the earth is the
Lord's and that love, not self-interest, is the first law of life.
Yet the church has become entangled with capitalist civilization to such an extent that it has compromised with capitalist
faith and morality and become a servant of the world. So intimate have the bonds between capitalism and Protestantism
become that the genealogists have suspected kinship. Some
have ascribed the parentage of capitalism to Protestantism
while others have seen in the latter the child of the former.[2]
But whatever may have been the relation between the modest
system of private ownership which a Calvin or a Wesley allowed and the gospel they proclaimed, that which obtains between the high capitalism of the later period and the church
must fall under the rule of the seventh and not of the fifth commandment, as a Hosea or a Jeremiah would have been quick

---

ernment, law, the established religion. Neither are we intent upon defending the principle of private property as an adequate basis for the modern
economic structure. But we are implying that modern capitalism does not
represent the inevitable product of the private property system in which
early democracy and Puritanism were interested, that it has corrupted and
perverted that system, making of it something which it was never intended
to be nor was bound to be. We believe that the economic interpretation of
history is itself a product and a statement of the economic faith and that
communism is in many ways a variant form of capitalist religion.

[2] Niebuhr is referring, of course, to the large literature on these relationships which was stimulated by the writings of Max Weber and Ernst
Troeltsch, and before them by Marx. Robert W. Green, ed., *Protestantism
and Capitalism: The Weber Thesis and Its Critics* (Boston: D. C. Heath
and Company, 1959) provides an introductory sampling and bibliography
of the controversy. Niebuhr's *Social Sources of Denominationalism* (1929),
The Kingdom of God in America (1937), and *Christ and Culture* (1951) are
all very relevant to the discussion. [Ed.]

to point out.[3] The entanglement with capitalism appears in the great economic interests of the church, in its debt structure, in its dependence through endowments upon the continued dividends of capitalism, and especially in its dependence upon the continued gifts of the privileged classes in the economic society. This entanglement has become the greater the more the church has attempted to keep pace with the development of capitalistic civilization, not without compromising with capitalist ideas of success and efficiency. At the same time evidence of religious syncretism, of the combination of Christianity with capitalist religion, has appeared. The "building of the kingdom of God" has been confused in many a churchly pronouncement with the increase of church possessions or with the economic advancement of mankind. The church has often behaved as though the saving of civilization and particularly of capitalist civilization were its mission. It has failed to apply to the morality of that civilization the rigid standards which it did not fail to use where less powerful realities were concerned. The development may have been inevitable, nevertheless it was a fall.

The bondage of the church to nationalism has been more apparent than its bondage to capitalism, partly because nationalism is so evidently a religion, partly because it issues in the dramatic sacrifices of war—sacrifices more obvious if not more actual than those which capitalism demands and offers to its god. Nationalism is no more to be confused with the principle of nationality than capitalism is to be confused with the principle of private property. Just as we can accept, without complaint against the past, the fact that a private property system replaced feudalism, so we can accept, without blaming our

---

[3] Niebuhr is using the Catholic-Lutheran not the Reformed-Anglican numbering of the Decalogue: fifth commandment, Thou shalt not kill; seventh commandment, Thou shalt not steal. [Ed.]

ancestors for moral delinquency, the rise of national organization in place of universal empire. But as the private property
system became the soil in which the lust for possessions and
the worship of wealth grew up, so the possibility of national
independence provided opportunity for the growth of religious
nationalism, the worship of the nation, and the lust for national
power and glory. And as religious capitalism perverted the
private property system, so religious nationalism corrupted the
nationalities. Nationalism regards the nation as the supreme
value, the source of all life's meaning, as an end-in-itself and a
law to itself. It seeks to persuade individuals and organizations
to make national might and glory their main aim in life. It even
achieves a certain deliverance of men by freeing them from
their bondage to self. In our modern polytheism it enters into
close relationship with capitalism, though not without friction
and occasional conflict, and sometimes it appears to offer an
alternative faith to those who have become disillusioned with
wealth-worship. Since the adequacy of its god is continually
called into question by the existence of other national deities,
it requires the demonstration of the omnipotence of nation and
breeds an unlimited lust for national power and expansion. But
since the god is limited the result is conflict, war and destruction. Despite the fact that the nationalist faith becomes obviously dominant only in times of sudden or continued political
crisis, it has had constant and growing influence in the West,
affecting particularly government and education.

The antithesis between the faith of the church and the nationalist idolatry has always been self-evident. The prophetic
revolution out of which Christianity eventually came was a
revolution against nationalist religion. The messianic career of
Jesus developed in defiance of the nationalisms of Judaism and
of Rome. In one sense Christianity emerged out of man's dis-
illusionment with the doctrine that the road to life and joy and
justice lies through the exercise of political force and the growth
of national power. The story of its rise is the history of long

struggle with self-righteous political power. Yet in the modern world Christianity has fallen into dependence upon the political agencies which have become the instruments of nationalism and has compromised with the religion they promote. The division of Christendom into national units would have been a less serious matter had it not resulted so frequently in a division into nationalistic units. The close relation of church and state in some instances, the participation of the church in the political life in other cases, has been accompanied by a syncretism of nationalism and Christianity. The confusion of democracy with the Christian ideal of life in America, of racialism and the gospel in Germany, of Western nationalism and church missions in the Orient, testify to the compromise which has taken place. The churches have encouraged the nations to regard themselves as messianic powers and have supplied them with religious excuses for their imperialist expansions and aggressions. And in every time of crisis it has been possible for nationalism to convert the major part of the church, which substituted the pagan Baal for the great Jehovah, without being well aware of what it did, and promoted a holy crusade in negation of the cross. The captivity of the church to the world of nationalism does not assume so dramatic a form as a rule, yet the difficulty of Christianity in achieving an international organization testifies to the reality of its bondage.

Capitalism and nationalism are variant forms of a faith which is more widespread in modern civilization than either. It is difficult to label this religion. It may be called humanism, but there is a humanism that, far from glorifying man, reminds him of his limitations the while it loves him in his feebleness and aspiration. It has become fashionable to name it liberalism, but there is a liberalism which is interested in human freedom as something to be achieved rather than something to be assumed and praised. It may be called modernism, but surely one can live in the modern world, accepting its science and engaging in its work, without falling into idolatry of the modern. The rather too technical term "anthropocentrism" seems to be the best designation of the faith. It is marked on its negative side by the rejection not only of the symbols of the creation, the fall and the salvation of men, but also of the belief in human dependence and limitation, in human wickedness and frailty, in divine forgiveness through the suffering of the innocent. Positively it affirms the sufficiency of man. Human desire is the source of all values. The mind and the will of man are sufficient instruments of his salvation. Evil is nothing but lack of development. Revolutionary second-birth is unnecessary. Although some elements of the anthropocentric faith are always present in human society, and although it was represented at the beginning of the modern development, it is not the source but rather the product of modern civilization. Growing out of the success of science and technology in understanding and modifying some of the conditions of life, it has substituted veneration of science for scientific knowledge, and glorification of human activity for its exercise. Following upon the long education in which Protestant and Catholic evangelism had brought Western men to a deep sense of their duty, this anthropocentrism glorified the mortal sense of man as his natural possession and taught him that he needed no other law than the one within. Yet, as in the case of capitalism and nationalism, the faith which grew out of modern culture has modified that culture. During the last generations the anthropocentric faith has entered deeply into the structure of society and has contributed not a little to the megapolitanism and megalomania of contemporary civilization.

The compromise of the church with anthropocentrism has come almost imperceptibly in the course of its collaboration in the work of culture. It was hastened by the tenacity of Christian traditionalism, which appeared to leave churchmen with no alternative than one between worship of the letter and worship of the men who wrote the letters. Nevertheless, the compromise is a perversion of the Christian position. The more obvious expressions of the compromise have been frequent but perhaps less dangerous than the prevailing one by means of which Christianity appeared to remain true to itself while accepting the anthropocentric position. That compromise was the substitution of religion for the God of faith. Man's aspiration after God, his prayer, his worship was exalted in this syncretism into a saving power, worthy of a place alongside science and art. Religion was endowed with all the attributes of Godhead, the while its basis was found in human nature itself. The adaptation of Christianity to the anthropocentric faith appeared in other ways: in the attenuation of the conviction of sin and of the necessity of rebirth, in the substitution of the human claim to immortality for the Christian hope and fear of an after-life, in the glorification of religious heroes, and in the efforts of religious men and societies to become saviors.

The captive church is the church which has become entangled with this system or these systems of worldliness. It is a church which seeks to prove its usefulness to civilization, in terms of civilization's own demands. It is a church which has lost the distinctive note and the earnestness of a Christian discipline of life and has become what every religious institution tends to become—the teacher of the prevailing code of morals and the pantheon of the social gods. It is a church, moreover, which has become entangled with the world in its desire for the increase of its power and prestige and which shares the worldly fear of insecurity.

How the church became entangled and a captive in this way may be understood. To blame the past for errors which have brought us to this pass is to indulge in the ancient fallacy of saying that the fathers have eaten sour grapes and the children's teeth are set on edge. The function of the present is neither praise nor blame of the past. It is rather the realization of the prevailing situation and preparation for the next task.

II THE REVOLT IN THE CHURCH

The realization of the dependence of the church is wide-spread and has led to revolt. There is revolt against the church and revolt within the church. Both of these uprisings have various aspects. The revolt against the church is in part the rebellion of those who have found in Christianity only the pure traditionalism of doctrine and symbol which have become meaningless through constant repetition without rethinking and through the consequent substitution of symbol for reality. In part it is a revulsion against the sentimentality which substituted for the ancient symbols, with the realities to which they pointed, the dubious realities of man's inner religious and moral life. In part it is the revolt of those who see in the church the willing servitor of tyrannical social institutions and classes. On the one hand, the intellectuals abandon the church because of its traditionalism or romanticism; on the other hand, disinherited classes and races protest against it as the ally of capitalist, racial or nationalist imperialism. But these revolts against the church are not the most significant elements in the present situation, from the church's point of view. They represent desertions and attacks inspired not by loyalty to the church's own principles but rather by devotion to interests other than those of the church. Such desertions and attacks, however justified they may seem from certain points of view, serve only to weaken the church and to increase its dependence. Only a churchly revolt can lead to the church's independence.

The revolt within the church has a dual character. It is a revolt both against the "world" of contemporary civilization and against the secularized church. No other institution or society in the Western world seems to be so shot through with the spirit of rebellion against the secular system with its abuses, as is the church. No other institution seems to harbor within it so many rebels against its own present form. They are rebels who are fundamentally loyal—loyal, that is to say, to the essential institution while they protest against its corrupted form. They have no alternative religions or philosophies of life to which they might wish to flee. A few, to be sure, leave the church year by year, yet even among these loyalty is often manifest. Some of the rebels remain romanticists who try to build "a kingdom of God" with secular means. More of them are frustrated revolutionaries who hate "the world" which outrages their consciences and denies their faith but who know of no way in which they can make their rebellion effective or by which they can reconcile themselves to the situation.

Like every revolt in its early stages, the Christian revolution of today is uncertain of its ends and vague in its strategy. It seems to be a sentiment and a protest rather than a theory and a plan of action. It is a matter of feeling, in part, just because the situation remains unanalyzed. It issues therefore in many ill-tempered accusations and in blind enthusiasms. Sometimes it concentrates itself against some particular feature of the secular civilization which seems particularly representative of its character. Perhaps the crusade against the liquor traffic was indebted for some of its force to the uneasy conscience of a church which was able to treat this particular phase of the "world" as the symbol and representative of all worldliness. As in all such emotional revolts there is a temptation to identify the evil with some evildoer and to make individual men—capitalists, munitions-manufacturers, dictators—responsible for the situation. Thus early Christians may have dealt with Nero, and Puritans with popes. The confusion of the revolt in the church is apparent, however, not only in its emotionalism but also in its association with revolting groups outside the church. In the beginning of every uprising against prevailing customs and institutions disparate groups who share a common antagonism are likely to assume that they share a common loyalty. It was so when princes and protestants and peasants arose against the Roman church and empire; it was so also when Puritans, Presbyterians, Independents and sectarians rose against King

Charles. Dissenters and democrats united in opposing the established church in American colonies. Such groups are united in their negations, not in their affirmations. Their positive loyalties, for the sake of which they make a common rejection, may be wholly different. The revolt in the church against the "world" and against "the world in the church" is confused today because of such associations. This confusion implies perils and temptations which may lead to disaster or to the continued captivity of the church. For if it is a frequent experience that common antagonism is confused with common loyalty, it is also well known that allies are prone to fight among themselves because of their variant interests. One danger to the Christian revolt is that it will enter into alliance with forces whose aims and strategies are so foreign to its own that when the common victory is won—if won it can be—the revolutionary church will be left with the sad reflection that it supplied the "Fourteen Points" which gave specious sanctity to an outrageous peace and that its fruits of victory are an external prosperity based on rotting foundations and debts which it cannot collect without destroying its own life.

The danger of such alliance or identification is not a fancied peril. The eagerness with which some of the leaders of the Christian revolt identify the gospel with the ideals and strategies of radical political parties, whether they be proletarian or nationalistic, the efforts to amalgamate gospel and political movements in a Christian socialism or in a Christian nationalism indicate the reality of the danger. It is not always understood by the American section of the Christian revolt that a considerable section of the so-called German Christian movement, in which the confusion of gospel and nationalism prevails, had sources in just such a reaction as its own against an individualistic, profit-loving and capitalistic civilization, and against the church in alliance with that civilization. There are many social idealists among these Germanizers of the gospel; and their fervor is essentially like that of the other idealists who equate the kingdom of God with a proletarian socialist instead of a national socialist society.[4] The "social gospel," in so far as it is the identification of the gospel with a certain temporal order, is no recent American invention. In the history of Europe and America there have been many similar efforts which sought ideal ends, identified the church with political agencies, and succeeded in fastening upon society only some new form of power control against which the church needed again to protest and rebel. Christianity has been confused in the past, in situations more or less similar to the present, with the rule of the Roman Empire, with feudalism, with the divine right of kings, with the rule of majorities, with the dominance of the Northern States over the Southern, with the extension of Anglo-Saxon influence in the Orient. The confusion was as explicable and as specious in every instance as is the identification of Christianity with radical political movements today. Yet in every instance the result was a new tyranny, a new disaster and a new dependence of the church. It is one thing for Christians to take a responsible part in the political life of their nation; it is another thing to identify the gospel and its antagonism to the "world" with the "worldly" antagonism of some revolting group.

The common social ideal or hope of the West includes the establishment of liberty, equality, fraternity, justice and peace. Almost every revolting movement in the past as well as in the present has fought in the name of this ideal and sought to establish it. With the ideal, Christianity cannot but have profound sympathy, for Christianity taught it first of all to the Western world. But every political and social revolt is based on the belief that the ideal can be established through the exercise of power by a disinterested group or person, be it the feudal group, the monarch, the middle class or the proletariat. To identify Chris-

---

4 Hitler had come to power in Germany in 1933 and began his assault on the Church. This involved an effort to make an "Aryanized" Jesus serve National Socialist ends. [Ed.]

tianity with one form of the messianic delusion and of the philosophy of power, while rejecting another, is to be guilty of
emotional and wishful thinking. In so far as every new revolt is
an attack upon the philosophy and structure of power politics
and self-righteousness, Christianity cannot but sympathize
with it; in so far as it is itself a new form of the philosophy,
Christianity must reject it or at least refuse to identify itself
with it. So long, of course, as the church has no faith in a divine
revolution and no strategy of its own for participation in that
revolution it will need to commit itself to some other revolutionary faith and strategy or remain conservative. But in such
a case it can have no true existence as a church; it can function
only as the religious institution of a revolting society, serving
the interests of the society in the same way that a capitalist
church serves a capitalist society.

The revolt in the church faces another danger in consequence
of the tendency toward the identification of Christianity with
revolting secular movements. Multitudes of Christians who had
become aware of tension between the gospel and the world but
who are also aware of the irreconcilability of the Christian faith
with the faiths of communism, socialism or fascism are forced
to make a choice between impossible alternatives. The greater
part of them are driven into reaction, for the old identification
of Christianity with the prevailing "worldliness" is at least more
familiar to them than the new. The fruit of false action today
in Christianity as in civilization will be reaction, not a true revolution. Similar movements in the past offer unmistakable lessons on this point. The confusion of Christian and of political
Puritanism played no small part in bringing on the Restoration.
The identification of the protest against slavery with the interests of the Northern States drove many Christians in the South
to the defense of the "peculiar institution," made the Civil War
inevitable and contributed to the continuation of the race problem. There is no guarantee that reaction can be avoided under
any circumstances, but it may be held in check. There is no

guarantee that overt struggle can be avoided, but it is criminal to make civil, class or international war the more likely by confusing issues and by arousing the passions which religious fervor can awaken. And in the end the solution will be as little to the mind of Christians as the unsolved problem was.

The dangers and temptations which beset the Christian revolt offer no excuse for acquiescence. The danger which confronts the world in the midst of its idolatries and lusts is too real, the message of the church is too imperative, the misery of men is too actual to make quiescence possible. But the moment requires the church to stand upon its own feet, to do its work in its own way, to carry on its revolt against "the world," not in dependence upon allies or associates, but independently. In any case the revolt in the church against secularization of life and the system of "worldliness" points the way to the declaration of its independence.

III   TOWARD THE INDEPENDENCE OF THE CHURCH

The declaration of the church's independence, when it comes, will not begin on the negative note. A movement toward emancipation cannot become effective so long as it is only a rejection of false loyalties and entanglements. Loyalties can be recognized to be false only when a true loyalty has been discovered. Moreover, independence is not desirable for its own sake. To seek it for its own sake means to seek it for the sake of self and to substitute loyalty to a self-sufficient self for loyalty to an alien power. But the church can have no illusion of self-sufficiency. Neither can it trust itself to play a messianic role in the deliverance of mankind. It knows too well that hierocracies have not been shining examples of justice among the aristocracies, monarchies, democracies, plutocracies, race tyrannies and class rules which have oppressed mankind.

The church's declaration of independence can begin only with the self-evident truth that it and all life are dependent upon God, that loyalty to him is the condition of life and that to him belong the kingdom and the power and the glory. Otherwise the emancipation of the church from the world is impossible; there is no motive for it nor any meaning in it. There is no flight out of the captivity of the church save into the captivity of God. Such words must seem to many to be pious and meaningless platitudes, mere gestures of respect to the past and bare of that realism which the present moment demands. That this is so is but another illustration of the extent to which the faith of the church has been confounded with the belief in the ideas, wishes and sentiments of men, and to which the word *God* has been made the symbol, not of the last reality with which man contends, but of his own aspirations. It remains true that loyalty to the "I am that I am" is the only reason for the church's existence and that the recovery of this loyalty is the beginning of true emancipation. It is even more true that this loyalty is not our own creation but that through the destruction of our idols and the relentless pursuit of our self-confidence God is driving us, in the church and in the world, to the last stand where we must recognize our dependence upon him or, in vainglorious rebellion, suffer demoralization and dissolution. The crisis of modern mankind is like the crisis of the prophets, the crisis of the Roman Empire in the days of Augustine, and that of the medieval world in the days of the Reformation. The last appeal beyond all finite principalities and powers must soon be made. It cannot be an appeal to the rights of men, of nations or religions but only an appeal to the right of God.[5]

The appeal to the right of God means for the church an appeal to the right of Jesus Christ. It is an appeal not only to the grim reality of the slayer who judges and destroys the self-aggrandizing classes and nations and men. Such an appeal

---

[5] The influence of Edwards is discernible in this paragraph. This influence became more explicit in *The Kingdom of God in America* (pp. 113–116) and was elaborated with some detail in *Radical Monotheism and Western Culture* (1960). [Ed.]

would be impossible and such a loyalty out of question were not men persuaded that this reality, whose ways are again evident in historic processes, is a redeeming and saving reality, and did they not come to some understanding of the manner in which he accomplishes salvation. But such persuasion and such revelation are available only through the event called Jesus Christ. If the church has no other plan of salvation to offer to men than one of deliverance by force, education, idealism or planned economy, it really has no existence as a church and needs to resolve itself into a political party or a school. But it knows of a plan of salvation which is not a plan it has devised. In its revolt it is becoming aware of the truth which it had forgotten or which it had hidden within symbols and myths. There is in the revolt something of the restlessness that comes from a buried memory which presses into consciousness. In some of its aspects it seems to be the blind effort to escape from the knowledge that the church along with the world belongs to the crucifiers rather than to the crucified. It seems to represent the desire to avert the eyes from the cross which stands in the present as in the past, and to turn attention away from ourselves to some other culprits whose sins the innocent must bear. When this memory of Jesus Christ, the crucified, comes fully alive it will not come as a traditional formula or symbol, reminding men only of the past, but as the recollection of a most decisive fact in the present situation of men. The church's remembrance of Jesus Christ will come in contemporary terms, so that it will be able to say: "That which was from the beginning, that which we have heard, that which we have seen with our eyes, that which we have beheld and which our hands have handled concerning the Word of life—that declare we unto you."[6]

Without this beginning in loyalty to God and to Jesus Christ no new beginning of the church's life is possible. But the self-evident truths and the original loyalties of the church can be

---

[6] See I John 1:1. [Ed.]

recaptured and reaffirmed not only as the events in time drive
men to their reaffirmation, but as the labor of thought makes
intelligible and clear the vague and general perceptions we receive from life. The dependent church rejected theology or
found it unintelligible because it accepted a "theology" which
was not its own, a theory of life which was essentially worldly.
It wanted action rather than creeds because its creed was that
the action of free, intelligent men was good and that God's
action was limited to human agencies of good will. The revolters
in the church are learning that without a Christian theory or
theology the Christian movement must lose itself in emotions
and sentiments or hasten to action which will be premature and
futile because it is not based upon a clear analysis of the situation. They have learned from the communists that years spent
in libraries and in study are not necessarily wasted years but
that years of activity without knowledge are lost years indeed.
They have learned from history that every true work of liberation and reformation was at the same time a work of theology.
They understand that the dependence of man upon God and the
orientation of man's work by reference to God's work require
that theology must take the place of the psychology and sociology which were the proper sciences of a Christianity which
was dependent on the spirit in man. The theory of the Christian
revolution is beginning to unfold itself again as the theory of a
divine determinism, of the inevitable divine judgment, and of
the salvation of men by the suffering of the innocent. But whatever be the content of the theory a clear understanding of it is
needed for the work of emancipation, reorganization and aggression in the Christian community.

It is evident that far more than all this is necessary. There is
no easy way in which the church can divorce itself from the
world. It cannot flee into asceticism nor seek refuge again in the
inner life of the spirit. The road to independence and to aggression is not one which leads straight forward upon one level.
How to be in the world and yet not of the world has always

been the problem of the church. It is a revolutionary community in a pre-revolutionary society. Its main task always remains that of understanding, proclaiming and preparing for the divine revolution in human life. Nevertheless, there remains the necessity of participation in the affairs of an unconverted and unreborn world. Hence the church's strategy always has a dual character and the dualism is in constant danger of being resolved into the monism of other-worldliness or of this-worldliness, into a more or less quiescent expectancy of a revolution beyond time or of a mere reform program carried on in terms of the existent order. How to maintain the dualism without sacrifice of the main revolutionary interest constitutes one of the important problems of a church moving toward its independence.

Yet it is as futile as it is impossible to project at this moment the solution of problems which will arise in the future. If the future is pregnant with difficulties it is no less full of promise. The movement toward the independence of the church may lead to the development of a new missionary or evangelical movement, to the rise of an effective international Christianity, to the union of the divided parts of the church of Christ, and to the realization in civilization of the unity and peace of the saved children of one God. The fulfilment of hopes and fears cannot be anticipated. The future will vary according to the way in which we deal with the present. And in this present the next step only begins to be visible. The time seems ripe for the declaration of the church's independence. Yet even that step cannot be forced; how it will come and under what leadership none can now determine. We can be sure, however, that the repentance and faith working in the rank and file of the church are the preconditions of its independence and renewal.

INDEX

THE AMERICAN HERITAGE SERIES

THE COLONIAL PERIOD

THE REVOLUTIONARY ERA

THE YOUNG NATION

THE MIDDLE PERIOD

THE LATE NINETEENTH CENTURY

THE TWENTIETH CENTURY